FIFTEEN CENTURIES
OF
CHILDREN'S LITERATURE

FIFTEEN CENTURIES
OF
CHILDREN'S LITERATURE

An Annotated Chronology of British and American Works in Historical Context

JANE BINGHAM
and
GRAYCE SCHOLT

GREENWOOD PRESS

WESTPORT, CONNECTICUT • LONDON, ENGLAND

Library of Congress Cataloging in Publication Data

Bingham, Jane.
  Fifteen centuries of children's literature.

  Includes indexes.
    1. Children's literature, English—Bibliography.
2. Children's literature, American—Bibliography.
3. Children's literature, English—History and
criticism. 4. Children's literature, American—
History and criticism. 5. Books and reading for
children—History. I. Scholt, Grayce, joint author.
II. Title.
Z1037.A1B582 [PN1009.A1]   028.52   79-8584
ISBN 0-313-22164-2 lib. bdg.

Library of Congress Catalog Card Number: 79-8584
ISBN: 0-313-22164-2

First published in 1980

Greenwood Press
A division of Congressional Information Service, Inc.
88 Post Road West, Westport, Connecticut 06881

Printed in the United States of America

10 9 8 7 6 5 4 3 2 1

To the memory of Grace Durrin, Professor of English,
Bowling Green State University, 1925-1962,
teacher and friend

Contents

Illustrations

Preface

The purpose of this work is to provide a single, annotated chronological listing of significant or representative books written for or used with or appropriated by British and American children from the sixth century to 1945. The chronology is divided into six time segments: Anglo-Saxon, ca. 523-1099; Middle English, 1100-1499; Renaissance to the Restoration, 1500-1659; Restoration to American Independence, 1660-1799; Nineteenth Century, 1800-1899; and the first part of the Twentieth Century, 1900-1945. The starting point, ca. 523, was chosen as the starting point because it is the generally accepted date for the introduction of Boethius's *De Consolatione Philosophiae* to England, where it was used with young scholars in monastic schools. The end date of 1945 was chosen arbitrarily: we hope to continue annotating important children's books in this fashion for the postwar and contemporary periods, but because of the enormous proliferation in children's books published beginning in the mid-1950s, a reexamination and perhaps a restriction of the bases of selection may be in order. We also expect continually to refine the entries in the present volume, and we invite readers' suggestions in anticipation of a revised edition.

Each time period is introduced by a description of the historical background, the development of books, and attitudes toward and treatment of children in an attempt to provide a context for the annotations that follow. Additional features of this volume include a bibliography of secondary sources; chronologies of British and American children's periodicals; a key to book collections in Britain, Canada, and the United States that house books by certain authors included in the chronology; a list of facsimile editions with a key to the publishers; a name index to authors, illustrators, translators, and early publishers and printers; and an index to approximately 9,700 titles included in the work.

Entry in the chronology is by the date the book is thought to have been used first by English-speaking children; manuscripts and incunabula probably would have been read in the original language, usually Latin. For books written after translation into English became common (in the early Middle-English period), entry is made according to the date of the first publication in English. It will be noted that from the beginnings to ca. 1850, entries in the chronology are mainly "lesson book" manuscripts, books of manners and morals, religious tracts, textbooks, translations from foreign languages—particularly Latin, French, German, and Spanish—and books intended for adults but appropriated by children. Entries from 1850 to 1945 are generally children's "trade" publications—books and periodicals intended for enjoyment. Where there are multiple entries for a single date, the order is alphabetical by author (or by title if the author is unknown).

Each of the 735 main entries in the chronology includes date of publication, author if known (and/or editor, illustrator, translator), title, publisher or printer, and a brief annotation. While each annotation describes the book's contents, for some of the early entries the book's use is pointed out; often little-known facts about the book, author, or publisher are provided. Additional works by an author, along with the publisher or printer and dates of publication, if known, are included, so that one main entry may list multiple titles. In the case of prolific authors, the entry is by a significant work or the first popular work. Titles following the entry date are listed chronologically. For instance, the writings of Edward L. Stratemeyer and his "Stratemeyer Syndicate" are entered under 1895, the date of publication of one of his earliest popular boys' books, *Reuben Stone's Discovery: or the Young Miller of Torrent Bend;* the annotation then lists hundreds of titles put out by Stratemeyer under his name and pseudonyms, along with titles produced by his daughter, Harriet Stratemeyer Adams, under a variety of pseudonyms. The last main entries in the chronology are for 1945, but additional titles published as late as 1969 may be noted. Even though several authors have written books published since, no attempt was made to include books beyond 1969, which was selected as the arbitrary cut-off date.

Selection of works in the chronological listing is admittedly personal; however, most books included are cited in more than one major resource, ranging from textbooks, such as Huck's *Children's Literature in the Elementary School* (Holt, 1975) and Arbuthnot and Sutherland's *Children and Books* (Scott, Foresman, 1972) to critical histories, such as Darton's *Children's Books in England* (Cambridge, 1932), Meigs's *A Critical History of Children's Literature* (Macmillan, 1969), Thwaite's *From Primer to Pleasure* (Horn Book, 1975), and Muir's *English Children's Books 1600-*

1900 (Batsford, 1954). Popular literature, not always recommended in the major source books, is also included in order to give a more comprehensive picture of the reading material available during each historical period.

The limitations of this work are important to note. We do not claim to have listed every work by every author or to have included all authors read by or used with children during the indicated period. Nor, despite best efforts, do we claim accuracy of publishing information in every case. As anyone who has done historical work in the field of children's literature realizes, much controversy exists about editions of children's books and original publishers and dates of publication. Much verification of first editions remains to be done, as is documented in *Society and Children's Literature,* edited by James H. Fraser (Godine, 1978), particularly in Gerald Gottlieb's chapter, "Peculiar Difficulty: A Tale of the Eighteenth Century. . . ." We have attempted to compile information found in conventional resources, and we hope that scholars who have knowledge about a particular date of publication, wording of a title, name of a publisher, and so on, will share this with us, so that the chronology may become more exact and comprehensive.

Our mode of operation was not elaborate. Authors and titles of books mentioned in basic children's literature textbooks and reference books were selected and recorded on three-by-five cards. If publishers and publication dates were given, they too were included. Additional authors and other works written by each author were identified by using various listings and catalogues, such as Evans, Wing, Pollard and Redgrave, d'Alte Welch, *The Cumulative Book Index,* the *National Union Catalog,* and *Something About the Author* (see Bibliography of Secondary Sources). When discrepancies in the citations were found, the *National Union Catalog* was consulted most often as the final authority, though in full awareness of its limitations.

We recognize that the literature of any people (whether for children or adults) is a complex blend of all cultures or cultural stages that have gone into its making. If one were to attempt a "complete" chronological report of children's literature for English-speaking children, he or she would be obliged to include works from all the nations of Europe, North and South America, Asia, and Africa as well. While it is true that many cultural and national groups have contributed to the history of children's literature as known in Britain and the United States, we are attempting here to present only general patterns and specific landmarks produced largely by British and American writers, publishers, printers, artists, editors, booksellers, and educators. Even with this focus, we can at best merely suggest some of the more representative books, outline major political and social developments, indicate significant changes in the making of books, and trace the vacillating attitudes of adults toward children.

This work grew in part out of our long interest, both personal and professional, in the nature and history of childhood, the relationships of adults to children, and the creation and publication of books for the young. It also evolved out of an awareness of the diffusion of materials. As college teachers of children's literature, we have long recognized the desirability of a single resource that would provide a brief but clear political and social history, a summary of the development of printed materials, and a chronological guide to noteworthy books created for or used with children through the centuries.

We first presented much of this material to our students in the form of a time line, which pointed out a few landmark books and was supplemented by lectures providing social and historical background. But one point led to another until it became clear that a larger, more detailed view of the historical development of children's books was desirable for students and perhaps for other interested readers. As our research developed, the time line grew to its present state. No doubt this work could be lifelong. The temptation to continue research is attractive, as we know that some milestone books, historical curiosities, or readers' "favorites" are not included; not all bibliographical data are provided, and some inevitable errors are perpetuated. But given the constraints of time, we have tried to choose—without using a staff of trained researchers or computerized research services—main entries that seem to be the most significant and most representative books in the history of literature for the young. Listings of authors' additional works, while admittedly incomplete, as far as we know are more extensive than in any single reference book now available.

In dividing this chronology into six time periods and introducing each in terms of three major concepts, we are not suggesting that such divisions are exact or that such closely related topics are truly separable; neither do we imply that such compartmentalizing of knowledge is desirable or suggestive of life. Our intention is to give the reader an overview, helping him or her to see the development of children's books in a useful historical perspective. In no way have we written complete histories of Britain and America, exhaustive analyses of attitudes toward children, or a thoroughgoing survey of book publishing (nor even of children's book publishing). Such would require expertise in many disciplines and would produce a library of books. We are indebted to many scholars who have covered this ground; their works are listed in the Bibliography of Secondary Sources.

Our main attempt has been to synthesize. We have not attempted to judge the worth of the books included; and we have tried to refrain from judging the manner in which adults have structured their governments and families and the ways they have treated their offspring. In the latter case, we know that we have been only moderately successful. The tendency toward oppression and manipulation of the young, as often revealed in their literature, is not easy to report with indifference.

In summary, this volume is intended for students of children's literature seeking a comprehensive, capsule history of children's books in Britain and the United States; for scholars searching for children's books of a particular time period; for researchers seeking readily accessible information about authors, titles, early printers, publishers, and the like; and for the general reader with a specific interest in children's books. While lengthy critical histories, specialized bibliographies, and partial time lines of children's literature exist, this work attempts to be a single resource that not only provides an annotated chronological listing of British and American children's books from the sixth century to 1945, but also places them in historical context and offers supplementary information and finding aides in appendices and indexes.

JANE BINGHAM
Oakland University
Rochester, Michigan

GRAYCE SCHOLT
Charles Stewart Mott
    Community College
Flint, Michigan

Acknowledgments

The authors acknowledge the following for their assistance in the preparation of this work: Catherine Andresen, Elizabeth Andresen, Anna Bradley, Marilyn Brownstein, Irene Bleisch, Judith M. Costello, Diana Elshoff, Elizabeth Hovinen, Didi Johnson, Lynn Taylor, the Oakland University Research Committee, and the Charles Stewart Mott Community College Instructional Media Services.

We also thank the faculty, staff, and administration of our respective institutions, as well as the staff of the Osborne and Lillian H. Smith Collections, Toronto Public Library, especially Judith St. John and Margaret Maloney, for their many courtesies.

Special thanks to Ava Kerr, Executive Secretary, Research and Instructional Services Office, Oakland University, for her care in typing of this manuscript and to Susan Kilmer and Lena Johnson for their generous help.

Key to Book Collections in Britain, Canada, and the United States

AAS	American Antiquarian Society, 185 Salisbury Street, Worcester, MA 01609
AB	American Blake Foundation Research Library, Illinois State University, Department of English, Normal, IL 61761
ACL	Aberdeen County Library, 14 Crown Terrace, Aberdeen AB9 2BH, Scotland
AM	Ashmolean Museum of Art, Oxford University, Beaumont Street, Oxford OX1 2PH, England
BA	Boston Athenaeum, 10½ Beacon Street, Boston, MA 02108
BC	Bowdoin College, Longfellow Library, Brunswick, ME 04011
BCL	Belfast City Libraries, Central Library, Royal Avenue, Belfast BT1 1EA, Ireland
BECL	Buffalo and Erie County Library, Rare Book Room, Lafayette Square, Buffalo, NY 14203
BGSU	Bowling Green State University, Bowling Green Library, William Dean Howells Collection, Bowling Green, OH 43403
BKU	Bucknell University, Ellen Clarke Bertrand Library, Lewisburg, PA 17837
BL	British Library, 14 Store Street, London WC1E 7DG, England
BM	British Museum Library, Great Russell Street, London WCIB 3DG, England
BPL	Boston Public Library, Copley Square, Boston, MA 02117
BU	Brown University, John Carter Brown Library, Providence, RI 02912

BaU   Baylor University, Browning Collection, Waco, TX 76706

BuC   Bunyan Collection, Central Library, Harpur Street, Bedford MK40 3NY, England

CBE   County Borough of Eastbourne Public Libraries, Grove Rd., Eastbourne, Sussex, England

CC   Colby College, Waterville, ME 04901

CCBC   Cooperative Children's Book Center, 411 West, State Capitol, Madison, WI 53702

CL   Crawford Library, Haigh Hall, Wigan WN1 1DQ, England

CMU   Central Michigan University, Lucile Clarke Memorial Children's Library, Mt. Pleasant, MI 48858

CNM   Cowper and Newton Museum, Market Place, Olney, Buckinghamshire, England

CoU   Cornell University, Olin Research Library, Rare Book Department, Ithaca, NY 14850

CPL   Cleveland Public Library, 325 Superior Street, Cleveland, OH 44114

CSC   College of St. Catherine, 2004 Randolph Avenue, St. Paul, MN 55116

CTC   Columbia Teachers College Library, Harvey Darton Collection, 525 West 120th Street, New York, NY 10027

CU   Columbia University, Special Collections Division, 654 Butler Library, New York, NY 10027

CUNY   City University of New York, City College Library-Special Collection, Convent Avenue & West 135th Street, New York, NY 10031

ChPL   Chicago Public Library, 78 East Washington Street, Chicago, IL 60602

DC   Dartmouth College, Special Collections Division, Baker Library, Hanover, NH 03755

DePL   Denver Public Library, 1357 Broadway, Denver, CO 80203

DL   Dallas Public Library, Rare Book Room, 1954 Commerce Street, Dallas, TX 75201

DPL   Detroit Public Library, Rare Book Division, 5201 Woodward Avenue, Detroit, MI 48202

DU   Duke University, William R. Perkins Library, Durham, NC 27706

DUL   Durham University Library, Palace Green, Durham DH1 3RN, England

EC   Emmanuel College, Cambridge CB2 3AP, England

ECL   Exeter Cathedral Library, Bishop's Place, Exeter EX4 4QJ, England

EI   Essex Institute, James Duncan Phillips Library, 132-134 Essex Street, Salem, MA 01970

EU   Emory University, Woodruff Library, Atlanta, GA 30322

FIL   Franklin Institute Library, 20th Street and The Parkway, Philadelphia, PA 19103

FSU   Florida State University, Childhood in Poetry Collection, Tallahassee, FL 32306

GL   Guildhall Library, London BN 21 4TL, England

GPM   Gunnersbury Park Museum, Sadler Collection, London W3 8LQ, England

HH   Henry E. Huntington Library, 1141 Oxford Road, San Marino, CA 91108

HPL   Houston Public Library, 500 McKinney Avenue, Houston, TX 77001

HS   New York Historical Society Library, 170 Central Park W., New York, NY 10024

HU   Harvard University, Houghton Library, Cambridge, MA 02138

ISU   Indiana State University, Cunningham Memorial Library, Department of Rare Books, Terre Haute, IN 47809

IUL   Indiana University Library, 10th and Jordan Streets, Bloomington, IN 47401

ISU   Illinois State University, Milner Library, Normal, IL 61761

JGC   John Greene Chandler Memorial, 57 East George Hill Road, South Lancaster, MA 01561

JHU   Johns Hopkins University, John Work Garrett Library, 4545 North Charles Street, Baltimore, MD 21210

JLI   Jones Library, Inc., 43 Amity Street, Amherst, MA 01002

JPL   Jacksonville Public Library, 122 North Ocean Street, Jacksonville, FL 32202

JRUL   John Rylands University Library of Manchester, Oxford Road, Manchester MI3 9PP, England

KSC   Kansas State Teachers College, William Allen White Library, Emporia, KS 66801

LBC   London Borough of Camden, Hampstead Central Library, Swiss Cottage, London NW3 3HA, England

LBL   London Borough of Lambeth, Tate Central Library, Streatham High Road, London SW16, England

LC   Library of Congress, Rare Book Division, Main Building, Second Floor, East Side, Room 256, Washington, DC 20540

LCP   Library Company of Philadelphia, 1314 Locust Street, Philadelphia, PA 19107

LPL   Liverpool City Libraries, William Brown Street, Liverpool L3 8EW, England

MC   Milton's Cottage, Chalfont St. Giles, Buckinghamshire, England

MCh   Museum of Childhood, 38 High Street, Edinburgh EH1 1TG, Scotland

MH   Massachusetts Historical Society Library, 1154 Boylston Street, Boston, MA 02215

MaPL   Manchester Public Library, St. Peter's Square, Manchester M2 5PD, England

MiPL   Minneapolis Public Library, 300 Nicollet Avenue, Minneapolis, MN 55401

MTL   Mark Twain Shrine Library, Stoutsville, MO 65283

NL   Newberry Library, 60 West Walton Street, Chicago, IL 60610

NU   Northwestern University, Evanston, IL 60201

NYPL   New York Public Library, Fifth Avenue and 42nd Street, New York, NY 10018

NYPL-A New York Public Library, Arents Collection, Fifth Avenue and 42nd Street, New York, NY 10018

NYPL-B New York Public Library, Berg Collection, Fifth Avenue and 42nd Street, Room 320, New York, NY 10018

NYPL-SC New York Public LIbrary, Spencer Collection, Fifth Avenue and 42nd Street, Room 324, New York, NY 10018

OHS   Ohio Historical Society, 71st and 17th Avenues, Columbus, OH 43211

PFL   Philadelphia Free Public Library, Rare Book Department, Logan Square, Philadelphia, PA 19103

PI   Pratt Institute Library, Ryerson Street, Brooklyn, NY 11205

PLC   Public Library of Cincinnati and Hamilton County, Department of Rare Books and Special Collections, 800 Vine Street, Cincinnati, OH 45202

PLP   Providence Public Library, The Edith Wetmore Collection, 150 Empire Street, Providence, RI 02903

PM   Pierpont Morgan Library, 29 East 36th Street, New York, NY 10016

PPL   Pomona Public Library, Pomona CA 91766

PSL   Pennsylvania State Library, Education Bldg., Box 1601, Walnut and Commonwealth, Harrisburg, PA 17126

PU   Princeton University, Rare Books and Special Collections, Firestone Library, Princeton, NJ 08540

RC   Rosenbach Collection, Philadelphia Free Public Library, Logan Square, Philadelphia, PA 19103

RHL   Rutherford B. Hayes Library, 1337 Hayes Avenue, Fremont, OH 43420

RLA   Rosenberg Library Association, Fox Rare Book Room, 2310 Sealy, Galveston, TX 77550

RPL   Revere Public Library, 179 Beach Street, Revere, MA 02151

SCSC   Southern Connecticut State College, Carolyn Sherwin Bailey Collection, 501 Crescent Street, New Haven, CT 06515

SDPL   San Diego Public Library, Wangenheim Room, 820 E Street, San Diego, CA 92101

SFPL   San Francisco Public Library, Department of Rare Books and Special Collections, Civic Center, San Francisco, CA 94102

SiC   Simmons College, School of Library Science, 300 Fenway, Boston, MA 02115

SIU   Southern Illinois University at Carbondale, Morris Library, Carbondale, IL 62901

SPL   South Portland Public Library, South Portland, ME 04106

SU   Syracuse University, E. S. Bird Library, George Arents Research Library for Special Collections, Syracuse, NY 13210

ST   St. Bride Foundation Institute, Printing Library, London ECH Y8EE, England

TC   Trinity College Library, College Street, Dublin 2, Ireland

TCL   Trinity College Library, Watkinson Library, 300 Summit Street, Hartford, CT 06106

TPL   Toronto Public Library, Osborne Collection, Boys and Girls House, 40 St. George Street, Toronto, Ontario M55 2E4, Canada

TUL   Temple University Library, Berks and 13th Streets, Philadelphia, PA 19122

UBC   University of British Columbia, Vancouver V6T 1W5, British Columbia, Canada

UC   University of Colorado, Rare Books Room, Norlin Library, Boulder, CO 80302

UCB   University of California at Berkeley, Bancroft Library, Berkeley, CA 94720

UCL   University of Cambridge Library, Cambridge CB3 9DR, England

UCLA   University of California at Los Angeles, William Andrews Clark Memorial Library, 2520 Cimarron Street at West Adams Boulevard, Los Angeles, CA 90018

UCSB   University of California at Santa Barbara, Department of Special Collections, University Library, Santa Barbara, CA 93106

UF   University of Florida, Department of Special Collections, University of Florida Library, Gainesville, FL 32601

UI   University of Illinois, Rare Book Room, 346 Library Building, Urbana, IL 61801

UIo   University of Iowa, Iowa City, IA 52240

UL   University of Louisville, Rare Book Room, Belnap Campus, Louisville, KY 40208

UM   University of Michigan, Department of Rare Books, 711 Hatcher, Graduate Library, Ann Arbor, MI 48104

UMi   University of Minnesota, Kerlan Collection, Wilson Library, Minneapolis, MN 55455

UNC   University of North Carolina at Chapel Hill, North Carolina Collection, University Library, Chapel Hill, NC 27514

UNCG   University of North Carolina at Greensboro, Walter Clinton Jackson Library, Greensboro, NC 27412

UO   University of Oklahoma Library, Rare Book Division, Norman, OK 73069

UOr   University of Oregon, 15th and Kincaid Streets, Eugene, OR 97403

UOx   University of Oxford, Bodleian Library, Oxford OX1 3BG, England

UP   University of Pittsburgh, Special Collections Department, 363 Hillman Library, Pittsburgh, PA 15260

UPa   University of Pennsylvania, Van Pelt Library, Rare Book Division, 3420 Walnut Street, Philadelphia, PA 19104

USF   University of San Francisco, Rare Books Room, Richard A. Gleeson Library, 2130 Fulton Street, San Francisco, CA 94117

UTA-L   University of Texas at Austin, Harold A. Larabee Collection, Harry Ransome Center, Austin, TX 78712

UW   University of Washington, Seattle, WA 98105

UWi   University of Wisconsin, Memorial Library, 728 State Street, Madison, WI 53706

WC   Williams College, Chapin Library, Williamstown, MA 01267

WCE   Whitelands College of Education, West Hill, Putney, London SW15, England

WCL   Wheaton College Library, Norton, MA 02766

WKU   Western Kentucky University, Louisville, KY 40201

WPL   Westerly Public Library, Box 356, Broad Street, Westerly, RI 02891

WU   Washington University, 6600 Millbrook, St. Louis, MO 63130

YES   York Elementary School, Alexis I. DuPont Special School District, Greenville, DL 19807

YU   Yale University, Beinecke Rare Book and Manuscript Library, Wall and High Streets, New Haven, CT 06520

Figure 1. A medieval scribe at work. Woodcut from Perceforest's *Histoire du Roy*, Paris, 1528; Newberry Library, Chicago. Shows typical writing materials used by the scribes as well as the room in which they worked. Note the window at the scribe's left; candles were not permitted, as they were considered too dangerous to the manuscripts. Two codices lie on the table in the foreground.

Figure 2. Lindisfarne Gospel manuscript, before A.D. 698; the Incarnation Initial from the Gospel of St. John begins: "In principio . . ." showing the text written in the majuscule hand, five rows of decorative capitals. The complex pattern contains many details, such as the girl's head in the letter C and the small dog's head at the lower left interlaced border, as well as the open passageway in the lower right indicating the continuing of the message on the next page. Original in color. Cotton Nero D. IV, f. 211; reproduced by permission of the British Library.

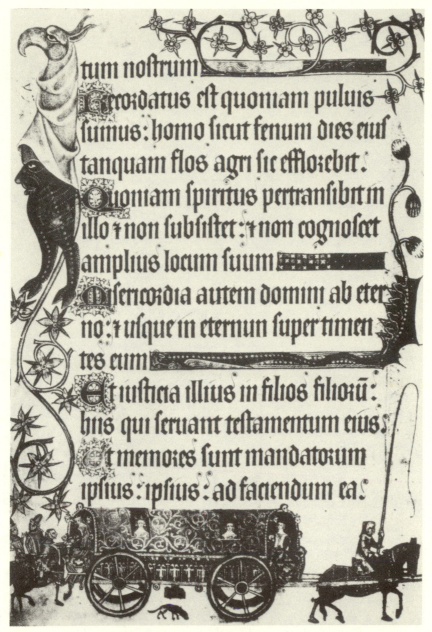

Figure 3. From the Luttrell Psalter, a fourteenth-century illuminated manuscript made for Sir Geoffrey Luttrell; includes, along with religious mattter, fabulous beasts as well as scenes from everyday life. In the original, the horse shown here is preceded by four other beasts, all decorated in elaborate harnesses and heavily shod. Original in color.

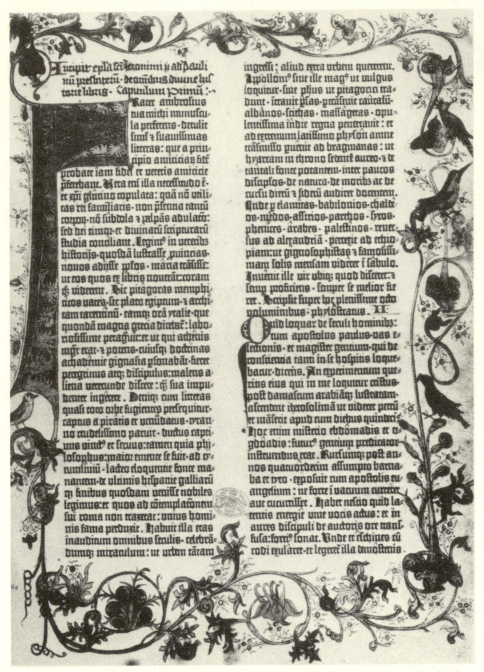

Figure 4. Gutenberg Bible, Mainz, ca. 1456. First book printed with movable type; illuminations added by hand.

ranne in to the forest / And whanne the wyld beestes sawe
hym come / they were so ferdfull that they alle beganne to flee /
For they wend / that it had be the lyon / And the mayster of
the asse serched and soughte his asse in every place al aboute
And as he had soughte longe / he thought that he wold go in
to the forest for to see yf his asse were there / And as soone as

Figure 5. Part of a page from William Caxton's *Aesop's Fables*, showing woodcut with typeface, 1484. From *Illustrating Children's Books* by Henry C. Pitz, Watson-Guptill Publications, New York, 1963.

Figure 6. Frontispiece and first page of The Gospel of St. Matthew from Tyndale's New Testament, Cologne, 1525, by Peter Quentell. By permission of the British Library.

Hys ys the boke of the generaciõ of Jesus Christ the sonne of David/The sonne also of Abra Chā. � Abraham and David are fyrst rehearsid/ because that christe was chefly promysed vnto them.

☞Abraham begatt Isaac:

Isaac begatt Jacob:

Jacob begatt Judas and hys bre= (thren:

Judas begat Phares: (thren:
  and Zaram of thamar:

Phares begatt Esrom:

Esrom begatt Aram:

Aram begatt Aminadab:

Aminadab begatt naasson:

Naasson begatt Salmon:

Salmon begatt boos of rahab:

Boos begatt obed of ruth:

Obed begatt Jesse:

Jesse begatt david the kynge:

☞David the kynge begatt Solomon/of her that was the (wyfe of vry:

Solomon begat roboam:

Roboam begatt Abia:

Abia begatt asa:

Asa begatt iosaphat:

Josaphat begatt Joram:

Joram begatt Osias:

Osias begatt Joatham:

Joatham begatt Achas:

Achas begatt Ezechias:

Ezechias begatt Manasses:

Manasses begatt Amon:

Amon begatt Josias:

Josias begatt Jechonias and his brethren about the tyme of the captivite of babilen

☞After they were led captive to babilon/Jechonias begatt

Saynct mathew leveth out certeyne generacions/ z describeth Christes linage from solomõ/after the lawe of Moses/ but Lucas describeth it accordyng to nature/frõ nathan solomõs brother. For the lawe calleth them a mannes childrẽ which his broder begatt of his wyfe lefte behynde hym after his death.deu.xv.c.

the place of execution, was there tied to the ſtake, and then ſtrangled firſt by the hangman, and afterward with fire conſumed in the morning at the towne of Filford, an. 1536. cry-

ing thus at the ſtake with a feruent zeale, and a loude voice, Lord open the King of Englands eyes.

Such was the power of his doctrine, and ſinceritie of his

The Martyrdome and burning of maiſter VVilliam Tindall, in Flaunders, by Filford Caſtle.

Figure 7. From Foxe's *Book of Martyrs*, printed in London by John Day, 1563. Woodcut shows William Tyndale, translator of the first Bible printed in English, being strangled and burned at the stake in the castle of Vilvorde on October 6, 1536.

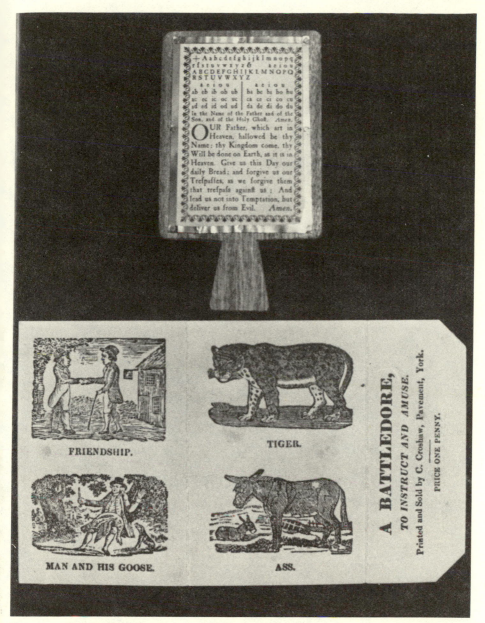

Figure 8. Hornbook and battledore, early forms of children's lesson books. A typical hornbook of about 1450, approximately three by five inches. The hornbook is thought to be the first lesson book designed for children's use. Below, a battledore; a refinement of the hornbook. The battledore is thought to have been designed in John Newbery's workshop about 1746. Used by permission of The Horn Book, Inc. Original of battledore is in the Boston Public Library.

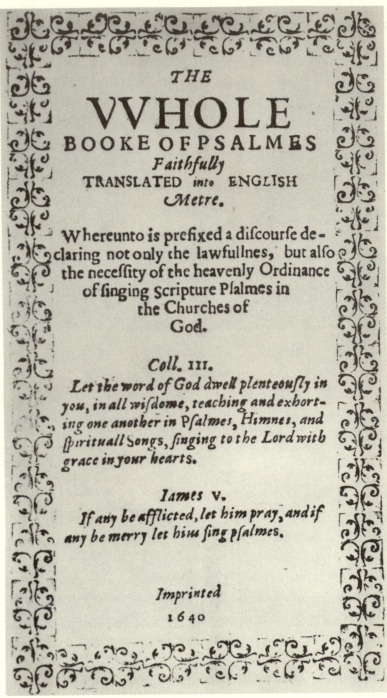

Figure 9. Title page from *The Whole Booke of Psalmes* (Bay Psalm Book), which is thought to be the earliest surviving piece of book printing in North America; printed by Stephen Daye, 1640. Original in the New York Public Library.

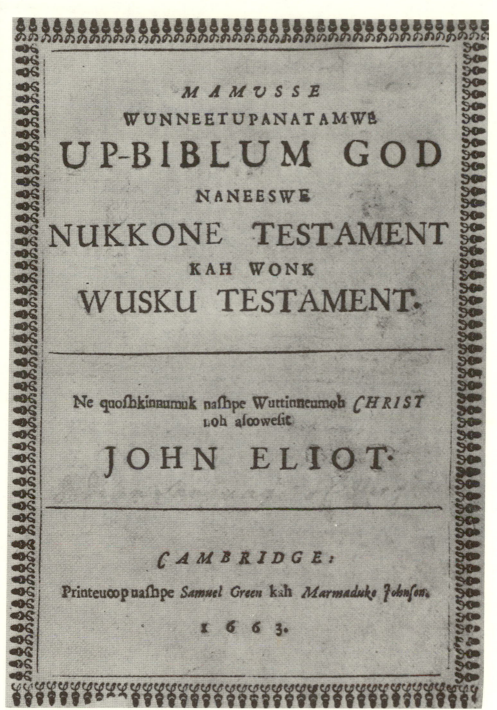

Figure 10. Title page from *Mamvsse Wunneetupanatamwe Up-Biblum God*, an Indian language translation of the Bible by the Rev. John Eliot, 1663; printed by Samuel Green and Marmaduke Johnson. By permission of the British Library.

Thus thou hast seen in short, all things that can be shewed, and hast learned the *chief Words* of the *English* and *Latin* *Tongue*.	Ita vidisti summatim res omnes quæ poterunt ostendi, & didicisti *Voces primarias* *Anglicæ* & *Latinæ* *Linguæ*.
Go on now and read other good *Books* diligently, and thou shalt become *learned, wise,* and *godly*.	Perge nunc & lege diligenter alias bonos *Libros,* ut fias *doctus, sapiens,* & *pius*.
Remember these things; fear God, and call upon him, that he may bestow upon thee the *Spirit of Wisdom*. Farewell.	Memento horum; Deum time, & invoca eum, ut largiatur tibi *Spiritum Sapientiæ*. Vale.

Figure 11. Last body page and first index page of the 1728 edition of Johann Comenius' *Orbis Sensualium Pictus* (Visible World); translated by Charles Hoole; printed in London by John and Benjamin Sprint; approximately 3¼ by 5½ inches.

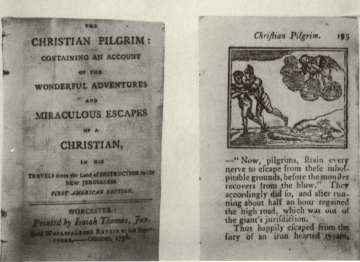

Figure 12. Title page of the 1678 edition of Bunyan's *Pilgrim's Progress*, printed for Nathaniel Ponder in London; approximately 3½ by 5¼ inches. Below, title page (on left) and typical body page (on right) of the first American edition, printed by Isaiah Thomas, Jr., Worcester, Mass., 1798; approximately 2½ by 4 inches. Originals in the Pierpont Morgan Library, New York.

A Little Pretty
POCKET-BOOK,
Intended for the
INSTRUCTION and AMUSEMENT
OF
LITTLE MASTER *TOMMY*,
AND
PRETTY MISS *POLLY*.
With Two Letters from
JACK the GIANT-KILLER;
AS ALSO
A BALL and PINCUSHION;
The Ufe of which will infallibly make *Tommy*
a good Boy, and *Polly* a good Girl.

To which is added,
A LITTLE SONG-BOOK,
BEING
A *New Attempt* to teach Children the Ufe of
the *Englifh Alphabet*, by Way of Diverfion.

LONDON:
Printed for J. NEWBERY, at the *Bible and Sun*
in St. *Paul's Church-Yard.* 1767.
[Price Six-pence bound.]

Delectando monemus
Instruction with Delight

Figure 13. Frontispiece and title page of the 1769 edition of John Newbery's *A Pretty Little Pocket-Book*; the 1744 edition is thought to be Newbery's first publication for children's amusement; approximately 2½ by 4 inches.

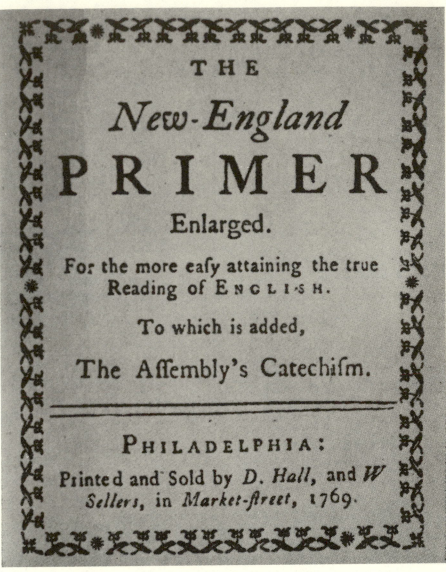

Figure 14. Title page and first page of *The New England Primer* showing the beginning of the alphabet, "In Adam's Fall . . ."; printed in Philadelphia by Hall and Sellers, 1769.

A   In *Adam*'s Fall,
We finned all.

B   Thy *Life* to mend,
This Book attend.

C   The *Cat* doth play,
And after flay.

D   A *Dog* will bite,
A Thief at Night.

E   An *Eagle*'s flight,
Is out of fight.

F   The idle Fool,
Is whipt at School.

Harlequin in a forest with the Taylor
Going to cut of his Head with his Shears.

A Proclamation being made
That Harlequin was seen at Dover
A Taylor with his Sheers displayd
Would cut his Head off soon as over.
Moral.
Yet tho' this Man was strong & Stout
Turn up, you'll find what came about.

Figure 15. Typical page from Robert Sayer's *Harlequin's In-*

Harlequin taken Prisoner.

Ha! Ha! my Friends a pretty Scene o
The like was ne'er before
The charming witty Harlequino
Is fastned Sure and Sure.
Moral.
Tricking you find will ne'er prevail
Turn up and then persue the Tale.

vasion, 1770, a representative eighteenth-century harlequinade.

HISTORIES
OR
TALES
OF
PAST TIMES,

TOLD BY
MOTHER GOOSE.

WITH
MORALS.

Written in French by M. PERRAULT.
And Englished by G. M. Gent.

The SIXTH EDITION, corrected.

SALISBURY:

Printed and fold by B. COLLINS; alfo by
CARNAN and NEWBERY, in St. Paul's
Church-Yard; and S. CROWDER, in Pater-
nofter-Row, London, M,DCC,LXXII.
(Price 9d. neatly bound.)

Figure 16. Frontispiece and title page from Perrault's *Histories or Tales of Past Times, Told by Mother Goose*; translated from the French by G. M. Gent; sixth edition, 1772, printed by B. Collins; approximately 2 3/8 by 3 3/8 inches.

Figure 17. Double-page spread from Randolph Caldecott's *The Diverting History of John Gilpin*, a poem by William Cowper. Routledge, 1878. Original in color. Used by permission of Frederick Warne & Company, Inc.

Figure 18. Frontispiece from *The Baby's Bouquet*, arranged and decorated by Walter Crane, 1878. Original in color. Used by permission of Frederick Warne & Company, Inc.

The wonderful music with shouting and laughter.

Figure 19. From Robert Browning's *The Pied Piper of Hamelin*, illustrated by Kate Greenaway, 1888. Original in color. Used by permission of Frederick Warne & Company, Inc.

Figure 20. Facing page to Chapter One of *The Story of King Arthur and His Knights*, written and illustrated by Howard Pyle, 1903. Used by permission of Charles Scribner's Sons.

Figure 21. Cover from Wanda Gág's *Millions of Cats*. Used by permission of Coward, McCann and Geoghegan, New York. Copyright, 1928.

Figure 22. From Hans Christian Andersen's "The Emperor's New Clothes," illustrated by Fritz Kredel in *The Complete Andersen*, translated by Jean Hersholt, Heritage, 1942.

FIFTEEN CENTURIES
OF
CHILDREN'S LITERATURE

Chapter 1

Anglo-Saxon Period (ca. 523–1099)

HISTORICAL BACKGROUND

Before the Roman occupation (ca. 55 B.C.-A.D. 410), Celtic tribes had swept into Britain from central Europe, beginning about 600 B.C., in three waves: first, the Gaels, who penetrated the north and west; next, the Britons, who about 400 B.C. pushed back the Gaels and occupied the eastern and northern portions of the islands; and last, the Belgae, the most advanced of the invading tribes, who in the first century B.C. drove back the Britons and occupied much of their land. By the time of Julius Caesar's expedition in 55 B.C., the Romans found a single Celtic race, but one divided into warring tribes with organized governments and social classes consisting of priests (druids), warriors, wealthy farmers and cattle owners, small farmers and craftsmen, and slaves. The Celts lived in fortified homes and villages, dressed well, and owned expertly wrought objects of metal and clay—utensils, jewelry, and weapons. Spinning, weaving, and dyeing cloth were common. The tribes traded with one another as well as with other countries. The earliest merchants to visit Britain were the Phoenicians, who traded in metals. About 330 B.C., the Greeks opened up extensive trading in tin, lead, enamels, and jewels—paid for at first by barter and later by coinage.

When the Romans conquered Britain in A.D. 43, they took over an artistic, sometimes bellicose people who had attained a relatively high degree of civilization as evidenced in their arts, crafts, and literature. The Celts' literature was oral and largely unconscious but distinctive, consisting of ballads, lays, songs, and legends, usually recounting battles. The Roman invaders brought with them the concept of centralized government. Christianity also arrived during their rule. Although the development of the Christian church would remain sporadic, Christian monasteries and schools, which would become firmly established in Ireland by the fifth century, helped to temper warlike impulses. Thriving Romano-British towns grew up, including London, which absorbed most of the influx of merchants and artisans. Although the central government administered taxation and legislation, local governments (citizens' councils) held most of the power. Residences, fortifications, town designs, and roads—which would bind Britain for centuries—as well as Roman art and crafts, reflected the degree to which Roman culture had permeated the region. For the most part, Roman Britain lived at peace: the Roman period would be the longest peaceful time in British history.

About A.D. 250, raiders from the north, the Scots, began to attack the western coasts. Soon the eastern and southern coasts were attacked by Saxons from mainland Europe. Britain suffered severely. When the Roman forces were recalled in the fifth century to defend the empire at home, the Britons, who were mostly scattered farmers, were vulnerable to the ever-increasing attacks from the Angles, the Saxons, and the Jutes. In 367 these three tribes made simultaneous attacks on the north, west, and east. Despite the frenzied efforts of the Britons to stop the invasions and the subsequent migrations, these Germanic tribes spread rapidly across the land, and Roman civilization was destroyed almost totally in most of Great Britain.

It is thought that during this period one Christian Briton chief, King Arthur, defeated the invaders temporarily (ca. 520). But the migrations continued, finally driving the Romanized Celts into the fringes of the land or absorbing those who remained. Between 450 and 800, the main island, the largest portion of which is now called England because of the power of the ruling Angles, became almost entirely Germanic (Anglo-Saxon), with Germanic language, laws, and social customs. Pagan worship of northern gods dominated, but eventually (ca. 563-664) Celtic (Irish) missionaries from the north, led by Saint Columba in 563, with their dauntless faith and devotion, and Roman missionaries, led by Saint Augustine in 597, with their strong sense of church organization, brought about the conversion of the Anglo-Saxon tribes to Christianity, resulting in a refinement of pagan beliefs and a general expansion of civilization. Social and cultural progress, however, was retarded by the bitter struggles for supremacy among the Anglo-Saxon kingdoms.

In spite of the political struggles, by the seventh century Northumbria had become a recognized seat of learning, attracting scholars from much of Europe. A few small libraries existed in monasteries. By the eighth century, the work of scholars and poets such as Caedmon, Bede, Alcuin, Cynewulf, and Anselm is well documented. About 900, an anonymous poet (probably an Anglican monk) wrote an epic poem called *Beowulf*, which reveals the mixing of Christian and pagan beliefs, as well as the everyday life of the people. The narrative relates the story of a Germanic hero who had supposedly flourished at the same time as the Celtic Arthur.

Just as a unified, Christian, Anglo-Saxon society was beginning to take shape, a new wave of invasions from the north began. In the last decade of the ninth century, raiding Danes stimulated Alfred the Great of Wessex (871-899) to defiance, with some success. Under Alfred, the Danish kingdoms were consolidated into a single kingdom of England. Alfred's victory also resulted in a revival of law, schools, and books. Significantly Alfred favored the use of the vernacular over Latin for writing literature. Under Alfred, the *Anglo-Saxon Chronicle*—a compilation of the annals of English history from the start of the Christian era and the first major work to be written in Anglo-Saxon (that is, English)—was begun in 891. Alfred also translated Latin classical writings into Anglo-Saxon and encouraged the use of the vernacular for the portions of the Bible given to lay people. But the use of the language of the people as the language of literature was soon to give way; the last surviving poem in Anglo-Saxon, *The Battle of Maldon,* was written about 991.

When Saint Dunstan, archbishop of Canterbury (960-988), restored the Benedictine monasteries in the tenth century, Latin was acclaimed once more as the language of learning and literature. Priests were ordered to help the poor and to teach Latin to boys in monastery schools "freely and for nothing." And learning advanced; a few libraries held as many as two or three hundred volumes, but Anglo-Saxon translations played a minor role. During Dunstan's time, defenses of the kingdom were strengthened, respect for law grew, and economic activity, including trade, increased.

In order to carry out expanding trade, learning—that is, reading, writing, and ciphering—revived somewhat, but the general status of England as a nation was not advanced. Its chief business was agriculture, which was administered by village communities, not individuals. Manufacturing was not widespread and was carried on in homes. Dwellings were generally primitive (rough stones, thatched roofs), although noblemen lived in large halls. Dress was coarse even for the rich, but garments often were decorated with ornaments.

Repeated Danish raids at the end of the tenth century devastated most churches and monasteries, especially in Northumbria and Mercia, severely curtailing the advancement of civilization, wreaking havoc in church organization, and sweeping away almost every trace of northern high culture. For a time, a Danish king, Canute, ruled all England. But on his death in 1035 his two inept sons ascended his throne. By 1042 England returned to the rule of an English king, Edward the Confessor.

In spite of a short period of relative calm, the northern raiders had so weakened England that another invasion was inevitable. In 1066, William of Normandy conquered the Saxons (the English) at the Battle of Hastings, and Britain was once again an occupied nation. Even before the conquest, Edward the Confessor had introduced the new (Norman) culture, for he had a Norman mother and a Norman education.

Through shrewd use of administrative power, William managed to centralize the government by requiring firm allegiance to the Crown. One of his most strategic moves was to order in 1086 a survey of all landholdings, properties, freemen, oxen, horses, sheep, and pigs in the whole of England, except the north. The resulting document, known as the *Domesday Book,* enabled the king to know what obligations every landowner owed him. Its influence would last for centuries.

Ironically, this fourth and last takeover to date, the Norman Conquest, with its military might, law courts, business acumen, organized church, and particular culture and language (French), would sow the seeds of a permanent English civilization.

DEVELOPMENT OF BOOKS

The literature (legends, ballads, songs, lays, and tales) of the early Celts was entirely oral; however, by the third century, the northern invaders had brought a runic alphabet of twenty-four characters made up of non-cursive letters which could be carved in stone, metal, wax tablets, or on bark. (*Book* comes from the Anglo-Saxon word *boc,* meaning tree bark.) Roman incursions first brought the Roman alphabet. It would be further established by Irish missionaries after the mid-sixth century. By the ninth or tenth century it would replace completely pagan runes. In Northumbria, preachers taught their flocks that the Word should be written in letters more pleasing to God than the heathenish runes.

The geometric Roman alphabet of the Latin language was first carved into stone, but gradually gave way to handwriting on a soft surface, which permitted rounding off certain angles. The first calligraphy (handwriting) was done in a large uncial style (*uncia* meaning inch) in the fourth century. As writing surfaces improved, the uncial style gave way to the smaller, rounded half-uncial (in about the sixth century) and to the minuscules (in about the eighth century), the size most familiar to us today.

The uncial style of calligraphy had a long history. It was first inscribed on ancient book rolls (scrolls), which had been used in Europe, North Africa, and Asia. The first book rolls, in fact, were made from papyrus, invented by the Egyptians about 4000 B.C.; papyrus was a material soft enough to be rolled. Later, parchment, made of goat and sheep skins, was used as the writing surface. The supple parchment sheets were pasted end to end, rolled up on cylinders of wood, ivory, or metal, and sometimes fitted with elaborate knobs for handles. Some of these rolls were short, from one to three feet; others were as long as forty feet. These rolls, which were stored on shelves, in cupboards, or in vases, were identified by small projecting labels called *tituli.* Because the roll was wrapped or "revolved" around its cylinder, it was called a *volume,* meaning a thing that is rolled around something else.

Although the codex, the precursor of the modern book, had originated in China and was known in Greece and Rome for centuries, it was first brought to Britain during the Roman occupation in the second century. Even as early as the first century before Christ, a collection of Roman laws, inscribed in wax on wooden tablets and fastened along one side, was referred to as a codex. (In Latin, the word *codex* means the trunk of a tree.) As the codex system developed, its leaves changed from a few wax tablets, perhaps six or eight, to a group of folded leaves, usually made of parchment, bound at one side. Eventually these leaves were protected by heavy covers of wood or leather attached on one side with leather thongs and later with coarse thread. By the fourth century, vellum (from the Old French meaning *calf*) found the highest favor with scribes in Britain, as well as elsewhere, because of its superior writing surface and ability to take gouache (opaque water colors mixed with gum); papyrus had taken only line drawings and water-colors. Vellum, that is, calf skin—although vellum would eventually come to mean almost any kind of animal skin—provided a better surface for writing and paint than parchment, and it became the most sought-after material for manuscripts.

The leaves of the early codex were usually squarish with several columns of calligraphy on each page; occasionally pictures, drawn or painted by the scribes, were fitted into the columns. Later codices were taller and narrower with two columns of writing usual; thus, the illustration, if there were one, was either a single-column picture (sometimes full page) or two miniature pictures placed side by side. In some cases, pictures filled the upper half of the page with the writing underneath, but some pages were divided into four rectangular picture blocks. Some illustrations were executed in outline drawings only, such as in the *Utrecht Psalter* of the ninth century; others were in plain ink or opaque paint based on a tempera medium made from egg and gum, such as was used in a copy of the *Utrecht Psalter* made at Canterbury about A.D. 1000. Although red usually dominated, the illumina-tion might be done in gold, silver, and other brilliant colors. The illuminated portions of the pages, which consisted of gilded painted illustrations, be-came known as "miniatures" (from the Latin *miniare,* which means "to paint with vermilion").

As manuscripts became more elaborate and more likely to be influenced by styles brought from Europe, the decorations, which were now often done by illustration specialists, became more heavily illuminated with fluid gold and contrasting silver—all written in graceful styles of calligraphy. At their best, illuminated manuscripts in codex form were works of art, per-haps conceived and executed by a single person, or by scribe and illustrator working closely. Other manuscripts were assembly-line duplications that were done by copyists, proofreaders, and illustrators, each monk doing his separate job somewhat independently of the others.

Of all the religious book types, Gospel books (evangeliaries) were the most typical illuminated books until about 1000. In the following two centuries, the Psalter (a book of psalms) was the most lavishly decorated book.

Although there were a few exceptions, the illuminated manuscript of the Middle Ages was almost exclusively a monastic work. Monasteries, often remote sanctuaries, provided a quiet, relatively safe life for scholars and artists who sometimes assumed the task of creating books, but more often copied the Bible and other sacred works for their own monastery's library or for other scholars elsewhere. While methods and facilities differed, the *scriptores* (monks or nuns) worked in the monastery's *scriptorium,* a workshop room usually located above the main house, or in separate rooms with a window for light. Candles were considered too dangerous because of possible fire damage to the manuscripts, so all work was done in the daylight hours, usually six hours at a time. Vellum or parchment, pens, inks, paint, knives, awls, and rulers were provided by the *armarius* (or *librarius*), the presiding officer, who also took care of the cataloging and shelving. Scribes were not permitted to talk; they could ask for materials but only by an elaborate set of signals. In every way they were protected from interruption in order to avoid errors; only the highest official could interrupt them at work. And scribes were valued. It was as serious a crime to kill a scribe as a bishop. (*See figure 1.*)

Each monk was given his vellum or parchment in sections; the sheets were folded and arranged in the order in which the book would be completed. The limits of the writing and decoration were ruled in with marginal lines; the vellum was held to a board by awls. Guide rules for the lines of calligraphy were ruled onto the vellum with a blunt tool. The vellum was arranged so that the two facing pages matched, that is, both were hair side, or both were flesh side. After the scribe's work of four sheets in eight leaves was finished, a proofreader compared the copy with the original, a *rubricator* inserted the "rubrics" (from the Latin *ruber,* meaning red) in red ink. Rubrics consisted of the opening lines of the text, the initial letters of the sections, the title, and the colophon which came at the end of the book and provided the name of the scribe, the place of copying, and the date. If the book was to be illustrated, the sheets were then sent to an illuminator or decorator, and finally to the *ligator* (binder). All of this work was regarded as a form of religious worship. Until the fourteenth century, illumination would be almost exclusively confined to religious manuscripts, since religion was considered the most worthy subject for glorification. As bearers of the Holy Word, illuminated manuscripts themselves became venerated objects. All through the Middle Ages, illumination was never regarded as mere illustration; its purpose was sacred adornment.

In the sixth century, the first great development of illuminated manuscripts began in Ireland, which had become a refuge for classical culture. It had been Christianized in the fifth century by Saint Patrick, who had come from Gaul. By the sixth century, there were over three hundred monasteries in Ireland and Scotland. The Irish monks, schooled in Oriental and Byzantine cultures through study, pilgrimages to Rome, and visits to French and Italian monasteries, were artists and scholars of the highest order. That they should be the leading makers of books is not surprising.

By the seventh century, Irish-style manuscripts had found their way to northern England, to the monasteries of Wearmouth and Jarrow, and especially to Lindisfarne. The resulting Hiberno-Saxon style was marked by elaborate linear ornamentation made of spirals that formed intertwining monsters and ornate, complex, interlacing initials. Such ornamentation, especially at the beginnings of books, or of sections of books, dominated manuscript production in Britain well into the ninth century. While early examples of the Hiberno-Saxon style date back to the sixth century, such as *Cathach of Saint Columba,* better known examples come from the seventh century, including the *Book of Durrow,* and from the eighth century, including the *Book of Kells,* produced at Saint Columba's monastery and said to contain the finest example of Irish calligraphy. The *Book of Kells* has been called the most beautiful manuscript book ever created.

As noted, the Irish school of calligraphy and illuminating reached England through Irish monks. At the oldest of these northern English monasteries, Lindisfarne, one of the most characteristic examples of the Hiberno-Saxon style of manuscripts produced in England, the *Lindisfarne Gospels,* was made about 700. The *Gospels* contains 258 leaves, each measuring about thirteen by ten inches and made of heavy vellum. The Latin text is beautifully designed in half-uncial characters. Five full pages of the *Gospels* are elaborately decorated in cruciform design; six pages contain highly ornamented text; four full-page miniatures show the Evangelists as scribes seated at desks, complete with cushions and footstools; sixteen pages contain the Canon tables fully ornamented; many other pages contain elaborate initials in various sizes. One ornamented page, for example, contains designs of eighty-eight birds arranged in a symmetrical pattern, as well as four single birds ingeniously interwoven between the points of the cross and corresponding panels. From such work, it is clear that manuscript artists took their work seriously; they cared enormously about color arrangement, detail, balance, and total design. (*See figure 2.*)

That such manuscripts were revered cannot be doubted. The *Lindisfarne Gospels,* for example, was held in such respect that a legend about its rescue from the sea is still remembered. According to the story, the *Gospels* was washed overboard in a storm and thought to be lost. After many attempts to recover the book and much lamentation by the patrons of the book, the manuscript was finally found, washed ashore completely intact, "exhibiting all of its outer splendor of jewels and gold and all the beauty of its pages and writing within, as though it had never been touched by water . . . and this is believed to be due to the merits of Saint Cuthbert himself and those who made the book. . . ."

By the tenth century, probably because of monastic reforms taking place at the time, famous schools of illumination developed in southern England, especially at Winchester. The Winchester style was marked by leafy foliage, decorative rosettes, and double frameworks, as seen in the *Benedictional of Saint Aethewold*. Most manuscripts in this style were in full color, but some miniatures were done in outline only; still others used only decorative initials composed of interlaced animals' heads.

Although it occurred in many distinctive styles, the illuminated manuscript in codex format would remain the most common form of the book until the introduction of movable-type printing in the fifteenth century. But the illuminated manuscripts would undergo many stages of development.

ATTITUDES TOWARD AND TREATMENT OF CHILDREN

In the earliest days children were not greatly valued. It was not uncommon in Britain and on the continent to dispose of sickly or unwanted offspring through abandonment, killing, or selling into slavery. Although well-to-do children were far more likely to survive than the poor, records of recurring legislation from the earliest Christian times to as late as the eighth century indicate that practices of infanticide and child sale must have been deeply ingrained and widely practiced. Clearly, the coming of Christianity tempered attitudes toward children, but throughout the Middle Ages the newborn child was far from secure. Empathy for infants was not part of the early British parents' psychological charge.

In fact, life in early Britain was hard for everyone. Frequent wars, first among the Celtic tribes themselves and then with northern invaders, rampant disease, and inadequate food and shelter made survival paramount.

Before the coming of the Romans, early Britons did not cluster in towns. Adults and children lived in scattered family units; the *sibb* consisted of paternal and maternal kinships, that is, a family composed of blood relations on both sides. Several families together made up a tribe. With the departure of the Romans in the fifth century, the Britons moved into the deserted Roman towns, and life became somewhat more settled. Before long, however, invaders began their relentless forays into the relatively undefended islands.

In spite of almost continual warfare, British civilization began to take hold. Even the earliest Britons (the Celts) revered music, the recital of history, and poetry. We know that Celtic princes took bards with them on journeys to fight or hunt or colonize. Few refinements existed in even upper-class households; life was generally hard for young and old alike. Certain customs which were passed down from antiquity, such as sending infants out to wet nurses, prevailed. Mortality was high; if the children survived, some received certain kinds of training in their own homes—household and country duties, for instance. Others were placed in monasteries or in other households as servants, pages, ladies-in-waiting, oblates, or clerks.

Children of all classes heard oral literature (ballads, songs, lays, stories) of adults, but only upper-class children had what might be called formal education. In the earliest times the teaching had been done by druid priests who chanted their laws and theology in meters; later, teaching was taken over by Christian priests. After the establishment of Christian monastic schools in the sixth century, more formalized education began, with girls receiving schooling as well as boys, although boys were favored in general. As early as age seven, privileged children might go to Canterbury, Jarrow, Malmesbury, York, or one of the other monastic schools.

With the coming of schools came schoolbooks. The medieval monk, often poorly educated himself, had to decide if heathen philosophers were proper authors for his charges to study. Before long, the monks themselves—in particular Bede, Alcuin, Aelfric, and others—began writing books for the purpose of educating the young, and the curriculum became set: *trivium* (grammar, logic, rhetoric) and *quadrivium* (music, arithmetic, geometry, and astronomy). In practice, many young scholars often learned little more than some Latin grammar from meager textbooks, but most knew at least one admirable text—a fragment of the *Consolations of Philosophy* by Boethius. Although Boethius was at first considered a heathen, he was accepted as a Christian, at least in spirit; by the eighth century he was canonized. His work was taught to the young from the Middle Ages onward; still popular eight hundred years later, it was printed by England's first printer, William Caxton, in 1497.

Few other manuscript books were available for children's learning, for they were far too valuable. Children were generally taught by writing letters and words on slates from dictation or from seeing them in reading-lesson manuscripts.

In the monastic schools the monk sat, usually elevated, facing the young people, holding an open manuscript book (a codex) before him on a lectern. The children sat or knelt before him. Some early illuminated manuscripts show lay schoolmasters instead of monks who hold rods as well as books. If a monk had a corrective instrument, it was usually a ladle-shaped stick for beating the palm of the hand. Mixed schools of girls and boys were taught by nuns, and both nuns and monks used whippings when deemed necessary.

Music, that is, the chanting of Psalms, was an important part of the medieval child's schooling, as was the study of numbers, although monks were often more interested in the mystical application of numbers than numbers for calculating. Poetry, too, particularly after the introduction of Aldhelm's *De Laude Virginitatis,* was an important part of schooling. Aldhelm also wrote on the mystical significance of the number seven, but more importantly for education, he used what might be called the first method, that is, the classical use of dialogue or conversation, to impart information. Sometimes the dialogues were between the *Discipulus* and *Magister* or, as in Aelfric's *Colloquy,* between master and laborer, or between two famous people such as Alcuin and Pepin, Charlemagne's son. Other methods of educating were riddles and puzzles, especially scriptural puzzles.

The great teacher of the Middle Ages was the Venerable Bede, "the father of English learning," who produced forty-five books, mostly commentaries on the Scriptures; he also wrote on history, grammar, physics, astronomy, medicine, and music. His greatest work in Latin was the *Ecclesiastical History of the English Nation,* but he also translated the Gospel of Saint John into English. *De Natura Rerum* was probably his monumental work. It contained all that was known of natural science, natural history, botany, and astronomy; it would remain a standard textbook used with the young for centuries.

Other important teachers were Egbert of York, who collected the finest library of the time which was visited by scholars from all over Europe, and Alcuin, a disciple of Egbert, who founded monasteries and schools, and wrote textbooks. It was Alcuin who took the learning of Britain to France; before long, Alfred the Great would bring European scholars to Britain.

By the time of Alfred (ninth century), Danish incursions had brought learning and civilization to a low level in Britain. Desiring to promote learning, Alfred imported scholars, while he himself translated many books into the Anglo-Saxon vernacular for the edification of all. Other important educators were Aelfric, who compiled the first English grammar, *Vocabulary,* for the boys of Winchester Cathedral School, and wrote *Colloquy,* which reveals important keys to the life of children in medieval Britain. Aelfric told, for example, of the use of the rod as a correction for laziness, of the importance of proper diet, and of the importance of pitying the poor serf who was attached to the soil; the *Colloquy* also provided information about most occupations of the time. The *Colloquy* was introduced as an easy-reading book to promote the speaking of Latin which would be required of English schoolboys for the next four centuries, even at play.

Although the concept of a parent-child relationship as we have come to know it in later centuries did not then exist, few promising sons would have been denied the right to a monastic school education by their noble Anglo-Saxon fathers. But monastic education was only part of such a boy's life.

Although a few Anglo-Saxon towns existed, people in general favored life in isolated homesteads which in time developed into villages. Sturdy folk with hardy dispositions, the Anglo-Saxons were also capable of creating beauty in jewelry, trinkets and utensils, and beautifully illuminated manuscripts. But life for most people meant spending much of their time outdoors at work, with rich and poor children alike expected to be industrious. Girls were expected to know how to run a household and do needlework, while boys tended herds of cattle, drove oxen, and carried out other country duties.

In the house of a nobleman of the period, the whole household ate the main meal together with the family and guests sitting to one side of the saltcellar and the servants and chance wayfarers to the other. Only sharp knives and bowls were used for eating, while ale or wine was drunk from polished drinking horns trimmed in silver. The table, surrounded by talkative, often singing diners, would have been loaded with large dishes of loaves of bread, fish, fruits, and joints of mutton or beef, all in sharp contrast to the barley porridge served to school boys on bare monastery school tables surrounded by rows of silent monks. In their homes the children would have been dressed like their elders, with the boys, for example, wearing heavy fur or woolen tunics which were sometimes embroidered with gold on the hem, and clasped at the shoulder with a flat buckle or brooch. Both sexes wore jewelry— rings, beads, buckles, pendants, and necklaces often adorned with Christian symbols; they also owned combs and other useful personal objects.

Anglo-Saxon adults and children reveled in sports, especially hunting, hawking, horse racing, archery, chess, draughts, and other tests of skill that were played with wooden bats and wooden balls.

By the tenth century, the hardy though often-besieged Anglo-Saxons remained essentially simple, out-of-doors people; yet it seems clear that at least the upper classes were concerned that their promising children know some of the gentle virtues. (Learning was not wasted on the less-promising child.) While the training of the young consisted of knowing school subjects as well as practical knowledge, adults also saw to it that their offspring learned reverence for God and for parents, knowledge of Scriptures, self-control, and diligence in scholarship. Clearly, adults hoped that their progeny would be able to take up positions as military leaders, landholders, logicians, bards, musicians, and clergy.

ANNOTATED CHRONOLOGY

ca. 523

Anicus Manlius Severius Boethius's *De Consolatione Philosophiae* (an enormously popular Latin manuscript in four parts which introduced Platonic ideas and the nature of Christ to Europeans; the work was used by clergy sent to Britain to teach young scholars in monastic schools; young people probably found the parts containing the fable of the giants warring against Jupiter and other similar dramatic accounts the most interesting, although their teachers probably urged them to pay most attention to the parts telling of such things as the vanity of an overly eager pursuit of fame and the power and goodness of the Creator in governing and upholding the university; the author, a Roman statesman and scholar, grew in disfavor with the government until he was imprisoned; he wrote this work during that time; an Anglo-Saxon loose translation, made by Alfred the Great ca. 895, was one of the first books given to the Anglo-Saxons in their own tongue; Geoffrey Chaucer's translation, *The Consoloacion of Philosophie,* ca. 1380, was printed by William Caxton in 1478; Boethius translated many philosophical, rhetorical, and mathematical works from Greek; his translations from Aristotle greatly influenced the development of European scholasticism; the author is often cited as the last Roman writer of any note to show a good knowledge of Greek language and literature; the author's other work includes manuals of geometry, arithmetic, and music which were used in monastic schools throughout the medieval period). BM, UCL, YU

ca. 680

Aldhelm's *De Septenario, de Metris, Aenigmatibus, ac Pedum Regulis* (a lengthy manuscript in Latin verse which discusses the Biblical meaning of the number seven and includes one hundred riddles and puzzles which are closely connected to the ones found in *The Exeter Book* and the old Latin tract, *Symposii Aenigmata*; the author was probably the first to write a lesson book especially for children and to establish the pattern of writing for children in verse and in question-answer form; the author was Abbot of Malmsbury ca. 673 and Bishop of Sherborne in 705; the author's other work includes *De Laude Virginitatis*).

ca. 698

The Venerable Bede's *De Natura Rerum* (an informational manuscript in clear, understandable Latin which embodies all that was known in Bede's time about astronomy, botany, natural history, and science; the text is pervaded by a mystical spirit and contains fabulous stories in which mermaids and other fanciful creatures are "scientifically" described; portions served as a text for children for more than three hundred years; the Roman poet, Lucretius, wrote a six-book didactic poem titled *De Rerum Natura,* or *On the Nature of Things,* ca. 45 B.C., which outlined the complete science of the universe based on the philosophies of Democritus and Epicurus; the author's other work includes *Book of the Art of Poetry,* ca. 700; *Book of Orthography Digested in Alphabetical Order,* ca. 700; *Ecclesiastical His-*

tory, ca. 731, which contains "The Hymn of Caedmon," one of the earliest pieces of poetry in the English (Northumbrian dialect) language; the author, known as one of Europe's greatest historians, probably also wrote various textbooks such as a grammar book based on Donatus, a rhetoric book, a music book, and a book of arithmetic puzzles; Benedict's unparalleled library, ca. 674, made Bede's historical work possible). BL, BM, HH, UOx

ca. 760

Alcuin's *Disputatio Pippini cum Albino Scholastico* (a manuscript written in Latin strongly influenced by Virgil and organized in a question-answer format; the author studied at Egbert of York's famous cloister school; the author-theologian-scholar was a tutor for Charlemagne's sons and several girls of the household, ca. 781; the author's other work includes *De Orthographia,* ca. 770; *De Rhetorica et Virtutibus,* ca. 770; *De Dialectica,* ca. 785; the author spent his life furthering the cause of education; his Anglo-Saxon name was Ealhwine).

ca. 900-1100

Beowulf (anonymous; an Anglo-Saxon manuscript in poetic form which records an epic hero's deeds and reflects the everyday life and values of the people of the period; the story of Beowulf was popular in the oral tradition before being recorded in superior verse by an unknown monk; both poetic and prose versions of the Beowulf epic are available to today's children). BM

ca. 985

Aelfric's *Vocabulary* (a Latin–Anglo-Saxon manuscript dictionary which consists of lists of words from colors to farming gear which are arranged alphabetically; the author's other work includes *Colloquy,* ca. 980, a book of simple questions and answers on everyday subjects designed to teach pupils Latin using interlinear Anglo-Saxon gloss, which contains a collection of riddles and puzzles written in Latin hexameters for pupils to solve, and *De Grammatica,* ca. 990, a grammar designed for the boys of Winchester Cathedral School based on parts of Priscian's *Priscian Major* and *Priscian Minor* and on Aelius Donatus's *Ars Minor* and *Ars Grammatica,* ca. 350, which were the basic Latin grammars used for hundreds of years and often referred to as *The Donat,* which is thought by some authorities to be the first book printed from moveable type, preceding Gutenberg's Bible, under the title *De octo partibus orationis,* 1448; the author, who translated Latin into understandable Anglo-Saxon prose, was the last of the prominent Anglo-Saxon educators; the author's pupil, Aelfric Banta, enlarged some of his works; the author is also known as "Grammaticus").

ca. 1046

The Exeter Book (anonymous; a manuscript collection of Anglo-Saxon poetry which includes "Widsith," "Deor," "The Wanderer," and "The Seafarer"; the manuscript also includes a father's instructions to his child, riddles and puzzles in verse, and popular songs such as the ballad of John Barleycorn; the collection was presented to the Cathedral of Exeter, ca. 1070, by Loefric, Exeter's first bishop). ECL

ca. 1060

Saint Anselm's *Elucidarium* (a manuscript book of general information, that is, an encyclopedia, designed for young students by the Archbishop of Canterbury under William Rufus; an incomplete extant copy is thought to have been recorded by a Norman monk about 1197; a version of Anselm's work also exists in Icelandic; although many other works titled "Elucidarium" or "Lucydarye" were *cathechisms,* some versions, such as the *Elucidarius Liber,* give a simple account of animals, plants, and other common things; William Caxton produced a small "Elucidarium" or "Lucydarye" thought by some to have been translated from the French by Alexander Chertsey; a thirteenth-century illuminated manuscript "Elucidarium" is titled *Elucidarium Magistri Alani*). DC

ca. 1071

John de Garlande's *Dictionarius* (a manuscript dictionary resembling a phrase book; items are not arranged alphabetically, and the organization of the lists of items, such as parts of the body or occupations or trades, is not clear; the author used interlinear Anglo-Saxon gloss sparsely, adding some explanatory notes; the author's other work includes *Verborum Explicatio et Synonyma,* ca. 1068).

Chapter 2

Middle-English Period (1100–1499)

HISTORICAL BACKGROUND

The Normans who conquered England in 1066 were descended from Vikings who had invaded France in 912, assimilating the best of French culture. By the time of Duke William, they had produced such strong laws, organized religion, and military might that the Normans were thought of as among the most enterprising people of Europe. Although the Normans were at this time fighting in Germany, Spain, and Italy (with some of their knights participating in the Crusades), they were able to establish with only a small population a solid government in England based on might and order, but one that was also concerned with education, business, religion, craftsmanship, and the arts, especially architecture. The decisive Norman Conquest revolutionized England by retaining the best of English institutions, reforming the Church, and creating a strong central government. At least part of this civil strength lay in William's development of the vassal system in which persons of every class except the lowest and the highest (the king) had others depending on them; most English lived as minor vassals.

Society was also divided into religious and nonreligious groups. Religious groups were monastic brotherhoods, monks, secular clergymen, and the powerful friars, who dominated theological thought. As in the rest of Europe, the Roman Catholic Church reigned supreme; it had its own language—Latin—its uniform rituals, and its highly structured organization. While it demanded full allegiance from individuals, it also fostered art and learning which transcended national boundaries.

There were four nonreligious classes: (1) noblemen (mostly of Norman descent) who felt that reading and writing were "clerk's work" but who lived relatively extravagant lives and enthusiastically played elaborate games of chivalry; (2) the minor noblemen (knights or country gentlemen) who owed allegiance to overlords, administered landholdings from their great estates, and trained squires to follow in their footsteps; (3) the common people or freemen (small farmers, yeomen, seamen, artisans, craftsmen) who usually lived in villages near the manor house of the knight and generally performed the work of the world; and (4) the serfs (laborers, plowmen, shepherds) who were bound to the land on which they were born and did society's most menial tasks. If not bound to the land, a man could join the military as a professional soldier, the lower ranks of the Church, or the education profession; or he could become a clerk or a servant to a person of a higher rank. As the centuries passed, this land-tenure system would gradually die and feudalism and chivalry with it. Trade and industry would eventually shift wealth to merchants and manufacturers. Craftsmen in organized guilds would further advance the rise of the middle class. But these changes would take hundreds of years.

Gradually the Normans intermarried with the English and both began to speak a Germanic dialect (Middle English), although English would not be established as the literary language for nearly four centuries. Other shifts toward "things English" began to be evident, especially the trend toward self-government. Although the Crown remained strong, this tendency toward self-government, inherited from Anglo-Saxon tribal traditions, grew. In spite of the drift toward the use of English as the national language and the organizing of district councils and local citizens' assemblies, the vassal system originated by the Normans generally held firm throughout the Middle-English period.

Against this societal structure, certain political and social changes slowly emerged. Some of the most important of these changes came about when the first of the Plantagenet kings, Henry II (1154-1189), instituted trial by jury and reformed certain tax laws; he also extended England's power over its neighbors, forcing both Ireland and Wales to accept English rule; only Scotland managed to cling to independence, but border skirmishes continued for centuries. Although the papacy was at the height of its power, rising opposition to the Church grew, reflected especially in the assassination of Thomas à Becket in 1170.

Although the Anglo-Saxon language, first favored by Alfred the Great, was considered the literary language well into the tenth century, the increasing influence of the Church brought the return of Latin as the language of philosophers, poets, and scholars; the writing of the *Anglo-Saxon Chronicle* stopped in 1154. As would be expected, ecclesiastical Latin literature produced theological works, but it also produced scientific and educational treatises, bestiaries, lives of saints, satires, hymns, and histories; the most important history was written by Geoffrey of Monmouth who collected Anglo-Saxon legends in Latin. Along with this growth of Latin literature,

Anglo-Norman literature arose, consisting of historical romances, histories, legends, love songs, lays, and *fabliaux* (comic verse tales). Such works, significantly, introduced French meters and rhymes. About 1200 literature written in English began to reappear, but its sound and substance were softened by Anglo-Norman influences, such as polysyllabic words, gentler and more varied meters, and a notable refinement in manners and ideas.

Changes developed in many areas of life. At Runnymede in 1215 a group of powerful barons, partly to benefit themselves, forced King John to grant the "great charter" (Magna Carta) which contained concessions to the Church, recognized certain rights of freemen, and placed certain restraints on the king's power. This charter would become the base of English, and eventually American, common law. In 1295 Parliament was organized as a representative body with the power to participate in government. A slowly growing interest in education, first evident in cathedral schools, resulted in the forming of Oxford University in the late twelfth century and Cambridge in the early thirteenth century; by the fourteenth century, both universities would be the unassailable seats of learning in the Western world. Though learning was monopolized by clergymen, an increase in intellectual interest and activity occurred in many areas of study. During the thirteenth century, advances were made in science, philosophy, art, and law. Among the most notable scholars were Edmund Rich who introduced the study of logic at Oxford, Roger Bacon who experimented in chemistry and optics, and Henry de Bracton who created a fundamental system of law based on vague and undefined Saxon and Norman customs. Although learning advanced somewhat (even in small towns, schoolmasters, generally civil servants, were at work), illiteracy was widespread. People of all classes, however, enjoyed a rich oral literature (legends, ballads, tales, fables, myths) garnered from Celtic traditions as well as the Roman, Norse, and Norman; the common people also attached much meaning to heraldic symbols. Meanwhile, the population increased and domestic trade expanded. By the end of the century, approximately two hundred cities and boroughs existed. Even international trade was increasing, with wool, hides, lead, tin, cheese, and coal the leading exports.

Although the fourteenth century marked the beginning of the Renaissance in Italy, its effect would not be felt much in Britain for nearly two hundred years. The work of the poet Geoffrey Chaucer (1340-1400) more or less established English as the permanent national language, but the people continued to speak a mixture of dialects, holdovers from the mixture of peoples that had invaded Britain. Daily life remained severe and full of risks. Abroad, Edward III's claim to the French throne started the Hundred Years' War. At home, the Black Death (bubonic plague) swept the country repeatedly from 1348 to 1379, causing great suffering and thousands of deaths, particularly among children.

Farming declined, in part because of the lack of workers caused by the loss of population from the plague. In demand for the first time in English history, workers had their appetites whetted for higher wages, and the restlessness created by the Hundred Years' War increased their consciousness of their situation. In 1381 they marched on London in the Peasants' Revolt led by Wat Tyler, burning homes of officials and landlords as they went, and demanding their rights. Although Richard II promised relief, the riots continued. Only when Tyler died did the revolt collapse.

Rumblings for reform within the Church began to be heard, but reformers were not tolerated. John Wycliffe (1320-1384) was the first to voice opposition. Although the full effect of his influence would not be felt for over a century, he was the first to attack openly the collection of papal taxes in England, ownership of property by the Roman Church, transubstantiation, and the authority of the pope. As a teacher at Oxford, his preachings and teachings were often in English. His greatest work, however, was his translation of the Old and New Testaments, the first translation of the Bible into English, and he gave portions to his followers, the Lollards, called "poor preachers," to read to the people. Although his movement, with its subsequent Lollard uprisings, was stopped by the Crown and Wycliffe was condemned and executed as a heretic, his influence spread to Europe where it finally touched Luther. Wycliffe clearly was an important forerunner of the Reformation.

The threat of war continued when Henry V (1413-1432) attempted to conquer France. The Hundred Years' War with France finally collapsed under the advance of Joan of Arc, but the conditions that resulted eventually led to a civil war, the Wars of the Roses (1455-1485), which broke out between the rival houses of York and Lancaster. The climax of that war, the Battle of Bosworth Field, destroyed the power of the feudal nobles and paved the way for the Tudor dynasty, beginning with Henry VII in 1485. The Tudors would reign until 1603, bringing with them despotism but also stability in government.

In spite of much political, religious, and social unrest, the fifteenth century was a period of increasing interest in education, as evident in the founding of song schools, English reading schools, grammar schools, colleges, and expanding Inns of Court (academies of English law). While the arts in general did not immediately flourish after Chaucer (even the writing of church history diminished), architecture, especially building parish churches, did. In economics, the shift from a totally agrarian economy to a manufacturing one (for example, raw wool to woolen cloth) would bring major changes. And although it was not evident at the time, the introduction of the printing press to England by William Caxton in 1476 prepared the way for a growth of learning.

In 1497 and 1498 John Cabot and sons were sent to explore the northeastern coast of North America; these voyages would become the basis of English claims in the New World. Such explorations, along with the coming of the printed word, would revolutionize Europe. The spirit of the Renaissance with its emphasis on inquiry had at last begun to find its way into British thought, but its real impact would not be realized until the sixteenth century.

The Middle Ages had brought profound changes to England: the decay of feudalism, the increase of trade and manufacturing, and the creation and rising importance of a generally law-abiding middle class. The period was a vital transitional stage in the development of English civilization. At the beginning of the age, England was an occupied territory without even its own language. By the end of the age, England was about to become one of the leading political and cultural powers of the world. In particular, the development of the English language and its subsequent printed literature would prove to be of enormous consequence.

DEVELOPMENT OF BOOKS

The Norman Conquest of England in 1066 caused no break in the development of illuminated manuscripts, but it served to bring together continental and English styles. The general agreement is that the English style (Hiberno-Saxon) was superior.

Monks in monasteries were creating illuminated manuscripts of varying degrees of excellence all over Europe during the eleventh century. But continuing monastic reforms during the period produced many new orders and brought substantial increases in libraries; by the twelfth century, schools of illumination were flourishing. Large-scale painting and sculpture, which had become fashionable in Europe, influenced book design. Books became very large and heavily decorated with enormous initials of great variety and splendor. Ornamental motifs abounded, including interlacing, complex border designs, sometimes abstractions, sometimes specific, detailed pictorial representations, such as biting men and monsters locked in struggle.

The *Winchester* and *Lambeth Bibles* (ca. 1150) were the monumental works in England. The *Winchester Bible,* for example, contained work of many artists of varying talents, reflecting both the Utrecht style of hot color and violent motion and the Byzantine style of classical cool colors and gently flowing draperies. It contained illuminated initials covering the whole length of the nearly twenty-inch pages, called "historiated" initials because they incorporated scenes from history rather than being merely decorative. Gradually, as the number of non-monastic readers increased, the size of books was reduced to make them more portable and more practical, thus accommodating readers who used books outside the monastery setting.

Toward the end of the twelfth century, monks remained the chief creators and copyists of books, but as methods became more painterly and subjects tended toward the secular, more and more lay artists became book illuminators. Developments in techniques included the discovery that gold leaf, instead of fluid gold, produced brilliant effects, especially when burnished. New attention was paid to painted bar borders often executed in rich opaque gouache pigments, with ultramarine made of powdered lapis lazuli dominating. The colorful borders often showed birds and other natural objects; the textual area was frequently filled out with ornamental bands so that the whole surface of the page was decorated—a custom that would be imitated in some of the first printed books in the fifteenth century. Pages, which now were often very large or very small, usually depicted biblical scenes reminiscent of stained glass windows of the period, but foliage scrollwork was also popular, especially inside the initial frames; this fashion would last for nearly two hundred years. Marginal sketches, "drolleries," which were often totally unrelated to the text but revealed life and customs of the period, were common; animal grotesqueries showing real animals from which moral lessons might be drawn (such as the fox symbolizing slyness or the Devil, or the salamander symbolizing imperviousness to the fires of temptation, since lizards were supposedly insensible to fire), as well as mythical creatures (dragons, centaurs, satyrs), also contributed to the decorative effects. (*See figure 3*.)

As noted, as early as the twelfth century, more and more laymen were becoming copyists. Stationers, which at first meant anyone connected with the book trade, were emerging as important producers of books. (*Stationer* originally referred to a tradesman in a "fixed position," in a shop or stall.) By the mid-thirteenth century, such book-production centers, usually located in stalls near one of the rising universities, were thriving. When children needed schoolbooks and students needed textbooks, the stationer provided them. The stationer either accepted orders for copies to be made by a layman-scribe or hired out volumes that could be copied by the customer before they were returned. In a stationer's stall, there might be several craftsmen working together: the man who prepared the parchment, the scribe, the illustrator if the manuscript was to be illustrated, the binder, and the man who was the business agent for all, the stationer himself. He took the orders and sold the materials (parchment and quills). It is in this last role as a seller of stationery that we know the term today. The demand for lawbooks, the classics, textbooks, grammars, romances, and handbooks on many subjects (that is, books that were not the principal concern of the monasteries' *scriptoria*) continued to grow. By 1357 the Stationers' Company was formed. This guild would eventually become a powerful force, but not until books were no longer made by hand.

In the mid-fourteenth century, illuminated manuscripts were still in demand, albeit in a new phase. Many artists continued to work on the same book, but they now used an illumination scheme based on the cycle system originating in antiquity. (A cycle was a series of consecutive pictures depicting every part of a story such as the Apocalypse, or they showed many scenes in the bestiaries or herbals, or in other popular forms of books, which could be easily "read" by illiterates.) When this cycle concept began to give way, book illumination was taken over even more by virtuosos, non-monastics who painted books. Though this new trend accounted for many splendid books, cheap imitations of fine books also abounded. For example, several imitations of the Limburg brothers' *Book of Hours,* belonging to the Duke of Berry who owned a magnificent library in France, found their way to England. By the end of the fifteenth century, the book of hours type of prayer book, used by laymen for private devotions, was immensely popular. It far outnumbered all other categories of illuminated manuscripts.

Although the contents and the illustrations of the many kinds of books of hours varied considerably, such a book usually contained a calendar illustrated by the occupations characteristic of the months and the hours of the Office of the Virgin in eight miniatures, each connected with a particular hour: Matins, *Annunciation;* Lauds, *Visitation;* Prime, *Nativity;* Tierce, *Annunciation to the Shepherds;* Sext, *Adoration of the Magi;* None, *Presentation in the Temple;* Vespers, *Flight into Egypt* or *Massacre of the Innocents;* Compline, *Coronation of the Virgin* or *Flight into Egypt.* Many of these pictures were copies from psalters. Other prayers were also illustrated, such as the Hours of the Cross, showing a crucifixion scene, the Office of the Dead, showing a funeral service, and the Commendation of Souls, showing scenes from the Last Judgment.

The production of illuminated books continued to increase until the Black Death, which swept England from 1348 to 1379. From then until the end of the century, only a few good books were made.

As the effects of the plague faded and living conditions improved, the demand for books grew once again. To meet this demand, professional laymen joined once more with scholars in copying books to create book "factories." Although standards declined, experimentation increased. With the coming of paper to Europe (paper was first used in China about A.D. 105), experiments with printing began. Experiments in block printing were successful and soon provided playing cards, pictures of the saints, scenes from the life of Jesus or the Virgin, and New Year's greetings. (It should be noted that the earliest extant block-printed book is from China, ca. 868; the earliest dated European woodblock print, produced by rubbing the paper against the inked block, is one done in 1423 showing Saint Christopher bearing the infant Christ.) Block books were intended for those who could neither read nor afford the highly treasured manuscripts. Direct ancestors of the first books printed from movable type, these books were pages (a picture with a small amount of text) carved directly on the block from which pages were printed and crudely bound together. When religious stories were used, these books were called "paupers' Bibles." Although the printing of these block books, as well as the printing of illustrations surrounded by manuscript writing, was considered respectable, experiments with efficient printing of words on pages (imitating manuscripts) were carried on largely in secret. But secret or not, the printing of whole books was about to occur.

The Chinese had used movable type made from terra cotta as early as 1040, and printing from metal sets of type was known as early as 1403 in Korea. Even Leonardo da Vinci had made designs of printing presses, but they never left his drawing board. It is to Johann Gutenberg, a German, that credit must go for discovering a practical method of using movable type. Probably his earliest work is a seventy-four-page *Fragment of the World Judgment* printed between 1444 and 1447. He also possibly printed a portion of a Latin grammar and a calendar for the year 1448. In 1455 copies of an indulgence of Pope Nicholas V also issued from this press, but whether these early pieces were the work of Gutenberg is impossible to know, since he did not sign his name. His experiments with designing fonts of type, based on the Gothic, block-letter manuscript writing of the period, of joining together various letters in composing sticks of his own invention in order to produce uniform and pleasing appearance, of composing printed pages that rivaled the hand-lettered volumes so universally respected were no small achievements. His methods would go essentially unchanged for three centuries. Although, as noted, he is thought to have printed other materials, his forty-two line (per page), full-length Bible remains his monument. No less than six hand presses were used to print the 641 leaves composed of double columns without numbers, catch words, or signatures. The pages are characterized by extraordinary evenness in the printing and accurate alignment of the letters; the glossy black ink and sharp impressions are remarkable even by modern standards. (*See figure 4.*)

But Gutenberg could not recover the 800 guilders he had borrowed from a Mainz lawyer, Johannes Fust, to finance creation of his printing press. His work stopped abruptly when his creditors, Fust and Peter Schoeffer, himself a talented printer, took over Gutenberg's equipment and methods and went on to become the leading printers in Mainz. Gutenberg's Bible established their reputation, although they went on to print some beautiful books of their own. Thus, by 1456, printing began its somewhat shaky journey toward respectability.

In an attempt to gain the trust of the church whose monasteries had been the centers of book production for centuries, as well as the patronage of the gentry, the earliest printed books (*incunabula,* meaning swaddling clothes) imitated manuscripts. Typefaces were fashioned to look like the calligraphy of leading scribes; initial letters were painted by hand after the pages were printed, and title pages (when they were included) were painted and lettered, at least in part, by hand. The functions of typesetter, printer, publisher, editor, and bookseller were not generally differentiated; often one person did all these jobs.

With the influence of printing spreading on the continent, William Caxton, an Englishman, decided to go to Europe to learn the trade. In Bruges about 1475 he published a book which he had recently translated from the French, *The Recuyell of the Historyes of Troy,* according to his own tastes. When he returned to England in 1476, he established England's first printing press in London at the Sign of the Red Pale, near Westminster Abbey. Although not a great printer, Caxton can hardly be blamed for a lack of style, as he had only English calligraphy and illuminating on which to base his work, and English culture, as noted before, was in a distinct decline because of the French wars, the Black Death, and the Wars of the Roses. Nevertheless, Caxton printed about 100 books, or 18,000 copies, in black-letter Gothic type, 74 of them in English. They were generally of high quality. His first book to be published in England is thought to be *The Dictes or Sayengis of the Philosophres,* 1477; his first illustrated book is thought to be *Mirrour of the World* (ca. 1481). In addition to publishing books and doing other small printing jobs that could be done quickly, Caxton was also the first English seller of printed books. All other London booksellers of the period were Dutch, German, or French. He was also a reputable translator. Twenty of his books were his own translations. These, along with his concern for "hardening" the form of the English language, his writing of prologues and epilogues, his skill in selecting titles, and his literary style, secure him a lasting place in English literature. (*See figure 5.*)

Like most early printers who were imitating manuscripts, Caxton did not use a title page. (An isolated exception in Germany was "Ein Mahnung," a small calendar printed in 1454.) The first experimental uses of title (or half-title) pages were tried by Schoeffer in 1463, who gave it up after one attempt, and Therhoernen of Cologne in his *Sermo de Praesentatione Beatae Mariae.* The first full title page was made by Erhard Ratdolt of Augsburg who printed an astronomical and astrological calendar in 1476, supplying the title information we expect today. Title pages were not regularly used in English books until about 1560. Caxton, following the fashion of the day, included the title in the colophon, a statement at the end of the book.

Somewhere around 1480, Wynken de Worde joined Caxton in his workshop near Westminster Abbey. Upon Caxton's death in 1491, de Worde inherited the business and went on to print about eight hundred books of varying quality. Among his best works are *All the Proprytees of Things* (1495), and reissuings of Caxton's *The Golden Legend* (1493) and *Canterbury Tales* (1498). But two-fifths of de Worde's work was for students, lawbooks especially, or schoolboys, including the well-known *Eight Parts of Speech* by Aelius Donatus, thus establishing de Worde as the first publisher to make a business of textbooks. Perhaps de Worde's greatest contribution, however, was that he carried on Caxton's attempt to help standardize the English language.

By the beginning of the sixteenth century, many improvements in the printing of books had come about. A few books even had illustrations; the first illustrated book, *Edelstein,* a collection of fables, was done in Bamberg, Germany, in 1461, by Alfrecht Pfister. Erhard Ratdolt even issued in 1487 a book, the *Obsequiale,* with a woodcut printed in colors. While a few other books with colored woodcuts were printed by Ratdolt thereafter, his great technical achievement did not immediately become a part of book production. The uncolored woodcut, which was printed as a separate impression from the type, was almost the sole method of book illustration for many years. By this time, books were also commonly paginated, and they usually had title (or half-title) pages which provided some information about the publisher as well as the date of printing. In Venice, however, even greater improvements were being made through the work of Nicolas Jensen, a Frenchman, and Aldus Mantius, an Italian. Jensen, who began his career in 1470, was creating typefaces—Greek, Gothic, and Roman—of such high quality that some say his work has never been surpassed. And Aldus Mantius, a scholar as well as a printer, had designed an inexpensive, small book done in an efficient style convenient enough for a student to carry; it would soon take the place of the large, inefficient codex. He was also about to introduce the first cursive type, the *italic,* in his *Virgil* and *Juvenal.* Thus, by 1500, Jensen and Mantius, as well as countless other early printers, were firmly laying the foundations for modern book design. The printed word would soon replace the manuscript, but not without a struggle.

In many countries, especially Italy, scribes and often their patrons were utterly contemptuous of printed books, that is, imitations of handwritten and illuminated manuscripts. For the professional copyists, the *scrittori,* as well as the ordinary *copisti* (clerks, schoolmasters, and scholars), the coming of printing meant the loss of their livelihoods. For the patrons, the acceptance of new forms of the book meant changing their attitude toward honoring books and their contents. When one considers the aesthetic difference between a resplendent illuminated manuscript bound in crimson velvet with silver clasps, and the inelegant, sparse, usually unillustrated or crudely illustrated printed page, it is perhaps easy to understand why Duke Frederick of Urbino was "ashamed to own a printed book."

But the time for printing was ripe. A reawakened Europe was demanding books that were practical to use and accessible to more people. It was clear that the process for creating multiple copies inexpensively, that is, printing, was firmly established, albeit, except in rare instances, in a somewhat primitive state. And printers were eager to work. Presses, however, were in no way standardized, nor were type faces. Type faces, in particular, would be undergoing almost continual change as printers and the rest of society made the transition from calligraphy to print.

In short, the development from manuscript to printed page was slow, but it was very certain. Until the early fifteenth century, Europe had an international style in manuscripts, derived from the evolution of writing the geometric Roman alphabet, that is, capitals cut in stone. Such carving found its way into manuscript writing, probably with a flat brush (about the first century A.D.). As writing surfaces changed from stone and wood to papyrus and parchment, the brush evolved to reeds and sharpened quills. By the fourth century, the Roman alphabet was softened into rounded letters, uncials, which were faster to write on parchment and often easier to read. By the sixth century, the half-uncial, or lower case, had come into being; by the eighth century, the minuscule, a true small letter, often credited to Alcuin of York, Abbot of Saint Martin's from 796 to 804, became the most fashionable style for calligraphy. The combination of majuscules (capitals) which started a sentence that continued in minuscules (lower case) set the pattern, one that has carried to the present day. But by the eleventh century, more condensed letters called Gothic script became widely used, probably to economize on parchment. The Gothic script underwent many forms; the most prominent in England from the fourteenth century on was black-letter, on which the first type face was based. With the coming of print, continual experimentation in type faces would occur. Although black-letter, or Gothic, would continue to be popular, evolutions of type faces would be patterned after humanistic script, *scrittura umanistica,* the calligraphy generally used by scholars, which was based on early classical capitals, and after chancery script, *cancellaresca,* calligraphy generally used by religious scribes, based on cursive forms and known for its beauty and speed of writing. Thus, type designers from the beginning imitated predominant styles of calligraphy. Broadly stated, these can be called, because of letter-shape and arrangement, the Ecclesiastical (black-letter) and the Renaissance-Classical (Roman). Today's letter forms, which began with Roman capitals chiseled in stone eighteen centuries before, were perfected in the humanistic script of the fifteenth century. It is largely on these Renaissance forms that present aesthetics of type design are based.

ATTITUDES TOWARD AND TREATMENT OF CHILDREN

After the Norman Conquest, English life changed very little, at least at first. The sibb-structured family from Anglo-Saxon times declined somewhat, but the extended family household remained. Infanticide was still practiced, particularly if the child was deformed or if it cried excessively. Such children were thought to be possessed by the Devil. Although there were many exceptions, parent-child affection was generally low. Children were not valued, at least not in the modern sense, probably because the high death rate made caring too great a psychological risk. Infant mortality was high because of poor sanitation, poor diet, and disease; only three or four out of a dozen or more children in a family were likely to reach maturity.

With death ever present, the child was born into an atmosphere of death and attempts to prevent it. From antiquity, various purification rites (fire, blood, urine, salt, wine, cold water) and even mutilations (the cutting of cheeks, the burning of the back of the neck with hot wax, the clipping of the tongue string) were used to stave off death and the Devil. Swaddling, that is, wrapping the child tightly with cloth bands and sometimes binding it to a board, was probably, at least in the beginning, an attempt to protect the child, with length of swaddling time varying from a few months to two years. It was thought that if the infant was not swaddled, it would scratch out its eyes, break its arms and legs, pull off its ears, or even crawl. Crawling was considered animal-like and was to be avoided at all costs. Various devices were designed from Roman times on to restrain the child as soon as it passed the swaddling period—back boards, corsets, stays, stools with braces—all used to keep the child sitting or standing upright. Other restraints were also used.

Ghosts, witches, and devils were deep fears of most medieval people. Children were kept in check by being told that such supernatural beings would steal them away or suck their blood or bone marrow. Even babies were sometimes restrained by beatings. In the few countries where swaddling was not generally used, such as Scotland, various "hardening" practices were applied, such as dipping the infant in ice water or rolling it in snow. Not until John Locke wrote against swaddling in 1693 would it begin to disappear in England, but it would not completely die out until the end of the eighteenth century.

Another custom originating in antiquity was the practice of sending an upper-class infant, at about three days of age, to a wet nurse; the child might remain there for one to three years. Such children spent little of their lives with their own families, only that time between being returned from the wet nurse at age two or three to being sent to school at about six or seven. School was either a monastery school or a cathedral choir school or, later, a university grammar school. Although a few children were tutored in the homes of their parents or their surrogate parents, this practice was not usual. More likely, the child would be sent to a feudal lord's manor house to learn virtue, service, and manners. This practice of "exchanging" upper-class children to act as servants (pages or ladies-in-waiting) in other households formed strong economic links. Few children ever returned home but eventually made profitable, often prearranged marriages in the exchange households.

A boy who went to a feudal lord's household at age seven or eight might learn to become a knight. Although knighthood was frowned upon by the lower classes, the clergy, and even the king, it remained a highly desirable vocation among the nobility. Probably every noble son had heard the *Song of Roland*. In spite of the church's disapproval of romantic love without marriage, the combination of chivalric love and high adventure was heady indeed.

The young future knight began as a page, where he learned to perform menial tasks courteously; he also learned some reading and writing along with hunting, falconry, riding, and perhaps singing, dancing, and playing the harp. He learned the "rudiments of love," that is, the art of chivalry. At age fourteen or perhaps later, he became a squire and learned to tilt and use a lance, a sword, and a battle-axe. He also accompanied his lord to tournaments where he bore the shield and led the spare chargers. Most importantly, he assisted his heavily armored patron by maintaining the smallest details of his lord's armament and by dressing him. Although not all squires became knights (it cost a considerable amount), most of them did. They entered knighthood in an elaborate ritual. The young man took his vows, put on the white tunic, symbol of honor, and the red rose, symbol of a man's mortality. He also received his own armor, shield, lance, and horse. He then gave gifts to the church, the poor, his friends, and to all those who had served him.

Young girls of noble birth were also sent to manor houses where they learned etiquette, music, needlework, and household management; sometimes they learned to read. There is evidence that some high-born young women even knew astronomy, arithmetic, geometry, rhetoric, and "clergy" (clerical skills). Not all upper-class children went to exchange households. Some were sent to monasteries and convents instead. Even lower-class children could go into the church.

All upper-class people spoke French, while the lower classes used English. Upper-class children, the educated ones, were supposed to speak Latin only, even while playing; if Latin was not possible, they were at least to speak French. English was not considered worthy until the fourteenth century when a few books were published in the vernacular. Even then French was the preferred substitute for Latin as the language of instruction.

A good deal is recorded about upper-class children, but little is known about children of the lower classes because they do not figure much in the writings of the time. They certainly fared less well than children of the wellborn, although more of them remained in their own homes and most were nursed by their own mothers. Country children usually shared the hard, meager life of their parents, but sometimes superfluous daughters were sent to neighboring farms. If the child of a poor family was able to learn to read, he might elevate himself, especially in the church. In 1392,

William Langland complained in *Piers Plowman* that, "The child of a cobbler or beggar has but to learn his book. He will become a bishop . . . in spite of his origin. . . ." But the chances of a poor boy's "learning his book" were slim.

Although town boys, too, went into the church, many of them, at age seven to nine, went to work in a master's household as apprentices. The apprenticeship would last for seven to nine years. An apprentice might expect to learn a trade, but his work consisted of the most menial tasks and his well-being depended on the charity of his master. Craft guilds, which were developing at this time, depended on the apprentice system. Although it varied from place to place, the purpose of the system was the same: to provide a young boy, in return for specific obligations, a bed, board, and training in a craft. Sometimes the master was also required to provide training in reading and writing; sometimes he provided clothing. But masters were always required to care for the boys if they were ill, and they were responsible for their behavior; thus, the master was another sort of surrogate parent. At the end of the young man's apprenticeship, he became a journeyman (from the Old French *journee,* meaning "by the day"). Craft guilds, like the guild merchants who regulated trade, were important to medieval life. Guilds had their own patron saints and their own rules, and they had the respect of society. Young men who succeeded in making the journey from apprentice to master were some of the most fortunate in medieval society.

While the apprentice was at the mercy of his master, upper-class children, royal wards, were also at the mercy of their surrogate parents. Wardships, however, were a deeply ingrained part of medieval life, and the system was accepted on all levels of society. Some girls, as young as seven or eight, were even sent abroad to work in the homes of the French nobility. But not all young girls left home. Lower-class girls were sometimes kept at home to do the menial tasks of the meager household; especially in the fourteenth century, parents sometimes kept upper-class girls at home to be educated. They were likely to have governesses who probably acted as chaperones, but they also had tutors to teach the gentle arts—music, language, reading Scriptures, and needlework. It is unlikely that girls of this period were educated either at home or at school if they were not of high station.

Discipline of children in all classes was harsh throughout the Middle Ages. It was generally believed that failure to discipline severely meant ruining the child. Although a thirteenth-century law forbade beating a child to death, it acknowledged that a child who was beaten at least until it bled would remember it. There were, however, a few voices that spoke against harsh treatment. Saint Anselm, for example, was far in advance of his time when he pleaded for "gentle beating." He asked, "Are they not human?" But cruel instruments of all kinds were used on children: whips, including cat-o'-nine-tails and chains; shovels; canes; iron and wooden rods; and school devices, such as the flapper, which was shaped like a pear with a hole in it, specifically made to raise blisters.

In spite of strict rules and the threat of severe punishment, medieval children clearly acted like children. They participated in fairs and festivals, scuffled in the street, and grinned, chattered, and shoved each other during choir practice. One writer records that boys played tricks on each other in their dormitory at school. Discipline could be psychological as well as physical. Children were required to serve both parents and surrogates "instantly" and without question. The custom of "asking blessing" of parents was widespread and represents the total subservience the child was expected to pay to his elders.

Submission was also required by schoolmasters, who were sometimes civil servants and often brutal disciplinarians. The clergy, often poorly educated themselves, continued to dominate education. The chief school subjects were the classics, often made so intolerable through poor translations and relentless drill that they lost their power as literature. Philosophy, which remained the focus of the curriculum, was used largely for disputations on inconsequential but mystical points. The most frequently used educational method was versification to aid memorizing. Popular stories, romances, fables, and bestiaries made up some of the few delights of children's reading, but substantial manuscript books were far too valuable to be used to any extent for such purposes. More likely, children were given brief tracts—advice on morals and manners, deportment, social intercourse, and the "affections."

In spite of the oppression of children which was evident in all social classes, instances of parental concern abound. Mothers worried, for example, over the selection of a suitable wet nurse: that she be strong, healthy, and of good temperament; they worried about the general well-being of the child: that it be bathed and kept safe; they even worried over the proper astrological influences: that the times of conception and birth be favorable. It is well to remember that bringing up children under crowded feudal conditions with no privacy at all was not easy. A crying infant was upsetting to the entire household. (The infant Christ was said to have never cried at night.) Although nurses often sang to the infants to quiet them, they also used opium and liquor. Swaddling also kept down the din, as the process of swaddling reduced the heart rate and fostered passivity.

That many parents loved their children there can be no doubt. Many accounts tell of mothers playing games with their children or singing to them; of parental joy and gratitude when a child miraculously recovered from a grave illness, or when a child, returning home after long absence, showed affection for its parents. There is also evidence that many child deaths from overlaying—the practice of taking a child to bed with the parents or nurse—were accidental; the child had been taken to bed to suckle, or for warmth. Intentional infanticide was practiced but probably most often for reasons of great poverty, that is, the inability of the parent to provide food. By the twelfth and thirteenth centuries, there were strict laws and severe punishments for killing and abandoning children. In many cases on record the women who killed their children stated that they had baptized them before committing the act.

The insecurity of all people of the period, both physical and mental, must not be overlooked. The birth of a child, for example, could be extremely dangerous to both mother and child. Although midwives used potions to soften the uterus and had instruments (hooks of various types) to expedite delivery, the birthing process and the period immediately following were often fatal. If the mother and child survived the birth ordeal, there was always the danger that one or both would die of illness.

All classes and all ages in the Middle Ages had work to do. A favorite maxim was *laborare est orare*, meaning "to work is to pray." Survival required that everyone be involved in work. For most people that meant raising and preparing food (plowing, sowing, harvesting, butchering, cooking, baking), making cloth (carding, spinning, weaving), and producing crafts (smithing, potting, carpentry). For princes and princesses, work was learning how to govern; for aristocratic children, it was learning royal service; for children of the lower classes, it was farming, manufacturing, or a trade. Idleness for all people, even little children, was considered a sin, and the sin of sloth, one of the seven deadliest.

By the end of the age, certain reforms began to occur, especially in education. John Cornwall, an Oxford schoolmaster, insisted on the desirability of using English instead of Latin (or French) as the language of instruction. He was successful because of rising nationalism and pride in "things English."

On all social levels there was a growing interest in learning to read, which would soon be enhanced by the coming of the printed word, especially "Englished" books printed by William Caxton. In general, learning was more favored than before with the church providing education, although often of poor quality, freely without regard to class distinction. While the upper classes continued the study of the *trivium* and the *quadrivium*, humanistic studies were growing in importance. Although the "Donat," the popular shortened form of the classical text, *Donatus Ars Grammatica*, was still the most widely used textbook, standard texts were *Cato* (a collection of adages and proverbs), the *Aeneid*, and Ovid's *Metamorphoses*. Even the severe disciplining of children, although still in effect for centuries, was about to be questioned by a few important men. In short, although the chief thrust of education on all levels was to produce a generation which would merely renew the cycle of trade, religion, and social customs, by the end of the fourteenth century there were movements in the direction of a more humane society.

In the next century, the wisdom of antiquity would be reborn under the name of the New Learning. Explorations in the New World would touch the imagination and the lives of all, and the roughness of medieval life would begin to fade. While traditional attitudes toward children would be slow to die, they would begin to be challenged, and even changed, during the next 160 years called the Renaissance.

ANNOTATED CHRONOLOGY

ca. 1100

Bestiaries (anonymous manuscript collections of legends about animals and their spiritual attributes, often illuminated; certain elements of the bestiaries have been preserved in stories for children to the present). BM, HH, TC

1147

Goeffrey of Monmouth's *Historia Regum Britanniae* (a reworking of an earlier collections of Cymryic and Brythonic traditions, legends, myths, and ballads which served to record the history of the Britons; the work is composed of twelve Latin manuscript books which took fifteen years to complete; children's history lessons were based on Geoffrey's work for hundreds of years). BM

ca. 1180

Alexander Neckham's *De Utensilibus* (an easy Latin manuscript reading book for children, describing the everyday life of the period, especially domestic manners and customs; author's other work includes *De Naturis Rerum,* ca. 1185, one edition in verse and one edition in prose; the author, who was Richard I's foster brother, was in charge of the famous school at Dunstable before becoming an eminent professor at the University of Paris).

ca. 1225

Batholomaeus Anglicus's or De Glanvilla's *De Proprietatibus Rerum* (a religious lesson book in manuscript form probably written in Latin; provides such useful information as the names of God, the parts of the body and their uses, diseases and remedies, and the nature and uses of plants, mountains, beasts, and virtues; translated into English as *All the Proprytees of Things* by John Trevisa and printed by Wynken de Worde in 1495; numerous editions followed). HH, UCL

ca. 1270

Walter de Biblesworth's *French-English Lesson Book* (a manuscript lesson book written at the request of the author's pupil, the Kentish heiress, Dionysia de Montchensi of Swanescombe; the events of a child's earliest years are described as simply as possible with difficult French words explained in the Anglo-Saxon glosses).

ca. 1290

Gesta Romanorum (anonymous; a manuscript collection of folktales and fables in Latin, with morals; some tales such as the "Bidpai" are from the Eastern tradition; Greek myths are given Christian interpretations; the collection was originally intended for "ignorant adults," but the stories were appropriated by children; later writers borrowed heavily from this collection; the earliest extant manuscript is dated 1326; the first illustrated printed edition was in Dutch, 1481; an English version was printed by Wynken de Worde, ca. 1517). CPL

ca. 1330

Holkham Bible Picture Book (anonymous; a manuscript written in Anglo-Norman, the language of the upper laity; the apocryphal infancy stories are told with captioned illustrations which provide a unique panorama of medieval life; written for and used by friars who defended the Apocrypha; the book condemned by the Lollards who regarded the stories as superstitious; portions of the text read: "How Jesus led the children of Egypt to the water and climbed upon it. They could not do so and were drowned and he raised them from the dead," and "How Jesus came to seek the children of the Jews with whom he used to play. And their fathers had hidden them in an oven. And Jesus asked what was in the oven and they said it was pigs. And Jesus said let it be pigs."). DPL

ca. 1385

The Wycliffe Bible (the first translation of the Old and New Testaments with the Apocryphal Books from the Latin Vulgate into Middle English by John Wycliffe; in manuscript form until 1850; many manuscript copies must have been made because approximately 170 copies of this manuscript, or fragments, still survive; the work was read to the common people by Wycliffe's followers, the Lollards or "poor preachers," to acquaint them with the Scriptures; the translation is of such high quality that the author has been called "the father of English prose"; the 1850 printed edition, *The Holy Bible, containing Old and New Testaments, with the Apocryphal Books, in the Earliest English Versions, made from the Latin Vulgate by*

John Wycliffe and his followers, was edited by the Reverend Josiah Forshall and Sir Frederick Madden and published by Oxford University Press in four volumes; author's other work includes numerous manuscripts which explain religious doctrines).

1392

Geoffrey Chaucer's *Treatise on the Astrolabe* (a translation and adaptation of the extant *Compositio et Operatio Astrolabii* by Messahala, an eighth-century Egyptian astronomer; written for Chaucer's ten-year-old son, Lewis; thought to be the earliest English-language description of the workings and capabilities of a scientific instrument, the astrolabe; the text is written in clear, often colloquial Middle English and provides many concrete examples; the author's other work includes *The Canterbury Tales,* 1387, a collection of verse narratives written in Middle-English vernacular which made the tales comprehensible to the common folk of the period; *The Canterbury Tales* was printed first by William Caxton in 1498; later editions include that of Wynken de Worde, 1498; the first sound edition of *The Canterbury Tales* did not appear until 1775, printed by Tyrwhitt; portions of these tales are used with children to the present). BL, HH, UCL, UOx

ca. 1430

The ABC of Aristotle (anonymous; a manuscript courtesy book which cautions the reader to "Be not—A too Amorous, too Adventurous, nor Argue too much. B too Bold, too Busy, nor Babble too long . . ."; ends with the familiar directive: "Learn this or go lacking").

How the Good Wife Taught Her Daughter (anonymous; a manuscript in poetic form in which a daughter, who sells homespun in the market, is given admonishments by her mother designed to help her lead a good life, including advice about not getting drunk; variant manuscripts which include *A Northern Mother's Blessing* along with the poem, *The Way To Thrift,* were printed in 1597).

Stans Puer Ad Mensam or *The Boy Standing at the Table* (anonymous, but often attributed to John Lydgate because his name is mentioned in the text: "If aught be amiss . . . , Put all the default upon John Lydgate"; a manuscript courtesy book full of popular maxims with many manuscripts still surviving; the text was founded on the Latin *Carmen juvenile de moribus puerorum,* of Johannes Sulpitius; printed by William Caxton in 1479 as *Stans puer ad mensam, with Anholy Salve in English and some moral distichs;* the text which was included in Hugh Rhodes's *Boke of Nurture,* ca. 1550, was popular until the seventeenth century). UCL

ca. 1435

The Boke of Curtasye (anonymous; a manuscript book of manners or courtesy written in poetic form and divided into three parts; based in part on John Garland's supplement to Dionysius Cato's fourth-century(?) set of maxims printed during the late Middle Ages; Cato is referred to in the *Boke of Curtasye* as Facet; complete title is: *Liber Faceti: docens mores hominum, precipue iuuenum, in supplementum illorum qui a moralissimo Cathone erant omissi iuuenibus utiles,* which translated reads: *The Book of the Polite Man, teaching manners for men, especially for boys, as a supplement to those which were omitted by the most moral Cato;* contains advice about how young men should act in the home of a nobleman, the duties of all servants in a nobleman's household, and numerous moral instructions; content is similar to *The Babees Book,* ca. 1430, and other courtesy books popular during the period; text was printed by William Caxton in 1477 in London, titled *The Booke of Curtesye or Lytylle John*). PM, UCL

ca. 1450

Hornbooks (lesson "books" designed especially for children to teach them the fundamentals of reading; usually a single printed sheet of text mounted on a paddle-shaped piece of wood protected by a covering of translucent animal horn; the paddle shape made the hornbook easy for children to handle, but other shapes were also used; the text most often consisted of the alphabet, Arabic numerals, the Lord's prayer, and a syllabary; a cross was often added to the upper left hand corner of early hornbooks which might account for their being referred to as "Criss-Cross-Row"). BM, NYPL, TPL

ca. 1453

Urbanitatis, or *Politeness* (anonymous; a manuscript courtesy book popular at the court of Edward IV; advice offered in poetic form is similar in content to other courtesy books of the period).

ca. 1456

The Gutenberg Bible or The Forty-Two-Line Bible (the first Bible, Latin Vulgate translation, and first large book to be printed in movable metal type, appeared in England soon after it was printed by Gutenberg or his creditors, Fust and Schoeffer, in Mainz, Germany; this edition of the Bible is also known as the Mazarin Bible because the first copy to be described was found in the Mazarin Library, Paris, in 1760). HH, IUL, LC, PM, YU

ca. 1460

John Russell's *Book of Nurture* (a manuscript courtesy book in poetic form which was probably based on part three of the *Book of Courtesy* that the author is said to have used as a youth; not to be confused with Hugh Rhodes's *Boke of Nurture,* ca. 1550).

ca. 1475

The Babees Book (anonymous; a manuscript courtesy book written in rhyme royal and probably addressed to young princes, subtitled *A Little Report of How Young People Should Behave;* originally written in Latin; provides advice to young men, not babies, on how to act as pages in their lords' households; often printed separately but sometimes included with other works throughout the fifteenth and sixteenth centuries; printed by William Caxton in London).

Raoul Le Fevre's *Recuyell of the Historyes of Troy* (translated by William Caxton from the 1464 French manuscript, *Le recueil des histoires de Troyes;* the first book printed by William Caxton in English in Bruges, Belgium; it contained slightly over a hundred folio pages; author's other work includes *The Historyes of Jason,* Westminster, 1477). BM, PML, UOx

1476

Jacques de Cessolis's *The Game and Playe of the Chesse* (translated from the author's two French versions of *Liber de ludo scaccorum* with dedication, interpolation, and epilogue by William Caxton; contains 148 folio pages; printed in Bruges, Belgium, by William Caxton; reprinted by Caxton in 1484 in London).

1477

The Dictes or Sayengis of the Philosophres (anonymous; translated from the Latin by Earl Rivers; a folio volume of 156 pages; probably was Caxton's first book set up in England; printed in London by William Caxton). ULC, YU

ca. 1480

The Little Children's Little Book (anonymous; a manuscript courtesy book in both prose and poetry versions; explains that courtesy came down from heaven when Gabriel greeted the Virgin, and Mary and Elizabeth met; similar in content to other courtesy books of the period; ends with the familiar "Learn or be Lews," *lews* meaning ignorant).

1481

Reynart the Foxe (anonymous; a prose translation of the "beast-epic" done by William Caxton from the poet Willem's Flemish text; a popular political satire of oppression and tyranny with a roguish fox as hero; stories of Reynard used with children up to the present; printed in London by William Caxton). BM, JRUL

Bellovacensis Vincentius's *The Myrrour of the worlde* (translated by William Caxton from the French prose version of Gautier de Metz's poem which deals with God and the liberal arts, the four elements, and astronomy; an encyclopedia illustrated with woodcuts). BM, JRUL, UCL, UOx

1484

The book of the subtyl historyes and fables of Esope (translated by William Caxton from a French edition by Machault, which was based on Steinhowel's German *Esopand;* printed in English by William Caxton and embellished with woodcuts; cautionary animal tales with morals; originally attributed to a sixth-century B.C. Samian slave, although some scholars doubt his existence; evidence exists that ca. 300 B.C. a Greek, Demetrius of Phalerum, recorded about two hundred fables which were later translated by a Greek slave, Phaedrus, ca. A.D. 30, into Latin verse which was commonly memorized during the Middle Ages and by English schoolchildren; prose paraphrases of Phaedrus's verses were written by tenth-century writer, Romulus; the first English edition for children was probably done by Sir Roger L'Estrange, in two volumes, 1692 and 1699; fables were endorsed as good learning fare by the English philosopher, John Locke, in his *Thoughts on Education,* 1693; enjoyed by children to the present). BM, UOx

Geoffrey de la Tour Landry's *The Knyght of the Tour or Knight of the Tower; The Booke of the Enseynments and Teachynge that the Knight of the Toure made to his Doughters. And spedketh of many faire ensamples* (translated from the French manuscript, written ca. 1371; printed by William Caxton; a book of advice to young women outlining their duties and giving examples in story form). UCL

1485

Sir Thomas Malory's *Le Morte D'Arthur* (translated into prose ca. 1470 from several Norman-French romances and an English alliterative epic, *Morte Arthur;* traces the life and death of Arthur, possibly a heroic cavalry general named Arturis who died in 538; Malory's work was edited by William Caxton into one long story instead of the eight separate stories originally written by Malory; printed in London by Caxton; the story extolls the legendary deeds of King Arthur and his courageous knights; numerous retellings of the Arthur stories exist; the stories are used with children to the present). JRUL, PM

Chapter 3

Renaissance to Restoration (1500–1659)

HISTORICAL BACKGROUND

In Britain the ascension of Henry VII (1485-1509) to the throne brought the absolute authority of the Tudors. Henry's task was to reconstruct a population exhausted from war and disorder. At home, he established the rule of law, repressed the feudal nobility, and conserved the national finances; abroad, he encouraged international exploration and commerce, while intimidating rivals. In short, he responded to the forces of the Renaissance and steered England into the Modern Age.

Enlightened though despotic, Henry VIII (1509-1547) raised England to a position of first importance by maintaining the balance of power in Europe and understanding the importance of sea power. He opposed the papacy openly by divorcing Catherine of Aragon in 1529, thus taking steps to found a national church with the king as the spiritual head. This action also resulted in the destruction of the monastic system and the transfer of its wealth from Rome to the Crown. With the formation of the Church of England in 1543, England became a unitary realm subject to a single ruler and governed by a single common law of the land alterable only by the sovereign authority of the king-in-Parliament. The spirit of the Reformation (which started in Germany because of deep-seated religious abuses, political unrest, and heavy taxation) swept England. One result was an order for Bibles for all churches.

Edward VI's short reign (1547-1553) was marked by inflation and economic collapse. He was controlled by the Earl of Somerset, a supporter of humane Protestantism, and the Earl of Northumberland, a supporter of violent Protestantism who attempted to secure the succession of Lady Jane

Grey to the throne. The ascension of Mary, Catherine of Aragon's daughter, to the throne in 1553 restored Roman Catholicism to power, and her marriage to Phillip II of Spain sacrificed England's political independence. An ardent Catholic, Mary viciously persecuted Protestants, firm believers in the reformist religion of Luther and Calvin, burning about three hundred dissidents as heretics in less than three years. Her reign was the cruelest in British history; her early death in 1558 most probably prevented a major rebellion.

Elizabeth's long, stable reign (1558-1603) brought a great calm to England as well as a resurgence of art and learning. She ably extricated England from foreign intrigues with Scotland, France, and Spain. And she removed Romanism from the English church, thus bringing about a settlement with middle-of-the-road Protestantism; in 1559 she established the Anglican church as the national church. While Elizabeth abhorred the Church of Rome, she also abhorred the fanaticism of Puritanism. Such dislike of the Calvinists would seem to have made her sympathetic to Mary, Queen of Scots, a Catholic who had been driven from her throne by her Calvinist subjects. But Mary made claims to the throne of England. When a rebellion in Scotland drove Mary into Elizabeth's hands, Elizabeth kept Mary in "honorable captivity" for the rest of her life. When Catholic plots thickened and Mary pressed her claim to the throne, Elizabeth had her beheaded.

Under Elizabeth, who resolved to stabilize the national church, John Whitgift (1530-1604) was made archbishop of Canterbury in 1583. Whitgift, like Elizabeth, was as strongly anti-Puritan as he was anti-Roman. Immediately following his appontment, an anonymous Puritan reform tract, printed by Robert Waldegrave, attacked Whitgift. The Crown reacted with increased censorship of the press. In 1586 Whitgift procured an extension of the existing censorship from the Star Chamber, and he and the bishop of London were given the power to control the press and forbid publication of seditious works. Although subsequent anonymous attacks on the established order occurred from time to time, royal censorship of books remained restrictive.

Although Elizabeth parried the Spanish power by flirting with powerful Phillip II of Spain and even hinting at her possible conversion to Roman Catholicism, she privately encouraged piratical adventurers such as Walter Raleigh, John Hawkins, and Francis Drake who sapped the strength of Spain by attacking its treasure fleets. When fear of Spain was ended by defeat of the famous Spanish Armada in 1588, a wave of exultation swept England.

Generally thought to have been an extraordinary political leader, Elizabeth knew that her ultimate strength came not from "divine right" but from her people. Near the end of her life she could say with confidence in the House of Commons, "Though God hath raised me high, yet this I count the glory of my crown, that I have reigned with your loves!"

The Elizabethan Age was noted for its increase in national prosperity through trade and manufacturing, its attempts to colonize Ireland, Newfoundland, and Virginia, its institution of the Poor Law in 1601 (which attempted to minimize vagrancy by finding work for the able-bodied unemployed and providing workhouses for the old and unemployable), and its mingling of economic classes and diverse social elements.

The splendor of the age was evidenced in the revival of learning—in the support of universities and grammar schools (although most Elizabethans were probably illiterate), in extensive building in the new architectural style of the Renaissance, and in the works of many of England's greatest poets, playwrights, and essayists: Shakespeare, Spencer, Johnson, Marlowe, Lyle, Sidney, and Francis Bacon—all assisted by the dissemination of printed matter which helped to establish English supremacy in language and literature.

By the end of the Tudor dynasty, England had become Protestant without a civil war and it held a firm position in world affairs. As a nation, most people knew an increase in material comforts. For the middle and upper classes, food, for example, was more plentiful than ever before. For the wealthy, life was abundant and luxurious, as evidenced in their clothes, furniture, armor, ornaments, jewelry, and fashionable homes. Even peasants yeoman farmers were relatively comfortable, eating regularly and dwelling in substantial cottages of brick or stone with wooden framework and sometimes erected on masonry foundations. Although the age was one of inconsistencies and excesses, most people were employed and had leisure time to enjoy their favorite recreations—games, the theater, and animal fights.

Elizabeth's death brought about the union of England and Scotland in that she left the crown to the first of the Stuart kings, James VI of Scotland, a country that had long been a dangerous rival. The Stuarts would reign, with one brief intermission, for a little over a century.

Although Elizabeth had attempted to put down the growth of Puritanism (in 1593 Parliament had passed an act which threatened to exile all those who refused to attend the Church of England), religious troubles were far from being settled. Under fear of torture and even death, some Puritans conformed outwardly but others emigrated. James, a Presbyterian, found himself in a difficult position. At first, he was friendly to the Catholics, but he was finally forced to take repressive measures when Guy Fawkes, a Catholic, in the Gunpowder Plot of 1605 attempted to blow up the Houses of Parliament. Weakened further by poorly selected advisors, James's rule deteriorated into increasing political and religious strife as he moved toward royal absolutism. He did, however, grant a charter to the London Company to settle in the New World, which resulted in the founding of Jamestown, the first permanent English settlement in North America, in 1607.

Charles's ascent to the throne in 1625 brought hope of a stronger ruler than James had been. But like his father, Charles had exalted notions of kingship. And like his father, he also selected the wrong advisors. Under Charles, English soldiers fought bitter battles in France while he wrangled at home over inflation and a failing economy with Parliament, which he dissolved in 1629. His distance from his subjects grew as he continued to favor the rival Spanish court life and collect expensive art objects, particularly the paintings of Reubens, Titian, and Van Dyke, from all over Europe. Although Charles remained a devout Anglican, he married a French Catholic, further widening the gap between the Royalists and the Parliamentarians-Puritans-Presbyterians. Although he recalled Parliament in 1640, domestic strife mounted until civil war broke out in 1642, a war which was fought somewhat reluctantly by both sides but which was to determine who would rule, the king or Parliament. The military success of the Parliamentarians over the Royalists and the subsequent beheading of Charles for treason in 1649 marked the first execution of a king by his people in Europe. Although Charles's death would later be interpreted as martyrdom, the absolutist tradition that had come with the Stuarts collapsed. At the time, the transference of power from the king to the Parliament seemed to signal a great victory for the people. But Oliver Cromwell, the head of the new Commonwealth government, was a Puritan who only appeared to be a republican; he would, in fact, become a military despot.

During Cromwell's reign, sober, rural traditions were praised. Theaters were closed and the press censored. Royal estates were sold, paintings were destroyed or sold, and sculpture was melted down. People wore plain clothes and cut their hair short. But although the Puritans experimented with governing for eleven years, Cromwell failed to establish a workable organization which could rule through its elected representatives. At his death in 1658, there was no one to take his place; his son, who succeeded him briefly, voluntarily resigned. As intense religious and political disputes continued, the nation grew tired of the wrangling. When Charles II, a friend of young Louis XIV of France, was restored to the throne in 1660, there was much rejoicing. Charles's return promised more flexibility. From the start, it was clear that life would be "more French," more elegant in dress and manners. Native English products were soon outclassed, at least in London society.

In short, the seventeenth century was an age of struggle, especially between king and Parliament and between religious groups. The two greatest literary figures of the period exemplify the extremes of the struggle. John Milton, Latin secretary to the Council of State and brilliant defender of Puritanism and native English rural traditions, stood for Parliament; John Dryden, a Roman Catholic critic, dramatist, and poet laureate of the court, stood for the monarchy.

But political, social, and intellectual groupings were not clear-cut. Englishmen were often mixtures of royalist sentiments while defending the institution of Parliament with religious, social, and intellectual differences equally mixed. In spite of such contradictions, most Englishmen welcomed the return of the monarchy, hoping for greater stability than the Commonwealth had produced.

Meanwhile, the Separatists, a persecuted band of religious Puritan zealots who felt that separation from the national Church of England was the only way for them to practice their beliefs in safety, fled to Holland. Twelve years later, largely because they feared losing their English culture, they decided to establish a colony in the New World. Even though they had read Captain John Smith's glowing accounts of the Massachusetts coast, they determined to settle in Virginia where an English colony already existed. Since they had little money, they turned to a company of merchants who recognized their industry and agreed to finance them. At the last minute, the company's unscrupulous changes in the contract caused many to remain in Holland, and their places were taken by non-Puritans, mostly Anglicans. After several false starts and a harrowing sixty-five days at sea, the 102 voyagers, only 35 of whom were actually Separatists, arrived at Cape Cod, Massachusetts. Too tired and too ill to proceed to Virginia, they decided to establish their colony where they had landed. Although over half of their number died during the first cruel winter, this hardy band persevered.

It should be noted that the English men and women who settled in the New World for whatever reasons were determined people set on making their way in the wilderness of North America. Although the Virginia settlers would not make their intellectual mark until the eighteenth century, the Puritan nonconformists who followed the earlier Pilgrim Separatists to New England made their cultural mark early. Many of their energies were absorbed by the hard work of creating a colony against tremendous odds— inclement climate, Indian attacks, rocky soil, and thick forests—but the intellectual caliber of the New Englanders was remarkably high, and they intended from the start to educate their young. In spite of their rigid moral codes and devotion to their particular faith, they had much of the spirit of the Renaissance in their zeal for knowledge. Some of their number were Oxford and Cambridge graduates. Not surprisingly, ships plying the seas between England and New England carried books.

Before long these same colonists, along with the grueling work of clearing massive forests and planting fields in virgin soil, were printing books. But that these colonials, and the thousands who followed, would in the next century establish a nation independent of the monarchy was beyond most men's imaginations.

DEVELOPMENT OF BOOKS

In Britain

Despite the contributions of William Caxton and Wynken de Worde and their contemporaries Richard Pynson, John Barbiar, John Lettou, Julian

Notary, and William de Machlinia (the latter four, like de Worde, had produced countless volumes to meet demands from students, schoolmasters, and lawyers), printing in England in the early sixteenth century was in a decline. Because its interests were almost totally economic and not aesthetic, it did not compare favorably with the great advances in design and illustration taking place on the continent, notably in Italy in the typography of Aldus Mantius and his successors, and in Germany in the woodcuts of Dürer and Holbein. Although England had produced some fine books in the late 1500s, such as the anonymous *Book of St. Albans* (1486) on hunting, hawking, and heraldry, which used two or three blocks for printing initials in color, the best of them reflected foreign influences. Caxton's best illustrated book, *Speculum Vitae Christi* (ca. 1486), for example, is thought to have contained imported woodcuts; Machlinia's *Primer* (ca. 1458) showed French influence. While Pynson, himself a Frenchman working in London, published more than three hundred works on theology, morality, grammar, language, and law, his best work, the *Morton Missal,* which is said to be the most beautiful book published in England before 1500, was illustrated with the work of a German artist, Hans Holbein.

Probably because Caxton and others had learned their art abroad, reliance on imported books and craftsmen was widely accepted at first. But the European connection began to fade when an Act of Parliament of 1484, which had permitted the foreign trade of books in England, was repealed. Foreign influence was further curtailed when successive acts of 1523 required young printers to be of English birth. Such laws were an attempt to protect English printers from foreign competition but, more to the point, they were an attempt to control the content of printed material. Imported religious matter often contained attacks on the Church or disseminated the doctrines of Luther. Such books were considered heretical and were frowned upon by the authorities. To impress upon the public how wicked these doctrines were, Luther was denounced as a heretic, and Lutheran books were publicly burned in London in 1521 and 1525. Booksellers were ordered not to handle such works without official approval. Wynken de Worde, for example, was questioned about one of his publications, *The Image of Love,* which was alleged to contain heretical implications. Other printers, even the king's printer, Thomas Berthelet, were questioned for no greater offence than failing to get official approval.

In spite of restrictions, the authorities were well aware that Lutheran pamphlets continued to be circulated and that copies of William Tyndale's translation of the New Testament, the first printed Bible in English which he began in Cologne and completed in the Protestant city of Worms, Germany, in 1525, were finding their way to England. (*See figure 6.*) Although John Wycliffe in the 1380s had translated the Bible into English, its suppression by the authorities and limited circulation (in manuscript) curbed its influence. But with printed material ever more readily available, by 1530 it was clear that the people were demanding a printed Bible in the vernacular. Coverdale's Bible of 1535, "Matthew's" Bible of 1537, and the Great Bible of 1539 were steps toward an "open Bible." But the way to the concept of widespread Bible reading by individuals was a tortuous one. For his part in the early translating and circulating of the Bible, Tyndale, for example, had been strangled and burned at the stake at Vilvorde Castle near Brussels in 1536. His last words were, "Lord, open the King of England's eyes." (*See figure 7.*)

Once the separation from the Church of Rome had been established by Parliament, the demand for a Bible in English began in earnest. Even then, Miles Coverdale, aware of Tyndale's fate, decided to do his work outside England. He translated the Old and New Testaments and published the first complete English Bible in Zurich in 1535. He based his New Testament largely on Tyndale's, but he modified the terms that were objectionable to the authorities and removed controversial notes; he based his Old Testament largely on Vulgate Latin and German texts. By 1537, a second edition of the Coverdale Bible, dedicated to the king, was being printed in England. In the same year a royal license also permitted another translation of the Bible, "Matthew's" Bible, printed in Antwerp, attributed to a nonexistent Thomas Matthew, but in fact the work of John Rogers, a disciple of Tyndale. Because of his work Rogers would be burned at the stake, along with nearly three hundred other dissidents, by the Catholic queen, Mary Tudor. In 1539, a revision of the "Matthew's" Bible was published by Richard Tavener, with a second revision in 1541. Both revisions were compilations of the work done by Tyndale and Coverdale. In 1539, the Great Bible, so named because of its size, edited largely by Coverdale, a friend of Thomas Cromwell, the king's vicar-general, became the first Bible "apoynted to the use of the churches." Its frontispiece, thought to have been designed by Holbein, shows Henry VIII handing a Bible to Thomas Cromwell and Archbishop Cranmer. By 1557, thirty editions of the complete Bible and fifty editions of the New Testament had been published in England.

In spite of the wide circulation of the Bible, not all people were considered equally well-equipped to read "this boke with judgement"; an act of 1543 forbade the reading of the Bible in English by women ("except noble or gentle women" who could read it to themselves only), apprentices, journeymen, artificers, servingmen, husbandmen, and laborers. These restrictions seem to indicate that literacy was fairly widespread among the social classes; it has been estimated, probably incorrectly, that 60 percent of the population could read. Although many people could read a "scant piece of the title," probably the reading level of most of the population was low, if they could read at all. It is also clear that interest in learning to read was indeed widespread and, at least in some areas such as Oxford, many people of all classes were literate.

The best sales records of the period are from the accounts of an Oxford bookseller of 1529, John Dorne. (But Oxford was a university town; Dorne's records might be atypical.) Although many of his 1,850 sales during ten months of that year were Latin works of a theological or classical nature, with 150 volumes by Erasmus, he also sold many books to beginning readers, both adults and children: ABC's, books of carols, ballads, poems, romances, lives of the saints, handbooks on cookery, carving, husbandry, treatment of horses, French and English vocabularies, and even fortune-telling. Some of Dorne's books were acquired abroad, but many were bought from London printers.

During the reign of Elizabeth, schools increased in number; clearly, people wanted to learn. Grammar schools, or petty schools, commonly provided the first stages—reading, writing, and sometimes arithmetic. Reading usually began with the hornbook which was generally a single sheet of print, containing the ABC's, the vowels, simple combinations of letters (ab, ba, and so on), and the Lord's Prayer. The printed sheet was pasted onto a wooden board in the shape of a paddle and covered with a thin sheet of transparent horn (the antlers from animals). (*See figure 8.*) From this the beginning reader went to the "Absey book," *The ABC with the Catechism*, which contained the alphabet, catechism, and prayers. This, in turn, led to the primer and catechism. Schools in which such beginning books were used were generally taught by the clergy. Where the clergy was industrious, learning flourished, as there was no lack of scholars. Many churches had chantry schools, at least partly taught by parishioners, in which boys and perhaps girls were trained to sing (and read) the Mass.

Although interest in learning to read in general and to read the Bible in particular continued to grow, Bible reading often had to be done in private as political changes occurred. For example, the ascension of Catholic Queen Mary to the throne in 1553 had brought the printing of Bibles to a complete stop, and Bible reading by individuals was considered heretical. But although Mary destroyed the Bibles used in churches, she was not able to rout out privately owned Bibles. Her persecutions caused many Protestant Bible scholars to flee to the continent to translate the Bible in comparative safety. When political fortunes changed again and Elizabeth came to the throne, these scholars made another translation in 1560 (the Old and the New Testament together with the Apocrypha) which popularly became known as the Geneva Bible. (The Geneva Bible was sometimes referred to as the "Breeches Bible" because its translation of Genesis 3:7 says that Adam and Eve covered themselves with fig-leaf breeches.) Although immensely popular with the common people, the Geneva Bible was not accepted officially by the Church of England because of its nonconformist leanings. In 1568 the archbishop of Canterbury, Matthew Parker, undertook to do a more acceptable translation based on the Great Bible; this translation was accepted by the Church of England where it became known as the Bishop's Bible. Fearing persecu-

tion under Protestant Elizabeth, many Catholic scholars fled to the continent, to Douai in France. These exiles printed their version of the New
Testament, in 1582, and of the Old Testament, in 1593. All of these translations would to some degree influence the Authorized (King James) Version
in 1611.

Throughout the sixteenth century, the demand for all kinds of books
continued to grow. The most popular subjects were religion, law, medicine,
practical manuals, education, arithmetic, astronomy, science, geography,
news, and literature. The range of religious books went from full translations of the Bible, as discussed above, to expensive folio volumes of over a
hundred sermons, or a broadside of a single sermon bought for a few pence.
These sermons, many of which were reprinted over and over, reveal the
period's spirited religious conflicts and zeal, and as such they were con-
sistent best sellers in the booksellers' stalls. Legal books were also in great
demand, from the *Statutes of the Realm* and *Year Books,* printed by Richard
Totell, to booklets on how to hold court or carry out the duties of constables.
Medical books, particularly herbals and recipes for good health, especially
those offering help in case of the dreaded plague, were extremely popular.
Manuals which provided practical instruction in such household matters as
planting, cooking, blood-letting, grafting, keeping bees, writing letters,
serving at table, acquiring a foreign language, playing musical instruments,
and cultivating the memory, took the place of the encyclopedias of information that had been popular from medieval days. Educational books, such as
Latin-English dictionaries, vocabularies, and grammar, were sought, but
new educational ideas based on Erasmus's "rational studies" also demanded
that composition, that is, the writing of prose, was essential to Latin studies,
and his many works translated into English provided that assistance. Books
on arithmetic that taught the use of spheres, the compass, and the astrolabe,
as well as astronomy and science (almanacs, the weather, eclipses), and
geography (sea travel was especially exciting to the Elizabethan imagination)
were all in great demand. But the "news" was probably the most popular
printed item. Ballad writers and cheap pamphleteers deluged the periodical market, that is, the "small copies" market which was published by "small"
printers, with often lurid accounts of trials and executions, exposure of
witches, the antics of those who were possessed by the Devil, the births of
monstrous animals and human beings, and the like. The Elizabethans,
however, also enjoyed a high quality of literature: poems, sonnets, verses,
translations of classical works, chivalric romances, stories and tales of all
sorts. Although the publishing of plays had not been taken seriously by the
early printers (only twenty-seven plays were printed by 1558), their publication increased enormously during the last decade of the century. Between
1590 and 1602, one hundred and three plays were published; many of them,
even Shakespeare's, were printed "unlawfully," that is, pirated for profit.

By the end of the sixteenth century, England had nineteen printers with thirty-three printing machines, and at least two hundred booksellers in London alone.

From the beginning, printing books was extremely competitive, first because of pirating and later because of monopolies. When a book sold well, it was often stolen or pirated by another printer almost at once, with profits to the originator of the work diminishing with every copy sold by another printer. Not until the printers joined with the booksellers' Stationers' Company (which had been founded in 1403) did their combined forces bring some control over pirating. The control, licensing by the Crown, was not one-sided, however. Although the King's Proclamation of 1538 offered protection against pirating, it also demanded that books be officially approved as fit, that is, not seditious to Crown nor derogatory to Church. In 1557, the Stationers' Company was granted a royal charter giving its membership the sole right to publish books that had secured a license. All seemed well, but out of this approval by the Crown, certain printers gained extraordinary privileges.

As early as 1485, Peter Actors had called himself "Stationer to the King"; he was followed by "Official Printers to the King"—William Faques, Richard Pynson, Thomas Berthelet, Richard Grafton, John Cawood, Richard Jugge. Such printers were singled out to do public service books for the Crown as well as manuals, prayer books, catechisms and the like, all of which established reputations and turned substantial profits. After the rise of the Stationers' Company, internal wranglings over the right to be official printers of the basic books (religion and education) brought great monopolistic power to certain printers. John Day, for example, one of the richest stationers and favored by the Crown, held many valuable patents, including Cunningham's *Cosmographical Glasse* (1559), Foxe's *Book of Martyrs* (1563), *Book of Christian Prayers* (1589), and the catechism, the ABC and primers, psalm books, and *Lily's Grammar.*

In addition to courting favor from the Crown, printers sought out patrons from the upper classes, who often commissioned a translation, the reprinting of an already published work, or the printing of a new work, which would then be dedicated to the sponsor. Patrons were actively sought by printers for financial support and as encouragement to the general reader, but they were also secured by authors as protection from critics. Dedicatory letters to patrons invoking protection were common.

Probably the most notable book patron of all times was James I, for it was to him that the Authorized Version of the Bible of 1611 was dedicated. Although the design of the Authorized Version cannot be compared to the beautiful folio Bibles that were being published abroad at the time, the Authorized Version was a remarkable achievement, and its translation was one of the great literary works of all time.

When James I ascended the throne in 1603, the Bishop's Bible, as noted before, was the official version used in churches, but the Bible used in homes continued to be the Geneva, which carried distinctly Calvinist theories in its marginal notes. In spite of his Calvinist beliefs, John Reynolds, a prominent Puritan, proposed to the king that because both translations were deficient, a new, conclusive translation should be made which could be used in church and home. James was enthusiastic about the venture, and forty-seven biblical scholars were chosen to do the translation without regard to theological or ecclesiastical bias; they were divided into six committees, two to work at Cambridge, two at Oxford, and two at Westminster, each group working on assigned portions. The resulting translation, published by the king's printer, Robert Barker, met amazing acceptance. In a short time, more than 150 editions were available for home reading although many editions were hastily, or perhaps spitefully, printed and consequently of poor quality. Omission of words, phrases, and sometimes whole lines was common. The 1631 edition, for example, printed by Barker, omitted *not* from the Seventh Commandment: "Thou shalt not commit adultery." Editions of this "Wicked Bible" were immediately called in and burned, but not soon enough to prevent the ruin of Barker's reputation. Most observers today believe the "error" was intentionally committed by a jealous printer, Bonham Norton, who was angry over missing out on Barker's lucrative Bible patent, and who induced proofreaders to allow the blasphemous misprint to go undetected. Norton, however, did not live to benefit; he died soon after in disgrace. But quarreling over monopolies was common, especially in regard to the Bible. When the Puritan Parliament came to power, it opposed the monopoly of Bible printing and its subsequent scandals as "wicked and intolerable."

The political-religious upheavals of seventeenth-century England brought many restrictions; one of the most affecting was censorship of the press. In the first years of printing when most printed matter was translations of classics and ecclesiastical writings accessible to only a few scholars and clergy, printing was not considered a threat to established authority. But as printing spread and literacy along with it, the Crown realized the power of the press. To restrain such power, the number of print shops and foundries was limited, in 1637, by royal decree. Only four cities—London, Oxford, Cambridge, and York—were allowed to have presses. The most severely restricted printers were those in London who worked nearest the royal censor, the Star Chamber, and the Stationers' Company. Restrictions were relaxed only when during the Civil War (1642-1646), Charles I took the king's printers and some of their presses from London to York and to Shrewsbury to produce royalist propaganda.

The results of censorship were deplored by many, the most eloquent of whom was John Milton when he addressed Parliament in 1643, speaking out for freedom of the press and against the restrictions on papers, pamphlets, and books. But his plea had no immediate effect. Restriction continued. Printing in all areas was tightly contained, but it would not be so forever.

The first feeble sparks signaling freedom of the press were ignited with the coming of newspapers, although their immediate effect was short-lived. The first newspaper, *Avisa Relation oder Zeitung,* was published in Germany in 1609. England's first news-type publication was not issued until 1622 by Nathaniel Butter, Nicholas Bourne, and Thomas Archer, and then it landed Archer in Holland, a refuge for journalists. From Holland, journalists operated clandestine presses that served countries where censorship was in force, such as England. With the coming of the Commonwealth in 1646, journalists hoped to gain more freedom, but Cromwell immediately instituted restrictions as repressive as those of any of the kings who preceded him. Restrained once more, the newspaper press was forced to lie dormant for the time, but it was far from dead.

In spite of censorship, patent quarrels, suppression, and even book burning, people continued to expand their reading interests at home and in public; when they were free to read the Bible in public, they read copies chained to desks or rails. Such chained libraries (a famous one is in Hereford Cathedral) were well used until about 1625.

Interest in book buying also continued, as literary masterpieces by such writers as Bacon, Milton, Bunyan, Herrick, Browne, and Walton were produced in abundance. But the quality of English book work in general was so low that even the Scriptures, as mentioned before, were affected by feuding among printers and by a general carelessness, brought on perhaps by the speed often needed to escape censorship. In addition to the Wicked Bible already mentioned, other notorious examples of slipshod work of the period were the Judas Bible of 1611 in which Judas, not Jesus, prays in Gethsemane, the Vinegar Bible of 1617 which changes the Parable of the Vineyard to the Parable of the Vinegar, and the Printers' Bible of 1702 which says "Printers have persecuted me" instead of "Princes have. . . ."

Not until Dr. John Fell of Oxford began the reformation of English printing did England begin to produce fine books once again. Although the king had appointed Oxford University the official Bible publisher of the realm as early as 1636, only when Fell acquired Dutch type matrices in 1675 and established a type foundry at Oxford in 1676 did the course of English printing turn in a new direction.

In America

Meanwhile, printing had found its way to America. When the English Puritans migrated to America, they took books, especially religious books, and they continually ordered more from England. Although the colony of

Virginia had been the first one settled, those colonists were not in general as scholarly as the New England settlers, and when they read, they read historical and travel books. But the New England settlers, largely educated Puritans, were adamant readers who demanded books of substance on religion, law, and politics.

In 1638 the first printing press was established in America. In that year, Joseph Glover, a nonconformist clergyman from Sutton in Surrey, imported a printing press from Cambridge, England, to Cambridge, Massachusetts. Although Glover died on the voyage, Stephen Daye, a locksmith that Glover had indentured to operate the press, and his son Matthew set up the press under the auspices of the president of Harvard and began work. Probably Stephen Daye was not a printer at all, but a qualified locksmith able to erect and maintain a press. Matthew, his nineteen-year-old son, had acquired some printing experience before coming to America; by 1647 he printed an *Almanack* under his own name.

The first printed piece the Dayes issued was the "Freeman's Oath, an Oath of Allegiance to the King" (1638), printed on a half sheet of small paper; it was followed by *An Almanack for 1639.* It is generally believed that their next work, *The Whole Booke of Psalmes,* in 1640, a reprint of a popular English text first published in 1562, was the first book printed in the New World; still extant, it is a plain but useful volume set in mixed type styles with a border of scrolled ornaments around its title page. (*See figure 9.*) Although four other publications (not extant) followed quickly, it was a *List of Theses* (1643), published for the Harvard College Commencement, which revealed the first considerable improvement in typography.

Twenty years later a second press was imported from England to Cambridge, Massachusetts, the city which held the sole privilege for printing. In 1654, John Eliot published a primer of an Indian language, *Catechism, in the Indian Language of Massachusetts.* In 1661, Eliot's translation of the New Testament into the language of the Natick Indians was printed by Marmaduke Johnson, the first master printer in America. Such a book presented many problems. The language had to be translated into sounds represented by the English alphabet, and into concepts that were meaningful to the Indians. Some Indian words even had to be invented, such as the title. Difficult as it was, the project reveals the lengths to which the colonists went to convert the native population. The entire *Mamvsse, Wunneetupana-tamwe, Up-Biblum God, naneesive, Nukkona Testament, kah wonk, Wusku Testament,* that is, the Old and New Testaments, was completed in 1663 by the Dayes' successor, Samuel Green, with the help of Marmaduke Johnson and an Indian youth later christened James Printer. (*See figure 10.*)

Most colonial books were printed in English, but some were printed in German, Dutch, and French. While many of these books were of an ecclesiastical nature, the colonials also kept historical records, and they wrote on social compacts, law, and politics; their main literary techniques were logic, allegory, satire, and invective.

Books published for children in the colonies were almost exclusively religious books, particularly catechisms. It is thought that the first book for children printed in America was John Cotton's *Milk for Babes, Drawn Out of the Breasts of Both Testaments, Chiefly for the spiritual nourishment of Boston Babes in either England . . .* in 1646. By the end of the century, eleven different catechisms in twenty editions were available. Other books for children (hornbooks, battledores, primers, ABC's, religious tracts, lesson books on manners and morals) also abounded, including a translation of one of the most famous German books of the seventeenth century, Comenius's *Orbis sensualium pictus, or Visible World—for the Use of Young Latin Scholars.* Possibly later colonial children also knew the *Book of Art and Instruction for Young People,* a translation of *Kunst und Lehrbüchlein,* first published by Feyerbend in Germany in 1580. Certainly seventeenth-century English children knew the book and its fine full-page woodcuts done by Jost Amman. The work is credited by some authorities with being the true picture book designed for children. (*See figure 11.*)

Censorship in England's colonies resembled censorship in the ruling country. Although not as restricted, printers were subject to approval by the royal governors. If a printer did not find favor with the authorities, he could lose his equipment, be fined, and even be imprisoned. As in England, the number of presses in the colonies was limited. At first, as mentioned above, the sole city for printing in America was Cambridge, Massachusetts, but this limitation would gradually be revised as the Americans edged toward independence.

ATTITUDES TOWARD AND TREATMENT OF CHILDREN

In Britain

Children in sixteenth- and seventeenth-century England were not valued, at least not by present-day standards. For one thing, they were not regarded as individuals with special child status; they were thought of no differently from adult members of the family. But the advancement of any individual was not considered important, regardless of age or class. Personal affections and ambitions of both young and old were of minor concern compared with the family's economy and well-being. Second, with the life span at about thirty years, infant mortality remained high although amulets and charms were used as protections against disease, death, the "evil eye," and the Devil. The probable death of offspring surely restricted parental affection. For centuries it had been necessary to breed many children because it was certain that only a few would survive. For this and other reasons, the size of a middle- or upper-class family might be as large as forty or even more. The family unit included one's own children and their spouses, first-born grandchildren, sisters, the elderly, and sometimes cousins, spinster aunts, as well as servants in a noble's house and apprentices in a master's household. This unit needed frequent realignment as deaths and births occurred. Much like the family in the Middle Ages, all members usually ate and lived together; later on, some of the upper-class families began to set aside servants' quarters, and some merchants and farmers began to build smaller houses, leading to smaller family units. In general, the family was large, with members of many ages who even dressed similarly, but with no special affectional status due anyone. Under such circumstances, focused sentimental attachments were limited. Because life, especially for the young, was so precarious, the age of the child had little importance. Although parish registers of birth were introduced in 1538, not until the Registration of Birth Act in 1836 did registration take place with regularity.

Infanticide was still practiced by all classes through exposure, strangulation, bruising, or whatever, but it was especially practiced by the poor who abandoned children in city streets or along country roads, most often because they could not feed them. When children of the poor survived, they were put to work at a very young age, usually as apprentices. The population boom of the late sixteenth and early seventeenth centuries brought a spate of apprentice laws, both as a protection for poor children and also as a protection for society against the potential threat of these "sturdy beggars." In 1536, for example, every parish was required to put beggar children between five and fourteen to work in unskilled jobs, with justices of the peace as overseers. Another act in 1598 made each parish responsible for putting its destitute orphaned children to work. Under cruel overseers, such children were often gravely mistreated. Even though some early schools had been started for the children of the poor (for example, at Canterbury), most such children were in fact not given education but were instead made to sort wool, tend sheep, knit, spin, weave, and so on—in short, to work at any menial task which might contribute to their upkeep.

Children generally, in all classes, were considered "miniature but trouble-some men and women." Because of the high death rate, parents of all classes often had superfluous children; these children were frequently sent to school simply because they were "troubling the house at home" and not because "they should learn anything in effect." Well into the eighteenth century schools were often used as dumping grounds for poor and rich children alike and also served to give employment to schoolmasters who were often older, lower-class, surplus people themselves.

The idea of the child as a developing human being was not yet born, perhaps in part because Elizabethan society believed that life did not progress; it repeated itself in cycles and spirals, each cycle repeating the last at a more complicated level. An individual's life was not thought of as a steady progression, but rather a sequence of short time periods, such as is described in Shakespeare's speech on the seven ages of man in *As You Like It*. The child accepted the fact that when he was ready to marry, he would establish his own household, the goal of his growth. He accepted the narrowness of his prescribed place in society, knowing that everyone had tasks suited to age and station. The common man did not expect life to improve or change, only to recycle. Nor did Elizabethan thinkers conceive of education as a progressive exercise or "ladder." It was instead something that occurred like life itself, in stages, each one more complex than before. The university curriculum, for instance, repeated the grammar school curriculum, but it amplified it; by the same token, the university student received floggings the same as the grammar school boy, perhaps even more rigorously. Only the lowest form of schooling, primary education, was not a dilution of the stage above; it was a place to acquire reading and writing, the mechanical foundations on which grammar school and university education was based.

Children were introduced into the adult world of school or work at the earliest possible age, usually between seven and nine. When children were accounted for in a specific way, it was almost always in regard to legal matters, such as the terms of an inheritance which would affect the family's fortunes.

As in the Middle Ages, infants were swaddled, although by the end of the seventeenth century there would be warnings against the practice. And children were sent to wet nurses almost immediately after birth. As before, children were also sent to exchange households, as an apprentice to a master, or a page or maid to a lord. During this period children were more likely to be sent to friends or acquaintances rather than strangers, but the purpose of sending children away from home was the same: to teach children skills or give them training by unrelated adults who might also arrange for economic benefits, that is, marriage. In upper-class households, children were taught manners and courtesy, music, matters of rank, the skill of serving—to carve meat was a great responsibility—all menial tasks, but generally without the taint of servility, affording experiences in practical matters not covered by education in schools or universities.

Girls in such exchange situations were trained to be good wives, that is, they were taught to manage a household by knowing how to preside over servants and over the working of the estate in case of widowhood, to ensure food and clothing for the entire household, to make drugs, and even to practice surgery and midwifery—as well as sometimes learning to read, write, do needlework, sing, and play an instrument. In some of the more scholarly families, girls pursued intellectual studies, learning Latin and Greek as well as the romance languages, reading the Scriptures and history, and doing translations. While most girls of all classes were sent away from their families, a few were tutored at home, sometimes by excellent teachers.

But for some upper-class boys of the period, educational practices stemming from the social order of the Middle Ages were beginning to change. Roger Ascham, one of the most famous tutors of the period, thought that noble boys should be educated in new ways along with the old; that is, along with tilting, hunting, hawking, and so on, they should also learn law and international languages, and they should be taught to make correct moral judgments.

With the expansion of trade both international and domestic, it was becoming clear that knowledge afforded power. If the next generation were to have power, educators realized that males must be adequately guided both as scholars and gentlemen. As the middle class began to grow, moral rectitude and a sense of propriety in social and economic affairs grew along with the notion of spiritual salvation, which was never out of mind in English education. As these ideas developed, so did the notion of an organized grammar school education and, along with it, the concept of childhood, per se, slowly emerged.

Classical studies and religious instruction based on logic had long been the basis of right ways of conduct in English society, but gradually moral training would become "practical." Grammar schools came to rely heavily on highly moralistic courtesy books (books on good manners). Along with books on domestic relations, these courtesy books which combined manners with virtue, as well as psalms and prayers, were highly favored by the middle class. Advice on all matters of behavior, admonitions against gambling, swearing, lying, malice, and so on, and arguing for the virtues of charity, love, and patience—always reflecting the duties of children on each level of society—were the main thrust of sixteenth-century education.

Educational reformers began to have some influence: Erasmus argued that parents should treat their children more humanely, paying special attention to their interests; John Colet urged gentleness; Roger Ascham crusaded against teaching based on the rod and urged that children be brought to learning through desire, although he did not think that all children should be trained equally. Probably the most important was John Mulcaster who advocated reforms in diet and clothing; he also prescribed programs of exercise. Of discipline he said that gentleness was "more nedefull than beatings." He also believed that girls should have the full advantages of the best education—reading, writing, music, and, if desired, language and medicine. Other important schoolmasters were Charles Hoole, who, along with editing several textbooks, translated Comenius's *Orbis Pictus* into English, and Richard Brinsley, who wrote *Ludus Literarius,* a treatise for adults admonishing them for sending their children away from home when they were too young. He too spoke against excessive flogging and suggested that the rod be only a "little twig."

With the growing interest in education came a new consciousness of the responsibility of parents toward their children. Children were finally beginning to be noticed; they were beginning to have an educational system that paid some small attention to their special needs rather than focusing exclusively on a system of service to society. Part of this development stemmed from a waning of the practice of exchanging children. If the child went to school in his own village, for example, the parent might even rehearse him in his lessons. Even if the child went to boarding school, he returned home often, thus linking the child to his family. Increased contact gradually brought about closer ties, and more frequent concern for the child's well-being. But the notion that the child was a developing human being would be slow to evolve. Throughout the period, parents were advised to keep their distance from their offspring, lest their children undermine parental authority and thereby grow irreverent. But the fact that manuals on domestic relations began carrying such admonitions suggests that changes were beginning to occur.

In spite of such development, children generally continued to be thought of as unimportant. Perhaps this was the reason why a few precocious children pushed themselves into adult affairs. Although fifteen was the usual age to enter university, some boys at age twelve or thirteen went to Cambridge and Oxford. Often these boys were accompanied by a parent who supervised them. Nonscholarly boys, as early as age seven, often distinguished themselves in other ways, particularly in archery (which was far more favored in English life than handball, football, or hockey). Other boys, as young as twelve, even accompanied adults—that is, their lords or their fathers—to battle. Girls, too, were expected to embark on their domestic duties in noble households at age twelve or thirteen.

The basic theme of Elizabethan life was belief in the necessity of order and the need for unquestioned obedience to authority—children to parents, apprentice to master, scholar to teacher, and the individual to the church and the state. Not surprisingly, children who were on the lowest level in all classes felt the sting of enforced obedience, that is, the discipline of the rod, most keenly.

The rod prevailed. The seal of the Louth Grammar School, founded in 1552, for example, carried the Latin inscription "Spare the rod and spoil the child"; it shows the master beating a child with a birch rod. Children were psychologically restricted as well; the school day was long. Children who went to grammar schools (which had increased in number rapidly between 1502 and 1515) were admitted at about seven or eight years of age, the same age that the upper-class boy was sent off to be a page. Such children began school at six in the morning with Latin recitation (homework given the day before) beginning before seven; class work went on till nine when pupils were given fifteen minutes for breakfast or for "honest recreation," that is, preparing for their next hours of work; they continued work until eleven o'clock. After a noon intermission they started again at one o'clock, continuing until 3:30 when they recessed for another fifteen-minute intermission; they worked again till 5:30 when the day ended with the singing of psalms and Bible reading till approximately 6:00 P.M. Even then, detractors objected to the two fifteen-minute breaks although they were assured that whatever games were played were carefully supervised with no "perilous" or "clownish sports" and no "playing for money." At some grammar schools—Saint Paul's, for instance—children also said prayers in the morning, at noon, and in the evening. Sundays were spent attending church, where the pupils took notes on the sermon, knowing they would be questioned on it the following day. No holidays were permitted except those allowed by the king or archbishop or bishop. Whippings were commonplace. According to an account by schoolmaster Henry Peacham, one master beat his pupils to warm himself on cold mornings. Birch rods were so much a part of life that peddlers sold "fine Jemmies . . . London Tartars" on the street, with the cost of the rods often charged to the boys themselves. Although some enlightened schoolmasters of the day, such as Roger Ascham and Richard Mulcaster, argued against excessive flogging, their advice went largely unheeded. Because children were considered diminutive adults and "troublesome," the rod was accepted as a necessary and important instructive instrument for inculcating obedience, work, manners, and religion. Even such humanists as Erasmus and Comenius wondered if the education of children had much real worth.

In spite of living under the threat of severe discipline, schoolboys did experience the lighter side of life on some occasions, especially when they participated in sports. Some sports, such as the popular bearbaiting, which even Queen Elizabeth enjoyed, and cockfighting, bullbaiting, cockthrowing, and frogthrowing, would be far too cruel for modern tastes. In Elizabethan England, however, bearbaiting and cockfighting might even be held in schoolrooms as part of the Shrove Tuesday celebrations. Boys, and girls in some instances, also played games such as archery, wrestling, leapfrog, stone throwing, ice skating (on sharpened animal bones which were attached to the feet), prisoner's base, hoodman-blind (blind man's buff), hot cockles, bob-cherry, dancing at moonrise and dancing around maypoles, hoop-and-hide (hide and seek), stool-ball (probably a forerunner of cricket), rounders (probably a forerunner of baseball), battledore and shuttlecock (forerunners of badminton), tennis, fencing, swimming, fishing, riding the see-saw, and many others.

Schools were always under the eye of the authorities. Roman Church-connected chantry schools, for example, had been abolished as "superstitious" when Henry VIII ascended the throne. And grammar schools underwent difficult times during the Reformation, suffering purges and counter-purges during that period of religious change. But universities suffered the most under the watchful eyes of vacillating leadership. Under some regimes, university scholars were purged and books were burned. Not until

Elizabeth's ascent to the throne in 1553 did some stability return, and university life began to improve: rooms, for example, were provided for students as well as for the dons, and some even had heat. Extravagance, however, especially in dress (although the period emphasized fashions) was frowned upon for students.

The curriculum in the free grammar school and the university was still based on the *trivium* (grammar, logic, rhetoric) and the *quadrivium* (music, arithmetic, geometry, astronomy) with Latin grammar the base. But the coming of the printed word along with the Reformation and the New Learning brought changes. Students no longer depended entirely on lectures; they now had printed texts to read themselves. Printed books also brought a growing concern for literary style and subsequent development of taste. In the Middle Ages, logic had been the base of theological study; now the printed English Bible became the focus of divinity studies and religious instruction. Once entirely theoretical, mathematics was becoming "practical" in that it was needed by businessmen negotiating increased trade and by navigators exploring the New World. The study of astronomy proper, however, lay in the future along with the soon-to-be-discovered telescope; Copernican theories went unheeded. Little of the natural sciences was known, except zoology as it related to the breeding of horses and dogs, and botany as it related to the making of Elizabethan gardens. Certain scientific discoveries were also making their mark on education, such as the study of the earth's magnetism. But the study of music declined, probably because of its being too "popish." It was, in fact, all but abolished in churches and was taught mostly in the home. Explorations in the New World made geography popular, geography being "cosmography"—a factual and fictional mixture of geography, anthropology, natural philosophy, history, astrology, and navigation. Many people, such as schoolmaster Richard Mulcaster, were calling for use of English as the language of instruction, but proficiency in Latin remained the standard test of an educated person.

Ideally, grammar schools and universities were available, financially and geographically, to all sixteenth- and seventeenth-century boys; Elizabethan education was based on the concept that schools be available to all for the good of the state. There are many accounts, however, of "free" grammar schools in which the schoolmasters were allowed to charge admission fees, sometimes based on ability to pay; some schools allowed the masters to receive tips from the pupils' relatives; some schools had special places allotted to the poor, but the number of such students was limited; some schools had entrance requirements, ranging from the pupil's knowing how to write his own name to his knowing English grammar perfectly; still others required the catechism. In practice, the children of the poor were often excluded. Not until 1699 were charity schools established explicitly for the poor. Girls, too, were often excluded. When educated, they generally received only a primary education, although in some cases this was very respectable. Primary education varied greatly; it often fulfilled the requirement for admission to the grammar school. And many large grammar schools insisted that the child have basic knowledge before being admitted. Such knowledge supposedly could be attained in a petty school (for little children) or sometimes in a dame school (schools run by old women who were often as ignorant of education as the children they taught). Small grammar schools usually took all pupils, the ill-prepared as well as others, and thus used a much diluted curriculum.

Primary education usually consisted of learning the alphabet, putting vowels and consonants together (ag, eg, ig, og, ug), learning diphthongs and longer letter combinations, first from a hornbook and later from primers. Writing with quill and ink was learned by copying examples made by the schoolmaster or a scrivener, written in English cursive script called Secretary or in the Italian style, an influence of the New Learning. Sometimes special writing teachers were brought in for a few weeks during the year to teach penmanship.

Although the teaching of French was not part of the usual school curriculum, it was taught in many private schools which existed for sons of the nobility and for sons of well-to-do merchants who traded abroad. Middle- and upper-class boys and girls in intellectual families were sometimes tutored in French at home by refugees from France and the Low Countries, who were much in demand.

Although the post-Renaissance schools on the continent had predominantly classical goals, English schools did not necessarily follow suit. While the English school curriculum contained classical authors, and Latin and Greek speech and composition, its main impulse was always religious. In fact, grammar schools in the first half of the sixteenth century were based on Dean Colet's Statutes of 1518 stating that schools were intended "to increase knowledge and worshipping God and Our Lord Jesus Christ and good Christian life and Manners in the children." The rise of Puritanism from 1559 to 1660 provided a distinctly religious thrust in English schools and society.

Although Puritanism in England had culminated in a civil war, the Puritans made a great impact on British education. They had also taken education to the American colonies. Sternly moralistic in their treatment of and attitudes toward children, but not as apt to use the rod as some of their forebears, they, like other Elizabethans, believed in obedience to authority, and they demanded such from their children. They also taught the rewards of moral virtue along with the results of sin. They sermonized against vice and lewdness and wrote and preached long sermons on the dangers of indolence, frivolity, and wickedness, all leading to eternal torment in the fires of Hell. While Puritan children were not appreciated and understood according to present-day notions, there is much evidence that Puritan parents rejoiced over their children's recoveries from illness and wept over their deaths. It is clear that they were much concerned with the lives of their children, especially their spiritual lives, and they were completely sure that they were properly preparing their children for the life hereafter.

With the coming of the Reformation, the Church of England had assumed the religious and political controls relinquished by the Church of Rome. Ecclesiastical control shifted again when Catholic Queen Mary ascended the throne. But after experiencing the death of nearly three hundred martyrs at the hand of Mary Tudor, Protestant parents of all sects under Elizabeth insisted that their children be trained in Protestantism so that a Catholic monarch would never suppress them again; thus, children were taught religion in the school as well as the home. Even when Elizabeth became repressive and Puritan scholars fled to the continent, religious instruction of a Protestant nature continued to be taught to the children.

Religious strife, culminating in the Civil War which started in 1642, plagued seventeenth-century English society. Only after the Restoration in 1660 did Puritan scholars dare to devise their own schools and colleges, "academies," for the purpose of training their own ministers. The academies would lead a precarious existence, but by the eighteenth century they would be among the soundest of all educational institutions in England.

Meanwhile, many Puritan and other dissenters fled to the New World, and prisoners, apprentices, the poor and the children of the poor, vagrants, and destitute orphans followed.

The fluctuations of English social and educational change continued. Charity schools, for example, designed for the education of the poor at first flourished, especially in the cities where wealthy merchants contributed to them proudly. (By 1729 there were over 1600 such schools. But similar movements, such as the creation of Foundling Hospital in 1741 for destitute children, were not so well received; the predicted reformation of manners and morals among the poor who went to school had not occurred.)

Idealistic Elizabethan reformers had tried to end poverty through education and law, particularly laws relating to the apprentices. Through such improvements they had tried to raise up the poor to become responsible citizens of the state. But these hopes grew feeble with the rise of the workhouses of the mid-seventeenth century. Although the concept of giving poor children a combination of education and work skills was laudable, workhouses soon provided little primary education and more and more became places where children were used as workers at minimal wages. When children, because of lack of stamina, frequent illness, and often early deaths could not turn a profit, many were returned to idleness and even starvation.

By the time of the Restoration, the idealism of the sixteenth- and seventeenth-century educational and social reformers had spent itself. Education was generally inadequate for both rich and poor on both sides of the Atlantic. But there was a growing consciousness of at least the presence of the child in all classes. Although educational principles in no way reflected our present system's concern for the child's growth and development, at the very least the schools in Britain and shortly, in America, provided a separate institution created especially for the young.

In America

From the first it was clear that the American colonists, like their English counterparts, desired education for their offspring. By 1636, only six years after the settling of Boston, the General Court, the governing body, gave half of the annual income of the entire colony of Massachusetts to the establishment of Harvard College. Conditions in Virginia, however, were not as good although many Virginians desired education for their young. The governor of that colony so mistrusted schools and the press that he forbade the establishment of both, fearing that they would bring "disobedience and heresy." But New England was controlled by Puritan ministers who believed in instruction. Before long, all New England colonies had schools supported at the expense of the parents. It was not until the time of the Revolution that schools in Boston were paid for entirely by town taxes; shortly after, such means of support became the norm.

Colonial educational modes were similar to those in England, but the schoolrooms were even more sparsely furnished, supplies severely limited. Because paper was scarce, birch bark and slates were often substituted. Although most colonial boys were provided schooling, the girls fared less well. As in England, the female was usually trained in domestic duties first. Even in the best families, colonial girls seldom learned more than basic reading, writing, and arithmetic, and occasionally music. Dame schools, however, for small boys and girls, existed almost from the beginning. In these schools, old widows, for very low wages, kept school in one room of their homes. Some upper-class girls had private tutors in their own homes; still others went to cities such as Boston which had private boarding schools where favored young girls were taught by private teachers. In most cases, even these schools stressed good behavior and how to carry out domestic duties rather than intellectual studies.

As in England, discipline was severe. Using Proverbs 22:15 as their guide, parents, teachers, and ministers employed the rod, as well as other types of whips. They also used split birch branches to pinch the end of a culprit's nose. Ferules and thimbles were used to rap pupils' heads; offending children were sometimes yoked together; talking children were quieted by wooden gags, "Whispering sticks," placed in the mouth. Children were also punished by having to sit on one-legged stools (unipods), by standing on dunce stools, by wearing dunce caps or heavy leather spectacles, and wearing placards hung from their necks which proclaimed their misdeeds. Other punishments included having to hold heavy loads and being placed in the pillory, like common criminals.

Like English children, colonial children learned their lessons from hornbooks, reading-boards (wooden tablets), and primers. In short, colonial education varied only in degree from its English origin. From the beginning, however, it was clear that climbing the social scale was a realistic goal in the colonies. Although sharp divisions existed between the rich and the poor, hard work, ambition, acquired skills (usually through apprenticeships), and good luck enabled many colonial boys to leave home early (it had long been an English tradition) and strike out on their own.

ANNOTATED CHRONOLOGY

ca. 1500

Bevis of Hampton (anonymous; a famous medieval romance from the oral tradition; the story tells of a child who is sold into slavery by his mother and later becomes a king who defends his land and his beloved princess from their enemies; the oldest complete extant text with woodcuts was printed by William Copeland; numerous versions of this popular story were published with some being appropriated by children). BM, UCL, UOx

Guy of Warwick (anonymous; a popular medieval romance about the son of the steward of the Earl of Warwick who did heroic deeds, won the love of the earl's daughter, and died a pious hermit; numerous versions were published, with some being appropriated by children; first printed in London by Wynken de Worde).

A Lytell Geste of Robyn Hode (anonymous; a traditional hero story in verse about the legendary Robin Hood of Sherwood Forest in Nottingham; printed in London by Wynken de Worde; *Robin Hood's Garland. Being a complete history of all the notable and merry exploits performed by him and his men, etc.* was a popular chapbook edition of the traditional ballads, which was printed in London by Sympson Warehouse, 1770?; both the stories and songs are used with children to the present). BCL, CPL, UCL

The Young Children's Book (anonymous; a manuscript courtesy book for "young children that bide not long at school"; possibly based in part on Dionysius Cato's fourth-century work).

ca. 1504

Valentine and Orson (anonymous; a popular romantic French tale probably based on the oral tradition: the story of twin princes, sons of the emperor of Greece, one of whom is raised by a bear; translated from a ca. 1498 French edition by Henry Watson, an apprentice to Wynken de Worde, printed in London by Wynken de Worde; William Copeland printed an edition ca. 1566; appropriated by children). TPL

1511

Demaundes Joyous (an early collection of riddles printed in London by Wynken de Worde). UCL

1525

The Tyndale Bible (the New Testament translated primarily from Erasmus's edition of the Greek Testament by William Tyndale; first printed by Peter Quentell in Cologne and Worms; *The Pentateuch* translation was printed ca. 1531 in Marburg, Hesse, with part of the Old Testament following; revisions of the New Testament were issued in 1534 and 1535; Tyndale's version of the Bible fixed the style and tone of the English Bible with about 90 percent of his translation being retained in the 1611 Authorized Version of the Bible; Tyndale was put to death by the enemies of the Reformation as a heretic in 1536; the Geneva Bible was a revision of the Tyndale Bible and the Great Bible, undertaken by English Protestant exiles in Geneva during the Marian persecutions, first published in Geneva in 1560; the Geneva Bible was the first Bible in which the chapters were divided into verses, the first in which italics were used, and the Bible most commonly used in homes; Shakespeare is known to have used the Geneva Bible; the 1578 edition of the Geneva Bible was printed in London by C. Barker).

1532

Robert Whittington's *A Lytell Book of good Manners for Chyldren* (translated from Desiderius Erasmus's *De civilitate morum puerilium,* ca. 1526; reveals Erasmus's true consideration for other people, including children; printed in both Latin and English in London by Wynken de Worde).

1533

Nicholas Udall's *Floures for latine speakying selected and gathered oute of Terence, and the same translated into Englyshe, together with the exposicion and settyng foorth as well of suche latine wordes, as were thought nedefull to be anoted, as well as also of diverse grammaticall rules . . .* (translated from the Latin and based on a similar compendium by Cornelius Graphius, 1530; Latin phrases are followed by English translations; a 1553 edition was printed in London by Thomas Berthelet; the author, who became headmaster at Eaton, was noted for his severity; the author's other work includes the earliest extant English comedy, *Ralph Royster Doyster,* registered at the Stationers' Company by Thomas Hacket in 1556; *A Pleasant Plain and Pithie Pathway leading to vertues and an honest lyfe, no less profytable than delectable,* London, ca. 1540).

1536

The Prymer of Salysbury Use, both in Englyshe and in Laten (an early primer for children with devotions; printed in London by John Gough). UCL

1537

The Coverdale Bible (the first approved, licensed edition of the complete Bible printed in England; translated by Miles Coverdale, an English priest converted to Protestantism, and his associates; from Tyndale's translation and Latin and German texts; printed in Southwarke by James Nycolson; Coverdale's 1539 revision was collated with the Tyndale Bible, printed in Cologne and Worms, 1525, and the "Matthew's" Bible, printed in London by E. Whitchurch, 1537, at the request of Thomas Cromwell; Coverdale edited The Great Bible, printed in London by R. Grafton and E. Whitchurch, 1539; this version was called The Great Bible because of its large size and it was the first Bible to be appointed for use in churches). JRUL, TC, UCL

1538

The BAC [sic] bothe in Latyn and in Englysshe (anonymous; the earliest extant example of a genuine ABC or child's reading book; its eight pages include the alphabet, syllabary, prayers, graces, and the Ten Commandments in verse; printed in London by Thomas Petyt). EC

1540

The Boke of Demaundes, of the Scyence of Phylosophye and Astronomye betwene Kyng Boccus and the philosopher Sydracke (a question and answer book set in the form of conversation between King Boccus and Sydrake, a philosopher; printed in London by R. Wyer).

1549

"Lily's Grammar" (a composite Latin grammar by John Colet and William Lily, with Colet providing a treatise in English on the eight parts of speech, and Lily providing the rudiments on construction, based on Erasmus's rational studies, with the two parts, the *Aeditio* and the *Rudimenta,* affording beginners the elements of accidence and syntax; published in one volume by R. Wolfium; parts were published as early as ca. 1510; the 1527 edition was entitled *Ionnes Coleti . . . aedito, una cum quibusdam G. Lilii Grammatices rudimentis;* another part was used by Wolsey in his school at Ipswich in 1529 under the title *Rudimenta grammatices it docendi methodus,* with the title page stating that the work had been prescribed for all schools in England; in another part, Lily's *Latin,* the syntax in Latin was so thoroughly revised by Erasmus that Lily disclaimed it, but it was finally published as *Libellus de constructione,* 1513, anonymously; a further part by Lily, *De generibus nominum, ac verborum praeteritis,* ca. 1520, gives rules for genders of nouns and inflections of verbs; these works, along with the *Aeditio* and *Rudimenta,* made up *An introduction to the eygth partes of speche,* or "Lily's Grammar," as it was known in 1542 when the King himself ordered that all "schoolemaisters" use this text only, which was printed by T. Berthelet). BL, UOx

ca. 1550

Hugh Rhodes's *The Boke of Nurture, or School of Good Manners for Men, Servants, and Children, with Stans Puer Ad Mensam, newly corrected, being necessary for all youth and children* (a popular courtesy book written in long, rhyming couplets; similar in content to other courtesy books of the period providing advice such as "Belch near no man's face . . . ," "Blow not your nose in the napkin . . . ," and "Avoid slanderous and bawdy tales . . ."; author was probably master of chapel children, "whose duty it was to direct their singing"; printed in London by H. Jackson). BL, HH, UOx

1551

An ABC wyth a Cathechisme (a primer entirely in English which included the Litany, suffrages, and graces; was intended as instruction before confirmation; used clear, large, well-spaced type which was more suitable for young children than most other early books; printed in London by Edward Whitchurch).

1553

John Withals's *A Shorte Dictionaire for Yonge Begynners* (a book designed to familiarize young children with Latin equivalents for common English words; probably for the use of four- or five-year old ABC or petty school children, who were expected to know their ABC's before being accepted at a grammar school or being apprenticed; published in London by T. Berthelet).

1557

Francis Seager's *School of Virtue and Book of Good Nurture for Children and Youth to Learn their Duty by. Newly perused, corrected and augmented by the first Auctor, F. W., with a brief declaration of the duty of each degree* (a book of courtesy written in rhyming couplets by a poet and translator who may also have been known as Francis Nicholsen; printed in London by William Seares; two seventeenth-century versions were written by Richard Weste, London, 1619, and Robert Crowley, London, ca. 1660; other versions printed as late as the nineteenth century include *The Book of Demeanor and Allowance* and *Disallowance of Certain Misdemeanors in Companie,* London, 1817).

1559

Robert Smith's *The complaynt of veritie, made by John Bradford. An exhortation of Mathew Rogers, unto his children . . .* (the farewell message of John Rogers, a Protestant martyr, who was burned at the stake while his wife and nine children looked on; a later edition titled *The exhortation that a father gave to his children which he wrot a few days before his burning. Being godly admonitions, fit for all Christians to follow;* ascribed to John Rogers, nicknamed ''Matthew'' Rogers because he helped Tyndale translate the Bible under the pseudonym of Thomas Matthews; included in Benjamin Harris's *The Protestant Tutor;* printed in London by Benjamin Harris, 1679; also included in *The New England Primer,* probably published by Benjamin Harris ca. 1700 in Boston). UOx

1563

John Foxe's *Book of Martyrs* (also known as *Actes and Monuments;* recounts the deaths of several Protestant martyrs, including John Rogers's; was Foxe's zealous attempt to spread the fire of the Protestant revolt against the Church of England; the text became required reading for Puritan children in England and in America; printed in London by John Day). AAS, BM, UCL, UOx

Thomas Newbery's *A Booke in Englysshe Metre; of the great Marchante Man called Dives Pragmaticus, very preaty for Children to reade* (a lighthearted, unillustrated, eight-page catalog of merchandise in rhymed couplets designed to help children learn to read and write; the text urges traders and shopkeepers to buy the merchant's wares, some of which are presented in the verse: ''Dripping pans, pot hooks, old cats and kits / And preaty fine dogs, without fleas or nits. Axes for butchers, and fine glass for wives / medicines for rats to shorten their lives''; printed in London for Alexander Lacy). HH, JRUL

1564

James Canceller's *An A.B.C. or holy alphabet, conteyning some plaine lessons gathered out of the word, to the number of the letters in the English alphabet, to enter young beginners in the schoole of Christ* (an alphabet book in twenty-four sections, one under each letter, dealing with reading and hearing the Word, excess and abuse in sports, fasting and drinking, and daily devotions and other "Christly acts"). BM

1570

An enterlude for children to play named Jack Jugler, bothe wittie and very plesant (anonymous; a children's play founded on the *Menaechmi* of Plautus, which was also the source of one part of Shakespeare's *The Comedy of Errors;* printed in London by John Allde).

John Hart's *A Method or comfortable beginning for all unlearned, whereby they may be taught to read English, in a very short time with pleasure* (probably the earliest extant pictured alphabet which was also a spelling book "on the phonic principle"; book printed in London by H. Denham).

Robert Henryson's *The Morall Fabillis of Esope the Phrygian* (an early free translation of Aesop in poetic form; continuation of title reads: *in Scottis meter, be maister Robert Henrisone . . . Newly imprentit . . . ;* printed in Edinburgh by Robert Lekpreuik for Henrie Charteris). BM

1585

William Bullokar's *Aesopz Fablz in Tru Ortography with Grammar-notz* (a school version of the fables by a spelling reformer and moralist; continuation of the title reads: *Her-untoo ar also jooined the short sentencez of the wyz Cato . . . translated out-of Latin in-too English by William Bullokar;* first published by Edmund Bollifant in London). BM, HH, UOx

1586

A Little Dictionarie for Children (an early attempt to create a usable dictionary for children; printed in London by Thomas Purfoote, to be sold at his shop "without Newgate, over againste Saint Sepulchers Churche").

1590

Lawrence Vaux's *A catechisme or Christian doctrine necessarie for children and ignorante people, briefly compiled by Laurence Vaux, bacheler of divinitie: with an other later addition of instruction of the laudable ceremonies used in the Catholicke church. Whereunto is adjoined a brief forme of confession (necessary for all good Christians) according to the use of the*

Catholicke church (a catechism first published in Louvain, 1567, and then in Antwerp, 1574; the author was a Roman Catholic divine who brought a papal degree from Rome which forbade attendance at Anglican services; he died in a London prison). BL

1591

John Browne's *The Marchants Aviso, Verie Necessairie For Their sonnes and servants, when they first send them beyond the seas, as to Spayne, and Portingale or other Countreyes. Made by their hartie well-willer in Christ. J. B. Marchant.* (a typical merchant manual of the day often used by youth who were educated by means of travel; printed in London by Thomas Orwin for William Norton). HH

1595

Children of the Wood; or the Norfolk Gentleman's Last Will and Testament (anonymous; a traditional ballad about the death of two children; the first printed edition was probably printed by Thomas Millington who entered the title at the Stationers' Company; the story was much anthologized in later collections both in ballad and prose forms; numerous versions exist, and are sometimes entitled *The Babes in the Wood;* appropriated by children).

1605

The vertuous Life and memorable Death of Sir Richard Whittington (anonymous; the earliest record of a print copy of this popular folk ballad; the first edition was probably printed by John Wright who entered the title at the Stationers' Company; included in many subsequent collections as both ballad and story; story popular to present; appropriated by children).

1607

Edward Topsell's *The historie of foure-footid beastes collected out of all the volumes of C. Gesner, etc.* (an early illustrated book purporting to be a natural history for childrer., but like the bestiaries it contained cuts of dragons and unicorns along with exaggerated descriptions of real animals; printed in London by W. Jaggard; many versions of this popular "informational book" followed). CU, HH, HU, NL

1611

The Holy Bible, Conteyning the Old Testament and the New: Newly Translated out of the Original tongues, with the former Translations diligently compared and revised, by his Majesties special commandment. Appointed to be read in Churches (scriptures translated by six committees of forty-seven biblical scholars, authorized by James I, and rendered into a masterpiece of Elizabethan prose; used by various English-speaking Protestant sects; printed in London by the king's printer, Robert Barker; commonly called

The Authorized Version, also commonly referred to in America as the King James Version; read in Protestant churches and by the common people, including children, to the present). UOx

1612

Miguel de Saavedra Cervantes's *History of the Valorous and Witty knight-errant, Don Quixote of the Mancha* (from the Spanish, *El ingenioso Hildalgo Don Quijote de la Mancha, 1605,* translated by Thomas Shelton, printed in London by William Stansby for Edward Blount and W. Barret; exciting adventure story elements were appropriated by children). D, LC, NL

1614

John Taylor's *Verbum Sempiternum* (a popular miniature Old Testament Bible, written in doggerel rhyme by England's "Water Poet"; New Testament version called *Salvator Mundi* [a thumb-Bible] printed in London by J. Beale for J. Hamman; first American edition printed ca. 1760; a ca. 1768 edition printed in Boston by Mein and Fleeming; reprinted many times throughout the 1800s). ACL, CL

1616

Mrs. Dorothy Leigh's *The mother's blessing; or, the godly counsaile of a gentle-woman, not long since deceased, left behind for her children. Containing many good exhortations, a godly admonition profitable for all parents, to leave as a legacy to their children* (a popular didactic, puritanical plea of a British mother to her sons to seek a life of devotion and to write a book for their children telling them how to be happy; printed in London for J. Budge; this work was even more popular than Mrs. Elizabeth Joceline's *The mother's legacy to her unborn child,* London, 1624, which was reissued six times in seven years). HH, UOx

1621

The History of Tom Thumbe the Little, for his small stature surnamed King Arthur's Dwarfe (anonymous; the adventures of the popular nursery tale hero; one of the earliest printed editions of a nursery tale in English; first American edition was entitled *Tom Thumb's Folio, for Little Giants. To which is prefixed An Abstract of the Life of Mr. Thumb. . . . Together with Some Anecdotes respecting Grumbo, the Great Giant,* printed in Boston by T. J. Fleet, ca. 1780, and copied from John Newbery's 1768 edition, *Tom Thumb's Folio; or, A New Play-thing for little Giants. To which is prefixed, an Abstract of the Life of Mr. Thumb*).

1624

John Brinsley's *Aesop's Fables* (an outstanding English school version of the fables by a famous Puritan schoolmaster; used by scholars from seven to fifteen; includes textual notes; printed by H. Lownes for Thomas Mann, and sold in London by Thomas Pavier; the author's other work includes *Pueriles Confabulatiunculae, Children's Dialogues, little conferences, or talkings together . . .* , London, 1617). BM

1629

The book of meery riddles; together with proper questions and witty proverbs, to make pleasant pastime; no lesse usefull then behoouefull for any young man, or child, to know if he be quick-witted, or no (anonymous; unusual in that this book of riddles, popular with adults at this time, is addressed to children; extant copy is probably a later edition of a late sixteenth-century collection titled *The book of Riddels,* referred to in Shakespeare's *Merry Wives,* I.i.; numerous editions appeared throughout the seventeenth century; this edition printed in London by T. Cotes for M. Sparke). HH

Francis Lenton's *The young gallants whirligig: or youths reakes. Demonstrating the inordinate affections, absurd actions, and profuse expenses, of unbridled and affected youth; with their extravagant courses, and preposterous progressions, and aversions* (a British poet's story of an Inns of Court student's discovery of vice; printed in London by M. Flesher for R. Bostocke). BM

ca. 1630

John Penkethman's *The fairest fairing for a school-bred sonne; whereby praise, ease, and profit may be wonne. That is to say, the schoole-masters precepts, or Lillies lesson to his schollers teaching them good manners* (a poetic version of Johannes Sulpitius's *Carmen Juvenile de moribus puerorum* printed in book form by J. Kingston, 1572, and also included at the beginning of Lily's *Latin Grammar;* designed to regulate the child's school conduct; author's other work includes a translation of Cato's *Distiches,* a collection of moral aphorisms in Latin composed in the fourth or fifth centuries, entitled *A Handful of Honesty, or Cato in English Verse,* 1623).

1637

John Milton's *A maske (Comus) presented at Ludlow Castle, 1634* (a melodramatic, didactic, romantic masque by a major English poet; thought by some to have been written for the instruction and delight of children; printed in London for H. Robinson). NYPL, UCLA, UI, UOx

1640

The Whole Booke of Psalmes faithfully Translated into English Metre (the first book printed in America, although the original book was published in England in 1562; a volume of 147 unnumbered pages which contained psalms along with a prefix extolling the "lawfullness, but also the necessity of the heavenly Ordinance of singing Scripture Psalmes in the Churches of God"; not well printed although the title page is ornamented with a scroll border; generally referred to as the "Bay Psalm Book"; printed in Cambridge, Massachusetts, by Stephen Daye, or more probably his son, Matthew). BU

1644

The Rule of the New-Creature To be Practiced every Day, in all the Particulars of it which are ten (anonymous; a popular Puritan spiritual guidebook for children first published in England; first American edition published in Cambridge, Massachusetts, by Samuel Green, 1668, with a second American edition published in Boston in 1682 by Mary Avery, said to be New England's first woman printer).

1646

John Cotton's *Milk for Babes. Drawn out of the Breasts of both Testaments. Chiefly, for the Spirituall nourishment of Boston babes in either England: But may be of like use for any children* (a catechism designed for Puritan children by Cotton Mather's grandfather; first printed in London by J. Coe for Henry Overton; the New England edition was titled *Spiritual Milk for Boston Babes in Either England: Drawn out of the breasts of both Testaments for their Souls nourishment,* printed in Cambridge, Massachusetts, by Samuel Green for Hezekiah Usher, 1656, and was probably the first book specifically printed for children in North America; in 1617 William Crashaw wrote *Milke for Babes. Or, A North-Countrie Catechisme* printed in London by Nicholas Oakes; in 1641, Hugh Peters's *Milke for Babes, and Meat for Men . . .* was printed in London by E. P. for J. W.; Grindal Rawson translated *Spiritual Milk* into a New England Indian language in 1691, *Nashauani Hue Meninnunk Wutch Mukkiesog, Wussesemun Wutch Sogkodtunanash Naneeswe Testamentsash . . . ,* printed in Cambridge for Samuel Green by Bartholomew Green; another Indian language translation of *Spiritual Milk* was appended to *The Indian Primer* or *The Indian Primer or the First Book By which Children may know truely to read the Indian Language. And Milk for Babes or Indiane Primer Asuh Negonneyeuuk. Ne nashpe Mukkiesog Woh tauog wunnamuhkuttee ogketamunnate Indiane Unnontoowaonk. Kah Meninnunk wutch Kukkiesog,* printed in Boston for B. Green, 1720; Robert Abbot, vicar of Southwick, wrote *Milk for babes; or, a mother's catechism for her children,* published in London, 1646). AAS, NYPL

ca. 1650

Chapbooks (usually anonymous; crude, folded "booklets," illustrated with inferior woodcuts, which made available to the unsophisticated masses a great variety of material—from coarse jests to a 1,000-line adaptation of the

Bible; their immense popularity was enhanced by the passing of the Licensing Acts after the Restoration, prohibiting the erection of printing presses except in London, Oxford, and Cambridge which meant no new books were available in the provinces except those peddled for a penny or two by chapmen, called "running stationers"; included rhymes, legends, superstitions, etc., as well as many famous stories, especially those from the oral tradition, such as Tom Hickathrift, Jack the Giant Killer, Tom Thumb, Dick Whittington, etc., also those from complete printed sources such as *Robinson Crusoe, Gulliver's Travels,* etc.; first printed in England, but later published in America). AAS, BM, UCL, UOx

1651

John Ogilby's *The Fables of Aesop, Paraphras'd in Verse* (an Irish author's versions of fables in verse; known as the first "polite edition meant for children as well as grownups" and "adorned with sculpture"; subsequent editions contained engravings by Wenceslaus Hollar, W. Stoop, and Francis Barlow; in two volumes, published by Andrew Crook).

ca. 1652

Albert Durer revived: or a book of drawing, limning, washing, or colouring of maps and prints: and the art of painting, with the names and mixtures of colours used by the picture-drawers. With directions how to lay and paint pictures upon glass. Or, the young man's time well spent. In which he hath the groundwork to make him fit for doing anything by hand, when he is able to draw well. . . . Very useful for all handicrafts, and ingenious gentlemen and youths (a folio of 20 engravings and accompanying text which attempts to explain what the title promises; n.p.).

Thomas Mayhew's *Indian Catechism* (a manuscript used by Mayhew to teach Martha's Vineyard Indians; Mayhew's wife, Experience, may have actually prepared the manuscript; an Indian language alternates with English from page to page; the manuscript was never published).

1654

John Eliot's *Catechism, in the Indian Language of Massachusetts* (compiled in 1651 and first used in manuscript form; published in Cambridge for the Corporation for the Propagation of the Gospel in New England; the author's other work includes *Mamvsse, Wunneetupanatamwe, Up-Biblum God, naneeswe, Nukkone Testament, kah wouk,* Wuskuu Testament, *Ne quoshkinnumuk nashpe Wuttinneumoh Christ,* the first complete Bible published in America, printed in Cambridge, Massachusetts, by Samuel Green and Marmaduke Johnson, 1663; *The Indian Primer; or, The way of training up of our Indian Youth in the knowledge of the Scriptures and in an ability to Reade,* published in Cambridge, Massachusetts, 1669). NYPL

1656

Francis Osborne's *Advice to a son* (a popular work typical of the many books of advice about how to lead a happy and moral life; reprinted many times, with many other works being based on or imitating it; work was first published anonymously in Oxford for Thomas Robinson; the misogyny evidenced in the author's chapter on love and marriage angered so many readers that subsequent editions bore an apology to the reader, especially to women; John Heydon's *Advice to a daughter, in opposition to the advice to a son,* originally published under the name Eugenius Theodidactus, was written in ridicule of Osborne's work). MHS, SC

C. W.'s *A schoole of nurture for children or the duty of children in honouring their parents, unfolded, proved, and applied. Very usefull in all families for parents to teach their children. That the dutifull may be encouraged, and the disobedient reclaimed. Occasioned by the many late disasters as sad effects of children disobedience* (an encyclopedic religious manual of 172 pages with eleven illustrations; contains prayers, a catechism, many poems, directions, and admonitions for the whole life of man, meditations and pious sentences from many sources, and "Comfort from Scripture both in Life and in Death" and "A Discourse betwixt *Adam and Eve,*" both in verse, concerning the conduct of their children on Earth; written in a plain style so that "the meanest capacity, may receive and understand my meaning").

1657

Thomas Brooke's *Apples of gold for young men and women: and a crown of glory for old men and women. Or, the happiness of being good betimes, and the honour of being an old disciple. Clearly and fully discovered, and closely and faithfully applyed. Also the young man's objections answered and the old man's doubts resolved* (a popular book of advice that was in print until at least 1816; the second edition was printed in London by R. I. for John Hancock).

Francis Cockin's *Divine blossomes. A prospect or looking-glass for youth. Wherein and whereby he may plainly behold and see a supereminency and superexcellency of grace and religion, beyond the world's honor, glory, fame, repute, pleasure, joy, delight, love, and all other lower accommodations whatsoever. Laid down to youth by exciting parallel between earths honor carnal pleasure inordinate love and heavens glory spiritual pleasure divine love. Under every of which particulars, the author exemplarily expresseth himself in a varied verse. Composed by a hearty wel-wisher to the youthful generation, Francis Cockin, alias Cokayne* (as the title indicates, even though the author attempts to describe his youthful experiences of pleasure and sin, he nowhere reveals that he quite knows what he's talking about; the book is dedicated to Mr. George Wither; a second part of the work was intended for young women: *A glass for virgins. Wherein also every Soul may see . . . the duty of every soul to Christ. Held forth by a continued parallel, between, virgins behaviours to their suitors, and the Christian souls to Christ*; n.p.) BM

1659

Johann Amos Comenius's *Orbis Sensualium Pictus, the world of Sensible Things drawn; that is the Nomenclature of Fundamental Things in the World and Actions in Life reduced to Ocular Demonstration* (translated from the Dutch edition, 1658, by Charles Hoole and printed in England for J. Kirton; first published by Michael Endter in Nuremberg, Germany, 1658? with woodcuts by Paul Kreutzberger; the first American edition, printed from the twelfth London edition by T. & J. Swords in New York in 1810, contains wood engravings by Alexander Anderson; a picture book of general knowledge designed to be "a brief of the whole world . . . a little encyclopedia of things subject to the senses" to make the teaching of Latin to children easier; pictured objects were given both Latin and English labels; often called the first picture book designed for children, other than ABC books; [however, a German picture book for children, *Kunst und Lehrbuchlein, A Book of Art and Instruction for young people wherein may be discovered all manner of merry and agreeable drawings,* was published by Sigmund Feyeraband in Frankfurt as early as 1580, which contained ninety-four full-page woodcuts by Jost Amman, a Swiss artist]; in subsequent editions, the original woodcuts were replaced with copper-plate engravings; the work became the pattern for hundreds of such books published during the next two hundred years; similar in content to the author's popular *Janua Linguarum Reserata,* 1631; author was invited by Parliament in 1641 to reform the English system of public education; in ca. 1654, he was invited to come to Cambridge to become president of Harvard University). BM

Rev. Abraham Pierson's *Some Helps for the Indians. Showing them How to improve their natural Reason, To know the True God, and the true Christian Religion . . .* (a Quiripi Indian Catechism used in southwestern Connecticut; English is printed in small type interlined with the Quiripi Indian language; printed in Cambridge, Massachusetts, by Samuel Green). BM

Chapter 4

Restoration to American Independence (1660–1799)

HISTORICAL BACKGROUND

In Britain

After a ten-year exile in Holland, Charles II was restored to the throne in 1660. The Commonwealth, a minority government that had depended on force and the leadership of one man, Oliver Cromwell, had never been popular. Its stern, moral code which had upset established traditions made for confusion and error. Not surprisingly, the rule of the Commonwealth ended in anarchy.

Remembering the tragic death of Charles I, England was ready for the return of his son who would quickly be dubbed the "Merry Monarch." Instead of being scornful of his excesses, his subjects seemed to delight in them, at least at first. Under Cromwell, all royal art objects and accoutrements, including the sceptre and the crown, had been melted down or sold. When the monarchy was restored, extravagant gifts of jewels, silverware, tankards, furniture, mirrors, and paintings were offered to the king. His palaces were refurbished with elaborate murals and architectural decorations. Charles, in turn, to the great delight of the people, revived dancing, games, and drama. The theaters had been closed since 1642. Horse racing, one of Charles's favorite pastimes, also became popular.

Politically, Charles also delighted the people at first. He promised leniency (in the Declaration of Breda) to all those who had participated in the rebellion and, with the help of his chief minister, Clarendon, he succeeded in putting down a general revenge on the Puritans. Unlike his father, Charles was not aloof in his dealings with his people; he was a shrewd, capable administrator. Like his father, he appreciated the arts. He also increased the influence of Parliament by not resisting the formation of two parties, the Whigs, who were opposed to the Crown, and the Tories, who supported the Crown. During his reign, he increased the navy's strength as he engaged in a running war with the Dutch. And under Charles the empire in America began to develop, but not without some pains to the colonists. It should be noted, however, that he did honor William Penn's request to make Pennsyvania a refuge for persecuted English Quakers.

Always a patron of the arts, Charles was not especially interested in the sciences; as a yachting enthusiast, he favored the study of navigation and shipping. But in 1662, Charles established the Royal Society of London for "the improvement of natural knowledge through experiments." Among the many notables who belonged to the Society were Robert Boyle, said to be the father of modern chemistry; William Petty, demographer, founder of population statistics; John Williams, mathematician and astronomer; Robert Hooke, physicist and inventor who was regarded the greatest mechanic of his age; Christopher Wren, the architect who built the Royal Observatory in 1673 and would eventually be responsible for rebuilding a great part of the City of London; and Isaac Newton, mathematician.

However, all was not jubilation. Affairs abroad did not always go well. England, for example, was involved in a naval war with Holland (1665-1667) it could not win; however, the settlement at Breda which forced the Dutch to give up the colonies of New York, New Jersey, and Delaware ultimately proved to be invaluable to the English. At home, there was an uneasy calm. The restored Anglican church, which had reestablished its supremacy, came down hard on nonconformists and dissenters; one of the thousands it persecuted was John Bunyan who wrote *Pilgrim's Progress* (1678) while imprisoned for attending non-Anglican meetings. (*See figure 12.*) Even disasters, particularly the Great Plague which killed 68,000 in London alone and the Great Fire of 1666 which destroyed vast amounts of commercial property in the capital, were somehow blamed on the Crown. In a few short years the joy had gone out of the Restoration. By the end of Charles's reign, he and Parliament were wrangling over waste and misspent money.

The ascension of James II, an ardent Catholic, brought open rebellion by the Protestants as he tried to catholicize all of England, even the Church of England. Although James quelled the revolts for a while, the rebels rose again in the Glorious Revolution of 1688 (also called the Sensible Revolution because no blood was shed), and James had to flee to France, dropping the Great Seal of the Realm in the Thames as he left as a final insult to his rebellious subjects. It is noteworthy that John Locke's *Treatise of Government* served as the "bible" of this uprising; in it he declared that men establish government to preserve their property and their lives, and that they may change government when it fails to serve those ends. (Locke would shortly find favor with the American colonists.)

James's son-in-law, William of Orange, succeeded him, accepting the call of Parliament to save English Protestantism. From this point on, no English king would rule against the wishes of Parliament. During William's rule, which ended in 1702, Jacobite rebellions in Ireland and Scotland favoring the restoration of James II were suppressed.

By the end of the seventeenth century, a more stable balance had been achieved between Parliament, the king, and the people, England had become a great commercial and maritime nation, the Bank of England had been founded along with the East India Company, and the turbulent social and religious strife during most of the century had taught England something of the value of tolerance and freedom of thought. But living conditions were mixed. The population was low because of high infant mortality, rampant disease, bad sanitation, and poor diet for most people. For the middle and upper classes, however, food was generally plentiful, with meat and bread the staple foods. When coffee was introduced in 1656, coffee houses quickly became fashionable gathering places where the elite discussed the new plays, read newspapers (which were just developing), wrote letters, and gossiped.

As mentioned earlier, the English upper classes were greatly influenced by French culture during the latter part of the seventeenth century. Perhaps as a defense against the Reformation's tendency to liberalize, most governments on the continent were concentrating power in the monarchy; this was especially true in France where Louis XIV, friend of Charles II, *was* the state. Glad to put the republican experiment behind them, most Englishmen looked to the manners and style of French society with relief, often aping French elegancies to an absurd extent. French styles in the visual arts, music, and architecture soon overshadowed native English products. For the rich, pursuing the "art of leisure" became the goal of life, a goal which often led to extravagant concoctions of entertainment, debauchery, depravity, whoring, and outrageous forms of buffoonery.

But not all Englishmen were of the urbane upper classes. The farming population, which made up a large part of English society, was divided into definite classes: squires, yeomen, cottagers, and laborers. England was still largely countryside, although common lands and wastelands were rapidly being enclosed. Roads were not much improved over former times, with road upkeep a local and often neglected concern. The tollgate system never was efficiently developed. Horsedrawn carts and stagecoaches were common on the mud roads, with horseback the quickest way to travel.

The chief cities of the seventeenth and eighteenth centuries were London and Bristol. In London, the Thames with its heavy traffic of boats and barges formed the nucleus of the city. The town was filled with raucous cries of animals, noise of carts and carriages, constables, pitchmen, and citizens visiting or more likely arguing on the street corners. The lack of sewers, the open slaughtering of animals, the dumping of refuse onto thoroughfares made for a filthy city, and such filth eventually brought the Great Plague in 1665. In 1666, the Great Fire consumed one third of the commercial section of London, but it was probably a "fortunate" disaster because the reconstruction was presided over by the master architect, Christopher Wren. In spite of often horrendous social conditions, London was also colorful with some of its citizenry planting flowers and trees; at any rate, the city throve. The wool industry, trade with the American colonies and the West Indies, banking, and the introduction of new crafts and industries made London an important city of the world.

More grammar schools existed than ever before. The Renaissance had called for a practical reexamination of accepted morals, and the rising middle class had called for more practical uses of education. Where medieval schools had emphasized the liberal arts, seventeenth-century schools and tutors emphasized the study of modern languages, writing, and even dancing and fencing. Although new educational interests and methods were relatively successful, the universities, the traditional places of learning, went into a decline from which they did not recover for over a century; they were mostly places of leisure for the aristocracy.

In literature, prose dominated with political pamphleteering a popular art. Lyricism in poetry had all but disappeared with the heroic couplet the principal verse form. Theaters, which had reopened under the patronage and encouragement of the king, played lusty pieces to select audiences of the rich and were totally dependent on court favor. Important writers were Dryden, Pepys, Wycherley, and Congreve; important philosophers were Thomas Hobbes and John Locke. Writers hostile to the court, such as John Milton who had brilliantly defended the Commonwealth, lived in poverty.

Most Englishmen were Protestants with Anglicans making up 70 percent of the population. The main pivots of local government were appointed justices of the peace who dealt with petty offenses, administered the Poor Law, issued begging licenses, collected taxes, and generally kept order.

The seventeenth century was a period of many changes, but the next century would bring even more. Under Queen Anne (1702-1714), England won many military victories, resulting in the Treaty of Utrecht (1713) which established the supremacy of Britain in North America and formed the prelude to the eighteenth-century struggle between France and America for commercial greatness. Perhaps even more importantly, Queen Anne, a devout Anglican, achieved the Act of Union in 1707 between England and Scotland, establishing the United Kingdom of Great Britain.

During this period, which was often referred to as the Augustan Age because it was thought that English civilization was duplicating the ancients— especially the period of Augustus Caesar—several eminent writers were at work: Richard Steele and Joseph Addison, essayists; Jonathan Swift, satirist; Samuel Johnson, critic; Daniel Defoe, Samuel Richardson, Henry Fielding,

Tobias Smollett, and Laurence Sterne, novelists; Oliver Goldsmith and Alexander Pope, poets. And Britain was experiencing a glowing period in other arts as well, especially in the painting of Joshua Reynolds and Thomas Gainsborough, the music of Georg Handel, and the architecture of Christopher Wren and others. The impressive Queen Anne style of architecture called for large, comfortable homes with Dutch gardens and Palladian facades. The countryside and fields surrounding the elaborate houses were fenced with hedgerows for privacy and beauty. Upper-class homes were usually made of brick and stone, with elaborate windows, plastered ceilings and walls, and marble fireplaces. Life in the cities for the well-to-do was more urbane than ever before (with coffeehouses still the center of intellectual life—by 1708 there were over 3,000 of them in London), but life in the country with its elaborate hunting parties and county balls was almost as extravagant. For the prosperous, the Augustan Age under Queen Anne and the subsequent Hanoverian kings was one of opulence, order, and stability.

The first of the Hanoverian kings, George I (1714-1727) who had been maneuvered onto the throne by the Whigs through the Act of Succession in 1701, was a German who could not speak English. He was interested chiefly in European affairs, usually leaving the task of governing to his ministers. Because of his Whig connections, the power passed to them and eventually to their leader, Robert Walpole. A clever politician, Walpole, who as the first prime minister (the term originally was one of abuse, not an official appointment) established the cabinet system. Walpole favored maintenance of the peace at all costs in order to increase business and commerce, and he sought friendly relations with many countries, even France, England's traditional rival. When George II ascended the throne in 1727, Walpole was favored by George I's wife Caroline and remained prime minister and continued his policies. But his opposition to foreign entanglements, along with the growth of manufacturing in the colonies and the growth of colonial trade, set the stage for revolt.

Britain was entering an age of many kinds of trouble. In spite of Walpole, foreign intrigues had so entangled Britain's political power, which was based upon influence, that its strength fluctuated with great rapidity, as evidenced in the Jacobite uprisings of 1715 and 1745, the wars against Spain (1739-1743), the War of the Austrian Succession (1740-1748), and the struggles with France in America and the Far East.

Britain was also entering an age of extreme class consciousness. The gentlemen at the top of the social scale were there by birth alone, with the landed gentry next in line. Oldest sons inherited estates and titles, while younger sons entered the clergy, the military, or trade. Merchants formed the middle class, a niche previously denied to them. Yeoman farmers were next on the scale, but their numbers were rapidly decreasing, while artisans and rural laborers made up the lower group. Court life, especially during the time of Walpole, was coarse and immoral. Vice, crime, and immorality were common. While coffee was still popular, drinking gin had become widespread among all the classes; more than 11 million gallons were consumed annually by the middle of the eighteenth century, most of it by the miserable poor.

The second half of the century was under the influence of a new spirit, one which ran counter to the Augustan Age; it was a time of revolutionary changes. The French writer, Jean Jacques Rousseau, heralded the new ideas which slowly made themselves felt in growing concerns for the natural man and his emotions, for distant times and places, and for a new view of the essential worth of ordinary people. Literary men in particular began to praise the humble life, while preachers such as John Wesley and George Whitefield taught that religion was for winning men's hearts, not for promoting organized creeds. The industrial revolution was just beginning, but new inventions, especially the mechanical loom and the spinning machine, along with the coming of steam power, were drastically changing the cloth industry; similar changes were soon to be found in mining, in the iron and steel industry, and even in the making of pottery. More efficient methods of agriculture also brought new wealth, but not to the small farmers. Large landowners eventually forced out the small farmers, who moved to industrial centers by the thousands.

Politically, the new spirit was felt in George III's attempt to regain the power for the Crown. For a while he succeeded in strengthening Tory control and keeping the Whigs at bay, but his mismanagement of the American colonies brought about his downfall. George's antagonizing of the colonists through a series of unpopular taxes, particularly the Stamp Tax and the tax on tea, caused the Americans to revolt in open fighting in 1775. They were further emboldened when France came to their aid in 1778. When Britain was forced to make peace in a treaty secured by the redoubtable American, Benjamin Franklin, in 1783, it had to recognize the complete independence of the thirteen Atlantic seaboard colonies as a new nation, the United States of America, one which was built on English foundations, but was totally free from British rule.

In America

The new nation's boundaries were set at the Great Lakes, the Mississippi River, and northern Florida. Shortly, there were several new states: Vermont in 1791, Kentucky in 1792, Tennessee in 1796, and Ohio in 1803. A strong central government was finally recognized as necessary in the new country to make the American flag and American trade respected. In spite of growing pains, the new nation made its way. In 1789 George Washington was inaugurated as the first president. The first Congress provided for a banking system, a federal court system, and a coinage system. Shortly after, two political parties emerged, the Republicans and the Federalists. During John Adams's presidency, 1797-1801, conflict between Napoleonic sympathizers and British sympathizers led to Congress's passing of the controversial Alien and Sedition Acts. During the later decades of the eighteenth century, Puritan influence, which had once been strong, continued to decline, but learning, reason, law and order, propriety, moderation, good manners, and respectability were still valued.

The dominant industry in the new country was agriculture, except for shipbuilding, commerce, and fishing on the New England coast. Most domestic manufacturing was carried on in homes. Some intellectual life was fostered by immigrants who had been educated at Oxford or Cambridge, and there were some good private libraries, especially among wealthy planters and professional men in the South. Thomas Jefferson, for example, owned 6,000 books. But education for the common man was not widespread in the South or elsewhere. Indentured servants and slaves from Africa (first imported to Virginia in 1619, but found in all colonies, especially south of Pennsylvania) played significant parts in the development of industry and commerce. Indian tribes who at first tried to maintain their lands were pushed farther and farther west, or eliminated by massacre, poverty, and disease.

While strides were made in religious toleration, complete religious freedom existed only in Rhode Island. Catholics, Unitarians, Deists, and Jews were denied the right to vote or hold office in all other areas. But the coming of the Constitution, adopted in 1787, served to establish and preserve the liberty of individuals and of local autonomy; its Bill of Rights was designed specifically to protect individual basic freedoms and the democratic processes.

DEVELOPMENT OF BOOKS

In Britain

The Restoration of the monarchy in 1660 brought great hope to the English people who were tired of the turmoil of war, religious strife, and its subsequent restrictions, including censorship. But censorship of the press was not soon to be lifted. Instead, in 1663 a newly created post, surveyor of the press, was given to the fanatical Roger L'Estrange; under the monarchy his censorship was often harsher than before. But the English people were determined that the monarchy would not fall again. After a civil war and the uneasy period of the Commonwealth, they were more than willing to accept the power of the Crown, even if it meant royal surveillance. Although press restrictions had been heavy during the Commonwealth period, Oliver Cromwell had allowed the number of printers to increase somewhat. When Charles II assumed power, he ordered that printers be reduced to the number specified in the 1637 Star Chamber Decree, twenty; they were to be reduced by "death or otherwise."

Despite these circumstances and a general barrenness of design which typified seventeenth-century books throughout Europe, production of books continued to grow as literacy slowly increased. The new literates, which began to include women and children of the gentry, demanded adventure stories, ballads, translations of Greek and Roman classics, books on medicine, surgery, exploration of newly discovered lands, manners, moral and religious instruction (including an emphasis on martyrdom), and child nurturing. Improved schools brought about the need for better textbooks (grammars, arithmetics, histories, geographies, books on navigation and the natural sciences). As part of the growing trade, university presses would soon make an impact. Oxford and Cambridge maintained their right to publish books in spite of attempts by the Stationers' Company to prohibit them, and were in large part responsible for the reformation of printing in England. In particular, the procurement of Dutch types in the 1670s by Dr. John Fell, bishop of Oxford and patron of the press, marked a turning point in English printing, away from a tendency toward carelessness, toward the printing of fine and scholarly books. With the publication of the first University *Almanack* in 1674, the Oxford University Press began its long history of high-quality work.

The lapse of the Licensing Act in 1695, which had restricted printing to London, Oxford, Cambridge, and York, also brought new life to printing. New companies, especially the successful houses of Baskerville in Birmingham, and Fry and Moore in Bristol, would bring many changes.

Other changes, especially the 1709 Copyright Law which established authors' rights for the first time in history, brought more improvements. Traditionally, the only payment to an author by a printer was the author's right to sell specified numbers of copies of his own work. In some cases, the author could earn from "subscription," which meant that the buyer agreed to pay the author a portion of the price of the book before it was completed, with the rest after completion. The Copyright Law established for the first time that an author's work was a valuable commodity that deserved to be protected by law. In practice, the idea of writing for prestige instead of money would persist well into the next century, but the coming of the Copyright Law brought profound developments. Until this time the only proof of ownership was entry into the Stationers' Register, which conferred perpetual copyright on a member of the Stationers' Company. This hardly helped the author who was seldom a stationer. While authors were much aided by the law, it also helped publishers in that it prohibited pirating and fixed prices. The social and economic changes that followed bought a decline in the need for patronage and court favor and also provided for the beginning of advertising to sell printed material. After a long decline, British printing began to change appreciably for the better.

Not until the eighteenth century did British printers begin to develop a national style. This style, reflecting an expanding empire and a rising middle class, would soon reveal a puritanical national attitude that would be executed in strong, sharp typography, and later in the moralistic illustrations of Hogarth and Blake.

One of the most influential eighteenth-century printers was William Caslon, probably the most successful British type founder. From 1722 on he developed new fonts based at first on Dutch models. His most famous style was Old Face, but he also produced numerous other fonts, Blackletter, as well as a wide range of Roman and *italic*. When Caslon died in 1766, his son took over the foundry. Caslon letters would remain throughout much of the century as the most popular type used in Britain and the American colonies.

Another important British printer was John Baskerville. He radically changed the look of the type page by reducing the use of capitalization, by recutting Caslon's letters into rounder and wider forms, by using generous spacing and wide margins without ornament, and by using specially formulated black ink on hot-pressed paper which made a silky finish. His first product, a Vergil in 1757, was a success, but his *Satyrae of Juvenal* and *Persius Flaccus* printed in 1761 were even more successful. Although he printed a few illustrated books, including an Aesop, his lasting contribution was to typography.

Another British printer dedicated to fine typography was William Bulmer. His best work was probably his folio edition of *Poems by Goldsmith and Parnell* in 1795 which contained wood engravings by Thomas and John Bewick, artists whose highly textured vignettes began a trend toward fine book illustrations. Thomas Bewick's *Gay's Fables, History of Quadrupeds,* and *British Birds* remain today as superb examples of the wood engraver's art. It should also be noted that in Bulmer's print shop the iron press was first used. Wooden presses, dating from the earliest days of printing, had remained virtually unchanged. The iron press, which doubled the size of the sheet that could be printed at one impression, was the first important improvement in two hundred years. It would be followed by the cylindrical steam press, first used on November 29, 1814, perhaps the most momentous day in printing since Gutenberg.

Against this background of brilliant mainstream printing, the maverick printer, William Blake, emerged. Although he was known by the general illustrated edition of Mary Wollstonecraft's *Original Stories from Real* his real genius is found in the poetic books that he wrote, designed, and printed. His pages are exceptionally beautiful illuminations for which his plates formed only the basis; he and his wife painted the total imprint. His exceptional talents were brought together in *Songs of Innocence* (1789) and *Songs of Experience* (1794), which have been used with children, as was his illustrated edition of Mary Wollenstonecraft's *Original Stories from Real*

Life. He also wrote, illustrated, and printed *America, a Prophecy; Europe, a Prophecy; Visions of the Daughters of Albion;* and *The Marriage of Heaven and Hell.* All of them use combined illustrative techniques—relief etching with watercolors, and woodcut with pen and wash. His most profound work is his *Illustrations to the Book of Job* (1825).

Another eighteenth-century artist who influenced the course of illustration was William Hogarth, although his best work was never published in books. His satiric series of prints, *The Rake's Progress,* marks him as a great moralist.

While major developments were occurring in British typography and book design, newspapers were rapidly becoming an important type of printed matter. England's first daily newspaper, the *Daily Courant,* was started by a woman, Elizabeth Mallet, in 1702. With financial aid from her partner, Samuel Buckley, the *Courant* ran for thirty years. As the quality of newspaper press work improved, so did the writing. The *Morning Chronicle,* for example, as well as the *Morning Post* carried writers of great talent. Among them were Coleridge, Hazlitt, and Lamb for the *Chronicle,* and Southey and Wordsworth for the *Post.* Clearly the spirit of liberty was at work on both sides of the Atlantic. A crusading newspaper, the *North Briton,* established by John Wilkes, fought to report news about governmental actions. Wilkes's enthusiasm cost him his paper and his seat in Parliament, but it made him a hero to his colonial sympathizers in the South Carolina Assembly who sent him 1,500 pounds to help him pay his debts.

While high-quality writing often appeared in newspapers, talented writers were also producing some of Britain's finest novels, plays, essays, and poems. The work of writers such as John Dryden, Jonathan Swift, Richard Steele, Joseph Addison, Alexander Pope, John Gay, William Collins, Thomas Gray, Samuel Johnson, Oliver Goldsmith, William Cowper, Robert Burns, Edmund Burke, and Daniel Defoe often provided printers with masterpieces to print.

While many of these writers produced works appropriated by children, it was Daniel Defoe's *The Life and Strange Surprising Adventures of Robinson Crusoe* (1719) that eventually became one of the great "children's classics" of all time. The book was addressed to adults, and children must have skipped the moralizing tucked in among the thrilling adventures, but read the book they did. The ever-popular theme, man against nature trying to control his world, especially satisfied the child's need for achievement. And because the moralizing fit into the popular educational philosophies of the time, it was not frowned upon by the children's elders.

Popular educational philosophies were based on either John Locke's *Thoughts Concerning Education* (1693) or Jean Jacques Rousseau's *Emile* (1762). Locke, an English pragmatist, gave advice to the strict but not unkindly British mothers about diet, clothes, exercises, self-denial, rational behavior, sleep, bowel habits, and the other "common-sense" details of raising children. Locke stressed the use of reason as well as the importance of environment in the molding of a child's life. But the French philosopher Rousseau stressed the glory of the natural man who would find God, as well as reason, in nature. When later educators tried to carry out these precepts, perhaps unconsciously, they often misinterpreted both philosophers. But it was followers of Rousseau who seized upon Robinson Crusoe as a splendid example of the natural man who, like a noble savage, innocently but reasonably and fearlessly worked out his design for living. The popularity of *Robinson Crusoe* was enormous as were the numerous imitations, "Robinsonades," that followed.

Technical innovations in illustrations, as well as in typography, continued to surface throughout the eighteenth century. Printers on the continent in particular tried to reproduce painting by printing. In France in 1729, the *Cabinet Crozat,* a series of reproductions of paintings, was printed in tones made from a combination of engraved plates and woodcuts. Another French innovation was the "crayon manner," a form of etching, which was an attempt to reproduce soft crayon effects by breaking up engraved lines into dots. At the end of the century, British printers were able to use effectively another form of etching, the aquatint, to resemble watercolors. But it was a German, Le Bon, working in Britain who applied Newton's three-primary-color theory to printing. Although colored woodcuts had been done as early as 1487, Le Bon produced the first three-color process book ever published. His book, *Coloritto,* which also explained his method, was not especially successful, but it marked a substantial step forward. It would, however, take 150 years before such a process would be perfected.

Along with the beginning of more sophisticated illustration methods, two other developments occurred in the eighteenth century that would affect book production: the rise of lending libraries, and the rise of books for children's entertainment as well as enlightenment.

In 1726 the concept of lending libraries was established when Allen Ramsay opened a small library as part of his bookshop in Edinburgh. In 1730 a lending library was opened in London. In America, Benjamin Franklin opened his "subscription library" in Philadelphia in 1731. Shortly thereafter, with the opening of the first free library in Boston, the American public library movement was launched. It grew quickly, especially when Massachusetts consolidated its public libraries in 1798.

The rise of books for children's "instruction and amusement" was largely the result of the work of John Newbery, a London bookseller and publisher, who realized the potential of a literature designed with children in mind; however, books for children had originated at least a century before. Bishop Johann Comenius, a visionary educator, instituted many innovations in the teaching of children, especially teaching concepts through pictures. His *Orbis Sensualium Pictus,* printed in 1658? in Nuremberg and shortly thereafter translated into English, is most often credited with being the first picture book designed especially for children. But books used by children that contained pictures were in existence at least as early as 1493, when a Swiss book, *Der Ritter von Turn,* illustrated with woodcuts, appeared. Caxton's 1484 *Aesop,* which was used by children as well as adults, also contained woodcuts. In 1580, a German picture book, *Kunst und Lederbüchlein,* with woodcuts by Jost Amman, was created for young people. In 1665, an elaborate edition of Aesop's fables was engraved by Wenzel Barlow, who is credited with being England's first major illustrator, but this expensive book was probably not much used by children. Puritan books, such as the crudely illustrated *The Young Man's Calling* by Nathaniel Crouch (1678), were much more likely to be given to the young.

Poorly illustrated chapbooks, which were often cheap, condensed editions of tales, legends of antiquity, and romances from the Middle Ages, were sold by peddlers called "running stationers." More than likely they were read by children although at first they were intended for uneducated adults who loved the often gory or lusty stories and wondrous events from the past. After chapbooks were designed for the juvenile trade in the eighteenth century, they became an important part of children's reading.

One popular type of chapbook that dates from the seventeenth century was books of street cries of London (in America, the cries were of Philadelphia, Boston, and New York). Pictures of the vendors of herring, cod, oysters, fruits and vegetables of all kinds, as well as toys and trinkets, with accompanying lighthearted verses, must have delighted children. But the reader was also frequently admonished to be kind to the poor vendors and to their children who were often vendors themselves and not as fortunate as the reader. Poorly printed on cheap paper, few chapbooks have survived, but some have been found carefully sewn or bound with ribbons and string, perhaps by the children who owned them.

Thus, children's books existed before John Newbery, but it was his 1744 publication of *A Little Pretty Pocket-Book* that ostensibly began a new line of books for children. Although his work reflected the didactic tone of the time, his books were not intended to be textbooks. Their gilt-paper covers, attractive pages, engaging stories and verses—and sometimes toys which were offered with the books—provided "diversion" for children of the English-speaking world. (*See figure 13.*)

About 1745, one of Newbery's assistants, Benjamin Collins, is credited with designing the battledore, a refinement of the hornbook. The first battledores, like the hornbooks, were ABC "books" made in the shape of a paddle used for playing an early form of badminton. In its earliest state, the battledore's letters were engraved directly onto wood, ivory, or silver, but eventually the letters were printed on a cheap, three-leaved piece of cardboard which folded into an oblong pocket-book shape. It contained easy reading lessons, small woodcuts, alphabets, and numerals, but unlike the hornbook, had no religious teaching.

In America

By the end of the seventeenth century, printing of all sorts was also developing in the colonies. As mentioned earlier, the first press had been established in Cambridge, Massachusetts, in 1638. With the addition of a second press imported from England in 1656, the printing output of Cambridge alone was greatly increased. In 1674, Marmaduke Johnson succeeded, after nine years of work to repeal the law restricting printing to Cambridge, in moving his press to Boston. In 1685, a Quaker from London, William Bradford, set up a press in Philadelphia, but he printed material that was not to the liking of the authorities and was arrested. It was not until the governor of New York, in 1693, arranged for his release that he was able to move his press to New York, where he remained the Royal Printer of New York for the next fifty years. By the end of the century, Boston had many printers and several booksellers. The first bookseller was Hezebiah Usher who, as early as 1652, had versions of the psalms printed for his distribution.

By 1690 the first newspaper in the New World, *Publick Occurences both Foreign and Domestick,* was printed by Richard Pierce for publisher Benjamin Harris. Only one issue was printed, however, as it was immediately banned by the provincial council. Not until 1704 was a newspaper, issued weekly, established by John Campbell, a bookseller and postmaster, called the *Boston News-Letter;* the first issue (a half-sheet of paper) contained an extract from a London newspaper. The *News-Letter* was published until 1723.

Although books were not as widely sought in Virginia as in Massachusetts, William Nuthead attempted to establish a press in Jamestown in 1682. But he never printed anything, as the press was closed down before he could get started. It took until 1703 to get official approval for a printing press in Virginia, and then it was in the capital at Williamsburg.

Early books in America were usually copies of English books often printed under pioneer circumstances. Types were imported from England, and styles of documents, business forms, legal papers, books, and newspapers were copies of English printed matter. Although illustrations were rare and often crudely done, colonial books' title pages were often decorated, usually with borders of flowers. The first illustration in a colonial book (a woodcut made by the printer John Foster) was a map of New England. It was published in Hubbard's *Narrative of the Indian Wars* (Boston, 1677). Frontispieces of Increase Mather (a copperplate-engraved portrait) were used for two of Mather's works, in 1701 and 1702.

Other presses came into prominence. Boston and Philadelphia remained important centers, but the press of William Parks in Williamsburg, Virginia, which began in 1730, achieved distinction also; among Parks's works was the first practical manual, *The Compleat Housewife* (1742). Another important press was established in Boston in 1717 by James Franklin, older brother of Benjamin Franklin, where he printed the *Boston Gazette.* Here the younger Franklin, an apprentice from 1718 to 1723, learned the printer's trade. In 1721 the elder Franklin began publishing the *New England Courant,* a single-page weekly journal based on the popular British publication, *The Spectator,* by Addison and Steele. For this journal Benjamin, at age sixteen, wrote his "Do-Good Papers." But the *Courant* ran into difficulties with the authorities for being too outspoken and after five years was finally closed down. In 1728 Benjamin Franklin set up his own print shop in Philadelphia where he published the *Pennsylvania Gazette* from 1729 to 1766.

Along with the *Pennsylvania Gazette,* Franklin published *Poor Richard's Almanack* from 1733 until 1757; it had wide distribution in America and later in Europe. Franklin also published *The American Instructor* (1742), the first compendium dealing with information on the practical arts and sciences. He also published the *General Magazine* which was to have been the first magazine in the colonies, but he was beaten out by a rival printer, the son of William Bradford, who brought out the *American Magazine* three days before Franklin issued his. It is interesting to note that by 1800 a total of ninety-eight magazines and periodicals were being published, primarily in Boston, New York, and Philadelphia. Among Franklin's other printing ventures were Richardson's *Pamela* (1744), the first novel published in the New World, translations of Cato's *Moral Distichs* (1735) and Cicero's *Cato Major* (1744); the latter was considered by Franklin to be his best work.

Newspapers were springing up all over the colonies. In 1775 there were five newspapers published in Boston, seven in Massachusetts, fourteen in New England, with a total of thirty-seven in the American colonies. By 1800 this number had grown to 150. Between 1690 and 1820, 2,120 newspapers were published in the thirty colonies and states, but only 461 of them maintained publication for ten years or more. The high mortality rate gives some notion of the difficulties printers encountered in the new country. That publishers persevered at all indicates how great was the American need to keep informed on events in the rapidly developing nation.

As newspapers were established, so was the reputation, and eventual influence, of their publishers. For example, William Bradford's grandson, publisher of the *Pennsylvania Journal and Weekly Advertiser,* a strong opponent of the Stamp Act, would become printer to the first Continental Congress. Another important printer was John Peter Zenger of New York, who was arrested and tried for "seditious libels." His acquittal in August

1735 was hailed as a resounding triumph for liberty in Britain as well as the colonies; it was an important step forward in the fight for freedom of the press which almost from the first days of printing had been highly restricted for religious and political reasons.

In addition to newspapers, almanacs, assembly laws and proceedings, primers, chapbooks, broadside ballads, literature (some appropriated by children), history, books on the arts (especially sacred music), and theology were printed in America. Between 1639 and 1791, over 24,000 titles were published. While books on theology led the list, there was a growing interest in literature and politics. But there was no colonial Bible. No Bible was printed in America, except for John Eliot's Indian translation of 1663 and other translations from foreign languages, such as a translation of Luther's German version for the Pennsylvania Germans in 1742, until America was independent.

Although William Bradford in 1688 and John Fleming in 1770 proposed the publication of an American Bible, they met with apathy, probably because of a thriving legitimate import trade from Britain, as well as a vigorous smuggling trade from Holland. And there was always the possibility of interdiction from the Crown. Apparently there was no need for an American Bible until the Revolution. At first, Congress took care of this matter by simply ordering more copies from Holland. Finally, Robert Aitken of Boston recognized the commercial possibilities and in 1777 published the first Bible in English printed in America. By 1781 he had published four more editions, with his 1781 edition receiving a recommendation from Congress, the so-called "Bible Congress"; this edition became the forerunner of many American editions.

By the end of the eighteenth century, printed material was in great demand in both Britain and America, and it was widely disseminated both privately and publicly. The most popular forms of printed material were Bibles, prayer books, histories, books of poems, novels, fables, travelogues, text-books on many subjects, periodicals, much-sought-after newspapers, and even books for children.

The success of Newbery's publications for children had spread quickly to Europe and America. As early as 1760, Hugh Gaine of New York was importing Newbery's books, and in 1762 he began reprinting them. In 1780, Jacob Johnson was publishing reprints and revisions of other British books, some of them for children, that went back as far as 1688. Most of the material that had been written and illustrated for children in both Britain and America had been and would continue to be the work of routine writers and illustrators. It was not until the work of such artists as William Blake (1757-1827) and Thomas Bewick (1755-1828) appeared in Britain, along with Alexander Anderson (1775-1870) in America, although his work was of lesser quality, that illustrated books, that is, beautiful books for children, began in earnest.

From this point, children's books were firmly established as an important part of the history of the development of printing and illustration.

ATTITUDES TOWARD AND TREATMENT OF CHILDREN

In Britain

During the late seventeenth and early eighteenth centuries changes began to occur in many areas—family life, child rearing, education, medicine, child labor—which would ultimately affect the way that adults thought of and treated children. But these changes were slow in coming and often contradictory. In some ways this period, often called the Age of Reason, revealed the brilliance of mankind, his compassionate nature, and his potential for human perfectability. In other ways, especially in his treatment of the coarser elements of society, this period was anything but enlightened. Although wealth increased for some, for the less fortunate conditions were such that they could not escape from their abject poverty even through traditional ways, such as education; the mobility that the school had provided for the poor in Elizabethan times was no longer available. For the middle and upper classes, however, life had new dignity and refinement. In fact, improving manners and doing philanthropic works were common goals of most eighteenth-century gentlemen and ladies.

The political stability and general economic prosperity of the time gave all but the lower class the feeling that mankind could endlessly improve, but to do so men must be practical, use their common sense, and sharply define their goals. To accomplish these ends, the purpose of science would be utilitarian and the purpose of literature, didactic.

On the one hand, eighteenth-century English society was enlightened, forward-looking, and brilliant; on the other, it was vice-ridden, degrading, and shabby. For children, as in former times, their elders sought means of handling them in such a way as to perpetuate the society the adults chose to pass on. Treatment of children in the eighteenth century differed only slightly from earlier times, except that those who dealt directly with them became keenly aware of children for the first time in history, not as autonomous individuals, but as objects to be molded systematically according to prescribed goals.

It is important to realize that for countless thousands life in post-Restoration England was hard. Indicative of the conditions was the life expectancy of children from ages one to fourteen: it was lower in the late seventeenth century than it had been in the 1500s. And it was even worse by the middle of the eighteenth century when the death rate of children under five years of age was probably as high as 75 percent in London, although in the rural areas it was considerably less. As in the past, midwifery was an undeveloped skill, and the nursing of sick children was left to careless, often indifferent women who treated children with alcohol, drugs, and magic.

Effective methods of medical therapy were slow in coming. The eighteenth century would, however, see for the first time the beginning of a concerted effort to study children's diseases, describe their symptoms, and prepare remedies. Although magic and folk remedies were often still employed, the new analytical spirit—which included surgical experimentation—began to grow, especially in preventive medicine regarding the plague. Throughout the century, however, the Almighty remained the most frequently invoked "cure," and infanticide was still practiced (although it had been outlawed), child neglect and cruelty were common, and most authorities still considered the rod the chief instrument of child rearing.

Not until medical practices changed in the late eighteenth century did life expectancy rise. As before, the most vulnerable years were the early ones, especially for poor children. With soaring death rates, parents of all classes knew it was likely that only one out of two of their offspring would survive. Perhaps because of the psychological risk of becoming too involved, many parents, as in former times, remained fatalistic, viewing the death of their young with indifference.

The valuing of children continued to be spurious, and most children, at least in the early part of the period, were put out into the world according to customs of the preceding generations. Although the practice of sending infants to a wet nurse had subsided for a while in the seventeenth century, the eighteenth century saw a return of the fashion to enhance the figures of upper-class women. Upper-class children were still being sent from home to other households, but not nearly as often. More often they were sent away to school; as in former times, some children were so rarely at home that their fathers could not recognize them. Some children of the lower classes, as before, were sent out as apprentices at early ages, but on the whole, ejections into the world outside the home were declining. A new concern for family life was growing as evident in the great number of books on child rearing that began to be published in the late seventeenth century. They clearly show that some parents wanted to raise their own children and raise them well. From letters and diaries of the period, it is also obvious that some parents loved their children.

While child-rearing books frequently reminded parents that too much fondness would breed contempt and irreverence in their children, the drive toward leniency grew, especially when tempered with restraint. Children were still reared according to the established social and moral codes. Mothers were urged to be close to their daughters, teaching them diligence, chastity, and piety, while fathers were encouraged to talk with their sons, preparing them for the rigors of life. Even among the unschooled, the young were admonished to be self-reliant, with fines imposed on apprentices, for instance, for indolence, for missing prayers, for playing games without the consent of their masters, and similar offences.

Self-control, the aristocratic ideal of the late seventeenth century, became the goal for eighteenth-century children as well as adults. John Locke (1632-1704), philosopher and physician, articulated this objective in treatises on child care and education. His thoughts on moderation and self-discipline, especially concerning the "lasting consequences" of the early years, became the foundation of child training. He believed that infants were neither innocent nor depraved, but that they had "blank" minds (tabula rasa) on which experience was to write. His comments on the bad effects of swaddling and the good effects of allowing children to crawl (which he did not consider animalistic as had most of his forebearers), to wear loose clothing, and to exercise in the open air, brought considerably more freedom of movement to young children. He also felt that the young should undergo "hardening" to strengthen character; this process included getting their feet wet and keeping them wet, sleeping on hard beds, and not being allowed to cry. He stated that the denial of luxury, especially that of rich foods, and the toleration of hardship would strengthen the mind as well as the body. While he warned parents against too much tenderness, which he felt would bring about weakness in children, he also cautioned them to be less free with the rod. He pointed out that coercion could come about equally well through shame. The disciplines of "esteem and disgrace," he said, "are . . . the most powerful incentives of the mind." He saw the possibilities of play when controlled, especially dancing, and advocated that parental example, particularly friendship between the father and son, be encouraged. He also recognized that reading for entertainment could have good results and advocated such books as *Aesop's Fables* along with religious material. He regarded learning foreign languages as a method of strengthening the mind. Locke's admonition to parents that they pay attention to children and spend time overseeing their learning, which at first meant merely a new form of control, sowed the seeds for a new interest in children per se, even if it did not attend to their autonomous development.

Along with new ideas in child rearing came changes in family life. Seventeenth-century households had been very large, often numbering between thirty and forty or more. By the beginning of the eighteenth century, increased wealth in the middle and upper classes enabled the separation of servants' quarters from the family itself, and thus relationships among immediate family members were allowed to deepen. Even in rural areas, it became the custom for the domestic servants to live outside the well-to-do farmer's house as the gentleman-farmer preferred not to have his children sit at table with common folk. But even in the homes of poor farmers, whose numbers had steadily increased since the Napoleonic Wars, the incidence of the help "living in" declined, although the cause was more likely dire poverty rather than class consciousness. Regardless of the reasons, a greater intimacy developed among family members, and increased concern for children by their parents grew, especially in the middle class where lineage and children's potential for profitable marriage were no longer essential for extending status. But in the upper classes, traditions continued much as before. For example, legal attempts in the late seventeenth century to restrict arranged child marriages for economic purposes failed. Thus, the middle class was by far the most likely group to see the child not as property to be used for profit and social status, but as a personality to be molded.

Although increased wealth might have brought improved education, such was not necessarily the case. Although many aristocratic boys did attend such prestigious schools as Eton, Winchester, Westminster, and Harrow, local grammar schools often served, although not always well, upper-class boys as well as the sons of yeomen and shopkeepers. Children were also tutored at home. In general, the established grammar schools of the eighteenth century had fallen into decay. Even Oxford and Cambridge, which excluded all who were not churchmen, became so expensive and provided such a low level of education that their enrollments shrank drastically. Their faculties rarely taught, and students often had to study under private tutors. Not until the end of the eighteenth century did internal reform begin to correct the poor conditions of English universities. In spite of such decadence in secondary education, the age produced brilliant literary men (Edmund Burke, Edward Gibbon, Alexander Pope, Joseph Addison, Richard Steele, Samuel Johnson, and others).

As in earlier times, both grammar and private schools advocated stern discipline. Open almost year around, their students attended from 6 in the morning to 5:30 P.M. with one two-hour mid-day break and one fifteen-minute break in the morning and afternoon. Educational goals were self-control, punctuality, and the acquisition of moral virtues largely through knowledge of the classics, although a strictly classical education was being questioned.

In upper-class families, firstborn sons, who were usually educated away from home, received the most education, as they were the ones who by law would inherit the estates. Succeeding sons often went into the army, the diplomatic service, the law, or the church. Upper-class girls were usually educated at home, often learning to read, write, sew, and manage the household from their mothers. Although girls were only rarely taught the classics or foreign languages, many grew up to manage large households and advise their menfolk, sometimes with unusual intelligence and insight.

While education for the rich was at best middling to fair, for poor children it was almost nonexistent. The ordinary parish in the late seventeenth century had no endowed schools, and although some villages offered dame schools, the dames who held them charged fees for their services. Not until charity schools were founded in the reign of Queen Anne was there any concentrated mass attempt to teach the poor reading, writing, moral discipline, and the principles of the Church of England. Probably because the notion that "idleness breeds mischief" (that is, poverty and wickedness are inextricable) was firmly planted in English thought, the charity school movement, founded in 1699, was viewed as a suitable and inspired means of dealing with the poor. While in former times (even as late as the mid-seventeenth century), the grammar school had been the chief vehicle to promote poor children lucky enough to be educated, the eighteenth century provided no such schooling.

In the charity schools humanists saw the means of educating the poor and at the same time keeping them "in that station of life wherein Providence hath placed them." Charity schools, which were often financed by subscription by men of moderate means, offered a method of administering "practical piety" which provided a great sense of satisfaction to the donors. Royal patronage added prestige. Along with providing basic education, charity schools clothed the poor children and eventually sent them out as apprentices. In return, the schools demanded submission to the system, gratitude, and reformation of manners. By 1729 over 1,600 such schools had been established, and Addison called them the "glory of the age."

Critics, such as Bernard Mandeville, disagreed, noting that the charity schools were a threat to the established order of things and that the working class should not be educated beyond their status because the structure of society would be upset. Unpopular at first, such criticism grew. And charity schools became less and less institutions of learning and more and more institutions of work, especially when the reformation of manners and morals of the poor, which had been predicted by the originators, did not necessarily occur.

As public support gradually withdrew from the charity schools, their proponents had to find ways to finance them, and to this end some of the schools became connected with workhouses. Training for industry, which in the beginning was only one part of the curriculum, eventually took over the educational scheme. But the work-for-profit curriculum was not successful, except in some girls' schools where domestic labor could be combined with basic education. Most of the children were either too inexpert or too weak to turn a profit, and gradually the movement for the education of the poor came to an end. By the last decade of the eighteenth century, the pupils of the charity schools which still existed were no longer the children of the really poor; pupils who attended these schools could afford to go to a school where no wages were paid, and only training in reading, writing, and cipher-ing was provided. These fortunate boys eventually worked for tradesmen. The less able poor were sent to industrial schools for manual work, while other poor children, if educated at all, were sent to Sunday schools, another charity voluntarily financed by the middle class in an attempt to rescue the very poor by teaching them the catechism and some reading and writing, but on Sundays only. Thus, the work patterns of society were not affected, the poor received some learning, and the "wild, ignorant children" were kept off the streets on the Sabbath.

The experience of the charity schools indicated quite clearly that provisions for the poor children of the eighteenth century were most heavily supported in situations where the children were expected to help support themselves. The Elizabethan poor laws had been established to promote national stability, while eighteenth-century reformers, humane but far more materialistic, hoped that poor-law reforms would promote national wealth.

Even John Locke, chief among those who had changed society's thinking about the treatment of children, suggested that poor children as early as age three be put to some useful work; thus their upkeep would cost the parishes nothing. But work prevented children from receiving education. Child labor for the poor, rather than education for the poor, became an established eighteenth-century social pattern, accepted even by humanists.

While the exploitation of children in factories was taken for granted as the common lot of the urban poor, rural children, hidden away in cottage industries, fared no better. Urban children of three or four were taught to handle bobbins; by five they worked full time in the lace schools; or they sorted straws at four, and earned regular wages at straw-plaiting by six. In some schools (workshops), reading from the Bible was taught once a day, but the purpose of the schools was not education. Poor rural children from age four on were expected to contribute their mites to the family's support in agriculture and mining, sometimes under brutal conditions.

In spite of such problems, eighteenth-century Britain witnessed a develop-ing sense of philanthropy, albeit erratic, and humanitarianism, albeit limited. Philanthropic and humane works were carried out by many in-dividuals and religious denominations, particularly the Methodists and the Quakers. Both groups taught the importance of self-control and fostered the humanitarian spirit. The founding of hospitals and improved medical service, especially for children, made for real advancement. But as noted, the charity schools, followed by the Sunday school movement especially after 1780, which tried to give some education to the masses, were not successful. Clever poor boys, who formerly had been given the chance to rise out of their class via the old grammar schools, were no longer able to do so. Excessive emphasis on class consciousness locked the poor in their "proper station." Yet, although the reasons for philanthropy were mixed, it was obvious that concern for improving the lot of the poor was genuine. For various reasons much of society was concerned about the "molding" of children, about rescuing them from abuse, and about providing them with basic skills with which to work when they were grown. It is also clear that British society was truly concerned about the unwanted child; schemes for training unwanted children surfaced throughout the century, but such children were viewed as the proper concern of individuals, not of the state.

It must be remembered that throughout these fluctuations in attitudes toward and treatment of children, knowledge of and concern for the nature of childhood was still largely unknown. In spite of such thinkers as Jean Jacques Rousseau who said that a child should be allowed to develop naturally, children were still expected to think and act as much like grown-ups as possible. Even the dress of children was "adult" until the end of the century when special dress for children was designed but considered by many to be an affectation. Demands of adult maturity from children sometimes resulted in precociousness, but for many children the requirements were too heavy, the frustrations enormous, and the tasks impossible.

Adult goals were reflected even in books that were given directly to children, such as Perrault's *Histories or Tales of Past Times, Told by Mother Goose (with morals). (See figure 16.)* Few eighteenth-century books succeeded in diverting and entertaining children. Most children's reading was done for some purpose, usually improvement in manners and morals. Not until John Newbery, a London publisher, began in 1744 to print some two hundred attractive, often illustrated books to "amuse" children, did young people have a literature conceived to be their own. Even then, Newbery's books resembled the moral tracts from the past.

In America

Growing up in the colonies—particularly New England—meant, at least for the first colonists, being faithful to English educational and moral principles, especially self-control. But colonial children early realized some benefits from the move to the new land. In the colonies, where population was low, every person who could work had to contribute to the general survival. Pioneer children worked hard and were soon recognized as valuable members of the community. Probably because of this new importance, the first colonial parents were especially obliged to see that their children were not too assertive or willful and that they looked to parental and divine guidance for the proper molding of their character.

Although mental restraints were often severe, it is well known that colonial children, even infants, experienced more physical freedom than their English counterparts. Swaddling, for example, was not used in the colonies although some newborn babies were bound to a stiff rod against the back and neck to keep the spine straight. And colonial mothers took care of their own children.

Leaving children in the care of wet nurses was scorned because the milk the child drank supposedly directly affected the child. Colonial mothers wanted to influence their own offspring. Nor were children given to servants for care; such practice was viewed as not carrying out the mother's proper duties. Although babies were seldom bathed, they were kept well covered so as not to take cold. Because of the fear of colds and other diseases, taking infants to the beds of parents was not uncommon and sometimes resulted in tragic "overlaying." When infants sickened, as they frequently did, the same remedies used for adults—bleeding, dosing, and purging—were used with children. Because of disease, lack of sound medical treatment, poor nutrition, and poor sanitation, less than half of colonial children under five survived.

Puritan parents especially coped with their offsprings' deaths by reminding themselves that life was not intended to be pleasant but only a means to the hereafter, "an error to be rectified," that a child was only "lent" by God and it was foolhardy to grow too attached to him. Many accounts reveal Puritan parents' grief over children's illnesses and deaths, but the accounts also encourage parents to strive to gain self-control, knowing that infants' souls would go to the "easiest room in Hell."

Infanticide was almost nonexistent in the colonies, but children, especially those of Puritan parents, were expected to be grateful for birth and indebted forever for causing trouble, that is, being a child. Puritan parents were obliged to give their children every chance to be saved, or their own fates would be even worse than those of their children. The goal of every Puritan's life was rigid self-control in order to make "war with the Devil." Both adults and children were therefore required to strive for divine guidance, self-discipline, and the avoidance of Hell. Fatherhood was thought of as being God-appointed; there was to be no parleying or excusing. Obedience to the father's will was unquestioned. Although the mother's role was more passive, her influence made for some moderation in the household. Children's misbehavior was correctable by a series of prescribed steps. Guilt, shame, sermonizing, and threats of everlasting punishment in fire and brimstone were advocated as the first steps toward correction of faults. The final step, the rod, could be administered by either the father or the mother, but the father, as the supreme earthly authority, was the most likely parent to do the "correcting." Discipline and appropriate steps toward correction were acknowedged as a large part of the serious emotional burden of the family and the whole community. During periods when the faith seemed to be weakening, ministers in resounding tones rekindled the hope of Heaven and the fear of Hell by preaching vehement sermons on the terrors in store for unrepentant sinners who lingered in total depravity.

By age seven, Puritan children were already well schooled in traditional manners and duties—both religious (exact knowledge of the Scriptures) and domestic. Boys had to learn the principles of farming or trade; girls had to learn the household tasks of cooking, spinning, weaving, and sewing. Some children attended school away from home from about age six to fourteen, but most schooling took place in the home where great emphasis was placed on learning to read the Bible, a necessity for going to Heaven; the Bible was also used to teach spelling. Numerous "goodly Godly books" such as *The New England Primer* (*see figure 14*) were published specifically for children, some extolling martyrdom; but the young were admonished to refrain from wasting time on fairy tales, fantasies, rhymes, ditties, ballads, and the like. In spite of churchmen's opposition, chapbooks and nursery rhymes prevailed both in written form and in the oral tradition. Such fare became increasingly popular around 1750 when British peddlers began to deluge colonial children with cheap editions, even abridgments of such novels as Fielding's *Pamela*. In the latter part of the eighteenth century, the printer Isaiah Thomas began to circulate pirated copies of John Newbery's books which were designed to amuse children.

By age six, Puritan children were dressed as miniature adults and were expected to use adult measures of self-control, but they were not legal adults. Like their elders, children were expected to follow rigid codes of behavior, to examine their consciences every day, and to say grace privately and in family gatherings. With their parents they attended six hours of sermons and psalms on Sunday as well as lectures on Thursday evenings, always hoping for the Experience (five steps) which would enable them to join the Church. Playing or falling asleep in church was discouraged by a tithing man who rapped backsliders on the head with a stout switch.

Some Puritan communities permitted celebrations such as weddings, ordinations, and funerals (when festive eating and drinking by all ages was expected), but Training Day, the mustering of the militia, was the most colorful day of the whole year. Christmas was not celebrated by the Puritans, but it was celebrated by the Dutch in New York as well as the Anglican English in other colonies who were far more frivolous than the New Englanders—allowing dancing, skating, promenading, and even kissing games. In most sexual matters, however, the Puritans were more open than many other groups—allowing bundling (to keep warm) and encouraging children to read sometimes erotic versions of Bible stories (to learn the consequences of sin). By the end of the 1700s, Puritan young people were sent out of the home well-schooled in the Protestant ethic that became dominant in America, that is, the "calling" to do honest labor growing out of rigorous discipline.

But Puritan standards gradually faded. As life became more commercial, it was impossible for the Puritan merchants to worship God on the Sabbath and on every other day of the week remind their unregenerated customers of their sinfulness. In order to survive in business, the merchants had to learn toleration of other creeds. As prosperity increased, Puritan principles declined. The liberalism which emerged opened the doors to a new humanitarianism, especially in the growing Anglican church and Unitarian and Universalist sects. Even the Presbyterians, whose beliefs were founded on Calvinism, softened their stands, but not enough. They soon lost their potential power to the Methodists and Baptists. The subsequent evangelism carried by circuit riders and preached at camp meetings would become a dominant civilizing influence on the coarse, ever-widening frontier.

Although the first colonial children closely resembled their European counterparts, succeeding generations grew increasingly different from them. The New World offered freedoms never dreamed of in the Old. While the colonial thinkers continued to urge that the family remain the basic social unit, churchmen had to work hard to keep it intact. At first, the terrors of the wilderness had caused families and communities to huddle together for comradeship and defense. Under such conditions rigid self-control had been absolutely necessary; it was easy to show children the need for obedience. But as life became more certain and communities spread, restraints began to break down. Some pioneer parents simply did not have the energy or patience necessary to hold tight reins on their offspring because of their own struggle to overcome adverse physical conditions. Mere survival often superseded the patient teaching of the old wisdoms. Children with their energy and curiosity often grew up quickly in the new life, and they frequently became more experienced and more adept in the new ways than their exhausted parents. While girls were more likely to follow traditional ways taught by their mothers (domestic skills do not change much whatever the setting), eighteenth-century boys were far more likely to break with the past and set out on their own.

While economic and social conditions in America encouraged children to grow up early, the colonial youth also had space. A continent wanting conquering lay to the west. By the thousands, pioneer lads with their young wives, often as young as fourteen, started off on the westward trek.

While the eighteenth-century British youth was still locked into class and its traditions, the American youth was breaking ties with church authority, social station, and the subsequent restraints. Sometimes foolhardy but full of energy and determined to pass the test, young Americans of the late eighteenth century set out with confidence in their mission and belief in their own self-sufficiency.

ANNOTATED CHRONOLOGY

1660

Thomas White's *Little Book for Little Children. Wherein are set down several Directions for Little Children. And Several Remarkable Stories both Ancient and Modern, of little Children. Divers whereof are of those Lately*

Deceased (appended to White's *A manual for parents. Wherein is set down very particular directions in reference to the baptising, correcting, instructing, and chusing a calling for their children;* printed in London by Joseph Cranford; the mayor of London and aldermen were admonished in the dedication "to put poor children in school . . . to buy good books, and give them to poor people that can read them . . . to send two or three hundred [of the books] to the Barbados . . . to maintain itinerary preachers," and to keep "youth at the universities whose parents cannot"; subtitled: *Wherein are set down several directions for little children; and several remarkable stories both ancient and modern of little children, divers whereof are of those who are lately deceased;* the gruesome text, which warned children against ballads and foolish books and recommended Richard Baxter's *Call to the Unconverted* and Foxe's *Book of Martyrs,* was intended as light literature to bring joy to children by saving their souls from perdition; the only extant edition is the twelfth of 1702 and included *Youth's alphabet; or, Herbert's morals;* the first American edition was reprinted by T. Green for Nicholas Buttolph at the corner of Gutteridges Coffee-House, 1702). GPM

1664

Samuel Crossman's *The Young Man's Monitor, Or a Modest Offer Toward the Pious, and Vertuous Composure of Life from Youth to Riper Years* (a Puritan work designed to save children from their evil natures; tenor of the work is comparatively gentle; uses a Bible format with Hebrew and Latin marginal glosses; printed in London by J. H. to be sold by S. Thompson and T. Parkhurst; author's other work includes *The Young Man's Calling; or, The Whole Duty of Youth,* printed in London, 1678; *The Young Mans Meditation, or Some Few Sacred Poems Upon Select Subjects and Scriptures,* printed by J. H. for S. Thompson, 1664).

1671

James Janeway's *Token for Children; being an exact Account of the Conversion, holy and exemplary Lives and Joyful Deaths of several young Children* (a popular religious book for children exhorting them to be good, love God, and die well; printed in London for Dorman Newman and issued in two volumes; the second volume, 1672, is titled: *A Token for Children. The Second Part. A Farther Account . . . ;* earliest extant copy is dated 1676; contains a total of thirteen deathbed scenes; written by a nonconformist English clergyman and Puritan divine; thirteen additional deathbed scenes were issued in a third volume by James Mathews, who was the author of an account of the death of his daughter; Cotton Mather, a colonist clergyman, added *A Token for the Children of New England; or some Examples of Children in whom the Fear of God was remarkably budding before they dyed: in several parts of New England . . .* to the American editions of Janeway's volumes of which Vol. 1 was printed in Boston for Nicholas

Boone, 1700, and Vols. 2 and 3 were printed by Timothy Green for Benjamin Eliot, 1700). UOx

H. Punchard's *A looking-glass for children. Being a narrative of God's gracious dealings with some little children; recollected by Henry Jessey in his lifetime. Together, with sundry seasonable lessons and instructions to youth, calling them early to remember their creator: written by Abraham Chear, late of Plymouth. The second edition, corrected and amended. To which is added many other poems very suitable. As also some elegies on departed friends: made by the said Abraham Chear. All now faithfully gathered together, for the benefit of young and old: by H. P.* (a collection of religious sayings, verses, and the histories of pious, suffering children; edited by Punchard and printed in London; both Jessey and Chear were English Baptist clergymen; Chear's ten-stanza poem to be memorized by young virgins ends with the well-known line, " 'Tis pity, such a pretty maid as I, should go to Hell"; in 1709 John Allen printed a copy in Boston for N. Boone which had the following added to the main title: *Together, with Sundry seasonable lessons and instructions to youth . . . by Abraham Chear, late of Plymouth . . .*).

1674

Giambattista Basile's *The Tale of the Tales* (translated from the Italian *Il Pentamerone* and first published in Naples in 1634-1636, in two volumes; not intended specifically for children, but parts were appropriated by them and known via the oral tradition; a fuller edition of the earliest known collection of European folktales, Straparola's *Le Tredici Piacevolissime Notti,* 1550, 1553, was published in France, 1585, and possibly influenced Perrault in that it contained an early form of "Puss in Boots"; also "Beauty and the Beast"; the first edition specifically for children, *The Pentamerone: or, The Story of Stories: Fun for the Little Ones,* was translated by John Edward Taylor, illustrated with six plates by George Cruikshank, and printed in London by D. Bogue, 1848). BM

The history of Prince Erastus son of the Emperor Dioclesian and those famous philosophers called the seven wise masters of Rome (anonymous; a romance published by Francis Kirkman who was a bookseller and also had a circulating library; additional stories were added to the basic text and the book was illustrated with copper cuts; the preface states that the book was "of so great esteem in Ireland that next to the Horn-book and knowledge of Letters, Children are in general put to read in it, and I know that only by that Book several have Learned to read well, so great is the pleasure that young and old take in reading thereof"; an earlier edition, *The history of the seven wise masters of Rome,* was printed by Wynken de Worde in 1520).

1675

The living words of a dying child, being a true relation of some part of the words that came forth, and were spoken by Joseph Briggins on his deathbed (anonymous; an eleven-and-one-half-year-old English Quaker boy's dying words of wisdom are paraphrased by his deathbed witnesses).

1678

John Bunyan's *The Pilgrim's Progress From This World, To That Which is to come: Delivered Under the Similitude of a Dream Wherein is Discovered, The manner of setting out, His Dangerous Journey; and safe Arrival at the Desired Countrey. I have used Similitudes* (an allegorical Puritan masterpiece written by a dissident English clergyman; intended for adults but appropriated by children because of its adventure element; printed in London for Nathaniel Ponder at the Peacock in the Poultry near Cornhil; issued in three parts, 1678, 1684, 1693, author's other work includes *A Book for Boys and Girls; or Country Rhimes for Children,* printed for Nathaniel Ponder, 1686; an unillustrated emblem book in which seventy-four everyday devices or objects which were, on the whole, of interest to children were used to illustrate divine truths or moral ideas; some of the verses are gentle, some reflect a true understanding of the child; the illustrated edition's title was changed to *Divine Emblems; or, Temporal things spiritualized,* and was printed in London by John Marshall in 1724 and in New York by James Carey for Mathew Carey, Philadelphia, 1794?; Bunyan's was the first collection of emblems, or parables in verse, designed for children although emblem books for adults had long been popular, beginning in England with Francis Quarles's *Embleme,* with engravings by William Marshall, and printed in London in 1635 by G. M. for I. Marriots; emblem books probably originated in Italy with Alciati's *Emblemata,* 1531; Isaiah Thomas printed a two-volume abridgement of *Pilgrim's Progress* for children, *The Christian Pilgrim: Containing an Account of the Wonderful Adventures and Miraculous Escapes of a Christian in His travels from the Land of Destruction to the New Jerusalem,* in Worcester, Mass., in 1798). AAS, BM, LC, HU, NYPL, PM, UCLA

Nathaniel Crouch's *The Young Man's Calling* (a pirating in chapbook form of Samuel Crossman's 1678 work to which Crouch affixed a miscellaneous collection of rather exciting semi-historical stories of famous young people, e.g. Isaac; Queen Elizabeth; Henry, Prince of Wales; crude but lively illustrations show beheadings, burning of martyrs, and a party of debauchers; printed in London by T. James for N. Crouch; author's other work under pseudonym R. B. includes *The Apprentice's Companion,* printed in London in 1681 and largely pirated from Wingate's *The Clerks Tutor,* printed by S. G. for Henry Twiford in London in 1671; *The Extraordinary Adventures*

and Discoveries of Several Famous Men, printed in London by J. Richardson for N. Crouch, 1683; *Delights for the Ingenious, in About Fifty Select
and Choice Emblems*, printed for N. Crouch in London in 1684; *England's
Monarchs,* 1685; *The English Heroe, or Sir Francis Drake Revived,* printed
in London for N. Crouch in1687; *Winter Evening's Entertainments,* printed
for N. Crouch in London in 1687, with short stories and fifty riddles illustrated in such a way that the answers are readily apparent; *Female Excellency,
or The Ladies of Glory,* printed for N. Crouch in London in 1688; *Martyrs
in Flames,* printed in London for N. Crouch in 1688; *Youth's Divine Pastime,*
the third edition printed in London for N. Crouch in 1691; *The Unhappy
Princess,* printed in London for N. Crouch in 1710; the author often published under the pseudonyms Richard Burton and Robert Burton). BM, UOx

*The fathers legacy: or counsels to his children. In three parts. Containing
the whole duty of man, I. to God, II. to himself, III. to man of all conditions.
Useful for families* (anonymous; the author takes John Locke's position
that children are not born evil or good, but that their environment imprints
good or evil upon them; he urges parents to treat children as friends and to
become intimate with them; he also maintained that there is no conflict
between religion and science, and said that the child's reading of romances
would be good for him because, "It is almost impossible to read a good
romance without feeling in ourselves an adversion from vice, or our desires
touched with the emulation of the brave actions which we read therein";
printed in London by Henry Brome).

1679

Benjamin Harris's *The Protestant Tutor. Instructing Children to Spel and
Read English and Grounding Them in the True Protestant Religion and
Discovering the Error and Deceits of the Papists* (an anti-Catholic primer
intended for religious instruction; published anonymously; some believe
that Benjamin Keach is the author; printed by Harris in England "under the
Piazza of the Royal Exchange in Cornhil"; the book contains, in part,
upper- and lower-case alphabets, syllables, the Lord's Prayer, the Creed,
and the Ten Commandments, and an account of the burning of the Reverend
John Rogers, an English Protestant martyr; an American abridgement was
printed by Samuel Green in Boston, 1685; thought to be a forerunner of
The New England Primer; author's other work includes *The Holy Bible in
Verse,* London, 1698, which may have been the first Bible designed for
children; first complete American edition was probably printed by Harris's
partner, John Allen, in Boston, 1717). AAS, NYPL, UCLA

1682

*The young-man's warning-piece: or, the extravagant youths pilgrimage and
progress in the world. Being a faithful relation of the remarkable life of*

J. Bradwill, son of W. Bradwill, merchant of the city (anonymous; a broadside ballad presenting a young rake's progress and conversion; illustrated with twelve woodcuts).

1688

Habits and Cryes of the City of London, drawn after the Life. P. Tempest excudit (anonymous; an illustrated collection of some cries of London; an attempt to amuse and to instruct children about the people and objects in the world around them; said to be the first of many such popular "cries" books printed in both England and America). AAS, RC, UCLA

1690

Cotton Mather's *Early piety, exemplified in the life and death of Mr. Nathaniel Mather, who having become at the age of nineteen, an instance of more than common learning and virtue, changed earth for heaven, Oct. 17, 1688. Whereto are added some discourses on the true nature, the great reward, and the best season of such a walk with God as he left a pattern of* (preface by the author's brother Samuel Mather, son of Increase Mather and grandson of Joseph Cotton; one of famous colonial clergyman's powerful sermons addressed to youth; printed in Boston; author's other works include *Early religion, urged in a sermon, upon the duties wherein, and the reasons wherefore, young people, should become religious. Whereto are added, the extracts of several papers, written by several persons, who here dying in their youth, left behind them those admonitions for the young survivers; with brief memoirs relating to the exemplary lives of some such, that have gone from hence to their everlasting rest,* printed in Boston in 1694; *A family well-ordered. Or an essay to render parents and children happy in one another. Handling two very important cases I. What are the duties to be done by pious parents, for the promoting of piety in their children. II. What are the duties that must be paid by children to their parents, that they may obtain the blessings of the dutiful,* printed in Boston in 1699; *A token, for children of New-England. Or, some examples of children, in whom the fear of God was remarkably budding, before they dyed; in several parts of New-England Preserved and published, for the encouragement of piety in other children. And added as a supplement, unto the excellent Janeways token for children: upon the re-printing of it, in this country,* printed in Boston by Timothy Green for Benjamin Eliot, 1700, containing previously published stories of deaths of five children, Nathanael Mather, the author's brother, John Clap, Priscilla Thornton, Ann Greenough, and John Baily, in addition to the deaths of two other children, Daniel Williams and Bethiah Longworth; *Another Tongue brought in, to Confess the Great Saviour of the World. Or, Some Communications of Christianity, Put into a Tongue used among the Iroquois Indians, in America,* printed in Boston by B. Green, n.d.; *Youth Under a Good Conduct,* Boston, 1704). BA

1692

Roger L'Estrange's *The Fables of Aesop and Other Eminent Mythologists: with Morals and Reflections* (five hundred fables, said to be the largest collection of fables in the English language; includes Aesop, Avianus, Phaedrus, La Fontaine; collected, retranslated, but unillustrated, with morals rewritten by popular pamphleteer, journalist, and colorful literary figure nicknamed "Dog Towzer" and renowned for his severities as licenser of the press after the Restoration; printed by R. Sare, T. Sawbridge, and others; fables were appropriated by children; some evidence exists that the fables were rewritten with children in mind, such as the statement "Children are but Blank Paper" included in the introduction; the 1788 American edition is titled *A History of the Life of Aesop* and was published in Philadelphia; the fables in the 1898 American edition, *A Hundred Fables of Aesop*, published by Dodd, Mead, were taken from L'Estrange, and illustrated by Percy J. Billinghurst with an introduction by Kenneth Grahame; author's other work includes *Machiavil's Advice to His Son . . . ,* London, 1681). BM

1694

J. G.'s *A Play-book for children, to allure them to read as soon as they can speak plain. Composed of small pages, on purpose not to tire children, and printed with a fair and pleasant letter. The matter and method plainer and easier than any yet extant* (anonymous; an early book designed to attract children to learning by creating a pleasing format—small pages, wide margins, large type; contained alphabets, one- to six-syllable words, short sentences arranged alphabetically, and sentences dealing with concrete things arranged in order of difficulty; printed in London by John Harris).

1698

The Young man's guide to a virtuous life: in many pleasant little tales or allegories: with moral explanations (anonymous; thirty-eight tales taken from the *Gesta Romanorum* [see ca. 1290]; illustrated with woodcuts).

1699

Comtesse Marie Catherine d'Aulnoy's *Tales of the Fairys* (translated from the 1697 French edition, *Contes de Flées;* published by T. Cockerill; four volumes of literary fairy tales including "The White Cat" and "The Blue Bird"; author's other work includes *Norwelles contes de flées,* 1698, which includes an adaptation of "Beauty and the Beast"; first comprehensive collection of author's works published in England, 1707, by J. Nicholson, entitled *The Diverting Works of the Countess D'Amois, Containing I. Memoirs of her own Life. II. All her Spanish Novels and Histories. III. Her Letters. IV. Tales of the Fairies in Three Parts complete;* first illustrated

English edition *"Tales of the Fairies in three parts, compleat" as extracted from the second edition in English of her "Diverting Works,"* E. 1715; *Queen Mab: Containing a Select Collection of Only the Best, most Instructive and Entertaining Tales of the Fairies,* 1770, which contains "Graciosa and Percinct," "The Fair One with the Golden Locks," "The Blue Bird," "The Invisible Prince," "The Princess Verenata," "The Princess Rosetta," "The Golden Bough," "The Orange Tree and the Bee," "The Little Good Mouse"; the American edition, *The History of the Tales of the Fairies,* was published in Wilmington, Delaware, by Peter Brynberg in 1800). BM, BPL

Joseph Harris's *The Fables of Pilpay* (English version of the ancient Indian Brahmin fables,*Bidpai,* which have come down through the Arabic translation of ca. 750 A.D.; edited and printed in London by Joseph Harris for D. Brown, C. Conningsby, D. Midwinter, and T. Leigh).

ca. 1700

The New England Primer (author disputed, but probably written by the printer Benjamin Harris, who lived in Boston, Massachusetts, 1686-1695; believed by some to be an abridgement of *The Protestant Tutor,* which may have been written by Benjamin Keach, and was printed by Harris first in London, 1679, and later in Boston, 1685; in 1691 Harris advertised *The New England Primer enlarged* as "forthcoming," but there is no extant copy; a fragment exists which was printed by Bradford in New York, ca. 1700; a copy which refers to King George is conjecturally dated 1690, but references date it not before 1714; earliest extant whole book, though imperfect, is a 1727 edition printed in Boston by S. Kneeland and T. Green, often said to be the first book both written and printed for children in America; although John Cotton's *Spiritual Milk,* 1656, is earlier, it was first printed in England; contains all or, in part, proverbs, pages of letters of the alphabet, easy syllables, one-syllable words to words of several syllables, the Lord's Prayer and the Creed, an illustrated alphabet, a rhymed alphabet, animal pictures with rhymes, Isaac Watts's "Cradle Hymn" and other poems, rhymed admonitions and prayers, a woodcut showing John Rogers being burned at the stake while his wife and children watch, questions and answers, a catechism, John Cotton's "Milk for Babes," and a dialogue between Christ, a youth, and the devil; translated into an American Indian language, 1691; between 1749 and 1766, Benjamin Franklin and his partner David Hall recorded that they sold 37,000 copies; it is estimated that in total at least 3 million copies were sold in America; a 1737 Boston edition contains "Now I lay me down to sleep"; *The Royal Primer; or, An easy and pleasant Guide to the Art of Reading,* anonymous, which was printed for Newbery and Collins in London, 1755, was much like *The New England Primer,* but was more Anglican in content and tone than its Puritan forerunner). BPL, FLP, HH, LC, NYPL

L. C.'s *Youth's pleasant recreation, or merry pastime. Containing delightful stories and novels; merry jests, sayings, and tales; the original of the word cocknee, and throwing at cocks; bulls and blundering discourses; pindaric odes on love matters; short epigrams and satyrs; banter, or sharp repartees; puns and drollery; riddles; witty fables; familiar letters; merry dialogues; directions for training up youth; the art and mystery of love, etc.* (anonymous; a collection of miscellaneous matters to interest youth; 1704 edition titled *Youth's recreation*).

1700-1701

François de Salignac de La Mothe Fénélon's *The Adventures of Telemachus, the Son of Ulysses* (translated from the French *Suite du IVe livre d'Odyssée, ou les adventures de Télémaque,* by Isaac Littlebury and Mr. Boyer; in five parts in two volumes; the didactic romance tells the story of young Telemachus's search for his father and displays the lessons he learned from the wise teacher, Mentor, on the subject of how to be a good king; *The Adventures of Aristonous,* written by archbishop of Cambrai, was added to the third edition; printed by A. and J. Churchill; first four and one-half books published in France in 1699, with the first part of the English translation issued in England in 1699). BM, LPL

1706-1708

Scheherazade's *The Arabian Nights' Entertainments: consisting of 1001 Stories told by the Sultaness of the Indies . . .* (from the Arabic, translated from Antoine Galland's 1558 French edition *Mille et une nuits;* published in seven successive volumes by A. Bell; these Persian, Egyptian, Turkish, Arabian tales were intended for adults, but stories such as "Aladdin," "Ali Baba," and "Sinbad the Sailor" were appropriated by children; Scheherazade is the collective pseudonym for the many tellers of tales from several countries; the collection is popularly known as *The Arabian Nights;* expurgated editions were written for children by E. W. Lane in 1839 and 1841, and by Andrew Lang in 1898; the first American edition was published in Philadelphia by Rice in 1794). AAS, BM

ca. 1712

T. W.'s *A Little Book for Little Children* (author unknown; contains an illustrated alphabet with rhymes containing "A was an Archer" which is thought to be the earliest nursery rhyme to be included in a printed book for children; the rhyme "I saw a Peacock with a fiery Tail" is also included; one of the earliest examples of a textbook which approaches education from the child's point of view rather than the adult's; not to be confused with Thomas White's more somber book of 1660 with the same title; printed for George Conyers). BM

1715

Eleazer Moody's *The School of Good Manners . . . rules for children's behavior, at the Meeting House, at Home, at the Table, in Company, in Discourse, at School, etc.* (an American pirating of an English courtesy book which served for many years as a guide to proper etiquette; printed and sold in New London, Connecticut, by T. Green and sold by B. Eliot in Boston; the entire text was lifted from J. Garretson's *The School of Manners. By the Author of the English Exercises. The Fourth Edition,* published in London in 1685).

Isaac Watts's *Divine Songs, Attempted in easy language for the Use of Children* (a collection of easy-to-learn, rhythmical verses by English dissenting clergyman; printed for M. Lawrence; provided religious lessons to be memorized by children; two moral songs, "'Tis the voice of the sluggard" and "How doth the little busy bee," were further immortalized in parodies written by Lewis Carroll in *Alice's Adventures in Wonderland* in 1865; a conservative estimate places total copies over 8 million, not including chapbook editions; used for nearly two hundred years; Thomas Foxton's *Moral Songs, composed for the use of Children,* London, 1728, praised by Watts, serves as a companion volume of emblems, fables, and stories with morals drawn for each; the author's other work includes *Prayers composed for the use and imitation of children . . . ,* printed in London in 1728; *The second sett of catechisms and prayers . . . ,* 1730; *A preservative from the sins and follies of childhood and youth . . . ,* printed in London ca. 1730; humorous American editions of *Divine Songs* were published; the earliest extant American edition of *Divine Songs* is the seventh edition published in Boston in 1730 and reprinted sixty-six times to 1819; Isaiah Thomas printed and sold *Divine and Moral Songs for Children; Revised and Altered . . . ,* in Worcester, Massachusetts, in 1738). BU, FPL, LC, TPL, YU

1717

A Legacy for Children (anonymous; story of Hannah Hill who lived to be eleven years and three months old before dying "a praiseworthy death"; published in Philadelphia by Andrew Bradford).

1719

Daniel Defoe's *The Life and Strange Surprising Adventures of Robinson Crusoe of York, Mariner . . .* (an adventure story by a British novelist appropriated by children; printed in London for W. Taylor; abridged and chapbook editions helped popularize the novel; "Robinsonades," imitations of Defoe's work about the self-reliant man's coming to grips with the wilderness and learning moral lessons therefrom, followed; the most popular imitation was *The Hermit, or the unparrallelled Suffering and surprising Adventures of Mr. Phillip Quarll, an Englishman, who was lately discovered . . . ;* reissued in chapbook form as *The English Hermit;* reprinted as *The Wonderful Life and Most Surprising Adventures of Robinson Crusoe . . .* in New York by Hugh Gaine in 1774; a Rousseauian version, *The New Robinson Crusoe,* was published in London in 1841 and 1842; the earliest printing of *Robinson Crusoe* in the Colonies by Samuel Keimer in Philadelphia, ca. 1725). BM, BP, DPL, RC, UCLA, UI, UM, YU

Thomas Fleet's *Mother Goose's Melodies* (a possible edition of Mother Goose collected by an American who married Elizabeth Goose, 1715; the collection is said to have arisen from hearing his mother-in-law repeat nursery rhymes to his children; although it was characteristic of Fleet to make such a collection, no copy of the book has ever been found; its existence is highly disputed).

1722

Reverend Samuel Croxall's *Fables of Aesop and Others* (fables "newly done into English with an Application to each Fable," illustrated with "Cuts," which were oval in shape and in rectangular frames, and later adapted by Thomas Bewick; printed for J. Tonson and J. Watts; the moral reflections are rather tedious, but some of the tellings are so pleasing that some twentieth-century editions, as well as earlier ones, are based on Croxall's; dedicated to five-year-old Baron Halifax; vied with Roger L'Estrange's larger but unillustrated and "Popish" collection of fables which remained popular although it was published sixty years previously; the 1777 American edition was published in Philadelphia). BM

1726

William Penn's *Fruits of a Father's Love. Being the Advice of William Penn to His Children, Relating to their Civil and Religious Conduct* (a typical book of advice by the well-known Quaker and founder of Pennsylvania; published posthumously, first in London in 1726, and then in Philadelphia by William Bradford in 1727). PFL

Jonathan Swift's *Travels into several remote nations of the world in four parts by Lemuel Gulliver* (better known as *Gulliver's Travels;* an English clergyman's adventure story told in highly satiric form which attacks the baseness of society; children appropriated adventure elements, which became immensely popular in chapbook form; printed in London for Benjamin Motte; reprinted in America as *The Adventures of Captain*

Gulliver, in Philadelphia, by Young and McCulloch in 1787). BM, LPL, UCLA, UM

1727

John Gay's *Fifty One New Fables in Verse* (fifty-one original verse-fables with moral lessons incorporated into the verse; invented for the six-year-old Duke of Cumberland; engravings for each episode were based on Samuel Croxall's edition; print was well spaced with generous margins; printed in London by J. Tonson and J. Watts; Gay's fables were popular to the Victorian period; Thomas Bewick imitated Croxall's cuts when he illustrated the 1779 edition of *Fables,* printed in Newcastle by T. Saint). BM, YU

1729

Charles Perrault's *Histories or Tales of Past Times* (translated by Robert Samber from the 1697 French edition *Histories ou Contes du Temps passé. Avec des Moralitez, par le Fils de Monsieur Perreault [sic],* published by Claude Barbin; included eight folktales: "The Sleeping Beauty," "Red Riding Hood," "Blue Beard," "Puss in Boots," "The Fairy," [later known as "Diamonds and Toads"], "Cinderella" or "The Glass Slipper," "Riquet with the Tuft," and "Little Thumb" [later known as "Hop O' My Thumb"]; a rhymed moral follows each tale; illustrated with woodcuts; frontispiece credits the tales to Mother Goose as "contes de ma mère l'Oye," or "Mother Goose's tales"; many scholars believe that Perrault's seventeen-year-old son, Pierre Perrault-Darmancour, was the collector and reteller of the tales with his father's help; advertised in England as printed by J. Pote; first American edition printed in Haverhill, Massachusetts, by Peter Edes in 1794). AAS, NYPL, PLP, PM

1730

A Description of Three Hundred Animals; viz. Beasts, Birds, Fishes, Serpents, and Insects (author uncertain, but may have been book's publisher, Thomas Boreman; a compilation of natural history lore; two other works on natural history followed which were published by Thomas Boreman, *A Description of a Great Variety of Animals and Vegetables,* 1736, and *A Description of some curious and uncommon Creatures, Omitted in the Description of Three Hundred Animals,* 1739). BM

1736

Martyrology; or, A Brief Account of the Lives, Sufferings and Deaths of those two holy Martyrs, viz. Mr. John Rogers, and Mr. John Bradford (anonymous; subject matter was reprinted in *The New England Primer;* published in Boston by S. Kneeland and T. Green in 1736).

ca. 1737-1741

The Prodigal Daughter . . . who because her parents would not support her in all of her Extravagance, bargained with the Devil to poison them, . . . (anonymous; the story of a young girl's death, her return from the grave, and her tales of what life after death is like; many popular chapbook and broadside editions were known in both Britain and America, though it is known primarily through its numerous American editions, many of which are extant; Thomas Fleet published copies from 1737 to 1741, which were illustrated with woodcuts by Fleet's black slave, Pompey Fleet; Isaiah Thomas published a 1769 edition as well as subsequent editions). AAS

1740-1741

Thomas Boreman's *The Gigantick History of the Two Famous Giants, and other Curiosities in Guildhall, London* (first of a series of some of the tiniest books ever made, barely two inches high, of which two volumes were addressed to "little Masters and Misses" and covered with Dutch flowered paper; designed as a guidebook to the sights of London for the amusement as well as the instruction of children; includes poems, stories, and crude woodcuts; list of subscribers given at book's end, with Gogmagog listed as taking a hundred copies; eight volumes published by Boreman in London followed: *Curiosities of the Tower of London* in two volumes, 1741; *The History and Description of the famous Cathedral of St. Paul's* in two volumes, 1741; *The History of Sejanus the Swedish Giant from his Birth to the present Time,* 1742; *Westminster Abbey* in three volumes, 1742-1743). GL

1741

Samuel Richardson's *Pamela; or Virtue Rewarded in a Series of Familiar Letters . . . Now first published in order to cultivate the Principles of Virtue and Religion in the Minds of the Youth of both Sexes* (in four volumes; the first two were printed in London for C. Rivington and J. Osborn, 1741, the last two were printed for Samuel Richardson, 1742; *Pamela* was the first novel to be printed in America, and was printed by Benjamin Franklin; it was intended as a novel for adults but was abridged for young people and published in London in 1756 as *The Paths of Virtue delineated; or the History in miniature of the celebrated Pamela, Clarissa Harlowe, and Sir Charles Grandison;* the author's other work includes the unabridged edition of *Clarissa; or the History of a Young Lady,* seven volumes, London: printed for S. Richardson, and sold by A. Millar, J. and Ja. Rivington, 1748; *The History of Two Good Boys and Girls, To Which is Added the Story of Three Naughty Girls and Boys,* printed in Boston by N. Coverly, 1793; *Aesop's Fables: with instructive Morals and Reflections. Abstracted from all party Considerations, adapted to all Capacities . . . containing two hundred and forty Fables . . .* , London: Printed for J. Osborn, 1740). BM, YU

1743

The Child's New Plaything (anonymous; intended "to make the learning to read a diversion instead of a task"; contains "A was an apple-pie"; published in London by Mrs. M. Cooper; published in Boston by J. Edwards in 1744; the extant American fourth edition was published in Boston by Draper for J. Edwards in 1750). BM, NYPL

1744

A Little Pretty Pocket-Book intended for the Instruction and Amusement of little Master Tommy and Pretty Miss Polly, With Two Letters from Jack the Giant-Killer; As Also a Ball and Pincushion; The Use of which will infallibly make Tommy a good Boy, and Polly a good Girl (author not established, nor is the date certain because no copy prior to the tenth edition, 1760, has been found, though advertisements and a letter praising the book, asking that a number of calf and gilt bound copies be sent, are dated 1744; known as the first of many children's books specifically intended for amusement as well as instruction; published by John Newbery, a British bookseller, generally accepted as the publisher who made children's books a permanent part of the book trade; to honor Newbery, the John Newbery Medal has been awarded annually since 1922 by the American Library Association to the author of the most distinguished contribution to literature for children published in the United States in the preceding year; the author must be a resident or citizen of the United States; the medal was donated by the Frederic G. Melcher family in honor of Melcher's efforts as chairman of the first Children's Book Week Committee, which became the Children's Book Council, established by the American Booksellers Association in 1919, and for his work as editor of *Publisher's Weekly;* an American edition published by Isaiah Thomas in Worcester in 1787). AAS, BM

Tommy Thumb's Song Book for all little Masters and Misses . . . by Nurse Lovechild (anonymous; the first known English nursery rhyme book for children's enjoyment; published in London by Mrs. M. Cooper; includes "Hickory, Dickory, Dock," "Little Tommy Tucker," "Baa Baa, Black Sheep," "Ladybird, Ladybird," "Mary, Mary," "Sing a Song of Sixpence," "Oranges and Lemons," "Cock Robin," "Great A, Little a," "There Was a Little Man," and thirty other rhymes, includes musical directions for singing; the 1744 sequel was titled *Nancy Cock's Song Book . . . a Companion to Tommy Thumb's and the Second Volume of that great and learned Work . . . by Nurse Lovechild;* a colonial edition, *Tommy*

Thumb's Song Book, was pirated from Mrs. Cooper by Isaiah Thomas in 1788; Mrs. M. Cooper also published in London *The Child's New Plaything: being a Spelling Book, intended to make the Learning to Read a Diversion instead of a Task . . . ,* 1743, and *The Court of Queen Mab,* 1752, "for the innocent amusement of children" as well as adults). BM

ca. 1745

Battledores (variant of the hornbook; the term is often used interchangeably with hornbook when reference is made to their use as lesson books; a folded paper or cardboard lesson-book designed for children on which is usually printed an illustrated alphabet, rhymes, numerals, sometimes a proverb or short prayer; the battledore eventually superseded the hornbook; the earliest known example was issued by John Newbery's associate, Benjamin Collins, who credited himself with inventing this teaching device; battledores were also printed and used in America). AAS, BM, TPL

History of the Holy Jesus (anonymous; probably of American origin; the life of Jesus presented in rhymed doggerel illustrated with crude woodcuts; the sixth edition was printed in Boston by J. Bushell and J. Green in 1749; yet, a tenth edition exists which was printed in Boston by Fleet and Crump for Buttolph in 1718; other editions include the third by Gray in Boston, 1746, the fifth by T. Green in Boston, 1748, the seventh in New London, Connecticut, 1754, the eighth by Fowle and Draper, 1762, and an edition printed by Hall in Boston in 1796; the book flourished in numerous editions for about seventy years). AAS, EI, RC

1745

The Circle of the Sciences: Or, the Compedious Library (anonymous; a ten-volume set of books, published over a three- to four-year period, which dealt with basic school subjects such as spelling, grammar, handwriting, arithmetic, poetry, logic, and geography; the *Circle* titles include *An Easy Introduction to English Language; Or, a Pretty entertaining Spelling-Book for little Masters and Misses,* 1745; *An Easy Introduction to the English Language; Or, a Compedious Grammar for the Use of young Gentlemen, Ladies and Foreigners,* 1745; *A Spelling Dictionary on a Plan entirely new,* 1745; *The Art of Writing; illustrated with Copper-plates; to which is added a Collection of letters . . . ,* 1746; *The Art of Arithmetick made familiar and easy to every Capacity . . . ,* 1746; *The Art of Rhetorick, laid down in an easy, entertaining Manner . . . ,* 1746; *The Art of Poetry made easy, and Embellish'd with great Variety of the most shining Epigrams, Epitaphs, Songs, Odes, Pastorals, etc.,* 1746; *Logick made familiar and easy to young Gentlemen and Ladies,* 1748?; *Chronology made familiar and easy to Young Gentlemen and Ladies,* 1748?; all published in London by John Newbery).

The Royal Battledore: being the first introductory Part of the Circle of the Sciences etc. (anonymous; a battledore with one lesson side which contains the saying: "He that ne'er learns his ABC / For ever will a Blockhead be / But he that learns these Letters fair / Shall have a Coach to take the air"; it also contains the alphabet and vowel-consonant combinations, two short blessings and the Lord's Prayer, followed by numerals 1 to 10, and woodcuts illustrating each letter of the alphabet; the reverse side is gilt-embossed, cream with blue Dutch paper; published by John Newbery; a French version, also printed by Newbery around 1745, was titled *Alphabet Royale: ou, Guide commode et agréable dans l'art de lire;* this battledore served as an introduction to Newbery's *Circle of the Sciences* series). UOx

1749

Sarah Fielding's *The Governess, or little Female Academy* (the stories of the lives of nine girls and the fairy tales they share under the tutelage and moralizing of their governess, Mrs. Teachum; published in London by A. Millar; *The Story of the Cruel Giant Barbarico,* one of the fairy tales in *The Governess,* was published separately in 1767 and printed in Boston by Mein and Fleeming; the author was sister of the novelist Henry Fielding; author's other work includes *David Simple,* 5 volumes, printed in London for A. Millar, 1744-1753; *The Lives of Cleopatra and Octavia,* printed in London by A. Millar, 1757; *The History of The Countess Dellwyn,* printed in London by A. Millar, 1759; *The History of Ophelia,* printed in London for R. Baldwin, 1760; *The History of Betty Barnes,* printed in London for J. Fleming, 1770). BM, UOx

1750?

A New Gift for Children (anonymous; a collection of ten entertaining stories, often cited as the earliest known children's book in America which was non-Biblical in content and tone, marking the beginning of secular literature for children in America; printed by D. Fowle in Boston). HH

1750

A Museum for young Gentlemen and Ladies (Youth): Or, A private (compleat) Tutor for little Masters and Misses . . . (anonymous; an advertisement described the book as being the second volume to *The Pretty Book for Children;* published in London by John Newbery).

Nurse Truelove's Christmas-Box: Or, The Golden Plaything for Little Children . . . Adorned with Thirty Cuts (anonymous; described as "given gratis by J. Newbery, only paying one Penny for the Binding . . . printed in London and sold by Carnan and Newbery"). UOx

The Pretty Book for Children: Or, An Easy Guide to the English Tongue . . . (anonymous; advertised as being printed in London for J. Newbery, J. Hodges, R. Baldwin, and B. Collins). BM

ca. 1752

A Pretty Book of Pictures for little Masters and Misses; or, Tommy Trip's History of Birds and Beasts; with a familiar Description of each in Verse and Prose. To which is added, the History of little Tom Trip himself, of his Dog Jowler, and of Woglog the great Giant (author not established; the text stresses kindness to animals; bound and gilt, numerous editions were published by John Newbery and his successors). ST

1752

The Lilliputian Magazine: Or, The Young Gentleman and Lady's Golden Library (anonymous; advertised as a monthly, but only a few volumes were published; collected volumes were frequently reprinted; printed and published in London by T. Carnan at Mr. Newbery's; illustrated with copperplate cuts; the first American edition is dated 1770). BM

1753

An Historical Account of the Curiosities of London and Westminster in 3 parts. Part 1. Contains a full Description of the Tower of London, and everything curious in and belonging to it. Part 2. Contains the History of Westminster Abbey from its foundation to the present time. . . . Part 3. Treats of the old Cathedral of St. Paul's and the New . . . (ascribed to David Henry; the work was not specifically for children, but it may have been suggested by Thomas Boreman's series about London for children; published in London by John Newbery). GL

ca. 1754

The Famous Tommy Thumb's Little Story-Book (anonymous; first published in England by Benjamin Collins, the book contains stories, fables, and nursery rhymes, including "This little pig went to market," and "Little Boy Blue"; printed in Boston in 1771).

1755

The Royal Primer: Or, An Easy and pleasant Guide to the Art of Reading . . . (anonymous; a basic lesson book "authorized by His Majesty King George II. To be used throughout His Majesty's dominions"; illustrated with twenty-seven cuts; published by John Newbery in London; James Chattin published the first American edition in Philadelphia, 1753, and

William McAlpine published an edition in Boston in 1768 which was more faithful to the original than Chattin's; the Boston edition is closest to Newbery's). PM, TPL

1756

Jeanne Marie Le Prince de Beaumont's *Le Magasin des enfants* (a French magazine in four volumes; the first volume was in French, with subsequent volumes in English titled *The Young Misses' Magazine,* which was similar in content to Fielding's *The Governess;* contained literary tales, "Beauty and the Beast" and "Prince Desir"). BM

(A Little Book of) Letters (and Cards) on the most common as well as important Occasions of Life, by Cicero, Pliny, etc., etc. . . . for the Use of young Gentlemen and Ladies (anonymous; a smaller, cheaper edition of this work which directed children how to live was available "for those who are very young"; published in London by John Newbery).

The Little Lottery Book for Children: containing a new Method of playing them into a Knowledge of the Letters, Figures, etc. Embellished with above fifty (forty) Cuts, and published with the Approbation of the Court of Common Sense (anonymous; a bound lesson book, with gilt, published in London by John Newbery). UOx

Tommy Tagg's *A Collection of Pretty Poems, for the Amusement of Children Three Foot High* (anonymous pseudonym; a first edition of verses facetiously described on the title page as the "fifty-fourth edition" and "printed for the Booksellers of Europe, Asia, Africa, and America"; illustrated "with above sixty Cuts"; published in London by John Newbery). St

1757

Fables in Verse, for the Improvement of Young and Old, by Abraham Aesop, Esq.; to which are added Fables in Verse and Prose, with the Conversations of Birds and Beasts at their several Meetings, Routs, and Assemblies, by Woglog the (great) Giant. . . . Illustrated with a Variety of curious Cuts, and an Account of the Lives of the Authors (author unknown, perhaps John Newbery; the preface mentions such authorities for the tales as Addison, Boileau, LaFontaine, the Bible, and Roman history; illustrated with rough woodcuts; published in London by John Newbery). BM

1758?

(A Collection of) Pretty Poems for the Amusement of Children Six Foot High . . . Calculated with a Variety of Copperplate Cuts designed and engrav'd by the best Masters (anonymous; the verses were interspersed with

a series of letters from "Cousin Sam to Cousin Sue" in which the subjects of criticism, poetry, and politics are discussed; published for "the Booksellers of Europe, Asia, Africa and America" by John Newbery in London). BM

1758

A Compendious History of England, from the Invasion of the Romans to the present Time. Adorned with a Map of Great Britain and Ireland, Colour'd; and embellished with Thirty-one Cuts of all the Kings and Queens, who have reign'd since the Conquest: drawn chiefly from their Statues at the Royal Exchange (anonymous; a history designed to be read by youth; published in London by John Newbery). BM

The Holy Bible abridg'd: Or, The History of the Old and New Testament, illustrated with Notes, and Adorned with Cuts, for the Use of Children (author unknown; a Bible for children; bound and gilt, published in London by John Newbery; published in Boston by R. Hodge for N. Coverly, 1782?). St

1759

The Infant Tutor: Or, An easy Spelling-Book for little Masters and Misses . . . (anonymous; a speller which was advertised as being designed as an introductory part to *The Circle of the Sciences;* bound and gilt, published in London by John Newbery). BM

The Mosaic Creation: Or, Divine Wisdom displayed in the Works of the first six Days (anonymous; an account of the Creation which may be the work listed at the end of *The History of Little Goody Two-Shoes,* 1765, as *The History of Creation;* published in London by John Newbery). BM

A Pretty Play-Thing for Children of all Denominations Containing, I. The Alphabet in Verse for the Use of little Children. II. An Alphabet in Prose, interspersed with proper Lessons in Life for the Use of great Children. III. The Sound of the Letters explained by visible Objects. IV. The Cuz's Chorus set to Music; to be sung by Children in order to teach them to join their Letters into Syllables, and pronounce them properly. The Whole embellish'd with Variety of Cuts, after the Manner of Ptolemy (anonymous; a language lesson book; bound and gilt, probably first published by John Newbery in London; an American edition was printed by Benjamin Johnson in Philadelphia in 1794). AAS, St

ca. 1760

The Top Book of All, for Little Masters and Misses (a collection of verses, containing the rhyme, "A gaping, wide-mouthed, waddling frog"; published in London by John Newbery).

ca. 1760

Toy books (term refers to standard picture books, such as those designed by Walter Crane in the nineteenth century and published by George Routledge, as well as those books which include moving parts of some sort; the latter include:

Harlequinades: A novelty "book" composed of a single sheet of paper folded perpendicularly into four parts; hinged to the head and foot of each fold is a picture divided in the center so as to make two flaps which, when raised, reveal another picture below; often doggerel verse on each section tells a simple story, with concluding instructions to turn down one flap for the continuation of the story; when the flap is turned down, a new scene is revealed and the story continues; other names for harlequinades are *metamorphoses* and *turnups;* the term *harlequinade* was first used ca. 1760 by Robert Sayer of Fleet Street, London, to describe his novelty books which summarized the pantomimes or harlequinades playing at the leading London theaters; the term *turnups* was popular from ca. 1816 on;

Manikin or paper doll books: Booklets consisting of a figure or a series of figures with interchangeable costumes or heads which are usually accompanied by a short story or verse; paper doll books were first put on the market by S. and J. Fuller at their "Temple of Fancy" in Rathbone Place, London, 1810;

Peep show or vista books: Books, which began to appear around 1825, in which the pages are arranged in hinged planes which open like a concertina, out of which holes are cut to form a tunnel for viewing; format suggests eighteenth-century peep shows that consisted of a large box on wheels with peep holes that viewers looked through to see the scene inside; their attraction was the long panoramic view that was created by making the scenery and figures diminish in size from front to back and so create the illusion of distance;

Dissolving picture books: Popular in the 1860s, these books began merely as single printed sheets cut horizontally in such a way that when one of the horizontal pieces is moved, by the pulling of a tab, a new scene appears; eventually the single sheets were gathered into books; Dean and Co. in England specialized in such toy books which also were known as *transformations;*

Pop-up books: Also referred to as surprise books, such books, which became popular in the latter part of the nineteenth century, are often folded in such a manner that their stand-up pieces "pop up" when the book is opened;

Toy theater books: These books, which began as juvenile drama sheets around 1810, were extremely popular between 1820 and 1830; they consist of pages showing theatrical stars of the period against the scenery of their plays, sometimes in color, sometimes uncolored so the buyer could add the color; the cutouts were to be used on a permanent table-model stage; a script called a Book of Words was also often provided). FLP, JCG, PPL, TPL

1761

Robert Dodsley's *Select Fables of Aesop, and Other Fabulists* (an English translation of fables printed by John Baskerville for R. and J. Dodsley which along with Croxall's and L'Estrange's helped to create animals who are stock human characters, i.e., wise owl, vain peacock, silly monkey, etc., by using language suitable to each animal's character; twelve small, round engravings are numbered to correspond to the fables; author was a book seller, a publisher, and a personal friend of Samuel Johnson; an American edition was printed by James in Philadelphia, ca. 1790). AAS

A New History of England, from the Invasion of Julius Caesar to the present Time. Adorned with Cuts of all the Kings and Queens who have reigned since the Norman Conquest (anonymous; a history of England designed for children; bound and gilt, published in London by John Newbery).

The Newtonian System of Philosophy, adapted to the Capacities of young Gentlemen and Ladies, and familiarized and made entertaining by Objects with which they are intimately acquainted. Being the Substance of six Lectures read to the Lilliputian Society by Tom Telescope, A.M., and collected and methodized for the Benefit of the Youth of these Kingdoms, by their old Friend, Mr. Newbery, in St. Paul's Churchyard: who has added Variety of Copper-plate Cuts, to illustrate and confirm the Doctrine advanced (anonymous; a treatise explaining Newtonian philosophy designed for children; often advertised under the title, *The Philosophy of Tops and Balls;* published in London by John Newbery). BM

1762

The Art of Poetry on a New Plan, illustrated with a great Variety of Examples . . . as may tend to form in our Youth an elegant Taste and render the Study of this Part of the Belles Lettres more rational and pleasing (author uncertain; a two-volume work attributed to John Newbery who dedicated it to Robert, Earl of Holderness; published in London by John Newbery). BM

Oliver Goldsmith's *Plutarch's Lives, abridg'd from the original Greek, illustrated with Notes and Reflections, and embellish'd with Copperplate*

Prints (a five-volume "Compendium Biography" which was never completed because of the competition of Dilly's *British Plutarch;* bound in the vellum manner; published in London by John Newbery). PFL, YU

1763

John Newbery's *A Compendious History of the World from the Creation to the Dissolution of the Roman Republic. Compiled for the Use of young Gentlemen and Ladies by their old Friend, Mr. Newbery* (a two-volume history designed for youth embellished with a variety of "copper-plates"; published in London by John Newbery). BM, St

1764

An History of England in a Series of Letters from a Nobleman to his Son (two volumes of letters originally attributed to Lord Chesterfield, but according to M. F. Thwaite, proof exists that Oliver Goldsmith was the author; published in London by John Newbery). BM, UOx

An History of the Life of our Lord and Saviour Jesus Christ, to which is added the Life of the blessed Virgin Mary (the story of the lives of Jesus and the Virgin ascribed to Oliver Goldsmith; the work forms Volume 2 in the Young Christian's Library; "adorned with a variety of copper-plate cuts"; published in London by John Newbery). St

An History of the Lives, Actions, Travels, Sufferings and Deaths of the most eminent Martyrs and primitive Fathers of the Church . . . (biographies of the Church fathers ascribed to Oliver Goldsmith; the work forms Volume 4 in the Young Christian's Library; "adorned with a variety of copper-plate cuts"; published in London by John Newbery). St

The (Renowned) History of Giles Gingerbread: a little Boy who lived upon Learning (author not established, but probably was John Newbery though he facetiously alleged it to be the work of Tommy Trip; various scholars have attributed it to Oliver Goldsmith, Griffith Jones, or Giles Jones; it is the story of a young boy who wants to learn to read in order to improve his economic station in life—as a reward, his father daily gives him fresh gingerbread with a letter of the alphabet imprinted on it; bound, gilt, and "adorned with Cuts"; fifteen woodcuts by "*Goody Two-Shoes* woodcutter"; published in London ca. 1764 by John Newbery; an American edition issued by Mein and Fleeming in Boston in 1768). BM

1765

The Easter Gift; Or, The Way to be (very) good. A book much wanted (anonymous; a book designed to direct children's lives toward goodness;

bound, gilt, and "adorned with Cuts"; published in London by John Newbery).

The Fairing: Or, (A) Golden Toy (Present) for Children, In which they may see all the Fun of the Fair, and at Home be as happy as if they were there . . . (anonymous; a pleasant pastime book; bound, gilt, and "adorned with Cuts"; published in London by John Newbery).

The History of Little Goody Two-Shoes; Otherwise Called Mrs. Margery Two-Shoes. With the Means by Which She Acquired Her Learning and Wisdom, and In Consequence Thereof Her Estate (author not established, but work is often attributed to Oliver Goldsmith; generally believed to be the first sustained piece of English fiction written especially for children; a story of a virtuous peasant girl who triumphs over adversity by marrying the lord of the manor; published in London by John Newbery; the first American edition was published by Hugh Gaine in 1775; a second American edition was published by Isaiah Thomas in 1787). BM, PFL, St, UOx

The Valentine's Gift: Or, a Plan to enable Children of all Sizes and Denominations to behave with Honour, Integrity and Humanity: very necessary in a Trading Nation (anonymous; a book designed to direct children to virtuous lives; bound, gilt, and "embellish'd with Cuts"; published in London by John Newbery). BM

The Whitsuntide Gift: Or, the Way to be (very) happy: A Book necessary for all Families . . . (anonymous; designed to show children the path to happiness; bound, gilt, and "embellish'd with Cuts"; published in London by John Newbery). UOx

1767

The Happy Child (anonymous; a popular chapbook published in Boston and sold at the Heart and Crown in Cornhill; the subtitle reads: *Or, a Remarkable and Surprising Relation of a Little Girl, Who Dwelt at Barnart;* the title-page woodcut was printed by Thomas and John Fleet and appeared in a *New England Primer* which used the cut to illustrate the alphabet verse "Job feels the Rod Yet Blesses God"; the woodcut was first used in Benjamin Harris's *The Holy Bible in Verse,* 1729). AAS

Sixpennyworth of Wit: Or, Little Stories for little Folks of all Denominations (anonymous; a collection of stories; bound, gilt, and "adorn'd with cuts"; published in London by John Newbery). St

The Twelfth Day Gift: Or, the Grand Exhibition . . . (anonymous; a typical Newbery "holiday book"; published in London by John Newbery).

James Ridley's *The Adventures of Urad* (an English fanciful tale taken from his *Tales of the Genii,* published in London in 1764; purported by the author to have been faithfully translated from a Persian manuscript by Charles Morell; also printed by Mein and Fleeming in Boston, ca. 1768).

1769

Frances Brooks's *The History of Emily Montague* (considered by some to be the first Canadian, as well as the first North American, novel, though printed in London by J. Dodsley; written in the same epistolary form as Richardson's *Pamela;* a novel of upper-class manners set in Quebec; this English author lived in Quebec for five years; author's other work includes *The History of Lady Julia Mandeville,* London: J. Dodsley, 1762; *All's Right At Last,* London: Printed for F. and J. Noble, 1774; *The Excursion,* London: Printed for T. Cadell, 1777; *The History of Charles Mandeville,* London: Printed for W. Lane, 1790).

1771

Thomas Bewick's *The New Lottery book of Birds and Beasts* (one of the earliest instances of a master illustrator putting his name to a work for children; an American edition was printed in Worcester by Isaiah Thomas in 1788; this English artist's other work includes *A Pretty Book of Pictures for Little Masters and Misses; or, Tommy Trip's History of Beasts and Birds,* London, 1779; *Fables,* 1779; *Selected Fables,* Newcastle: T. Saint, 1784; *Quadrupeds,* London: Walker, 1790; *History of British Birds,* London: Beilby and Bewick, 1797-1804; *Fables of Aesop and Others,* London, 1818; the artist's brother, John, also illustrated books, such as Berquin's *Blossoms of Morality,* 1796). BM, LC

1775

The New Testament adapted to the Capacities of Children, to which is added An Historical Account of the Lives, Actions, Travels, Sufferings, and Deaths of the Apostles and Evangelists . . . (anonymous; illustrated by Mr. Raphael and engraved by Mr. Walker; the book later appeared as two separate works, *The New Testament of our Lord and Savior Jesus Christ,* 1764, and *An History of the Lives, Actions, Travels, Sufferings and Deaths of the Apostles and Evangelists,* 1763; published in London by John Newbery). St. TPL

Nurse Truelove's New-Year's Gift: Or, The Book of Books for Children. Embellish'd with Cuts; and designed for a Present to every little Boy who would become a great Man, and ride upon a fine Horse; and to every little Girl who would become a great Woman, and ride in a Lord-Mayor's gilt

Coach (anonymous; it contained "The House That Jack Built"; bound and gilt; published in London by John Newbery; an American edition was published by Isaiah Thomas, 1786, at Worcester, Massachusetts; similar to *Nurse Truelove's Christmas-Box,* London: Carnan and Newbery, 1750). UOx

1777?

Toby Ticklepitcher's *The Hobby-Horse, or Christmas Companion* (anonymous pseudonym; Elizabeth Newbery's 1784 edition of Francis Newbery's edition, advertised in the *London Chronicle* in 1771, is the earliest copy of the book that has been traced; the subtitle of the 1790 edition, printed for Elizabeth Newbery, summarizes the book's contents: *Containing among other interesting particulars, The Song of a Cock and a Bull, A Canterbury Story, and a Tale of a Tub. Faithfully Copied from the Original Manuscript, in the Vatican Library;* Hosea Sprague printed and sold illustrated copies in Boston in 1804; and an earlier edition is thought to have been issued by Isaiah Thomas in 1786). AAS

1777

Thomas Thumb's *A Bag of Nuts Ready Cracked* (anonymous; Thomas Thumb may have been a pseudonym of John Newbery; the first and second edition of the book were printed for Francis Newbery; the title page text of the ninth edition, which was printed for Elizabeth Newbery, explains the book's contents: *A Bag of Nuts Ready Cracked, or, Instructive Fables, Ingenious Riddles, and Merry Conundrums. By the Celebrated and Facetious Thomas Thumb, Esq. Published for the Benefit of all Little Masters and Misses Who Love Reading As Well As Playing;* Isaiah Thomas printed copies in Worcester, Massachusetts, in 1786).

1779

Benjamin Franklin's *The Story of the Whistle* (a narrative written in both French and English and printed by the author in Passy, France, while he was the American ambassador; the story is titled *The Whistle: A True Story, Written to His Nephew* in a 1793 edition of Franklin's published works; author's other work includes *Maxims and Morals from Dr. Franklin,* 1807, which contains excerpts from Franklin's "words of wisdom," illustrated by the London publisher, William Darton; *Franklin's Way To Wealth,* Jacob Johnson of Philadelphia, 1808; *The Art of Making Money Plenty,* Samuel Wood of New York, 1811). FIL, HH, LC, UPa

ca. 1780

Entertaining Traveller (anonymous; a chapbook subtitled *A Brief Account of the Voyages and Travels of Master Tommy Columbus, in Search of the*

Island of Wisdom; with a description of that island: as also of the Rock of Curiosity, the Court of Ambition, the Field of Luxury, and the Desert of Famine; published in London by Elizabeth Newbery, wife of John; the subtitle describes the book's contents).

1780

Mary Ann (Maze) Kilner's *The Adventures of a Pincushion Designed Chiefly for the Use of Young Ladies* (two volumes of moralistic tales by Dorothy Kilner's sister-in-law; published in London by John Marshall; the subtitle states: "Imagination here supplies, What Nature's sparing hand denies, A, by her magic powers dispense, To meanest Object's thought and sense"; the author's other work includes *Adventures of a Peg-Top,* London: J. Marshall, ca. 1780; *Jemima Placid; or, The Advantage of Good Nature, Exemplified in a Variety of Familiar Incidents,* London: J. Marshall, 1783; *William Sedley; or, The Evil Day Deferred,* London, 1783).

Mrs. Teachwell's *Fables in Monosyllables* (a popular edition of fables with morals set up in dialogue form between a mother and her children; reissued in Philadelphia in 1798; "Mrs. Teachwell" is the pseudonym of Lady Eleanor Fenn; Fenn's other pseudonyms include Mrs. Lovechild, Nurse Lovechild, and Solomon Lovechild; the second part of an American edition of fables titled *Morals to a Set of Fables;* illustrated with numerous woodcuts; the author's other work includes *Juvenile Correspondence,* London: J. Marshall, 1783; *The Fairy Spectator,* London: J. Marshall, 1788; *Tommy Thumb's Song Book, for All Little Masters and Misses to be Sung to Them By Their Nurses, Until They Can Sing Themselves,* Worcester, Mass., 1788; *The Juvenile Tatler,* London: J. Marshall, 1789; *Cobwebs to Catch Flies; or, Dialogues in Short Sentences, Adapted for Children from the Age of Three to Eight Years,* London: J. Marshall, 1796?; *The Little Vocabulary,* London, 1814; *Mrs. Lovechild's Book of Two Hundred and Sixteen Cuts, Designed by the Late Lady Fenn, To Teach Children the Names of Things,* London: Darton, 1824; *The Child's Grammar,* London, 1831; *Talk About Indians,* Concord: Merrill, 1849; *The Clever Boy,* Philadelphia: Ball, 1850; *Sketches of Little Boys; the Well-Behaved Little Boy; the Covetous, the Dilatory, the Exact, the Attentive, the Inattentive, the Quarrelsome, and the Good Little Boy,* London: Dean, 1852?; *Sketches of Little Girls, Containing the Good-natured, the Thoughtless, the Vain, the Orderly, the Untidy, the Forward, and the Persevering Little Girl,* London: Dean, 1852; *The Poetical Alphabet,* Concord: Merrill, 1855). LC

1781

Mother Goose's Melody; or Sonnets for the Cradle (author not established; this work may have been Newbery's first publication of Mother Goose rhymes, but first extant edition of Newbery publication is dated 1791; contains fifty-two nursery rhymes, including "Hush a-bye Baby," "Crosspatch," "Two little dicky-birds," "Ding dong, bell," "Three Wise Men of Gotham," "Hey diddle, diddle," "Jack and Jill," "See-saw, Margery Daw," "One, two, three, four, five," "Pease pudding hot," "Robin and Richard were two pretty men," and sixteen songs from Shakespeare's plays; Newbery's earliest compilation of rhymes may have been ca. 1765; a pirated American edition was printed in Boston by Isaiah Thomas, 1786).

ca. 1782

William Cowper's *The History of John Gilpin* (a popular ballad-sheet published by Joseph Johnson for adults in the *Public Advertizer,* November 14, 1782, but appropriated by children; Randolph Caldecott's color illustrations for the ballad were published in his toy book by Edmund Evans, 1878; the Caldecott Medal is embossed with a picture of Gilpin galloping through town; other editions of Cowper's work are titled *The History of Johnny Gilpin,* ca. 1810; W. Belch's *Diverting History of John Gilpin,* ca. 1815; *The Diverting History of John Gilpin: Showing How He Went Farther Than He Intended, and Came Safe Home Again. With Six Illustrations by George Cruikshank,* 1828; *The Diverting History of John Gilpin, Showing How He Went Farther Than He Intended, and Came Safe Home Again,* ca. 1830; *Cowper's Diverting History of John Gilpin with Twenty Illustrations by Percy Cruikshank,* ca. 1850; *The History of John Gilpin Showing How he Went Further Than He Intended and Came Safe Home Again,* ca. 1850; *John Gilpin* [Aunt Louisa's London Toy Books No. 8], ca. 1870; an early American edition titled *The Facetious Story of John Gilpin* published in Philadelphia by Wrigley and Berriman for Stephens and M'Kenzie, 1794). NYHS, PU, TPL

1783

Arnaud Berquin's *The Children's Friend* (translated from the French, *L'Ami des Enfans;* a twenty-four-part monthly series of moral tales, letters, dramas and dialogues published in various forms; the first English translation was published in London by T. Cadell and P. Elmsley; another popular translation by Mark Anthony Meilan was published in London by J. Stockdale, 1786; selections from *L'Ami des Enfans* were translated, compiled and adapted by Richard Johnson, published by Elizabeth Newbery under Johnson's pseudonym, the Reverend W. D. Cooper, and titled *The Looking-Glass for the Mind; or, Intellectual Mirror, Being An Elegant Collection of the Most Delightful Little Stories and Interesting Tales,* 1787; the second edition, 1792, was illustrated by John Bewick; an American edition illustrated by Alexander Anderson was published in Boston by J. Folsom ca. 1789; Bewick also illustrated Berquin's *Blossoms of Morality*, London, 1796). BM, TPL

Thomas Day's *The History of Sandford and Merton* (a popular moralistic story for children based on Rousseau's principles for educating children as set forth in *Emile*, 1762; first published as a long short story in 1783, then extended to second volume in 1786, and then to third volume in 1789; a typical didactic device [contrasting behaviors] is used to show the effects of education on rich, spoiled Tommy and on poor but self-reliant Harry; another popular Rousseauian story by this English author was *History of Little Jack*, embellished with twenty-three cuts said to be by John Bewick; originally published in Stockdale's *Children's Miscellany*, 1787; the author's other work includes *The Grateful Turk*, 1789).

Comtesse de Stéphanie Félicité du Crest de Saint Aubin Genlis's *Adèle et Théodore; ou, lettres sur l'éducation;* published in London by Bathurst and Cadell; the author's other work includes *Tales of the Castle*, translated by Thomas Holcroft, 1784; and *The Beauty and the Monster*, the first children's book to be issued by Isaiah Thomas in Worcester, Massachusetts, 1785, advertised as a comedy from the French of Madame de Genlis). AAS, BM

Dorothy Kilner's *Life and Perambulations of a Mouse* (a popular moral tale designed "no less to instruct and improve, than . . . to amuse and divert"; the author's works are sometimes confused with her sister-in-law Mary Ann (Maze) Kilner's similar writings for children; the author's other work published in London includes *Short Conversations; or, An Easy Road To the Temple of Fame; Which All May Reach Who Endeavor To Be Good*, ca. 1785; *The Rotchfords' or, The Friendly Counsellor: Designed for the Instruction and Amusement of the Youth of Both Sexes*, 1786; *The History of a Great Many Little Boys and Girls, for the Amusement of All Good Children of Four and Five Years of Age*, ca. 1790; *The Village School . . . ,* John Marshall, ca. 1795; *The Rational Brutes: or, Talking Animals*, Vernor & Hood, 1799; *The Holiday Present . . . ,* Wilson and Spence, 1803; *First Going To School: or, The Story of Tom Brown and His Sisters*, Tabart, 1804). BM, TPL

Noah Webster's *A Grammatical Institute, of the English Language . . . Part I* (a famous spelling book, the "Blue-backed Speller" as it came to be known; popular for over a hundred years in America; published in Hartford, Connecticut, by Hudson and Goodwin). NYPL

1784

Gammer Gurton's Garland (anonymous; a 1784 chapbook containing numerous nursery rhymes including "There was an old woman, who lived in a shoe," "Bye baby bunting," "Ride a cock horse," "Hark, hark, the dogs do bark," "Goosey, goosey gander," "A diller a dollar," "Come let's to bed, says Sleepy Head"; an 1810 edition, subtitled *The Nursery Parnassus* and published in London by Stockton, contains 136 traditional rhymes edited by Joseph Ritson; it has been an important source for later collectors; the latter contains, among other rhymes, "Little Bo-Peep," "Old chairs to mend," "Humpty Dumpty," "I love sixpence, jolly little sixpence").

1786

Mother Goose's Melody (thought to be first American printing of Newbery's English publication as pirated by Isaiah Thomas; among other works pirated by Thomas from Newbery were *Nurse Truelove's New Year's Gift,* ca. 1755; *Little Pretty Pocket-Book,* 1787; *Be Merry and Wise; or, the Cream of Jests,* ca. 1786).

Sarah Trimmer's *Fabulous Histories . . . Designed for the Instruction of Children respecting their Treatment of Animals* (the title was changed in a later edition to *The History of the Robins;* heavily moral in tone, this work was designed to instruct children on how to treat animals kindly; the writer believed children to be naturally evil and campaigned against what she felt to be wrong for them; she especially disliked giving children fairy tales, and said so in her periodical titled *The Guardian of Education,* 1802-1804; the author's other work includes *Sacred History,* in six volumes, 1782-1784, which covers English and Roman history and includes a number of engravings with an explanatory text to be displayed in classrooms and nurseries). BM, TPL

ca. 1788

Mary Wollstonecraft's *Original Stories from Real Life* (a collection of stories reprinted, with engravings by William Blake; the author was an early feminist whose daughter Mary became Percy B. Shelley's wife; her other work published in London includes *Tales for Youth, Thoughts on the Education of Daughters,* and *Vindication of the Rights of Women;* the author's husband, William Godwin, also wrote for children).

1788

Jacky Dandy's Delight; or, the History of Birds and Beasts (anonymous; a collection of animal stories which includes "Androcles and the Lion," "The Death and Burial of Cock Robin," and "A Visit at Homely Hall"; printed by Isaiah Thomas).

The Juvenile Magazine; or an instructive and entertaining miscellany for youth of both sexes (existed for only one year; published in London by J. Marshall).

1789

William Blake's *Songs of Innocence* (lyrical poems about children, but not necessarily addressed to them; illustrated by this English master with hand-colored copper etchings, hand-printed and bound by Blake and his wife, Catharine; author-artist's other work related to children is *Songs of Experience*). BM, LBL

The Entertaining and Affecting History of Prince Lee Boo: With An Account of the Pelew Islands, and the Manners and Customs of the Inhabitants (the story of a Pelew Islands prince who was brought to England after the wreck of *The Antelope* in 1783; the Pelew Islands, or Palau Islands as they are now called, are part of the Caroline Islands in the Pacific Ocean east of the Philippines).

Jean de La Fontaine's *Fables Calculated for the Amusement and Instruction of Youth* (translated from the French, *Fables Chaisis,* published in Paris ca. 1672, by J. Poole and printed by Taunton; La Fontaine's fables were dedicated to seven-year-old Louis XIV and are based on Latin versions of Aesop; others are based on the fables of Bidpai; other early editions of La Fontaine's fables include *Fables and Tales from La Fontaine. In French and English,* London: Bettsworth, Hitch, and Davis, 1734; *Fables* translated into English verse by Walter Thornbury, with illustrations by Gustave Doré, London: Cassell, 1800?).

1792

John Aikin and Anna Laetitia Barbauld's *Evenings At Home* (a collection of stories by Unitarian brother and sister published in six volumes; Anna Barbauld's other work includes *Lessons for Children,* London, ca. 1780; *Hymns in Prose for Children,* London, 1781; *Cobwebs to Catch Flies,* London, ca. 1783; *Rational Sports,* London, ca. 1783; *Fables by Mrs. Teachwell,* London, ca. 1783; *Morals to a Set of Fables,* London, ca. 1783; author's sister, Lucy Aiken, wrote *Juvenile Correspondence,* London, 1816). TPL

1793

Mrs. Pinchard's *The Blind Child* (one of the author's popular books about an unfortunate but pious child; published in Philadelphia by Spotswood and Rice; the author's other work includes *The Two Cousins,* Boston: Etheridge, 1796; *Dramatic Dialogues for the Use of Young Persons,* Boston: Spotswood, 1798; *The Little Trifpler*, Boston: Spotswood, 1798). AAS

1795

Hannah More's *Cheap Repository Tracts: The Shepherd of Salisbury Plain [in two parts]. Black Giles the Poacher, and the History of Tawny Rachel the Fortune Teller, Black Giles' Wife, The History of Tom White, the Postilion [in three parts].* (chapbook-like tracts, with some parts written by More's sister, designed to show English children and adults the values of religion and industry through vigorous narratives; first published under the pseudonym "Z"; an attempt to counteract Jacobin influence and atheism; these verses and short sermons were to be read at home and in school; although published by J. Marshall, London, millions of copies were distributed through the Religious Tract Society which was founded in London in 1799; the author's other work includes other Cheap Repository Tracts: *Bear Ye One Another's Burthens, The Black Prince, The Good Mother's Legacy, The Grand Assizes, The Happy Waterman, The History of Diligent Dick, The History of Charles Jones, The Footman, The History of Hestor Wilmont,* in two parts, *The History of Mary Wood, The History of Mr. Bragwell, The History of Mr. Fantom, The History of Two Shoemakers,* in three parts, *The Hubbub, The Life of William Baker, Parley the Porter, Sorrowful Sam; or The Two Blacksmiths, The Strait Gate and The Broad Way, "'Tis All for the Best," The Troubles of Life, The Two Soldiers, The Wonderful Advantages of Adventuring in the Lottery;* a play, *Percy, A Tragedy,* Cadell, 1778; *The Fatal Falsehood,* Cadell, 1779; *The Plum-Cakes,* Marshall, 1796; *The Cottage Cook; or Mrs. Jone's Cheap Dishes,* Marshall, 1797; *Hints Toward Forming the Character of a Young Princess,* Cadell, 1805; *Bible Rhymes,* Wells, 1821; *Stories for Young People,* T. Allman, 1840). BM, JRUL

1796

Maria Edgeworth's *The Parent's Assistant* (the first of many editions of this three-volume collection of popular stories for children who are rewarded for honesty, cheerfulness, and hard work; its prolific Irish author was a skillful describer of character and is today considered to be one of the best of the children's moralists, especially as seen in her popular story "The Purple Jar"; the author's other work includes *Early Lessons,* ten volumes, London, 1801, which are stories for younger children, some of them reprinted from *The Parent's Assistant and Practical Education; Moral Tales,* London, 1801; *Popular Tales,* 1804; *Frank: A Sequel to Frank in Early Lessons,* two volumes, London, 1822; *Harry and Lucy Concluded: Being the Last Part of Early Lessons,* four volumes, London, 1825; *Little Plays for Children,* including "The Grinding Organ," "Dumb Andy," and "The Dame Holiday School," London, 1827; *Helen, A Tale,* three volumes, London, 1834; *Orlandino,* Edinburgh, 1848; *The Most Unfortunate Day of My Life: Being a Hitherto Unpublished Story, Together With The Purple Jar and Other Stories,* London, 1931; early American editions of Edgeworth's books were published by Jacob Johnson and were illustrated by Alexander Anderson, sometimes called "the father of wood engraving in

America''; the author's father, Richard L. Edgeworth, wrote the Rousseauian book, *Practical Education: or, The History of Harry and Lucy,* with the help of his wife, Honora Sneyd, and daughter Maria; it urges children to be their own teachers and includes a glossary of difficult words). BM, LC,D TPL, UOx, YU

Lady Templetown's *The Birth-day Gift or The Joy of a New Doll* (a brief story accompanied by seven illustrations engraved from paper cuttings made by the author, Elizabeth Broughton Upton; James Girton did the calligraphy and Tompkins did the engravings; the book is dedicated to Princess Amelia). TPL

Chapter 5

Nineteenth Century
(1800–1899)

HISTORICAL BACKGROUND

In Britain

In England the nineteenth century was a period of change centered on the machine age. The earliest stages of the Industrial Revolution were based on a system of canals, improved roads, and waterpower. But by 1781 James Watt had developed a rotating engine powered by steam. At first, steam power was used only on a small scale in the textile industry. But when George Stephenson applied the principle of the stationary engine to the locomotive in 1814, the age of the railroad and subsequent mechanization began.

Although locomotives were first used only in coal mines to pull heavy loads short distances, the concept of long-distance hauling soon developed. By 1835 the first long-distance railway line from London to Birmingham, Liverpool, Manchester, and Preston was completed. By 1844 the outline of the present British railway system was complete; although the pattern resembled the canals of fifty years before, there the resemblance ended. Where canal hauling had been slow and cargoes small, the railroad was fast and could carry huge loads. The coming of the locomotive meant the dawn of the Age of Iron which meant enormous progress in mechanization, greater production of goods, and better communication. In 1851, the Great Exhibition, organized by Queen Victoria's consort, Prince Albert, showed 6 million Englishmen the triumphs of the Industrial Revolution. Although the profits of these triumphs would be unevenly distributed, the dream of progress and prosperity based on mechanization was firmly fixed.

The Age of Steel followed the Age of Iron when, in 1856, Henry Bessemer invented a process for making steel cheaply in almost unlimited amounts.

Eleven years later William Siemans invented the open-hearth process for smelting iron ore. At first only non-phosphorous ore, which had to be imported from Sweden and Spain, could be used, but in 1879 Sidney Gilchrist Thomas modified the process to include phosphoric ores. Steel production increased in England, but not as much as in Germany where there was an almost unlimited supply of such ores. After 1879, England's industrial competitors, Germany and the rapidly industrializing United States, surpassed it in coal and steel production.

Meanwhile, England's population was growing. By 1851 only two-thirds of the food needed in the island nation could be supplied by British farmers. Although this shortage at first meant great prosperity for farms, newly equipped with steam-powered machinery, later in the century the farm economy collapsed as steamships brought cheap wheat produced on the virgin soil of America's prairies.

Steamships at first were clumsy; they had heavy engines and little cargo space because so much of their space had to be used for carrying coal. But in 1854 an engine was devised that provided more power with less fuel, thus increasing available cargo space. Sailing ships quickly went into a decline, and they never recovered. By 1880 the British merchant navy was equally divided between sail and steam, but soon after, steamships replaced sailing vessels rapidly. Sailing ships, for example, could not use the Suez Canal, which opened in 1869 and became one of the major trade routes of the world. International trade was Britain's life blood. In the 1870s the British merchant fleet supplied two-thirds of the world's imports of manufactured goods. Britain not only carried its own trade in its ships, but was also carrier—and banker and insurer—to the world.

In general, Britain flourished, and even for the poor, life gradually improved through the century. But the poor had been exploited to create the industrial system. Social changes, though great, were slow to come. Some reforms such as the Factory Act of 1833 and the New Poor Law of 1834, which were meant to provide initiative to the poor by making poverty disgraceful, in reality brought new hardships. It was thought that cash welfare grants encouraged the poor to beget more children to get more money, and the new laws brought no real relief; in fact, they authorized the well-off to herd the poor into workhouses. From the 1830s on, the employment levels of the laboring class fluctuated with each new technical achievement, often throwing thousands into deepest poverty while business in general flourished.

The population continued to grow. By 1871 London was a city of 3,250,000 people, and other large cities increased almost as fast. Middle- and upper-class people enjoyed rising wealth from the machine age and even called for increased growth. But some critics, such as Benjamin Disraeli in his Crystal Palace speech in 1872, pleaded for attention to the health of millions of working people herded together in the overcrowded slums. Other critics, such as the radical John Bright, thought that attention should also be paid to the voting rights of these people, and that they should participate in electing Parliament. But most people, even the serious, thought of the working class as a "mob" and their "violence" was greatly feared. While the poor frequently evoked sympathy—often patronizing to be sure—and even genuine charity, they were seen almost universally by their "betters" as "ignorant" and unfit to take part in government.

But reform was in the air. The vote had long been confined to a small class of property owners, but now attempts began to include more people in the democratic process. The first bill to give voting rights to the working class was made by John Russell in 1831. Although it failed, in 1867 a similar bill passed and doubled the total number of working-class male voters, their eligibility based on sex and rental as well as ownership of property. Other reforms followed, especially after William Gladstone became prime minister.

Gladstone also attempted to make peace with Ireland. Although he energetically tried to persuade Parliament to extend self-government to Ireland, he failed. Ireland would remain deeply discontented.

Gladstone admired thrift, self-control, and hard work; he tried to provide freedom to the individual so that the individual, without government aid, could make a decent life for himself. Under Gladstone, for example, the civil service was opened to competitive examinations so that many young men of the lower classes could find work; he also reformed the army. The Education Act of 1870 laid the foundations for a national system of education, and the Ballot Act of 1872 provided for the use of the secret ballot.

Nevertheless, for some, especially the trade unions, the Liberal party's reforms came too slowly, while others thought the changes were too rapid. In the elections of 1874 victory went to the Conservatives, and Disraeli, Queen Victoria's favorite, became prime minister. Largely because of Disraeli's support, Victoria evolved as the beloved head of a great empire both at home and abroad while a new series of reforms began. The 1875 Public Health Act improved sanitation and fought infectious diseases. There followed provisions to pull down the worst slums and build better housing; to procure pure water, parks, and recreation; to prevent wealthy landowners from absorbing public lands; to protect trade unions by allowing picketing and strikes; to protect workers by regulating hours and working conditions, and by regulating the loading and insuring of ships to protect sailors, who had been at the mercy of the shipping-line owners. All these reforms reflected a tendency away from the notion of individual self-control and toward government control.

Even when the Liberals were returned to power, reforms continued. Voting rights were extended again in 1884, giving male farm workers the same voting privileges as male city workers. (Not until 1928 would women get the vote.) Nominated justices of the peace, who had traditionally carried out the work of local governments, were replaced by elected county councils. Thus, by the end of the nineteenth century, democracy had come to Britain, and at least the middle and upper classes led agreeable lives.

Life for the poor was not agreeable. In 1889, 30 percent of the population of London, the richest city in the world, lived in dire poverty. Such misery also prevailed in other cities and on farms. Private charities and voluntary groups tried to cope with many social problems. Some of these groups later developed into international organizations, such as the Salvation Army which was started in London's East End in 1865 by William Booth. Such efforts often aroused the wrath of politicians who wanted to maintain the status quo, the liquor trade for interfering with business, and even the Church of England which resented upsetting the social scale. Poor children were fed, housed, and trained for jobs, but they were often exploited for profit, and the workhouses in which they lived and were supposedly educated were frequently shabby and disreputable. Millions of youth emigrated, especially to Canada.

Meanwhile, the economy was faltering. In 1875 an agricultural depression had set in when cheap grain from the United States (and Canada in 1891) began to pour in. Industry went into a decline as Germany and the United States surpassed British production of manufactured goods. As conditions grew worse, socialism, touted through the trade unions, attracted many people. By the late 1880s a new direction in the working class was clear. The trade unions took firmer stands than ever before as the labor movement entered politics. By 1875 eleven working-class candidates had been elected to Parliament. In 1893, the workers formed the Independent Labour party under the leadership of Keir Hardie who wore his miner's cap and rough tweed suit to Parliament. Although the party made little immediate impact, by 1906 it had managed to get twenty-nine members elected to Parliament. By 1924, the Labour party had the power to form a government and make its leader, Ramsay MacDonald, the prime minister.

In the United States

By the beginning of the nineteenth century, the political break with Great Britain was complete. The United States had survived the War of Independence (1775-1783) and the critical reconstruction period (1783-1789) that followed. At first the central government was weak; it was merely a congress of representatives from thirteen separate state governments held together by the Articles of Confederation. Congress had no control over the foreign trade of each state, nor could it coin money or levy taxes. When John Adams, as envoy, went to England to discuss a commercial treaty, he was asked to bring representatives from the thirteen states. Britain thus began by dealing with each state separately, as if there were no united government, as indeed there was not.

In addition to problems abroad, the thirteen states had lands with indefinable claims that stretched westward. When settlers began moving west, it was clear that these claims had to be settled if domestic peace was to be maintained. The weaknesses of the central government quite naturally led some Americans to lean toward a monarchial system in order to bring more stability to the new country. Finally, a constitutional convention was called in 1787 in Philadelphia. After a difficult period of hammering out the details, the Constitution of the United States emerged. In 1788, the first Congress under the new Constitution met in New York.

The problem of supremacy of the federal government, which appeared to be settled, and the problem of slavery, which would be even more difficult, would greatly affect the development of the new country. Slavery began early in the New World. As early as the 1490s the Spaniards had enslaved Indians in the Caribbean. In the Pequot War of 1637, more Indians were enslaved. There is some evidence that captured Indians were used to work in mines and on plantations as late as the Revolutionary War. The slavery of blacks had its origins when a Dutch ship sold indenture contracts for twenty Africans at Jamestown in 1619, but these people were freed when their terms of service were over. It was not until the middle of the century that blacks became slaves for life.

Almost from the start men of conscience were troubled about the slave trade. Thomas Jefferson, who owned slaves himself, openly accused Great Britain of preventing every attempt on the part of the colonists to check the importation of slaves because of their commercial value to that nation. The trade did not stop. Britain, along with Spain and Portugal, had large landholdings in America and needed laborers to work the lands. The labor of slaves meant great commercial advantage to these nations and to American landholders as well. Many colonists, however, who accepted slavery on plantations had trouble accepting the cruelties of the hunts in western Africa and the horrors of the trans-Atlantic voyages. From the first, there were protests by some, but the enormous economic advantage to others overrode conscience.

In eighteenth-century Britain, as well as in America, there was great agitation against the slave trade. In 1770 there were 15,000 slaves in Britain, many of whom were brought from the New World by their owners; but in 1771, after a test case, slavery in Britain was abolished. In a similar test case in Massachusetts, slavery was abolished in 1783, but slaves were not permitted to enter the state's borders. Many Southern states condemned the trade as did many Southern statesmen such as Thomas Jefferson and George Washington; yet presumably because the slaves were their only domestics, these leaders, like many other plantation owners, kept slaves. While there was always a strong group in Virginia that favored freeing the slaves, other groups feared that freeing these people so recently arrived from Africa would wreak havoc in the new country. Still others enjoyed the great economic profits realized from slaves too much to give them up. The question of slavery was a plague upon America from the start. Its influence would profoundly affect the course of the nation's development.

Although the question of a strong central government would go on being debated, during George Washington's presidency (1789-1797) a sound federal government was organized. But fears of an overly strong central government persisted. The election of Democrat-Republican Thomas Jefferson (1801-1809) ensured the triumph of democratic ideals. Jefferson believed that government should rest in the hands of those who labored and applied capital directly to the natural resources and stressed simplicity in running the government. Under Jefferson the new nation expanded rapidly. The Louisiana Territory, purchased from France, added the area between the Mississippi River and the Rocky Mountains. And Alexander Hamilton organized a workable banking system.

The years following Jefferson's presidency were characterized by a period of nationalism, most obvious in the War of 1812 with Great Britain, ostensibly over violations on the high seas. The outcome of the war was inconclusive, but political maneuvering succeeded in breaking Indian power, in giving impetus to the factory system in New England by keeping out foreign goods, and in providing a sense of national unity. Because of a need for capital, Republicans sought financial aid from Federalist bankers, and the result was a trend toward a one-party system. Abroad, the decline of Spanish influence in the world led to American absorption of Florida in the treaty of 1819. But when Britain suggested that the United States help stop France from recovering its colonies, President James Monroe issued the doctrine of no interference in Europe's internal affairs.

By the mid-1820s an era of relative domestic stability ended when sectionalism began to divide the nation. One of the most bitter sectional debates centered on the admission of Missouri to statehood in 1818. Its settlers, most of whom came from the South, expected Missouri to become a slave state, but the House of Representatives passed a bill in 1819 forbidding importation of slaves and providing ultimate emancipation of all slaves born in Missouri. The Senate, however, did not pass the bill. Various congressional compromises tried to balance the number of free states with the number of slave states, but they were sharply debated until the Missouri legislature pledged that nothing in its constitution would be interpreted to abridge the rights of citizens, that is, to place restrictions on slavery. After long wranglings and countless compromise moves, Missouri was admitted to the Union in 1821, but the Missouri Compromise would remain a volatile issue.

Other forms of sectionalism were also evident. Industrial states often competed. Factional politics and diverse economic interests, including the slavery issue, characterized Andrew Jackson's term in office. A westerner, Andy Jackson, hero of the War of 1812 and an Indian fighter, sparred openly with Republican John Quincy Adams and won the presidency. Jackson symbolized the new democratic spirit.

Economic changes included the coming of the first locomotive in 1829 and the expansion of canals into the Middle West. By 1835 the national debt was extinguished, but by 1837 a severe panic was in progress; it was brought on partly because of banking instability and by President Andrew Jackson's suppression of the Bank of the United States, but mainly by irresponsible monetary operations of lands in the West.

Economic changes paralleled political changes. When Jackson's successor, Democrat Martin Van Buren, was unable to recoup his party's power, the opposing Whigs united in 1890 to elect William Henry Harrison, who died after serving one month. John Tyler, the first vice-president to ascend to the presidency, soon found himself a president without a party when his rift with Henry Clay, the party leader, over Tyler's vetoing of a national bank, caused the resignation of his cabinet.

In 1845, under James Polk, Texas was admitted as a state, but quarrels with Mexico over the annexation of Texas and settlement of claims arising from injuries and property losses sustained by Americans in the various Mexican revolutions, along with America's desire to acquire California, brought about the breakdown of diplomatic relations between the United States and Mexico. Although Polk sent a representative to negotiate a settlement, thereby purchasing California and New Mexico and assuming liability for the claims of United States citizens in return for boundary adjustments, Mexico would not negotiate. After armed clashes on both sides, war broke out in 1846. Unable to present a united front because of internal strife, Mexico lost the war. The treaty of 1848 gave the United States two-fifths of Mexico's territory, $15 million, and the assumption of American claims against Mexico. Although the question of the territory was now settled, whether or not that territory would be free or slave revived the slavery issue.

A rising spirit of equality and democracy called for the abolition of property qualifications for voting, for direct election of more officials, and for liberalizing state constitutions. The immigration of more than 5 million aliens, mostly European, from 1820 to 1860 to nonslave states added greatly to the power of the North, which generally favored abolition.

Public education in the North and the Middle West was expanding and improving, as evidenced in the new middle class's support of the founding of 174 colleges and universities between 1820 and 1860. Cultural societies proliferated; temperance lecturers and feminists usually faced at least polite listeners; romantic novels, periodicals, and "ladies' magazines" flourished. The California gold rush of 1849-1850 stirred the nation's imagination. Imprisonment for petty crimes was abolished; utopian socialists as well as doomsday predictors got sympathetic hearings.

Leaders of widespread reform movements more and more debated the issue of slavery. William Lloyd Garrison's publication of the *Liberator* in Boston in 1831, the Underground Railroad's assistance to escaping slaves who told of slavery's cruelties, and the lynching and murder of slaves and abolitionists emphasized the seriousness of the slavery issue. Westward expansion was also linked to the question of slavery in the Wilmot Proviso of 1846 which implied that no new states could be slave. Henry Clay's Compromise of 1850, which divided the West into slave and free, tempered the matter for a time, but neither slave nor nonslave supporters were satisfied. The issue was reopened when the Kansas-Nebraska Bill, repealing the Missouri Compromise, aimed to admit Kansas as a slave state. A new party, the Republicans, established in 1854, opposed the expansion of slavery. Violence over the issue became increasingly frequent throughout the land, and in 1859 John Brown raided the federal arsenal in Harper's Ferry, Virginia (now West Virginia).

In 1860, with feelings running high, Republican Abraham Lincoln was elected president. As a result, in 1861, South Carolina seceded from the Union, and the Confederate States of America was launched. The move was supposedly based on the constitutional right of voluntary secession, but more realistically it was the result of irreconcilable economic conflicts, including slavery. When Fort Sumter was fired upon, the North took up arms. The Civil War, or War Between the States, had begun.

Because both sides were ill prepared, the war was predicted to be short, and it was to be fought by volunteers. By the end of the long, bloody conflict in 1865, both sides had been forced to use conscription, involving nearly 4 million men, and the war had cost the North 5 billion dollars and the South 3 billion. Both sides had lost their finest young men to battle and disease.

Because of war production, the North boomed. The building of new factories and railroads, which would eventually provide stable currency and the backbone of the American industrial system, was a direct outgrowth of the struggle. The South, however, did not fare so well. Much of the war was fought on Southern soil, and most Southern states were decimated; much of their accumulated wealth was lost. Heavy destruction of property and great suffering and loss of life caused profound internal strife. But the war had at least settled two legal problems that had plagued the nation since its inception: slavery, and the ultimate supremacy of the federal government.

The assassination of Lincoln in April 1865 ended attempts to reestablish the Union quickly. Under Reconstruction (1865-1870), the Southern states were placed under military governments. Blacks were granted suffrage, slavery was abolished, and Freedman's Bureaus were established. Almost at once, unscrupulous entrepreneurs from the North and inexperienced former slaves took over the Southern states' governments. In the ensuing confusion, secret white societies (most prominently the Ku Klux Klan) incited disruption and violence, turning many Northerners against Reconstruction. By 1876, most conservative Confederate leaders were back in power with former slaves playing smaller and smaller roles.

The dominant elements in the last quarter of the century were economic and social. At home, the nation was extending its industrial system, and the federal government was subsidizing private enterprise by granting 131 million acres of land to individuals and companies. The first transcontinental railroad, completed in 1869, along with subsequent ones in the 1880s, stimulated migration westward and helped develop Great Plains farms and western ranches. At the same time devastation of Indian lands resulted in more than two hundred bloody battles between 1869 and 1876. Meat packing, petroleum, steel production, and flour milling were among the largest industries, but textiles were also important. The shift of textile companies from New England to the South in search of raw material and cheap labor created a new economic empire. Abroad, the United States intervened in Cuba in 1895, when revolt against Spanish control threatened American sugar interests. As a result of the Spanish-American War, the United States acquired Puerto Rico, Guam, and the Philippines as colonies.

After a brief depression, the United States under William McKinley and his gold-standard Republicanism enjoyed an upward swing in business, and by the end of the 1800s the nation's mood was buoyant. But in spite of the general optimism, the conversion of the United States into the world's leading manufacturing nation had brought profound social changes. From the Civil War on, shifting social patterns fostered the relentless and highly approved pursuit of wealth, labeled by Mark Twain as the Gilded Age. The rich were more extravagant than ever, while the poor (mostly newly arrived immigrants and former slaves) were wretched. Life for middle-class Americans, however, seemed relatively secure. By the end of the century, most Americans looked forward eagerly to the ever-expanding prosperity that the next century promised.

DEVELOPMENT OF BOOKS

In Britain

In the 1800s Britain led the world in book production. Receptive to new techniques created by the Industrial Revolution, British printers made many innovations throughout the period. In 1800, the finest printer in Britain, William Bulmer, was experimenting with the iron Stanhope press which would almost double production. Another well-known printer, Thomas Bensley, was promoting the cylindrical press. By 1814, the *London Times* was printed on steam-powered presses, after steam was first applied to the printing press by Friedrich Koenig in 1812 in Germany; books, however, would not be printed by steam press to any extent before mid-century. A papermaking machine, invented by Didot in France in the late eighteenth century, was in commercial operation in England by 1812. In 1820 cloth bindings were introduced; by the end of the century almost all books were cloth-bound and machine-assembled. In 1822 William Church invented a letter-founding machine which cast letters mechanically rather than by hand. In 1828 Applegarth and Cowper invented the four-cylinder press which evolved to the rotary press by 1866. Book jackets came into use in 1833. By 1840, wood pulp, although it produced inferior paper, was being used to make continuous rolls; until this time, paper was manufactured mostly from rags as single sheets.

While advances in technology were many, changes in typography were few as British printers such as Bulmer and Bensley continued the traditions established in the eighteenth century, the production of neat and classical typefaces. Charles Whittingham, however, who came to the Chiswick Press in 1824, revived the Caslon old-style and helped to make Chiswick one of the most influential presses of the Victorian period. Whittingham's partner, William Pickering, promoted the first cloth-bound book and designed the first modern title page, avoiding the characteristic long title but setting the necessary letters in careful arrangement. The Chiswick Press printed many fine books, especially their "Aldine Edition of the British Poets" series. They also printed books reminiscent of earlier times, using woodcuts, ornaments, and black-letter type printed in red and black on beautiful paper. *Queen Elizabeth's Prayer Book* (1869) with woodcuts by Mary Byfield is considered their masterpiece.

Throughout the century various composing machines were patented, such as the linotype and the intertype, machines which cast type in one-piece "slugs" for each line from matrices assembled at the touch of a keyboard. But the most important composing machine, the monotype, was invented by an American, Tolbert Lanson, in 1889; it cast type in individual letters from banks of matrices, guided by a perforated tape made on a keyboard. Along with advances in composing machines came experimentation with photography, eventually resulting in the application of photographic methods to all types of pictorial reproduction, line engraving, photogravure, lithography, collotype, and finally offset.

Methods for illustration, particularly in color, were also undergoing experimentation. Early in the century, aquatints, which reproduced the colors of the English romantic landscape paintings that were so popular at this time, were made by many artists, including J. M. W. Turner. William

Blake was also using color in his graphic processes, but Blake was going his solitary way of genius. Although the moody symbolism of his great books was not understood by the public of his time, his work, especially his hand-colored plates, is a landmark in British illustration.

A more important event for the future of printing in color was the coming of lithography. Although lithography had been invented about 1796 and was widely used on the continent by many artists (Daumier, Goya, Gericault, Charlet, Delacroix), few quality lithographs had been produced in Britain until the 1830s. Wood engraving, perfected by Thomas Bewick at the end of the eighteenth century, remained the most common illustration medium. If color was used, until about 1840 it was almost always applied by hand, often by amateurs, usually children, who filled in the colors according to a guide—one child painting the red, one the yellow, and so on. While some notable English lithographers were at work, among them Edward Lear whose children's book, the *Book of Nonsense* (1846) is a landmark, most lithography was used for commercial work, maps, labels, and cheap editions of toy books for children, starting with the English publication of the German cautionary tale, *Struwwelpter* in 1848. It should be mentioned that Edward Lear, often credited with the creation of the limerick, was probably inspired as a young boy by a set of anonymous books containing limericks and brightly colored drawings, *Anecdotes and Adventures of Fifteen Gentlemen* (1820), published by John Marshall.

Improved methods of engraving (on copper and steel) intrigued many English artists, particulary book and magazine illustrators with a bent for social commentary. Nonsense, caricature, and satire seem to have been particularly English. In the eighteenth century, Hogarth had commented on British life in his great satiric series, *The Rake's Progress.* In the early nineteenth century, Thomas Rowlandson published a rollicking commentary in *The Tour of Dr. Syntax in Search of the Picturesque.* Artists such as George Cruikshank and "Phiz" (Hablot K. Browne), both well-known illustrators for the humor magazine *Punch* as well as *The Illustrated London News,* began to do book illustrations; their work in Dickens's novels is especially memorable. George Cruikshank is also credited with what was probably the first book illustrated in the modern style for children, *Grimm's Fairy Tales* (1823). Other artists such as John Tenniel, who illustrated Lewis Carroll's *Alice's Adventures in Wonderland* (1865), and John Leech and Richard Doyle were also doing illustrations for children's books, but much book illustration remained in the hands of hacks.

As the reading population increased, so did the demand for all types of printed material. Much of the demand was filled with cheap editions of popular novels, tracts, and "catnachery." The latter was the work of James Catnatch and successors, printing jobbers who published broadsides, song sheets, sensational stories about royalty, murderers, and the like, penny

ABC's, ballads, fairy tales, and rhymes for children. Although poorly printed from worn blocks, these products were cheap and widely read. Even though increased mechanization had reduced printing costs, well-printed books remained too expensive for the lower classes.

While some producers of nineteenth-century children's books published for commercial reasons only, others created children's books to promote educational or religious beliefs, manners, behavior, and morals. The rise of didactic literature, that is, moral tales and verses intended to instruct, made for thousands of titles. While such writers supposedly followed the admonitions of Rousseau to allow the child to develop naturally according to his interests, in practice youngsters were often burdened with the pressure of information. Fairy tales, as well as other works of the imagination, were considered a waste of time by many educators and by some, even dangerous. Every activity was turned into a lesson in geography, mathematics, or other school subject, and every thought or deed had some moralistic overtone. Didactic tales and verses were produced by a determined group of such lesser talents as Mrs. Elliott, Mrs. Barbauld, Mrs. Sherwood, and Mrs. Trimmer—and even by writers of greater talent such as Maria Edgeworth. Well-intentioned but relentless, these writers impressed upon the child the practical side of life, and many of their themes were humane ones, especially their sermons against the cruelty of slavery and the mistreatment of animals.

The Sunday school movement in Britain and America gave additional impetus to the rise of didactic literature. The Religious Tract Society, the Society for Promoting Christian Knowledge, the Christian Tract Society, the Church Missionary Society, the Sunday School Union, Protectors of Children and Animals, temperance societies, slavery abolitionists, and many church-related groups all provided thousands of publications—magazines, books, and tracts—to promote their religious and social beliefs.

Books of high literary quality were also being produced. British writers of great children's books of the nineteenth century include such illustrious names as Charles Dickens, Lewis Carroll, George MacDonald, Edward Lear, Christina Rossetti, Anna Sewell, Robert Louis Stevenson, Lucretia Hale, Frances Hodgson Burnett, E. Nesbit, and Rudyard Kipling; still others, such as Joseph Jacobs and Andrew Lang, who were influenced by the German Brothers Grimm, collected the folk fairy tales.

Books with fine illustrations were also produced. Although illustration developed somewhat later in children's books than in adult books, the rise parallels the course of British mainstream printing. Although, as noted, some children's books before 1835 had hand-colored illustrations, few had printed colored pictures. Some exceptions were Mary Elliott's *Tales for Boys* and *Tales for Girls,* which had colored frontispieces, Mrs. Sherwood's *Caroline Mordaunt,* which is the first recorded use of the Baxter color-printing process from woodblocks, and the Chiswick Press's Home Treasury series by Felix Summerly. But most illustrations in books for children before 1855 were not in color; as in adult books, most books for children contained traditional woodcuts or wood engravings, which were generally mediocre.

Chromolithography, several colors printed from a series of lithographic plates, had been invented in Britain by Charles Hullmandel in 1836. This process eventually became the chief method used, but it was often combined with woodblocks. Fine art books, that is, reproductions of paintings such as those in Henry Shaw's books produced by the Chiswick Press and those by Henry Noel Humphreys who made beautiful "illuminated" gift books, were printed in chromolithography. But at mid-century chromolithography was not widely used for general printing.

Although color printing from wood became an industry after 1850, the most notable book illustrators of the 1860s relied almost exclusively on wood engraving in black and white and the skill of such engravers as the Dalziel brothers, W. J. Linton, and John Swain. During this period wood engraving made two important advances: drawing on the block directly, and photographing drawings on wood, the latter pioneered by Henry Fox Talbot. (Photography would bring many changes: the first photoengraving appeared in 1851; the first halftones in 1881.)

The greatest advances in color printing came in the innovative woodcuts of Edmund Evans, the period's leading wood engraver, who improved the woodblock color process of Baxter and other pioneers. Evans's first book with full-color wood engravings was *Sabbath Bells* (1856), illustrated by Birket Foster. It was followed by *The Poems of Oliver Goldsmith* and *Common Wayside Flowers*. In addition to producing beautiful books for adults, Evans was much interested in creating high-quality books for children.

In the 1860s Evans began to print toy books, published by Routledge and Warne and illustrated at first by anonymous artists. But Evans succeeded in drawing the attention of great talents as it became clear that he was genuinely concerned with producing children's books of real beauty. Fortunately, Evans's toy books attracted Walter Crane, a first-rate designer, who had apprenticed with W. J. Linton.

It should be noted that the term "toy book" had come to mean any books for children that had pictures. But toy books, that is, books for fun, went back at least to 1760 when harlequinades, or turnups, first appeared. They consisted of pages covered with fold-overs that could be moved up or down to make other scenes. Verses or stories were sometimes printed on sheets with slots, with pockets fastened on the backs. Cutouts could be slipped through the slot and held in the pocket, thus changing the faces or limbs or costumes of the characters. (*See figure 15.*) From 1840 on, books with movable or removable parts—tabs, panels, flaps, fold-overs, cutouts, pop-ups —had a wide audience. Many artists were also creating illusion, shadow, and silhouette books. One of the most popular creators was Charles Henry Bennett. All his illusion books were well received, but his first book, *Shadows* (1856), was probably his best.

Walter Crane was the first of the serious toy-book illustrators who wanted children's books to be works of art. Impressed by Japanese woodblock prints, Crane at first designed his books with attention to large areas of white space, flat color, and harmonious patterns; later, his work tended to a pre-Raphaelite, that is, richly ornamented, style. Crane's contribution to the development of color illustration was immense, not only for his toy books, but also for his adult work, such as his collaborations with William Morris of the Kelmscott Press. (*See figure 18.*)

Another artist who worked with Evans was Randolph Caldecott. Caldecott, following the high standards set by Crane and personally encouraged by him, experimented with various methods of reproduction—with his drawings usually being "photographed on the block and then passed through the engraver's hands." His style, especially his free, economical use of line, suited well the illustrating of active, robust stories for children. Although he published many works for adults, particularly the popular Washington Irving's *Sketch Book,* his children's picture books of the 1870s best reveal his characteristic engaging spirit. Today, the Caldecott Medal is given annually in America in his honor to the illustrator of the most distinguished children's picture book. (*See figure 17.*)

While Caldecott's characters usually cavort joyously across the eighteenth century British countryside, Kate Greenaway's work generally shows proper British children in old-fashioned costumes promenading in tidy gardens. Although her earliest works were undistinguished lithographs, her association with Edmund Evans and her use of his method of reproducing illustrations launched her career—one that was filled with prizes, commissions, and acclaim, even from such an astute art critic as John Ruskin.

There is no question that Greenaway was Evans's special protége. From the beginning he had such faith in her work that the first edition of their first publication, *Under the Window* (1878), ran to the then astronomical number of 20,000 copies. His faith was well directed. Her illustrations in both books and magazines, reflecting her serene, cheerful personality, made her name a household word. At her death, tributes came from thousands not only in Britain but in America, Germany, and France as well. Today, the Greenaway Medal is given annually in Britain to the illustrator of the best children's picture book. (*See figure 19.*)

Thus, the last quarter of the nineteenth century saw children's books becoming firmly established in the history and development of printing and illustration in England. Other notable achievements were also occurring. Just as new methods were being refined in photochemical processes, certain designers, such as William Morris and Aubrey Beardsley representing the private press, looked to the past and revived interest in the primitive wood-cut, with Morris going back to the fifteenth century for inspiration. Morris's elaborate edition of *The Works of Geoffrey Chaucer,* with eighty-seven woodcuts by Edward Burne-Jones (1896), was probably his greatest achievement in decorative but (according to some critics) not especially readable books. Morris's Kelmscott Press (which used only the best paper, ink, and printing and binding methods) was followed by other private presses such as the Doves and the Ashendene Press, which helped to raise standards of craftsmanship.

Throughout the century, much attention was paid to bindings, with the first cloth-bound book, as noted earlier, coming in 1820. But expensive and elaborate bindings were popular throughout the 1800s. In the 1840s and 1850s vellum, velvet, silk, leather, porcelain, tortoiseshell, gilt, papier-mâché, and varnished tartan paper on wood bindings were especially sought after. Children's books and cheap editions of adult books, however, were almost always bound in paper or imitation cloth throughout the period.

In the United States

In America, as in Britain, the nineteenth century marked the beginning of care in book production; only crude woodcuts had appeared in typical American books before 1800. At first, American wood engravers copied British originals for reprints, but experiments with steel engraving (for bank notes) began as early as 1810. Book illustration in America, however, would develop slowly with the years between 1840 and 1870 marking the first significant growth.

As in Britain wood engraving remained the dominant medium for most of the century. Alexander Anderson (1775-1870), considered the "father of wood engraving in America," was America's first professional illustrator. Anderson, intrigued by Bewick's "white-line" engraving, copied many of his blocks, including those from his *Quadrupeds* (1790), but he also reinterpreted Bewick. And he worked in his own style. Although most of his work was for adults, for children he did *Mother Goose* and *Children's Friend.*

In the 1840s the first American illustrator of consequence, Felix Darley (1882-1888), came on the scene. While he illustrated the adult works of Dickens, Poe, Irving, Longfellow, and others, he also illustrated the work of Mary Mapes Dodge, a popular American editor and writer of children's stories, as well as the work of Maria Edgeworth, Britain's foremost moralist for the young. Other important American illustrators of this period were William Croome, John McLenan, and Winslow Homer.

Although, as in Britain, wood engraving remained the most common medium for book illustration, other methods were being tried, including lithography. One early and immense achievement in lithography was J. J. Audubon's publication of *The Birds of America* in London between 1827 and 1838. The elephantine-size, lithographed plates of the first edition accommodated the natural sizes of the American eagle, the wild turkey, and other large birds; a smaller-size edition was published in America in 1860. Another achievement was the work of the famous American firm of Currier and Ives which produced a large number of series as well as single-print lithographs of American landscapes.

Series books for children were popular in America throughout the century, but the 1830s saw the rise of two of the greatest series of all—the Peter Parley books by S. G. Goodrich, which began in 1827, and the Rollo books by Jacob Abbott, which began in 1835. If illustrated at all, series books almost always had undistinguished steel engravings.

The 1850s saw the origin of many illustrated magazines, such as *Harper's,* which increased the demand for wood engravers. But magazines, tracts, and annuals for children were known in England much earlier and were often of an evangelical nature. *The Juvenile Magazine* was one of the first in 1788; it was followed by *The Youth's Magazine or Evangelical Miscellany* in 1805. These early magazines contained sheets of music (often hymns), maps, religious exhortations, tales of travel, verses, biographies, and informational articles, and were usually illustrated with woodcuts or copperplate engravings. Many of these magazines were bound into annuals designed to catch the Christmas-gift trade, such as *Blossoms at Christmas and the First Flowers of the New Year* (1825), *The Children's Friend* (1824), and *The Child's Companion; or Sunday Scholar's Reward* (1824). But there were dozens more, usually profusely illustrated and often with colored covers with colors having been added by hand. Magazines such as *The Boy's Penny Magazine* (1863) were priced cheaply so poor children, for whom they were produced, could afford a subscription. By 1890 the British market was saturated with scores of inexpensive reading materials, from evangelical tracts to blood-and-thunder thrillers, the latter enjoying tremendous popularity. As early as 1850 American publishers were hijacking these "shilling shockers."

Even earlier, in the 1840s, some American publishers who recognized the popularity of such fare were selling twenty-five-cent paper-covered novels which were full of sensationalism, romance, and adventure. The Beadle Publishing Company launched the American "dime novel." Irwin Beadle's first book, *Malaeska, or Indian Wife of the White Hunter,* by Ann S. Stephens, was published in 1860. Ann S. Stephens, who was a popular magazine writer and novelist in her own time, had produced a story which was not typical of the dime novel as it would later develop, for it was a story of Indian life. But it was full of action, and it opened the flood gates.

Malaeska sold 300,000 copies, and within five years it had been translated into five languages.

Beadle's second novel, *Seth Jones, or the Captive of the Frontier* by Edward Sylvester Ellis, was far more typical of what was to come. It would be the most successful title in the entire Beadle empire, selling over 600,000 copies; it was translated into six languages. Subsequently, once a month or oftener the Beadle presses rumbled off poorly written but exciting thrillers, such as *Apollo Bill, The Frontier Detective, Deadwood Dick on Deck,* or *Calamity Jane, the Heroine of Whoop-Up,* and hundreds more.

The "Beadles" and their successors swept the nation, feeding both adults' and children's appetites for action on the frontier, for belief in the importance of the individual, and for belief in an ideal world in which the patriot could achieve. Along with frontier fiction, detective thrillers, such as Halsy's *Old Sleuth Stories* and Coryell's *Nick Carter* series, sold millions of copies.

Magazines, usually priced at two or three cents, also enjoyed tremendous growth during this period; among them, *Our Young Folks* (1865), *The Riverside Magazine for Young People* (1867), *Harper's Young People* (1879), and *St. Nicholas* (1873) greatly influenced interest in writing and illustrating for the juvenile market. While much magazine material was the work of unknowns, many famous American and English artists and writers such as Charles Dickens, Thomas Bailey Aldrich, Frances Hodgson Burnett, Mark Twain, Winslow Homer, Thomas Nast, A. B. Frost, and Howard Pyle also contributed.

In the last quarter of the century, American press work, at least for quality books, improved substantially. Daniel Updike of the Merrymount Press, influenced by the standards set by the Kelmscott Press, produced some outstanding books. Frederick Goudy was the most prolific type designer, Bruce Rogers the best typographer. As in England, the coming of photoengraving in the 1870s created a demand for photographing on wood. The coming of the halftone, which at first temporarily reduced standards, eventually attracted great talents. Even such a fine wood engraver as Howard Pyle began in the 1880s to paint illustrations which required the use of halftones for reproductions in books. (*See figure 20.*)

Pyle's influence on book illustration, especially on books for children, was enormous. As a practicing artist and teacher, he set high standards of art and craftsmanship. Pyle's vigorous approach to art and life influenced countless artists, including A. B. Frost, Frederick Remington, Jessie Willcox Smith, Maxfield Parrish, Frank E. Schoonover, Thornton Oakley, Pyle's sister Katharine, and especially N. C. Wyeth. Such artists along with talented writers, including Mark Twain, Nathaniel Hawthorne, Louisa May Alcott, and Mary Mapes Dodge, formed near the end of the century the "Golden Age of Children's Books" in America.

ATTITUDES TOWARD AND TREATMENT OF CHILDREN

In Britain

While the Age of Reason had produced the practical wisdom of the English philosopher John Locke, the subsequent Age of Enlightenment produced the French philosopher Jean Jacques Rousseau, who called attention to the worth of the child and to the importance of child nurturing. Assisted by the public turmoil following the French Revolution and the Napoleonic Wars which turned families toward idealizing private life and domesticity, Rousseau's doctrines found great following first on the continent and later in England. He believed that the child, who was born in innocence, should be allowed to develop naturally; such thinking helped to bring new freedom to children. Like Locke, he attacked swaddling, but he also pleaded that mothers nurse their own children and that both parents pay attention to their offspring. From Rousseau onward, a new commitment to childhood was developing, at least among enlightened parents. But for a great part of Britain's population the effects of the new thought were slow in coming. Not until the nineteenth century were the subsequent social and educational reforms observable and then, though far-reaching, the immediate effects were not widespread.

The poor were still very poor in the early 1800s. Successive Enclosure Acts passed by Parliament in the eighteenth century had caused increased poverty among the rural poor, driving them to cities in search of employment. But the newly industrialized towns were unable to handle the influx of rural people, whose birthrates had soared during the Napoleonic Wars when there had been great demand for female and child labor. The resulting city slums were wretched. The new city dwellers, those fortunate enough to find work, worked long hours at machines driven by steam. Both adults and children, many having been recruited like soldiers, were part of the labor force. With no child labor laws in view for half a century, many of the ill-kempt and ill-fed children, especially orphans and foundlings, lived in barracks under grossly inadequate conditions, completely at the mercy of their employers. If poor children were schooled at all, they received only minimal training in reading and writing, usually in the barracks in which they lived.

In the first decades of the nineteenth century, 80 percent of the English cotton mill workers were children. Such cheap labor was highly desirable to the proprietors, one of whom said that the children were like "lively elves . . . whose work seemed to resemble a sport." But criticism of such "sport" existed early. The poet Robert Southey, for instance, who visited a cotton factory in Manchester in 1807, likened the children at work on the machines to a scene in Dante's *Inferno*. In 1833, he said the ". . . slave trade is a mercy compared to it [the factory system]." The criticism grew.

By 1841 the Select Commission reported that some children were kept at lace-making machines twenty-four hours a day; in 1843 the Miners Commission reported that mine-working children and women were "chained, belted, harnessed like dogs in a go-cart." Such workers, often wet and half naked, were used to open and close the ventilator shafts in the mines (a dangerous job) and also pulled or shoved heavy coal carts. If they refused to work they could be sent to prison. Chimney sweeping was another common occupation for poor boys until 1875 when legislation finally forbade boys to be so employed. The young were preferred as sweeps because their narrow shoulders and hips, aggravated by malnutrition, were good for lowering them into the chimneys in which they sometimes died of suffocation. Much exploitation of this sort was regarded with complacency because of the generally accepted notion that society had a place for everyone and everyone should accept his lot according to the laws of creation.

Poor children were commonly dealt severe punishments for minor infractions. As late as 1833, a child of nine was hanged for stealing five halfpence worth of paint. Child hangings, sometimes in public, were not uncommon, nor was the "transportation" of children overseas, a well-established practice first authorized in 1718. In 1834, for example, a boy of fourteen was sentenced to "transportation" for stealing a silk handkerchief, and a girl of ten for stealing a shawl and a petticoat; both were sentenced to seven years. Prisons, which often held children, were so overcrowded that many persons both young and old were kept in the "hulks," old ships lying in the harbors of the Thames in London and the Medway in Portsmouth. With no sanitary facilities, conditions aboard the "hulks" were the most horrible recorded in the history of British prisons.

Other offenses against poor children were child stealing, not punishable by law until 1814, and acts commonly committed by the children's own parents who legally owned them. Children of both sexes, for example, were often sold into prostitution by their own parents as late as 1886, when the age of consent was finally raised to sixteen. Parents commonly defended drinking by children and children's buying beer and gin, and parents commonly had children "fetch" their liquor from the pubs. Attempts to restrict parents from using their children as they saw fit were considered dangerous by many who felt that such intervention would undermine parental authority and upset the balance of society.

Even proposals of compulsory education, as well as meals for grossly undernourished children, were at first strenuously opposed as infringements of the rights of parents. Opponents felt that such assistance would also, along with undermining the family, lower personal initiative. Even the Charity Organization Society opposed such action, not wishing to imperil the principle of the sanctity of the family. Not until the end of the century were laws passed that protected children from their parents—in particular, the Prevention of Cruelty Act and the Poor Law Adoption Act of 1889, and the Custody of Children Act of 1891, which gave the "poor child the same protection given by the Court of Chancery to wealthier children who have property bestowed upon them." The creation of the National Society for the Prevention of Cruelty to Children in 1895 brought about further reforms which eventually gave children the first legal protection in history. Along with the passage of laws for children's rights came advances in medicine and sanitation which would shortly improve the life of the young.

Changes in societal attitudes, especially toward the poor who committed crimes, were nevertheless slow to develop. From the mid-eighteenth century on there had been numerous rescue societies which attempted to assist poor, uneducated children who had drifted into crime. Voluntary foster parent plans, asylums, and reformatories were all tried, with varying results. The first real attempt to get at the causes of juvenile crime did not come about until the founding of the Society for Investigating the Causes of the Alarming Increase of Juvenile Delinquency in the Metropolis, in 1815. Its work, along with that of similar organizations, helped to reveal the flaws in society that caused children to do criminal acts and finally brought slow but inevitable changes in the public's attitude toward poor children.

Like crime, death was rampant throughout the 1800s, especially for the poor. Although registration of births and deaths for all classes was imprecise, it was estimated that, for example, half of the children born in 1831 died before age two. Among the working classes the infant death rate caused by starvation, unsanitary conditions, and unsuitable foods—and often drugs—soared. Opium was an especially common remedy to "calm" babies and was often used from the first day of life. Countless thousands of infants died from overdosing either by mothers or by those left in charge while the mothers worked, or from prolonged use which eventually resulted in death or in a "half-idiotic" life or a "ruined constitution." Among the aristocracy, on the other hand, life expectancy was rising, having jumped from forty-two years in the early eighteenth century to fifty-four years in the mid-nineteenth, with the middle-class life expectancy almost as high. But for the majority of the laboring classes, that is, 85 percent of the population, the loss of children was a fundamental expectation of life.

The upper classes, meanwhile, were experiencing an improvement in all aspects of life, with the exception of education. Many children of the well-off were more and more being viewed in the light of Rousseauian principles—especially by the Romantic poets who, like William Wordsworth, assumed that the child was in a state of grace coming straight from heaven "trailing clouds of glory." But the education of these children was far from ideal. Training for the professions was expensive and genrally of low quality. The public schools had become the dumping grounds for sons of the gentry and the middle class who had no prospects of going to the universities and were in school only for social polish before entering the army, going to the colonies, or going into the civil service or business. Private boarding schools had a long tradition in British education; they were known as early as 1380. But even such schools, especially before the reforms of 1830 under Thomas Arnold, offered only fair education at best with discipline sometimes brutally severe or utterly lax. Parents felt that schoolmasters were unscrupulous, as indeed many were, and were far more interested in getting students for their business than in educating them. Some schoolmasters, on the other hand, felt that the parents did not care anyhow and that schools were only used for getting rid of surplus children at home, the results of improved medical practices and high fertility. It is clear that in certain schools living conditions, as well as education, were deplorable. After 138 children died from cholera in 1849 in a private school in Tooting, guardians were legally forbidden to send children to such institutions. But although the private school issue continued to be debated throughout the century, the English boarding school survived restraining legislation.

Education in general was still largely classical. When it did succeed in educating youth, it trained them almost exclusively for the clergy, law, medicine, and civil service. Even then, the professions were overcrowded, with agriculture and commerce not considered desirable. Talented young men, frustrated at not being able to procure the right sort of positions in society, often ended up as private tutors and intellectuals who spent their time in clubs and lodges, such as freemasonry, planning adolescent pranks, and carrying out, at least temporarily, experiments in living the Bohemian life and establishing utopian communities. By the end of the century, however, conditions in upper-class education had improved. Outwardly at least the English schoolboy was a serious and polished student dedicated to his school.

Throughout the nineteenth century, the moral improvement of youth through work and diligence, not education, was the life goal as set by their elders. Punctuality and exemplary behavior—that is, reformation of manners and morals—were taught as the means to success for all classes and, as such, took precedence over instruction. Educationalists, particularly women writers of the period who often had high ideals but little talent, championed materialistic values and practicality, while scorning "irrational influences" on the child's mind, such as fairy tales and nursery rhymes.

Regardless of class, discipline of children still tended to be severe. Although the incidences of caning began to diminish in the 1840s, not until the end of the century did even enlightened parents give it up and then with frequent misgivings. There are instances of children being whipped at age two for dirtying a frock, and at equally tender ages for falling, stumbling, crying, not being able to spell a word, and disobeying—all done by upper-class parents. Other punishments included withholding food. Food for children was at best simple and monotonous, since most educated parents followed Locke's theories that fancy food was bad for children's bodies and minds. Children were never allowed to ask for food, but were expected, sometimes forced, to eat what was placed before them. As part of the hardening process long felt to be important in childrearing, upper-class children, who always ate away from their parents, were sometimes asked to join their parents at the end of the meal; but often they were given nothing, or perhaps a slice of fruit while the parents ate rich desserts, or they were given cake that was snatched away before they could eat it, or they were made to crack nuts for guests without eating any themselves, and so on. Although some parents were proud to handle their children without such coercion or without corporal punishment, such instances were unusual. But parental concern about the best disciplinary methods to use was in itself an enormous change in attitude over previous times. While some authorities continued to argue for severe punishment, more and more educators and parents argued for leniency.

Along with simple food, such as bread and milk, cold baths were advocated as health builders, especially by John Locke. Some Victorian parents tried to follow his cold-bath theory by submerging their offspring promptly upon arising, in some cases for as long as an hour—but first having to break the ice on the tub. In spite of the child's protests, the bath continued until the child was finally dried and wrapped in a light frock and then set down to a cold breakfast; hot porridge was sometimes offered in winter.

While the bath gown was almost always light, the usual dress was heavy, with little girls always wearing a chemise (vest), because it was "nice" to do so, underneath the rest of their clothes. Both sexes wore stays, boys till about seven, girls for the rest of their lives. Children were dressed in garters, drawers, flannel petticoats, white crinoline petticoats, black stockings, frocks, pinafores, and sashes—until boys were finally considered old enough to be permitted to wear "manly breeches." While some of these practices seem unenlightened and even cruel by present-day standards, it is well to remember that they were carried out according to the best authorities of the time; and they do indicate concern for children's welfare unknown to previous generations.

In the early part of the century, the evils of the Industrial Age were not recognized and the Age of Steam was even romanticized. The power of the mercantile classes was not yet threatening to the rich and, as in former times, the poor were largely ignored. The Georgians were in large part innocent of conditions of the world around them; the worst that wealthy children of that period were warned against was the possible sin of "false pride" in extravagant nobles.

Attitudes toward and the treatment of upper-class children of the Georgian period are clearly recognized in such children's books as Thomas Day's fictionalizing of Rousseauian theories in *Sandford and Merton*. The book also laid down methods for teaching manners and morals, which were repeated in the hordes of such books that followed in the next thirty years: the use of characters (children) with contrasting behaviors in illusive story settings; innumerable instructional facts and moral lessons on behavior dispensed by all-knowing adults; sermonizing on the evils of fashionable life, on the dignity of labor, on the importance of rational principles (that is, allowing children to learn the consequences of their actions), on kindness—especially to animals—and on the blessings of living the simple life. Like Day, Maria Edgeworth, the most gifted of these didactic writers, expounded a rational approach through the popular "instruction-through-conversation" method, but she also advocated lessons in natural science, education for girls, and "modern" rather than classical training. These books taught duty to parents and patronizing benevolence toward the poor, who by the laws of nature were "bound to their station." Sensibility was frowned upon, and self-control took precedence over all emotional states.

By the Victorian period, duty to parents had become a dominant theme in all books for children. When fairy tales as well as other allegories were allowed, they were often used to point out moral principles. While the Georgians had largely ignored religion, pointing out the physical consequence of bad behavior (the rod), the early Victorians stressed the importance of a peaceful conscience, with correction coming through mental pressure and discussion of one's duty to ultimate authority, that is, to parents (on earth) and to God (in heaven). While submission to authority was a cardinal principle, sensibility (often rhapsodic), particularly in girls, was now acclaimed. In those decades, swooning was fashionable.

The middle years of the century produced a spate of tract books which revealed the evangelistic Victorian preoccupations with the sufferings of the poor (as individuals) and the evils of drink, gambling, and bad company that brought the benighted poor (as a class) low. Death was often lingered over; fictional characters were often either near death or at least recently ill. The themes and settings of stories frequently revealed extreme intolerance of other religions, social systems, and points of view; at the same time they taught carefulness, temperance, and the importance of the fixed social caste system ("do what you are intended to do"), as well as the necessity of working hard to achieve perfection.

Not until after 1860 did changes in the treatment of children begin in earnest. Then, a new appreciation of childhood is evident in many books given to them—fantasy, history, adventure, biography—but even then these stories were often touted to keep boys away from the popular "Penny Dreadfuls," not for their intrinsic value.

By the end of the century, British children of all classes were beginning to be thought of as people with enthusiasms and emotions worth noting and encouraging. Even the lot of poor children was improving. Medical inspection and the feeding of pauper children by educational authorities in the industrial schools and workhouses where the children lived resulted in better living conditions and better education.

Important advances in education, influenced by developments on the continent, had occurred throughout the period. After visiting Switzerland in 1815, Robert Owen, for instance, had established the first British infant school for children from "as soon as they could walk" to age six. Improvements in teacher training, based on the work of Pestalozzi and Fellenberg, had also occurred. But because British democracy had long insisted that schools were outside of the sphere of government, a national system of education was slow to develop. Milestones along the way were the Factory Act of 1802 for apprentices, but it was evaded when proprietors refused to call their child laborers "apprentices." Further reforms were blocked by those who feared that education of the masses would bring about rebellion. Not until 1833 did Parliament vote any money for schools, and not until 1841 did teacher training institutions receive any government grants. Thus, education remained hard for many to achieve. In Liverpool as late as 1870 one-fourth of the children never attended school. But in that same year the Elementary Education Act was passed, providing elementary schools at public expense. For the first time school districts would have elected boards for the purpose of establishing schools where none existed. While the government continued to aid private schools, it had at last established a system of public schools for the "school-less multitudes," as Matthew Arnold called them. By 1880 England had compulsory attendance laws for all children under twelve.

In 1871 another educational reform came with the passing of the University Tests Act, which opened Oxford and Cambridge to non-Anglican students. Oxford and Cambridge had been the only universities in England until the founding of the University of London in 1828 and the University of Durham in 1832, although Scotland had long had four universities. Near the end of the century other universities were organized in the larger provincial towns, providing higher education for a much wider spectrum of English students.

By the end of the century, British children were being raised in urban and industrial conditions unknown before: the old social order was disintegrating, and the social system was in great flux. Advice on all matters came from many quarters. One writer suggested seriously that even speaking in the proper accent, especially if accompanied with conformity to the usages of polite society, might assist one in rising from his class in order to become acceptable to "those above."

In the United States

Meanwhile in America, British influences, which had been strong until about 1820, were undergoing "Americanization." Until this time, English writers with English "messages" had filled the demand for juvenile books.

But experimentation, especially concerning "little Americans," was in the air. English things no longer seemed suitable or desirable, and changes occurred rapidly. Educators worked diligently at producing American spellers, dictionaries, and histories; stories of democratic American youths visiting foreign lands were popular. And books on rearing children which were aimed at American parents appeared. In them Locke's influence was obvious; they gave advice on giving children cold baths, simple foods, light clothing, and so on, but they also contained references to the importance of submitting in proper amounts to the "restraint of government," that is, American federalism, and they reflected the buoyant optimism and patriotism of the new land.

Life for country children (97 percent of the population at the beginning of the nineteenth century was rural) was still similar to pre-Revolutionary days; there was much emphasis on hard work, Bible reading, and correction by the rod. But as religious revivals became common in the rural areas, their enthusiasm and evangelical fervor, along with new political developments and economic opportunities, caused many a young farmer to grow restless under the yoke of tradition and move on to better lands and new life-styles.

The public school movement, with all of its problems of bad and often cruel schoolmasters and uncomfortable conditions, was spreading even into isolated regions. Although the public school did not teach religious doctrine, religious tracts were widely distributed by Sunday schools which often touched the lives of even the poorest children—as did chapbooks, broadsides, and cheap editions which brought inexpensive entertainment to the urban "street Arab" as well as to the lonely rural child. Families who could afford them preferred private tutors in the home; many parents balked at the school's taking over the intellectual and moral demands made on the child. This rivalry along with complaints against the "overloaded" schoolchild working in crowded, unsavory conditions brought on an anti-intellectualism that plagued the public school well into the twentieth century. But more and more children of all classes went to school; the first compulsory attendance law was passed in Massachusetts in 1854.

Almost paralleling the growth of the public school was the rise of the American Sunday school. Although Sunday schools had originated in Britain, the movement in the United States was a powerful educational force throughout the century. Like the British Sunday school, the American version aimed to instruct poor children in primary education. Recognizing the declining religious zeal in the new country, Sunday school proponents also hoped to provide religious instruction through the churches for those who were no longer receiving it in their homes. The American Sunday School Union, formed in 1824, represented many denominations which attempted to provide all children with suitable oral instruction and juvenile reading material both at school and at home. The Union published hundreds of volumes as well as thousands of tracts, magazines, and journals, which generally were cheerful in tone and provided instruction about religious matters, the importance of charity to the poor, kindness to animals, the dangers of idleness, and the virtues of work. Far from being subtle, the material reflected the spirit of reform which was abroad in the land and the hope the future held for good, hardworking people.

Although the Sunday schools flourished, the public schools continued to have problems. The change to women schoolmarms about 1840 brought some hope for a more nurturing education for the young. But the idea of submitting to secular authority outside the home rankled many patriots (and their offspring) who had so recently been triumphant through self-assertion.

Traditional child-rearing methods brought from Europe held fast, but after about 1830, mothers, on whom the business of child rearing was squarely placed, were admonished by growing numbers of child-care advisors (mostly clergymen) to teach their children patriotism along with religion, hygiene, and refinement of manners. Many advisors still advocated firmness and obedience to parents, but more and more they began to plead for tenderness and diversion before resorting to whippings. Mothers, in particular, were admonished to produce sons fit to become the nation's leaders and daughters to become the mothers of suitable sons.

For the young, the colonial objectives of religious education and training for a vocation were rapidly fading as secularization, advances in transportation and communication, the growth of cities and towns—all coupled with the frontier spirit—changed the focus of education to facilitate the "rise of the common man."

Infant mortality was still high, and great numbers of Americans suffered from poor hygiene, lack of competent medical care, improper clothing, and poor diet. Throughout the nineteenth century, however, living conditions, particularly sanitation, slowly improved. Dependence on medicine, which had also improved, gradually developed, although many Americans, particularly in the rural areas, were suspicious of the new ways and clung to folk wisdom and "kitchen physick."

In general, the 1800s brought substantial changes for the better in the American child's life. Play, for example, which had been frowned upon and scorned as idleness in colonial times, was by the 1830s looked upon as a necessary part of invigorating the child's mind and body. Although not all parents accepted Rousseau's call to "look kindly on the child's play," controlled or "rational" play was gaining acceptance. The nineteenth-century child was also beginning to realize other types of emancipation: holidays were more frequently and joyously celebrated, organized sports and games were permitted and encouraged, and hygiene was improved. Bathing remained a problem in poorly heated homes in cold weather, but American parents were not as apt to follow Locke's advice to plunge children into cold baths as were their English counterparts. Although children's dress had traditionally imitated adult fashions (the first costume for a child was created in 1770), garments designed for children's special use began to appear. Although the fashions moved through high collars, ruffles, crinoline petticoats, bustles, high heels, flowered waistcoats, tight knee breeches, and the rest, the tendency ran toward simpler, looser clothing as the century progressed. Although some advisors still advocated that children wear light clothing to harden them against disease, others advised the opposite practice, that of protecting children against every draft—through the use of woolen coats, woolen drawers, flannels worn next to the skin, nightcaps, mufflers, and so on. Throughout the century, concern over every sort of child welfare grew, from toilet training to moral education. Improved management of the young had at last become a widespread interest.

One of the most important nurturing books of the second half of the century was Jacob Abbott's *Gentle Measures in the Management and Training of the Young* (1871). By interpreting Darwin's evolutionary theories to mean that mankind's development was in a positive direction, Abbott helped to establish that the child was a developing individual: changes in the child resulted, he said, because of his inherited tendencies but also because of his surroundings. He pointed out that the child's mental and moral development as well as his physical development came about slowly and could not be forced. He believed in authority "without violence or anger" and "right development" integrated with the qualities particular to the child's mind. He said that play and the imagination had useful purposes which the parent must understand, and that "bad tendencies" resulted from heredity while "bad action" resulted from improper training. Natural depravity, or sin, was at last removed as the prime cause of children's wrongdoings, with the responsibility being shifted from supernatural causes to the parents' backgrounds and teachings. *Gentle Measures,* like many nurturing books to come, concentrated on how to deal with specific subjects: lying, wishes, money, religious teaching, punishment, and others. While Abbott insisted on the supreme authority of the parents and advocated the use of corporal punishment as a last resort, his advice, as well as the advice of most of the child observers to come, implied the child's rationality and inherent goodness when properly trained. Although "proof" of success was grossly exaggerated and the "science" upon which Abbott's case studies were based was far from scientific, his and other nurturing books caught the attention of the public and deepened interest in children on both sides of the Atlantic.

Although eclectic and lacking in uniform direction, publications on child study increased rapidly between 1880 and 1900. Among the most notable writers of this period were John Dewey, William James, Edward Lee Thorndike, James McKeen Cattell, and G. Stanley Hall. As a result of new ideas on the nature and training of children, child-study clubs sprang up in many communities. Two of the most important of these were the Society for the Study of Child Nature (later called the Child Study Association), founded in 1890, and the National Congress of Mothers, formed in 1897.

By the end of the century, many groups specifically created to aid children and their parents had been formed. But influences prior to this period had laid the groundwork. At mid-century, for example, important changes in the American family had occurred, particularly increased wealth. The coming of immigrants, who formed a supply of cheap labor, meant that many established American families could move out of the laboring class. As cheap labor increased, the middle class in the North gradually became infected with the notion that ladies and gentlemen did not work with their hands. In the South, the child of gentility had long been accustomed to servants, especially to the "play-child" slave who was at his white master's or mistress's beck and call and was expected to serve without question and with delight. Girls on plantations were expected to know how to keep household accounts and learn to supervise "a whole village of slaves," while boys were expected to excel in horsemanship, strength, eloquence, and bravery, as well as to be "as autocratic as the czar." To visiting foreigners, American children of the middle and upper classes in all regions seemed unruly, noisy, and disrespectful to their elders in spite of the inordinate amount of attention paid to their rearing.

Throughout the century, child-advice tracts proliferated, giving advice on everything from medical "cures"—often more killer than cure—to religious training, although the advice grew less and less religious in tone. As mentioned before, ideas on child rearing were often in conflict. Effects of the theory of evolution, the Civil War, the westward movement, the growth of cities, the decline of Calvinist doctrines, the rise of extreme wealth and extreme poverty all made for much indecision. Some experts advised being "gentle" and "unoppressive," advocating even "absolute freedom," while other critics argued for the exact opposite. In spite of such fluctuations the family continued to be the center of life, particularly the farm family. And middle-class parents grew more and more tolerant of children's whimsies although they still, for the most part, exercised firm control.

Books for children, both English and American, were in great favor, with children's fantasies, poetry, romances, and historical fiction especially well received. Children's periodicals were also extremely popular and were distributed to city and country children alike.

As the wealth of the upper classes increased, there was a growing tendency away from "hardening" and from robustness. Both educators and parents seemed to favor instilling sensibility and "delicacy" in children, particularly pertaining to physical matters; the body was frequently referred to as a "temple." If children were "indelicate," the cause was thought to be "bad company" or "bad blood." Clearly British Victorian sensibility had become the fashion, indicating that nineteenth-century America had not cast off its European ties. Europe had, in fact, regained its aura. For upper-class Americans, travel to Europe as wealthy visitors was a celebration not to be denied.

Although medical advances (vaccinations, anesthesia, antiseptics, and others) increased life expectancy and brought new interest in health and hygiene, American children of the period were surprisingly pale, sickly, and lacking in muscle tone. While such pallid coloring was to be expected in the very poor who increased in number with each wave of immigrants, that rich children were sickly was not easily explained. (In New York in 1853, 49 percent of deaths of all classes were children under five.) Some authorities blamed poor diet, while others blamed lack of exercise, stuffy rooms, too much study, and bad climate. Funerals of children of all classes were common; probably as a defense, death was often romanticized, especially in the case of a handsome young person who "faded." In 1862 the first pediatric clinic was established in New York City, but not until pasteurization of milk became widespread near the end of the century did infant mortality subside.

Throughout the century, the American poor were poor indeed. As in England, the children of poverty labored long hours in factories or on the farms, with some beginning work at age three. Some were abandoned. Because the infant mortality rate in foundling homes was extremely high, many unwanted babies were "dropped" on the doorsteps of the rich, usually to little avail. By 1854 the Children's Aid Society had begun to find places for a few indigent children by sending them to the frontier, but the problem of the poor child remained enormous. Although children's books repudiated snobbishness, particularly the "sin" of the fortunate looking down on the less fortunate, the realities of life were far different from the ideals presented in stories. While merit supposedly superseded money, difference in rank was acknowledged. But the only difference that "counted" was said to be in moral behavior.

In spite of such pleasant teachings, thousands of poor adults, almost always women, were legally sterilized to prevent the "filthy stream" of immigrants and former slaves from mingling with the "purer water of our communities." Under such conditions it is easy to see how far some Americans had fallen from the egalitarian ideals on which the country had been founded. Model, priggish children of the "purer water" were instilled with the notion that perfection was possible in their own persons, and that in America such perfection was possible through unswerving loyalty to stridently democratic ideals and through self-reliance. Children were taught to believe in the importance of charity toward the less fortunate, temperance, kindliness, and the possibility of reform. Both school and church preached that temptation in a hostile world of immoral nations (not America) and men (not Americans) could be overcome if democratic, Christian values were maintained, and that moral dignity commensurate with material possessions was attainable and desirable.

With such idealism, it seems clear why "right development" gradually won out over the discipline of the rod; moral instruction and Christian nurturing became the "gentle persuasion." Thus, by the end of the century, hopes for the future were high—at least among the upper classes. Although poor children, including children of minority groups, grew poorer, they were, as in former times, largely ignored. Upper-class children were attending dancing schools, "coming out" to join society, traveling to Europe to take on "polish," attending the best schools, and enjoying a proper, elegant, "gilded" life based on imported pseudo-aristocratic ideas. Without a hereditary aristocracy which set the standards, Americans had to exhibit their wealth and prestige through displaying their riches, belonging to correct clubs, attending proper schools, dressing according to the latest European fashions, and arranging proper and economically sound marriages for their offspring.

By the end of the century even the middle class lived in comparative ease. Many middle-class homes had electricity, bathrooms, and even telephones. Middle-class children attended church with their families, dined with them, visited lyceums and chautauquas, and attended denominational colleges. Parents belonged to fraternal groups and social clubs, while their offspring belonged to singing societies, bicycle clubs, and other organizations. Almost all middle-class children attended free public schools, although work was still generally preferred over schooling as the most expedient means of getting ahead. While levels of economic worth clearly existed, there were, in fact, no hard class lines. If ambition, hard work, and good fortune prevailed, it was possible for the diligent youth to cross class lines, especially if he started out in the middle class. Without question, "moving up" was the aspiration of all ambitious American youth. But the very fluidity of American society made it subject to capriciousness. While the rewards of success were great, failure was disastrous.

Throughout most of the century the formal education of offspring had played a small role in career making. Promotion came through the world of work, the child often learning his craft, or business, or running a farm from his elders. But as agriculture and industry moved from family concerns to complex corporations and landholdings ceased to be the most important avenues of advancement, children were encouraged to become formally educated as an entry into the rapidly growing professions. By the end of the century even industry was calling for men with dependable credentials from recognized institutions of higher learning.

The poor, now including immigrants, former slaves and children of slaves, and native Americans, still lived in wretched but relatively stable niches of society with few choices available: boys usually followed their fathers and continued the occupations of family members, or struck out on their own to pursue similar occupations. Girls usually married these boys or took jobs as domestics or as factory or shop workers. But middle- and upper-class children looked to a future fraught with choices. Thus, the turn of the twentieth century marked the first time in human history that millions of young people had some measure of control over their own destinies.

ANNOTATED CHRONOLOGY

1800

Mrs. Pilkington's *The Asiatic Princess* (a pseudo-Eastern moralistic tale in which a Siamese princess, Princess Merjee, discovers the West and receives an education "befitting a future ruler"; her European traveling companions are a black girl rescued from slavery and an English couple; published in London in two volumes; the author's other work includes *Tale of the Hermitage*, E. Newbery, 1798; *Biography for Boys . . . ,* E. Newbery, 1799; *Biography for Girls . . . ,* E. Newbery, 1799; *New Tales of the Castle; or, The Noble Emigrants: A Story of Modern Times,* J. Harris, 1800; *Marvellous Adventures, or The Vicissitudes of a Cat. In Which Are Sketches of the Characters of the Different Young Ladies and Gentlemen into Whose Hands Grimalkin Came,* London, 1802; *Mentorial Tales, for the Instruction of Young Ladies Just Leaving School and Entering Upon the Theatre of Life,* London, 1802; *Parental Care Producing Practical Virtue . . . : Interspersed with a Description of the Inhabitants of Russia, and a Variety of Interesting Anecdotes of Peter the Great,* London, 1810; *A Reward for Attentive Studies; or, Moral and Entertaining Stories,* Stroud, ca. 1815; *The Shipwreck; or, Misfortune the Inspirer of Virtuous Sentiments,* W. Darton, 1819; Mrs. Pilkington is the pseudonym of Mary [Hopkins] Pilkington).

1804

Ann and Jane Taylor's *Original Poems for Infant Minds* (two volumes of "moral songs or short tales in verse" designed to appeal to children's interests; although moralistic, the authors' work was light, simple, and based on children's experiences; *Rhymes for the Nursery,* Darton and Harvey, 1806, contained Jane Taylor's "Twinkle twinkle little star"; Jane Taylor wrote under the pseudonym Q. Q.; the authors' other work includes *Signor*

Topsy Turvey's Wonderful Magic Lantern, or The World Turned Upside Down, Tabart, 1810; *Limed Twigs to Catch Young Birds, being Easy Reading for Children: Sketches from a Youthful Circle,* Darton and Harvey, n.d.; Ann Taylor's popular poem, "My Mother," was published in book form with illustrations in 1815). LC, PFL

1805

Edward Baldwin's *Fables Ancient and Modern* (a collection of fables adapted for the use of children and published in London; Edward Baldwin is pseudonym of William Godwin; author's other work published in London includes *Gaffer Gray,* n.p., 1806, and a sequel to the 1803 edition of *Old Dame Trot and Her Comical Cat,* titled *A Continuation of Old Dame Trot and Her Comical Cat,* n.p., 1806).

The Comic Adventures of Old Mother Hubbard and Her Dog (a traditional sixteen-page chapbook version of a popular nursery rhyme; contains three-quarter page copper illustrations with neat, bold, legible, and well-spaced engraved verses; a sequel followed; the first of a series of chapbooks published in London by John Harris, former manager of Elizabeth Newbery's bookshop; other popular chapbooks published by Harris include *The Talking Bird; or, Dame Trudge and Her Parrot,* 1806; *The Courtship and Marriage of Jerry and Kitty,* 1814; *Little Rhymes for Little Folks,* 1823).

The Silver Penny, for the Amusement and Instruction of Good Children (anonymous; pseudonym J. Horner, Esq., a Fellow of the Royal Society of ABC; an ABC chapbook which features a key word for each letter of the alphabet; a quatrain and an attractively framed woodcut illustrate each letter; a moral concludes the work; printed from Sidney's Press, New Haven, Connecticut; a British edition was printed by James Kendrew in York ca.1820).

1806

Mason Locke Weems's *The Life of Washington the Great* (the fourth augmented edition of "Parson Weems'" biography of George Washington; published in Augusta, Georgia, but the first edition, *A History of the Life and Death, Virtues, and Exploits, of General George Washington,* was published in Georgetown, D.C., 1800; this fourth edition is embellished with such inventions as the story of Washington cutting down the cherry tree with his hatchet and declaring, "Father, I cannot tell a lie"; the author's work includes *The Life of General Francis Marion,* n.p., 1809; *God's Revenge Against Drunkenness,* n.p., 1812; *The Life of Doctor Benjamin Franklin,* Philadelphia, 1815; *The Life of William Penn,* Carey and Lea, 1822).

1807

Charles and Mary Lamb's *Tales from Shakespeare* (in two volumes; twenty of Shakespeare's plays cast into short prose tales; probably illustrated by William Mulready and engraved by William Blake, printed for Thomas Hodgkins in London; authors' other [combined] work includes *Mrs. Leicester's School,* London, 1809; *Poetry for Children,* M. J. Godwin, 1809; Charles Lamb wrote for children *The King and Queen of Hearts,* Thomas Hodgkins, 1805; *The Adventures of Ulysses,* M. J. Godwin, 1808; *Prince Dorus,* M. J. Godwin, 1811).

Sir William Roscoe's *The Butterfly's Ball* (the first of a series of entertaining books in a "Cabinet of Amusement and Instruction" published in Britain by John Harris, reprinted from the *Gentlemen's Magazine;* a rhymed fantasy written by a prominent attorney and member of Parliament for his young son; first illustrated with colored engravings by William Mulready, who later became a member of the Royal Academy and a designer of Britain's first postage stamp; many imitations followed in Britain and America). NYPL

Elizabeth Turner's *The Daisy; or Cautionary Stories in Verse* (typical of the cautionary or moralistic verse of the period; published in Philadelphia by Jacob Johnson; author's other work includes *The Cowslip; or, More Cautionary Stories in Verse,* J. Harris, 1811; *The Pink; or, Child's First Book of Poetry,* London, 1823; *The Blue-Bell; or, Tales and Fables,* Derby, 1838; *The Crocus: Another Series of Cautionary Stories,* London, 1844; *Short Poems for Young Children,* London, 1850).

1808

The Cries of New York (anonymous; a distinctively American street-cries book; such books were popular in both England and America; it was first issued by Samuel Wood; an 1825 edition by Mahlon Day and illustrated with woodcuts is titled *New York Street Cries in Rhyme*).

Mrs. Dorset's *The Peacock at Home* (a popular successor to Roscoe's *The Butterfly's Ball* which sold forty thousand copies in one year and was followed by numerous imitations such as this; the author's full name is Catherine Ann Turner Dorset; published in London).

1813

The History of the Celebrated Nanny Goose (probably the earliest printed folktale version of the popular ballad "The Fox and the Goose," which shares similar elements of plot with "The Story of the Three Little Pigs,"

1813 *continued*

but the latter did not appear in print until James Halliwell-Phillips's fifth edition of *The Nursery Rhymes of England,* 1853; printed for S. Hood in Soho, London, by Jones; in 1833, the tale was retold as *The History of the Prince Renardo and the Lady Goosiana* and published in London at Leicester Square). TPL

Peter Piper's Practical Principles of Plain and Perfect Pronunciation (anonymous; printed in London; an unusual and imaginative use of words and subjects, presented in alliterative alphabet verses; colored illustrations; first published in America ca. 1830 by Carter Andrews and Co., Lancaster, Pennsylvania; a poor companion piece which dealt with the multiplication tables was *Marmaduke Multiply's Merry Method of Making Minor Mathematicians, or The Multiplication Tables,* London, 1817).

1814

Mrs. Sherwood's *Little Henry and His Bearer* (a moralistc story set in India which was designed to show the worth of women missionaries, but features the conversations of five-year-old Henry and his bearer; translated into many languages; published by the American Tract Society; the author's work reflects the belief that the child is inherently evil; the author's other work includes a popular four-part work, *The Fairchild Family,* published between 1818 and 1847 in New York by F. A. Stokes; *Caroline Mordaunt,* published in London by W. Darton in 1835, which contains a colored frontispiece, the first recorded use of the Baxter color process, using woodblocks, as adapted by the Kronheims; *The Traditions,* W. Lane, 1795; *Shanty the Blacksmith,* Darton, 1800; *The Infant's Progress,* 1809-1810; *The Child's Pilgrim's Progress*, n.p., ca. 1816; *The History of Henry Milner*, 1823-1837; *The De Cliffords,* n.p., 1847; *The Ayah and the Lady,* n.p., 1813; *The Indian Pilgrim,* n.p., 1817; *The History of Theophilus and Sophia,* Houlston, 1818; *A Drive in the Coach Through the Streets of London,* Houlston, 1819; *History of Henry Fairchild and Charles Trueman,* Sunday and Adult School Union, 1819; *The Little Woodman, and His Dog Caesar,* Houlston, 1819; *The Governess; or, The Little Female Academy,* Houlston, 1820; *The Hedge of Thorns,* S. Wood, 1820; *The History of Emily and Her Brothers,* Sunday and Adult School Union, 1820; *The History of Little George and His Penny,* William Hyde, 1820; *The Two Sisters,* Houlston, 1820; *Memoirs of Sergeant Dale, His Daughter and the Orphan Mary,* Houlston, 1821; *Mrs. Sherwood's Primer,* Houlston, 1821; *The Busy Bee,* Flagg and Gould, 1821; *The Errand-Boy,* Lincoln and Edmands, 1821; *The Infant's Progress,* Armstrong, 1821; *The May-Bee,* Houlston, 1821; *The Orphan Boy,* Armstrong, 1821; *The Re-Captured Negro . . . ,* Armstrong, 1821; *Dazee, or The Re-captured Negro,* Gilman, 1822; *The History of Henry Milner, A Little Boy Who Was Not Brought Up According to the Fashions of This World,* Hatchard, 1822; *The Orphans of Normandy,* Hatchard, 1822; *The Village School Mistress,* J. Offor, 1822; *Charles Lorraine,* Armstrong, 1823; *The Blind Man and Little George,* Armstrong, 1823; *The Lady of the Manor,* Houlston, 1823-1829; *Little Robert and the Owl,* Armstrong, 1824; *The History of Little Lucy and Her Dhaye,* Armstrong, 1824; *The Penny Tract,* W. Tyler, 1824; *The Rose; A Fairy Tale,* Armstrong, 1824; *The Shawl,* Darton, 1824; *The Wishing-Cap . . . ,* Houlston, 1824; *Juliana Oakley,* Cooke, 1825; *My Three Uncles and The Swiss Cottage,* Darton, 1825; *My Uncle Timothy,* Knight and Lacey, 1825; *The History of Susan Gray,* Bacon, 1825; *The Pink Tippet, or The Contrast in Sabbath Scholars Displayed,* Loring, 1825; *Julian Percival,* Houlston, 1826; *Mary Anne,* Religious Tract Society, ca. 1826; *Clara Stephens; or, The White Rose,* Sunday School Union, 1827; *Edward Mansfield,* Whipple and Lawrence, 1827; *Susannah,* Longman, 1827; *The Happy Choice,* Sunday School Union, 1827; *The Shepherd of the Pyrenees,* Sunday School Union, 1827; *The Youth's Casket; or, A Teacher's Present to the Most Studious Scholars in School,* Loring, 1827; *Mary Grant; or, The Secret Fault,* Sunday School Union, 1828; *My Aunt Kate,* Houlston, 1828; *Procrastination,* Fauntleroy and Burton, 1828; *The Broken Hyacinth; or Ellen and Sophia,* Sunday School Union, 1828; *The History of Lucy Clare Hartford,* Robinson, 1828; *The History of Mary Saunders,* D. F. Robinson, 1828; *The Juvenile Wreath,* Houlston, 1828; *Arzoomund,* Houlston, 1829; *Emancipation,* Wellington, 1829; *The Butterfly,* Melrose, 1829; *The Millennium,* Leavitt, 1829; *The Orange Grove,* Houlston, 1829; *The Rainbow,* Houlston, 1829; *Abdallah,* Religious Tract Society, 1830; *A Visit to Grandpa,* Houlston, ca. 1830; *Intimate Friends,* Houlston, 1830; *The Children of the Hartz Mountains,* Sunday School Union, 1830; *The Father's Eye,* T. Melrose, 1830; *The Improved Boy,* S. Babcock, 1830; *The Golden Chain,* T. Melrose, 1830; *The Little Beggars,* General Protestant Episcopal Sunday School Union, 1830; *The Red Book,* Religious Tract Society, 1830; *The Two Dolls,* Houlston, 1830; *Easy Questions,* Sidney's Press, 1831; *Obedience,* T. Melrose, 1831; *Poor Burruff,* Houlston, 1831; *Roxobel,* Houlston, 1831; *The Babes in the Wood of the New World,* Day, 1831; *The Fawns,* Houlston, 1831; *The Hills,* Houlston, 1831; *Emmeline,* T. Melrose, 1832; *Home,* S. Babcock, 1833; *Victoria,* J. Hatchard, 1833; *The Flowers of the Forest,* George, Latimer & Co., 1833; *The History of Mrs. Catherine Crawley,* Houlston, 1833; *Social Tales for the Young,* Whetham, 1835; *The Lofty and Lowly Way,* T. Melrose, 1835; *The Violet Leaf,* B. Olds, 1835; *A Rustic Excusion for Tarry-At-Home Travellers,* J. S. Horton, 1836; *Little Arthur,* Houlston, 1836; *Katharine Seward,* Houlston, 1837; *The Thunderstorm,* Cecil Mortimer, 1837; *Seaside Stories,* Darton, 1838; *The Little Negroes,* Houlston, 1838; *Biography Illustrated,* Darton, 1839; *Grandma Parker; or, The Father's Return,* Darton, 1839-1847; *Scenes from Real Life for the Young,* Darton,

1814 *continued*

1839; *The Former and the Latter Rain,* Melrose, 1839; *The Little Girl's Keepsake,* Darton, 1839; *The Last Days of Boosy; or, Sequel to Little Henry and His Beaver,* Sunday School Union, ca. 1840; *The Traveller,* Darton, 1840; *The History of John Marten, A Sequel to The Life of Henry Milner,* Hatchard, 1844; *Think Before You Act,* Darton, 1845; *Duty Is Safety; or Troublesome Tom,* Appleton, 1847; *Joys and Sorrows of Childhood,* Darton, 1847-1862; *The Golden Garden of Inestimable Delights,* Hatchard, 1849; *Family Tales,* Darton, 1850; *The Heron's Plume and Other Tales,* Darton, ca. 1850; *Clever Stories for Clever Boys and Girls* [containing *Think Before You Act, Jack the Sailor Boy, Duty is Safe*], Appleton, 1851; *The De Cliffords,* Darton, 1851; *The Mirror Maidens in the Days of Queen Bess,* Hatchard, 1851; *Robert and Frederick; A Book for Boys,* Bohn, 1853; *Boys Will Be Boys,* Darton, 1854; *The Story Book of Wonders,* T. Nelson, 1855; *Popular Tales,* S. Marshall, 1861; *The Idiot Boy,* Houlston, ca. 1870; *Frank Beauchamp; or, The Sailor's Family,* Darton, 1877; *The White Pigeon,* Darton, 1877; *English Mary,* J. Loring, 18__; *Jack the Sailor Boy,* Darton, 184__; *The Cloak,* Darton, 18__; *The Gipsy Babes,* Houlston, n.d.; *The Poor Man of Colour,* n.p., n.d.; Mrs. Sherwood is the pseudonym of Martha Mary Butt). LC, TPL

Johann David Rudolph Wyss's *The Swiss Family Robinson* (translated from the German *Der Schweizerische Robinson* by William Godwin; published at Zurich in two parts in 1812 and 1813 by the author's son; published in England by William Godwin under his wife Mary's name, a French author, Mme de Monotholieu, expanded the story into five volumes between 1824 and 1826; in 1879, William H. G. Kingston made a new translation which omitted "the long sententious lectures" in the original to which he objected; Audrey Clark used H. Firth's 1878 translation from the French and German sources as the basis for her rendering of the story for the 1957 "Children's Illustrated Classics" series, published by J. M. Dent in England).

1819

Geoffrey Crayon's *The Sketch Book* (a collection of essays and tales based on folklore, in two volumes, published in London by John Miller; includes "Rip Van Winkle" and "The Legend of Sleepy Hollow"; appropriated by children; Geoffrey Crayon is the pseudonym of Washington Irving, a popular American author; Irving's *Knickerbocker's History of New York* was edited for children by Anne C. Moore and published in 1928). CU, YU

1820

Sir Walter Scott's *Ivanhoe: A Romance* (in three volumes, published by Constable in Edinburgh; a novel presenting English medieval life, sometimes inaccurately; often used as school reading assignments by older children; the author's other work includes *The Lady of the Lake,* Edinburgh, 1810; *Waverly: Or, 'Tis Sixty Years Since,* three volumes, Edinburgh, 1814; *Guy Mannering; or the Astrologer,* three volumes, Edinburgh, 1815; *Rob Roy,* three volumes, Edinburgh, 1818; *The Monastery,* three volumes, Edinburgh, 1820; *The Abbot,* Edinburgh, 1820; *Kenilworth,* Edinburgh, 1821; *The Fortunes of Nigel,* Edinburgh, 1822; *Peveril of the Peak,* Edinburgh, 1822; *Quentin Durward,* three volumes, Edinburgh, 1823; *Redgauntlet: Tales of the Crusaders,* three volumes, Edinburgh, 1825; *Woodstock,* three volumes, Edinburgh, 1826; *Tales of a Grandfather,* three volumes, Cadell, 1828-1831; under pseudonym of Jebediah Cleisbotham, the author wrote *Tales of My Landlord* series). TUL

1821

James Fenimore Cooper's *The Spy: A Tale of the Neutral Ground* (the first of the Leatherstocking novels about Indians living in the forests and on the prairies of North America, published in New York by Wiley and Halstead; the rest of the series includes *The Pioneers,* Wiley, 1823; *The Prairie,* Carey, Lea and Carey, 1827; *The Pathfinder,* Lea and Blanchard, 1840; *The Deerslayer,* Lea and Blanchard, 1841; the author's other work includes *Tales for Fifteen; or, Imagination and Heart,* Wiley, 1823; *Lionel Lincoln; or, The Leaguer of Boston,* Wiley, 1825; *The Last of the Mohicans: a Narrative of 1757,* Carey and Lea, 1826; *The Red Rover: A Tale,* Carey, Lea and Carey, 1828; *Notions of the Americans: Picked Up by a Travelling Bachelor,* Carey, 1828; *The Wept of Wish-ton-Wish: A Tale,* Carey, 1829; *The Water Witch; or, The Skimmer of the Seas: A Tale,* Carey, 1830; *The Bravo: A Tale,* Carey, 1831; *Homeward Bound; or, The Chase: A Tale of the Sea,* Carey, 1838; *Home As Found,* Lea and Blanchard, 1838; *Mercedes of Castile; or, The Voyage of Cathay,* Lea and Blanchard, 1840; *The Two Admirals: A Tale,* Lea and Blanchard, 1842; *The Wing-and-Wing; or, Le Feu-Follet: A Tale,* Lea and Blanchard, 1842; *Le Mouchoir: An Autobiographical Romance,* Wilson & Co., Brother Jonathan Press, 1843, also published as *Autobiography of a Pocket Handkerchief; Wyandotté; or, The Hutted Knoll: A Tale,* Lea and Blanchard, 1843; *Ned Myers; or, A Life Before the Mast,* Lea and Blanchard, 1843; *Afloat and Ashore; or, the Adventures of Miles Wallingford,* J. F. Cooper, 1844; *Satanstoe; or, The Littlepage Manuscripts: A Tale of the Colony,* Burgess, 1845; *The Chainbearer; or, The Littlepage Manuscripts,* Burgess, 1845; *Lives of Distinguished Naval Officers,* Carey, 1846; *The Redskins; or, Indian and Injin: Being the Conclusion of the Littlepage Manuscripts,* Burgess, 1846; *The Crater; or, Vulcan's Peak: A Tale of the Pacific,* Burgess, 1847; *Jack Tier; or, The Florida Reef,* Burgess, 1848; *The Oak Openings; or The Bee-Hunter,* Burgess, 1848; *The Sea Lions; or The Lost Sealers,* Stringer, 1849; *The*

1821 *continued*
Ways of the Hour: A Tale, Putnam, 1850; Susan Fenimore Cooper wrote *Mount Vernon: A Letter to the Children of America,* Appleton, 1858). NYPL, YU

1822

Mary Belson Elliott's *The Orphan Boy, or A Journey to Bath* (a popular moralistic tale of how an orphan boy made good; typical of author's numerous artless and "edifying" tales and verses published by the Quaker firm of Darton; author's other work, published in London by Darton except as noted, includes *The History of Tommy Two-Shoes,* Litchfield: Hosmer, 1808; *The Mice and Their Picnic. A Good Moral Tale. By a Looking-Glass Maker,* 1810; *Grateful Tributes; or Recollections from Infancy,* 1811; *The Baby's Holiday,* 1812; *Industry and Idleness,* 1816; *Simple Truths,* 1816; *Little Lessons for Little Folks,* 1818; *The Modern Goody Two- Shoes . . . ,* 1819; *The Rambles of a Butterfly,* 1819; *The Wax Taper; or, the Effects of Bad Habits,* 1819; *The Gift of Friendship,* 1822; *The Sunflower,* 1822; *The Two Edwards,* 1823; *The Rose,* 1824; *The Bird's Nest,* 1825?; *Dumb Animals; or, Cruelty Punished,* ca. 1825; *The Greedy Child Cured,* 1825; *The Little Meddler; or, One Fault Leads To Many,* 1825; *Gems in the Mind, or Traits and Habits of Childhood in Verse,* Lancaster, Pennsylvania: Buffam, 1828; *Amusement for Little Girls' Leisure Hours,* Philadelphia: Ash, 1838; *The Contrast; or, How To Be Happy,* 1840?; *Tales for Boys,* 1846; *Tales for Girls,* 1846; *Beauty But Skin Deep,* McLoughlin, 1856).

1823

Jacob and Wilhelm Grimm's *German Popular Stories* (translated from the German *Kinder und Haus Märchen* by Edgar Taylor; volume one was published by C. Baldwin in London, 1823; volume two was published in London by J. Robins, 1826; illustrated with twenty-two etchings by George Cruikshank; the original two volumes, *Hausmärchen,* which were printed in Berlin by Georg Reimer, 1812-1824, marked the beginning of serious folktale collecting on the continent; the many translators of the Grimm collection include Lucy Crane, Margaret Hunt, and Wanda Gág).

Clement G. Moore's *A Visit from St. Nicholas* (the first American "classic" poem for children, written for the author's own children and originally published anonymously in New York in the *Troy Sentinel,* subsequently in other newspapers, and in the *Citizen's and Farmer's Almanack* for 1825 published in Philadelphia by Griggs and Dickinson, 1824, pp. 17-18; not published under author's name until 1844; popularly referred to as "The Night Before Christmas"; numerous editions exist including Louis Prang's 1864 edition). IU, LC

1824

Mother Goose's Quarto; or, Melodies Complete (published in Boston by Munroe and Francis; contains 180 rhymes, drawn from the Isaiah Thomas reprint of the Newbery collection of rhymes and the Tabard Company's *Songs for the Nursery,* 1805; a subsequent edition, *The Only True Mother Goose Melodies,* contains 170 rhymes; most of the short rhymes were taken from Newbery's *Melody,* while the longer ones were taken from *Gammer Gurton's Garland, or The Nursery Parnassus,* compiled in 1784 by Joseph Ritson, the first collector inspired by the *Melody,* which he had bought in 1781; Ritson's *Garland* was greatly enlarged by 1810; the Munroe and Francis edition continues to be an important source book for collectors to the present).

1826

The Juvenile Miscellany (the first important children's magazine in America; emphasized history and biography; edited by Lydia Maria Child until she was forced to resign because of her abolitionist views; Sarah Josepha Hale, who wrote "Mary Had a Little Lamb," published in *Juvenile Miscellany* in 1830, took over the editorship; the magazine expired in 1834). NYPL

1827

Peter Parley's *The Tales of Peter Parley about America* (the first of a series of travel books in which an old man tells some children about his experiences in Boston, New York, Hartford, and Charleston, introduces the children to the life of some American Indians living around 1750, describes the countries of Peru and Brazil, and gives a brief history of America from Columbus to the Revolutionary War; illustrated with forty-four woodcuts by Abel Bowen and George L. Brown, and published in Boston by Carter, Hendee and Co.; the author edited and published the periodicals *Parley's Magazine,* 1833-1834, and *Robert's Merry Museum,* 1841-1850; the author's other work includes *Peter Parley's Stories About Curious and Wonderful Birds,* Mahlon, 1803; *The Adventures of Billy Bump on the Pacific,* Williams, n.d.; *The Child's Arithmetic . . . ,* Goodrich, 1818; editor, *Cabinet of Curiosities, Natural and Artificial, and Historical, Selected from the Most Authentic Records, Ancient and Modern,* Hartford, 1822; *The Tales of Peter Parley About America,* Goodrich, 1827; *The Child's Botany,* Goodrich, 1828; *The Tales of Peter Parley About Europe,* Goodrich, 1828; *Peter Parley's Story of the Bird Nest,* Goodrich, 1829; *Peter Parley's Story of the Faithful Dog,* Goodrich, 1829; *Peter Parley's Story of Little Prisoners,* Goodrich, 1829; *Peter Parley's Story of the Little Soldiers,* Goodrich, 1829; *Peter Parley's Winter Evening Tales,* Carter, 1829; *Stories About Captain John Smith of Virginia,* Huntington, 1829; *One of Peter Parley's Winter Evening*

1827 *continued*

Stories, Carter, 1830; *Peter Parley's Juvenile Tales. A New-Year's Present for Children,* Carter, 1830; *Peter Parley's Stories About Balloons,* Mahlon, 1830?; *Peter Parley's Story of the Mocking Bird,* Carter, 1830; *Peter Parley's Story of the Pleasure Boat,* Boston, 1830; *Peter Parley's Story of the Soldier and His Dog,* Boston, 1830; *Peter Parley's Tales About Asia,* Gray and Bowen, 1830; *Story of the Little Drummer Boy,* Boston, 1830; *Story of the Trapper,* Carter, 1830; *The Tales of Peter Parley About Europe,* Hendee, 1830; *The First Book of History for Children,* Richardson, 1831; *Peter Parley's Tales About the Islands in the Pacific Ocean,* Gray, 1831; *Peter Parley's Tales About Great Britain,* Jewett, 1832; *Peter Parley's Tales About South America,* Jewett, 1832; *Peter Parley's Tales About the Sun, Moon, and Stars,* Gray, 1832; S. Goodrich, *A Book of Mythology for Youth,* Richardson, 1832; *A Book of Quadrupeds for Youth,* Hill, 1832; *The Child's Geology,* Peck, 1832; *Peter Parley's Tales About Ancient and Modern Greece,* Collins, 1832; *Peter Parley's Tales About the State and City of New York,* Pendleton, 1832; *A Present from Peter Parley to All His Friends,* Pomeroy, 1832; *Peter Parley's Story of the Orphans,* Allen, 1833; *Peter Parley's Story of the Freshet; or, the Morning Walk,* Allen, 1833; *Peter Parley's Story of the Little Gardener,* Allen 1833; *Peter Parley's Story of the Little Wanderers,* Allen, 1833; *Peter Parley's Story of Robert Seaboy, the Bird Robber,* Allen, 1833; *Peter Parley's Story of Two Friends; or, Harry and His Dog,* Allen, 1833; *Peter Parley's Story of the Umbrella and the Tiger,* Allen, 1833; *Peter Parley's Tales About Ancient Rome,* Carter, 1833; *The Every Day Book for Youth,* Carter, 1834; *Peter Parley's Book of Bible Stories,* Lilly, 1834; *Peter Parley's Short Stories for Long Nights,* Boston, 1834; *The Tales of Peter Parley About Africa,* Desilver, 1835; *Parley's Ancient History and Customs,* Mahlon, 1836; *Parley's History of the Manners of the Jews,* Mahlon, 1836; *Parley's Juvenile Lectures on Insects,* Mahlon, 1836; *The Tales of Peter Parley About Asia,* Desilver, 1836; *Peter Parley's Arithmetic,* Hendee, 1837; *Peter Parley's Common School History,* American Stationers', 1838; *Peter Parley's Picture Book,* Colman, 1839; *Peter Parley's Rambles in England, Wales, Scotland and Ireland,* Colman, 1839; *Peter Parley's Farewell,* Colman, 1840; *Peter Parley's Wonders of the Earth, Sea, and Sky,* Colman, 1840; *Moral Tales,* Littlefield, 1840; *Peter Parley's Common-School Primer,* Morton, 1840; *Curiosities of Human Nature,* Bradbury, 1843; *Famous Men of Ancient Times,* Bradbury, 1843; *Famous Men of Modern Times,* Bradbury, 1843; *Lives of Benefactors,* Thompson, 1843; *Lives of Celebrated American Indians,* Bradbury, 1843; *Make the Best of It,* Wiley, 1843; *History of the Indians of North and South America,* Bradbury, 1844; *Lights and Shadows of African History,* Bradbury, 1844; *Lights and Shadows of American History,* Bradbury, 1844; *Lights and Shadows of Asiatic History,* Bradbury,

1844; *Lights and Shadows of European History,* Bradbury, 1844; *Lives of Celebrated Women,* Bradbury, 1844; *The Manners, Customs, and Antiquities of the Indians of North and South America,* Bradbury, 1844; *Manners and Customs of the Principal Nations of the World,* Thomas, 1844; *Peter Parley's Little Leaves for Little Readers,* Munroe, 1844; *Persevere and Prosper; or, The Life of a Siberian Sable Hunter,* Sheldon, 1844; *Dick Boldhero; or, A Tale of Adventures in South America,* Sorin, 1845; S. Goodrich, *A Home In the Sea; or, The Adventures of Philip Brusque,* Sorin, 1845; *The Truth-Finder; or, The Story of Inquisitive Jack,* Sorin, 1845; *Right Is Might,* Sorin, 1846; *Tales of Land and Sea,* Sorin, 1846; *Life of Louis Philippe, Late King of the French,* Ball, 1848; *Take Care of Number One; or, Good To Me Includes Good To Thee,* Darton, 1848; *Recollections of a Lifetime,* n.p., 1851; *Stories About New York,* Leavitt, 1853; *The Balloon Travels of Robert Merry and His Young Friends,* Derby, 1855; *The Book of Trades, Arts and Professions Relative To Food, Clothing, Shelter, Traveling and Ornament,* Darton, 1855; *The Life and Adventures of Thomas Titmouse, and Other Stories,* Knight, ca. 1855; *Peter Parley's Book of Travels and Adventures Over Various Countries in Europe,* Derby, 1857; *Peter Parley's Kaleidoscope,* Barnitz, 1857; *Peter Parley's Thousand and One Stories of Fact and Fancy, Wit and Humor, Rhyme, Reason and Romance,* Miller, 1857; *Parley's Four Quarters of the World,* Desilver, 1860; *The American Child's Pictorial History of the United States,* Butler, 1861; *Peter Parley's Own Story,* Sheldon, 1864; *Peter Parley's Merry Stories,* Miller, 1869; *The Adventures of Billy Bump,* Sheldon, 1871; Peter Parley books were published and many imitations appeared in England; Peter Parley is pseudonym of Samuel Griswold Goodrich). DPL, DU, FLP, LC

The Youth's Companion (a four-page-weekly children's paper started by Nathaniel Willis; publication appealed to the entire family and achieved the highest circulation of any nineteenth-century magazine; merged with *The American Boy* in 1929). NYPL

1829

Mrs. Cameron's *The Warning Clock* (a moralistic, didactic story by Mrs. Sherwood's sister; published in London by Day; the author's other work includes *The Mother's Grave,* Houlston, 1819; *The History of Fidelity and Profession,* Samuel Wood, 1820; *The Holiday Queen,* Houlston, 1820; *The Polite Little Children,* Newman, 1820; *Martin and His Two Little Scholars at Sunday School,* Houlston, 1821; *The History of Susan and Esther Hall,* Sunday School Union, 1821; *The Caskets,* Boston, 1822; *The Sister's Friend,* Armstrong, 1824; *The Story of a Kind Little Boy,* Sunday School Union, 1825; *The Baby and the Doll,* Houlston, 1826; *Emma and Her Nurse,*

1829 *continued*
Sunday School Union, 1827; *Amelia,* Houlston, 1828; *The History of Margaret Whyte,* Houlston, 1829; *Memory,* Houlston, 1830; *Dialogues for the Entertainment and Instruction of Youth,* Houlston, 1837; *The Fruits of Ed.,* Houlston, 1837; *The Use of Talents,* Houlston, 1837; *The Raven and the Dove,* Sunday School Union, 1842; *The Farmer's Daughter,* Appleton, 1843; *The Pastor's Stories,* Waite, 1845; *I Can Do Without It,* Sunday School Union, n.d.; *The Bee-Hive Cottage,* Sunday School Union, n.d.; *The Seeds of Greediness,* Sunday School Union, n.d.; *The Two Lambs,* Mahlon Day, 18__). TPL

1831

Eleanor Mure's *The Story of the Three Bears* (an early Canadian manuscript of a popular nursery story often attributed to Robert Southey because he was the first to publish the story in London in 1837 in his literary magazine, *The Doctor;* this verse version features, as does Southey's, a silver-haired old woman instead of the well-known Goldilocks who was first used in a volume of tales, *A Treasury of Pleasure-Books for Young People,* edited and collected by Joseph Cundall, 1856, illustrated by the author in color; first published in book form by the Friends of the Lillian H. Smith and Edgar Osborne Collections, Toronto Public Library, in 1967). TPL, YU

1834

The Baptist Children's Magazine, and Sabbath Scholars' Reward (a monthly edited by J. F. Winks of Leicester; editor also edited the *Baptist Youth's Magazine,* 1859-1861).

1835

Jacob Abbott's *The Little Scholar Learning To Talk: A Picture Book for Rollo* (the first of the Rollo series, by an American minister, in which a child's experiences are described in order to teach the reader particular concepts or values; published in Boston by John Allen; other books in the Rollo series include *Rollo Learning To Read,* Allen, 1835; *Rollo At Work,* Webb, 1837; *Rollo At Play,* Carter, 1838; *Rollo At School,* Webb, 1839; *Rollo's Vacation,* Webb, 1839; *Rollo's Experiments,* Allen, 1839; *Rollo's Museum,* Weeks, 1839; *Rollo's Travels,* Webb, 1840; *Rollo's Correspondence,* Carter, 1840; *The Rollo Reader,* n.d.; *The Rollo Code of Morals,* Crocker, 1841; *The Rollo Philosophy,* in four parts: *Part I: Water,* Gould, 1842, *Part II: Air,* Webb, 1842, *Part III: Fire,* Otis, 1843, *Part IV: The Sky,* Otis, 1843; *Rollo on the Atlantic,* Reynolds, 1853; *Rollo in Paris,* Reynolds, 1854; *Rollo in Switzerland,* Reynolds, 1854; *Rollo's Tour in Europe,* Reynolds, 1855; *Rollo in London,* Reynolds, 1855; *Rollo on the Rhine,* Reynolds, 1855; *Rollo in Scotland,* Reynolds, 1856; *Rollo in Holland,* Brown, 1857; *Rollo in*

Geneva, Brown, 1857; *Rollo in Naples,* Brown, 1858; *Rollo in Rome,* Brown, 1858; the popular Rollo storybooks, which contained stories from the books in the Rollo series, were published, some by Phillips and some by Sheldon, between 1857 and 1864: *Labor Lost,* Phillips, 1857; *The Two Wheelbarrows,* Sheldon, 1861; *Causey Building,* Sheldon, 1864; *Rollo's Garden,* Phillips, 1857; *The Apple Gathering,* Phillips, 1857; *Georgie,* Sheldon, 1857; *Rollo in the Woods,* Sheldon, 1864; *The Steeple Trap,* Sheldon, 1864; *The Halo Around the Moon,* Phillips, 1857; *The Freshet,* Sheldon, 1863; *Blue-Berrying,* Phillips, 1857; *Trouble on the Mountains,* Sheldon, 1857; *The Rocking Horse; or, The Rollo and Lucy First Book of Poetry,* Childs, 1863; *Carlo; or, The Rollo and Lucy Second Book of Poetry,* Childs, 1863; *The Canary Bird; or, The Rollo and Lucy Third Book of Poetry,* Childs, 1863; under the pseudonym of Erodore, the author's other work includes *The Little Philosopher,* 1829; *Early Piety,* 1831; *The Mount Vernon Reader for Junior Classes,* 1838; *The Family Story Book,* Volume II, Harvard, 1835; *The Sabbath Day Book for Boys and Girls,* 1835; under the pseudonym of Marianna, the Children's Fireside series which includes *Every Day Duty,* Leavitt, 1834; *Right and Wrong . . . ,* Pierce, 1834; *The Way for a Child to be Saved,* Leavitt, 1835; *The Way of Salvation Explained,* Leavitt, 1835; the Caleb and Jonas series which include *Caleb in Town,* Crocker, 1839; *Caleb in the Country,* Crocker, 1839; *Jonas's Stories Related to Rollo and Lucy,* Ticknor, 1839; *Jonas as a Judge,* Ticknor, 1840; *Jonas on a Farm in Summer,* Ticknor, 1842, *Jonas on a Farm in Winter,* Ticknor, 1842; the Lucy series published by Mussey which includes *Cousin Lucy at Study,* 1842; *Stories Told to Rollo's Cousin Lucy,* 1842; *Cousin Lucy's Conversation,* 1842; *Cousin Lucy Among the Mountains,* 1842; *Cousin Lucy on the Sea-Shore,* 1842; the Marco Paul series published in New York by T. Harrington Carter in 1843, which includes *Marco Paul in the City of New York, Marco Paul on the Erie Canal, Marco Paul in the Forests of Maine, Marco Paul in Vermont, Marco Paul in the City of Boston, Marco Paul at the Springfield Armory;* the Franconia series published in New York between 1850 and 1853 by Harper Brothers, which includes *Malleville, Mary Bell, Ellen Linn, Wallace, Beechnut, Stuyvesant, Agnes, Mary Erskine, Rodolphus, Caroline;* the Harper Story Book series published by Harper between 1854 and 1857 which includes *Bruno,* 1854; *Willie and the Mortgage,* 1854; *The Strait Gate,* 1855; *The Little Louvre,* 1855; *Frank,* 1855; *Emma,* 1855; *Virginia,* 1855; *Timboo and Joliba,* 1855; *Timboo and Fanny,* 1855; *The Harper Establishment,* 1855; *Franklin,* 1855; *The Studio,* 1855; *The Story of Ancient History,* 1855; *The Story of English History,* 1856; *The Story of American History,* 1856; *John True,* 1856; *Elfred,* 1856; *The Museum,* 1856; *The Engineer,* 1856; *Rambles Among the Alps,* 1856; *The Three Gold Dollars, 1856; The Gibraltar Gallery,* 1856; *The Alcove,* 1856; *Dialogues for . . . Young People,* 1856; *The Great Elm,* 1856; *Aunt Margaret,*

1835 *continued*

1856; *Vernon,* 1857; *Carl and Jocki,* 1857; *Lapstone,* 1857; *Orkney the Peacemaker,* 1857; *Judge Justin,* 1857; *Minigo,* 1857; *Jasper,* 1857; *Congo,* 1857; *Viola and Her Little Brother Arno,* 1857; *Little Paul,* 1857; The Little Learner or Harper's Picture Books for the Nursery series, published by Harper, which includes *Learning to Talk,* 1855, *Learning to Think,* 1856, *Learning to Read,* 1856, *Learning About Common Things,* 1857, *Learning About Right and Wrong,* 1857; the Science for the Young series, published by Harper, which includes *Heat,* 1871, *Light,* 1871, *Water and Land,* 1871, *Force,* 1872; story books about children which include *Madeline,* 1857, *Handie,* 1859, *Rainbow's Journey,* 1860, *The Three Pines,* 1860, *Selling Lucky,* 1860, *Up the River,* 1861; the Florence series which includes *Florence and John,* 1860, *Grimkie,* 1860, *Excursion to the Orkney Islands,* 1860, *The English Channel,* 1860, *Visit to the Isle of Wight,* 1864, *Florence's Return,* 1864; the Harlie series, published by Sheldon, except as noted, in 1863 includes *The New Shoes, The French Flower,* Worthington, *Harlie's Letter,* Worthington, *Wild Peggie, The Sea-Shore, Friskie, the Pony;* the *Gay* series published by Hurd and Houghton between 1865 and 1876 which includes *Mary Gay, or Work for Girls,* four seasonal volumes, 1865, *William Gay, or Play for Boys,* in four seasonal volumes, 1869, *John Gay, or Work for Boys,* in four seasonal volumes, 1876; the Juno series published by Dodd, Mead in 1870 which includes *Juno and Georgie, Mary Osborne, Juno on a Journey, Hubert;* the August series published by Dodd, Mead which includes *August and Elvie,* 1871, *Hunter and Tom,* 1871, *The Schooner Mary Ann,* 1872, *Granville Valley,* 1872; the Biographical Histories, later called the Makers of History series published by Harper which includes *Charles the First,* 1848, *Mary, Queen of Scots,* 1848, *Alexander the Great,* 1848, *Julius Caesar,* 1849, *Hannibal the Carthaginian,* 1848, *William the Conqueror,* 1848, *Charles the Second,* 1848, *Elizabeth, the Queen of England,* 1848, *King Alfred of England,* 1849, *Xerxes, the Great,* 1849, *Cyrus, the Great,* 1849, *Darius the Great,* 1850, *Cleopatra, Queen of Egypt,* 1851, *Romulus,* 1851, *Nero,* 1853, *Pyrrhus,* 1853, *King Richard the First,* 1857, *King Richard the Second,* 1858, *King Richard the Third,* 1858, *Peter the Great,* 1859, *Genghis Khan,* 1860, *Margaret of Anjou,* 1861; the author's brother John Abbot [*sic*] wrote ten "Histories": *Henry IV of France; Hernando Cortez; Hortense, Mother of Napoleon III: Joseph Bonaparte; Josephine; King Philip; Louis XIV; Louis Phillippe; Madame Roland; Marie Antonette).* AAS, BC, CC, LC, TPL

1836

William Holmes McGuffey's *The Eclectic First Reader* (the first of a series of graded readers, containing stories with strong moral tones, which strongly influenced three generations of Americans, published in Cincinnati by Truman and Smith). DePL, LC

Catharine Parr Traill's *The Backwoods of Canada* (a well-known Canadian immigrant writer tells about her life in Upper Canada [now Ontario]), published in Toronto by McClelland; before coming to Canada, the author wrote *The Young Emigrants; or Pictures of Canada. Calculated to Amuse and Instruct the Minds of Youth,* Darton, 1826; the author's other work includes her first Canadian children's book, edited by her sister Agnes Strickland, *Canadian Crusoes* [also published as *Lost in the Backwoods*], 1852; *Lady Mary and Her Nurse; or, A Peep Into Canadian Forests,* Hall, 1856 [also published as *Afar in the Forest* and *In the Forest*]; *Cot and Cradle Stories*; and *Little Downy, or The History of a Field Mouse: A Moral Tale,* Dean, 1822; *The Tell-Tale,* Harris, 1923; *The Flower Basket; or Poetical Blossoms,* Newman, ca. 1825; *Happy Because Good*, Dean, ca. 1830). TPL

1837

Lady Charlotte Guest's *The Mabinogion* (translated from the fourteenth- and fifteenth-century Welsh manuscript, *Llyfr Coch O Hergest, the Red Book of Hergest,* a collection of tales that were once songs of the bards, many dealing with King Arthur and his court [*Mabinogion* means bards' narrative songs]; a second edition was published by Quaritch in 1877).

1839

Catherine Sinclair's *Holiday House* (intended as a relief from didactic books: Mrs. Crabtree, the governess, is disliked not only by the children but by their grandmother and uncle as well; light treatment of misconduct is unusual for the period and the "Wonderful Story About Giant Snap-'em-up," who had to stand on a ladder in order to comb his own hair, is probably the earliest example of nonsense literature for children; published in Edinburgh by M. Whyte; the author's other work includes *Charlie Seymour; or, The Good Aunt and the Bad Aunt,* Carter, 1832; *Frank Vansittart; or, The Model Schoolboys,* London, 1853; *The Picture Letter by Catherine Sinclair,* n.p., 1861; the first of a series of six "hieroglyphic stories in letter form," with pictures printed in color by W. H. McFarlane; others in the series are *Another Letter from Catherine Sinclair,* n.p., 1862; *A Bible Picture Letter,* n.p., n.d.; *A Crossman's Letter by Catherine Sinclair,* n.p., 1862; *A Sunday Letter by Catherine Sinclair,* n.p., 1862; *The First of April Picture Letter by Catherine Sinclair*, Edinburgh, 1864). TPL

Daniel Pierce Thompson's *The Green Mountain Boys* (a popular story set in Vermont; published in two volumes in Philadelphia by J.W. Bradley and by E. P. Walton; the author's other work includes *May Martin,* J. Clements, 1835; *Locke Amsden*, Boston, 1847; *Lucy Hosmer*, London, 1848; *The Rangers*, B. B. Mussey, 1851? *Gaut Gurley*, J. P. Jewett, 1857; *The Doomed Chief,* J. W. Bradley, 1860; *Centeola, and Other Tales*, Carleton, 1864; *The Demon Trapper of Umbagog*, Columbian, 1890; the author published all works anonymously).

1840

Richard Henry Dana, Jr.'s *Two Years Before the Mast* (a popular novel of a young seaman's experiences as he sails around Cape Horn to California; published in Boston by Caldwell; appropriated by children).

1841

Captain Frederick Marryat's *Masterman Ready* (the author's first book and one specifically for children though his adult novels were read by children; an attempt to improve on *The Swiss Family Robinson* which he, as a navy officer, felt was sadly lacking in the principles of navigation and geography; the author's other work includes *The Naval Officer; or, Scenes and Adventures in the Life of Frank Mildmay,* Colburn, 1829; *The King's Own,* Colburn, 1830; *Newton Forster,* Cochrane, 1832?; *Jacob Faithful,* Saunders, 1834; *Peter Simple,* Saunders, 1834; *Japhet in Search of a Father,* Trenton, 1835; *The Pirate and Three Cutters,* Longman, 1836; *Snarleyyow; or, the Dog's Friend,* Colburn, 1837; *Poor Jack,* Longman, 1840; *Joseph Rushbrook,* Longman, 1841; *Percival Keene,* Colburn, 1842; *The Settlers in Canada,* Longman, 1844; *The Mission, or, Scenes from Africa; Written for Young People,* Longman, 1845; *The Poacher,* Bentley, 1846; *The Privateer's Man One Hundred Years Ago,* Longman, 1846; *Children of the New Forest,* Hurst, 1847; *The Phantom Ship,* Bentley, 1847; *The Little Savage,* Hurst, 1848; *The Travels and Adventures of Monsieur Violet,* Bentley, 1849; *Mr. Midshipman Easy,* Bentley, 1852). UI

Felix Summerly's *Home Treasury of Pleasure Books for Young Children* (a series of twelve booklets bound in stiff ornamented paper covers, published by Joseph Cundall and Addey; the titles include *Jack the Giant-Killer, Jack and the Beanstalk, The Sleeping Beauty, Red Riding Hood, Cinderella, Beauty and the Beast, Chevy Chase, The Sisters and the Golden Locks, Grumble and Cheery,* [Peacock's] *Sir Hornbook, Dick Whitington, Bible Events;* the stories are written in literate fashion, and the pictures are taken from the work of such painters as Holbein, Raphael, and Titian; illustrators include William Mulready and J. C. Horsley in an attempt to expose children to the best art work possible; Felix Summerly was the pseudonym of Sir Henry Cole, one of the founders of the South Kensington Museum and first director of the Victoria and Albert Museum; the author's other work includes *Traditional Nursery Songs of England, with Pictures by Eminent Modern Artists,* Cundall, 1846).

1842

Richard Doyle's *The Marvellous History of Jack the Giant Killer* (an illustrated retelling of an old popular tale, published in London by Eyre and Spottiswood; the author-illustrator's other work includes *The Story of Jack and the Giants,* Cundall, 1851; with J. R. Planché; *An Old Fairy Tale. The Sleeping Beauty,* Routledge, 1868; illustrations for William Allingham's *In Fairy Land,* 1870, Anthony Montalba's *Fairy Tales of All Nations,* Dean, 1872, John Ruskin's *King of the Golden River,* Lovell, 1885, Theodore Martin's *The Book of Ballads,* Blackwood, 1903, Charles Dickens's *Christmas Books,* illustrated by Doyle and others, Chapman, 1910).

James Halliwell-Phillipps's *The Nursery Rhymes of England* (a collection of over 550 rhymes chiefly from the oral tradition; a major primary source for numerous subsequent nursery-rhyme collections; printed by T. Richards in London for the Percy Society; subsequent editions included tales and stories until *Popular Rhymes and Nursery Tales: a sequel to The Nursery Rhymes of England* was published in London by John Russell Smith in 1849).

The Magazine for the Young (a British magazine intended for children of the working class; contributors included Charlotte Yonge).

Edgar Allan Poe's *The Pit and the Pendulum* (a frightening short story by a famous American writer published in Philadelphia by Carey and Hart; the author's other work appropriated by children includes *The Tell-Tale Heart,* first published in *The Pioneer,* January 1843, and published in book form by Heartman; *The Gold Bug,* New York, 1845; *The Raven, and Other Poems,* Wiley, 1845).

1843

Charles Dickens's *A Christmas Carol* (a famous moral adult ghost story by a popular British writer; published in London by Chapman and Hall; the author's other work includes *Oliver Twist; or, The Parish Boy's Progress,* Richard Bently, 1838; *The Cricket on the Hearth. A Fairy Tale of Home,* Bradbury and Evans, 1846; *The Personal History of David Copperfield,* Bradbury and Evans, 1850; *Little Dorrit,* Bradbury and Evans, 1855-1857, published in parts; *The Tale of Two Cities,* Chapman and Hall, 1859; *Great Expectations,* Chapman and Hall, 1861; all these books were appropriated by children; the author's work specifically for children includes *A Child's History of England,* in three volumes, 1852-1854; *A Holiday Romance,* Bradbury and Evans, 1868; and four stories, one of which was "The Magic Fishbone," which appeared serially in 1868). FLP, JRUL, NYPL-B, PLC, YU

1844

Lydia Maria Child's *Flowers for Children* (a three-volume set of stories; *Part I: For Children Eight or Nine Years Old; Part II: For Children from Four to Six Years Old; Part III: For Children Eleven and Twelve;* published

1844 *continued*

by C. S. Francis; the author's other work includes the lyrics for "Over the River and Through the Woods"; *Emily Parker,* Bowles, 1827; *Biographical Sketches of Great and Good Men,* Putnam, 1928; *The Mother's Book,* Carter, 1831; *The Girl's Own Book,* Austin, 1933; *Rainbows for Children,* Francis, 1848; *Rose Marian and the Flower Fairies,* Francis, 1850; *The Brother and Sister,* Philadelphia, 1852; *The Magician's Show Box,* Ticknor, 1856; *A New Flower for Children,* Francis, 1856; *The R.B.R.'s: My Little Neighbors,* Walker, 1862; *The Christ-Child,* Lothrop, 1869; *The Children of Mt. Ida,* Francis, 1871; *The Adventures of Jamie and Jeannie,* Lothrop, 1876?; *Good Little Mitty,* Lothrop, 1880?; *The Little Girl's Own Book,* Carter, 1831; the author was founder and editor of *The Juvenile Miscellany,* 1826-1834).

Alexander Dumas's *The Three Musketeers* (from the French; a romantic adventure novel; author's other work includes *The Count of Monte Cristo,* in two volumes, published in London by W. S. Orr, 1846; *The Honey-Stew of the Countess Bertha. A Fairy Tale,* translated from the French by Mrs. Cooke Taylor, illustrated by W. Weir, published in London by Jeremiah How, 1846; the author's work has been appropriated by children).

Harriet Martineau's *The Crofton Boys* (the fourth part of the "Playfellow" series of four stories published in London by Charles Knight; the story of life in a boys' school from a child's point of view; the author's other work, published in London by C. Knight, includes *Feats on the Fjord,* the third part of the "Playfellow" series, 1841; *The Children Who Lived by the Jordon,* 1842; *The Peasant and the Prince,* part of the "Playfellow" series, 1841; *The Settlers at Home,* a part of the "Playfellow" series, 1841; *The Billow and the Rock*, 1846). TPL

Francis Edward Paget's *The Hope of the Katzekopfs* (sometimes called the first literary fairy tale written in English; the direct ancestor of Thackeray's *The Rose and the King* and other court fairy tales; intended as a moral allegory or fable, based on Church of England doctrine; published under the pseudonym William Chusne of Staffordshire; a shortened version reissued in 1908 as *The Self-Willed Prince;* the author's other work includes *Tales of the Village Children,* London, 1844 and 1845; *Luke Sharp,* London, 1845; the author edited *The Juvenile Englishman's Library,* twenty-one volumes, published between 1844 and 1849).

1845

Frederic William Naufor Bayley's *Comic Nursery Tales with Illustrations Humorous and Numerous* (a collection of retellings of such stories as "Little

Red Riding Hood," "Robinson Crusoe," and "Bluebeard"; illustrated by Arthur Crowquill, a pseudonym for Alfred Henry Forrester, who often shared the name with his brother, Charles Forrester, a writer, when they produced joint works; the author's other work includes *The New Tale of the Tub, An Adventure in Verse,* Wiley, 1842; *Little Red Riding Hood,* Wilson, 1844; *Blue Beard,* Burgess, 1845; *Drolleries for Little Folks,* Shepard, 1845; *Jack the Giant Killer,* illustrated by John Leech, Burgess, 1845).

1846

Hans Christian Andersen's *Wonderful Stories for Children* (ten of Andersen's tales translated from the Danish by Mary Howitt and published by Chapman and Hall; the original four stories in Danish, *Eventyr Fortalte for Born,* were published in Denmark by C. A. Reitzel in 1835, the first of a three-part series, with subsequent series being published in 1838 and 1845; the complete collection of the author's 168 tales appeared in Danish in two volumes: the first was *Eventyr or Historien,* Odense, 1862-1863, illustrated by Thomas Vilhelm Pedersen; the second was *Nye Eventyr Og Historien, Odense,* 1870-1874, illustrated by Lorenz Froelich; *Christmas Roses,* a popular American collection of a few of Andersen's tales, was translated by Mary Howitt and published by Wiley and Putnam in 1847; the author is sometimes credited with being the "father of modern fantasy," having perfected the literary fairy tale genre; numerous translations of the author's work have been made, including Caroline Peachey's *Danish Fairy-Legends and Tales,* Pickering, 1846; Charles Boner's *A Danish Story-Book* and *The Nightingale and OtherTales,* illustrated by Count Pocci, Cundall, 1846; M. R. James's *Forty Stories,* Faber, 1930, and his *Hans Andersen Forty-Two Stories,* illustrated by Robin Jacques, Faber, 1953; Rex Whistler's *Fairy Tales and Legends*, Bodley, 1935; R. P. Keigwin's *Fairy Tales*, four volumes, illustrated by Vilhelm Pedersen and edited by Svend Larsen, Ward, 1851-1960; Reginald Spink's *Hans Andersen's Fairy Tales*, illustrated by Hans Baumhauer, Dent, 1858; other translators and dates of their publications include: Anne S. Bushby, 1853; H. W. Dulcken, 1864; Jean Hersholt, 1942; Eva La Gallienne, 1959; numerous picture book editions of the author's work also exist). LC, UCB

Mrs. Fairstar's *Memoirs of a London Doll. Written By Herself* (edited by Mrs. Fairstar; Maria Poppet, a doll, recounts her adventures as she passes through the hands of many loving owners; Mrs. Fairstar is pseudonym of Richard Henry Horne; published in London by J. Cundall; the author's other work includes *The Good Natured Bear,* Cundall, 1846).

1846 *continued*

Edward Lear's *Book of Nonsense* (a conscious attempt by British author-artist to make children laugh through verses and sketches; one of the first children's books without instruction or moralizing; published in London by Thomas McClear; author's other work includes *A Book of Nonsense,* enlarged edition published by Routledge, Warne, and Routledge, 1861; *Nonsense Songs and Stories,* London, 1871; *More Nonsense,* Aylesbury, 1872; *Laughable Lyrics,* London, 1877; *Nonsense Botany,* Warne, 1888; *Queery Leary Nonsense,* Mills and Boon, 1911; *Teapots and Quails, and Other New Nonsense,* John Murray, 1953). LC, TPL

1847

The Snow Drop; or, Juvenile Magazine (the first Canadian magazine for children; contained moral and religious tales, verse, information and anecdotes on natural history, and a few riddles).

1848

Heinrich Hoffman's *The English Struwwelpeter; or Pretty Stories and Funny Pictures for Little Children* (translated from the German, *Der Struwwelpeter; oder, Lustige Geschicten und drollige Bilder,* Frankfurt, 1847?, probably by J. R. Planché, published in Leipzig by F. Volckmar; American edition, *Slovenly Peter,* published in Philadelphia by Winston in 1849; exaggerated didactic verses with colored lithographs of grotesque children—Shockheaded Peter, Harriet and the Matches, Fidgety Phillip; the book has both frightened and amused children to the present day; author's other work includes *King Nutcracker,* translated by J. R. Planché, Tagg, 1853; *The Little Sister,* translated by Charles Brooks, n.p., 1853; *In Heaven So On Earth,* n.p., ca. 1853; *Sebastian the Lazybones,* n.p., 1854; *Master Pigmy,* translated by Charles Brooks, n.p., 186__?; *Prince Greenwood and Pearl-of-Price,* translated by M. Despard, Peters, 1874; *A Visit To Madam Sun,* n.p., 1924).

Thomas James's *Aesop's Fables* (a prose translation of 203 fables chiefly from original sources, published in London by John Murray; many subsequent versions were based on James's *Aesop;* engravings by John Tenniel).

1849

Mary Howitt's *Our Cousins in Ohio* (a British author describes life in the American Midwest; published in London by Darton; the author's other work includes *Peter Parley's Fable of the Spider and the Fly,* Carter, 1830; *Sketches of Natural History,* Effingham Wilson, 1834; *Tales in Prose for the Young,* Darton, 1836; *Tales in Verse,* Harper, 1836; *Birds and Flowers and Other Country Things,* Darton, 1838; *The Christmas Library. . . .*

Hymns and Fireside Verses, Darton, 1839; *Hope On! Hope Ever! or, The Boyhood of Felix Law,* Munroe, 1840; *Sowing and Reaping; or, What will Come of It,* Monroe, 1840; *Strive and Thrive,* Munroe, 1840; *Who Shall Be Greatest?,* Munroe, 1841; *Little Coin, Much Care or, How Poor Men Live,* Appleton, 1842; *Which Is the Wiser or People Abroad,* Appleton, 1842; *Alice Franklin. A Tale,* Appleton, 1843; *Love and Money,* Tegg, 1843; *No Sense Like Common Sense,* Appleton, 1843; *Work and Wages or, Life in Service,* Appleton, 1843; *My Own Story, or The Autobiography of a Child,* Appleton, 1844; *The Child's Poetry Book,* Mowatt, 1844; *The Favorite Scholar,* Francis, 1844; *My Uncle the Clockmaker,* Appleton, 1845; *The Author's Daughter,* Harper, 1845; *The Two Apprentices,* New York, 1845; *Ballads and Other Poems,* Longman, 1847; *Bright Days; or Herbert and Meggy,* Lothrop, 1847; *Floral Gems,* Taylor, 1847; *Poetical Tales for Good Boys and Girls,* Livermore, 1847; *The Children's Year,* Lothrop, 1847, Longmans, 1847; translation from the Swedish of Fredrika Bremer's *Brothers and Sisters,* Harper, 1848; *The Four Sisters,* Peterson, 1860; *The Childhood of Mary Leeson,* Crosby Nichols, 1848, Darton, 1848; *Juvenile Tales and Stories,* Appleton, 1850; *Pictures from Nature,* Routledge, 1850; *Popular Moral Tales for the Young,* Appleton, 1850; *Story Book,* Francis, 1850; *The Stedfast Gabriel,* Chambers, 1850; *The Christmas Tree,* Francis, 1852; *Pictures and Verses,* Colby, 1853; *The Turtle Dove and Other Stories,* Francis, 1853; *Songs and Stories for Mother's Darling,* Lippincott, 1854; *Stories In Rhyme,* Brown, 1855; *Illustrated Library for the Young,* Tools, 1856; *The Picture Book for the Young,* Lippincott, 1856; *Jack and Harry, or Pictures of the Young,* Tilton, 1859; *Hans Andersen's Story Book. With a Memoir,* Francis, 1860; *Little Arthur's Letters to His Sister Mary,* London, 1861; *The Blackbird and Parrot and the Cat and Other Stories,* 1861; *The Golden Casket. A Treasury of Tales for Young People,* Hogg, 1861; *The Story of Little Cristal,* London, 1863; *Mr. Rudd's Grandchildren* [*Timothy Cossington, The Painter's Little Model, Little Dick Appleton*], London, 1864; *Peter Drake's Dream,* Miller, 1865; *The Angel Unawares,* Miller, 1865; *New Story Book,* Miller, 1866; *John Oriel's Start in Life,* London, 1868; *Little Dick and the Angel,* Tilton, 1869; *Adventures of Jack and Harry,* London, 1869; *Natural History Stories for My Juvenile Friends,* Partridge, 1874; translation from the Danish of H. C. Andersen, *The Improvisatore,* Houghton, 1879; *Mabel on Midsummer Day,* Osgood, 1881; *The Little Peacemaker; Prince Hempseed on His Travels; and William and His Teacher,* Cassell, 1885; *Mary Howitt; an Autobiography,* W. Isbister, 1889; *A Birthday Gift,* Darton, 185__; *Lillieslea,* Routledge, n.d.; *The Artist-Wife and Other Tales,* Stringer,, 18__; *The Child's Delight; or, The Three Wishes, and Other Entertaining Stories,* Miller, 18__; the author's husband William Howitt also wrote books for children; his works include *The Boy's Country Book,* Longman, 1839; *The*

1849 *continued*

Life and Adventures of Jack of the Mill; Commonly Called Lord Othmill,
Longman, 1844; *The Miner's Daughters,* Dewitt, 1850; *Madam Darrington
of the Dene,* Colburn, 1851; *A Boy's Adventures in the Wilds of Australia,*
Hall, 1855; *The Man of the People,* Hurst, 1860).

Mark Lemon's *The Enchanted Doll* (a fairy story of one of the founders of
Punch; published in London; foreshadows *Pinocchio;* illustrated by Richard
Doyle; author's other work includes *Fairy Tales,* London, 1865; *Tinykin's
Transformations: A Child's Story,* illustrated by C. Green, Stark, ca. 1870).

Herman Melville's *Redburn: His First Voyage* (the story of a sailor-boy's
life in the merchant service; published by Richard Bentley; the author's
other work includes *Narrative of a Four Months' Residence Among the
Natives of a Valley of the Marquesas Islands; Or, A Peep At Polynesian
Life,* J. Murray, 1846; *Typee,* Routledge, 1846; *The Story of Toby, A Sequel
To "Typee,"* J. Murray, 1846; *Omoo; A Narrative of Adventures in the
South Seas,* J. Murray, 1847; *Mardi: And a Voyage Thither,* Richard
Bentley, 1849; *White Jacket; Or, The World in a Man-Of-War,* Richard
Bentley, 1850; *The Whale; Or, Moby-Dick,* Richard Bentley, 1851; *Pierre;
Or, The Ambiguities,* Harper, 1852; *Bartleby, the Scrivener: A Story of
Wall-Street,* New York, 1853; *Cock-a-Doodle-Do! Or, The Crowing of the
Noble Cock Beneventano,* New York, 1853; *The Piazza Tales,* New York,
1856; *The Refugee,* Peterson, 1865; *John Marr and Other Sailors,* De Vinne,
1888).

Francis Parkman, Jr.'s *The California and Oregon Trail* (a trained historian's
account of the passage westward, published in New York by G. P. Putnam;
author's other work includes *Pioneers of France in the New World,* Little,
Brown, and Co., 1865; *The Jesuits in North America,* Little, Brown and
Co., 1867; *LaSalle and the Discovery of the Great West,* Little, Brown and
Co., 1879; *The Old Regime in Canada,* Little, Brown and Co., 1874;
Montcalm and Wolfe, Little, Brown and Co., 1884).

ca. 1850

H. C.'s *The Picture Alphabet for the Amusement and Instruction of Boys
and Girls* (anonymous; an ABC chapbook which begins, "A was an Angler,
and caught a fine fish"; each letter of the alphabet is illustrated with an
attractive woodcut; published in Otley, England, by William Walker).

*The Galloping Guide to the ABC; or the Child's Agreeable Introduction to
a Knowledge of the Gentlemen of the Alphabet* (anonymous; an ABC
chapbook which uses "He who ne'er learns his ABC / For ever will a blockhead be" as an introduction; the ABC's begin with "A was an ass / with

his panniers and load''; detailed woodcuts illustrate each letter; published by J. G. Rusher in Banbury, England).

The Golden Pippin (anonymous; an ABC chapbook with four letters per page; begins with ''A was an Arch Boy / B a Beauty was''; woodcuts illustrate the verses; published in London by Ryle and Company).

The Picture Alphabet (anonymous; a sophisticated ABC chapbook which begins with ''A was an Archer / And Shot at a frog / But missing his mark / Shot into a bog''; each letter also features one line from ''A apple-pie''; the subject for each letter of the alphabet is incorporated into the woodcut design; published by Thomas Richardson of Derby, England).

1850

Elizabeth Wetherell's *The Wide, Wide World* (the story of a girl's growing up in unpleasant surroundings and under the care of a bad-humored aunt; in two volumes, published in New York by G. P. Putnam; popular in Britain as well as America; has strong religious tone; gives a picture of life in rural America as well as in a large city; Elizabeth Wetherell was the pseudonym of Susan Warner; the author's other work includes *Queechy,* G. P. Putnam, 1852; *The Hills of Shatemac,* Constable, 1856; *The Old Helmet,* R. Carter Brothers, 1863; *Melbourne House,* DeWolfe, Fiske and Co., 1864; *Daisy,* Lippincott, 1868; *Diana,* G. P. Putnam, 1877; the author also wrote the well-known Protestant Sunday school hymn, ''Jesus Loves Me''; the author's younger sister, Anna Warner, collaborated with her on *The Wide, Wide World*; *Mrs. Rutherford's Children*, G. P. Putnam, 1853; *Wych Hazel*, G. P. Putnam, 1876; Anna Warner's pseudonym was Amy Lathrop).

1851

Margaret Gatty's *The Fairy Godmothers* (retellings of fairy tales with morals, published in London; author was mother of Juliana H. Ewing; edited *Aunt Judy's Magazine,* 1866-1885, an important English children's magazine, which contained the work of such writers as Hans C. Andersen, Lewis Carroll, Juliana Ewing, Mrs. Molesworth, and was the first magazine to feature regular reviews of children's books; the author's other work includes *Parables from Nature,* Bell, 1855-1871; *Worlds Not Realized,* London, 1856; *Proverbs Illustrated,* London, 1857; *Legendary Tales,* London, 1858; *Aunt Judy's Tales,* London, 1859; *Aunt Judy's Letters,* London, 1862; *The Mothers' Poetry Book,* London, 1872; the author's books are illustrated by such artists as J. Tenniel, J. Millais, H. Hunt, and E. Burne-Jones).

William Henry Giles Kingston's *Peter the Whaler* (the first of over one hundred exciting adventure stories for boys, all of which used a heavy-handed

1851 *continued*

moral tone; published in London; the author was first editor of Sampson Low's periodical, *Union Jack,* 1880, succeeded by G. A. Henty; the author's other work includes short stories published in *Kingston's Magazine for Boys,* 1859-1862; *Mark Seaworth,* London, 1852; *Manco, the Peruvian Chief,* London, 1853; *Salt Water,* London, 1857; *Old Jack,* Nelson, 1859; *Round the World,* London, 1860; *Digby Heathcote,* London, 1860; *Will Weatherhelm,* London, 1860; *The Three Midshipmen,* Dutton, 1862; *Washed Ashore,* London, 1866; *The Perils and Adventures of Harry Skipworth,* London, 1868; *The Three Lieutenants,* Beccles, 1874; *The Three Commanders,* Beccles, 1875; *The Wanderers,* Beccles, 1876; *The Three Admirals,* Beccles, 1878; *The Rival Crusoes,* Beccles, 1878; *The Frontier Fort,* London, 1879; *Arctic Adventures,* Routledge, 1882).

John Ruskin's *King of the Golden River* (a literary fairy tale by a famous art critic; written in the style of a folktale; published in London; illustrated by Richard Doyle; the author's other work includes *Dame Wiggins of Lee and Her Seven Wonderful Cats,* illustrated by Kate Greenaway, Allen, 1885). JRUL, SDPL, YU

The Monthly Packet (a magazine for girls and young women planned for the home schoolroom rather than the village school; for forty-two years it was edited by Charlotte Yonge).

1852

Francis Robert Goulding's *Robert and Harold; or, The Young Marooners on the Florida Coast* (a boy's adventure story, published in London; sequel was *Marooner's Island; or Dr. Gordon in Search of His Children,* Claxton, 1869; this Presbyterian minister's other work includes *Little Josephine,* American Sunday School Union, 1844; *Frank Gordon,* London, 1869; *Woodruff Stories,* Claxton, 1870; *Nacoochee,* Claxton, 1871).

Nathaniel Hawthorne's *A Wonder-Book for Boys and Girls* (a free adaptation of Greek myths for children by famous American novelist; first published in London in 1851; the author's other work for children includes *Grandfather's Chair,* Peabody, 1841; *Tanglewood Tales, for Girls and Boys; being a Second Wonder Book,* Ticknor, 1853). NYPL-B

Susannah Moodie's *Roughing It in the Bush* (a Canadian classic by a Canadian immigrant author; published in New York by G. P. Putnam; the author's other work, with her sister, Catherine Parr Traill, includes *Hugh Latimer,* Dean, 1828; *The Little Prisoner,* Newman, 1828; *The World Before Them,* Bentley, 1868). TPL

Harriet Beecher Stowe's *Uncle Tom's Cabin; or Life Among the Lowly* (a persuasive adult novel, published in Boston by J. P. Jewett, about the plight of slaves in the American South, appropriated by children; the author's other work includes *Little Pussy Willow,* London, 1871, which was intended for children; *A Dog's Mission,* London and New York, 1857).

The Youth's Casket. An Illustrated Magazine for the Young (published in Buffalo, New York, by Erastus Beadle and edited by Mrs. H. E. G. Arey, in six volumes; in 1857 it merged with *Forrester's Magazine of Boston*).

1853

George Cruikshank's *Fairy Library* (three volumes of well-known fairy tales selected and illustrated by Cruikshank; published in London by David Bogue; selector-illustrator's other work includes *Cries of London,* Robins, ca. 1828; *The Comic Alphabet,* London, ca. 1832; *The Bottle,* Bogue, 1847; *The Drunkard's Children. A Sequel to the Bottle,* Bogue, 1848; *Puss in Boots,* Arnold, 1864; *The History of Jack in the Beanstalk,* Routledge, 1865). PU

1854

Maria Susanna Cummins's *The Lamplighter* (a popular novel originally published anonymously, which tells the story of a poor girl who is rescued by a lamplighter and eventually marries a wealthy man; published by Jewett; the author's other work includes *Mabel Vaughan,* Jewett, 1857).

Charlotte Yonge's *The Little Duke* (the story of Richard the Fearless as a young boy; one of a series of suspenseful historical novels for young people; first published serially in the author's literary magazine, *The Monthly Packet,* 1851; published in Boston by D. Lothrup, 1881; this English author published over 150 novels for both adults and children; the author's other work includes *Henrietta's Wish,* Munro, 1850; *Langley School,* London, 1850; *The Heir of Redclyffe,* London, 1853; *The Lances of Lynwood,* London, 1855; *The Two Guardians,* Masters, 1855; *The Daisy Chain,* Parker, 1856; *Richard the Fearless,* Appleton, 1856; *Dynevor Terrace,* Parker, 1857; *Heartsease,* Appleton, 1861; *Hopes and Fears,* Appleton, 1861; *Countess Kate,* London, 1862; *The Stokesley Secret,* Tauchnitz, 1862; *History of Christian Names,* Parker, 1863; *A Book of Golden Deeds,* Macmillan, 1864; *The Trial,* Appleton, 1864; *Biographies of Good Women,* Mozley, 1865; *The Clever Woman of the Family,* Appleton, 1865; *The Dove in the Eagle's Nest,* Appleton, 1866; *The Prince and the Page,* Macmillan, 1866; *The Danvers Papers,* Macmillan, 1867; *Landmarks of History,* Leypoldt and Holt, 1867-1868; *The Six Cushions,* Mozley, 1867; *Cameos from English History, From Rollo to Edward II,* Macmillan, 1868; *A Book of Worthies,* Macmillan, 1869; *The Chaplet of Pearls,* Appleton, 1869;

1854 *continued*

The Caged Lion, London, 1870; *A Storehouse of Stories,* Macmillan, 1870; *Beechcraft,* Appleton, 1871; *Lady Hester,* Macmillan, 1874; *My Young Alcides,* Macmillan, 1876; *Unknown to History,* Macmillan, 1882; *Aunt Charlotte's Stories of American History,* Appleton, 1883; *Story Pearls,* Harper, 1883; *The Armourer's Prentices,* Munro, 1884; *Nuttie's Father,* Munro, 1885; *The Two Sides of the Shield,* Munro, 1885; *Chantry House,* Munro, 1886; *A Modern Telemachus,* Harper, 1886; *Scenes and Characters,* Macmillan, 1886; *The Herb of the Field,* Macmillan, 1887; *Beechcraft At Rockstone,* Munro, 1889; *The Penniless Princess,* Macmillan, 1891; *That Stick,* Macmillan, 1892; *Grisby Grisell,* Macmillan, 1893; *The Treasurers in the Marshes,* Whittaker, 1893; *Aunt Charlotte's Stories of Bible History for Young Disciples,* Philadelphia, 1898; *The Herd Boy and His Hermit,* Whittaker, 1899; *Little Lucy's Wonderful Globe,* Harper, 1927). TPL

1855

Thomas Bulfinch's *The Age of the Fable; or, Stories of Gods and Heroes* (popular retellings of Greek myths; published in Boston by Sanbor, Carter and Bazin; author's other work includes *The Age of Chivalry,* in two parts, "King Arthur and His Knights" and "The Mabinogion; or Welsh Popular Tales," Crosby, 1859).

Henry Wadsworth Longfellow's *Hiawatha* (a long narrative poem written in the same metre as the Finnish epic, *The Kalevala;* published in Boston by Ticknor and Fields; inspired by Native American history and customs as the author idealized them).

Oliver Optic's *The Boat Club; or The Bunkers of Rippleton, A Tale for Boys* (the first of the *Yacht Club* adventure series, published in Boston by Brown, Bazin, and Company; the author wrote 116 series books, including the Army and Navy series; the Starry Flag series; the Upward and Onward series; the Lake Shore series; and the Katy books; Oliver Optic was pseudonym for William Taylor Adams, a New England school teacher and children's magazine editor who encouraged Horatio Alger to write and published Alger's "Ragged Dick" in his *Student and Schoolmate* in 1876; the author edited *Oliver Optic's Magazine for Boys and Girls,* published by Lee and Shepard, which ran from 1867 to 1875, and *Our Little Ones and the Nursery, Illustrated Stories and Poems for Young People,* which began around 1880 and ran until about 1889; the author's other work includes, under pseudonym of Warren T. Ashton, *Hatchie, the Guardian Slave; or, The Heiress of Bellevue,* Mussey, 1853; *In Doors and Out,* Brown, 1854; *All Aboard; or, Life on the Lake. A Sequel To "The Boat Club,"* Brown, 1865; *Poor and Proud, or The Fortunes of Katy Redburn,* Phillips, 1856; *Now or Never;*

or, The Adventures of Bobby Bright, Brown, 1857; *Try Again, or The Trials and Triumphs of Harry West,* Brown, 1858; *The Birthday Party, A Story for Little Folks,* Lee, 1863; *Careless Kate,* Lee, 1863; *The Christmas Gift,* Lee, 1863; *The Do-Somethings,* Lee, 1863; *Dolly and I,* Lee, 1863; *Little By Little; or, The Cruise of the Flyaway,* Lee, 1861; *The Gold Thimble,* Lee, 1863; *The Little Merchant,* Lee, 1863; *The Picnic Party,* Lee, 1863; *Proud and Lazy,* Lee, 1863; *Robinson Crusoe, Jr.,* Lee, 1863; *The Young Voyagers,* Lee, 1863; *In School and Out; A Tale for Wide-Awake Boys,* Lee, 1864; *The Soldier Boy; or, Tom Somers in the Army,* Lee, 1864; *Rich and Humble,* Lee, 1864; *Watch and Wait; or, The Young Fugitives,* Lee, 1864; *Brave Old Salt,* Lee, 1865; *Fighting Joe; or, The Fortunes of a Staff Officer,* Burt, 1865; *The Sailor Boy; or, Jack Somers in the Navy,* Lee, 1865; *A Young Lieutenant,* Lee, 1865; *The Yankee Middy,* Lee, 1865; *Hope and Have; or, Fanny Grant Among the Indians,* Lee, 1866; *Stem To Stern; or, Building the Boat,* Lee, 1866; *Work and Win; or, Noddy Newman on a Cruise,* Lee, 1866; *The Way of the World,* Lee, 1866; *Whip-poor-will. A Sad Story of a Naughty Boy,* Boston, 1866; *Haste and Waste; or, The Young Pilot of Lake Champlain,* Lee, 1867; *Outward Bound, or, Young America Afloat,* Lee, 1867; *The Starry Flag, or, The Young Fisherman of Cape Ann,* Lee, 1867; *Dikes and Ditches, or, Young America in Holland and Belgium,* Lee, 1868; *Breaking Away,* Lee, 1868; *Freaks of Fortune; or, Half Round the World,* Lee, 1868; *Our Standard Bearer; or, The Life of General Ulysses S. Grant,* Lee, 1868; *Palace and Cottage; or, Young America in France and Switzerland,* Lee, 1868; *Red Cross; or, Young America in England and Wales,* Lee, 1868; *Seek and Find; or, The Adventures of a Smart Boy,* Lee, 1868; *Shamrock and Thistle; or, Young America in Ireland and Scotland,* Lee, 1868; *Uncle Ben,* Lee, 1868; *Bear and Forbear; or, The Young Skipper of Lake Ucayga,* Lee, 1869; *Down the River; or, Buck Bradford and His Tryants,* Lee, 1869; *Make or Break; or, The Rich Man's Daughter,* Lee, 1869; *Brake Up; or, The Young Peacemakers,* Lee, 1870; *Cringle and Cross-Tree, or, The Sea Swashes of a Sailor,* Lee, 1870; *Down the Rhine; or, Young America in Germany,* Lee, 1870; *Lightning Express; or, The Rival Academies,* Lee, 1870; *On Time; or, The Young Captain of the Ucayga Steamer,* Lee, 1870; *Switch Off; or, The War of the Students,* Lee, 1870; *Through the Daylight; or, The Young Engineer of the Lake Shore Railroad,* Lee, 1870; *Bivouac and Battle,* Lee, 1871; *Desk and Debit; or, The Catastrophes of a Clerk,* Lee, 1871; *Plane and Plank; or, The Mishaps of a Mechanic,* Lee, 1871; *Little Bobtail; or, The Wreck of the Penobscot,* Lee, 1872; *Northern Lands; or, Young America in Russia and Prussia,* Lee, 1872; *Sea and Shore; or, The Tramps of a Traveller,* Lee, 1872; *Cross and Crescent, or a Young American in Turkey,* Lee, 1873; *Money-Maker; or, The Victory of the Basilisk,* Lee, 1874; *The Yacht Club; or, The Young Boat-Builder,* Lee, 1874; *The Coming Wave; or, The Hidden Treasure of*

1855 *continued*

High Rock, Lee, 1875; *The Dorcas Club; or, Our Girls Afloat,* Lee, 1875; *Ocean-Born; or, The Cruise of the Clubs,* Lee, 1875; *Sunny Shores; or, Young America in Italy,* Lee, 1875; *Going West,* Lee, 1876; *Vine and Olive; or, Young America in Spain and Portugal,* Lee, 1876; *Isles of the Sea; or, Young America Homeward Bound,* Lee, 1877; *Just His Luck,* Lee, 1877; *Out West; or, Roughing It on the Great Lakes,* Lee, 1877; *Going South; or, Yachting on the Atlantic Coast,* Lee, 1879; *Lake Breezes,* Lee, 1879; *Down South; or, Yacht Adventures in Florida,* Lee, 1881; *Up the River; or, Yachting on the Mississippi,* Lee, 1881; *All Adrift, or, The Goldwing Club,* Lee and Shepard, 1882; *Making a Man of Himself; or, Right Makes Might,* Lothrop, 1884; *Snug Harbor; or, The Champlain Mechanics,* Lee, 1884; *His Own Helper; or, Stout Arm and True Heart,* Street, 1885; *All Taught; or, Rigging the Boat,* Lee and Shepard, 1887; *Honest Kit Dunstable,* Lothrop, 1887; *Ready About; or Sailing the Boat,* Lee, 1887; under the pseudonym of Brooks McCormick, *Nature's Young Nobleman,* Munsey, 1888; *Taken by the Enemy,* Lothrop, 1888; *Among the Missing,* Lothrop, 1890; *Within the Enemy's Lines,* Lee, 1890; *A Missing Million,* Lee, 1891; *On the Blockade,* Lee, 1891; *Three Millions! or, The Way of the World,* Lee, 1891; *The Young Actor; or, The Solution of a Mystery,* United States Book Co., 1891; *Fighting for the Right,* Lee, 1892; *Stand By the Union,* Lee, 1892; *American Boys Afloat,* Lee, 1893; *Strange Sights Abroad; or, A Voyage in European Waters,* Lee, 1893; *A Victorious Union,* Lee, 1893; *A Young Knight-Errant,* Lee, 1893; *Brother Against Brother,* Lee, 1894; *Up and Down the Nile; or, Young Adventurers in Africa,* Lee, 1894; *The Young Navigators; or, The Foreign Cruise of the Maud,* Lee, 1894; *Across India; or, Live Boys in the Far East,* Lee and Shepard, 1895; *Asiatic Breezes; or, Students on the Wing,* Lee and Shepard, 1895; *Half Round the World; or, Among the Uncivilized,* Lee, 1895; editor, *In the Saddle, A Collection of Poems on Horseback-riding,* Lee, 1895; *A Lieutenant At Eighteen,* Lee, 1895; *Field and Forest; or, The Fortunes of a Farmer,* Lee, 1896; *Four Young Explorers; or, Sight-Seeing in the Tropics,* Lee, 1896; *On the Staff,* Lee, 1896; *At the Front,* Lee, 1897; *Pacific Shores; or, Adventures in Eastern Seas,* Lee, 1898; *An Undivided Union,* Lee, 1899; *The Rival Battalions,* Street, 1900; *Building Himself Up; or, The Cruise of the "Fish Hawk,"* Lothrop, 1910). LC, NYPL-A, UMi

William Makepeace Thackeray's *The Rose and the Ring* (a burlesque fairy tale about the royal families of Paflagonia and Crim Tartary which makes the possessors of both the rose and the ring most attractive and lovable; published in London by Smith, Elder and Co.; originally illustrated by the author, who sometimes used the pseudonym M. A. Titmarsh; the author's other work read by children includes *Rebecca and Rowena,* Chapman, 1850; *The Kickleburys on the Rhine,* Smith, 1850). NYPL-B, YU

1856

Robert Michael Ballantyne's *Snowflakes and Sunbeams; or, the Young Fur Traders* (thought to be the first of the author's numerous adventure stories which, in 1901, was published by T. Nelson and Sons in London, titled *The Young Fur Traders;* the author sometimes used the pseudonym of Comus; the author's other work includes *Hudson's Bay; or, Life in the Wilds of North America,* Blackwood, 1848? [1858, 3rd edition known]; *Coral Island,* Nelson, 1857; *Mr. Fox,* Nelson, 1857; *My Mother,* Hazard, 1857; *Ungava,* Nelson, 1857; *Martin Rattler; or, A Boy's Adventures in the Forests of Brazil,* Nelson, 1858; *The Robber Kitten,* Miller, 1858; *Mee-A-Mow; or, Good Advice to Cats and Kittens,* Nelson, 1859; *The World of Ice: Adventure in the Polar Regions,* Nelson, 1859; *The Golden Dream; or Adventures in the Far West,* Shaw, 1860; *The Dog Crusoe: A Tale of the Western Prairies,* Nelson, 1861; *The Gorilla Hunters: A Tale of the Wilds of Africa,* Nelson, 1861; *Red Eric; or, the Whaler's Last Cruise,* Routledge, 1861; *Man on the Ocean,* Nelson, 1862; *Gascoyne, the Sandal-Wood Trader,* Nisbet, 1863; *The Kitten Series: The Three Little Kittens, The Butterfly's Ball, and The Life of a Ship,* Nelson, 1862; *The Lifeboat,* Nisbet, 1864; *The Light-House,* Nisbet, 1865; *Shifting Winds,* Nisbet, 1866; *Fighting the Flames,* Nisbet, 1867; *Silver Lake; or, Lost in the Snow,* Jackson, 1867; *Deep Down: A Tale of the Cornish Mines,* Nisbet, 1868; *Erling the Bold: A Tale of the Norse Sea-Kings,* Nisbet, 1869; *The Floating Light of the Goodwin Sands,* Nisbet, 1870; *The Iron Horse,* Nisbet, 1871; *The Norsemen in the West,* Nisbet, 1872; *The Pioneers,* Nisbet, 1872; *Life in the Red Brigade,* Routledge, 1873; *Jarwin and Cuffy,* Warne, 1873; *Tales of Adventure; or, Wild Work in Strange Places,* London, 1873; *The Story of the Rock,* Nisbet, 1875; *Black Ivory: Adventures Among the Slavers,* Nisbet, 1873; *The Ocean and Its Wonders,* Nelson, 1874; *The Pirate City: An Algerian Tale,* Nisbet, 1874; *Rivers and Ice,* Nisbet, 1874; *Wrecked But Not Ruined,* London, 1875; *Under the Waves,* Nisbet, 1876; *The Settler and the Savage: A Tale of Peace and War in South Africa,* Nisbet, 1877; *In the Track of the Troops,* Nisbet, 1878; *Six Months at the Cape; or Letters from Periwinkle in South Africa,* Nisbet, 1879; *Post Haste: A Tale of H. M. Mails,* Nisbet, 1879; *Digging for Gold,* Nisbet, 1879; *Philosopher Jack,* Nisbet, 1880; *The Lonely Island,* Nisbet, 1880; *The Red Man's Revenge,* Nisbet, 1880; *The Giant of the North,* Nisbet, 1881; *The Battery and the Boiler; or, Adventures in the Laying of Submarine Electric Cables,* Nisbet, 1881; *My Doggie and I,* Nisbet, 1881; *The Kitten Pilgrims; or Great Battles and Grand Victories,* Nisbet, 1882; *Battle with the Sea,* Nisbet, 1883; *Dusty Diamonds Cut and Polished; A Tale of City Arab Life,* Nisbet, 1883; *The Madman and the Pirate,* Nisbet, 1883; *The Thorogood Family,* Nisbet, 1883; *Twice Bought: A Tale of the Oregon Gold-Fields,* Nisbet, 1884; *Young Trawler,* Nisbet, 1884; *Freaks on the Fells,* Routledge, 1885; *Island Queen; or Dethroned by Fire and Water,* Nisbet, 1885; *The Rover of the Andes,*

1856 *continued*

Nisbet, 1885; *Wild Man of the West,* Nisbet, 1885; *Big Otter,* Routledge, 1886; *The Lively Poll,* Nisbet, 1886; *Prairie Chief,* Nisbet, 1886; *Red Rooney,* London, 1886; *The Fugitives; or, the Tyrant Queen of Madagascar,* Nisbet, 1887; *Blue Lights; or, Hot Work in the Soudan,* Nisbet, 1888; *The Middy and the Moors: An Algerian Story,* Nisbet, 1888; an eighteen-volume periodical series, *Ballantyne's Miscellany,* was published between ca. 1863 and 1886).

1857

Charles Bennett's *The Fables of Aesop, Translated in [sic] Human Nature* (the traditional fables are retold and illustrated by author-illustrator, who anticipated colored wood engravings, sometimes handling color in a more original way than Caldecott or Greenaway; published in London by W. Kent; illustrations aptly reflect "animals as human beings" in the Grandville manner; compiler-illustrator's other work includes *Shadows,* London, 1856; *Old Nurse's Book of Rhymes, Jingles, and Ditties,* London, 1858; *The Nine Lives of a Cat,* Griffith, 1860; *Quarles Emblems,* London, 1861; *The Stories that Little Breeches Told, and the Pictures which Charles Bennett Drew for Them,* Sampson Low, 1863; *The Sorrowful Ending of Noodldoo, with the Fortune and Fate of Her Neighbors and Friends,* Sampson Low, 1865).

Tom Brown's *Tom Brown's Schooldays* (a "classic" British novel about boys' lives in Rugby, an English public school: this story began a spate of books about the codes, teams, and rivalries in boarding-school life; published by Macmillan, illustrated by Arthur Hughes; author's other work includes *The Scouring of the White Horse,* Macmillan, 1859; *Tom Brown at Oxford,* Macmillan, 1861; Tom Brown is the pseudonym of Thomas Hughes).

Frances Browne's *Granny's Wonderful Chair and the Tales It Told* (a popular collection of children's stories by an Irish author, published in London by Griffith and Farrow; reissued by Frances Hodgson Burnett as *The Story of the Lost Fairy Book,* London, 1887; author's other work includes *Pictures and Songs from Home,* Nelson, 1856; *Our Uncle the Traveler,* Kent, 1859; *The Young Foresters,* London, 1860).

George Eliot's *Adam Bede* (the first of several novels exploring the world of English townfolk and peasantry; strongly moral in tone; published in London by Blackwood; the author's other work appropriated by children includes *Silas Marner,* Blackwood, 1860; *The Mill on the Floss,* Blackwood, 1860; George Eliot is the pseudonym of Mary Anne Evans).

1858

Frederic William Farrar's *Eric, or Little By Little* (a popular boys' story which emphasized the horrors of "Roslyn School"; published in Edinburgh; author's other work includes *Julian Home: A Tale of College Life,* Edinburgh, 1859; *St. Winifred's, or The World of School,* Edinburgh, 1862; *The Three Homes: A Tale for Fathers and Sons,* Cassell, Peter, and Galpin, 1873; *Darkness and Dawn, or Scenes in the Days of Nero,* Longmans, 1891; *Gathering Clouds,* Longmans, 1895).

1859

A.L.O.E.'s *The Story of a Needle* (one of the author's instructive stories for children published by Nelson; the author's other work includes *The Rambles of a Rat,* Nelson, 1860; A.L.O.E. stands for A Lady of England and is the pseudonym of Charlotte Maria Tucker).

Peter Asbjörnsen and Jörgen Engebretsen Moe's *Popular Tales from the Norse* (translated from the Norwegian *Norske Folkeeventyr,* 1842, by George Webbe Dasent; published in Edinburgh by Edmunston and Douglas; the first collection of Norse folktales appropriated by children; the translator's subsequent edition, *Selections,* London, 1862, was intended for children; the translator's other work includes *Tales from the Fjeld*, Chapman, 1861).

Charles Reade's *The Cloister and the Hearth* (a story about the parents of Erasmus, which also provides information about the Renaissance in Europe; illustrated by Gordon Browne and published in London by Chambers; the author's other work includes *Christie Johnstone,* Bentley, 1853; *Griffith Gaunt; or, Jealousy,* Chapman, 1866; *Good Stories,* Harper, 1884; *Hard Cash,* Chatto, 1892).

ca. 1860

Dime novels (sensational blood-and-thunder adventure stories in paperback form; the stories were usually set on the American frontier and extolled the virtues of American individualism; first published by Irwin Beadle, the dime novels were probably an outgrowth of the English "shilling shockers" which contained exciting but thin plots). UMi

1860

Edward Sylvester Ellis's *Seth Jones; or the Captives of the Frontier* (one of the popular Beadle's dime novels offering "thrilling romance"; published by Irwin P. Beadle company, New York, and bound in orange paper wrappers lettered in black; author's other work, published in New York by Irwin P. Beadle except as noted, includes *The Life and Times of Colonel Daniel*

1860 *continued*

Boone, the Hunter of Kentucky, 1860; *The Life and Times of Christopher Carson, the Rocky Mountain Scout and Guide,* New York Publishing, 1861; *The Life of Pontiac, the Conspirator, Chief of Ottawas,* 1861; *The Life and Adventures of Colonel David Crockett,* 1862; *Kent, the Ranger; or The Fugitives of the Border,* 1863; *Oonomoo, the Huron,* 1863; *The Hunter's Escape: A Tale of the Northwest in 1862,* 1864; *Indian Jim: A Tale of the Minnesota Massacre,* 1864; *Nathan Todd; or, The Fate of the Sioux Captive,* 1864; *The Rangers of the Mohawk: A Tale of Cherry Valley,* 1864; *The Mystic Canoe: A Romance of One Hundred Years Ago,* 1865; *The Rival Scouts; or, The Forest Garrison,* 1865; *The Haunted Wood: A Legend of the Mohawk in 1778,* Chapman, 1866; *Monowano, the Shawnee Spy,* ca. 1866; *Prairie Trail,* Irwin, 1867; *Phantom Horseman,* 1869; *Chewacho,* Munro, 1870; *Fugitives of the Chatachoochie,* Munro, 1870; *Jack's Horseshoe; or, What the Waugroo Bitters Did,* 1883; *Ned in the Blockhouse: A Tale of Early Days in the West,* Porter, 1883; *Jack's Horseshoe,* National Temperance Society, 1883; *Life on the Mountain and Prairie,* Munro, 1884; *The Lost Trail,* 1884; *Ned in the Woods; A Tale of Early Days in the West,* Porter, 1884; *Ned on the River,* Porter, 1884; *Campfire and Wigwam,* Porter, 1885; *Up the Tapajos; or, Adventures in Brazil,* 1886; *Down the Mississippi,* Cassell, 1886; *Lost in the Wilds,* Cassell, 1886; *Up the Tapajoes,* Cassell, 1886; *Footprints in the Forest,* Porter, 1886; *The Last War Trail,* Porter, 1887; *The Hunters of the Ozark,* Porter, 1887; *The Camp in the Mountains,* Porter, 1887; *Adrift in the Wilds; or, the Adventures of Two Shipwrecked Boys,* Burt, 1887; *Wyoming,* Porter, 1888; *The Star of India,* Munsey, 1888; *A Young Hero; or, Fighting To Win,* Burt, 1888; *Storm Mountain,* 1889; *A Jaunt Through Java: The Story of a Journey to the Sacred Mountain by Two American Boys,* Burt, 1889; *The Cabin in the Clearing: A Tale of the Frontier,* Porter, 1890; *Arthur Helmuth,* United States Book Co.,* 1891; *Tad; or, "Getting Even" with Him,* Cassel, 1891; *Through Forest and Fire,* Porter, 1891; *Lost in Samoa: A Tale of Adventure in the Navigator Islands,* Cassell, 1891; *Check 2134,* United States Book Co., 1892; *On the Trail of the Moose,* United States Book Co., 1892; *From the Throttle to the President's Chair: A Story of Railway Life,* Cassell, 1892; *The River Fugitives,* Price-McGill, 1893; *The Campers Out; or, The Right Path and the Wrong,* Penn, 1893; *The Wilderness Fugitives,* 1893; *Lena-Wingo, the Mohawk,* Price-McGill, 1893; *Across Texas,* 1893; *Among the Esquimaux; or, Adventures Under the Arctic Circle,* Penn, 1894; *The Great Cattle Trail,* Porter, 1894; *Righting the Wrong,* Merriam, 1894; *Honest Ned,* Merriam, 1894; *Brave Tom; or, The Battle That Won,* Merriam, 1894; *Makers of Our Country,* 1894; *The Young Ranchers; or, Fighting the Sioux,* Coates, 1895; *The Young Scout: The Story of a West Point Lieutenant,* Burt, 1895; *Comrades True; or, Perseverance Versus Genius,*

Penn, 1895; *Jack Midwood; or, Bread Cast Upon the Waters,* Merriam, 1895; *The Path in the Ravine,* Porter, 1895; *The Phantom of the River,* Coates, 1896; *Shod with Silence: A Tale of the Frontier,* Coates, 1896; *Uncrowning a King: A Tale of King Philip's War,* New Amsterdam, 1896; *Young Conductor,* Merriam, 1896; *True To His Trust,* Penn, 1897; *Eye of the Sun,* Rand, 1897; *A Strange Craft and Its Wonderful Voyage,* Coates, 1897; *In the Days of Pioneers,* Coates, 1897; *Lives of the Presidents of the United States,* 1897; *Cowmen and Rustlers: A Story of Wyoming Cattle Rangers in 1892,* Coates, 1898; *Lost in the Rockies,* Burt, 1898; *Two Boys in Wyoming: A Tale of Adventure,* Coates, 1898; *Klondike Nuggets, and How Two Boys Secured Them,* Doubleday, 1898; *Captured by Indians: a Tale of the American Frontier; and Daughter of the Chieftan: A Story of an Indian Girl,* Cassell, 1899; *Tales Told Out of School,* Bardeen, 1899; *Through Jungle and Wilderness,* Mershon, 1899; *Dorsey, the Young Inventor,* Fords, 1899; *From Tent to White House,* 1899; *Iron Heart, War Chief of the Iroquois,* Coates, 1899; *The Land of Wonders,* Mershon, 1899; *Secret of Coffin Island,* Coates, 1899; *The Boy Patriot: A Story of Jack, the Young Friend of Washington,* Burt, 1900; *Blazing Arrow,* Coates, 1900; *A Waif of the Mountains,* Mershon, 1900; *Red Plume,* Mershon, 1900; *Red Jacket,* Dutton, 1900; *Our Jim; or The Power of Example,* Estes, 1901; *Red Eagle: A Tale of the Frontier,* Coates, 1901; *Lucky Ned,* Estes, 1902; *Logan the Mingo,* Dutton, 1902; *Jim and Joe, Two Brave Boys,* Coates, 1902; *Limber Lew, the Circus Boy; or, The Battle of Life,* 1903; *Old Ironsides, the Hero of Tripoli and 1812, and Other Tales and Adventures on Sea and Land,* Hurst, 1903; *The Jungle Fugitives: A Tale of Life and Adventure in India, including Also Many Stories of American Adventure, Enterprise and Daring,* Hurst, 1903; *True Blue: A Story of Luck and Pluck,* Estes, 1903; *The Last Emperor of the Old Dominion,* Coates, 1904; *Patriot and Tory,* Estes, 1904; *The Telegraph Messenger Boy; or, The Straight Road to Success,* Mershon, 1904; *The Cromwells of Virginia: A Story of Bacon's Rebellion,* Coates, 1904; *Plucky Jo,* Estes, 1905; *Deerfoot on the Prairies,* Winston, 1905; *Deerfoot in the Mountains,* 1905; *Deerfoot in the Forest,* 1905; *Among the Redskins,* Street, 1906; *The Hunt of the White Elephant,* Winston, 1906; *From Low to High Gear,* Estes, 1906; *A Hunt on Snow Shoes,* Winston, 1906; *Lost in the Forbidden Land,* Winston, 1906; *River and Jungle,* Winston, 1906; *Tracked Through the Wilds,* Street, 1906; *The Cruise of the Firefly,* Winston, 1906; *Black Partridge,* Dutton, 1906; *Fighting to Win: The Story of a New York Boy,* Burt, 1907; *The Forest Messengers,* Winston, 1907; *Low Twelve: "By Their Deeds Ye Shall Know Them." A Series of Striking and Truthful Incidents Illustrative of the Fidelity of Free Masons to One Another in Times of Distress and Danger,* Ellis, 1907; *Princess of the Woods,* Cassell, 1907; *The Queen of the Clouds,* Winston, 1907; *The Mountain Star,* Winston, 1907; *Brave Billy,* Winston, 1907; *The Lost Dragon,* Estes,

1860 *continued*

1907; *Plucky Dick; or, Sowing and Reaping,* Winston, 1907; *Tam: or, Holding the Fort,* Winston, 1908; *The P.Q. & G.: or, "As the Twig Is Bent the Tree's Inclined,"* Estes, 1908; *The Phantom Auto,* Winston, 1908; *Off the Reservation; or, Caught in an Apache Raid,* Winston, 1908; *The Story of Red Feather: A Tale of the American Frontier,* McLoughlin, 1908; *The Young Pioneers; or, Better To Be Born Plucky Than Rich,* Burt, 1908; *The Round-Up; or, Geronimo's Last Raid,* Winston, 1908; *Alden Among the Indians; or, The Search for the Missing Pony Express Rider,* Winston, 1909; *Alden the Pony Express Rider; or, Racing for Life,* Winston, 1909; *Boy Hunters of Kentucky,* Cassell, 1909; *Unlucky Tib,* Estes, 1909; *Upside Down: An Automobile Story for Boys,* Winston, 1909; *Catamount Camp,* Winston, 1910; *Captain of the Camp; or, Ben the Young Boss,* Winston, 1910; *The Frontier Angel: A Romance of Kentucky Rangers' Life,* Hurst, 1910; *The Forest Spy: A Tale of the War of 1812,* Hurst, 1910; *Work and Win: Story of a Country Boy's Success,* Burt, 1910; *The Ranger; or, The Fugitives of the Border,* Hurst, 1911; *Irona: or, Life on the Southwest Border,* Hurst, 1911; *The Hunter's Cabin: An Episode of the Early Settlements of Southern Ohio,* Hurst, 1911; *The Flying Boys to the Rescue,* Winston, 1911; *The Flying Boys in the Sky,* Winston, 1911; *Adrift on the Pacific: A Boy's Story of the Sea and Its Perils,* Burt, 1911; *Riflemen of the Miami,* Hurst, 1912; *The Worst Boys,* American Tract Society, 1912; *The Launch Boys' Adventure in Northern Waters,* Winston, 1912; *The Launch Boys' Cruise in the Deerfoot,* Winston, 1912; *High Twelve,* Macoy, 1912; *The Boy Patrol Around the Council Fire,* 1913; *The Boy Patrol,* Winston, 1913; *"Remember the Alamo,"* Winston, 1914; *The Three Arrows,* Winston, 1914; under the pseudonym of B. H. Belnap: *Pegleg Smith: A Tale,* 1866; under the pseudonym of J. G. Bethune: *Hands Up! or, The Great Bank Burglary,* United States Book Co., 1890; *The "F" Cipher,* Price-McGill, 1892; *The Great Berwyck Bank Burglary,* Collier, 1893; *The Third Man,* Cassell, 1893; under pseudonym of Captain L. C. Carleton: *The Hunter,* ca. 1893; *The Trapper's Retreat: A Sequel to "The Hunter,"* 1893; *Scar-Cheek: The Wild Half-Bred,* Munro, 1864; *The Three Daring Trappers,* Munro, 1865; *Old Norte the Hunter: or, Adventures in Texas,* Munro, 1866; *Buffalo Jack,* Munro, 1866; *Hank Wiggins, Esq.,* 1867; *Cooney Bush, Trapper and Scout,* Munro, 1876; *Spotted Day,* Munro, 1867; *Marksman the Hunter,* Munro, 1867; *Hunter Scouts,* Munro, 1869; *Hunters and Redskins,* 1869; *Brimstone Jake,* Munro, 1869; *Small-Pox Dave,* Munro, 1869; *Red Hand,* Munro, 1870; *Club-Foot,* Munro, 1879; *Mysterious Hunter; or, The Man of Death,* Munro, 1885; *The Wild Man of the Woods,* Munro, 1892; under the pseudonym of Colonel H. R. Gordon: *Pontiac, Chief of the Ottawas: A Tale of the Siege of Detroit,* 1897; *Tecumseh, Chief of the Shawanoes: A Tale of the War of 1812,* Dutton, 1889; *Osceola, Chief of the Seminoles,* Dutton, 1899; *Red Jacket, the Last of the Senecas,* Dutton, 1900; *Logan the Mingo: A Story of the Frontier,* Dutton, 1902; *Black Partridge; or, The Fall of Fort Dearborn,* Dutton, 1906; under the pseudonym of Captain R. M. Hawthorne: *Hurricane Gulch: A Tale of the Aosta and Bufferville Trail,* Collier, 1892; under the pseudonym of Lieutenant R. H. Jayne: *Perils of the Jungle: A Tale of Adventure in the Dark Continent,* Munsey, 1888; *The White Mustang: A Tale of the Lone Star State,* Lovell, 1889; *The Land of Mystery,* Lovell, 1889; *On the Trail of Geronimo; or, In the Apache Country,* Winston, 1889; *Lost in the Wilderness,* Price-McGill, 1892; *Through Apache Land,* Price-McGill, 1893; *The Cave in the Mountain,* Merriam, 1894; *In the Pecos Country,* Merriam, 1894; *The Golden Rock,* American Publishers, 1896; under the pseudonym of C. E. Lassalle: *Buffalo Trapper,* 1870; *Burt Bunker, Trapper,* 1870; *Forest Monster,* 1870; under pseudonym of Seward D. Lisle: *Teddy and Towser: A Story of Early Days in California,* Coates, 1904; *Up the Forked River; or, Adventures in South America,* Coates, 1904; under pseudonym of Billex Muller: *River Rifles,* Starr, 1870; under the pseudonym of Lieutenant J. H. Randolph: *Buck Buckram,* Starr, 1869; *The Phantom Chief,* 1867; under the pseudonym of Captain Wheeler: *The Track of Fire,* 1864; under pseudonym of Emerson Redman: *Mad Anthony's Scouts,* Starr, 1870; under the pseudonym of Seelin Robins: *The Phantom Chief,* Irwin, 1867; editor: *Golden Days,* ca. 1880; author of numerous adult biographies, histories, school textbooks, and reference works). LC, PFL, UMi

Ann S. Stephens's *Malaeska, or Indian Wife of the White Hunter* (the first of a series of enormously popular "dime novels" published by the Beadle Publishing Co. in New York; although this unhappy story of Indian life lacked the "blood-and-thunder" sensationalism of the stories in the series that followed, its format set the patterns for Beadle's "dime novels"; a pocket-sized booklet of about 25,000 words on 128 pages printed on white rag paper; its salmon-colored paper cover bore a steel engraving of the heroine and the ten-cent piece which was to become the emblem of the series). UMi

1861

Jane Andrews's *The Seven Little Sisters Who Live on the Round Ball That Floats in the Air* (a story popular with several generations of young readers about seven little girls who live in seven different parts of the world; published by Ticknor and Fields; author's other work includes *Each and All; or, How the Seven Little Sisters Prove Their Sisterhood,* Lee, 1878; *Ten Boys Who Lived on the Road from Long Ago Till Now,* Ginn, 1885; *Only a Year, and What It Brought,* Lothrop, 1887; *The Stories Mother Nature Told Her Children,* Ginn, 1888). CCBC

1861 *continued*

Norman Macleod's *The Golden Thread* (an allegorical tale by a Scottish author, published in Edinburgh; similar to George MacDonald's *The Golden Key;* author was MacDonald's friend and editor; the author's other work includes *The Old Lieutenant,* Partridge, 1910).

1862

Christina Georgina Rossetti's *Goblin Market* (exquisite fairy poems expressing the ancient motif of evil fairies being overcome by love; published in Cambridge; illustrated by Arthur Hughes; the author's other work includes *Sing Song,* Routledge, 1872; *Speaking Likenesses,* Macmillan, 1874). PU

1863

The Boys' Journal: a magazine of literature, science, adventure, and amusement (British published monthly by Henry Vickers and edited by C. P. Brown; incorporated with the *Youth's Play-Hour* in February 1871).

Charles Kinglsey's *Water Babies: a Fairy Tale for a Land-Baby* (a modern moralistic fairy tale which attempts to show children the divine element in nature; reveals the author's hatred of child labor through the chimney sweep hero; designs by Noel Paton; printed in London; the author's other work includes *Glaucus, or the Wonders of the Shore,* Cambridge: Macmillan, 1855; *Westward Ho!* Cambridge, 1855, appropriated by children; *The Heroes, or Greek Fairy Tales for My Children,* Cambridge, 1856; *Hereward the Wake,* London, 1866; *Madame How and Lady Why,* Bell, 1870).

Coventry Patmore's *The Children's Garland from the Best Poets* (a collection of poems carefully selected with children in mind; published in London by Macmillan; poems include those by Blake, Poe, Tennyson, Browning, Shelley, and Keats).

William Brighty Rands's *Lilliput Levee* (a collection of fantastic and nonsense verses; the author is best known for his verse "Great, wide, beautiful, wonderful world / With the wonderful water round you curled" and "The Pedlar's Caravan"; the author's other work includes *Lilliput Lectures,* London, 1871; *Lilliput Revels,* Routledge, 1871; *Lilliput Legends,* London, 1872; *Lilliput Lyrics,* J. Lane, 1899).

Mrs. A. D. T. Whitney's *Faith Gartney's Girlhood* (a popular girls' story which includes a rendering of "The Little Small Red Hen" in an Irish dialect; published in Boston by A. K. Loring; the author's other work includes *The Lamplighter,* Boston, 1853; *Sights & Insights,* Osgood, 1876; *Boys at Chequasset,* Houghton, 1862; *The Gayworthys,* Loring, 1865; *A*

Summer in Leslie Goldthwaite's Life, Ticknor, 1866; *We Girls,* Fields, 1870; *Real Folks,* Osgood, 1871; *Pansies,* Osgood, 1872; *The Other Girls,* Osgood, 1873; *Odd or Even,* Houghton, 1880; *Bonnyborough,* Houghton, 1886; *A Golden Gossip,* Houghton, 1892; *White Memories,* Houghton, 1893; *Friendly Letters to Girl Friends,* Houghton, 1896; the author's full name is Adeline Dutton Train Whitney).

1864

Horatio Alger's *Frank's Campaign* (the first of a popular series of stories set in America in which the heroes climb from "rags to riches"; published in Boston by Loring; the author's other work, published by Loring except as noted, includes *Bertha's Christmas Vision,* Brown, 1856; *Nothing To Do,* French, 1857; *Paul Prescott's Charge,* 1865; *Helen Ford,* 1866; *Timothy Crump's World,* first published anonymously in 1866, but later rewritten and published as *Jack's Ward,* 1875; *Charlie Codman's Cruise,* 1867; *Fame and Fortune,* 1868; *Ragged Dick, or, Street Life in New York with the Boot Blacks,* 1868; *Mark the Match Boy,* 1869; *Rough and Ready,* 1869; *Ralph Raymond's Heir,* Gleason, 1869; *Luck and Pluck,* 1869; *Sink or Swim,* 1870; *Ben the Luggage Boy,* 1870; *Rufus and Rose,* 1870; *Paul the Peddler,* 1871; *Strong and Steady,* 1871; *Slow and Sure,* 1872; *Strive and Succeed,* 1872; *Bound to Rise,* 1873; *Try and Trust,* 1873; *Brave and Bold,* 1874; *Julius: or, the Street Boy Out West,* 1874; *Risen from the Ranks,* 1874; *Grand'ther Baldwin's Thanksgiving and Other Ballads and Poems,* 1875; *Herbert Carter's Legacy,* 1875; *Seeking His Fortune,* 1875; *Young Outlaw,* 1875; *Sam's Chance,* 1876; *Shifting for Himself,* 1876; *Wait and Hope,* 1877; *Young Adventurer,* 1878; *The Western Boy,* Street, 1878, reprinted as *Tom the Bootblack; The Telegraph Boy,* 1879; *The Young Miner,* 1879; *Tony the Hero,* Ogilvie, 1880; *Young Explorer,* 1880; *From Canal Boy to President, or the Boyhood and Manhood of James A. Garfield,* Anderson, 1881; *Ben's Nugget,* Porter, 1882; *From Farm Boy to Senator; Being the History of the Boyhood and Manhood of Daniel Webster,* Ogilvie, 1882; *The Train Boy,* Street, 1883; *The Young Circus Rider,* Porter, 1883; *Abraham Lincoln, the Backwoods Boy,* Anderson, 1883; *Do and Dare,* Porter, 1884; *Dan the Detective,* Street, 1884; *Hector's Inheritance,* Porter, 1885; *Helping Himself,* Porter, 1886; *Joe's Luck,* Burt, 1887; *Frank Fowler, The Cash Boy,* Burt, 1887; under the pseudonym of Arthur Lee Putnam: *Number 91 or The Adventures of a New York Telegraph Boy,* Munsey, 1887; *The Store Boy,* Porter, 1887; *The Young Acrobat,* Munsey, 1888; *Tom Tracy, or The Trials of a New York Newsboy,* Munsey, 1888; *Tom Thather's Fortune,* Burt, 1888; *Tom Temple's Career,* Burt, 1888; *Bob Burton,* Porter, 1888; *The Errand Boy,* Burt, 1888; *Luke Walton,* Porter, 1889; *The $500 Check,* Lovell, 1890; *Ned Newton,* Lovell, 1890; *Mark Stanton,* Lovell, 1890; *A New York Boy,* Lovell, 1890; *The Odds Against*

1864 *continued*

Him, Penn, 1890; *Struggling Upward,* Porter, 1890; *Dean Dunham,* United States Book Co., 1891; *The Young Boatman,* Penn, 1892; *Digging for Gold,* Porter, 1893; *Facing the World,* Porter, 1893; *In a New World,* Porter, 1893; *Victor Vane,* Porter, 1894; *Only An Irish Boy,* Porter, 1894; *Adrift in the City,* Coates, 1895; *Young Salesman,* Coates, 1896; *Frank Hunter's Peril,* Coates, 1896; *Frank and Fearless,* Coates, 1897; *Walter Sherwood's Probation,* Coates, 1897; *A Boy's Fortune,* Coates, 1898; *Young Bank Messenger,* Coates, 1898; *Mark Mason's Victory,* Burt, 1899; *Rupert's Ambition,* Coates, 1899; *A Debt of Honor,* Burt, 1900; *Falling in With Fortune,* Mershon, 1900; *Out for Business,* Mershon, 1900; *Jed the Poorhouse Boy,* Coates, 1900; *Making His Mark,* Penn, 1901; *Tester's Luck,* Coates, 1901; *Ben Bruce,* Burt, 1901; *Tom Brave,* Street, 1901; *Striving for Fortune,* Street, 1901; *Nelson the Newsboy,* Mershon, 1901; *Young Captain Jack,* Mershon, 1901; *Wren Winter's Triumph,* Thompson, 1902, also published as *A Rolling Stone* by Arthur Lee Putnam; *Andy Grant's Pluck,* Coates, 1902; *Tom Turner's Legacy,* Burt, 1902; *The World Before Him,* Penn, 1902; *Adrift in New York,* Street, 1903; *Bernard Brooks' Adventures,* Burt, 1903; *Chester Rand,* Coates, 1903; *Forging Ahead,* Penn, 1903; *Finding a Fortune,* Penn, 1904; *Jerry the Backwoods Boy,* Mershon, 1904; *Lost At Sea,* Mershon, 1904; *From Farm To Fortune,* Stitt, 1905; *Young Book Agent,* Stitt, 1905; *Mark Manning's Mission,* Burt, 1905; *Randy of the River,* Chatterton-Peck, 1906; *Joe the Hotel Boy,* Cupples, 1906; *Young Musician,* Penn, 1906; *In Search of Treasure,* Burt, 1907; *Wait and Win,* Burt, 1907; *Ben Logan's Triumph,* Cupples, 1908; *Robert Coverdale's Struggle,* Street, 1910; the author also used the pseudonyms Arthur Hamilton and Caroline F. Preston). DC, HPL, LC, RPL, UMi

Harry Castlemon's *Frank on a Gunboat* (one of the Gunboat series books based on author's United States Navy experiences; the author's other work includes *Frank Before Vicksburg,* 1864; *Frank, the Young Naturalist,* 1864; *No Moss; or, The Career of a Rolling Stone,* 1864; *Frank Among the Ranchers,* 1865; *Frank in the Woods,* 1865; *Frank on the Prairie,* 1865; *Go-Ahead; or, The Fisher Boy's Motto,* 1867; *Tom Newcombe; or, The Boy of Bad Habits,* 1867; *Frank at Don Carlos' Rancho,* 1868; *Frank in the Mountains,* 1868; *Frank on the Lower Mississippi,* 1868; *Our Duck Hunt,* Miller, 1873; *Sportsman's Club in the Saddle,* 1873; *The Sportsman's Club Afloat,* 1874; *The Sportsman's Club Among the Trappers,* 1874; *Frank Nelson in the Forecastle,* 1876; *Snowed Up,* 1876; *The Boy Traders,* Porter, 1877; *The Buried Treasure,* 1877; *The Boy Trapper,* Porter, 1878; *George in Camp,* 1879; *The Mail Carrier,* 1879; *George At the Wheel,* 1881; *George At the Fort,* 1882; *Don Gordon's Shooting Box,* 1883; *The Young Wild-Fowlers,* 1885; *Joe Wayring At Home,* 1886; *Julian Mortimer,* Burt, 1887;

Guy Harris, the Runaway, Burt, 1887; *Our Fellows,* Coates, 1887; *Snagged and Sunk; or, The Adventures of a Canvas Canoe,* 1888; *The Steel Horse; or, The Rambles of a Bicycle,* 1888; *True to His Colors,* 1889; *Marcy, the Blockade-Runner,* 1891; *Rodney the Partisan,* 1891; *Marcy, the Refugee,* 1892; *Rodney, the Overseer,* 1892; *Two Ways of Becoming a Hunter,* 1892; *The Camp in the Foothills,* 1893; *Sailor Jack, the Trader,* 1893; *Oscar in Africa,* 1894; *Elam Storm, the Wolfer,* 1895; *The Haunted Mine,* Coates, 1895; *The Missing Pocket-Book; or, Tom Mason's Luck,* Coates, 1895; *The Rod and Gun Club,* 1895; *The Mystery of Lost River Canyon,* Coates, 1896; *The Young Game-Warden,* Coates, 1896; *A Rebellion in Dixie,* Coates, 1897; *The Ten Ton Cutter,* Coates, 1897; *A Sailor in Spite of Himself,* Coates, 1898; *The Pony Express Rider,* Coates, 1898; *Carl the Trailer,* Winston, 1899; *The White Beaver,* Coates, 1899; *The First Capture,* Saalfield, 1900; *Floating Treasure,* Coates, 1901; *Winged Arrow's Medicine,* Saalfield, 1901; *White Horse Fred; or, Julian Among the Outlaws,* Coates, 1901; *A Struggle for a Fortune,* Saalfield, 1902; Henry Castlemon was the pseudonym of Charles Austin Fosdick). DC, IUL, LC

John Townsend Trowbridge's *Cugjo's Cave* (a story of the adventures of an abolitionist Quaker schoolmaster in Tennessee before the Civil War; published in Boston by Lothrop; appropriated by children; the author's other work, published in Boston by Lothrop except as noted, includes *Father Brighthopes,* Lee and Shepard, 1853; *Neighbor Jack Wood,* Sampson, 1857; *The Vagabonds,* Gregory, 1864; *Lucy Arlyn,* Ticknor, 1866; *Lawrence's Adventures Among the Ice-Cutters, Glass-Makers, Coal Miners, Iron Men and Ship Builders,* Porter, 1870; *The Story of Columbus,* Fields and Osgood, 1870; *Coupon Bonds and Other Stories,* Osgood, 1873; *The Emigrant's Story and Other Poems,* Osgood, 1875; *Fast Friends,* Osgood, 1875; *The Book of Gold and Other Poems,* Harper, 1878; *Bound in Honor,* Lee and Shepard, 1878; *A Home Idyl & Other Poems,* Houghton, 1881; *The Pocket Rifle,* Dillingham, 1882; *The Tinkham Brothers' Tide Mill,* Lee and Shepard, 1882; *The Jolly Rover,* Dillingham, 1883; *Phil and His Friends,* Dillingham, 1884; *Farnell's Folly,* Dillingham, 1885; *His One Fault,* Dillingham, 1887; *The Little Master,* Lee and Shepard, 1887; *Peter Budstone,* Dillingham, 1888; *The Adventures of David Vane and David Crane,* Lothrop, 1889; *Biding His Time,* Dillingham, 1889; *A Start in Life,* Lee and Shepard, 1889; *The Drummer Boy,* Lee and Shepard, 1891; *The Kelp-Gatherers,* Lee and Shepard, 1891; *The Scarlet Tanager,* Lee and Shepard, 1891; *The Three Scouts,* Lee and Shepard, 1892; *The Fortunes of Toby Trafford,* Lee and Shepard, 1893; *Woodie Thorpe's Pilgrimmage,* Lee and Shepard, 1893; *The Satin-wood Box,* Lee and Shepard, 1894; *The Lottery Ticket,* Lee and Shepard, 1896; *The Prize Cup,* Century, 1896; *A Question of Damages,* Lee and Shepard, 1897; *Two Bediccut Boys,* Century, 1898; *Jack Hazard*

1864 *continued*

and His Fortunes, Coates, 1899; *The Young Surveyor,* Coates, 1903; *Young Joe and Other Boys,* Lee and Shepard, 1907; *The Silver Medal,* Lee and Shepard, 1908; *His Own Master,* 1905; *A Pair of Madcaps,* Lee and Shepard, 1909; *A Chance for Himself,* Coates, 1900; *Doing His Best,* Coates, 1901; *Darius Green and His Flying Machine,* Houghton, 1910; the author edited *Our Young Folks,* 1865-1873, along with Lucy Larcom and Gail Hamilton, and many of his stories first appeared in the magazine; the author also published under the pseudonym of Paul Creyton).

1865

Lewis Carroll's *Alice's Adventures in Wonderland* (one of the most success-ful fantasies ever written; published by Macmillan in London, followed by *Through the Looking Glass,* Macmillan, 1872; Lewis Carroll was the pseudo-nym of Charles Ludwig Dodgson, an Oxford mathematician; both books were illustrated by Sir John Tenniel; the author's other work includes "Bruno's Revenge" in *Aunt Judy's Magazine,* 1867; *The Hunting of the Snark,* Macmillan, 1876; *Doublets, a Word Puzzle,* 1879; *Rhyme? and Reason?,* Macmillan, 1883; *A Tangled Tale,* 1885; *The Game of Logic,* 1886; *Alice's Adventures Underground,* Macmillan, 1886; *The Nursery Alice,* Macmillan, 1889; *Sylvie and Bruno,* Macmillan, 1889; *Sylvie and Bruno Concluded,* Macmillan, 1893; *Letters to Child Friends,* 1933; the author's poetry collections include *Phantasmagoria, and Other Poems,* Macmillan, 1869; *Three Sunsets and Other Poems,* 1898; *The Lewis Carroll Picture Book,* 1899; *Novelty and Romancement: A Story,* Brimmer, 1925; *For the Train: Five Poems and a Tale,* Archer, 1932; *The Rectory Umbrella and Mischmasch,* Cassell, 1932; *Instructive and Useful Poetry,* Macmillan, 1954; *The Mad Gardner's Song,* Bobbs-Merrill, 1967; *The Jabberwocky and Other Frabjous Nonsense,* Crown, 1967). LC, NYPL-B, UBC

Walter Crane's *The House That Jack Built* (the first of the author-illustrator's many "toy books" engraved by Edmund Evans which marked the beginning of the modern color era in illustration in children's books; the book is also the first title in Ward, Lock and Tyler's New Shilling series, published in London; other Crane titles in the series are *The Comical Cat*, 1865 and *The Affecting Story of Jenny Wren,* 1865; for the Aunt Mavor Series of Toy Books, published in London for George Routledge [later known as the Sixpenny Toy Series], Crane illustrated: *The Railroad Alphabet*, 1865; *The Farmyard Alphabet,* 1865; *Sing a Song of Sixpence,* 1865; *A Gaping-Wide-Mouth Waddling Frog,* 1865; *The Old Courtier,* 1867; *Multiplication Table in Verse,* 1867; *Chattering Jack,* 1867; *How Jessie Was Lost,* 1868; *Gram-mar in Rhyme,* 1868; *Annie and Jack in London,* 1869; *One, Two, Buckle My Shoe,* 1869; *The Fairy Ship,* 1870; *The Adventures of Puffy,* 1870; *This Little Pig Went To Market,* 1870; *King Luckyboy's Party,* 1870; *Noah's*

Ark Alphabet, 1872; *My Mother,* 1873; *Ali Baba and the Forty Thieves,* 1873; *The Three Bears,* 1873; *Cinderella,* 1873; *Valentine and Orson,* 1874; *Puss in Boots,* 1874; *Old Mother Hubbard,* 1874; *The Absurd ABC,* 1874; *Little Red Riding Hood,* 1875; *Jack and the Beanstalk,* 1875; *Bluebeard,* 1875; *Baby's Own Alphabet,* 1875; *The Sleeping Beauty in the Wood,* 1876; for the Routledge Shilling Series, Crane illustrated: *The Frog Prince, Goody Two Shoes, Beauty and the Beast, The Alphabet of Old Friends,* 1874; and *The Yellow Dwarf, Aladdin, The Hind in the Wood, Princess Belle Etoile,* 1875; other works by Crane contained collections of the stories or rhymes in the Shilling 'n Sixpenny Series, published by Routledge: *The Baby's Opera, A Book of Old Rhymes in New Dresses,* 1877; and *The Baby's Bouquet, A Fresh Bunch of Old Rhymes and Tunes,* collected and arranged by Lucy Crane, 1878, illustrated by Walter Crane, and printed by Marcus Ward; the author-illustrator's other work includes *Cock Robin,* Warne, 1866; The Marcus Ward Picture Books *Thoughts in a Hammock,* Ward, 1884; *Slate-andpencilvania; Being the Adventures of Dick on a Desert Island,* Ward, 1885; *Little Queen Anne and Her Majesty's Letters,* Ward, 1885; *Pothooks and Perseverance, or the ABC Serpent,* Ward, 1885; *Baby's Own Aesop, Being the Fables Condensed in Rhyme with Portable Morals Pictorially Pointed,* Ward, 1887; *Echoes of Hellas, The Tale of Troy and the Story of Orestes from Homer and Aeschylus,* Ward, 1887; *Legends for Lionel* [Crane's son] *in Pen and Pencil,* Cassell, 1887; *Mr. Michael Mouse Unfolds His Tale,* MS 1887, Yale University Press, 1956; *Flora's Feast: A Masque of Flowers,* Cassell, 1889; *The Turtle Dove's Nest and Other Nursery Rhymes,* Routledge, 1890; *Queen Summer,* Cassell, 1891; *A Floral Fantasy,* Cassell, 1898; Crane also illustrated numerous books by authors such as Henry Gilbert, E. J. Gould, Charles Lamb, Mary MacGregor, Mary de-Morgan, William Morris, William Shakespeare, Edmund Spencer, Oscar Wilde, and Nathaniel Hawthorne). NYPL-SC, YU

Mary Elizabeth Mapes Dodge's *Hans Brinker, or The Silver Skates, A Story of Life in Holland* (a popular novel for children which shows life in a foreign land; so realistic that this American author's story was accepted at the time as "Dutch" by the people of Holland; illustrated by F. O. C. Darley and Thomas Nast; published in New York by James O'Kane; the author's other work includes *The Irvington Stories,* O'Kane, 1865; *Rhymes and Jingles,* Scribner, 1874; *When Life Is Young,* New York, 1894; *Donald and Dorothy,* Roberts, 1883; *The Land of Pluck,* New York, 1894; *The Golden Gate,* Donohue, 1903; the author was editor of the *St. Nicholas Magazine,* 1873-1905, and also edited *Baby World,* Century, 1884, and *Baby Days,* 1883).

J. C. Edgar's *Cressy and Pointiers* (the story of the Black Prince based largely on Froissart; published in London by S. O. Beaton; one of the author's several short, historically based stories and biographies of great men).

1865 *continued*

Edward Everett Hale's *The Man Without a Country* (a well-known story published in Boston by Ticknor and Fields, but which originally appeared in the December 1863 issue of the *Atlantic Monthly;* with Susan Hale, the author wrote a series of travel books: *A Family Flight through France, Germany, Norway and Switzerland,* Lothrop, 1881; *A Family Flight Over Egypt and Syria,* Lothrop, 1882; *A Family Flight Around Home,* Lothrop, 1884; *A Family Flight through Mexico,* Lothrop, 1886; and by Susan Hale, *A Family Flight through Spain,* Lothrop, 1883; author's other work includes, under the pseudonym of Capt. Frederic Ingham, *Ten Times One Is Ten; The Possible Reformation,* Roberts, 1871; *His Level Best and Other Stories,* Roberts, 1872; editor, *Six of One By Half Dozen of the Other,* Roberts, 1872; *Christmas Eve and Christmas Day,* Roberts, 1873; *In His Name. A Christmas Story,* Boston, 1873; editor, *Ups and Downs,* Roberts, 1873; editor, *Stand and Wait,* Lockwood, 1875; *Spoons in a Wheery,* Boston, 1875; editor, *Silhouettes and Songs Illustrative of the Months,* Lockwood, 1876; *Mrs. Merriam's Scholars,* Roberts, 1878; *Crusoe in New York,* Roberts, 1880; *Stories of Discovery As Told By Discoverers,* Roberts, 1882; *Our Christmas in a Palace,* Funk, 1883; *Christmas in Narragansett,* Funk, 1884; *The Fortunes of Rachel,* Funk, 1884; *Boys' Heroes,* Lothrop, 1885; *Stories of Inventions Told By Inventors,* Roberts, 1885; *Red and White: A Christmas Story,* 1887; *The Life of George Washington Studied Anew,* Putnam, 1888; *Mrs. Tangiers Vacation,* Roberts, 1888; *Stories of Adventure As Told By Adventurers,* Roberts, 1888; *East and West; A Story of New-Born Ohio,* Cassell, 1892; *G.T.T.; or, The Wonderful Adventures of a Pullman,* Roberts, 1892; with Lucretia P. Hale, *The New Harry and Lucy; A Story of Boston in the Summer of 1891,* Roberts, 1892; *Sybil Knox; or, Home Again,* Cassell, 1892; *A New England Boyhood,* Cassell, 1893; editor, *Tales from the Travels of Baron Munchausen,* illustrated by Gustave Doré, Heath, 1900; *New England History in Ballads,* Little, 1903; editor, *The Only True Mother Goose Melodies; An Exact Reproduction of the Text and Illustrations of the Original Edition Published in 1833 by Munroe and Francis,* Lee, 1905).

Sophie May's *Dotty Dimple* (the first of a popular series of books about seven-year-old Alice Parlin, better known as Dotty Dimple; the author also wrote a series of Little Prudy books, about Dotty's sister Prudy, begun in 1863; author's other work, published by Lee and Shepard except as noted, includes the Dotty Dimple series: *Dotty Dimple at Grandmother's,* 1867; *Dotty Dimple At Home,* 1868; *Dotty Dimple At Play,* 1868; *Dotty Dimple At School,* 1869; *Dotty Dimple's Flyaway,* 1870; *Dotty Dimple Out West,* 1870; the Little Prudy series: *Little Prudy,* 1864; *Sister Susy,* 1864; *Cousin Grace,* 1864; *Captain Horace,* 1864; . . . *Fairy Book,* 1865; Little Prudy

Flyaway series: *Little Folks Astray,* 1871; *Prudy Keeping House,* 1871; *Aunt Madge's Story,* 1871; *Little Grandmother,* 1872; *Little Grandfather,* 1873; *Miss Thistledown,* 1873; *Doctor Papa,* 1877; the Little Prudy's Children series: *Wee Lucy; Little Prudy's "wee croodlin doo,"* 1894; *Jimmy Boy,* 1895; *Jimmy, Lucy and All,* 1900; *Lucy in Fairyland,* 1901; Little Prudy series: *Little Prudy's Captain Horace,* Lee, 1892; *Little Prudy's Cousin Grace,* Lee, 1892; *Little Prudy's Dotty Dimple,* Lee, 1893; *Little Prudy's Fairy Book,* Lee, 1908; the Flaxie Frizzle series: *Flaxie Frizzle,* 1876; *Flaxie Growing Up,* 1884; *Little Pitchers,* 1878; *The Twin Cousins,* 1880; the Quinnebasset series: *Quinnebasset Girls,* 1877; *In Old Quinnebasset,* 1891; *Joy Bells: A Quinnebasset Story,* 1903; *Little Prudy's Sister Susy,* 1864; *Baby Pitcher's Trials,* Clark and Fiske, 1869; *The Doctor's Daughter,* 1871; *Our Helen,* 1874; *The Asbury Twins,* 1875; *The Horn of Plenty of Home Poems and Home Pictures, with New Poems by Louisa M. Alcott,* W. F. Gill, 1875; *Drone's Honey,* 1878; *Janet: A Poor Heiress,* 1882; *Joe,* 1884; *Kittyleen,* 1884; *A Christmas Breeze,* 1886; *Kyzie Dunlee, "A Golden Girl,"* 1895; *The Campion Diamonds,* 1897; *Santa Claus on Snow Shoes,* DeWolfe, 1898; *Wee Lucy's Secret,* 1899; *Pauline Wyman,* 1898; Sophie May was the pseudonym of Rebecca Clarke). LC

Our Young Folks (an illustrated magazine published by Ticknor and Fields and edited by J. J. Trowbridge, Lucy, Larcom, and Gail Hamilton—the pseudonym of Mary Abigail Dodge; other authors include Mayne Reid, "Oliver Optic," Horatio Alger, Lucretia P. Hale, and Thomas Bailey Aldrich; merged with *St. Nicholas* in October, 1873). UW

1866

Aunt Judy's Magazine for Young People (a British monthly published from 1866 to 1885 in half-yearly Christmas and May-Day volumes; established by Margaret Gatty to provide a suitable outlet for the writings of her daughter, Juliana Ewing; edited by Mrs. Gatty until her death in 1874 when Juliana Ewing and her sister, Mrs. Horatia K. F. G. Eden, became the editors; in 1876, Eden took over the editorship until 1885; famous contributors included Lewis Carroll and Hans Christian Andersen; Gatty began a regular book-reviewing section by reviewing *Alice in Wonderland* and *What the Moon Saw, and Other Tales;* illustrations were engraved after such artists as George Cruikshank and Randolph Caldecott).

The Boys of England. A Young Gentleman's Journal of Sport, Sensation, Fun and Instruction (a penny weekly which continued under the title *Up-to-Date-Boys;* after the first nine numbers, which were edited by Charles Stevens, E. J. Brett became the "proprietor and conductor"; Brett first introduced Jack Harkaway to *Boys of England* readers in July 1871; beneath the title appeared: "Subscribed to by His Royal Highness Prince Arthur").

1866 *continued*

George Manville Fenn's *Hollowdell Grange* (one of the author's several books dealing with the exploration of interesting geographical areas; published in London by Routledge; the author's other work includes *Playing To Win,* Beadle, 1881; *Nat the Naturalist,* Blackie, 1882; *Bunyip Lane,* Blackie, 1885; *Brownsmith's Boy,* Blackie, 1886; *Off to the Wilds,* Crowell, 1886; *The Bag of Diamonds,* Ward, 1887; *Devon Boys,* Blackie, 1887; *Black Blood,* Lovell, 1888; *The Story of Antony Grace,* Lovell, 1888; *Three Boys of the Chiefs of the Clan Mackhai,* Dutton, 1888; *Quicksilver,* Blackie, 1889; *Ching, the Chinaman, and His Middy Friends,* Society for Promoting Christian Knowledge, 189__; *Mother Carey's Chickens,* Blackie, 189__; *Burr Junior,* Griffith, 1891; *The Crystal Hunters,* Appleton, 1891; *Blue Jackets,* Griffith, 1893; *Beneath the Sea,* Crowell, 1896; *The Black Fox,* Lippincott, 1896; *Roy Royland,* Chambers, 1896; *The King's Sons,* Dutton, 1901; *Stan Lynn; A Boy's Adventures in China,* Chambers, 1902; *Glyn Severn's School-Days,* Chambers, 1904; *The Boys At Menhardoc,* Blackie, 1911; *Coastguard Jack,* Sutton, 1902).

1867

Martha Farquharson's *Elsie Dinsmore* (the first of an eighteen-book series of American novels, published from 1867 to 1905 in New York by Dodd, Mead, which follow Victorian Elsie from childhood through widowhood; Martha Farquharson was the pseudonym of Martha Finley; the author's other work, published by Presbyterian Publications Board, except as noted, includes *Ella Clinton,* 1856; *Aunt Ruth,* Philadelphia, 1857; *Marion Harvie,* 1857; *Annadale,* 1858; *Lame Letty,* Philadelphia, 1859; *Mildred and Elsie,* 1861; *Try: Better Do It, Than Wish It Done,* 1863; *Little Joe Carter, The Cripple,* 1864; *Mysie's Work,* 1864; *Willie Elton,* Philadelphia, 1864; *Black Steve; or The Strange Warning,* 1865; *Brookside Farm-House,* 1865; *Hugo and Franz,* Philadelphia, 1865; *Robert and Daisy,* Philadelphia, 1865; *Allan's Fault,* 1866; *Anna Hand, the Meddlesome Girl,* Philadelphia, 1868; *Casella,* Dodd, 1868; *Grandma Foster's Sunbeam,* Philadelphia, 1868; *Little Dick Positive,* Philadelphia, 1868; *Little Patience,* Philadelphia, 1868; *Loitering Linus,* Philadelphia, 1868; *Maude's Two Homes,* Philadelphia, 1868; *Millie,* Philadelphia, 1868; *Stupid Sally, the Poor-House Girl,* Philadelphia, 1868; *Amy and Her Kitten,* Philadelphia, 1870; *Betty Page,* Philadelphia, 1870; *The Broken Basket,* Philadelphia, 1870; *Jamie By the Lake,* Philadelphia, 1870; *Rufus the Unready,* Philadelphia, 1870; *The White Dress,* Philadelphia, 1870; *An Old-Fashioned Boy,* Evans, 1871; *Lilian; or, Did She Do It Right?,* Evans, 1871; *Wanted—A Pedigree,* Dodd, 1871; *Contented Jim,* Philadelphia, 1872; *Honest Jim,* 1872; *How Jim Did It,* 1872; *Noll in the Country,* 1872; *Elsie's Holidays and Roselands,* Dodd, 1872; *Elsie's Girlhood,* Dodd, 1872; *The Twin Babies,* 1872; *Our Fred,*

Donohue, 1874; *The Peddler of La Grave,* 1875; *Aunt Hetty's Fowls,* 1876; *Elsie's Motherhood,* Dodd, 1876; *Harry and His Chickens,* 1876; *Harry and His Cousins,* 1876; *Harry At Aunt Jane's,* 1876; *Harry's Christmas in the City,* 1876; *Harry's Fourth of July,* 1876; *Harry's Grandma,* 1876; *Harry's Little Sister,* 1876; *Harry's Ride With Papa,* 1876; *Harry's Walk With Grandma,* 1876; *The Pewit's Nest,* 1876; *Rosa and Robbie,* 1876; *Elsie's Children,* Dodd, 1877; *Mildred Keith,* Dodd, 1876; *Mildred At Roselands,* Dodd, 1879; *Signing the Contract,* Dodd, 1879; *Elsie's Widowhood,* Dodd, 1880; *Grandmother Elsie,* Dodd, 1882; *Mildred's Married Life,* Dodd, 1882; *Elsie's New Relations,* Dodd, 1883; *Elsie At Nantucket,* Dodd, 1884; *Elsie At the World's Fair,* Dodd, 1884; *Mildred At Home,* Dodd, 1884; *The Two Elsies,* Dodd, 1885; *Elsie's Keth and Kin,* Dodd, 1886; *Mildred's Boys and Girls,* Dodd, 1886; *The Thorn in the Nest,* Dodd, 1886; *Elsie's Friends At Woodburn,* Dodd, 1887; *Christmas With Grandma Elsie,* Dodd, 1888; *Elsie and the Raymonds,* Dodd, 1889; *Elsie's Widowhood,* Routledge, 1889; *Elsie Yachting with the Raymonds,* Dodd, 1890; *Elsie's Vacation,* Dodd, 1891; *Elsie At Viamede,* Dodd, 1892; *Elsie At Ion,* Dodd, 1893; *The Tragedy of Wild River Valley,* Dodd, 1893; *Mildred's New Daughter,* Burt, 1894; *Elsie's Journey on Inland Waters,* Dodd, 1895; *Elsie At Home,* Dodd, 1897; *Elsie on the Hudson and Elsewhere,* Dodd, 1898; *Twiddledetwit, a Fairytale,* Dodd, 1898; *Elsie in the South,* Dodd, 1899; *Elsie's Young Folks in Peace and War,* Dodd, 1900; *Elsie's Womanhood,* Dodd, 1901; *Elsie's Winter Trip,* Dodd, 1902; *Elsie and Her Loved Ones,* Dodd, 1903; *Elsie and Her Namesakes,* Dodd, 1905). NYPL-A, DPL, LC, PFL

Elijah Kellogg's *Good Old Times* (a popular story of the author's grandfather's life as a Maine backwoodsman; published in Boston by Lothrop; author's other work includes *Lion Ben of Elm Island,* Lee, 1896, and other "Elm Island Stories" about Maine pioneers and fishermen). BC

Oliver Optic's Magazine for Boys and Girls (a periodical which began in January 1867 as a semiannual but became a monthly as of January 1871; published by Lee and Shepard and edited by William Taylor Adams; the magazine's editorial column was used to defend Oliver Optic's books for boys from attackers such as Louisa May Alcott and Edward Eggleston; Oliver Optic was the pseudonym of William Taylor Adams; the magazine was discontinued following Lee and Shepard's bankruptcy in 1875).

Hesba Stretton's *Jessica's First Prayer* (a tract telling the story of a poor waif's first realization of the meaning of religion; published in Boston by Bradley and Woodruff; first appeared in the periodical *Sunday At Home,* 1866; over a million and a half copies sold in fifty years; translated into

1867 *continued*

every European and most Asiatic and African languages; Hesba Stretton was the pseudonym of Sarah Smith; the author's other work includes *Little Meg's Children,* American Tract Society, 1868; *Alone in London,* American Tract Society, 1869; *Lost Gip,* London, 1873).

1868

Louisa May Alcott's *Little Women; or, Meg, Jo, Beth and Amy* (the first of a series of family-story "classics"; illustrated by the author's sister, Mary Alcott; the characters are real parents and true-to-life children; the story convincingly reflects New England life; published in Boston in two volumes by Roberts Brothers and in London by Sampson Low as *Little Women* and *Good Wives,* in two volumes, 1871; volume two of the Roberts edition was published in New York by Dutton in 1907 as *Good Wives;* the author's other work includes *Comic Tragedies, Written by "Jo" and "Meg" and Acted by the "Little Women,"* Roberts, 1893; *Flower Fables,* Briggs, 1855; *Hospital Sketches,* Redpath, 1863; *The Rose Family: A Fairy Tale,* Redpath, 1864; *On Picket Duty,* Redpath, 1864; *Morning-Glories and Other Stories,* Carleton, 1867; *Three Proverb Stories,* containing *Kitty's Class Day, Aunt Kipp,* and *Psyche's Art,* Loring, 1868; *Nellie's Hospital,* United States Sanitary Commission, 1868; *Concord Sketches,* Osgood, 1869; *An Old-Fashioned Girl,* Roberts, 1870; *Will's Wonder Book,* Fuller, 1870; *Little Men: Life At Plumfield with Jo's Boys,* Roberts, 1871; *Eight Cousins, or The Aunt-Hill,* Roberts, 1875; *Rose in Bloom: A Sequel to "Eight Cousins,"* Roberts, 1876; *Under the Lilacs,* Roberts, 1878; *Jack and Jill, A Village Story,* Roberts, 1880; *Jo's Boys, and How They Turned Out: A Sequel to Little Men,* Roberts, 1886; the author's collections of stories include *Aunt Jo's Scrap-Bag,* six volumes, Roberts, 1872; Vol. 1: *My Boys,* Vol. 2: *Shawl Straps,* Roberts, 1872; Vol. 3: *Cupid and Chow-Chow,* Roberts, 1874; Vol. 4: *My Girls,* Roberts, 1875; Vol. 5: *Jimmy's Cruise in the Pinafore,* Roberts, 1879; Vol. 6: *An Old-Fashioned Thanksgiving,* Roberts, 1882; *Lulu's Library,* three volumes, Roberts, 1886, 1887, 1889; *Silver Pitchers* [and] *Independence: A Centennial Love Story,* Roberts, 1876; *Meadow Blossoms,* Crowell, 1879; *Water Cresses,* Crowell, 1879; *Sparkles for Bright Eyes,* Crowell, 1879; *Proverb Stories,* Roberts, 1882; *Spinning Wheel Stories,* Roberts, 1884; *A Garland for Girls,* Roberts, 1888; the author's father, Bronson Alcott, wrote *Conversations with Children on the Gospel;* numerous stories from the author's collections were reprinted in book form and in a periodical for children, *Merry Museum,* 1867; the author contributed to numerous other periodicals including *St. Nicholas, Hearth and Home, Young Folks' Journal, The Youth's Companion, Atlantic Monthly, Saturday Evening Gazette,* and *Putnam's Magazine*). CMU, LC

Paul Belloni Du Chaillu's *Stories of the Gorilla Country* (an account of daring adventures in equatorial African jungles; published in New York by Harper; the author-explorer's other work includes *Wild Life Under the Equator,* Harper, 1869; *Lost in the Jungle,* Harper, 1869; *The Country of the Dwarfs,* Harper, 1871; *The Land of the Midnight Sun,* Harper, 1881; *The Viking Age,* Scribner, 1889).

Elizabeth Anna Hart's *Poems Written For A Child* (a collection of poems which reflect a genuine understanding of a child's world; some of the poems were written by the author's sister, Menella Bute Smedley; the author's other work includes *Child-World* with Menella Smedley, London, 1869; *Child-Nature,* London, 1869; *The Runaway,* London, 1872; *Paws and Claws,* Cassell, 1874; *Tiny Houses and Their Builders,* Cassell, 1876; *Poor Nelly,* London, 1880; *Two Four-penny Bits,* London, 1880; *May Cunningham's Trial,* London, 1883; *Mr. Burke's Nieces,* London, 1883; *He Conquers Who Endures,* London, 1886; *The Mystery of Shoncliff School,* London, 1888).

1869

R. D. Blackmore's *Lorna Doone* (a popular romance about Exmoor set in the seventeenth century; published in London by Sampson Low; appropriated by children).

Jean Ingelow's *Mopsa the Fairy* (a fantasy somewhat resembling *Alice's Adventures in Wonderland,* published in London by Longmans, Green and Co.; the author's other work includes *Tales of Orris,* Bath, 1860; *Studies for Stories,* Strahan, 1864; *A Sister's Bye-Hours,* London, 1868; *The Little Wonder Horn,* London, 1872; *Very Young and Quite Another Story,* Longmans, 1890).

Edward A. Knatchbull-Hugessen's *Stories for My Children* (retellings of fairy stories and wonder tales; published in London; followed by thirteen similar volumes; the author's works were illustrated by such artists as Richard Doyle, Gustave Doré, Ernest Griset, and Linely Sambourne; the author was also known as Lord Brabourne).

James de Mille's *The B.O.W.C.: A Book for Boys* (first book in Canadian author's B.O.W.C. [Brethren of the White Cross] series, published in Boston by Lee and Shepard; other books in the series published by Lee and Shepard include *The Boys of the Grand Pré School,* 1870; *Lost in the Fog,* 1870; *Picked Up Adrift,* 1872; *Treasure of the Sea,* 1873; the B.O.W.C. was the first series by a Canadian author and an early schoolboy series: the

1869 *continued*

author's other work includes *Among the Brigands*, 1871; *The Winged Lion; or, Stories of Venice*, 1876).

Florence Montgomery's *Misunderstood* (a popular story about a pathetic, misunderstood boy; even though the preface states that it is not a story for children but a story for those interested in children, many young people read the book; published by Bentley; the author's other work includes *A Very Simple Story; Being a Chronicle of the Thoughts and Feelings of a Child*, W. Kent, 1867; *Thwarted; or Ducks' Eggs in a Hen's Nest*, Bentley, 1873; *The Town-Crier, To Which Is Added The Children with the Indian-Rubber Ball*, Bentley, 1874; *Tony, a Sketch Being the Account of a Little Innocent on a Short Railway Journey*, Bentley, 1898).

1870

Thomas Bailey Aldrich's *The Story of a Bad Boy* (a realistic tale about author's own boyhood in New Hampshire; published in London by Sampson Low; forerunner of the Tom Sawyer type story, told with verve and humor; appeared first in serial form in *Our Young Folks' Magazine*, January to December 1869; the author edited the *Atlantic Monthly*, 1881-1890). HU, PU

William Allingham's *In Fairyland* (a collection of poems which contains "Up the airy mountain / Down the rushy glen"; published in London by Longmans; illustrated by Richard [Dicky] Doyle; the author's other work includes *The Music Master*, Routledge, 1855, illustrated by Arthur Hughes; *Rhymes for the Young Folk*, Cassell, 1887, illustrated by Helen Allingham, Kate Greenaway, Caroline Peterson, and Henry Furniss; editor, *Ballad Book*, Macmillan, 1865).

George Alfred Henty's *Out on the Pampas* (an adventure story set in Argentina, published in London by Griffith, Farrow, Okedan, and Welsh; first of the author's more than seventy books which present geographical and historical concepts based on the author's experiences as war correspondent, traveler, and "history buff"; the author's other work, published in London by Blackie except as noted, includes *A Search for a Secret*, Tinsley, 1867; *All But Lost*, Tinsley, 1869; *Young Franc-tireurs and their Adventures in the Franco-Prussian War*, Griffith, 1872; *March to Coomasie*, Tinsley, 1874; *The Young Burglers; a Tale of the Peninsular War*, Dutton, 1879; *The Cornet of Horse. A Tale of Marlborough's War*, Sampson, 1881; *In Times of Peril; A Tale of India*, Dutton, 1881; *Under Drake's Flag*, 1882; *Winning His Spears: A Tale of the Crusades*, Sampson, 1882; *The Boy Knight: A Tale of the Crusades*, Robert, 1883; *The Boy Knight Who Won His Spurs*

Fighting with King Richard of England, Robert, 1883; *By Sheer Pluck; A Tale of the Ashanti War,* 1883; *Friends, Though Divided. A Tale of the Civil War,* Griffith, 1883; *Jack Archer. A Tale of Crimea,* Sampson, 1883; *St. George for England: A Tale of Cressy and Portiers,* 1884; *With Clive in India: or, The Beginnings of the Empire,* 1884; *True to Old Flag,* 1885; *Yarns on the Beach; A Bundle of Tales,* Scribner, 1885; *The Young Colonists,* Routledge, 1885; *The Dragon and the Raven: Or, The Days of King Alfred,* 1886; *A Final Reckoning; A Tale of Bush Life in Australia,* 1886; *For Name and Fame: or, Through Afghan Passes,* 1886; *The Lion of the North: A Tale of the Times of Gustavus Adolphus and the Wars of Religion,* 1886; *Through the Fray: A Tale of the Luddite Riots,* 1886; *With Wolfe in Canada,* 1886; *The Young Carthaginian; A Story of the Times of Hannibal,* 1886; *Bonnie Prince Charlie: A Tale of Fontenoy and Culloden,* 1887; *For the Temple; A Tale of the Fall of Jerusalem,* 1887; *Orange and Green: A Tale of the Boyne and Limerick,* 1888; *Sturdy and Strong: or, How George Andrews Makes His Way,* 1888; *By Pike and Dyke; A Tale of the Rise of the Dutch Republic,* Scribner, 1889; *Captain Bayley's Heir; A Tale of the Gold Fields of California,* 1889; *The Cat of Bubastes; A Tale of Ancient Egypt,* 1889; *The Curse of Carne's Hold,* Blackett, 1889; *The Lion of St. Mark,* 1889; *With Lee in Virginia; A Story of the American Civil War,* 1889; *A Hidden Foe,* United States Book Co., 1890; *One of the 28th; A Tale of Waterloo,* 1890; *Stories of History,* Melbourne, 1890; *Tales of Daring and Danger,* 1890; *By Right of Conquest: or, With Cortez in Mexico,* 1891; *The Chapter of Adventures: or, Through the Bombardment of Alexandria,* 1891; *By England's Aid: or, The Freeing of the Netherlands (1585-1604),* 1891; *The Dash for Khartoum, A Tale of the Nile Expedition,* Scribner, 1891; *Maori and Settler: A Story of the New Zealand War,* 1891; *Stories of Peril and Adventure,* Ward, 1891; *The Fall of Sebastopol, A Tale of the Crimea,* Brown, 1892; *Fighting the Saracens,* Brown, 1892; *Held Fast For England: A Tale of the Siege of Gibraltar (1779-1783),* 1892; *In Greek Waters,* Scribner, 1892; *Redskin and Cow-Boy; A Tale of the Western Plains,* 1892; *To Herat and Cabul; A Story of the First Afghan War,* 1892; *Beric the Briton: A Story of the Roman Invasion,* 1893; *Condemned As A Nihilist: A Story of Escape from Siberia,* 1893; *In Greek Waters: A Story of the Grecian War of Independence (1821-1827),* 1893; *In the Days of Mutiny,* Taylor, 1893; *Rujub, the Juggler,* Chatto, 1893; *The Jacobite Exile: Being the Adventures of a Young Englishman in the Service of Charles XII of Sweden,* 1894; *Through the Sikh War: A Tale of the Conquest of the Punjaub,* 1894; *St. Bartholomew's Eve: A Tale of the Huguenot Wars,* 1894; *In the Heart of the Rockies; A Story of Adventure in Colorado,* 1894; *Two Sieges of Paris,* Fenno, 1895; *When London Burned; A Story of Restoration Times and the Great Fire,* 1895; *A Woman of the Commune; A Tale of Two Sieges of Paris,* White, 1895; *Wulf the Saxon; A Story of the Norman Conquest,* Blackie, 1895; *Dorothy's Double; The Story of a Great*

1870 *continued*

Deception, Rand, 1896; *The Tiger of Mysore; A Story of the War with Tippoo Saib,* 1896; *A Knight of the White Cross; A Tale of the Siege of Rhodes,* 1896; *Through Russian Snows; A Story of Napoleon's Retreat from Moscow,* 1896; *With Cochrane the Dauntless; A Tale of the Exploits of Lord Cochrane in South American Waters,* 1897; *At Agincourt; A Tale of the White Hoods of Paris,* 1897; *On the Irrawaddy; A Story of the First Burmese War,* 1897; *At Aboukir and Acre; A Story of Napoleon's Invasion of Egypt,* Scribner, 1898; *Colonel Thorndyke's Secret,* Chatto, 1898; *Girl of the Commune,* Fenno, 1898; *A March on London; Being a Story of Wat Tyler's Insurrection,* 1898; *The Queen's Cup,* Appleton, 1898; *Through Fire and Storm,* Partridge, 1898; *With Frederick the Great; A Story of the Seven Years War,* 1898; *With Moore at Corunna,* 1898; *Yule Logs,* 1898; *Both Sides of the Border; A Tale of Hotspur and Glendower,* 1899; *Cuthbert Hartington; A Tale of Two Sieges of Paris,* Partridge, 1899; *The Golden Cañon,* Hurst, 1899; *The Lost Heir,* Hurst, 1899; *Command, A Tale of the Peninsular War, 1899; Yule-Tide Yarns,* Longmans, 1899; *The Brahmin's Treasure,* Lippincott, 1900; *In the Hands of the Cave Dwellers,* Harper, 1900; *No Surrender! A Tale of the Rising in La Vendee,* 1900; *A Roving Commission; or, Through the Black Insurrection of Hayti,* 1900; *With Buller in Natal,* Scribner, 1900; *Won By the Sword; A Tale of the Thirty Years' War,* 1900; *Bears and Dacoits and Other Stories,* 1901; *In the Irish Brigade; A Tale of War in Flanders and Spain,* 1901; *Out with Garibaldi; A Story of the Liberation of Italy,* 1901; *Queen Victoria,* 1901; *At the Point of the Bayonet; A Tale of the Mahratta War,* 1902; *The Treasure of the Incas,* 1902; *With Roberts to Pretoria; A Tale of the South African War,* 1902; *With the British Legion,* Scribner, 1902; *The Young Midshipman; A Story of the Bombardment of Alexandria,* Street, 1902; *In the Reign of Terror,* Scribner, 1903; *With Kitchener in the Soudan; A Story of Atbara and Omdurman,* 1903; *With the Allies to Pekin,* Scribner, 1903; *With the British Legion: A Story of the Carlist Wars,* 1903; *Through Three Campaigns; A Story of Chitral, Tirah, and Ashantee,* 1904; *By Conduct and Courage; A Story of the Days of Nelson,* 1905; *In the Hands of the Malays,* 1905; *Redskins and Colonists,* Burt, 1905; *A Highland Chief,* 1906; *A Soldier's Daughter and Other Stories,* 1906; *Facing Death,* 1908; *The Bravest of the Brave,* 1914; *The Plague Ship,* Sheldon, 1923; *John Hawke's Fortune,* 1925; *Among the Bushrangers, from "A final reckoning,"* 1929; the author was editor of the Union Jack series, 1880-1883, and wrote extensively for *The Boy's Own Magazine).* HH, IU

Tom Hood's *Petsetilla's Posy* (similar to *The Rose and the Ring* but also contains nonsense verse and comic absurdities; published in London; the author was the son of Thomas Hood, the poet who wrote "The Song of the Shirt"; the author's other work includes *The Fairy Realm,* London, illustrated by Gustave Doré, 1865; *From Nowhere to the North Pole,* London, 1875; a story very similar to Lewis Carroll's *Alice;* author also contributed puzzles to *Good Things,* ca. 1875, a periodical for children).

Pansy's *A Christmas Time* (pseudonymous author; the first of a series of popular Sunday school stories typical of the period; the author was editor of a Sunday school magazine for children called *The Pansy,* 1874-1896; author's other work, published by Lothrop except as noted, includes *Ester Ried; or, Asleep and Awake,* Western Tract Society, 1870; *Three People,* 1872; *Bernie's White Chicken* [and] *The Diamond Bracelet,* 1874; *Helen Lester* [and] *Nannie's Experiment,* 1894; with Faye Huntington, pseudonym of Theodosia Toll Foster, *Modern Prophets: Temperance Stories,* 1874; *Cunning Workmen,* 1875; *Grandpa's Darlings,* 1875; with Faye Huntington, *Dr. Deane's Way, and Other Stories,* 1875; *Four Girls at Chautauqua,* 1876; *Pansy's Picture Book,* 1876; *Pansy's Picture Library,* four volumes, 1876; *The Randolphs,* 1876; *The Ester Ried Library,* five volumes, ca. 1876 [contains *Three People, Ester Ried, Julia Ried, King's Daughter,* and *Wise and Otherwise*]; *Chautauqua Girls at Home,* 1877; *Getting Ahead,* 1877; *Little People in Picture and Story,* 1877; *Mother's Boys and Girls,* 1877; *Pansies,* 1877; *Two Boys,* 1877; *A Lesson in Story: Pansy's Lesson-Book for Boys and Girls,* two volumes, 1878; *Links in Rebecca's Life,* 1878; *Our Darlings, What They Think, Say, and Do,* 1878; *Sidney Martin's Christmas,* 1878; *Six Little Girls,* 1878; with Faye Huntington, *From Different Stand-Points,* 1878; *Miss Priscilla Hunter,* 1879; *My Daughter Susan,* 1879; *Little Hands,* 1879; *Little by Little,* 1879; *New Graft on the Family Tree,* 1880; *People Who Haven't Time and Can't Afford It,* 1880; *The Teacher's Helper,* 1880; *What She Said, and What She Meant,* 1880; with Mrs. C. M. Livingston, *Divers Women,* 1880; with Faye Huntington, *That Boy Bob, and Other Stories,* 1880; *Mrs. Harry Harper's Awakening,* Lothrop, 1881; *Pocket Measure,* 1881; *Five Friends,* 1882; *Hall in the Grove,* 1882; *Mrs. Solomon Smith Looking On,* 1882; *Some Young Heroines,* 1882; *Ester Ried Yet Speaking,* 1883; *Man of the House,* 1883; *Side by Side* [and] *Leonora Claribel,* 1883; with others, *Mary Burton Abroad and Other Stories,* 1883; editor, *Pansy's Home Story Book,* 1883; *The Endless Chain,* 1884; *An Hour with Miss Streator,* 1884; *New Year's Tangles, and Other Stories,* 1884; *Tip Lewis and His Lamp,* 1884; *Christy's Christmas,* 1884; *A Hedge Fence,* 1884; *Pansy: Stories of Child-Life at Home and Abroad, and of Modern and Ancient History,* six volumes, 1884-1889; *Young Folks' Stories of American History and Home Life,* first series, 1884, second series, 1887; *Young Folks' Stories of Foreign Lands,* first series, 1884, second series, 1887; *Gertrude's Diary* [and] *The Cube,* 1885; *In the Woods and Out, and Other Stories,* 1885; *Interrupted,* 1885; *One Commonplace Day,* 1885; *The Browning Boys,* 1886; *Spun from Fact,* 1886; *Stories and Pictures from the Life of Jesus,* 1886; *Eighty-Seven,*

1870 *continued*

1887; *Little Fishers and Their Nets,* 1887; *Pansy's Story Book,* 1887; *Six O'Clock in the Evening,* 1887; editor, *At Home Stories,* 1887; *Pansy's Sunday-Book,* 1887; *Sunday Chat for Boys and Girls,* 1887; *A Dozen of Them,* 1888; *Judge Burnham's Daughters,* 1888; *Pansies for Thoughts,* edited by Grace Livingston, 1888, with Mrs. C. M. Livingston, *Profiles,* 1888; *Chrissy's Endeavor,* 1889; *We Twelve Girls,* 1889; *Young Folks Worth Knowing,* 1889; editor, with husband G. R. Alden, of *The Pansy,* five volumes, 1890-1894; *The Prince of Peace; or, The Beautiful Life of Jesus,* 1890; *Helen the Historian,* 1891; *Her Associate Members,* 1891; *Miss Dee Dunmore Bryant,* 1891; *Stephen Mitchell's Journey,* 1893; *Twenty Minutes Late,* 1893; with Mrs. C. M. Livingston, *Worth Having,* 1893; *Pansy's Stories of American History,* 1893; *Only Ten Cents,* 1894; *Wanted,* 1894; *What They Couldn't,* 1895; *Making Fate,* 1896; *Older Brother,* 1897; *Overruled,* 1897; *Agatha's Unknown Way: A Story of Missionary Guidance,* Revell, 1898; *As In a Mirror,* 1898; *Reuben's Hindrances, and How He Made Them Helps toward Progress,* 1898; *A Modern Sacrifice: The Story of Kissie Gordon's Experiment,* 1899; *Three Times Three: A Story for Young People,* Revell, 1899; *Yesterday Framed in To-Day: A Story of the Christ, and How To-Day Received Him,* 1899; *Missent: Story of a Letter,* 1900; with Mrs. C. M. Livingstone *[sic], By Way of Wilderness,* 1900; *Mag and Margaret: A Story for Girls,* illustrated by C. C. Emerson, 1901; *Pauline,* 1901; *Unto the End,* 1902; *Mara,* 1903; *Household Puzzles,* 1903; *Dorris Farrand's Vocation,* 1904; *David Ransom's Watch,* 1905; *Ester Ried's Namesake,* illustrated by Ernest Fosbery, 1906; *Ruth Erskine's Son,* illustrated by Louise Clark, 1907; *Ruth Erskine's Crosses,* 1907; *The Browns at Mt. Hermon,* illustrated by Elizabeth Withington, Lothrop, 1908; *Lost on the Trail,* illustrated by Elizabeth Withington, 1911; *Long Way Home,* illustrated by Withington, 1912; *Four Mothers at Chautauqua,* 1913; *Tony Keating's Surprises,* Donohue, 1914; *The Fortunate Calamity,* illustrated by Grace Norcross, Lippincott, 1927; *An Interrupted Night,* foreword by Grace Livingston Hill, Lippincott, 1929; *Memories of Yesterdays,* edited by G. L. Hill, Lippincott, 1931; author's other work includes *Docia's Journal, Daisy and Grandpa, Little Minnie, Robbie and the Stars, Pictures from Bobby's Life, Exact Truth, Glimpses of Girlhood, Grace Holbrook, Her Mother's Bible, Jessie Wells, Little Card, Monteagle, Next Things, Pansy's Scrap Book, Stories Told for a Purpose, Their Vacation;* with Mrs. C. M. Livingston *Aunt Hannah, Martha and John,* and *John Remington, Martyr* [with others] *Bobby's Wolf, and Other Stories,* and *Seven Fold Trouble;* Pansy is the pseudonym of Isabelle Alden).

Frank R. Stockton's *Ting-a-ling Tales* (a collection of literary fairy tales published in New York by Scribner, first published in *Riverside Magazine;* illustrated by E. B. Bensell; the author served as assistant to Mary Mapes

Dodge in editing the *St. Nicholas* magazine, 1873-1876, and wrote stories for it under the pseudonyms of Paul Fort and John Lewees, as well as under his own name; his popular short story, "The Lady or the Tiger?" was published in the *Century Magazine,* 1884, and was also published by Scribner in *The Lady and the Tiger and Other Stories,* 1884; the author's other work includes *The Floating Prince and Other Stories,* Scribner, 1881; *The Bee-Man of Orn and Other Fanciful Tales,* Scribner, 1887; *The Squirrels' Inn,* Century, 1891; *The Storyteller's Pack,* Scribner, 1897; *Buccaneers and Pirates of Our Coast,* Macmillan, 1898).

1871

George MacDonald's *At the Back of the North Wind* (a well-known British fantasy, serious and spiritual in tone; illustrated by Arthur Hughes; the author was editor of *Good Words for the Young,* 1869-1872; the author's other work includes five stories, *Dealing with the Fairies,* London, 1867, one of which was *"The Light Princess"; Works of Fancy and Imagination,* London, 1871; *Adela Cathcart,* 1864; *Ranald Bannerman's Boyhood,* London, 1871; *The Princess and the Goblin,* London, 1872; *Gutta Percha Willie,* London, 1873; *The Gifts of the Christ Child and Other Tales,* Low, 1882; *The Princess and Curdie,* Chatto, 1883; *The Wise Woman, or The Lost Princess,* London, 1882, which was serialized under the title "A Double Story" in the periodical *Good Things,* 1874, and also published as "Princess Rosamond" and "The Lost Princess," 1895; *A Rough Shaking,* Blackie, 1890). TUL, YU

John Greenleaf Whittier's *Child Life, A Collection of Poems* (an anthology of poems which combined "simplicity with a certain degree of literary excellence without on the one hand descending to silliness or, on the other, rising above the average comprehension of childhood"; poets included James Russell Lowell, Elizabeth Barrett Browning, Edward Lear, and George MacDonald; published in Boston by Osgood; the editor's other work includes *Child Life in Prose,* published by Osgood in 1874).

1872

Ouida's *A Dog of Flanders, and Other Stories* (a collection of stories, published in Philadelphia by Lippincott, which includes the life story of a Belgian work dog and his boy-artist would-be friend; the author's other work includes "The Nürnberg Stove" from her collection of stories, and *Bimbi Stories for Children,* Lippincott, 1882; Ouida was the pseudonym of Louise de la Ramée).

Jules Verne's *Around the World in Eighty Days* (a popular scientific adventure story which won the French Academy prize, published in New York by Street and Smith; adapted for the stage in 1874 and in 1948; a motion

1872 *continued*

picture based on the story appeared in 1956; the author's other work includes *From the Earth to the Moon,* Newark Printing, 1866; *Twenty Thousand Leagues Under the Sea,* Smith, 1869; *The Mysterious Island,* Lovell, 1875; *The Child of the Cavern,* Low, 1877).

1873

Susan Coolidge's *What Katy Did* (a popular story of family life based on the author's own childhood memories; published in Boston by Roberts; illustrated by Addie Ledyard; the author's other work, published by Roberts Brothers, except as noted, includes *The New-Year's Bargain,* 1871; *What Katy Did At School,* 1873; *Mischief's Thanksgiving, and Other Stories,* 1874; *Nine Little Goslings,* 1875; *For Summer Afternoons,* 1876; *Eyebright,* 1879; *The Guernsey Lily,* 1880; *Verses,* 1880; *Cross Patch and Other Stories,* 1881; *A Round Dozen,* 1883; *A Little Country Girl,* 1885; *What Katy Did Next,* 1886; *Clover,* 1888; *A Few More Verses,* 1889; *Just Sixteen,* 1889; *A Day's Message,* 1890; *In the High Valley,* 1891; *Rhymes and Ballads for Girls and Boys,* 1892; *The Barberry Bush,* 1893; *Not Quite Eighteen,* 1894; *An Old Convent School in Paris, and Other Papers,* 1895; *Curly Locks,* Little, 1899; *Little Tommy Tucker,* Little, 1900; *Two Girls,* Little, 1900; *Little Bo-peep,* Little, 19801; *Uncle and Aunt,* Little, 1901; *The Rule of Three,* Altmus, 1904; *Last Verses,* Little, 1906; *A Sheaf of Stories,* Little, 1906; Susan Coolidge is the pseudonym of Sarah Chauncey Woolsey).

St. Nicholas Magazine (probably the most significant American magazine for children; founded by Roswell Smith and published by Scribner and Co. as *St. Nicholas: Scribner's Illustrated Magazine for Girls and Boys;* planned, named, and edited by Mary Mapes Dodge from 1873 to 1905; William Fayal Clarke served as editor from 1905 to 1927; George F. Thompson was editor from 1927 to 1930; Albert G. Lanier was editor from 1930 to 1931, and May Lamberton Becker was literary editor from 1931 to 1933; in 1880 the Century Company took over publication, merging with *Our Young Folks* in January 1874, *Children's Hour,* July 1874, *The Little Corporal* and *Schoolday Magazine* in May 1875, and *Wide Awake* in September 1893; the American Education Press published the magazine from 1930 until 1934; in 1935, the Educational Press took over until it was sold to the Woolworth Company in 1939 and subsequently became a young children's picture magazine; *St. Nicholas* expired in June 1943; during its long run, its excellent stories, articles, and poems helped to bring about the decline of didacticism; in its heyday its contributors included Louisa May Alcott, Lucretia P. Hale, Mary Mapes Dodge, Cramer H. Burnett, Rudyard Kipling, Howard Pyle, and Palmer Cox; the St. Nicholas League, which was established in 1898, offered gold and silver badges to young people whose prose and verse were accepted for publication in the magazine; among the young contributors were Ring Lardner, Rosemary and Stephen Benét, Cornelia Otis Skinner, Babette Deutsch, Peggy Bacon, Elinor Wiley, Bennett Cerf, and Edmund Wilson). NYPL, SiC

1874

Juliana Horatia Ewing's *Lob-Lie-by-the-Fire* (one of a fairly sophisticated series of stories showing the warmth of an English family without preaching or sentimentality, by the daughter of Mrs. Gatty; illustrated by Randolph Caldecott; the author's other work, published in London by the society for the Promotion of Christian Knowledge except as noted, includes *Melchior's Dream, and Other Stories,* 1862; *Mrs. Overtheway's Remembrances,* London, 1869; *The Brownies, and Other Stories,* London, 1870; *A Flat Iron for a Farthing,* London, 1872; *Six to Sixteen,* Beccles, 1875; *Jan of the Windmill,* London, 1876; *A Great Emergency, and Other Tales,* London, 1877; *We and the World,* Bell, 1880; *Old-Fashioned Fairy Tales,* 1882; *Brothers of Pity, and Other Tales,* 1882; *Blue and Red,* 1883; *A Week Spent in a Glass Pond by the Great Water Beetle,* Worthington, 1883; *Jackanapes,* 1884; *Daddy Darwin's Dovecot,* 1884; *Story of a Short Life,* 1885; *Mary's Meadow,* 1886; *The Peace Egg,* 1887; *A Christmas Mumming Play,* 1887; *Dandelion Clocks, and Other Tales,* 1887; *Snapdragon and Old Father Christmas,* 1888; *Verses for Children,* London, 1888; nearly all the author's works were originally published in *Aunt Judy's Magazine,* or occasionally in *The Monthly Packet* or *Little Folks*). LC, HU, IUL, NYPL

Lucy Larcom's *Childhood Songs* (a collection of poems published by Houghton, written by a well-known poet who was a friend of J. G. Whittier; in addition to editing *Our Young Folks,* 1865-1873, the author's work includes *Leila Among the Mountains,* Hoyt, 1861; *Childhood Songs,* Houghton, 1874; *A New England Girlhood,* Houghton, 1889).

Charles Asbury Stephens's *The Young Moose Hunters* (a backwoods boy's story by the author of the *Camping Out* series, one hundred serials, and three thousand short stories; published in Boston by H. L. Shepard; the author's other work includes *Lynx Hunting,* Osgood, 1872; *Left on Labrador,* Osgood, 1872; *On the Amazons,* Osgood, 1872; *The Knockabout Club Alongshore,* Estes, 1882; *When Life Was Young,* Old Squire's Bookstore, 1912; *Stories of My Home Folks,* Mason, 1926; *Katahdin Camps,* Houghton, 1928; the author was on the staff of *Youth's Companion* from 1870 to 1929). BC

1875

Dinah Maria Mulock's *The Little Lame Prince* (an allegorical tale of little Prince Dolor and his magic traveling cloak; the author also published under

1875 *continued*

the name of Mrs. Craik after her marriage to George Lillie Craik, a partner of Macmillan Publishers; the author's other work includes *Alice Learmont,* London, 1852; *A Hero: Philip's Book,* London, 1853; *John Halifax, Gentleman,* London, 1856; *Our Year,* Cambridge, 1860; *The Fairy Book,* London, 1863; *A New Year's Gift for Sick Children,* Edinburgh, 1865; *Little Sunshine's Holiday,* London, 1872; editor, *Is It True?,* London, 1872; *The Adventures of a Brownie,* Low, 1872; *Children's Poetry,* Macmillan, 1881).

Horace Elisha Scudder's *Doings of the Bodley Family in Town and Country* (the first of a series of eight books, published between 1876 and 1884, about the Bodley family by the founder and editor of the *Riverside Magazine for Young Folks,* 1867-1870, and editor of the *Atlantic Monthly,* 1890-1898; the author's other work includes *Seven Little People and Their Friends,* Houghton, 1862; *Dream Children,* Sever, 1864; *Stories from My Attic,* Hurd, 1869; *The Bodleys Telling Stories,* Hurd, 1877; *The Bodleys on Wheels,* Houghton, 1878; *The Bodleys Afoot,* Houghton, 1879; *Stories and Romances,* Houghton, 1880; editor, *The Children's Book,* Houghton, 1881; *The Book of Fables,* Houghton, 1882; *The Bodley Grandchildren and Their Journey in Holland,* Houghton, 1882; *Mr. Bodley Abroad,* Houghton, 1882; *The Book of Fables,* Houghton, 1882; *The English Bodley Family,* Houghton, 1884; *The Viking Bodleys,* Houghton, 1885; *The Bodleys on Wheels, and the Bodleys Afoot,* Houghton, 1887; *The Book of Folk Stories,* Houghton, 1887; *Book of Legends,* Houghton, 1890; *The Book of Fables and Folk Stories,* Houghton, 1890; *Fables, Folk Stories and Legends,* Houghton, 1899).

Wide Awake (subtitled *An Illustrated Magazine for Boys and Girls;* founded by Daniel Lothrop, a Boston book publisher; the editors included Ella Fairman Pratt, 1875-1891; Ella Pratt and Charles Stuart Pratt, 1891-1893; Margaret Sidney began her Five Little Peppers series in the magazine in 1880; contributors included Sarah Orne Jewett, Edward Everett Hale, James Whitcomb Riley, Imogen Guiney, Charles Egbert Craddock, Louise Chandler Moulton, Edgar Fawcett, Mary H. Catherwood, Kirk Munroe, and John T. Trowbridge). SiC

1876

John Habberton's *Helen's Babies* (a novel for young ladies; subtitled *With Some Account of Their Ways Innocent, Crafty, Angelic, Impish, Witching, and Repulsive. Also, A Partial Record of Their Actions During Ten Days of Their Existence by Their Latest Victim;* published in Boston by Loring; the author's other work, published in New York by Putnam, includes *Other People's Children,* 1877; *Budge and Toddie,* 1878; *The Worst Boy in Town,* 1880).

Mark Twain's *The Adventures of Tom Sawyer* (the first adventure story that was totally American in tone; published in London by Chatto and Windus and in San Francisco by A. Roman; followed by *The Adventures of Huckleberry Finn: Tom Sawyer's Comrade,* Harper, 1884, often thought to be a sequel to *Tom Sawyer,* but themes, situations, and dialects make Huckleberry Finn difficult for children; the author's other work includes *The Celebrated Jumping Frog of Calaveras County,* Routledge, 1867; *The Innocents Abroad; or The New Pilgrims' Progress; Being Some Account of the Steamship Quaker City's Pleasure Excursion to Europe and the Holy Land,* American, 1869; *A Tramp Abroad,* American, 1880; *The Stolen White Elephant,* Osgood, 1882; *Roughing It,* American, 1872; *The Guilded Age, A Tale of Today,* Gilman, 1873; *The Prince and the Pauper,* Dawson, 1881; *Life on the Mississippi,* Osgood, 1883; *A Connecticut Yankee in King Arthur's Court,* Webster, 1889; *The American Claimant,* Webster, 1892; *Merry Tales and Other Stories,* Webster, 1892; *The $1,000,000 Bank Note,* Webster, 1893; *Pudd'nhead Wilson,* Chatto, 1894; *Tom Sawyer Abroad, by Huck Finn,* Webster, 1894; *Tom Sawyer, Detective,* Chatto, 1897; *The Man That Corrupted Hadleyburg and Other Stories and Essays,* Harper, 1900; *A Dog's Tale,* Harper, 1904; *The $30,000 Bequest, and Other Stories,* American, 1907; *Extract from Captain Stormfield's Visit To Heaven,* Harper, 1909; *The Mysterious Stranger,* Harper, 1916; *Mark Twain's Autobiography,* Harper, 1924; Mark Twain is the pseudonym of Samuel Longhorn Clemens). BECL, DPL, MTL, NYPL-B, PLC, PU, SU, UCB, Ulo, YU

1877

Charles Carleton Coffin's *The Boys of '76* (a history of the battles of the Revolution; published in New York by Harper Brothers; one of author's several books about war; the author's other work includes *My Days and Nights on the Battlefield,* Ticknor, 1864, 1887; *Four Years of Fighting,* Ticknor, 1866; *Abraham Lincoln,* Harper, 1893).

Mary De Morgan's *On a Pincushion, and Other Fairy Tales* (poetic, rather mysterious tales illustrated by author's brother William in which the etchings were made to resemble woodcuts; published in London by Seeley, Jackson and Halliday; a second volume of tales, *The Necklace of Princess Fiorimonde,* Macmillan, 1880, was illustrated by Walter Crane; the author's other work includes, with Edith H. Dixon, *Sixty Two,* 1873; *A Choice of Chance,* Unwin, 1887; *The Wind Fairies, and Other Tales,* Seeley, 1900).

Anna Sewell's *Black Beauty* (a popular horse story which helped to promote a more kindly treatment of horses; published in London by Jarrold and Sons; the 1890 American edition was subtitled *The Uncle Tom's Cabin of*

1877 *continued*

the Animal World, and was sponsored by the Humane Society; the author's mother, Elizabeth Sewell, began writing stories for children at age sixty and was assisted by her daughter in such stories as *Thy Poor Brother,* Jarrold, 1863).

1878

Randolph Caldecott's *The Diverting History of John Gilpin* written by William Cowper (the first of a series of sixteen picture books first issued singly and then together; the robust characters and action are done with great economy of line and expert use of color; in honor of this British artist, the Caldecott Medal has been given yearly in the United States, from 1938 on, to the illustrator of the most distinguished picture book for children published during the preceding year; the author-illustrator's other work, published by Routledge, except as noted, includes *The House That Jack Built,* 1878; *Oliver Goldsmith's Elegy on a Mad Dog,* 1879; *The Babes in the Wood,* 1879; *Sing a Song for Sixpence,* 1880; *Three Jovial Huntsmen,* 1880; *The Farmer's Boy,* 1881; *The Queen of Hearts,* 1881; *The Milkmaid,* 1882; *Hey Diddle Diddle and Baby Bunting,* 1882; *A Frog He Would A-Wooing Go,* 1883; *The Fox Jumps over the Farmer's Gate,* 1883; *Come Lasses and Lads, Ride a Cock Horse, and A Farmer Went Trotting,* 1884; Samuel Foote's *The Great Panjandrum,* 1885; Oliver Goldsmith's *Mrs. Mary Blaize,* 1885; collections of these books, which were published in pairs, were issued beginning ca. 1879; *Randolph Caldecott's Picture Books,* vols. 1 and 2; *Randolph Caldecott's Collection of Pictures and Songs,* 1883; *The Hey Diddle Diddle Picture Book,* 1883; *The Panjandrum Picture Book,* 1885; *Randolph Caldecott's Second Collection of Pictures and Songs,* 1885; Caldecott also illustrated Mrs. Ewing's *Jackanapes,* Christian Knowledge Society, 1884; *Daddy Darwin's Dovecot,* Christian Knowledge society, 1884; and a new edition of *Lob-Lie-by-The Fire,* London, ca. 1885; Washington Irving's *Old Christmas,* Macmillan, 1876, and *Bracebridge Hall,* Macmillan, 1877). JPL, NYPL-A

Kate Greenaway's *Under the Window* (the first of a series of "classic" picture books by a British illustrator who had influence similar to that of Crane and Caldecott; published in London by Routledge; in honor of the artist, the Kate Greenaway Medal has been given annually in Britain from 1955 on to the most distinguished artist working in the illustration of children's books published in the United Kingdom during the preceding year; the author-illustrator's other work, published in London by Routledge except as noted, includes *Children's Songs,* Ward, ca. 1875; with Walter Crane, *Quiver of Love: A Collection of Valentines,* 1876; *Trot's Journey,* Worthington, 1879; *Toyland, Trot's Journey, and Other Poems and Stories,* Worhtington, 1879; *Kate Greenaway's Birthday Book,* 1880; *A Day in a*

Child's Life, 1881; *Mother Goose,* 1881; *Kate Greenaway Almanacks,* 1883-1897 [excluding 1896]; *Kate Greenaway's Carols,* ca. 1884; *The Language of Flowers,* 1884; *Marigold Garden,* 1885; *Kate Greenaway's Alphabet,* ca. 1885; *Kate Greenaway's Album,* ca. 1885; *A Apple Pie,* 1886; *Baby's Birthday Book,* Ward, 1886; *Around the House,* Worthington, 1888; *Kate Greenaway's Book of Games,* 1889; Greenaway also did illustrations for Madame D'Aulnoy's *Book of Fairy Tales,* Gall, ca. 1871; *Diamonds and Toads,* London, 1871; Charlotte Yonge's *Heir of Redclyffe,* London, 1879; Andrew Lang's *The Library,* London, 1881; Jane and Ann Taylor's *Little Ann and Other Poems,* London, 1883; John Ruskin's edition of *Dame Wiggins of Lee and Her Seven Wonderful Cats,* Allen, 1885; Bret Harte's *The Queen of the Pirate Isle,* Cassell, 1886; William Allingham's *Rhymes for the Young Folk,* Cassell, 1887; Robert Browning's *The Pied Piper of Hamelin,* Routledge, 1888; Countess Von Arnim's *The April Baby's Book of Tunes,* Macmillan, 1900; author-illustrator also did illustrations for books by less well-known authors, as well as the artwork for songbooks, painting books, calendars, a spelling book, greeting cards, and numerous periodicals including *Little Folks, St. Nicholas, Little Wide Awake, Harper's Young People, The Girl's Own Paper).* DPL, NYPL-A, PFL, TPL, USM

Flora Shaw's *Castle Blair* (a story set during the Irish Revolution; published in London; the author's other work includes *Phyllis Brown,* Roberts, 1882; *Hector,* Bell, 1883; Flora Louisa Shaw is also known as Lady Lugard).

1879

The Boy's Own Paper (edited by G. A. Hutchinson and coedited by Talbot Baines Reed; a popular periodical dedicated to providing healthy, wholesome fare, Christian in tone but without religious emotionalism; published by the Religious Tract Society under James M. Macaulay's direction, authors such as R. M. Ballantyne, W. H. G. Kingston, G. A. Henty, and Jules Verne were included in *B.O.P.;* published until 1967).

Mrs. Molesworth's *The Tapestry Room* (one of more than a hundred collections of realism, fantasies, and fairy tales by a British author who has been called "the Jane Austen of the nursery"; published in London by Macmillan; under the pseudonym of Ennis Graham, the author wrote *Tell Me A Story,* illustrated by Walter Crane, London, 1875; the author's most famous book, *The Cuckoo Clock,* Macmillan, 1877, was also illustrated by Walter Crane; the author's other work, published in London by Macmillan except as noted, includes *Carrots,* 1876; *Grandmother Dear,* 1878; *A Christmas Child,* 1880; *The Adventures of Herr Baby,* 1881; *Hermy,* Routledge, 1882; *Hoodie,* Routledge, 1882; *Two Little Waifs,* 1883; *Christmas Tree Land,* 1884; *The Little Old Portrait,* Christian Knowledge Society, 1884; *Us,* 1885; *Four Winds Farm,* 1887; *Little Miss Peggy,* 1887; *Children of the Castle,*

1879 *continued*

1890; *Nurse Heatherdale's Story,* 1891; *An Enchanted Garden,* Unwin, 1892; *Imogen, or Only Eighteen,* Chambers, 1892; *The Carved Lions,* 1895; *My New Home,* 1894; *Shelia's Mystery,* 1895; *Greyling Towers,* Chambers, n.d.; *The House That Grew,* 1900; *The Woodpigeons and Mary,* 1901; *Peterkin,* 1902; *The Ruby Ring,* 1904; *Jasper,* 1906; *The Little Guest,* 1907; *Fairies-Of-Sorts,* 1908; *The Story of a Year,* 1910; *Fairies Afield,* 1911; Mrs. Molesworth's full name is Mary Louisa S. Molesworth). LC, TPL

1880

Hezekiah Butterworth's *Zigzag Journeys in Europe. Vacation Rambles in Historic Lands* (one of a series of seventeen travel books; published in Boston by Estes and Lauriat; the author was editor of *The Youth's Companion,* 1870-1894; the author's other work includes *The Story of the Hymns,* American Tract Society, 1875; *Songs of History,* New England Publishing Company, 1876; *Great Composers,* Lothrop, n.d.; *Poems for Christmas, Easter and New Years,* Estes, 1885; *The Knight of Liberty,* Appleton, 1895; *In the Boyhood of Lincoln,* Appleton, 1892; *The Patriot Schoolmaster,* Appleton, 1894; *In Old New England,* Appleton, n.d.; and the Zigzag series, which includes: *Zigzag Journeys in Classic Lands,* 1881; *Zigzag Journeys in the Orient,* 1882; *Zigzag Journeys in the Occident,* 1883; *Zigzag Journeys in Northern Lands,* 1884; *Zigzag Journeys in Arcadia and New France,* 1885; *Zigzag Journeys in the Levant,* 1886; *Zigzag Journeys in the Sunny South,* 1887; *Zigzag Journeys in India,* 1887; *Zigzag Journeys in the Antipodes,* 1888; *Zigzag Journeys in the British Isles,* 1889; *Zigzag Journeys in the Great Northwest,* 1890; *Zigzag Journeys in Australia or A Visit to the Ocean World,* 1891; *Zigzag Journeys on the Mississippi, From Chicago to the Islands of the Discovery,* 1892; *Zigzag Journeys on the Mediterranean,* 1893; *Zigzag Journeys in the White City,* 1894; *Zigzag Journeys Around the World,* 1895). LC

Lucretia P. Hale's *Peterkin Papers* (some of the first of American nonsense stories filled with eccentric characters and humorous events; published in Boston by J. R. Osgood; appeared serially as early as 1868 in *Our Young Folks* and later, in 1874, in *St. Nicholas;* a continuation, later collected as *The Last of the Peterkins* in 1866, published in Boston by Roberts Brothers, appeared originally in *St. Nicholas*).

Thomas Wallace Knox's *The Boy Travellers in the Far East* (one of journalist's Boy Travellers series of travel books; published in New York by Harper Brothers; the author's other work, published by Harper except as noted, includes *Campfire and Cotton-Field,* Blelock, 1865; *Overland Through Asia,* Gilman, 1870; *Backsheesh! or, Life and Adventures in the Orient,*

Worthington, 1875; *The Boy Travellers in the Far East,* 1879; *The Young Nimrods in North America,* 1881; *Adventures of Two Youths in the Open Polar Sea,* 1885; *The Boy Travellers in South America,* 1885; *The Boy Travellers in the Russian Empire,* 1886; *The Boy Travellers in the Congo,* 1887; *The Boy Travellers in Australia,* 1888; *The Boy Travellers in Central Europe,* 1889; *The Boy Travellers in Great Britain and Ireland,* 1890; *The Boy Travellers in Mexico,* 1890; *The Boy Travellers in Northern Europe,* 1891; *John Boyd's Adventurers,* Appleton, 1893; *The Boy Travellers in Southern Europe,* 1894; *The Boy Travellers in Levant,* 1895; *The Boy's Life of General Grant,* Merriam, 1896). SCSC

Sidney Lanier's *The Boy's King Arthur* (an important retelling of Thomas Malory's *Morte d'Arthur* for young people by an American poet; published in New York by Charles Scribner; the author's other work includes retellings of Welsh tales in *The Boy's Mabinogion,* Low, 1881; the author was editor of *The Boy's Froissart,* Low, 1879, and *The Boy's Percy,* Low, 1882). JHU

1881

Noah Brooks's *The Fairport Nine* (said to be the first baseball story for children; published in New York by Charles Scribner; the author's other work includes *The Boy Emigrants,* Scribner, 1877, serialized in *St. Nicholas,* 1876; *The Boy Settlers,* Scribner, 1891; *First Across The Continent,* Scribner, 1901).

Joel Chandler Harris's *Uncle Remus; His Songs and Sayings: The Folklore of the Old Plantation* (illustrated by Frederick S. Church and James S. Moser; published in Boston by J. R. Osgood; the author's other work includes *Nights with Uncle Remus,* 1883; *Mingo, and Other Sketches in Black and White,* Osgood, 1884; *Free Joe, and Other Georgian Sketches,* Scribner, 1887; *Uncle Remus and His Friends,* Houghton, 1892; *On the Plantation: A Story of a Georgia Boy's Adventures During War,* Appleton, 1892; *Little Mr. Thimblefinger and His Queer Country,* Houghton, 1894; *The Chronicles of Aunt Minervy Ann,* Scribner, 1899; *The Tar Baby and Other Rhymes of Uncle Remus,* Appleton, 1904; *Uncle Remus and Br'er Rabbit,* Stokes, 1906; *Uncle Remus Returns,* Houghton, 1918; the author was editor of *Uncle Remus's Magazine,* from June 1907 to July 1908). CPL, DPL, EU, LC, PFL, TUL

Rossiter Johnson's *Phaeton Rogers* (subtitled *A Novel of Boy Life;* first appeared serially in *St. Nicholas,* December 1880 to October 1881; published in New York by Charles Scribner; the author was editor of *Little Classics,* eighteen volumes, 1875-1880; the author's other work includes *Campfire and Battlefield,* Bryan, 1896; *Captain John Smith,* Macmillan, 1914).

1881 *continued*

James Otis's *Toby Tyler* (a popular story of a boy's ten-week adventure with a circus; published in New York by Harper Brothers; the author's other work includes *Jenny Wren's Boarding-House, A Story of Newsboy Life in New York,* Estes, 1881; *Mr. Stubbs' Brother,* Harper, 1882; James Otis is pseudonym for James Otis Kaler). SPL

Margaret Sidney's *The Five Little Peppers and How They Grew* (first of a series of books about the everyday life of a large family; published in Boston by D. Lothrop; the story was first published in *Wide Awake* magazine in 1878; Margaret Sidney is the pseudonym for Harriet Mulford Stone Lathrop; the author's other work, all published by Lothrop, includes *The Five Little Peppers Midway,* 1892; *The Five Little Peppers Grown-Up,* 1892; *Phronsie Pepper, the Youngest of the Five Little Peppers,* 1897; *The Stories Polly Pepper Told to the Five Little Peppers,* 1899; *The Adventures of Joel Pepper,* 1900; *Five Little Peppers Abroad,* 1902; *Five Little Peppers At School,* 1903; *Five Little Peppers and Their Friends,* 1904; *Ben Pepper,* 1905; *The Five Little Peppers in the Little Brown House,* 1907; *Our Davie Pepper,* 1916). CCBC

1882

F. Anstey's *Vice Versa* (the story of a father and son who change places and shapes; published in London by Smith, Elder and Co.; the author's other work includes *The Talking Horse,* Smith, Elder, 1892; *Paleface and Redskin,* Richards, 1898; *The Brass Bottle,* Smith, 1900; *Only Toys!,* Richards, 1903; and many adult works; F. Anstey is pseudonym for Thomas Anstey Guthrie).

James Baldwin's *The Story of Siegfried* (a highly regarded retelling of the Norse saga; published in New York by Charles Scribner; illustrated by Howard Pyle; the author's other work includes *The Story of Roland,* Scribner, 1883; *Old Greek Stories,* American Book Co., 1895; *Hero Tales Told in School,* Scribner, 1904; *John Bunyan's Dream Story,* American Book Co., 1913; *A Story of the Golden Age,* Scribner, 1887).

Daniel Carter Beard's *The American Boy's Handy Book: What To Do and How To Do It* (a book describing numerous activities with directions for carrying them out; published by Scribner; a companion volume was *The American Girl's Handy Book,* Scribner, 1887, by Lina and Adelia B. Beard; the author's other work includes *Dan Beard's Animal Book and Campfire Stories,* Moffat, 1907; *The Boy Pioneers,* Scribner, 1909; *The American Boys' Book of Sport,* Scribner, 1910; *The American Boys' Book of Bugs, Butterflies and Beetles,* Lippincott, 1915; *The American Boys' Book of Signs, Signals, and Symbols,* Lippincott, 1918; *The American Boys' Book of Wild Animals,* Lippincott, 1921; *The Black Wolf Pack,* Scribner, 1922; *The American Boys' Book of Birds and Brownies of the Woods,* Lippincott, 1923).

Robert Browning's *Pied Piper of Hamelin* (a popular story-poem by well-known British poet; published in New York by Lyman and Curtiss; illustrated by Livingston Hopkins; other illustrated editions include Kate Greenaway's, 1880; Hope Dunlap's, 1910; Arthur Rackham's, 1934; Roger Duvoisin's, 1936; Harold Jones's, 1962; Lieselotte Schwarz's, 1970; C. Walter Hodges's, 1971; the author's collected poems for children include *The Young Folks Browning,* Page, 1919; *The Brownings for the Young,* Smith, 1896; *The Boys' Browning: Poems of Action and Incident,* Estes, 1899; the author's wife, Elizabeth Barrett Browning, wrote *Sonnets from the Portuguese,* 1850, appropriated by youth). BaU

Richard Jefferies's *Bevis: The Story of a Boy* (issued in three volumes in London by Low, Marston, Searle, and Rivington; the adventures of two boys who alternately pretend to be living on a desert and to be waging war with Indians; the author's other work includes factual nature books such as *The Amateur Poacher,* Smith, 1880, and *The Game Keeper At Home,* London, 1878; *Wood Magic; A Fable,* Cassell, 1881; *After London; or, Wild England,* Cassell, 1885). IUL

Louise Clarke Pyrnelle's *Diddie, Dumps, And Tot* (story of child life on a Southern plantation, published in New York by Harper Brothers; the author's other work includes *The Marriage of Aunt Flora,* n.p., 1895, and *Miss Li'l Tweetty,* Harper, 1907).

1883

The Boys & Girls' Companion (an illustrated monthly published by the Church of England Sunday School Institute; a continuation of the *Sunday Scholar's Companion*).

Alfred Caldecott's *Some of Aesop's Fables* (a retelling which aimed to replace "the florid style of . . . older English versions and the stilted harshness of more modern ones, by a plainness and terseness more nearly like the character of the originals"; published by Macmillan; illustrations by Randolph Caldecott follow each fable and depict a humorous, modern scene with social or political implications instead of the traditional moral ending; the reteller was the brother of Randolph Caldecott).

Lizzie Williams Champney's *Three Vassar Girls Abroad* (a story of the rambles of three college girls on a vacation trip through France and Spain; published in Boston by Estes and Lauriat; illustrated by "Champ," i.e.,

1883 *continued*

J. Wells Champney; the author's other work includes *Three Vassar Girls on the Rhine,* 1884; *Three Vassar Girls in South America,* 1885; *Three Vassar Girls in Italy,* 1886; *Three Vassar Girls on the Rhine. A Holiday Trip of Three College Girls through Germany, by Way of This Celebrated River,* 1886; *The Vassar Girls at Home,* 1888; *Three Vassar Girls in France,* 1888; *Three Vassar Girls in Russia and Turkey,* 1889; *Three Vassar Girls in Switzerland,* 1890; *Three Vassar Girls in Tyrol,* 1891; *Three Vassar Girls in the Holy Land,* 1892; all published in Boston by Estes and Lauriat; the Witch Winnie series published in New York by Dodd, Mead: *Witch Winnie; the Story of a "King's Daughter,"* 1891; *Witch Winnie's Mystery; or, The Old Oak Cabinet,* 1891; *Witch Winnie's Studio; or, The King's Daughter's Art Life,* 1892; *Witch Winnie in Paris; or, The King's Daughters Abroad,* 1893; *Witch Winnie at Versailles,* 1895; *Witch Winnie in Holland,* 1896; *Witch Winnie in Venice, and the Alchemist's Story,* 1897; *Witch Winnie in Spain,* 1898).

Francis James Child's *The English and Scottish Popular Ballads* (a collection of five volumes of ballads with variants of the British Isles, collected by Child, published in Boston by Hampton; some of the best known have been appropriated by children).

Edward Eggleston's *The Hoosier School-Boy* (a popular story of an Indiana schoolboy, published in New York by Charles Scribner; appeared serially in *St. Nicholas* from December 1881 to April 1882; the author's other work includes *The Circuit Rider,* Ford, 1874; *Roxy,* Chatto, 1878).

George Wilbur Peck's *Peck's Bad Boy and His Pa* (a popular, humorous boy's story, published in Chicago by Belford, Clarke and Co.; illustrated by Gean Smith; the author's other work includes *Adventures of One Terrance McGrant,* Lambert, 1871; *The Grocery Man and Peck's Bad Boy,* n.p., 1883; *How Private Geo. W. Peck Put Down the Rebellion,* Belford, 1887; *Peck's Uncle Ike and the Red-Headed Boy,* Belford, 1899; *Sunbeams: Humor, Sarcasm, and Sense,* Jamieson-Higgins, 1900; *Peck's Red-Headed Boy,* Hurst, 1901; *Peck's Bad Boy Abroad,* Stanton, 1905; *Peck's Bad Boy with the Circus,* Thompson, 1906; *Peck's Bad Boy with the Cowboys,* Thompson, 1907).

Howard Pyle's *Merry Adventures of Robin Hood of Great Renown, in Nottinghamshire* (a robust adaptation of the adventures of the English folk hero, published in New York by Charles Scribner; illustrated by the author who was one of America's greatest book illustrators and teachers; his students included N. C. Wyeth, Maxfield Parrish, Jessie Willcox Smith;

the author-artist's other work includes *Yankee Doodle, An Old Friend in New Dress,* Dodd, 1881; *Within the Capes,* Scribner, 1885; *Pepper and Salt,* Harper, 1886; *The Wonder Clock,* Harper, 1888; *Otto of the Silver Hand,* Scribner, 1888; *The Rose of Paradise,* Harper, 1888; *Men of Iron,* Harper, 1892; *Twilight Land,* Harper, 1895; *The Story of Jack Ballister's Fortunes,* Century, 1895; *The Garden Behind the Moon,* Scribner, 1895; *The Price of Blood,* Badger, 1899; *Rejected of Men,* Harper, 1903; *The Story of King Arthur and His Knights,* Scribner, 1903; *Stolen Treasure,* Harper, 1907; *The Ruby of Kishmoor,* Harper, 1908; *Howard Pyle's Book of Pirates,* Harper, 1921). LC, PFL

Oscar Wilde's *The Happy Prince, and Other Tales* (a famous British author's first collection of allegorical literary fairy tales, published in New York by R. F. Fenno and Co.; followed by *A House of Pomegranates,* Osgood, 1891, which includes "The Selfish Giant"). UCLA

1884

Helen Hunt Jackson's *Ramona* (a romance, published in Boston by Roberts Brothers; one of the author's many novels appropriated by older children; the author's other work, published by Roberts, except as noted, includes *Bathmendi,* Loring, 1867; *Saxe Holme's Stories,* Scribner, 1874, 1878; *Mercy Philbrick's Choice,* 1876; *Hetty's Strange History,* 1877; *Nelly's Silver Mine,* 1878; *Letters from a Cat,* 1879; *Mammy Titleback,* 1881; *Zeph,* 1885). HH

Johanna Spyri's *Heidi; Her Years of Wandering and Learning* (translated from the German by Louise Brooks; published in Boston by DeWolfe; an early book in which the author shows children a captivating Swiss child in an appealing foreign setting; author's other work includes *Willis the Pilot, a Sequel to the Swiss Family Robinson,* Lee, n.d.; *Red-Letter Stories,* Lothrop, 1884; *Rico and Wiseli,* DeWolfe, 1885; *Uncle Titus,* Lothrop, 1886; *Veronica and Other Friends,* Cupples, 1886; *Gritl's Children, A Story For Children and For Those Who Love Children,* Cupples, 1887; *Swiss Stories for Children,* Lothrop, 1887; *Moni, the Goat Boy and Other Stories,* Ginn, 1906; *Heimatlos,* Gin, 1912; *Chel, A Story of the Swiss Mountains,* Eaton, 1913; *The Rose Child,* Crowell, 1916; *What Sami Sings With the Birds,* Crowell, 1917; *Little Miss Grasshopper,* Crowell, 1918; *Little Curly Head the Pet Lamb,* Crowell, 1919; *Cornelli,* Burt, 1920; *Erick and Sally,* Beacon, 1921; *The Story of Rico,* Beacon, 1921; *Tiss, a Little Alpine Waif,* Crowell, 1921; *Toni, the Little Woodcarver,* Crowell, 1920; *Trini, the Little Strawberry Girl,* Crowell, 1922; *Jo, the Little Machinist,* Crowell, 1923; *Vinzi,* Lippincott, 1923; *Dora,* Lippincott, 1924; *Jorli, the Story of a Swiss Boy,* Sanborn, 1924; *The Little Alpine Musician,* Crowell, 1924; *The New Year's Carol,* Houghton, 1924; *Arthur and Squirrel,* Crowell, 1925; *Children of the Alps,*

1884 *continued*

Lippincott, 1925; *The Children's Carol,* Crowell, 1925; *Francesca at Hinterwald,* Lippincott, 1925; *Eveli and Beni,* Crowell, 1926; *Eveli, the Little Singer,* Lippincott, 1926; *Peppino,* Lippincott, 1926; *Stories of Swiss Children,* Crowell, 1926; *Castle Wonderful,* Crowell, 1928; *Jorli; or, The Stauffer Mill,* Lippincott, 1928; *Boys and Girls of the Alps,* Crowell, 1929; *In the Swiss Mountains,* Crowell, 1929).

1885

H. Rider Haggard's *King Solomon's Mines* (a popular South African adventure story, published in London by Cassell and Co.; the author's other work includes a sequel, *Allan Quatermain,* Longmans, 1887; *She,* Longmans, 1887, and sequel, *Ayesha,* Lock, 1905; *Cleopatra,* Longmans, 1889; with Andrew Lang, *The World's Desire,* Longmans, 1890; *Eric Brighteyes,* Longmans, 1891; *Nada the Lily,* Longmans, 1892; *Montezuma's Daughter,* Longmans, 1893; *The People of the Mist,* Longmans, 1894; *Heart of the World,* Longmans, 1896; *Lysbeth: A Tale of the Dutch,* Longmans, 1901; *Pearl Maiden,* Longmans, 1903; *The Brethren,* Cassell, 1904; *The Ghost Kings,* Cassell, 1908; *The Yellow God, an Idol of Africa,* Cassell, 1908; *The Lady of Blossholme,* Hodder, 1909; *Morning Star,* Cassell, 1910; *Queen Sheba's Ring,* Nash, 1910; *Red Eve,* Hodder, 1911; *Marie,* Cassell, 1912; *Child of Storm,* Cassell, 1913; *The Wanderer's Necklace,* Cassell, 1914; *The Holy Flower, Lock,* 1915; *The Ivory Child,* Cassell, 1916; *Finished,* Paget, 1917; *When the World Shook,* n.p., 1919; *She and Allan,* Hutchinson, 1921; *The Virgin of the Sun,* Cassell, 1922; *Wisdom's Daughter,* Hutchinson, 1923; *Queen of the Dawn,* Hutchinson, 1921; *Allan and the Ice Gods,* Hutchinson, 1927; *Belshazzar,* Paul, 1930). TCL

Robert Louis Stevenson's *A Child's Garden of Verses* (published in Britain at Cambridge University Press as *Penny Whistles* in 1883; a "classic" book of poems which deals with a child's everyday experiences; a famous American edition was illustrated by Jessie Willcox Smith, 1905; the author also wrote *Treasure Island,* Cassell, 1883, [originally titled *The Sea Cook*], a famous American edition was illustrated by N. C. Wyeth in 1911; the author's other work includes *New Arabian Nights,* Chatto, 1882; *Prince Otto,* Chatto, 1885; with Fanny Stevenson, *The Dynamiter,* Holt, 1885; *Kidnapped,* Cassell, 1886; *The Strange Case of Dr. Jekyll and Mr. Hyde,* Longmans, 1886; *The Merry Men, and Other Tales,* 1887; *The Black Arrow,* Cassell, 1888; *The Master of Ballantrae,* Tauchnitz, 1889; with L. Osbourne, *The Wrong Box,* Scribner, 1889, and *The Wrecker,* concluded by A. T. Quiller-Couch, Scribner, 1892; *Catriona,* Cassell, 1893; *Island Night's Entertainment,* Cassell, 1893; with L. Osbourne, *The Ebb Tide,* Heinemann, n.d.; *Weir of Hermiston,* Chatto, 1896; *St. Ives,* Heinemann, 1897). TUL, YU

1886

Frances Hodgson Burnett's *Little Lord Fauntleroy* (an enormously popular account by a British-born author of an American boy who is heir to an English dukedom; published by Charles Scribner; illustrated by Reginald Birch; first appeared serially in *St. Nicholas,* November 1885 to October 1886; the author's other work includes *Editha's Burglar . . . ,* Marsh, 1888; *Sara Crewe: Or What Happened at Miss Minchin's,* Scribner, 1888; *The Pretty Sister of Jose,* Scribner, 1889; *Little St. Elizabeth and Other Stories,* Scribner, 1890; *Giovanni and the Other: Children Who Have Made Stories,* Scribner, 1892; *The One I Knew Best of All: A Memory of the Mind of a Child,* Scribner, 1893; *The Captain's Youngest, Piccino and Other Stories,* Warne, 1894; *Piccino and Other Child Stories,* Scribner, 1894; *Two Little Pilgrims' Progress,* Scribner, 1895; *The Prince of Osmonde,* 1896; *In the Closed Room,* McClure, 1904; *A Little Princess, Being the Whole Story of Sara Crewe, Now Told for the First Time,* Scribner, 1905; *Racketty Packetty House,* Century, 1907; *The Cosy Lion: As Told by Queen Crosspatch,* Century, 1907; *The Spring Cleaning,* Century, 1908; *The Good Wolf,* Moffat, 1908; with Katherine Birdsall and Vivian Burnett, *The Children's Book,* Moffat, 1909; *The Land of the Blue Flower,* Moffat, 1909; *The Secret Garden,* Stokes, 1911; *My Robin,* Stokes, 1912; *T. Tembarom,* Century, 1913; *The Lost Prince,* Century, 1915; *The Way to the House of Santa Claus: A Christmas Story for Very Small Boys in Which Every Little Reader is the Hero of A Big Adventure,* Harper, 1916; *The Little Hunchback Zia,* Stokes, 1916; *The White People,* Harper, 1917). LC, CPL

Charles Edward Carryl's *Davy and the Goblin; or, What Followed Reading "Alice's Adventures in Wonderland"* (a popular fanciful story illustrated by the author; published in New York by Houghton, Mifflin; first appeared serially in *St. Nicholas,* from December 1884 to March 1885; the author's other work includes *The Admiral's Caravan,* Century, 1892).

1887

Atalanta (a magazine published monthly from October 1887 to September 1898 by various publishers; edited by L. T. Meade [Mrs. E. T. M. Smith], Alicia Amy Leith, John C. Staples, Alexander Balfour Symington, and Edwin Oliver; outstanding writers of the day were contributors, including R. L. Stevenson, whose *Catriona* appeared serially as "David Balfour: Memories of His Adventures At Home and Abroad," from December 1892 to September 1893).

Alice Corkran's *Down the Snow Stairs* (a popular though didactic allegory about Kitty's adventures in dreamland; published in London by Blackie and Son; the author's other work includes *Bessie Lang,* Blackwood, 1876;

1887 *continued*

The Adventures of Mrs. Wishing-To-Be, and Other Stories, Blackie, 1883; *The Young Philistine, and Other Stories,* Burns, 1888; *Margery Merton's Girlhood,* Blackie, 1888; *Mischievous Jack,* Blackie, 1888; *The Fatal House,* Ward, 1889; *Joan's Adventures at the North Pole,* Blackie, 1889; *Meg's Friends,* Blackie, 1889; *Boppy's Repentance,* Blackie, 1896).

Palmer Cox's *The Brownies: Their Book* (the first of a series of eleven popular books written and illustrated by Cox and published in New York by Century and in London by Unwin; the rest of the series includes *Another Brownie Book,* 1890; *The Brownies At Home,* 1893; *The Brownies Around the World,* 1904; *The Brownies Through the Union,* 1895; *The Brownies Abroad,* 1899; *The Brownies in the Philippines,* 1904; *The Brownies' Latest Adventures,* 1910; *The Brownies' Many More Nights,* Century, 1913; *The Brownies and Prince Florimel,* Century, 1918; *The Brownies in Fairyland,* Century, 1925; author's other work includes *Squibs of California,* Mutual, 1874, Roman, 1874; *Hans Von Pelter's Trip To Gotham,* Art Printing, 1876; *How Columbus Found America,* Art Printing, 1877; *That Stanley!,* Art Printing, 1878; *Queer People with Paws and Claws,* Hubbard, 1888, Griffith, 1889; *Queer People Such As Goblins, Giants, Merry Men and Monarchs and Their Kweer Kapers,* Griffith, 1889; *Comic Yarns,* Hubbard, 1889; *Frontier Humor,* Edgewood, 1889; *Palmer Cox's Brownies, A Libretto,* Harmes, 1894; *The Brownies in Fairyland, A Libretto,* Harmes, 1894; *Brownie Year Book,* McLaughlin, 1895; *The Palmer Cox Brownie Primer,* text by Mary C. Judd, Century, 1906; *Brownie Clown of Brownie Town,* Century, 1908; *Bugaboo Bill,* Farrar, 1971, which first appeared in *St. Nicholas,* 1880; the author-illustrator's work was a regular feature of *St. Nicholas Magazine*). CPL, PFL

Talbot Baines Reed's *The Fifth Form At St. Dominic's* (a popular English public-schoolboy story published in London by R. T. S., the editor of *The Boy's Own Paper;* author's other work includes *Follow My Leader,* Cassell, 1885; *The Willoughby Captains,* Hodder, 1887; *My Friend Smith,* Religious Tract Society, 1889; *Sir Ludar,* Sampson, 1889; *Roger Ingleton, Minor,* Low, 1891; *The Cockhouse at Fellsgarth,* Religious Tract Society, 1893; *The Master of the Shell,* Religious Tract Society, 1894; *Tom, Dick and Harry,* Religious Tract Society, 1894; *A Dog with a Bad Name,* Religious Tract Society, 1894; *Reginald Cruden,* Religious Tract Society, 1894; *Kilgorman,* Nelson, 1895).

1888

Thomas Nelson Page's *Two Little Confederates* (the story of the tragedy of the Civil War as seen through the eyes of a child; appeared serially in *St.*

Nicholas, from May to October 1888; published in New York by Scribner; author's other work includes, with A. C. Gordon, *Befo' de War,* Scribner, 1888; *Santa Claus's Partner,* Scribner, 1899; *Robert E. Lee, Man and Soldier,* Scribner, 1911).

1889

Andrew Lang's *The Blue Fairy Book* (the first of this Scottish collector's series of "color books" of folktales edited and adapted especially for children and published in London by Longmans; the author's other work, published by Longmans except as noted, includes *The Princess Nobody,* 1884; *The Gold of Farnilee,* Arrowsmith, 1888; *Prince Prigio,* Arrowsmith, 1889; *The Red Fairy Book,* 1890; *The Green Fairy Book,* 1892; *Prince Richardo of Pantouflia,* Arrowsmith, 1893; *The True Story Book,* 1893; *The Yellow Fairy Book,* 1894; *The Red True Fairy Book,* 1895; *The Animal Story Book,* 1896; *The Nursery Rhyme Book,* illustrated by L. Leslie Brooke, Warne, 1897; *The Pink Fairy Book,* 1897; *Arabian Nights' Entertainments,* 1898; *The Red Book of Animal Stories,* 1899; *The Grey Fairy Book,* 1900; *The Violet Fairy Book,* 1901; *The Crimson Fairy Book,* 1903; *The Story of the Golden Fleece,* Kelley, 1903; *The Brown Fairy Book,* 1904; *The Red Book of Romance,* 1905; *The Story of Joan of Arc,* Dutton, 1906; *Tales of a Fairy Court,* Collins, 1906; *The Orange Fairy Book,* 1906; *Tales of Troy and Greece,* 1907; *The Olive Fairy Book,* 1907; *The Lilac Fairy Book,* 1910; the author also wrote many adult novels and nonfiction including poetry and introductions to such works as Walton's *Complete Angler,* 1896; Lamb's *Tales from Shakespeare,* 1889; Dumas's *The Three Musketeers,* 1903; Stevenson's *A Child's Garden of Verses,* 1907; Alleyne's *The Book of Princes and Princesses,* 1908; *The Red Book of Heroes,* 1909; *All Sorts of Stories Book,* 1911; *The Book of Saints and Heroes,* 1912; *The Strange Story Book,* 1913). IUL

1890

William Dean Howells's *A Boy's Town* (subtitled *Described for Harper's Young People;* published in New York by Harper; the author's other work includes thirty-eight adult novels and *The Flight of Pony Baker,* Harper, 1902). BGSU, BKU, RHL

Joseph Jacobs's *English Fairy Tales* (a two-volume set of eighty-seven tales published between 1890 and 1894 in London by D. Nutt; retold in the vernacular for children; notes on sources are included; the stories include such famous tales as "Childe Rowland," "Tom Hickathrift," and "Children of the Wood," as well as English variants of tales such as "Rumpelstiltskin"; the author-collector's other work includes *Aesop's Fables,* two volumes, Nutt, 1889; *Celtic Fairy Tales,* two volumes, Nutt, 1892, 1894;

1890 *continued*
Indian Fairy Tales, Nutt, 1892; *The Book of Wonder Voyages,* Macmillan, 1896; *The Story of Geographical Discovery,* Newnes, 1898; *Europa's Fairy Book,* Putnam, 1915).

Thomas Janvier's *The Aztec Treasure-House* (a romantic tale of a search for treasure in an ancient and lost city of the Aztecs; published in New York by Harper Brothers; the author's other work, published by Harper, includes *In the Sargasso Sea,* 1898; *Henry Hudson,* 1909; *Legends of the City of Mexico,* 1910).

Eliza Orne White's *Miss Brooks: A Story* (the first of the author's many stories for girls of all ages; published in Boston by Roberts Brothers; most of the author's books were written after she had become blind, but her descriptive passages may be all the more detailed because of it; the author's other work, published in Boston by Houghton, Mifflin except as noted, includes *Winterborough,* 1892; *When Molly Was Six,* 1894; *The Coming of Theodora: A Novel,* 1895; *A Little Girl of Long Ago,* 1906; *A Browning Courtship,* 1897; *A Lover of Truth,* 1898; *Ednah and Her Brothers,* 1900; *John Forsyth's Aunts,* McClure Phillips, 1901; *Lesley Chilton,* 1903; *An Only Child,* illustrated by Katherine Pyle, 1905; *A Borrowed Sister,* sequel to *An Only Child,* illustrated by Katherine Pyle, 1906; *The Wares of Edgefield,* 1909; *Brothers in Fur,* 1910; *The Enchanted Mountain,* 1911; *The First Step,* 1914; *The Blue Aunt,* illustrated by Katherine Pyle, 1918; *The Strange Year,* 1920; *Peggy in Her Blue Frock,* 1921; *Tony,* 1924; *Joan Morse,* 1926; *Diana's Rosebush,* 1927; *The Adventures of Andres,* 1928; *Sally in Her Fur Coat,* 1929; *The Green Door,* 1930; *When Abigail Was Seven,* 1931; *The Four Young Kendalls,* 1932; *Where Is Adelaide?,* illustrated by Helen Sewell, 1933; *Lending Mary,* 1934; *Ann Frances,* illustrated by H. Sewell, 1935; *Nancy Alden,* 1936; *The Farm Beyond the Town,* 1937; *Helen's Gift House,* 1938; *Patty Makes a Visit,* 1939; *The House Across the Way,* 1940; *I: the Autobiography of a Cat,* 1941; *Training Sylvia,* 1942; *When Esther Was a Little Girl,* 1944).

1891

Mrs. Cecilia Jamison's *Lady Jane* (a popular story for older girls; published in London by Osgood and McIlvaine; the author's other work includes *Something To Do,* Osgood, 1871; *Ropes of Sand, and Other Stories,* Osgood, 1876; *My Bonnie Lass,* Estes, 1877; *The Story of an Enthusiast,* Ticknor, 1888; *Toinette's Philip,* Century, 1894; *Thistledown,* Century, 1903; *The Penhallow Family,* Wilde, 1905).

James Whitcomb Riley's *Rhymes of Childhood* (nostalgic, popular verses about childhood written in a rural dialect; published in Indianapolis by

Bowen-Merrill; the best known verses include "The Raggedy Man" and "Little Orphan Annie"; the author's other work includes *The Old Swimmin'-Hole, and 'Leven More Poems*, Hitt, 1883; *The Boss Girl*, Bowen-Merrill, 1886; *Afterwhiles*, Bowen-Merrill, 1887; *Pipes o' Pan at Zekesbury*, Bowen-Merrill, 1888; *Old Fashioned Roses*, Bowen-Merrill, 1888; *Green Field and Running Brooks*, Bowen-Merrill, 1892; *Poems Here at Home*, Century, 1893; *Riley Child-Rhymes*, Bowen-Merrill, 1899; *The Book of Joyous Children*, Scribner, 1902; *Old Schoolboy Romances*, Bobbs-Merrill, 1909; *Knee-Deep in June*, Bobbs-Merrill, 1912). IUL

William Osborn Stoddard's *Little Smoke* (a popular tale of the Sioux, published in New York by Appleton; the author's other work includes *Verses of Many Days*, Miller, 1875; *Red Beauty, A Story of the Pawnee Trail*, Lippincott, 1877; *The Heart of It*, Putnam, 1880; *Dab Kinzer; A Story of a Growing Boy*, Scribner, 1881; *Esau Hardery*, White, 1881; *The Quartet; A Sequel to Dab Kinzer*, Scribner, 1881; *Saltillo Boys*, Scribner, 1882; *The Talking Leaves*, Harper, 1882; *Wrecked?*, White, 1883; *Winter Fun*, Scribner, 1885; *George Washington*, White, 1886; *George Washington's Fifty-Seven Rules of Behavior*, Lawrence, 1886; *Two Arrows*, Harper, 1886; *Ulysses S. Grant*, White, 1886; *James Madison, James Monroe and John Quincy Adams*, Stokes, 1887; *Abraham Lincoln and Andrew Johnson*, Stokes, 1888; *Grover Cleveland*, Stokes, 1888; *William Henry Harrison, John Tyler and James Knox Polk*, Stokes, 1888; *Zachary Taylor, Millard Fillmore, Franklin Pierce and James Buchanan*, Stokes, 1888; *Rutherford Birchard Hayes, James Arbram Garfield and Chester Alan Arthur*, Stokes, 1889; *Crowded Out O' Crofield; or, The Boy Who Made His Way*, Appleton, 1890; *The Red Mustang*, Harper, 1890; *Chuck Purdy, the Story of a New York Boy*, Lothrop, 1891; *Gid Granger; The Story of a Rough Boy*, Lothrop, 1891; *Mart Satterlee Among the Indians*, Bonner, 1891; *The Battle of New York*, Appleton, 1892; *Guert Ten Eyck; A Hero Story*, Lothrop, 1893; *On the Old Frontier; or, The Last Raid of the Iroquois*, Appleton, 1893; *Tom and the Monkey King*, Price-McGill, 1893; *The White Cave*, Century, 1893; *The Captain's Boat*, Merriam, 1894; *Chris, the Model Maker*, Appleton, 1894; *The Partners; the Story of an Every-Day Girl and Boy and How They Helped Along*, Lothrop, 1895; *The Swordmaker's Son; A Story of the Year 30 A.D.*, Century, 1896; *The Windfall*, Appleton, 1896; *The Red Patriot*, Appleton, 1897; *Walled In*, Revell, 1897; *The First Cruiser Out*, Stone, 1898; *The Lost Gold of the Montezumas*, Lippincott, 1898; *Success Against Odds*, Appleton, 1898; *With the Black Prince*, Appleton, 1898; *The Despatch Boat of the Whistle; A Story of Santiago*, Lothrop, 1899; *Ulric the Jarl; A Story of a Penitent Thief*, Eaton, 1899; *Ned, the Son of Webb*, Estes, 1900; *Running the Cuban Blockade*, Stone, 1900; *The Financier*, Penn, 1900; *Jack Morgan; A Boy of 1812*, Lothrop, 1901; *Montayne; or, The Slavers of Old New York*, Altemus, 1901; *Boys of*

1891 *continued*
Bunker Academy, Jacobs, 1902; *The Voyage of Charlemagne,* Estes, 1902; *The Spy of Yorktown,* Appleton, 1903; *The Village Champion,* Jacobs, 1903; *The Fight for the Valley,* Appleton, 1904; *Long Bridge Boys; A Story of 1861,* Lothrop, 1904; *Zeb, A New England Boy,* Jacobs, 1904; *The Boy Lincoln,* Appleton, 1905; *Dan Monroe, A Story of Bunker Hill,* Lothrop, 1905; *Two Cadets with Washington,* Lothrop, 1906; *In the Open,* Harper, 1908; *Longshore Boys,* Lippincott, 1909; *The Captain of the Cat's Paw,* Harper, 1914).

1892

John Kendrick Bangs's *The Tiddledywink's Poetry Book* (a collection of poems for children which includes several fanciful poems by Bangs; published by R. H. Russell; the author's other work includes *Tiddledywink Tales,* Russell, 1893; *The Young Folk's Minstrels,* Harper, 1897; *Binkey the Skicycle and Other Tales of Jimmieboy*, Riggs, 1902; *Mollie and the Unwiseman*, Coates, 1902; *Mollie and the Unwiseman Abroad*, Lippincott, 1910; *Santa Claus and Little Billee,* Browne, 1914; *Jarley's Thanksgiving,* Century, 1928).

Carlo Collodi's *The Adventures of Pinocchio* (translated from the Italian *Le Avventure di Pinocchio,* 1883, by M. A. Murray; perhaps the best puppet story ever written; first appeared in Rome's children's newspaper, *Giornale per i Bambini*, July 1881, with the title "Storia di un Burattino, The Story of a Puppet"; the first English edition was issued in 1891 as *The Story of a Puppet,* published by Unwin, but the title was soon changed to *The Adventures of Pinocchio;* Carlo Collodi is pseudonym of Italian author, Carlo Lorenzini).

Arthur Conan Doyle's *The Adventures of Sherlock Holmes* (a popular British detective story; published first in the *Strand Magazine* in London and later in book form in New York by A. L. Burt; appropriated first by British and later by American children; the author's other work includes *A Study in Scarlet,* Conkey, 1887; *Micah Clarke,* Longmans, 1889; *The Sign of Four,* Blackett, 1890; *The Firm of Girdlestone,* Chatto, 1890; *The White Company,* Smith, 1891; *The Doings of Raffles Haw,* Conkey, 1891; *The Great Shadow,* Arrowsmith, 1892; *The Refugees,* Longmans, 1893; *The Memoirs of Sherlock Holmes,* Newnes, 1894; *The Parasite,* illustrated by Howard Pyle, Harper, 1894; *The Exploits of Brigadier Gerard,* Newnes, 1896; *Rodney Stone,* Murray, 1896; *Uncle Bernace,* Cox, 1897; *The Man from Archangel,* Street, 1898; *The Tragedy of Korosko,* Smith, 1898; *The Hound of the Baskervilles,* Collier, 1901; *Adventures of Gerard,* McClure, 1903; *Sherlock Holmes,* Fenno, 1903; *The Return of Sherlock Holmes,*

Newnes, 1905; *Sir Nigel,* Smith, 1906; *The Crime of the Congo,* Hutchinson, 1909; *The Lost World,* Hodder, 1912; *The Poison Belt,* Hodder, 1913; *The Valley of Fear,* Smith, 1915; *His Last Bow,* Murray, 1917; *The Black Doctor and Other Tales,* Doran, 1919; *The Case Book of Sherlock Holmes,* Murray, 1927; *The Complete Sherlock Holmes,* Doubleday, 1927; *The Maracot Deep,* Doubleday, 1929). SFPL

Ernst Theodor Amadeus Hoffman's *The Nutcracker and the Mouse King and the Educated Cat* (translated from the German by Ascott R. Hope; well-known story which inspired Tschaikowsky to compose the "Nutcracker Suite" in 1892).

1893

Frances E. Crompton's *The Gentle Heritage* (a story with strong, realistic child characters in a garden setting; published in London by A. D. Innes; the author's other work includes *Friday's Child,* Dutton, 1889; *Master Bartlemy,* Innes, 1892; *Messire, and Other Tales,* Innes, 1894; *The Green Garland,* Innes, 1896; *The Voyage of the "Mary Adair,"* Nister, 1899; *The Rose Carnation,* Nister, 1900; *The Little Swan Maidens,* Nister, 1903; *The Children of the Hermitage,* Innes, 1903).

L. T. Meade's *Beyond the Blue Mountains* (a tale of how children successfully defeat their fearful enemies with the help of good angels; published in London by Cassell; the author's other work includes *The Autocrat of the Nursery,* Hodder, 1884; *A World of Girls,* illustrated by M. E. Edwards, Cassell, 1887; *Deb and the Duchess,* Hatchards, 1888; *Polly, a New-Fashioned Girl,* Cassell, 1889; *A Sweet Girl Graduate,* Cassell, 1891; *Daddy's Girl,* Newnes, 1891; *Bashful Fifteen,* Cassell, 1892; *The Rebel of the School,* illustrated by W. Rainey, Chambers, 1902; L. T. Meade is the pseudonym of Elizabeth Thomasina Meade Smith).

Wee Willie Winkie (a children's magazine started in England by Lady Aberdeen and carried on in Canada with the editorial assistance of her daughter, Lady Marjorie Gordon; when Lady Aberdeen's husband became governor-general of Canada, she moved to Ottawa to help establish a *Wee Willie Winkie* editorial office in Montreal in 1894; a Canadian edition was published until 1897; the magazine contained "competitions," i.e., puzzles, correspondence, and messages encouraging donations to the poor).

Stanley John Weyman's *A Gentleman of France* (one of the author's many English melodramatic historical romances, published in three volumes by Longmans in London; the author's works were praised by A. C. Doyle, R. L. Stevenson, H. Walpole, and R. Kipling; the author's other work

1893 *continued*

includes *The House of Wolf,* Tauchnitz, 1890; *The New Rector,* Smith, 1891; *The Story of Francis Cludde,* Cassell, 1891; *The Man in Black,* Cassell, 1894; *Under the Red Robe,* Methuen, 1894; *My Lady Rotha,* Innes, 1894; *From the Memoirs of a Minister of France,* Cassell, 1895; *A Little Wizard,* Fenno, 1895; *The Red Cockade,* Longmans, 1898; *Shrewsbury,* Longmans, 1895; *The Castle Inn,* Smith, 1898; *Sophia,* Longmans, 1900; *Count Hannible,* Smith, 1901; *In King's Byways,* Smith, 1902; *The Long Night,* Longmans, 1903; *The Abbess of Vlaye,* Longmans, 1903; *Starvecrow Farm,* Hutchinson, 1905; *Chippinge,* Smith, 1906; *Laid Up in Lavender,* Smith, 1907; *The Wild Geese,* Hodder, 1908; *Madam Constantia,* n.p., 1919; *The Great House,* Murray, 1919; *Ovington's Bank,* Murray, 1922; *The Traveller in the Fur Cloak,* Hutchinson, 1924; *Queen's Folly,* Murray, 1925; *That Lively Peggy,* Murray, 1928).

1894

The Aldine Garfield Boys' Journal (London weekly which was also published in monthly parts; incorporated with the *Aldine Cheerful Library* [begun in 1894] on August 7, 1895; the magazine named after James A. Garfield, a canal boy who became President of the United States).

Harold Avery's *The School's Honour* (a collection of short stories about life in a boys' school; published in London by the Sunday School Union; the author's other work, published in London by Nelson except as noted, includes *The Triple Alliance,* 1897, which was first serialized in the *Boy's Own Paper* in 1896; *Dormitory Flag,* 1899; *Heads or Tails,* 1901; *Play the Game,* 1906; *Not Cricket!,* Partridge, 1912; *Between Two Schools,* 1923; *Won for the School,* Collins, 1927; *The Cock House Cup,* 1933; *Chums At Charlhurst,* 1936).

Laurence Housman's *A Farm in Fairyland* (a collection of short romantic fairy tales for children by a well-known British writer; published in London for Keegan Paul; the author's other work includes retellings of *Stories of the Arabian Nights,* illustrated by Edmund Dulac, Hodder, 1907). CC, HU, ISU, USF

Rudyard Kipling's *The Jungle Books* (a sensitive treatment of animals by a famous English writer who was living in Vermont while writing the two volumes; published in London by Macmillan; the stories' moral code transcends the usual didacticism of period; the author's other work includes *Schoolboy Lyrics,* n.p., 1881; *Wee Willie Winkie, and Other Stories,* Wheeler, 1888; *Captains Courageous,* Tauchnitz, 1897; *Stalky & Co.,* Macmillan, 1899; *Kim,* Tauchnitz, 1901; *The Naulahka,* with Wolcott Balestier, Heinemann, 1892; *The Just So Stories,* Tauchnitz, 1902; *Puck of Pook's Hill,* Macmillan, 1906; *Rewards and Fairies,* Macmillan, 1910;

A History of England, with C. R. Fletcher, Clarendon, 1911; *Land and Sea Tales for Scouts and Guides,* Macmillan, 1923; *Thy Servant A Dog,* Macmillan, 1930). CoU, LC, PU

Amy Le Feuvre's *Eric's Good News* (the first of the author's many tracts, many of which are still distributed by some missionary societies; published in London by the Religious Tract Society; the author's other work, published by the Religious Tract Society except as noted, includes *Probable Sons,* 1895; *Teddy's Button!,* 1896; *Dwell Deep; or, Hilda Thorne's Life Story,* 1896; *On the Edge of a Moor,* 1897; *Odd,* 1897; *A Puzzling Pair,* 1898; *His Big Opportunity,* Hodder and Stoughton, 1898; *Bulbs and Blossoms,* 1898; *A Thoughtless Seven,* 1898; *The Carved Cupboard,* 1899; *Bunny's Friends,* 1899; *Roses,* 1899; *Legend-Led,* 1899; *Brownie,* Hodder and Stoughton, 1900; *A Cherry Tree,* Hodder and Stoughton, 1901; *Heather's Mistress,* 1901; *A Daughter of the Sea,* Hodder and Stoughton, 1902; *Odd Made Even,* 1902; *The Making of a Woman,* Hodder and Stoughton, 1903; *Two Tramps,* Hodder and Stoughton, 1903; *Jill's Red Bag,* 1903; *His Little Daughter,* 1904; *A Little Maid,* 1904; *Bridget's Quarter Deck,* 1905; *The Buried Ring,* Hodder and Stoughton, 1905; *The Children's Morning Message,* Hodder and Stoughton, 1905; *Christina and the Boys,* Hodder and Stoughton, 1906; *The Mender,* 1906; *Miss Lavender's Boy and Other Sketches,* 1906; *Robin's Heritage,* Hodder and Stoughton, 1907; *Number Twa!,* 1907; *The Chateau by the Lake,* Hodder and Stoughton, 1907; *A Bit of Rough Road,* 1908; *Me and Nobbles,* 1908; *Us, and Our Donkey,* 1909; *A Country Corner,* Cassell, 1909; *The Birthday: A Christmas Sketch,* 1909; *Joyce and the Rambler,* Hodder and Stoughton, 1910; *A Little Listener,* 1910; *Us, and Our Empire,* 1911; *Tested!,* Partridge, 1912; *Four Gates,* Cassell, 1912; *Laddie's Choice,* 1912; *Some Builders,* Cassell, 1913; *Her Husband's Property,* 1913; *Herself and Her Boy,* Cassell, 1914; *Daddy's Sword,* Hodder and Stoughton, 1915; *Joan's Handful,* Cassell, 1915; *Dudley Napier's Daughters,* Morgan and Scott, 1916; *A Madcap Family; or, Sybil's Home,* Partridge, 1916; *Us, and Our Charge,* 1916; *Tomina in Retreat,* 1917; *Joy Cometh in the Morning,* 1917).

C. Phillips-Wolley's *Gold, Gold in Cariboo; A Story of Adventure in British Columbia* (an adventure story published in London by Blackie, with a Canadian setting; this Canadian author's other work includes *Snap. A Legend of a Lone Mountain,* Longmans, 1890; *The Queensberry Cup,* Methuen, 1895; *The Chicamon Stone,* Bell, 1900).

Marshall Saunders's *Beautiful Joe* (a popular dog story which won the American Humane Education Society Prize Competition; Marshall Saunders is pseudonym for Margaret Marshall Saunders; published in Philadelphia by the American Baptist Publication Society and in London by Jarrold

1894 *continued*

and Sons; the author's other work includes *Charles and His Lamb,* Barnes, 1895; *For the Other Boy's Sake, and Other Stories,* Barnes, 1896; *The House of Armour,* Rowland, 1897; *The King of the Pack,* Crowell, 1897; *Deficient Saints,* Page, 1899; *For His Country,* Page, 1900; *Her Sailor,* Page, 1900; *Tilda Jane, An Orphan In Search of a Home,* Page, 1901; *Beautiful Joe's Paradise,* Page, 1902; *Nita, the Story of an Irish Setter,* Page, 1904; *The Story of Gravelys,* Page, 1904; *Princess Sukey; The Story of a Pigeon and Her Human Friends,* Eaton, 1905; *The Story of an Eskimo Dog,* Hodder, 1906; *My Pets,* Griffith, 1908; *Tilda Jane's Orphans,* Page, 1909; *The Girl from Vermont,* Griffith, 1910; *Pussy Black-Face,* Page, 1913; *"Boy," the Wandering Dog,* Grosset, 1916; *Golden Dicky,* Stokes, 1919; *Bonnie Prince Fetlar,* Doran, 1920; *Jimmy Gold-Cast,* McKay, 1924).

1895

Edward L. Stratemeyer's *Reuben Stone's Discovery; or, The Young Miller of Torrent Bend* (one of this prolific author's "boys' books" published by Merriam, and part of the Ship and Shore series, which also includes *The Last Cruise of the Spitfire,* Merriam, 1894; the author, along with his "Stratemeyer Syndicate" of writers including his daughter Harriet Stratemeyer Adams, has produced books from 1895 to the present, including *The Rival Bicyclists,* Donahue, 1897; *The Minute Boys of Lexington,* Estes, 1898; *The Minute Boys of Bunker Hill,* Estes, 1899; *Olive Bright's Search,* Lothrop, 1899; *The Last Cruise of the Spitfire; or, Luke Forster's Strange Voyage,* Lee, 1900; *On to Peking; or, Old Glory in China,* Lee, 1900; *True to Himself; or, Roger Strong's Struggle for Place,* Lee, 1900; *Between Boer and Briton; or, Two Boys' Adventures in South Africa,* Lee, 1900; *American Boy's Life of William McKinley,* Lee, 1901; *Tour of the Zero Club,* Street, 1902; *Under Scott in Mexico,* Estes, 1902; *The Young Bridge-Tender,* Street, 1902; *Bound to be an Electrician; or, Franklin Bell's Success,* Lee, 1903; *The Young Auctioneer; or, The Polishing of a Rolling Stone,* Lee, 1903; *Joe the Surveyor; or, The Value of a Lost Claim,* Lee, 1903; *American Boy's Life of Theodore Roosevelt,* Lee, 1903; *Under the Mikado's Flag,* Lee, 1903; *Larry the Wanderer; or, The Rise of a Nobody,* Lee, 1904; *Defending His Flag; or, A Boy in Blue and a Boy in Gray,* Lothrop, 1904; *Under Togo for Japan; or, Three Young Americans on Land and Sea,* Lee, 1906; *First at the North Pole; or, Two Boys in the Arctic Circle,* Lothrop, 1909; the Bound to Win series: *Richard Dare's Venture; or, Striking Out for Himself,* Merriam, 1894; *Fighting for His Own; or, The Fortunes of a Young Artist,* Allison, 1897; *The Missing Tin Box,* Allison, 1897; *Gun and Sled; or, The Young Hunters of the Snow-Top Island,* Allison, 1897; *Leo the Circus Boy; or, Life Under the Great White Canvas,* Lee, 1897; *Schooldays of Fred Harley; or, Rivals for All Honors,*

Allison, 1897; *Shorthand Tom; or, The Exploits of a Bright Boy,* Allison, 1897; *To Alaska for Gold; or, The Fortune Hunters of the Yukon,* Lee, 1899; the Colonial series, published by Lee and Shepard: *With Washington in the West; or, A Soldier Boy's Battles in the Wilderness,* 1901; *Marching on Niagara; or, The Soldier Boys of the Old Frontier,* 1902; *At the Fall of Montreal; or, A Soldier Boy's Final Victory,* 1903; *On the Trail of Pontiac; or, The Pioneer Boys of Ohio,* 1904; *The Fort in the Wilderness; or, The Soldier Boys of the Indian Trails,* 1905; *Trail and Trading Post; or, The Young Hunters of Ohio,* 1906; the Dave Porter series, published by Lothrop, Lee, and Shepard: *Dave Porter at Oak Hall; or, The Schooldays of an American Boy,* 1905; *Dave Porter in the South Seas; or, The Strange Cruise of the Stormy Petrel,* 1906; *Dave Porter's Return to School; or Winning the Medal of Honor,* 1907; *Dave Porter in the Far North; or the Pluck of an American Schoolboy,* 1908; *Dave Porter and His Classmates; or, For the Honor of Oak Hall,* 1909; *Dave Porter at Star Ranch; or, The Cowboy's Secret,* 1910; *Dave Porter and His Rivals; or, The Chums and Foes of Oak Hall,* 1911; *Dave Porter on Cave Island; or, A Schoolboy's Mysterious Mission,* 1912; *Dave Porter and the Runaways; or, Last Days at Oak Hall,* 1913; *Dave Porter in the Gold Fields; or, The Search for the Landslide Mine,* 1914; *Dave Porter at Bear Camp; or, The Wild Man at Mirror Lake,* 1915; *Dave Porter and His Double; or, The Disappearance of the Basswood Fortune,* 1916; *Dave Porter and His Great Search,* 1917; *Dave Porter Under Fire,* 1918; *Dave Porter and His War Honors,* 1919; the Lakeport series, published by Lothrop: *The Boat Club Boys,* 1908; *Boys of Lakeport; or, The Water Champions,* 1908; *The Gun Club Boys of Lakeport; or, The Island Camp,* 1908; *The Football Boys of Lakeport; or, More Goals Than One,* 1909; *The Automobile Boys of Lakeport; or, A Run for Fun and Fame,* 1910; *The Aircraft Boys of Lakeport; or, Rivals of the Clouds,* 1912; the Old Glory series, published by Lee and Shepard: *A Young Volunteer in Cuba; or, Fighting for the Single Star,* 1898; *Under Dewey at Manila; or, The War Fortunes of a Castaway,* 1898; *Under Otis in the Philippines; or, A Young Officer in the Tropics,* 1899; *Fighting in Cuban Waters; or, Under Schley on the Brooklyn,* 1899; *The Campaign of the Jungle; or, Under Lawton through the Luzon,* 1900; *Under MacArthur in Luzon; or, Last Battles in the Philippines,* 1901; the Pan American series published by Lothrop, Lee, and Shepard: *Young Hunters in Porto Rico,* 1900; *Lost on the Orinoco; or, American Boys in Venezuela,* 1902; *The Young Volcano Explorers; or, American Boys in the West Indies,* 1902; *Young Explorers of the Isthmus; or, American Boys in Central America,* 1903; *Young Explorers of the Amazon; or, American Boys in Brazil,* 1904; *Treasure Seekers of the Andes; or, American Boys in Peru,* 1907; *Chased Across the Pampas; or, American Boys in Argentina and Homeward Bound,* 1911; under the pseudonym Victor Appleton II: the Don Sturdy series, published by Grosset:

1895 *continued*

Don Sturdy Across the North Pole, 1925; *Don Sturdy in the Land of the Volcanoes,* 1925; *Don Sturdy in the Tombs of Gold,* 1925; *Don Sturdy on the Desert,* 1925; *Don Sturdy with the Big Snake Hunters,* 1925; *Don Sturdy in the Port of Lost Ships,* 1926; *Don Sturdy Among the Gorillas,* 1927; *Don Sturdy Captured by Head Hunters; or, Adrift in the Wilds of Borneo,* 1928; *Don Sturdy in Lion Land,* 1929; *Don Sturdy in the Land of the Giants; or, Captives of the Savage Patagonians,* 1930; *Don Sturdy on the Ocean Bottom,* 1931; *Don Sturdy in the Temples of Fear,* 1932; *Don Sturdy Lost in Glacier Bay,* 1933; *Don Sturdy Trapped in the Flaming Wilderness,* 1934; *Don Sturdy with the Harpoon Hunters,* 1935; the Movie Boys series, published by Garden City except as noted: *The Moving Picture Boys; or, The Perils of a Great City Depicted,* Grosset, 1913; *The Movie Boys and the Flood,* 1926; *The Movie Boys and the Wreckers,* 1926; *The Movie Boys At the Seaside Park,* 1926; *The Movie Boys At the Big Fair,* 1926; *The Movie Boys' First Showhouse,* 1926; *The Movie Boys in Earthquake Land,* 1926; *The Movie Boys in Peril,* 1926; *The Movie Boys in the Jungle,* 1926; *The Movie Boys in the Wild West,* 1926; *The Movie Boys' New Idea,* 1926; *The Movie Boys on Broadway,* 1926; *The Movie Boys on Call,* 1926; *The Movie Boys' Outdoor Exhibition,* 1926; *The Movie Boys Under Uncle Sam,* 1926; *The Movie Boys' War Spectacle,* 1927; the Tom Swift Series, published by Grosset: *Tom Swift and His Airship,* 1910; *Tom Swift and His Electric Runabout,* 1910; *Tom Swift and His Motor Boat,* 1910; *Tom Swift and His Motor-Cycle,* 1910; *Tom Swift Among the Diamond Mines,* 1911; *Tom Swift and His Electric Rifle,* 1911; *Tom Swift and His Sky Racer,* 1911; *Tom Swift and His Wireless,* 1911; *Tom Swift in the Caves,* 1911; *Tom Swift and His Air Glider,* 1912; *Tom Swift and His Great Searchlight,* 1912; *Tom Swift and His Wizard Camera,* 1912; *Tom Swift in Captivity,* 1912; *Tom Swift in the City of Gold,* 1912; *Tom Swift and His Giant Cannon,* 1913; *Tom Swift and His Photo Telephone,* 1914; *Tom Swift and His Aerial Warship,* 1915; *Tom Swift and His Big Tunnel,* 1916; *Tom Swift and His Submarine,* 1916; *Tom Swift in the Land of Wonders,* 1917; *Tom Swift in His Air Scout,* 1919; *Tom Swift in His War Tank,* 1919; *Tom Swift and His Under Sea Search,* 1920; *Tom Swift Among the Fire Fighters,* 1921; *Tom Swift and His Electric Locomotive,* 1922; *Tom Swift and His Flying Boat,* 1923; *Tom Swift and His Great Oil Gusher,* 1924; *Tom Swift and His Chest of Secrets,* 1925; *Tom Swift and His Airline Express,* 1926; *Tom Swift Circling the Globe,* 1927; *Tom Swift and His Talking Pictures,* 1928; *Tom Swift and His House on Wheels,* 1929; *Tom Swift and His Big Dirigible,* 1930; *Tom Swift and His Sky Train,* 1931; *Tom Swift and His Giant Magnet,* 1932; *Tom Swift and His Television Detector,* 1933; *Tom Swift and His Ocean Airport,* 1934; *Tom Swift and His Planet Stone,* 1935;

Tom Swift and His Magnet Silencer, 1941; the Tom Swift Jr. series: *Tom Swift and His Atomic Earth Blaster,* 1954; *Tom Swift and His Flying Lab,* 1954; *Tom Swift and His Giant Robot,* 1954; *Tom Swift and His Jet Marine,* 1954; *Tom Swift and His Rocket Ship,* 1954; *Tom Swift and His Outpost in Space,* 1955; the Young Pioneer series under the pseudonym of Harrison Adams, published by L. C. Page: *The Pioneer Boys on the Great Lakes; or, On the Trail of the Iroquois,* 1912; *The Pioneer Boys of the Ohio; or, Clearing the Wilderness,* 1913; *The Pioneer Boys of the Mississippi; or, The Homestead in the Wilderness,* 1913; *The Pioneer Boys of the Missouri; or, In the Country of the Sioux,* 1914; *The Pioneer Boys of the Yellowstone; or, Lost in the Land of Wonders,* 1915; *The Pioneers of the Columbia; or, In the Wilderness of the Great Northwest,* 1916; *The Pioneer Boys of the Colorado; or, Braving the Perils of the Grand Canyon Country,* 1926; *The Pioneer Boys of Kansas; or, A Prairie Home in Buffalo-Land,* 1928; the Boy Hunters series under the pseudonym of Captain Ralph Bonehill: *The Island Camp; or, The Young Hunters of Lakeport,* Barnes, 1904; *Four Boy Hunters; or, The Outing of the Gun Club,* Cupples, 1906; *Guns and Snowshoes; or, The Winter Outing of the Young Hunters,* Cupples, 1907; *Young Hunters of the Lake; or, Out with Rod and Gun,* Cupples, 1908; *Out with Gun and Camera; or, The Boy Hunters in the Mountains,* Cupples, 1910; the Flag of Freedom series under the pseudonym of Captain Ralph Bonehill: *A Sailor With Dewey; or, Afloat in the Philippines,* Mershon, 1899; *When Santiago Fell; or, The War Adventures of Two Chums,* Mershon, 1899; *The Young Bandmaster; or, Concert Stage and Battlefield,* Mershon, 1900; *Boys of the Fort; or, A Young Captain's Pluck,* Mershon, 1901; *With Custer in the Black Hills; or, A Young Scout Among the Indians,* Grosset, 1902; *Off for Hawaii; or, The Mystery of a Great Volcano,* Mershon, 1905; under the pseudonym of Captain Ralph Bonehill: *Young Hunters in Puerto Rico; or, The Search for a Lost Treasure,* Donohue, 1900; *For the Liberty of Texas,* Estes, 1900; *Boys of the Fort,* Mershon, 1901; *With Taylor on the Rio Grande,* Estes, 1901; *Three Young Ranchmen, or, Daring Adventures in the Great West,* Saalfield, 1901; *The Boy Land Boomer; or, Dick Arbuckle's Adventures in Oklahoma,* Saalfield, 1902; *Lost in the Land of Ice; or, Daring Adventures Around the South Pole,* Wessels, 1902; *Neka, the Boy Conjurer; or, A Mystery of the Stage,* McKay, 1902; *With Boone on the Frontier; or, The Pioneer Boys of Old Kentucky,* Mershon, 1903; *Pioneer Boys of the Great Northwest; or, With Lewis and Clark Across the Rockies,* Mershon, 1904; *Pioneer Boys of the Gold Fields; or, The Nugget Hunters of '49,* Chatterton-Peck, 1906; under the pseudonym Annie Roe Carr and published by Sully, the Nan Sherwood series: *Nan Sherwood at Lakeview Hall; or, The Mystery of the Haunted Boathouse,* 1916; *Nan Sherwood at Pine Camp, or, The Old Lumberman's Secret,* 1916; *Nan Sherwood's Winter Holidays; or, Rescuing the Runaways,*

1895 *continued*

1916; *Nan Sherwood at Rose Ranch; or, The Old Mexican's Treasure,* 1919; *Nan Sherwood at Palm Beach; or, Strange Adventures among the Orange Groves,* 1921; *Nan Sherwood's Summer Holidays,* n.d.; under the pseudonym of Allen Chapman: *Bound to Rise; or, The Young Florists of Spring Hill* and *Walter Loring's Career,* Mershon, 1900; under the pseudonym of Louis Charles: *Fortune Hunters of the Philippines; or, The Treasure of the Burning Mountain,* Mershon, 1900; *The Land of Fire,* Mershon, 1900; under the pseudonym of James A. Cooper: *Cap'n Abe, Storekeeper,* Sully, 1917; *Cap'n Jonah's Fortune,* Sully, 1919; *Tobias o' the Light,* Sully, 1920; *Sheila of Big Wreck Cove,* Sully, 1922; under the pseudonym Franklin W. Dixon, the Hardy Boys series, published by Grosset: *The Mark on the Door,* 1934; *The Sinister Signpost,* 1936; *The Twisted Claw,* 1939; *The Mystery of the Flying Express,* 1941; *The Flickering Torch Mystery,* 1943; *The Secret Panel,* 1946; *The Secret of Skull Mountain,* 1948; *The Wailing Siren Mystery,* 1951; *The Tower Treasure,* 1959; *The House on the Cliff,* 1959; *The Mystery of the Aztec Warrior,* 1964; under the pseudonym Robert W. Hamilton: *Belinda of the Red Cross,* Sully, 1917; under the pseudonym of Chester K. Steele: *The Mansion of Mystery,* Cupples, 1911; *The Diamond Cross Mystery,* Sully, 1918; *The Golf Course Mystery,* Sully, 1919; *House of Disappearances,* Clode, 1927; *The Crime at Red Towers,* Clode, 1927; under the pseudonym of E. Ward Strayer: *Making Good With Margaret,* Sully, 1918; under the pseudonym of Arthur M. Winfield: *The Missing Tin Box; or, The Stolen Railroad Bonds,* Allison, 1897; *By Pluck, Not Luck; or, Dan Granbury's Struggle to Rise,* Allison, 1897; *A Young Inventor's Pluck; or, The Mystery of the Willington Legacy,* Saalfield, 1901; *Bob, the Photographer; or, A Hero in Spite of Himself,* Wessels, 1902; *Larry Barlow's Ambition; or, The Adventures of a Young Fireman,* Saalfield, 1902; *Mark Dale's Stage Venture; or, Bound To Be An Actor,* Street, 1902; *The Young Bank Clerk; or, Mark Vincent's Strange Discovery,* Street, 1902; *The Young Bridge-Tender; or, Ralph Nelson's Upward Struggle,* Street, 1902; under the pseudonym Julia K. Duncan and published by Altmus except as noted, the Doris Force Mystery series: *Doris Force at Cloudy Cover,* 1931; *Doris Force at Locked Gates; or Saving a Mysterious Fortune,* 1931; *Doris Force at Barry Manor; or, Mysterious Adventures between Classes,* 1932; *Doris Force at Raven Rock,* 1932; under the pseudonym Alice B. Emerson and published by Cupples, the Betty Gordon series: *Betty Gordon at Pramble Farm,* 1920; *Betty Gordon at Mystery Farm,* 1930; *Betty Gordon on No-Trail Island,* 1920; *Betty Gordon at Boarding School,* 1921; *Betty Gordon at Mountain Camp,* 1922, *Betty Gordon at Ocean Park,* 1923; *Betty Gordon and Her School Chums,* 1924; *Betty Gordon at Rainbow Ranch,* 1925; *Betty Gordon in Mexican Wilds,* 1926; *Betty Gordon and the Lost Pearls,* 1927; *Betty*

Gordon on the Campus, 1928; *Betty Gordon and the Hale Twins,* 1929; *Betty Gordon at Mystery Farm,* 1920; *Betty Gordon on No-Trail Island,* 1931; *Betty Gordon and the Mystery Girl,* 1932; the Ruth Fielding series: *Ruth Fielding at Lighthouse Point; or Nita, the Girl Castaway,* 1913; *Ruth Fielding at Silver Ranch; or Schoolgirls among the Cowboys,* 1913; *Ruth Fielding at Snow Camp; or Lost in the Backwoods,* 1913; *Ruth Fielding of Briarwood Hall; or Solving the Campus Mystery,* 1913; *Ruth Fielding of the Red Mill; or Jasper Parloe's Secret,* 1913; *Ruth Fielding and the Gypsies; or The Missing Pearl Necklace,* 1915; *Ruth Fielding at Sunrise Farm; or What Became of the Baby Orphans,* 1915; *Ruth Fielding on Cliff Island; or The Old Hunter's Treasure Box,* 1915; *Ruth Fielding Down in Dixie; or Great Days in the Land of Cotton,* 1916; *Ruth Fielding in Moving Pictures; or Helping the Dormitory Fund,* 1916; *Ruth Fielding at College; or The Missing Examination Papers,* 1917; *Ruth Fielding in the Saddle; or College Girls in the Land of Gold,* 1917; *Ruth Fielding at the War Front; or The Hunt for a Lost Soldier,* 1918; *Ruth Fielding Homeward Bound; or a Red Cross Worker's Ocean Perils,* 1919; *Ruth Fielding Down East; or The Hermit of Beach Plum Point,* 1920; *Ruth Fielding in the Great Northwest; or The Indian Girl Star of the Movies,* 1921; *Ruth Fielding on the St. Lawrence; or The Queer Old Man of the Thousand Islands,* 1922; *Ruth Fielding Treasure Hunting; or A Moving Picture That Became Real,* 1923; *Ruth Fielding in the Far North; or The Lost Motion Picture Company,* 1924; *Ruth Fielding at Golden Pass; or The Perils of an Artificial Avalanche,* 1925; *Ruth Fielding in Alaska; or The Miners of Snow Mountain,* 1926; *Ruth Fielding and Her Great Scenario; or Striving for the Moving Picture Prize,* 1927; *Ruth Fielding at Cameron Hall; or A Mysterious Disappearance,* 1928; *Ruth Fielding Clearing Her Name; or The Rivals of Hollywood,* 1929; *Ruth Fielding in Talking Pictures; or The Prisoners of the Tower,* 1930; *Ruth Fielding and Baby June,* 1931; *Ruth Fielding and Her Double,* 1932; *Ruth Fielding and Her Greatest Triumph; or Saving Her Company from Disaster,* 1933; *Ruth Fielding and Her Crowning Victory; or Winning Honors Abroad,* 1934; under the pseudonym Alice Dale Hardy and published by Grosset, the Flyaway stories: *The Flyaways and Cinderella,* 1925; *The Flyaways and Goldilocks,* 1925; *The Flyaways and Little Red Riding Hood,* 1925; the Riddle Club books: *The Riddle Club at Home; How the Club Was Formed, What Riddles Were Asked and How the Members Solved a Mystery,* 1924; *The Riddle Club in Camp; How They Journeyed to the Lake, What Happened Around the Campfire and How a Forgotten Name was Recalled,* 1924; *The Riddle Club through the Holidays,* 1924; *The Riddle Club at Sunrise Beach,* 1924; *The Riddle Club at Shadybrook; Why They Went There, What Happened on the Way and What Occurred During Their Absence from Home,* 1926; *The Riddle Club at Rocky Falls,* 1929; under the pseudonym Mabel C. Hawley and published

1895 *continued*

by Sully except as noted, the Four Little Blossoms series: *Four Little Blossoms and Their Winter Fun,* 1920; *Four Little Blossoms at Brookside Farm,* 1920; *Four Little Blossoms at Oak Hill School,* 1920; *Four Little Blossoms on Apple Tree Island,* 1921; *Four Little Blossoms through the Holidays,* 1922; *Four Little Blossoms at Sunrise Beach,* Cupples, 1929; *Four Little Blossoms Indoors and Out,* Cupples, 1930; under the pseudonym Grace Brooks Hill and published by Barse and Hopkins except as noted, the Corner House Girls series: *The Corner House Girls; How They moved to Milton, What They Found and What They Did,* 1915; *The Corner House Girls at School; How They Entered, Whom They Met, and What They Did,* 1915; *The Corner House Girls Under Canvas; How They Reached Pleasant Cove and What Happened Afterward,* 1915; *The Corner House Girls in a Play; How They Rehearsed, How They Acted and What the Play Brought On,* 1916; *The Corner House Girls' Odd Find; Where They Made It, and What the Strange Discovery Led To,* 1916; *The Corner House Girls on a Tour; Where They Went, What They Saw, and What They Found,* 1917; *The Corner House Girls Growing Up,* 1918; *The Corner House Girls Snowbound,* 1919; *The Corner House Girls on a Houseboat,* 1920; *The Corner House Girls among the Gypsies; How They Met, What Happened, and How It Ended,* 1921; *The Corner House Girls on Palm Island,* 1922; *The Corner House Girls Solve a Mystery; What It Was, Where It Was, and Who Found It,* 1923; *The Corner House Girls Facing the World,* 1926; under the pseudonym Laura Lee Hope, and published by Grosset except as noted: the Blythe Girls series: *The Blythe Girls: Helen, Margy and Rose, or Facing the Great World,* 1925; *The Blythe Girls: Margy's Queer Inheritance, or The Worth of a Name,* 1925; *The Blythe Girls: Rose's Great Problem or Face to Face with a Crisis,* 1925; *The Blythe Girls: Three on Vacation, or The Mystery at Peach Farm,* 1925; *The Blythe Girls: Helen's Strange Boarder, or The Girl from Bronx Park,* 1925; *The Blythe Girls: Margy's Secret Mission, or Exciting Days at Shadymere,* 1926; *The Blythe Girls: Rose's Odd Discovery, or The Search for Irene Conroy,* 1927; *The Blythe Girls: The Disappearance of Helen, or The Art Shop Mystery,* 1928; *The Blythe Girls: Snowbound in Camp, or The Mystery at Elk Lodge,* 1929; *The Blythe Girls: Margy's Mysterious Visitor, or Guarding the Pepper Fortune,* 1930; *The Blythe Girls: Rose's Hidden Talent,* 1931; *The Blythe Girls: Helen's Wonderful Mistake, or The Mysterious Necklace,* 1932; The Bobbsey Twins series: *The Bobbsey Twins; or Merry Days Indoors and Out,* Mershon, 1904; *The Bobbsey Twins at the Seashore,* Cupples, 1907; *The Bobbsey Twins in the Country,* Cupples, 1907; *The Bobbsey Twins at Snow Lodge,* 1913; *The Bobbsey Twins at School,* 1913; *The Bobbsey Twins at Meadow Brook,* 1915; *The Bobbsey Twins on a Houseboat,* 1915; *The Bobbsey Twins at Home,* 1916; *The Bobbsey Twins in a Great City,* 1917; *The Bobbsey Twins on Blueberry Island,* 1917; *The Bobbsey Twins on the Deep Blue Sea,* 1918; *The Bobbsey Twins in Washington,* 1919; *The Bobbsey Twins in the Great West,* 1920; *The Bobbsey Twins at Cedar Camp,* 1921; *The Bobbsey Twins at the Country Fair,* 1922; *The Bobbsey Twins Camping Out,* 1923; *The Bobbsey Twins and Baby May,* 1924; *The Bobbsey Twins Keeping House,* 1925; *The Bobbsey Twins at Cloverbank,* 1926; *The Bobbsey Twins at Cherry Corners,* 1927; *The Bobbsey Twins and Their Schoolmates,* 1928; *The Bobbsey Twins Treasure Hunting,* 1929; *The Bobbsey Twins at Spruce Lake,* 1930; *The Bobbsey Twins' Wonderful Secret,* 1931; *The Bobbsey Twins at the Circus,* 1932; *The Bobbsey Twins on an Airplane Trip,* 1933; *The Bobbsey Twins Solve a Mystery,* 1934; *The Bobbsey Twins on a Ranch,* 1935; *The Bobbsey Twins in Eskimo Land,* 1936; *The Bobbsey Twins in a Radio Play,* 1937; *The Bobbsey Twins at Windmill Cottage,* 1938; *The Bobbsey Twins at Lighthouse Point,* 1939; *The Bobbsey Twins at Indian Hollow,* 1940; *The Bobbsey Twins at the Ice Carnival,* 1941; *The Bobbsey Twins in the Land of Cotton,* 1942; *The Bobbsey Twins in Echo Valley,* 1943; *The Bobbsey Twins on the Pony Trail,* 1944; *The Bobbsey Twins at Mystery Mansion,* 1945; *The Bobbsey Twins at Sugar Maple Hill,* 1946; *The Bobbsey Twins in Mexico,* 1947; *The Bobbsey Twins' Toy Shop,* 1948; *The Bobbsey Twins in Tulip Land,* 1949; *The Bobbsey Twins in Rainbow Valley,* 1950; *The Bobbsey Twins at Whitesail Harbor,* 1952; *The Bobbsey Twins and the Horseshoe Riddle,* 1953; *The Bobbsey Twins at Big Bear Pond,* 1953; *Meet the Bobbsey Twins,* 1954; *The Bobbsey Twins on a Bicycle Trip,* 1956; *The Bobbsey Twins' Own Little Ferryboat,* 1957; *The Bobbsey Twins at Pilgrim Rock,* 1958; *The Bobbsey Twins' Forest Adventure,* 1959; *The Bobbsey Twins at London Tower,* 1960; *The Bobbsey Twins' Search in the Great City,* 1960; *The Bobbsey Twins and the Mystery at Snow Lodge,* 1960; *The Bobbsey Twins' Big Adventure at Home,* 1960; *The Bobbsey Twins in the Mystery Cave,* 1960; *The Bobbsey Twins and The Circus Surprise,* 1960; *The Bobbsey Twins and the County Fair Mystery,* 1960; *The Bobbsey Twins of Lakeport,* 1961; *The Bobbsey Twins in Volcano Island,* 1961; *The Bobbsey Twins and the Goldfish Mystery,* 1962; *The Bobbsey Twins' Mystery at Meadowbrook,* 1963; *The Bobbsey Twins and the Big River Mystery,* 1963; *The Bobbsey Twins and the Greek Hat Mystery,* 1964; *The Bobbsey Twins' Search for The Green Rooster,* 1965; *The Bobbsey Twins' Mystery on the Deep Blue Sea,* 1965; *The Bobbsey Twins and Their Camel Adventure,* 1966; *The Bobbsey Twins' Visit to the Great West,* 1966; *The Bobbsey Twins' Mystery of the King's Puppet,* 1967; *The Bobbsey Twins and the Cedar Camp Mystery,* 1967; *The Bobbsey Twins' Adventures with Baby May,* 1968; *The Bobbsey Twins and the Four-leaf Clover Mystery,* 1968; *The Bobbsey Twins and the Secret of Candy Castle,* 1968; *The Bobbsey Twins and the Doodlebug Mystery,* 1969; *The Bobbsey Twins and the Talking Fox Mystery,* 1970; *The Bobbsey Twins: The Red, White*

1895 *continued*

and Blue Mystery, 1971; *The Bobbsey Twins and the Smoky Mountain Mystery*, 1977; the Bunny Brown stories: *Bunny Brown and His Sister Sue*, 1916; *Bunny Brown and His Sister Sue at Aunt Lu's City Home*, 1916; *Bunny Brown and His Sister Sue at Camp Rest-a-While*, 1916; *Bunny Brown and His Sister Sue on Grandpa's Farm*, 1916; *Bunny Brown and His Sister Sue Playing Circus*, 1916; *Bunny Brown and His Sister Sue in the Big Woods*, 1917; *Bunny Brown and His Sister Sue on an Auto Tour*, 1917; *Bunny Brown and His Sister Sue and Their Shetland Pony*, 1918; *Bunny Brown and His Sister Sue Giving a Show*, 1919; *Bunny Brown and His Sister Sue at Christmas Tree Cove*, 1920; *Bunny Brown and His Sister Sue in the Sunny South*, 1921; *Bunny Brown and His Sister Sue Keeping Store*, 1922; *Bunny Brown and His Sister Sue and Their Trick Dog*, 1923; *Bunny Brown and His Sister Sue at a Sugar Camp*, 1924; *Bunny Brown and His Sister Sue on the Rolling Ocean*, 1925; *Bunny Brown and His Sister Sue on Jack Frost Island*, 1927; *Bunny Brown and His Sister Sue at Shore Acres*, 1928; *Bunny Brown and His Sister Sue at Berry Hill*, 1929; *Bunny Brown and His Sister Sue at Sky Top*, 1930; *Bunny Brown and His Sister Sue at the Summer Carnival*, 1931; the Make Believe stories: *The Story of a Calico Clown*, 1920; *The Story of a Candy Rabbit*, 1920; *The Story of a Lamb on Wheels*, 1920; *The Story of a Monkey on a Stick*, 1920; *The Story of a Sawdust Doll*, 1920; *The Story of a White Rocking Horse*, 1920; *The Story of a Bold Tin Soldier*, 1920; *The Story of a China Cat*, 1921; *The Story of a Nodding Donkey*, 1921; *The Story of a Plush Bear*, 1921; *The Story of a Stuffed Elephant*, 1922; *The Story of a Woolly Dog*, 1923; the Moving Picture Girls: *The Moving Picture Girls or, First Appearances in Photo Dramas*, 1914; *The Moving Picture Girls at Oak Farm or, Queer Happenings While Taking Rural Plays*, 1914; *The Moving Picture Girls at Rocky Ranch or, Great Days among the Cowboys*, 1914; *The Moving Picture Girls at Sea or, A Shipwreck that Became Real*, 1914; *The Moving Picture Girls in War Plays or, The Sham Battles at Oak Farm*, 1914; *The Moving Picture Girls Snowbound or, The Proof on the Film*, 1914; *The Moving Picture Girls under the Palms or, Lost in the Wilds of Florida*, 1914; the Outdoor Girls: *The Outdoor Girls at Rainbow Lake*, 1913; *The Outdoor Girls in a Motor Car*, 1913; *The Outdoor Girls in a Winter Camp*, 1913; *The Outdoor Girls in Florida*, 1913; *The Outdoor Girls of Deepdale*, 1913; *The Outdoor Girls at Ocean View*, 1915; *The Outdoor Girls on Pine Island*, 1916; *The Outdoor Girls in Army Service*, 1918; *The Outdoor Girls at the Hostess House*, 1919; *The Outdoor Girls at Bluff Point*, 1920; *The Outdoor Girls at Wild Rose Lodge*, 1921; *The Outdoor Girls in the Saddle*, 1922; *The Outdoor Girls around the Campfire*, 1923; *The Outdoor Girls on Cape Cod*, 1924; *The Outdoor Girls at Foaming Falls*, 1925; *The Outdoor Girls along the Coast*, 1926; *The Outdoor Girls at Spring Hill Farm*, 1927; *The Outdoor*

Girls at New Moon Ranch, 1928; *The Outdoor Girls on a Hike,* 1929; *The Outdoor Girls on a Canoe Trip,* 1930; *The Outdoor Girls at Cedar Ridge,* 1931; *The Outdoor Girls in the Air,* 1932; *The Outdoor Girls in Desert Valley,* 1933; the Six Little Bunkers: *Six Little Bunkers at Aunt Jo's,* 1918; *Six Little Bunkers at Cousin Tom's,* 1918; *Six Little Bunkers at Grandma Bell's,* 1918; *Six Little Bunkers at Grandpa Ford's,* 1918; *Six Little Bunkers at Uncle Fred's,* 1918; *Six Little Bunkers at Captain Ben's,* 1920; *Six Little Bunkers at Cowboy Jack's,* 1921; *Six Little Bunkers at Mammy June's,* 1922; *Six Little Bunkers at Farmer Joel's,* 1923; *Six Little Bunkers at Miller Ned's,* 1924; *Six Little Bunkers at Indian John's,* 1925; *Six Little Bunkers at Happy Jim's,* 1928; *Six Little Bunkers at Skipper Bob's,* 1929; *Six Little Bunkers at Lighthouse Nell's,* 1930; under the pseudonym Frances K. Judd and published by Cupples, the Kay Tracey Mystery stories: *The Secret of the Red Scarf,* 1934; *The Strange Echo,* 1934; *The Shadow on the Door,* 1935; *The Mystery of the Swaying Curtains,* 1935; *The Green Cameo Mystery,* 1936; *The Six Fingered Glove Mystery,* 1936; *The Secret at the Windmill,* 1937; *Beneath the Crimson Brier Bush,* 1937; *The Message in the Sand Dunes,* 1938; *The Murmuring Portrait,* 1938; *In the Sunken Garden,* 1939; *When the Key Turned,* 1939; *The Forbidden Tower,* 1940; *The Sacred Feather,* 1940; *The Double Disguise,* 1941; *The Lone Footprint,* 1941; *The Mansion of Secrets,* 1942; *The Mysterious Neighbors,* 1942; under the pseudonym Carolyn Keene and published by Grosset, except as noted, the Dana Girls Mystery Stories: *By the Light of the Study Lamp,* 1934; *The Secret at Lone Tree Cottage,* 1934; *In the Shadow of the Tower,* 1934; *A Three-Cornered Mystery,* 1935; *The Secret at the Hermitage,* 1936; *The Circle of Footprints,* 1937; *The Mystery of the Locked Room,* 1938; *The Clue in the Cobweb,* 1939; *The Secret at the Gatehouse,* 1940; *The Mysterious Fireplace,* 1941; *The Clue of the Rusty Key,* 1942; *The Portrait in the Sand,* 1943; *The Secret in the Old Well,* 1944; *The Clue in the Ivy,* 1952; *The Secret of the Jade Ring,* 1953; *The Mystery at the Crossroads,* 1954; *The Ghost in the Gallery,* 1955; *The Clue of the Black Flower,* 1956; *The Winking Ruby Mystery,* 1957; *The Secret of the Swiss Chalet,* 1958; *The Haunted Lagoon,* 1959; *The Mystery of the Bamboo Bird,* 1960; *The Sierra Gold Mystery,* 1961; *The Secret of Lost Lake,* 1963; *The Mystery of the Stone Tiger,* 1963; *The Riddle of the Frozen Fountain,* 1964; *The Secret of the Silver Dolphin,* 1965; *The Mystery of the Wax Queen,* 1966; *The Secret of the Minstrel's Guitar,* 1967; *The Phantom Surfer,* 1968; *The Curious Coronation,* 1976; the Nancy Drew series: *The Secret of the Old Clock,* 1930; *The Hidden Staircase,* 1930; *The Bungalow Mystery,* 1930; *The Mystery at Lilac Inn,* 1930; *The Secret of Shadow Ranch,* 1931; *The Secret of Red Gate Farm,* 1931; *The Clue in the Diary,* 1932; *Nancy's Mysterious Letter,* 1932; *The Sign of the Twisted Candles,* 1933; *The Password to Larkspur Lane,* 1933; *The Clue of the Broken Locket,* 1934;

1895 *continued*

The Message in the Hollow Oak, 1935; *The Mystery of the Ivory Charm,* 1936; *The Whispering Statue,* 1937; *The Haunted Bridge,* 1937; *The Clue of the Tapping Heels,* 1939; *The Mystery of the Brass Bound Trunk,* 1940; *The Mystery at the Moss-Covered Mansion,* 1941; *The Quest of the Missing Map,* 1942; *The Clue in the Jewel Box,* 1943; *The Secret in the Old Attic,* 1944; *The Clue in the Crumbling Wall,* 1945; *The Mystery of the Tolling Bell,* 1946; *The Clue in the Old Album,* 1947; *The Ghost of Blackwood Hall,* 1948; *The Clue of the Leaning Chimney,* 1949; *The Secret of the Wooden Lady,* 1950; *The Clue of the Black Keys,* 1951; *The Mystery at the Ski Jump,* 1952; *The Clue of the Velvet Mask,* 1953; *The Ringmaster's Secret,* 1953; *The Scarlet Slipper Mystery,* 1954; *The Witch Tree Symbol,* 1955; *The Hidden Window Mystery,* 1957; *The Haunted Showboat,* 1958; *The Secret of the Golden Pavilion,* 1959; *The Clue in the Old Stagecoach,* 1960; *The Mystery of the Fire Dragon,* 1961; *The Clue of the Dancing Puppet,* 1962; *The Moonstone Castle Mystery,* 1963; *The Clue of the Whistling Bagpipes,* 1964; *The Secret of Shadow Ranch,* 1965; *The Phantom of Pine Hill,* 1965; *The Mystery of the 99 Steps,* 1966; *The Clue in the Crossword Cipher,* 1967; *The Spider Sapphire Mystery,* 1968; *The Invisible Intruder,* 1969; *The Mysterious Mannequin,* 1970; *The Crooked Bannister,* 1971; *The Secret of Mirror Bay,* 1972; *The Double Jinx Mystery,* 1973; *The Mystery of the Glowing Eye,* 1974; *The Secret of the Forgotten City,* 1975; under the pseudonym Helen Beecher Long and published by Sully, the Janice Day series: *Janice Day,* 1914; *The Testing of Janice Day,* 1915; *How Janice Day Won,* 1916; *The Mission of Janice Day,* 1917; *Janice Day, the Young Homemaker,* 1919; under the pseudonym Margaret Penrose and published by Cupples, except as noted, the Campfire Girls series: *The Campfire Girls of Roselawn or, A Strange Message from the Air,* Goldsmith, n.d.; *The Campfire Girls on the Program or, Singing and Reciting at the Sending Station,* Goldsmith, n.d.; *The Campfire Girls on Station Island or, The Wireless from the Steam Yacht,* Goldsmith, n.d.; *The Campfire Girls at Forest Lodge,* Goldsmith, n.d.; the Dorothy Dale series: *Dorothy Dale: A Girl of Today,* 1908; *Dorothy Dale at Glenwood School,* 1908; *Dorothy Dale and Her Chums,* 1909; *Dorothy Dale's Great Secret,* 1909; *Dorothy Dale's Queer Holidays,* 1910; *Dorothy Dale's Camping Days,* 1911; *Dorothy Dale's School Rivals,* 1912; *Dorothy Dale in the City,* 1913; *Dorothy Dale's Promise,* 1914; *Dorothy Dale in the West,* 1915; *Dorothy Dale's Strange Discovery,* 1916; *Dorothy Dale's Engagement,* 1917; *Dorothy Dale to the Rescue,* 1924; the Motor Girls series: *The Motor Girls or, A Mystery of the Road,* 1910; *The Motor Girls on a Tour or, Keeping a Strange Promise,* 1910; *The Motor Girls at Lookout Beach or, In Quest of the Runaways,* 1911; *The Motor Girls through New England or, Held by the Gypsies,* 1911; *The Motor Girls on Cedar Lake or, The Hermit of Fern*

Island, 1911; *The Motor Girls on the Coast or, The Waif from the Sea,* 1912; *The Motor Girls on Crystal Bay or, The Secret of the Red Oar,* 1913; *The Motor Girls on Waters Blue or, The Strange Cruise of the Tartar,* 1915; *The Motor Girls at Camp Surprise or, The Cave in the Mountains,* 1916; *The Motor Girls in the Mountains or, The Gypsy Girl's Secret,* 1917; the Radio Girls: *The Radio Girls of Roselawn; or, A Strange Message from the Air,* 1922; *The Radio Girls on Station Island; or, The Wireless from the Steam Yacht,* 1922; *The Radio Girls on the Program; or, Singing and Reciting at the Sending Station,* 1922; *The Radio Girls at Forest Lodge; or, The Strange Hut in the Swamp,* 1924; under the pseudonym Helen Louise Thorndyke and published by Grosset, the Honey Bunch books: *Honey Bunch, Just a Little Girl,* 1923; *Honey Bunch, Her First Visit to the City,* 1923; *Honey Bunch, Her First Visit to the Seashore,* 1924; *Honey Bunch, Her First Little Garden,* 1924; *Honey Bunch, Her First Day in Camp,* 1925; *Honey Bunch, Her First Auto Tour,* 1926; *Honey Bunch, Her First Trip on the Ocean,* 1927; *Honey Bunch, Her First Trip West,* 1928; *Honey Bunch, Her First Trip on an Island,* 1929; *Honey Bunch, Her First Days on the Farm,* 1929; *Honey Bunch, Her First Trip on the Great Lakes,* 1930; *Honey Bunch, Her First Trip in an Airplane,* 1931; *Honey Bunch, Her First Trip to the Zoo,* 1932; *Honey Bunch, Her First Big Adventure,* 1933; *Honey Bunch, Her First Big Parade,* 1934; *Honey Bunch, Her First Little Mystery,* 1935; *Honey Bunch, Her First Little Circus,* 1936; *Honey Bunch, Her First Little Treasure Hunt,* 1937; *Honey Bunch, Her First Little Club,* 1938; *Honey Bunch, Her First Trip in a Trailer,* 1939; *Honey Bunch, Her First Trip to a Big Fair,* 1940; *Honey Bunch, Her First Twin Playmates,* 1941; *Honey Bunch, Her First Costume Party,* 1943; *Honey Bunch, Her First Trip on a Houseboat,* 1945; *Honey Bunch, Her First Winter at Snowtop,* 1946; *Honey Bunch, Her First Trip to the Big Woods,* 1947; *Honey Bunch, Her First Little Pet Show,* 1948; *Honey Bunch, Her First Trip to a Lighthouse,* 1949; *Honey Bunch, Her First Visit to a Pony Ranch,* 1950; *Honey Bunch, Her First Tour of Toy Town,* 1951; *Honey Bunch, Her First Visit to Puppyland,* 1952; *Honey Bunch, Her First Trip to Reindeer Farm,* 1953; and Honey Bunch and Norman: *Honey Bunch and Norman Ride with the Sky Mailman,* 1954; *Honey Bunch and Norman Visit Beaver Island* (first published in 1949 as *Honey Bunch, Her First Trip to a Lighthouse*); *Honey Bunch and Norman Play Detective at Niagara Falls,* 1957; *Honey Bunch and Norman Tour Toy Town,* 1957; *Honey Bunch and Norman Visit Reindeer Farm* (first published in 1953 as *Honey Bunch, Her First Trip to Reindeer Farm*), 1958; *Honey Bunch and Norman in the Castle of Magic,* 1959; *Honey Bunch and Norman Solve the Pine Cone Mystery,* 1960; *Honey Bunch and Norman and the Paper Lantern Mystery,* 1961; *Honey Bunch and Norman and the Painted Pony,* 1962; *Honey Bunch and Norman and the Walnut Tree Mystery,*

1895 *continued*

1963; under the pseudonym Jerry West and published by Doubleday, the Happy Hollisters series: *The Happy Hollisters,* 1953; *The Happy Hollisters and the Indian Treasure,* 1953; *The Happy Hollisters at Sea Gull Beach,* 1953; *The Happy Hollisters on a River Trip,* 1953; *The Happy Hollisters and the Trading Post Mystery,* 1954; *The Happy Hollisters at Mystery Mountain,* 1954; *The Happy Hollisters at Snowflake Camp,* 1954; *The Happy Hollisters and the Merry-Go-Round Mystery,* 1955; *The Happy Hollisters and the Secret Fort,* 1955; *The Happy Hollisters at Circus Island,* 1955; *The Happy Hollisters and the Old Clipper Ship,* 1956; *The Happy Hollisters at Pony Hill Farm,* 1956; *The Happy Hollisters and the Scarecrow Mystery,* 1957; *The Happy Hollisters at Lizard Cove,* 1957; *The Happy Hollisters and the Ice Carnival Mystery,* 1958; *The Happy Hollisters and the Mystery of the Totem Faces,* 1958; *The Happy Hollisters and the Mystery in Skyscraper City,* 1959; *The Happy Hollisters and the Mystery of the Little Mermaid,* 1960; *The Happy Hollisters and the Cowboy Mystery,* 1961; *The Happy Hollisters and the Mystery at Missile Town,* 1961; *The Happy Hollisters and the Haunted House Mystery,* 1962; *The Happy Hollisters and the Secret of the Lucky Coins,* 1962; *The Happy Hollisters and the Castle Rock Mystery,* 1963; *The Happy Hollisters and the Swiss Echo Mystery,* 1963; *The Happy Hollisters and the Punch and Judy Mystery,* 1964; *The Happy Hollisters and the Sea Turtle Mystery,* 1964; *The Happy Hollisters and the Whistle-Pig Mystery,* 1964; *The Happy Hollisters and the Ghost Horse Mystery,* 1965; *The Happy Hollisters and the Mystery of the Golden Witch,* 1966; *The Happy Hollisters and the Mystery of the Mexican Idol,* 1967; *The Happy Hollisters and the Monster Mystery,* 1969; under the pseudonym Janet D. Wheeler and published by Sully, except as noted, the Billie Bradley Series: *Billie Bradley and Her Inheritance, or, The Queer Homestead at Cherry Corners,* 1920; *Billie Bradley at Three Towers Hall; or Leading a Needed Rebellion,* 1920; *Billie Bradley on Lighthouse Island; or, The Mystery of the Wreck,* 1920; *Billie Bradley and Her Classmates; or, The Secret of the Locked Tower,* 1921; *Billie Bradley at Twin Lakes; or, Jolly Schoolgirls Afloat and Ashore,* 1922; *Billie Bradley at Treasure Cove; or, The Old Sailor's Secret,* Cupples, 1928; *Billie Bradley at Sun Dial Lodge; or, School Chums Solving a Mystery,* Cupples, 1929; *Billie Bradley and The School Mystery; or, The Girl from Oklahoma,* Cupples, 1930; *Billie Bradley Winning the Trophy; or, Scoring against Big Odds,* Cupples, 1932; the Putnam Hall series under pseudonym of Arthur M. Winfield: *The Putnam Hall Cadets; or, Good Times in School and Out,* Stitt, 1905; *The Putnam Hall Rivals; or, Fun and Sport Afloat and Ashore,* Mershon, 1906; *The Putnam Hall Champions; or, Bound to Win Out,* Grosset, 1908; *The Putnam Hall Rebellion; or, The Rival Runaways,* Grosset, 1909; *The Putnam Hall Encampment; or, The Secret of the Old*

Mill, Grosset, 1910; *The Putnam Hall Mystery; or, The School Chums' Strange Discovery,* Grosset, 1911; the Rover Boys series under pseudonym Arthur M. Winfield: *The Rover Boys on the Ocean; or, A Chase for a Fortune,* Mershon, 1899; *The Rover Boys in the Jungle; or, Stirring Adventures in Africa,* Mershon, 1899; *The Rover Boys at School; or, The Cadets at Putnam Hall,* Mershon, 1899; *The Rover Boys Out West; or, The Search for the Lost Mine,* Mershon, 1900; *The Rover Boys on the Great Lakes; or, The Secret of the Island Cave,* Mershon, 1901; *The Rover Boys on the Great Lakes; or, The Search for the Lost Mine,* Mershon, 1901; *The Rover Boys in the Mountains; or, A Hunt for Fun and Fortune,* Mershon, 1902; *The Rover Boys on Land and Sea, or The Crusoes of Seven Islands,* Mershon, 1903; *The Rover Boys in Camp; or, The Rivals of Pine Island,* Mershon, 1904; *The Rover Boys on the River; or, The Search for the Missing Houseboat,* Grosset, 1905; *The Rover Boys on the Plains; or, The Mystery of Red Rock Ranch,* Mershon, 1906; *The Rover Boys in Southern Waters; or, The Deserted Steam Yacht,* Grosset, 1907; *The Rover Boys on the Farm; or, Last Days At Putnam Hall,* Grosset, 1908; *The Rover Boys in the Air,* 1912; *The Rover Boys in New York,* 1913; *The Rover Boys on Treasure Isle; or, The Strange Bonds,* Grosset, 1915; *The Rover Boys at Colby Hall; or, The Struggles of the Young Cadets,* Grosset, 1917; *The Rover Boys on Snowshoe Island,* 1918; *The Rover Boys Under Canvas; or, The Mystery of the Wrecked Submarine,* Grosset, 1919; *The Rover Boys on Sunset Trail; or, The Old Miner's Mysterious Message,* Grosset, 1925; two books by Horatio Alger, Jr., were completed under the pseudonym A. M. Winfield: *Out for Business,* Mershon, 1900, and *Nelson the Newsboy,* Mershon, 1901; the Holly Library series under the pseudonym of Edna Winfield, published by Mershon except as noted: *The Little Cuban Rebel,* Street, 1898; *Temptations of a Great City; or, The Love That Lived Through All,* 1899; *A Struggle for Honor; or, The World Against Her,* 1900; *An Actress' Crime; or, All for Name and Gold,* 1900; *Lured from Home; or, Alone in a Great City,* 1900; *The Girl from the Ranch; or, The Western Girl's Rival Lovers,* 1900; *Because of Her Love; or, The Mystery of a Spell,* 1900; other pseudonyms which appear to have been used by the "Stratemeyer Syndicate" include: Charles A. Beach, Jim Bowie, Lester Chadwick, John R. Cooper [James A. Cooper?], Elmer A. Dawson, Jim Daly, James Cody Ferris, Grahame Forbes, Hal Harkaway, Captain Wilbur Lawton, Mel Martin, Lt. Howard Payson, Nat Ridley, Roy Rockwood, Raymond Speery, Frank Webster, Nat Woods, Clarence Young). UMi

Bertha Upton's *The Adventures of Two Dutch Dolls and a Golliwogg* (the first of a popular series of "Golliwogg" picture books written in verse; published in London by Longmans; the stories feature the adventures of a Golliwogg, a black rag-doll character, and two Dutch dolls; other

1895 *continued*

books in the series are set in different countries; illustrated with lithographs by Florence Upton; as a result of the series, "golliwoggs" became popular dolls in England and have remained so to the present; the author's other work, published by Longmans, includes *The Golliwogg's Air-Ship,* 1902; *The Golliwogg in Holland,* 1904; *The Golliwogg's Fox-hunt,* 1905; *The Golliwogg's Desert Island,* 1906; *The Golliwogg's Christmas,* 1907; *Golliwogg in the African Jungle,* 1909).

H. G. Wells's *The Time Machine* (a popular work of science fiction by a well-known British journalist, propagandist, and reformer; published in New York by Holt; the author's other work includes *The Stolen Bacillus,* Tauchnitz, 1895; *The Island of Dr. Moreau,* Stone, 1896; *The Invisible Man,* Harper, 1897; *The War of the Worlds,* Harper, 1898; *When the Sleeper Wakes,* Harper, 1899; *Love and Mr. Lewisham,* Doran, 1900; *Kipps,* Scribner, 1905; *In the Days of the Comet,* Century, 1906; *Ann Veronica,* Unwin, 1909; *Tono-Bungay,* Duffield, 1909; *The History of Mr. Polly,* Duffield, 1910; *The Door in the Wall and Other Stories,* Kennerley, 1911; *The New Machiavelli,* Duffield, 1911; *The Country of the Blind,* Nelson, 1913; *Little Wars,* Small, 1913; *Joan and Peter,* Macmillan, 1918; *Christina Alberta's Father,* Macmillan, 1925).

1896

Hilaire Belloc's *The Bad Child's Book of Beasts* (one of author's several books of pithy verse illustrated by Basil T. Blackwell; published in Oxford by Alden; the author's other work includes *More Beasts for Worse Children,* Arnold, 1897; *The Modern Traveller,* Arnold, 1899; *A Moral Alphabet,* n.p., 1899; *Cautionary Tales for Children,* Nash, 1908; *More Peers,* Swift, 1911; *New Cautionary Tales,* Duckworth, 1930).

Eugene Field's *Poems of Childhood* (a popular collection of verses, tending to idealize childhood, which include "The Gingham Dog and the Calico Cat," "Wynken, Blynken and Nod," and "Barefoot Boy With Cheeks of Tan"; published in New York by Scribner; the 1904 edition is illustrated by Maxfield Parrish; the author's other work includes *With Trumpet and Drum,* 1892; *Songs of Childhood, with music by Reginald De Koven and Others,* 1896; *The Stars: A Slumber Story,* Amsterdam, 1901). DePL, JLI, NL, WU

Sarah Orne Jewett's *The Country of the Pointed Firs* (a collection of short stories which aptly reflect everyday life in Maine; published in Boston by Houghton, Mifflin and Company; the author's other work, published by Houghton, includes *Deephaven,* 1877; *Country By-Ways,* 1881; *A Country*

Doctor, 1884; *A Marsh Island*, 1885; *A White Heron*, 1886; *Betty Leicester*, 1890; *Betty Leicester's Christmas*, 1894; *Play Days. A Book of Stories for Children*, 1906).

Annie Fellows Johnston's *The Little Colonel* (the most popular of the twelve-volume Cosy Corner series, 1895-1912; published in Boston by J. Knight; illustrated by Etheldred B. Barry; the author's other work, published in New York by Page except as noted, includes *Big Brother*, Knight, 1894; *Joel: A Boy of Galilee*, Roberts, 1895; *The Little Colonel*, 1895; *Ole Mammy's Torment*, Page, 1897; *The Gate of Giant Scissors*, 1898; *The Little Colonel Stories*, 1899; *Two Little Knights of Kentucky Who Were the "Little Colonel's" Neighbors*, 1899; *The Little Colonel's House Party*, 1900; *The Story of Dago*, 1900; *Asa Holmes*, 1902; . . . *Aunt 'Liza's Hero, and Other Stories*, 1903; *Cicely, and Other Stories*, 1903; *"Islands of Providence,"* 1903; *The Little Colonel At Boarding School*, 1903; *The Little Colonel's Hero*, 1903; *In the Desert Waiting*, 1904; *The Little Colonel in Arizona*, 1904; *The Quilt That Jack Built*, 1904; *The Little Colonel's Christmas Vacation*, 1905; *The Three Weavers*, 1905; *Keeping Tryst*, 1906; *The Little Colonel: Maid of Honor*, 1906; *Mildred's Inheritance*, 1906; *The Legend of the Bleeding Heart*, 1907; *The Little Colonel's Knight Comes Riding By*, 1907; *The Little Colonel's Chum: Mary Ware*, 1908; *Mary Ware, the Little Colonel's Chum*, 1908; *The Rescue of the Princess Winsome: A Fairy Play*, 1908; *The Jester's Sword*, 1909; *Mary Ware in Texas*, 1910; *Travelers Along Life's Highway*, 1911; *Mary Ware's Promised Land*, 1912; *Miss Santa Claus of the Pullman*, Century, 1913; *Georgina of the Rainbows*, Britton, 1916; *Georgina's Service Stars*, Britton, 1918; *The Little Man in Motley*, 1918; *It Was the Road to Jericho*, Britton, 1919; *The Little Colonel's Holidays*, 1921; *The Road of the Loving Heart*, 1922; *The Land of the Little Colonel*, 1929; *For Pierre's Sake, and Other Stories*, 1934). SCSC, WKU

Mrs. K. Langloh Parker's *Australian Legendary Tales; Folklore of Noongahburrahs As Told To the Piccaninnies* (a volume of Australian folktales collected by Catherine Somerville [Field] Parker with an introduction by Andrew Lang; published in London by D. Nutt; the author's other work includes *More Australian Legendary Tales*, n.p., 1897).

Gilbert Patten's *Frank Merriwell on His Mettle* (one of the author's numerous popular "Merriwell" books written under the pseudonym of Burt L. Standish and published by Street and Smith except as noted; the author's other work includes *The Diamond Sport*, Beadle, 1886; *Daisy Dare, the Sport from Denver*, Beadle, 1887; *Captain Mystery*, Beadle, 1887; *Aztec Jack*, Beadle, 1891; under the pseudonym of William West Wilder: *Cowboy Chris in Cinnabar*, Beadle, 1897; *Cowboy Chris, the Vengeance Volunteer*,

1896 *continued*

Beadle, 1891; *Clear-Grit Cal,* Beadle, 1892; *Bicycle Ben,* 1893; *Fire-eye the Thugs Terror,* Beadle, 1894; *Frank Merriwell in New York,* 1896; *Frank Merriwell's Frolics,* 1896; *Frank Merriwell's Foe,* 1896; *Frank Merriwell's First Job,* 1896; *Frank Merriwell's Fault,* 1896; *Frank Merriwell's Fate,* 1896; *Frank Merriwell's Furlough,* 1896; *Frank Merriwell or, First Days At Fardale,* 1896; *Frank Merriwell at Yale,* 1897; *Frank Merriwell's Fame,* 1898; *Frank Merriwell's College Chums,* 1898; *Frank Merriwell's Cruise,* 1898; *Frank Merriwell's Chase,* 1898; *Frank Merriwell on the Road,* 1898; *Frank Merriwell's Generosity,* 1899; *Frank Merriwell's Fun,* 1899; *Frank Merriwell's Auto,* 1899; *Don Kirk's Mine,* 1899; *Frank Merriwell On the Boulevards,* 1899; *Don Kirk, the Boy Cattle King,* 1899; *The Boy from the West,* 1899; *Frank Merriwell's Stage Hit,* 1899; *Frank Merriwell's Victories,* 1900; *Frank Merriwell's Shrewdness,* 1900; *Frank Merriwell's Iron Nerve,* 1900; *Frank Merriwell's High Jump,* 1900; *Frank Merriwell's Faith,* 1900; *Dick Merriwell's Glory,* 1901; *Frank Merriwell's Search,* 1901; *Frank Merriwell's Support,* 1901; *Frank Merriwell's Strong Arm,* 1901; *Frank Merriwell's Club,* 1901; *Frank Merriwell As Coach,* 1901; *Dick Merriwell's Dash,* 1902; *Dick Merriwell's Delivery,* 1902; *Dick Merriwell's Diamond,* 1902; *Dick Merriwell's Wonders,* 1902; *Dick Merriwell's Ability,* 1902; *Dick Merriwell's Trap,* 1902; *Dick Merriwell's Ruse,* 1902; *Dick Merriwell's Revenge,* 1902; *Dick Merriwell's Rescue,* 1902; *Dick Merriwell's Racket,* 1902; *Dick Merriwell's Narrow Escape,* 1902; *Frank Merriwell's Winners,* 1902; *Frank Merriwell's Honor,* 1902; *Frank Merriwell's Chums,* 1902; *Frank Merriwell's Sports Afield,* 1903; *Dick Merriwell's Defense,* 1903; *Dick Merriwell's Disguise,* 1903; *Dick Merriwell's Marked Money,* 1903; *Dick Merriwell's Backstop,* 1903; *Dick Merriwell's Model,* 1903; *Dick Merriwell's Mystery,* 1903; *Dick Merriwell's Western Mission,* 1903; *Frank Merriwell's Daring,* 1903; *Frank Merriwell's Bravery,* 1903; *Frank Merriwell's Bicycle Tour,* 1903; *Frank Merriwell's Athletes,* 1903; *Dick Merriwell's Day,* 1904; *Dick Merriwell's Downfall,* 1904; *Dick Merriwell's Grit,* 1904; *Dick Merriwell's Long Slide,* 1904; *Dick Merriwell's Assurance,* 1904; *Dick Merriwell's Peril,* 1904; *Dick Merriwell's Persistence,* 1904; *Dick Merriwell's Threat,* 1904; *Frank Merriwell's Strategy,* 1904; *Frank Merriwell's Loyalty,* 1904; *Frank Merriwell's Secret,* 1904; *Frank Merriwell's Danger,* 1904; *Frank Merriwell's Triumph,* 1904; *Frank Merriwell's Champions,* 1904; *Frank Merriwell's Camp,* 1904; *The Deadwood Trail,* Appleton, 1904; *Dick Merriwell Abroad,* 1905; *Frank Merriwell's Endurance,* 1905; *Dick Merriwell the Wizard,* 1905; *Dick Merriwell's Cleverness,* 1905; *Dick Merriwell's Five,* 1905; *Dick Merriwell's Marriage,* 1905; *Dick Merriwell's Pranks,* 1905; *Dick Merriwell's Resource,* 1905; *Dick Merriwell's Stroke,* 1905; *Frank Merriwell in the Rockies,* 1905; *Frank Merriwell's Fag,* 1905; *Frank Merriwell's Son; or A Chip Off the Old Block,* 1906; *Dick Merriwell's Dare,* 1906; *Dick Merriwell's: Freshman,* 1906; *Dick Merriwell's*

Home Run, 1906; *Dick Merriwell's Influence*, 1906; *Dick Merriwell's Polo Team*, 1906; *Dick Merriwell's Staying Power*, 1906; *Dick Merriwell's Team Mate*, 1906; *Frank Merriwell's Leaguers*, 1906; *Frank Merriwell's Happy Camp*, 1906; *Dick Merriwell's Backers*, 1907; *Dick Merriwell's Best Work*, 1907; *Dick Merriwell's Black Star*, 1907; *Dick Merriwell's Close Call*, 1907; *Dick Merriwell Adrift*, 1907; *Dick Merriwell's Debt*, 1907; *Dick Merriwell's Distrust*, 1907; *Dick Merriwell's Joke*, 1907; *Dick Merriwell's Magnetism*, 1907; *Dick Merriwell's Mastery*, 1907; *Dick Merriwell's Regret*, 1907; *Frank Merriwell's Worst Boy*, 1907; *Frank Merriwell's Talisman*, 1907; *Frank Merriwell's Horse*, 1907; *Frank Merriwell's Air Voyage*, 1907; *Frank Merriwell's Lesson*, 1908; *Frank Merriwell's Steadying Hand*, 1908; *Dick Merriwell Doubted*, 1908; *Dick Merriwell in the Wilds*, 1908; *Dick Merriwell's Example*, 1908; *Dick Merriwell's Reputation*, 1908; *Dick Merriwell's Stanchness*, 1908; *Dick Merriwell's Stand*, 1908; *Dick Merriwell's Way*, 1908; *Frank Merriwell in Wall Street*, 1908; *Frank Merriwell's Hard Case*, 1908; *Frank Merriwell Facing His Foes*, 1908; *Frank Merriwell's Wizard*, 1909; *Dick Merriwell's Honors*, 1909; *Dick Merriwell's Power*, 1909; *Dick Merriwell's Race*, 1909; *Frank Merriwell's Encouragement*, 1909; *Bill Bruce of Harvard*, Dodd, 1910; *Dick Merriwell, Captain of the Varsity*, 1910; *Frank Merriwell in Peru*, 1910; *Cliff Sterling, Captain of the Nine*, McKay, 1910; *Cliff Sterling*, 1911; *Dick Merriwell's Commencement*, 1911; *Dick Merriwell's Reliance*, 1911; *Cliff Sterling Behind the Line*, McKay, 1911; *Dick Merriwell's Counsel*, 1912; *Dick Merriwell's Varsity Nine*, 1912; *Frank Merriwell, Jr.'s Helping Hand*, 1912; *Cliff Sterling, Stroke of the Crew*, McKay, 1912; *Cliff Sterling, Freshman At Stormbridge*, McKay, 1913; *Cliff Sterling, Sophomore at Stormbridge*, McKay, 1913; *Dick Merriwell Tricked*, 1914; *The College Rebel*, Barse, 1914; *Brick King, Backstop*, Barse, 1914; *Boltwood of Yale*, Barse, 1914; under the pseudonym Burt L. Standish: *Courtney of the Center Garden*, Barse, 1915; *Covering the Look-in Corner*, Barse, 1915; *Crossed Signals*, Barse, 1928; *The Call of the Varsity*, Barse, 1920; *Frank Merriwell's Trip West*, 1924; *Ben Oakman*, Barse, 1925). UMi

1897

John Bennett's *Master Skylark* (an historical novel which captures the spirit and beauty of Shakespearean England; published in New York by Century; the author's other work includes *Barnaby Lee*, Century, 1902; and *The Pigtail of Ah Lee Ben Loo*, Longmans, a collection of stories and ballads with silhouette illustrations, which was a runner-up for the Newbery Award in 1929).

Edward Verrall Lucas's *The Flamp, and Other Stories* (a collection of stories of which the fanciful tale of "The Schoolboy's Apprentice" is

1897 *continued*

probably best known; published in London by G. Richards; the author's other work includes a book of verses, *Four and Twenty Toilers,* illustrated by Francis D. Bedford, Dalton, 1900; *Anne's Terrible Good Nature, and Other Stories,* Chatto, 1908; *The Slowcoach,* Wells, 1910; *Playtime and Company,* Methuen, 1925; the author edited *A Book of Verses for Children,* Richards, 1897, and *Another Book of Verse for Children,* Wells, 1907). DC

William Nicholson's *An Alphabet* (a distinctively illustrated ABC book with a full-page lithograph for each letter of the alphabet; published in London by W. Heinemann; the author-illustrator's other work includes *An Almanac of Twelve Sports, Twelve Portraits, London Types, The Square Book of Animals,* Heinemann, 1898-1900; *Clever Bill,* Doubleday, 1926; *The Pirate Twins,* Coward, 1929).

Egerton Ryerson Young's *Three Boys in the Wild North Land* (a minister's account of an English, a Scottish, and an Irish boy who spend time in Canada as guests of a former Hudson's Bay Company member; published in Toronto by Briggs; this Canadian author's other work includes *Children of the Forest: A Story of Indian Love,* Revell, 1904; *Duck Lake,* Religious Tract Society, 1905).

1898

Alfred Ollivant's *Bob, Son of Battle* (an animal story in which both man and dog move inevitably toward their doom; published in Garden City, New York, by Doubleday; the author's other work, published by Doubleday except as noted, includes *Danny,* 1902; *The Gentleman,* Burt, 1908; *The Brown Mare,* Knopf, 1916).

Albert Bigelow Paine's *The Hollow Tree* (one of the author's many nature stories; published in New York by R. H. Russell; the author's other work includes, with William Allen White, *Rhymes by Two Friends,* Izor, 1893; with Ruth McEnery White, *Gobolinks,* Century, 1896; *The Dumpies,* Keegan Paul, 1897; *The Arkansas Bear,* Russell, 1898; *The Little Lady, Her Book,* Altemus, 1901; *The Wanderings of Joe and Little Em,* n.p., 1903; *The Lucky Piece,* Outing, 1906; *The Tent Dwellers,* Outing, 1908; *Elsie and the Arkansas Bear,* Altemus, 1909; *The Ship Dwellers,* Harper, 1910; *The Boy's Life of Mark Twain,* Harper, 1916; *Dwellers in Arcady,* Harper, 1919; *The Girl in White Armor,* Macmillan, 1927; the author was editor of *St. Nicholas* from 1899 to 1909).

Ernest Thompson Seton's *Wild Animals I Have Known* (one of the first attempts to present authentic, sympathetic accounts of animals in their natural environment to children; published in New York by Charles Scribner;

the author was naturalist to the government of Manitoba; the author's other work includes *The Trail of the Sandhill Stag,* Scribner, 1899; *Lobo, Rag, and Vixen,* Scribner, 1899; *Biography of a Grizzly,* Century, 1900; *Lives of the Hunted,* Scribner, 1901; *Krag and Johnny Bear,* Scribner, 1902; *Two Little Savages,* Doubleday, 1903; *How to Play Indian,* Curtis, 1903; *Woodmyth and Fable,* Century, 1905; *Animal Heroes,* Scribner, 1905; *The Birch-Bark Roll of the Outdoor Life,* Doubleday, 1908; *The Biography of a Silver Fox,* Constable, 1909; *The Book of Woodcraft and Indian Lore,* Doubleday, 1912; *Bannertail,* Scribner, 1922; *Katug the Snow Child,* n.p., 1922; *Billy,* Hodder, 1925; *Lives of Game Animals,* Doubleday, 1925; *Chink, A Woolly Coated Little Dog,* Hodder, 1929; *Famous Animal Stories,* Bretanos, 1932; *The Gospel of the Red Man,* Doubleday, 1936; *Biography of an Arctic Fox,* Appleton, 1937; *The Buffalo Wind,* Santa Fe, 1938).

1899

Helen Bannerman's *Little Black Sambo* (an early nursery picture-story which included black characters; this British author's "classic" became controversial in America, especially in the 1960s, because of the text and stereotypic illustrations by the author; the author's other work, published by Nisbet, except as noted, includes *Story of Little Black Mingo,* 1901; *Story of Little Black Quibba,* 1902; *Little Degchie-Head: An Awful Warning to Bad Babas,* 1903; *Little Kettle-head,* 1904; *Pat and the Spider,* 1905; *The Teasing Monkey,* Stokes, 1907; *Little Black Quasha,* 1908; *Story of Little Black Bobtail,* Stokes, 1909; *Sambo and the Twins,* Stokes, 1936; *Little White Squibba,* Chatto, 1965).

Ralph Henry Barbour's *The Half-Back* (an early sports story centering on school football and golf; published in New York by Appleton; illustrated by B. West Clinedinst).

Hamlin Garlin's *Boy Life on the Prairie* (a realistic account of everyday farm life in Iowa, published in New York by Harper; author's other work, published in New York by Harper except as noted, includes *The Eagle's Nest,* 1900; *Her Mountain Lover,* Century, 1901; *The Captain of the Grayhorse Troop,* 1902; *Hesper,* 1902; *The Moccasin Ranch,* 1909; *Cavanagh, Forest Ranger,* 1910; *Victor Ollnee's Discipline,* 1911). UMI

E. Nesbit's *The Story of the Treasure Seekers* (the first of a series of famous stories about the Bastable children; published in London by T. Fisher Unwin; the story first appeared in the *Illustrated London News,* 1897, under the pseudonym of Ethyl Mortimer; the author's other work includes *The Book of Dragons*, Harper, 1900; *The Would-Be-Goods*, Unwin, 1901;

1899 *continued*

Nine Unlikely Tales for Children, Unwin, 1901; *Five Children and It,* Unwin, 1902; *The New Treasure Seekers,* Unwin, 1904; *The Phoenix and the Carpet,* Newnes, 1904; *Oswald Bastable, and Others,* Wells, 1905; *The Railway Children,* Wells, 1906; *The Story of the Amulet,* Unwin, 1906; *The Enchanted Castle,* Unwin, 1907; *The House of Arden,* Unwin, 1908; *Harding's Luck,* Hodder, 1909; *The Magic City,* Macmillan, 1910; *The Wonderful Garden,* Macmillan, 1911; *The Magic World,* Macmillan, 1912; *Wet Magic,* Laurie, 1912; *Five of Us and Madeline,* Unwin, 1925). LC, TPL

James Macdonald Oxley's *Fife and Drum at Louisbourg* (one of this Canadian author's more than twenty boys' adventure stories, many of which are set in Canada; published in London by Ward; the author's other work includes *Fergus MacTavish,* Hodder, 1893; *Up Among the Ice-floes,* Nelson, 1894; *Standing the Test,* Religious Tract Society, 1898; *L'Hasa At Last,* Ward, 1900; *Norman's Nugget,* Partridge, 1902). TPL

William Allen White's *The Court of Boyville* (a boy's story by a well-known adult writer; published in New York by Doubleday, McClure; the author was owner and editor of *Emporia Gazette,* 1895-1944). KSC

Chapter 6
Twentieth Century (1900–1945)

HISTORICAL BACKGROUND

In Britain

The death of Queen Victoria in 1901 marked the end of an epoch. Britain, the greatest nation on earth, would never be the same. At home, the masses of people were demanding, often forcefully, better living conditions and higher wages, all of which alarmed the old ruling classes. But domestic struggles—national strikes, and women demanding suffrage—continued, as did foreign problems. Britain was having difficulty governing her far-flung Empire, especially in South Africa, India, and Egypt. And the Irish question remained unresolved. The worst problem of all was the threat of a rapidly growing Germany.

Although the British fleet was continuing to expand, Germany's navy doubled and redoubled. And while Britain's employment decreased, Germany's increased. In spite of rising concerns, many Britons liked to think that their nation could stand firm and in "splendid isolation." The Boer War, however, signaled things to come.

In 1886 gold had been discovered in South Africa. Almost as soon as the British and others joined the rush to mine it, tensions grew between the Boer (Dutch) farmers who wanted to keep their way of life and the *uitlanders*, the "outsiders" who wanted citizenship. Although the Boers succeeded in refusing to make concessions, they feared annexation by Britain, and tensions increased. Compromise was attempted, but war broke out in 1899. The British forces were defeated several times; not until volunteers from Canada, Australia, and New Zealand came to Britain's rescue was it (with a force of 448,000 men) able to crush the resistance (87,000 men) and extricate itself. The war showed the British the difficulties and brutalities of empire building and the need for assistance in time of crisis.

With the need for alliance clear, Britain made a treaty with Japan in 1902. A treaty with the rising Germany was even proposed, but Germany was allied to Austria-Hungary. And France and Russia were linked. When European tensions increased, Britain joined sides with France and Russia, and the three became the Triple Entente.

Meanwhile, German power grew. Its annexations, its build-up of military might, and its jealousy of Britain's and France's colonial empires made German interference in Balkan affairs, which were already tense, extremely serious. As rivalry between Austria and Russia heightened, ties between Britain and France increased. (When France expanded its power in Morocco, for example, it did so with British support.) The situation in the Balkan Peninsula of southeastern Europe grew worse when Austria annexed the Turkish provinces of Bosnia and Herzegovina, which enraged Russia. The resulting Balkan Wars, 1912-1913, permitted the Balkan states of Montenegro, Bulgaria, Greece, and Serbia to seize Turkey's remaining territory in Europe; but the states fought among themselves over the spoils, with Serbia profiting the most. Tensions increased even further as Bulgaria became an Austrian ally, and Serbia and Rumania joined with Russia. With the whole area about to explode, Archduke Francis Ferdinand, heir to the Austrian throne, was assassinated in Bosnia. The Austrian government was certain that the murder was committed by a Serbian, since the assassin had recently come from Belgrade, the Serbian capital. Against a background of complicated alliances in Europe and great strife in the Balkan Peninsula, the assassination touched off World War I, the first of its kind in history. It would engulf all Europe, involve dozens of nations, and take millions of lives.

Britain was pulled into the war when it went to the aid of Belgium, a small, neutral country which had been overrun by Germany. Fierce fighting continued until both sides reached an impasse. Locked in bloody trench warfare that spread across the entire continent, neither side was able to advance. As the war went on, the Allies were more and more hard pressed for supplies and munitions. The worst blow occurred when Russia, which had incurred enormous losses, pulled out of the war. Then in 1917, a workers' revolution overthrew the czar, and the Communist party made a separate peace with Germany.

Meanwhile, America had entered the war. Although the German surface navy was kept sequestered by the British, German submarines waged continual war on Allied merchant and passenger vessels. The submarine blockade of Britain might have starved the British into surrendering, but German U-boat attacks on American ships convinced the United States to join the Allies. With American money, machines, and over 4 million American men in arms, the back of the German defense was finally broken. On November 11, 1918, an armistice was signed. Casualties had been enormous: the United Kingdom had lost 750,00 men, the United States 115,000, France 1,400,000, Russia 1,700,000, and Germany nearly 2 million.

The peace was as hard to resolve as the war had been to win. Old Europe was gone: Germany had collapsed, the Austro-Hungarian Empire was fragmented, Russia was no longer a monarchy, and Turkey would soon lose its centuries-old Ottoman sultanate. Although the Treaty of Versailles attempted to thwart Germany permanently by forcing it to pay the costs of the war, it was not long before Germany would rise again.

Tired of foreign entanglements, the American Congress would not support President Woodrow Wilson and join the new League of Nations. Without American approval, the league fell into disrepute.

By 1922, Benito Mussolini, a Fascist, had taken over the government of Italy. By the mid-twenties, improved economic conditions in Italy made fascism attractive to many. Meanwhile, Germany continued to smart from inflation, unemployment, and deep humiliation. When Adolph Hitler, an anti-Communist nationalist, promised to destroy the Versailles Treaty, as well as the Jews on whom he blamed Germany's problems, he appealed to the passions of the German people, especially the middle class. In 1933 he became chancellor. By 1936 Hitler's Nazi party had become completely totalitarian.

Although Britain tried to stem the rise of fascism in Germany and Italy, it found that negotiation was impossible. Even while Hitler carried out annexation after annexation, Britain continued to attempt mediation. Finally, in 1939, when Germany overran Poland, Britain and France declared war.

For a while, Hitler's *Blitzkrieg* (lightning war) overwhelmed the Allies, and France collapsed. Britain stood alone, repelling attack after attack of German sea and air power. In 1941 Hitler attacked Russia and the scope of the war broadened. But not until December 7, 1941, did the war become worldwide. Wishing to control the economy of the South Pacific, Japan, which had joined Germany and Italy, attacked the United States's naval fleet at Pearl Harbor in Hawaii. The United States entered the war the next day.

Japanese power spread rapidly across the Pacific. But in 1942 the tide of the war turned when the Americans began a furious counterattack in the South Pacific. Meanwhile, through an immense industrial effort at home, the United States was able to replenish Britain's failing supplies. Shortly thereafter, Hitler's forces were defeated by the British in North Africa, and the Russians stopped the Germans at Stalingrad. From 1943 on, the Germans were slowly driven back, but it took two more brutal years before hostility ceased. The Allies' long drive north through Sicily and Italy severely crippled the remaining German armies, but the cost in suffering and death was heavy. Meanwhile, allied air raids on German industrial areas continued. In 1944, after Germany was attacked on three fronts, the Allies invaded Normandy; Germany surrendered on May 7, 1945.

In the South Pacific, the bombing of Japan itself, beginning in November 1944, at first had little effect. After incendiary attacks began, however, Japanese cities (mostly wooden structures) were soon in shambles. But not until the Americans dropped the first two atomic bombs, the first on Hiroshima on August 6 and the second on Nagasaki three days later, did the Japanese agree to "unconditional surrender."

With World War II over, most of the nations of the earth could disarm and begin to rebuild. But technical innovations hitherto unknown had caused mass slaughter, both military and civilian: the United Kingdom suffered 420,000 casualties, the United States 400,000, France 540,000, while the Soviet Union lost 20 million people, Germany 6,500,000, Japan nearly 2 million, and Italy 450,000. An estimated 6 million Jews were killed, more than 3 million in Poland alone, as a result of Hitler's design for extermination of all Jews.

While war dominated the history of the world during most of the first half of the twentieth century, there were nevertheless many social reforms. In Britain the changes were characterized by a movement toward socialism. Problems of poverty, slums, health, old age, and unemployment were slowly absorbed by the government. Lloyd George and his Liberal party, who at first were roundly condemned as radicals, began to convert the country to the notion of the welfare state. In 1906 the Labour party was formed which would push for greater reforms. Worried by too rapid social change, the upper classes resented the new directions, but the sacrifices made by common people in World War I had vastly improved their social station.

Reform was in the air. One of the most important of the reforms of the period following World War I was the Education Act of 1918. Improvement in education along with a demand for housing and greater trade brought immediate prosperity and boosted the morale of millions who were tired of war. Prospects were high for an improved future.

But by 1921, hopes had fallen again as the country's changeover from a wartime to a peacetime economy resulted in a prolonged industrial depression which grew more and more serious. Although unemployment acts were extended in 1920 and trade unions strove to aid workers, strikes were frequent (a nine-day general strike was called in 1926), and unrest and unemployment continued. Economic problems, which culminated in the American stock market crash of 1929 and the subsequent international depression, did not begin to be alleviated until Britain began to rearm for what became World War II.

In the United States

At the beginning of the twentieth century, the now heavily industrialized United States had risen to world-power status. But with profits came problems. The successful conclusion of the Spanish-American War just before the nineteenth century closed had caused America to move rapidly along the path of a worldwide empire. The treaty, the Peace of Paris, gave the United States the Philippines, Puerto Rico, and Guam, along with the annexation of Hawaii. The results of the war also emphasized the desirability of building a canal between the Atlantic and Pacific oceans. At first, the canal was to be run under the joint guarantee of Great Britain and the United States, but in 1901 the secretary of state, John Hay, acquired the rights for the United States alone. With construction of the canal starting in 1903, the United States became a strong military and economic force in the Caribbean.

The assassination of President William McKinley by a crazed anarchist in the autumn of 1901 gave the reins of government to the dynamic, young vice-president, Theodore Roosevelt. An aggressive nationalist, Roosevelt set out at once to remodel the structure of the government and make it more responsive to the ideals of social justice. Roosevelt's "progressive" ideas, feared most by the conservative leaders in his own Republican party, swept in a series of reforms. He criticized the evils of industrialism, and as "trust-buster" he acted to break up the giant corporations. He called for authority to regulate railroads, labor, and management, as well as public health and education. His "square deal" showed concern for all—capital, labor, and the public. And he was the first national leader to call for conservation of natural resources, along with a general awakening of social consciousness in the nation's churches.

Other changes that came about during the Teddy Roosevelt era were municipal and state welfare reforms. Several states enacted laws regulating wages, hours, industrial working conditions, and safety standards; granting public aid to the aged and mothers with dependent children; restricting the labor of women and children; establishing settlement houses and providing recreational facilities for the urban poor, and clearing slums. Although women's suffrage had been discussed as early as the 1840s, it was not until 1890 when Wyoming, the first suffrage state, was admitted to the union, that any American woman had the right to vote. Finally, in 1920 an amendment to the United States Constitution gave national suffrage to women.

Roosevelt's successor, William Howard Taft, who also sympathized with the political reformers but lacked the political skill to carry on Roosevelt's "progressivism," eventually brought about a split in the Republican party, into conservative and liberal wings. With the election of 1912, three parties were in contention; for the Democrats, Woodrow Wilson; for the Republicans, President Taft; and for the newly formed Progressives, Theodore Roosevelt. With schism in the Republican ranks, Woodrow Wilson easily became the next president.

Wilson, who called himself a "progressive with the brakes on" and who admired Roosevelt, carried out many reforms of his own, especially those that related to tariffs, banking, trusts, agriculture, and labor. Abroad, Wilson attempted to modify the growing imperialism of the United States and to support the democratic development of other countries. Wilson was far more interested in internal affairs, and his presidency was soon darkened by confusing developments in foreign policy: first, in a dispute with Great Britain over collecting tolls on the Panama Canal; then, in a confrontation with Mexico over the failure to recognize its new regime and the subsequent seizure of a squad of American marines. Although Wilson took a moral stance in his dealings with foreign nations and attempted peaceful negotiations rather than force, the United States was unalterably drawn into World War I through entanglements with Europe in providing munitions, foodstuffs, raw materials, and money. Although Wilson attempted to keep the United States a disinterested, neutral nation, public sympathy lay with the Allies because of ancestry and cultural ties and opposed the Germans because it distrusted Germany as authoritarian. After the German invasion of Belgium, many Americans were certain of the identity of the aggressor.

Although some antiwar movements surfaced in the United States, the likelihood of war became apparent, especially when German submarine warfare developed. In the spring of 1916 American preparations began in earnest. Although President Wilson proposed a settlement of the war as late as January 1917, German U-boat activity began again, and the United States broke off diplomatic relations. After four American merchant vessels were sunk by German submarines, Congress declared war on April 6, 1917.

With America's entry into the war, domestic reforms came to a standstill. But much had already been accomplished: legislation for the development of Alaska, the means of settling railway disputes, creation of banks to aid farmers, legislation to build interstate highways, and enlargement of the self-government of the Philippines and Puerto Rico.

With the Allies' forces at low ebb, the American armies of over 2 million combat soldiers marked the turning point in the bitterly fought war, which ended November 11, 1918. Winning the so-called "war to end wars" gave the United States unprecedented power, although America had lost 115,000 lives, with 236,000 wounded and over 22 million dollars in immediate costs.

Winning the peace would be even harder. From the beginning of the peace plans to "make the world safe for democracy" it was clear that the idealism voiced during the conflict would be hard to find when making the treaty. The spirit of nationalism on the part of American as well as European statesmen made Wilson's "Fourteen Points" difficult to achieve.

Among other things, he asked for freedom of the seas, removal of international barriers, reduction of arms, and establishment of a general association of nations. While most of the points of the peace treaty were eventually accepted by Congress, Wilson's most important point, the League of Nations, was turned down. With the treaty rejected, Congress passed a joint resolution declaring that the war with Germany was ended. Although Wilson vetoed it, President Harding, his successor, signed a similar resolution in July 1921; subsequent treaties negotiated with Germany, Austria, and Hungary were ratified at once.

War weariness brought about a revival of isolationism and a desire to return to peacetime interests—"normalcy"—but serious problems remained unsolved, among them the disparity of economic balance between industry and agriculture, large-scale immigration, and prohibition.

In 1921 old-guard Republican politicans took over with the election of Warren G. Harding as president. Although a weak president, his cabinet succeeded in developing a policy of containing Japan which was becoming a military threat in Asia, reducing the national debt, and creating an efficient commerce department, headed by Herbert Hoover, which catered to business and helped the growing prosperity.

After Harding's death in 1923, Calvin Coolidge became president. Under his administration, business continued to grow—particularly because of the rise of the automobile, the expanding use of electricity and electrical appliances, and the catch-up on shortages resulting from the war. Nationalism was strong, tariffs were high, and immigration quotas were established.

The 1920s, the "jazz age," was marked by an acceleration of American life. Tired of domestic reform movements and disillusioned by the failure of the war to bring real peace to the world, Americans sought relief from serious problems by amusing themselves. New leisure time brought about by new inventions and prosperity for most people made the search for recreation the goal in life. Growth of motion pictures, the car industry, radio, and sports, coupled with the jazz craze and fads—from marathon dancing to flagpole sitting—characterized life for the majority of the American people.

The decade of the 1920s was also an age of political radicalism. After the war there was much unrest in the labor movement, even a "Red Scare" when thirty people were killed in a bomb explosion on Wall Street. Labor unrest was mollified by the growth in jobs and increased wages, but radicalism or the fear of it continued throughout the decade, particularly in the Boston police strike and the Sacco-Vanzetti case. Reform, so recently popular, was in a decline; organizations for racial and religious intolerance, such as the Ku Klux Klan, grew rapidly after 1920. The national prohibition of the manufacture and sale of liquor in 1919, favored in the rural areas and opposed in the urban, also added to the lawlessness and political corruption.

Prohibition would not be repealed until 1933 when control of liquor regulations would be given to the states, but much would happen in American life in the interim.

When Coolidge refused to seek reelection, the Republican candidate was Herbert Hoover; he easily won over the Democrat (and Catholic) Alfred E. Smith. Hoover's term began in 1929 during a period of great prosperity, which fostered a feeling of carefree unconcern. But by autumn of the same year, the nation had sunk into a heavy gloom caused by the deepest economic depression in history. Among the many causes were the continuing decline of agriculture, industrial overexpansion, the failure of employment to keep pace with the growth of population and capital, labor's not getting its share of the new wealth, unwise consumer installment buying, extravagant speculation, and a deteriorating international situation which was caused in part by high tariffs and a drain on the world's gold to the United States. The resulting stock market crash of 1929 was chaotic.

Attempts to alleviate the situation met with little success until the new president, Franklin Delano Roosevelt, elected in 1932, aggressively put through a series of acts known as the New Deal. These reforms were aimed at curing the sick economy through a banking moratorium, improvement of the Federal Reserve System and correction of banking abuses, an end to specie payment, a call-in of gold securities and fixing the value of the dollar, a bolstering of agriculture and restoring farmers' purchasing power through controlled production, guaranteed prices, and subsidies, improving credit facilities, increasing loans to industry and increasing self-regulation, regulating business by widening powers of the Interstate Commerce Commission, regulating public utilities, supervising and regulating exchanges in securities and commodities, and reducing unemployment through subsidizing work projects. At the New Deal's height in 1936, its programs provided jobs for 3,800,000 people. Labor was strengthened by providing greater security and establishing minimum wages and maximum hours, and child labor was banned once and for all. A system of unemployment insurance and old-age pension, known as Social Security, was also established. Although highly unpopular with many of the affluent classes, such measures preserved the American social system.

Along with domestic reforms, many international changes occurred. The Soviet Union was recognized for the first time since the Communist Revolution of 1917. A good neighbor policy toward Latin America was extended. The Philippines were granted some self-rule. Foreign commerce was strengthened, while tariffs were reduced. Although some of the legislation was temporary, much of it was intended to be permanent reform.

At the outbreak of World War II in Europe in 1939, the United States was in a thoroughly isolationist mood. Taken up with severe domestic problems throughout the 1930s, Americans thought of Europe as far away. But Hitler's "annexations" were spreading throughout Europe. When Germany invaded Poland on September 1, 1939, Americans were profoundly shocked.

As in World War I, the United States was officially neutral at first, with representatives of Western Hemisphere nations meeting in Panama to proclaim both neutrality and solidarity but promising at the same time to defend Canada. Meanwhile, Congress sent overage destroyers to Britain, stationed men in Greenland and Iceland, leased military bases in many critical defense positions throughout the world, built a two-ocean navy, voted the largest peacetime budget for the military in history, and enacted a compulsory Selective Training and Service Act.

Breaking a long-established precedent that a president should be in office only two terms, Roosevelt ran for and was elected to a third term. During that term he convinced Congress to give him, through the Lend-Lease Act, power to sell, lease, lend, or exchange war equipment to any country as he thought necessary and to send it on American convoys protected by American naval and air forces. Although these convoys were attacked, war was not declared officially until the Japanese bombed the Pearl Harbor naval base on December 7, 1941, destroying much of the navy and killing 2,400 men. On December 8 the United States declared war on Japan; on December 11 on Germany and Italy; and on June 5, 1942, on their allies Bulgaria, Hungary, and Rumania.

Although the Americans fought a defensive war for the first six months in the Pacific, by August 1942, the United States took the offensive. In November 1942 the Americans joined the British in invasion of the Atlantic and Mediterranean coasts of Africa. Later, the United States played a major role in the successful invasions of Italy and France. In 1944 Roosevelt was reelected for a fourth term, but he did not live to finish it; on April 12, 1945, he died, leaving Harry S. Truman to order the dropping of the first atomic bomb on Hiroshima on August 6, 1945, killing 71,379 people, and the second on Nagasaki on August 9. Both cities were obliterated; the nuclear age had come; and the war ended a few days later.

After the war, which had cost millions of lives and billions of dollars, there was no return to isolation as there had been after World War I. The United States was the chief supporter of the United Nations, a peace-keeping assembly of nations, whose charter was formulated in San Francisco. But in spite of high hope for the United Nations, foreign entanglements continued: Truman asked for funds to protect Greece and Turkey from Soviet pressure, and the Marshall Plan was enacted to aid those nations who joined in economic cooperation to reconstruct Europe. When the Soviet bloc did not accept, the cold war was under way.

At home, the period following the war was highly prosperous, but it was also besieged with inflation, labor unrest, and myriads of domestic problems that foreshadowed the conflicts of the next decades.

DEVELOPMENT OF BOOKS

At first the coming of the machine age meant a reduction in printing and publishing standards. Although technical improvements brought certain advances, late Victorian books in general, on both sides of the Atlantic, were not especially pleasing aesthetically. But the technical accomplishments were decisive in the history of printing; eventually they would affect methods of production, publication procedures, distribution, and even the habits of the reading public. Mechanization, from letter-founding to book-binding, ultimately meant that greater numbers of books and better-quality books at lower prices were within reach of all readers. Because of growing universal education in both England and America, literacy increased, and all forms of printed material—books, periodicals, almanacs, newspapers—were being read by all social and economic classes. Thus, mechanization brought numerous advantages to the twentieth-century reading public, but for some printers the ensuing competition to see who could print the most cheaply called for rethinking.

Private presses in England near the end of the nineteenth century had helped to restore standards and set new ones. Inspired by the art and crafts movement of the 1880s, William Morris in particular originated and provided the momentum needed to restore high quality to printed works. After studying the calligraphy of the Middle Ages as well as the earliest printed materials, Morris, who was already well known as an artist, designer, craftsman, and poet, issued his first book from the Kelmscott Press in 1891, *The Story of the Glittering Plain*. Although he printed only fifty-three books in all, totaling eighteen thousand copies, his work began a new vogue for beautiful books. With type cast on his own designs based on medieval script and using heavily decorated borders, initials, and even a colophon, the way printers in the past had done, his pages were masterpieces of book design. Although some critics found his texts "unreadable" because of the distractingly beautiful borders, Morris's artistry set the tone for private presses to follow. Even commercial houses would feel the impact in the twentieth century. Using only the finest materials and the greatest care, all his books are works of the printer's highest art, but his Kelmscott Chaucer, with woodcuts by Edward Burne-Jones, is thought to be his greatest.

Other important private press printers were T. J. Cobden-Sanderson and Emery Walker of the Doves Press, 1900-1917; C. H. St. John Hornby of the Ashendene Press, 1894-1935; Lucien Pissaro of the Ergany Press, 1894-1914; and Charles Ricketts of the Vale Press, 1896-1903.

English printing, especially that of the private press, enjoyed a renaissance, but American printers, too, made profound contributions. From 1903 to 1912 Bruce Rogers, America's greatest typographer, directed the Riverside Press in Cambridge, Massachusetts. In addition to producing many beautiful books at Riverside, including a three-volume edition of Montaigne, he also acted as adviser to the Cambridge University Press and the Oxford University Press in England. One of the great works of the twentieth century, the Oxford University Press's *Lectern Bible,* was made under Rogers's direction.

Other fine American presses were the Merrymount in Boston, directed by Daniel Berkley Updike; the Grabhorn, founded by brothers Edwin and Robert Grabhorn in 1920 in San Francisco; the Limited Editions Club, founded by George Macy in 1929, which was followed by the Heritage Club and the commercial houses of Doubleday's Limited Editions; the Folio Club; and Random House's Illustrated Modern Library.

The first English attempt to mass-produce fine editions was J. M. Dent's "Everyman's Library" in 1906. Using Morris's design principles on the title pages and endpapers, the "Everyman" series marked the beginning of the attractive, low-cost books in British commercial printing.

After World War I, improved methods of typography and design were applied to commercial printing throughout England and America, and on the continent as well. In England, the Nonesuch Press, founded by Francis Meynell in 1923, was the first successful commercial house to use machines to produce fine books and thus overcome the criticism that beautiful books had to be handmade. Before long all publishing ventures were affected, and technical progress forged ahead.

From the beginning of this renaissance, children's books were an important part of the movement. From the 1860s on, when Edmund Evans determined to print toy books of high quality and engaged such talents as Randolph Caldecott, Walter Crane, and Kate Greenaway, the numbers of beautifully written and illustrated books for children increased.

Although inexpensive editions were still published in great numbers in both England and America, quality editions of children's books began in earnest in the United States in the 1870s and 1880s when photoengraving methods were developed. While Thomas Nast and Felix Darley did a great amount of the work, new artists, many of them working with Charles Parsons at Harper and Brothers, began to do work for children's books: Howard Pyle, Edwin A. Abbey, William A. Rogers, George Luks, Charles Stanley Reinhart, A. B. Frost, William Smedley, and Edward B. Kembly.

But the influence of Howard Pyle would be the most far-reaching. Already a popular painter, Pyle trained some of the greatest illustrators of the early twentieth century, most notably N. C. Wyeth. Although an artist in his own right, Wyeth will probably be best remembered for his illustrations for children's books. Other well-known American artists who devoted part of their work to children's books were Palmer Cox, Peter Newell, Oliver Herford, Reginald Birch, Walter Harrison Cady, Charles Dana Gibson, and T. S. Sullivant.

Other well-known illustrators of the early part of the century who also wrote for children were Ernest Thompson Seton, Dan Beard, Willy Pogany, and Charles Falls. While these illustrators used a variety of methods, only the last two returned to the earliest method of creating pictures in books, the woodcut. Falls' *ABC Book* (1923), cut in wood, is a landmark in the field of illustration.

The early 1920s, the period immediately following World War I, was a time of worldwide prosperity. Americans especially had more money than ever before, and they spent a considerable share of it on books. With child study in fashion, parents, relatives, and friends bought books for children. Responding to the market, publishers created for the first time separate juvenile departments with special editors. In 1919, for example, Louise Seaman was named the children's book editor at Macmillan, as was May Massee at Doubleday, Doran and Company in 1922. Distribution schedules were increased, providing new book lists all year, as well as during the traditional Christmas period. Improvements in bookmaking and illustration, selling and distribution began in earnest, but the criticism of children's books had just begun.

Not until Anne Carroll Moore became librarian at the Pratt Institute Free Library in Brooklyn in 1896 did any concerted effort to criticize, and thereby improve, children's books occur. With criticism came improvements in design, format, artistry, and literary qualities. And the promotion of "juveniles" came with some regularity: in 1918 the first Children's Book Week was launched by the American Library Association; in 1924 came the first issue of *The Horn Book Magazine,* a journal that would devote all its energies to children's literature; in 1929 the Junior Literary Guild, the first book club for children, was formed.

With so many improvements and so much new enthusiasm, talented artists in large numbers, both native and foreign-born, began to illustrate books for children; among them were Valenti Angelo, William Pene DuBois, Wanda Gág (*see figure 21*), Lois Lenski, Robert Lawson, Alice and Martin Provensen, Ingri and Edgar D'Aulaire, Fritz Kredel (*see figure 22*), Roger Duvoisin, Fritz Eichenberg, Feodor Rojankovsky, Kate Seredy, Gustaf Tenggren, and Nicolas Mordvinoff.

Although the 1930s were depressed economically for all businesses, children's book publication was only temporarily set back. The Great Depression brought declining sales and forced publishers to put out fewer books and even discontinue some juvenile departments. In an attempt to make up losses, inexpensive editions were offered for as little as ten or fifteen cents; even the "quality" houses had dollar books.

With the 1940s came new problems—especially wartime shortages of materials. To cope with these problems, books were printed on poor-quality paper, with narrow margins, unsubstantial bindings, few colored illustrations, and less artwork in general. With few toys available because of wartime restrictions, toy books (pop-ups, pull-outs, and so on) enjoyed a resurgence of popularity.

Although the 1940s was a relatively low period in the production of all books in America (and even lower in Europe), the end of World War II and the following prosperity would bring increased expansion during the 1950s and 1960s, along with the increased experimentation that comes from a flourishing economy. Such expansion would bring fine books of exceedingly high quality as well as mass-produced books, such as those from the Disney Studios, Golden Books, and paperbacks. As children's books moved into the second half of the twentieth century, new methods of illustration and printing would continue to be developed and new, more "permissive" themes in literature—and in life—would continue to be explored.

ATTITUDES TOWARD AND TREATMENT OF CHILDREN

By the end of the nineteenth century, in Britain and America childhood was a recognized stage of development, with emphasis on the adolescent years. While exemption from the world of work had long been permitted for upper-class British youth, such was not the case for the middle and lower classes, with poor children having so recently been a large part of the labor force. When the reformers finally began to make education available to all adolescent youth, its worth was seriously debated, especially by the lower classes themselves.

When the new science of psychology clearly pointed out the vulnerability of childhood and the years immediately thereafter, protective legislation followed. Along with the widespread concern came organizations such as the Boy Scouts, founded in 1908, and the Girl Guides (or Girl Scouts), founded in 1909, and new institutions such as special welfare agencies, juvenile courts, and juvenile prisons. Although the debate continued over whether or not the recognition of adolescence was good or bad, laws were passed and social changes followed.

In Britain the middle and upper classes tended to favor the extended education of youth, hoping that it would better prepare young people for adulthood and bring about a universal cure-all for society's ills, yet fearing that the teenagers would, when freed from work, spend their time in idleness and delinquency. The lower classes, on the other hand, resented the lengthening of childhood and keeping young people in school because these reforms took youth out of the work force, and poor families needed the income. When the middle class tried to thrust conformity on the poor in the form of schools, boys' clubs, and other organized activities, lower-class youth tended to resist. Along with poverty, poor housing, disease, and high death rates, crime increased; the reformers discovered that entering the world of "boys' fun" was no panacea for social ills; no simple formulas existed for dealing with adolescents—or with any phase of childhood. The recognition of children and their rights had brought new problems to replace the old.

With children no longer a particular asset to the family income, family size decreased, and there came a greater concern for those who were born. In the early decades of the century, medical assistance, along with better social services, raised standards of child care considerably. Along with attention to the child's physical health came concern for his mental well-being. Gradually the working classes began to press for a national system of education that had real worth and one in which they could play an important role. The first reform was the Education Act of 1918 which finally abolished fees for attendance at all elementary schools and raised the school-leaving age to fourteen. By the 1940s subsequent education and welfare legislation had brought needed reforms that finally, after hundreds of years, allowed British children of all classes to climb the "educational ladder." By World War II what had been the traditional privilege of the few had become the right of the masses.

In America, too, the rights of children were undergoing numerous changes at the turn of the century. Parents heard from all quarters that there were no absolute moral and behavioral standards to uphold and no absolute procedures to follow. In short, all children were different. Kate Douglas Wiggin in *Children's Rights* (1892) summed up the spirit of the time by pointing out that it was up to the parents to recognize the problems of childhood and deal with them according to their best knowledge. The child was not naturally depraved, but indeed had a sense of right and wrong and needed only "gentle guidance." She warned against "overmoralizing" the child. What he needed, she said, were right parental examples and "right mental conditions" in the home and school; and parents must not expect the child to be precocious intellectually or morally. The only way to educate children properly was to awaken their sensibility.

Charlotte Perkins Gilman, editor of *Childhood Magazine,* acknowledged that parents were confused because of the rapidly changing social conditions of the time (increase in wealth, imitation of supposed excellence in other nations, conflicting ideas on child rearing, and so on); she advocated that parents take on a new spirit of understanding the child by facing the facts that psychology had revealed. The Victorian ideal of children being "seen and not heard" no longer had meaning. Children of such homes, she said, were caricatures and lived unwholesome lives. In *Childhood,* Mrs. Birney said further that parents must balance obedience to the "universal laws" of the child's behavior with respect for the individual child, all part of the infinite plan of life.

Even conservative writers argued against excessive restraint and warned against too many "don'ts." Thus, American children, even the poor, by the beginning of the century were beginning to feel a lifting of bonds and confinements.

Like their English counterparts, American children had also worked in factories in the nineteenth century, as many as 100,000 in New York in 1873. And their homes were squalid tenements. When Jacob A. Riis's *The Children of the Poor* (1892) pointed out the exploitation of American children, journalists and social workers took up the cause. Although compulsory education laws already existed, child labor laws banning the employment of boys and girls had to be passed in order to abolish the system. By the 1920s most states had such laws. Although this legislation brought more humane treatment to children, poor families, as in England, were seriously affected by the reduced family income.

When social workers such as Jane Addams and Lillian Wald told the stories of the lives of slum children, the comfortable classes listened, sometimes in horror. Although confused and condescending at first, most Americans eventually believed the child savers and tried diligently to help. As in England, boys' clubs and other organizations designed for youth were viewed as splendid means to aid slum children by showing them alternatives; for immigrant children, they seemed the way to "Americanize" them.

Education, along with social welfare agencies, was also taking new directions. At the turn of the century, the National Education Association, which had been founded in 1857, was rapidly expanding. Teacher training institutions were increasing: in 1880 there had been 80 normal schools in the United States; by 1900 there were 264. Many experimental schools, along with the recently introduced kindergarten and the high school, would soon establish a nationwide educational system. Until 1900, American education had been conservative and interested only in teaching certain subjects. (It has been estimated that only 10 percent of American children had high school training.) After 1900, new educational theory provided for additional subjects (drawing, music, nature study, manual training, domestic science, gardening, and others). Such curricula revealed a rethinking about the role of the school in society and about the relationships between teachers and students.

Thus, with the emancipation of the child had come the emancipation of the school. Although new and old studies sometimes conflicted, changes in curricula came surprisingly quickly. Parents and teachers were generally eager to take on the new ways, since new methods did not disclaim the old ideal of character building, but rather took on the forming of character and good citizenship as their prime targets. Although it was more difficult to teach under the new "softening," children were admonished to do the "right thing" not out of fear of being punished, but as it related to their own interests and activities. Teachers, especially kindergarten teachers, were seen as surrogate parents and were respected accordingly. That they must be expert in their subject matter and knowledge of children was expected. Discipline was no longer based on the rod, but on humane recognition of the child's particular needs and the adult's knowledge of how best to deal with them.

The new ideas about education were borrowed from Thomas Jefferson's belief in the educability of all who possessed enough intelligence to take part in the social process and Horace Mann's belief that poverty, crime, bigotry, and selfishness would disappear if enough educational opportunities were made available. John Dewey, their intellectual heir, added the belief that the right environment, developed intelligently by those who cared, had to be part of the educational process. Dewey and his followers, therefore, devoted their attention to developing the school as a social institution. "Socializing" the child became the leading concept in American education and child rearing. Although generally accepted, the takeover was not without criticism.

Some critics said that such education was "spoonfeeding" and could only bring about laziness and dropping standards. Others said that the new education neglected difficult and demanding tasks and therefore was dishonest in its preparation of students for life. Against this latter charge defenders proclaimed that too much work was cruel; that school pressures, especially on the very young, produced "brain fag" which ultimately undid whatever good education might bring.

William James's *Talks to Teachers* (1900) summed up the situation and brought some calm to the great debate. He pointed out that the new freedom in education held great promise, but there were factors to be watched carefully. Foremost among them was the quality of the teacher and his or her knowledge and sensitivities. One must also acknowledge that not all learning could be exciting, some things by their nature were dull; that competition for grades seemed to be necessary and should not be eliminated thoughtlessly; that not all learning was interesting, but good teachers could challenge the students regardless; and that real character was formed on scruples, the surest way to build security. The new education then was not entirely "new" in that moral development was an important part of its base, but it was an approach far different from what any previous child, American or otherwise, had known before.

Even with improved and compulsory education, some American youth tended to be independent. From colonial days they had often "cut loose" from their homes, sometimes as early as age thirteen. Now with the new child labor laws prohibiting their work in factories and the like, even more youth joined gangs or became tramps, traveling salesmen, circus roustabouts, evangelists, and so on. Some ended up as vagrants or in prisons, missions, and reformatories. Girls too grew restless; many moved out of their homes and neighborhoods to become clerks, servants, dancers, and actresses; some ended up as beggars and streetwalkers, even prisoners.

Learning from experience was still considered desirable. Many of America's richest men had climbed from apprenticeships to great wealth, with Henry Ford the most notable example. To be in the world of work was still extremely attractive. Some combined school and work by cutting schooling short to study for vocations part time while still enrolled in conventional schools.

Child rearing, like education, also had many voices. Parents were admonished to know what the child-study experts had discovered, although the evidence might be conflicting. Parents were above all to set examples and create a proper atmosphere in every situation. They were to establish steady control at home and work constantly for improved family relationships. And they were to provide religious training.

Since 1900 the notion of infant depravity had been almost totally abandoned. Somewhat guardedly at first, Christian theologians, mostly Protestants, had come to agree with psychologists that the child's will, instincts, interests, energies, and temperament were to be considered only as psychological phenomena without moral overtones. The child was not to be overly idealized as born innocent, but neither was he bad. His neutrality, in addition to the evolutionary theory that life moved from the simple to the complex, made it possible for many theologians to see the development of children as part of the divine plan. The child had only to want to better himself and thereby improve the human race. Protestants, while still believing that the child possessed an immortal soul and that he deserved to have his "divine spark" recognized, accepted these notions as metaphoric ways of describing the spiritual development of the child. In practice, they pursued moral and social improvements rather than theological concerns.

Religious training no longer meant frightening the child by reminding him of his sinfulness or his powerlessness; while heaven was not stressed, neither was the torment of hell. Instead, children were to infer that they had no inherited guilt; they were, in fact, taught that Christ had special concern for them and gave them His protection. It was only that the child's spirit needed development and that was what he must attend do. For such training, precepts and examples were felt to be better than revival meetings and the experience of conversion, which was considered by some authorities to be too shocking. To be religious meant to have self-mastery and self-esteem along with being responsible for others in the community; thus, both school and church admonished the child to be a good citizen. The Sunday school and its literature were almost entirely devoted to moral development; old concerns with the nature of God, meditation, and the reading of the Bible were no longer primary.

Sectarianism was declining. The child was taught to believe in the fatherhood of God and the brotherhood of man. Although children had prayer books designed for them, the prayers emphasized the love, not fear, of God and his son, Jesus Christ. While children frequently memorized Bible verses and prayers, they were usually short and often stressed the importance of love, mercy, faith—and good hygiene.

Although religion was not taught in public schools, some groups insisted that school children from eight to fourteen should read the Old Testament for its heroes, history, and so on, while adolescents should concentrate on Jesus's teachings. Objections to such Bible reading in the school came quickly from some non-Christians, but especially from those groups who feared that reading the Bible would bring about the discontent of Jews, Catholics, women, the poor, and the downtrodden.

While immigrant children had particular problems, no group had a greater need to learn new skills than blacks, 90 percent of whom still lived on small Southern farms at the beginning of World War I. When segregated education provided no hope of necessary help, humanitarians, such as Booker T. Washington, began to form institutions for the improvement of the lives of black young people. Native Americans, too, especially those who wanted to learn the white man's ways, were beginning to be educated, as were immigrant youths of every ethnic and national background.

Most of these young people sought training in the vocations. Subsequently, land-grant colleges, funded by the federal government, were established to provide training in agriculture and the technical arts. In addition to the vocations, some of these institutions offered education in forestry, journalism, teaching, engineering, nursing, and the like, and thus some lower class youth began to enter the professions.

But many problems remained; one of the most serious and far-reaching was prejudice. Jews, women, blacks, Native Americans, and sometimes Catholics were frequent victims of discrimination. And wealth was not always a saving factor. Even well-off young Jews, for example, in the early years of the century had trouble gaining entrance to some universities and, if admitted, had difficulty with social encounters.

Although restrictions based on religion, race, and sex tended to break down as the century progressed, prejudice on all levels of society was far from abolished in American life, with blacks being the most discriminated against—a situation which would not openly erupt until the 1960s.

The coming of the Great Depression in the 1930s followed by World War

II did not dramatically change attitudes toward or the treatment of children and youth in America. While unemployment in the early 1930s caused untold suffering for millions, relative prosperity had returned to many by 1937 and to most by World War II. After the Great Depression, however, more and more young people had begun to work for government and non-political agencies such as health, social welfare, and educational organizations, while work in agriculture and the handicrafts declined. With these changes came a loss of independence. Once anxious to "cut loose" from home and highly organized family lives, American youth from the 1940s on looked more and more to organizations—business, industry, government, and education—for fulfillment.

The New Deal which immediately followed the Depression tended to discredit aristocratic trends and attempted to give new value to egalitarianism through an array of social programs. Although at first viewed with suspicion, especially by the affluent, the federal government's new concern for the health and welfare of the young became widely accepted; as years passed, Americans took it for granted that government would provide children with a more positive life. The schooling of children to promote further equality and a better life was also expected, and educationists set out boldly to take on the reform of an increasingly pluralistic society; schools, as the transmitter of skills and knowledge, molded their products as needed, and education became popular as never before. The "normal" expectation for childen's school lives would be that the child go through a four-level system: the elementary school, the secondary school, college, and the professional school. But millions remained far from the so-called norm. Some, as of old, chose to "cut loose" and pursue careers outside academia, while blacks, Native Americans, and the poor were often so handicapped by poverty and prejudice that they could not cope with mainstream education.

By 1945, in spite of the cataclysmic struggle of World War II when millions of youth died, most American children were valued and far better off than ever before in the history of the human race. Government provided protective laws against exploitation and assault; social agencies watched over their welfare, protecting them, at least in part, even against their own parents if necessary; educational institutions and churches provided for their intellectual and religious development; and parents, as never before, were attentive.

Child rearing followed well-established modes, although many variations existed. But the responsibility of parents for their children's well-being was unquestioned. In spite of the Depression of the 1930s and the World War of the 1940s, mainstream American children were secure. It would be almost two decades before excluded children—blacks, Native Americans, those of ethnic origin, and the poor—would become targets of intense concern. The struggle for their rights would be long and arduous.

ANNOTATED CHRONOLOGY

1900

L. Frank Baum's *The Wizard of Oz* (the first of a famous series of stories, published in Chicago by Hill, which are said to be the first American fantasies; the author attempted to omit disagreeable incidents; illustrated by W. W. Denslow; the author's other work, published by Reilly and illustrated by John R. Neill except as noted, includes *The Best of Hamburgs,* Stoddard, 1886; *Mother Goose in Prose,* Way, 1897, illustrated by Maxfield Parrish; *By the Candalabra's Glare,* illustrated by W. W. Denslow, privately printed, 1898; *Father Goose, His Book,* illustrated by W. W. Denslow, Hill, 1899; *The Songs of Father Goose,* illustrated by W. W. Denslow, Hill, 1900; *Dot and Tot of Merryland,* illustrated by W. W. Denslow, Hill, 1901; *American Fairy Tales,* illustrated by Harry Kennedy, Ike Morgan, and N. P. Hall, Hill, 1901; *The Master Key, An Electrical Fairy Tale,* illustrated by Fanny Y. Cory, Bowen-Merrill, 1901; *The Life and Adventures of Santa Claus,* illustrated by Mary Cowles Clark, Bobbs, 1902; *The Enchanted Island of Yew whereon Prince Marvel Encountered the High Ki of Twi and Other Surprising People,* Bobbs, 1903; *The Surprising Adventures of the Magical Monarch of Mo and His People,* illustrated by Frank Ver Beck, Bobbs, 1903; *The Marvelous Land of Oz,* 1904; *Queen Zixi of Ix,* illustrated by Frederick Richardson, Century, 1905; *The Woggle-Bug Book*, illustrated by Ike Morgan, 1905; *John Dough and the Cherub,* 1906; *Father Goose's Year Book,* illustrated by Walter J. Enright, 1907; *Ozma of Oz,* 1907; *Baum's American Fairy Tales: Stories of Astonishing Adventures of American Boys and Girls with the Fairies of their Native Land,* illustrated by George Kerr, Bobbs, 1908; *Little Dorothy and the Wizard of Oz,* 1908; *The Road to Oz,* 1909; *The Emerald City of Oz,* 1910; *Juvenile Speaker,* illustrated by Neill and M. W. Enright, 1910; *Baum's Own Book for Children,* illustrated by Neill and M. W. Enright, 1911; *The Daring Twins,* illustrated by Pauline Batchelder, 1911; *The Sea Fairies,* 1911; *Phoebe Daring: A Story for Young Folks,* illustrated by J. P. Nuyttens, 1912; *Sky Island,* 1912; *The Little Wizard Series,* six volumes: *Jack Pumpkinhead and the Sawhorse, Little Dorothy and Toto, Ozma and the Little Wizard, The Cowardly Lion and the Hungry Tiger, The Scarecrow and the Tin Woodman, Tik-Tok and the Nome King,* 1913; *The Patchwork Girl of Oz,* 1913; *Tik-Tok of Oz,* 1914; *The Scarecrow of Oz,* 1915; *Rinkitink in Oz,* 1916; *Babes in Birdland,* illustrated by M. W. Enright, 1917; *The Lost Princess of Oz,* 1917; *Glinda of Oz,* 1918; *The Tin Woodman of Oz,* 1918; *The Magic of Oz,* 1919; *Glinda of Oz,* 1920; *Oz-Man Tales,* Neill, 1920; *Jaglon and the Tiger Fairies,* illustrated by Dale Ulrey, 1953; *The Visitors from Oz,* 1960; *Animal Fairy Tales,* the International Wizard of Oz Club, 1969; *A Kidnapped Santa Claus,* illustrated by Frederick Richardson, Bobbs, 1969;

under the pseudonym of Floyd Akers, the author wrote: *The Boy Fortune Hunters in Alaska,* illustrated by Howard Heath, 1908, *The Boy Fortune Hunters in Egypt,* illustrated by Emile Nelson, 1908, *The Boy Fortune Hunters in the Panama,* illustrated by Howard Heath, 1908, *The Boy Fortune Hunters in China,* 1909, *The Boy Fortune Hunters in the Yucatan,* 1910, *The Boy Fortune Hunters in the South Seas,* 1911; under the pseudonym of Laura Bancroft the author wrote: *The Twinkle Tales,* six volumes: *Bandit Jim Crow, Mr. Woodchuck, Prairie Dog Town, Prince Mud-Turtle, Sugar-Loaf Mountain, Twinkle's Enchantment,* illustrated by M. W. Enright, 1906, reissued in one volume titled *Twinkle Chubbins; Their Astonishing Adventures in Nature-Fairyland,* illustrated by M. W. Enright, 1911; *Policeman Bluejay,* illustrated by M. W. Enright, 1908; reissued in 1911 and 1917 as *Babes in Birdland;* under the pseudonym of Capt. Hugh Fitzgerald, the author wrote: *Sam Steele's Adventures on Land and Sea,* illustrated by Howard Heath, 1906; *Sam Steele's Adventures in Panama,* illustrated by Howard Heath, 1907; under the pseudonym of Suzanne Metcalf the author wrote *Annabel; A Novel for Young Folks,* illustrated by H. Putnam Hall, 1906; under the pseudonym of Edith Van Dyne the author wrote: *Aunt Jane's Nieces,* illustrated by Emile Nelson, 1906; *Aunt Jane's Nieces Abroad,* illustrated by Emile Nelson, 1906; *Aunt Jane's Nieces at Millville,* 1908; *Aunt Jane's Nieces At Work,* 1909; *Aunt Jane's Nieces in Society,* 1910; *Aunt Jane's Nieces and Uncle John,* 1911; *The Flying Girl,* illustrated by J. P. Nuyttens, 1911; *The Flying Girl and Her Chum,* illustrated by J. P. Nuyttens, 1912; *Aunt Jane's Nieces On Vacation,* 1912; *Aunt Jane's Nieces Out West,* 1914; *Aunt Jane's Nieces in the Red Cross,* 1915; *Mary Louise,* 1916; *Mary Louise in the Country,* 1916; *Aunt Jane's Nieces on the Ranch,* 1917; *Mary Louise Solves a Mystery,* 1917; *Mary Louise and the Liberty Girls,* 1917; *Mary Louise Adopts a Soldier,* 1919; additional Oz titles by other authors, but published by Reilly, include: Ruth Plumly Thompson's *The Royal Book of Oz,* 1921; *Kabumpo in Oz,* 1922; *The Cowardly Lion of Oz,* 1923; *Grampa in Oz,* 1924; *The Lost King in Oz,* 1925; *The Hungry Tiger in Oz,* 1926; *The Gnome King of Oz,* 1927; *The Giant Hope of Oz,* 1928; *Jack Pumpkinhead of Oz,* 1929; *The Yellow Knight of Oz,* 1930; *The Purple Prince of Oz,* 1932; *Ojo in Oz,* 1933; *Speedy in Oz,* 1934; *The Wishing Horse of Oz,* 1935; *Captain Salt in Oz,* 1936; *Handy Mandy in Oz,* 1937; *The Silver Princess in Oz,* 1938; *Ozoplanning with the Wizard of Oz,* 1939; John R. Neill's *The Wonder City of Oz,* 1940; *The Scalawagons of Oz,* 1940; *Lucky Bucky in Oz,* 1942; *Jack Snow's Magical Mimics in Oz,* illustrated by Frank Kramer, 1946; *The Shaggy Man of Oz,* illustrated by Frank Kramer, 1949; Rachel R. Cosgrove's *The Hidden Valley of Oz,* illustrated by "Dirk" [Dirk Gringuis], 1951; Eloise Jarvis McGraw's and Lauren McGraw Wagner's *Merry Go Round in Oz,* illustrated by Dick Martin, 1963; the author's son, Frank J. (Joslyn)

1900 *continued*

Baum, wrote *The Laughing Dragon of Oz,* illustrated by Milt Youngren, Whitman, 1934). CU, LC, NYPL-A, YU

Frank Gelett Burgess's *Goops and How to Be Them: A Manual of Manners for Polite Infants Inculcating Many Juvenile Virtues both by Precept and Example* (the first of a series of "Goop" books, etiquette books based on negative principles as demonstrated by the "goops," who are unmannerly, whimsical creatures; published in New York by F. A. Stokes, written in verse and illustrated by the author with ninety drawings; the author's other work includes *Vivette,* Copeland and Day, 1897; *The Goop Directory,* Stokes, 1913; *The Goop Encyclopedia,* Stokes, 1916; *New Goops,* Random, 1940; the author wrote the popular verse, "The Purple Cow," for his magazine *The Lark*, which he edited, 1895-1897). UMi

Katherine Pyle's *The Christmas Angel* (a seasonal story, published in Boston by Little, by the co-author of *The Wonder Clock;* the author's other work includes *The Rabbit Witch,* Dutton, 1897; *The Counterpane Fairy,* Dutton, 1898; *Stories in Prose and Verse,* American, 1899; *As the Goose Flies,* Little, 1901; *In the Green Forest,* Little, 1902; *Careless Jane and Other Tales,* Dutton, 1902; *Where the Wind Blows,* Russell, 1902; *Childhood,* Dutton, 1909; *Theodora,* Little, 1907; *Nancy Rutledge,* Little, 1906; *Once Upon a Time in Delaware,* Mercantile, 1911; *Fairy Tales from Many Lands,* Dutton, 1911; *Tales of Two Bunnies,* Dutton, 1913; *Six Little Ducklings,* Dodd, 1915; *Wonder Tales Retold,* Little, 1916; *Two Little Mice,* Dodd, 1917; *Mother's Nursery Tales,* Dutton, 1918; *Tales of Folk and Fairies,* Little, 1919; *Three Little Kittens,* Dodd, 1920; *Tales of Wonder and Magic,* Little, 1920; *Matilda and Other Tales,* Dutton, 1921; *Fairy Tales from Far and Near,* Little, 1922; *The Pearl Fairy Book,* Hutchinson, 1923; *The Black-Eyed Puppy,* Dutton, 1923; *Tales from Greek Mythology,* Lippincott, 1928; *Wonder Tales from Many Lands,* Harrap, 1928; *Tales from Norse Mythology,* Lippincott, 1930; *Charlemagne and His Knights,* Lippincott, 1932; *Heroic Tales from Greek Mythology,* Lippincott, 1934; *Heroic Tales from the Norse,* Lippincott, 1934).

1901

John Burnham's *Jack Ralston; or, The Outbreak of the Nauscopees: A Tale of Life in the Far Northeast of Canada* (an adventure story by Canadian author has a vividly realistic Canadian setting, but conventional plot and unconvincing characters; published in London by T. Nelson).

Ralph Connor's *The Man from Glengarry: A Tale of the Ottawa* (a Canadian author's account of pioneer days in Glengarry County, Ontario; published in Toronto by Westminster; a sequel, *Glengarry School Days: A Story of Early Days in Glengarry,* was published in Chicago by Revell, 1902; Ralph Connor is the pseudonym of Charles W. Gordon).

Alice Caldwell Hegan's *Mrs. Wiggs of the Cabbage Patch* (a popular story, published in New York by Century, about a poor Irish widow who brings her children up in an atmosphere of cheerfulness, hard work, and godliness; written in dialect; each chapter begins with a thought in verse form, such as "In the mud and scum of things / Something always, always sings!"; the author's full name is Alice Caldwell Hegan Rice; the author's other work includes *Captain June*, Century, 1907, and several adult novels).

Josephine Diebitsch Peary's *The Snow Baby* (a story, illustrated by the author, and published in New York by F. A. Stokes; appeared originally in *St. Nicholas* as "Ahnighito"; the author's other work includes *My Arctic Journal,* Longmans, 1893; *Children of the Arctic,* Stokes, 1903).

Beatrix Potter's *The Tale of Peter Rabbit* (the first of a series of twenty-three famous picture-story, miniature books exquisitely illustrated by the author; this British author-illustrator's other work, published by Warne, includes *The Tailor of Gloucester,* 1902; *The Tale of Squirrel Nutkin,* 1903; *The Tale of Benjamin Bunny,* 1904; *The Tale of Two Bad Mice,* 1904; *The Tale of Mrs. Twiggy-Winkle,* 1905; *The Pie and the Patty-pan,* 1905; *The Tale of Mr. Jeremy Fisher,* 1906; *The Story of a Fierce Bad Rabbit,* 1906; *The Story of Miss Moppet,* 1906; *The Tale of Tom Kitten,* 1907; *The Tale of Jemima Puddle-Duck,* 1908; *The Roly-Poly Pudding,* 1908, retitled *The Tale of Samuel Whiskers,* 1908; *The Tale of the Flopsy Bunnies,* 1909; *Ginger and Pickles,* 1909; *The Tale of Mrs. Tittlemouse,* 1910; *Peter Rabbit's Painting Book,* 1911; *The Tale of Timmy Tiptoes,* 1911; *The Tale of Mr. Tod,* 1912; *The Tale of Pigling Bland,* 1913; *Tom Kitten's Painting Book,* 1917; *Appley Dapply's Nursery Rhymes,* 1917; *The Tale of Johnny Town-Mouse,* 1917; *Cecily Parsley's Nursery Rhymes,* 1922; *Jemima Puddle-Duck's Painting Book,* 1925; *Peter Rabbit's Almanac for 1929,* 1928; *The Fairy Caravan,* 1929; *The Tale of Little Pig Robinson,* 1930; *Sister Anne,* 1932; *Wag-by-Wall,* The Horn Book, 1944; *The Tale of the Faithful Dove,* 1955). PFL, TPL

1902

Lady Gregory's *Cuchulain of Muirthemme: The Story of the Men of the Red Branch of Ulster* (translated from the Celtic; published in London by John Murray; the story of the Cuchulain, legendary Irish hero, written in poetic English with touches of the Irish idiom; the author's other work includes *Gods and Fighting Men,* Murray, 1904). NYPL-B, SIU

1902 *continued*

Walter de la Mare's *Songs of Childhood* (the first major collection of this British poet's distinguished poems for children, originally published under the pseudonym of Walter Ramel; the author's other work includes *The Three Mulla Mulgars,* Duckworth, 1910; *A Child's Day,* Constable, 1912; *Peacock Pie,* Constable, 1913; *Memoirs of a Midget,* Collins, 1921; *Down-Adown-Derry,* Constable, 1922; *Crossings: A Fairy Play,* Beaumont, 1923; *Come Hither,* Constable, 1923; *Broomsticks, and Other Tales,* Constable, 1925; *Miss Jemima,* Blackwell, 1925; *Told Again,* Blackwell, 1927; *Stuff and Nonsense,* Constable, 1927; *Lucy,* Blackwell, 1927; *Tom Tiddler's Ground*, Collins, 1931; *A Froward Child*, Faber, 1934; *The Nap and Other Stories,* London, 1936; *This Year, Next Year,* Faber, 1937; *The Lord Fish, and Other Stories,* Faber, 1933; *Animal Stories,* Faber, 1940; *The Picnic and Other Stories,* London, 1941; *Bells and Grass,* Faber, 1941; *Mr. Bumps and His Monkey,* Lathrop, 1942; *The Magic Jacket and Other Stories,* Faber, 1943; *The Scarecrow and Other Stories,* Faber, 1945; *Collected Stories for Children,* Faber, 1946, was awarded the Carnegie Medal, 1947, which is the British equivalent of the Newbery Medal, given annually since 1936 for a children's book of outstanding merit written by a British subject; *Snow-White*, illustrated by D. Walsh, Hulton, 1952; *Cinderella*, illustrated by Ionicus, Hulton, 1952). TUL

Henry Augustus Shute's *The Real Diary of a Real Boy* (the first of a series of books attempting to capture the real thoughts and activities of children; published in Boston by Everett Press; the author's other work includes a sequel, *Sequil, or Things Which Ain't Finished in the First,* Everett, 1904; *Real Boys,* Donahue, 1905; *Plupy,* Grosset, 1910; *Misadventures of Three Good Boys,* Houghton, 1914; *The Lad with the Downy Chin,* Houghton, 1917; *Brite and Fair,* Cosmopolitan, 1918; *Plupy, the Wirst Yet,* Dorrance, 1929).

1903

Andy Adams's *The Log of a Cowboy: A Narrative of the Old Trail Days* (one of author's several books dealing with Texas cowboy life; illustrated by E. Boyd Smith; the author's other work, published by Houghton except as noted, includes *A Texas Matchmaker*, 1904; *The Outlet*, 1905; *Cattle Brands: A Collection of Western Campfire Stories,* 1906; *Reed Anthony, Cowman: An Autobiography,* 1907; *Wells Brothers: The Young Cattle Kings,* 1911; *The Ranch on the Beaver: A Sequel to "The Wells Brothers,"* 1927; *Why the Chisholm Trail Forks, and Other Tales of the Cattle Country,* 1956; *Trail Drive: A True Narrative of Cowboy Life from Andy Adams' "Log of a Cowboy" edited and illustrated by Glen Rounds,* Holiday House, 1965).

J. M. Barrie's *Peter Pan; or, The Boy Who Would Not Grow Up* (a play produced in London at the Duke of York Theatre and based on an excerpt from the author's book, *Tommy and Grizel,* Cassell, 1900, and the play *The Little White Bird; or, Adventures in Kensington Gardens,* Scribner, 1902, and published by Scribner in novel form in 1928; the author's other work includes *Peter Pan in Kensington Gardens,* illustrated by Arthur Rackham, Scribner, 1906; a narrative version of the play *Peter Pan, Peter Pan and Wendy,* Scribner, 1911, and *Peter Pan: An Afterthought,* or *When Wendy Grew Up,* a play produced in 1908 and later published in prose as *When Wendy Grew Up: An Afterthought,* Nelson, 1957; numerous retellings, adaptations, and illustrated editions have been published). YU

L. Leslie Brooke's *Johnny Crow's Garden* (the first of three Johnny Crow picture books of nonsense verse; the author-illustrator's other work, published by Warne, includes *The Story of the Three Bears,* 1904; *The Story of the Three Pigs,* 1904; *The Golden Goose Book,* 1905; *Johnny Crow's Party,* 1907; *The Tailor and the Crow,* 1911; *Oranges and Lemons,* 1913; *The Man in the Moon,* 1914; *A Nursery Rhyme Picture Book,* 1914; *Ring O' Roses,* 1922; *A Nursery Rhyme Picture Book, No. 2,* 1922; *Little Bo-Peep,* 1922; *Johnny Crow's New Garden,* 1935; *Wee Willie Winkie,* n.d.; illustrated Grimm's *The House in the Wood,* 1910, and Edward Lear's *The Jumblies and Other Nonsense Verse,* 1954). TPL

Jack London's *Call of the Wild* (one of the first American animal adventure stories that realistically presents the relationship between man and dog; published in New York by Macmillan; appropriated by children; the author's other work includes *Sophie Sutherland,* n.p., 1893; *The Son of the Wolf,* Grosset, 1900; *The People of the Abyss,* Grosset, 1903; *The Sea-Wolf,* Grosset, 1904; *The Game,* Donahue, 1905; *White Fang,* Macmillan, 1905; *The Road,* Macmillan, 1907; *Martin Eden,* Grosset, 1909; *South Sea Tales,* Donahue, 1911; *The Cruise of the Snark,* Regent, 1911; *The Son of the Sun,* Grosset, 1912; *John Barleycorn,* Century, 1913; *The Abysmal Brute,* Century, 1913; *The Strength of the Strong,* Grosset, 1914). UCB

Frances Trego Montgomery's *Billy Whiskers; the Autobiography of a Goat* (the first of a series of books about an adventuresome goat; illustrated by W. H. Fry and published by Saalfield; the author's other work, published by Saalfield except as noted, includes *Billy Whiskers' Kids, or Day and Night,* 1903; *The Wonderful Electric Elephant,* 1903; *Billy Whiskers Jr.,* 1904; *On a Lark to the Planets,* 1904; *Christmas with Santa Claus,* 1905; *Frances and the Irrepressibles at Buena Vista Farm,* 1905; *Billy Whiskers' Friends,* Brewer, 1906; *Billy Whiskers Jr. and His Chums,* Brewer, 1907;

1903 *continued*

under the pseudonym of F. G. Wheeler, *Billy Whiskers' Travels,* 1907; *Santa Claus' Twin Brother,* Brewer, 1907; *Dogs and Puppies,* Barse, 1908; *Billy Whiskers' Grandchildren,* Brewer, 1909; *Billy Whiskers Kidnapped,* 1910; *Cats and Kits,* Barse, 1910; *Pigs and Piggies,* Barse, 1910; *Billy Whiskers in an Aeroplane,* 1912; *Cows and Calves,* Barse, 1912; under the pseudonym F. G. Wheeler, *Billy Whiskers At the Circus,* 1913; *Billy Whiskers in Panama,* 1914; *Billy Whiskers in the South,* 1917; *Zip, the Adventures of a Frisky Fox Terrier,* 1917; *Billy Whiskers in Camp,* 1918; *Billy Whiskers in France,* 1919; *Billy Whiskers' Adventures,* illustrated by Paul Hawthorne, 1920; *Billy Whiskers in the Movies,* 1921; *Billy Whiskers Out for Fun,* 1922; *Billy Whiskers' Frolics,* 1923; *Billy Whiskers At Home,* illustrated by C. W. Frank and Frances Brundage, 1924; *Billy Whiskers' Pranks,* 1925; *Billy Whiskers in Mischief,* 1926).

Kate Douglas Wiggin's *Rebecca of Sunnybrook Farm* (a warm, farm-family story by the founder of the first free kindergarten on the Pacific Coast, 1878-1884; the author's other work, published by Houghton except as noted, includes a sequel of short stories about Rebecca, the *New Chronicles of Rebecca,* 1907, and a play based on both books, written with Charlotte Thompson: *Rebecca of Sunnybrook Farm: A State o' Maine Play,* French, 1932; *The Story of Patsy; A Reminiscence,* 1883; *The Birds' Christmas Carol,* 1887, and as a play, written with Helen Ingersoll, *The Birds' Christmas Carol,* 1914; *A Summer in a Canyon: A California Story,* 1889; with Nora Archibald Smith, *The Story Hour: A Book for Home and Kindergarten,* 1890; *Timothy's Quest: A Story for Anybody, Young or Old, Who Cares to Read It,* 1890, excerpt from *Timothy's Quest,* published as *Finding A Home,* 1907; *Polly Oliver's Problem: A Story for Girls,* 1893; *The Village Watch-Tower,* 1895; *Nine Love-Songs and a Carol,* 1896; *Marm Lisa,* 1896; *The Diary of a Goose Girl,* 1902; *Half-a-Dozen Housekeepers: A Story for Girls, in Half-a-Dozen Chapters,* Altmus, 1903; *Rose o' the River,* 1905; *The Flag-Raising,* 1907; *The Old Peabody Pew: A Christmas Romance of a Country Church,* 1907; *Susanna and Sue,* 1909; *Homespun Tales: Rose o' the River, The Old Peabody Pew, and Susanna and Sue,* 1909; *Mother Carey's Chickens,* 1911; *The Story of Waitstill Baxter,* 1913; *The Romance of a Christmas Card,* 1916; *Creeping Jenny, and Other New England Stories,* 1924; the author also edited, with her sister Nora A. Smith, *The Golden Numbers: A Book of Verse for Youth,* McClure, 1902; *The Posy Ring: A Book of Verse for Children,* 1903, McClure, reprinted as *Poems Every Child Should Know,* McClure, 1942; *The Fairy Ring,* McClure, 1906, reprinted as *Fairy Stories Every Child Should Know,* McClure, 1942; *Pinafore Palace: A Book of Rhymes for the Nursery,* McClure, 1907; *Magic Casements,* McClure, 1907; *Tales of Laughter: A Third Fairy Book,* McClure, 1908, reprinted as *Tales of Laughter Every Child Should Know,* McClure,

1939; *Arabian Nights: Their Best-Known Tales,* illustrated by Maxfield Parrish, Scribner, 1909; *Tales of Wonder: A Fourth Fairy Book,* Doubleday, 1909, reprinted as *Tales of Wonder Every Child Should Know,* Doubleday, ca. 1941; *An Hour with the Fairies,* Doubleday, 1911; *The Talking Beasts: A Book of Fable Wisdom,* Doubleday, 1911; *Twilight Stories: More Tales for the Story Hour,* 1925). BC

1904

William Frederick Cody's *The Adventures of Buffalo Bill* (a fictional account of the adventures of a colorful Western hero; published by Harper).

Dillon Wallace's *The Lure of the Labrador Wild* (an account of the author's experiences on an expedition to Labrador; published in Chicago by F. Revell; the author's other work includes *Ungava Bob,* F. Revell, 1907; *The Gaunt Gray Wolf,* Fleming and Revell, 1914; and *Grit-a-Plenty,* Fleming and Revell, 1918).

1906

Angela Brazil's *The Fortunes of Philippa* (the first of the author's many popular girl's school stories; published by Blackie; the author's other work, published by Blackie except as noted, includes *A Terrible Tomboy,* Gay and Bird, 1904; *The Third Class at Miss Kaye's,* 1908; *Bosom Friends: A Seaside Story,* Nelson, 1909; *The Nicest Girl in the School,* 1909; *The Manor House School,* 1910; *A Fourth Form Friendship,* 1911; *The New Girl at St. Chad's,* 1911; *A Pair of Schoolgirls,* 1912; *The Leader of the Lower School,* 1913; *The Youngest Girl in the Fifth,* 1913; *The Girls of St. Cyprian's,* 1914; *The School by the Sea,* 1914; *The Jolliest Term on Record,* 1915; *For the Sake of the School,* 1915; *The Luckiest Girl in the School,* 1916; *The Madcap of the School,* 1917; *The Slap-Bang Boys,* Nelson, 1917; *A Patriotic Schoolgirl,* 1918; *For the School Colours,* 1918; *A Harum-Scarum Schoolgirl,* 1919; *The Head Girl at The Gables,* 1919; *Two Little Scamps and a Puppy,* Nelson, 1919; *A Gift from the Sea,* Nelson, 1920; *Loyal to the School,* 1920; *A Popular Schoolgirl,* 1920; *The Princess of the School,* 1920; *A Fortunate Term,* 1921; *Monitress Merle,* 1922; *The School in the South,* 1922; *The Khaki Boys and Other Stories,* Nelson, 1923; *Schoolgirl Kitty,* 1923; *Captain Peggie,* 1924; *Joan's Best Chum,* 1926; *Queen of the Dormitory and Other Stories,* Cassell, 1926; *Ruth of St. Ronan's,* 1927; *At School with Rachel,* 1928; *St. Catherine's College,* 1929; *The Little Green School,* 1931; *Nesta's New School,* 1932, republished as *Amanda's New School,* Armada, 1970; *Jean's Golden Term,* 1934; *The School at The Turrets,* 1935; *An Exciting Term,* 1936; *Jill's Jolliest School,* 1937; *The School on the Cliff,* 1938; *The School on the Moor,* 1939; *The New School at Scawdale,* 1940; *Five Jolly Schoolgirls,* 1941; *The Mystery of the Moated Grange,*

1906 *continued*

1942; *The Secret of the Border Castle,* 1943; *The School in the Forest,* 1944; *Three Terms at Uplands,* 1945; *The School on the Loch,* 1946).

Edgar Rice Burroughs's *Tarzan of the Apes* (one of a popular series of stories about a jungle hero, Tarzan, invented by the author; published in New York by McClurg; the author's other work includes *Tarzan of the Apes,* McClurg, 1914; *Beasts of Tarzan,* McClurg, 1915; *A Princess of Mars,* McClurg, 1917; *The Son of Tarzan,* McClurg, 1917; *The Son of Tarzan,* McClurg, 1917; *The Gods of Mars,* McClurg, 1918; *Tarzan and the Jewels of Opar,* McClurg, 1918; *Jungle Tales of Tarzan,* McClurg, 1919; *The Warlord of Mars,* McClurg, 1919; *Tarzan the Untamed,* McClurg, 1920; *Thuvia, Maid of Mars,* McClurg, 1920; *The Mucker,* McClurg, 1921; *Tarzan the Terrible,* McClurg, 1921; *At the Earth's Core,* McClurg, 1922; *The Chessmen of Mars,* McClurg, 1922; *The Girl from Hollywood,* Macaulay, 1923; *Pellucidar,* McClurg, 1923; *Tarzan and the Golden Lion,* McClurg, 1923; *The Land that Time Forgot,* McClurg, 1924; *Tarzan and the Ant Men,* McClurg, 1924; *The Bandit of Hell's Bend,* McClurg, 1925; *The Cave Girl,* McClurg, 1925; *The Eternal Lover,* McClurg, 1925; *The Mad King,* McClurg, 1926; *The Moon Maid,* McClurg, 1926; *The Outlaw of Torn,* McClurg, 1927; *The Tarzan Twins,* Volland, 1927; *The War Chief,* McClurg, 1927; *The Master Mind of Mars,* McClurg, 1928; *The Monster Men,* McClurg, 1929; *Tarzan and the Lost Empire,* Grosset, 1929; *Tanar of Pellucidar,* Grosset, 1930; *Tarzan At the Earth's Core,* Grosset, 1930; *A Fighting Man of Mars,* Burroughs, 1931; *Tarzan the Invincible,* Burroughs, 1931; *Jungle Girl,* Burroughs, 1932; *Tarzan Triumphant,* Burroughs, 1932; *Apache Devil,* Burroughs, 1933; *Tarzan and the City of Gold,* Burroughs, 1933; *Pirates of Venus,* Burroughs, 1934; *Tarzan and the Lion Man,* Burroughs, 1934; *Lost on Venus,* Burroughs, 1935; *Tarzan and the Leopard Men,* Burroughs, 1935; *Swords of Mars,* Burroughs, 1936; *Tarzan and the Tarzan Twins with Jad-Bal-Ja, the Golden Lion,* Whitman, 1936; *Tarzan's Quest,* Burroughs, 1936; *Back To the Stone Age,* Burroughs, 1937; *The Oakdale Affair; The Rider,* Burroughs, 1937; *The Lad and the Lion,* Burroughs, 1938; *Tarzan and the Forbidden City,* Burroughs, 1938; *Tarzan's Revenge,* Whitman, 1938; *Carson of Venus,* Burroughs, 1939; *Tarzan the Magnificent,* Burroughs, 1939; *The Deputy Sheriff of Comanche County,* Burroughs, 1940; *Synthetic Men of Mars,* Burroughs, 1940; *Land of Terror,* Burroughs, 1944; *Escape on Venus,* Burroughs, 1946; *Tarzan and "The Foreign Legion,"* Burroughs, 1947; *Llana of Gathol,* Burroughs, 1948). LC, PLC, UMi

Norman Duncan's *The Adventures of Billy Topsail* (the first of a series of sea stories about the son of a Newfoundland deep-sea fisherman set at the beginning of the twentieth century; published in New York by Revell).

1907

Louis Maurice Boutet de Monvel's *Joan of Arc* (the well-known story of France's heroine, retold with illustrations done in the typical de Monvel manner; French edition published in 1897; published in English by Century; the author-illustrator's use of pastels, sometimes touched with gold, is also found in his interpretation of Anatole France's *Our Children,* first published in French in 1886; Anatole France is the pseudonym of Jacques Anatole Thibault). NYPL

Selma Lagerlöf's *The Wonderful Adventures of Nils* (translated from the Swedish by Velma S. Howard; illustrated by Mary Hamilton Frye; published in New York by Doubleday, Page; reveals the spirit of Sweden, but suggests the universality of man; originally commissioned as a textbook for Swedish children).

Charles Robinson's *Black Bunnies* (one of the well-known illustrator's books for very young children; the author-illustrator's other work includes *Aesop's Fables,* 1895; *Christmas Dreams,* under the pseudonym of Awfly Weirdly, 1896; *Ten Little Babies,* S.P.C.K., 1905; *Fanciful Fowls,* Dent, 1906; *Peculiar Piggies,* Dent, 1906; *Black Doggies,* Blackie, 1907; *Black Sambos,* Blackie, 1906, *Mother Goose Rhymes,* 1928; and illustrations for Stevenson's *A Child's Garden of Verses,* 1895; Rand's *Lilliput Lyrics,* 1898; *Fairy Tales from Hans Christian Andersen,* with brothers Thomas and William Heath Robinson, 1899; Perrault's *Tales of Passed Times,* 1900; the Lambs' *Stories for Children,* with W. Green, 1902; Jerrold's *The Big Book of Nursery Rhymes,* 1903; Carroll's *Alice's Adventures in Wonderland,* 1907; Burnett's *The Secret Garden,* 1911; Blake's *Songs of Innocence,* with Mary Robinson, 1912; Wilde's *The Happy Prince,* 1913; Irving's *Rip Van Winkle,* 1915; Milne's *Once on a Time,* 1925).

1908

Walter Camp's *The Substitute: A Football Story* (one of several football stories by "The Father of American Football," who rewrote football rules for safety and fair play; the author's other work, published in New York by Appleton, includes *Jack Hall at Yale: A Football Story,* 1909; *Old Ryerson,* 1911; *Danny Fists,* 1913; *Captain Danny,* 1914; *Danny the Freshman,* 1915; and numerous informational books on sports and games).

Kenneth Grahame's *The Wind in the Willows* (a British animal fantasy published in London by Methuen; well-known illustrated editions by E. H. Shepard, 1933 and 1960, and Arthur Rackham, 1940; the author's other work includes the introduction to *A Hundred Fables of Aesop,* collected by

1908 *continued*

Roger L'Estrange, Dodd, 1898; *Dream Days,* Lane, 1899; *The Golden Age,* illustrated by Maxfield Parrish, Stone and Kimball, 1900; *Bertie's Escapade,* Lippincott, 1949, reissued in 1977; the author served as editor for *The Cambridge Book of Poetry for Children,* Cambridge, 1916). UOx

Emerson Hough's *The Young Alaskans* (a four-volume series describing the life of two young boys in the Alaskan wilderness; published in New York by Harper; the author's other work includes *The Story of the Cowboys,* Appleton, 1897; *The Mississippi Bubble,* Grosset, 1902; *The Law of the Land,* Grosset, 1904; *The Sowing,* n.p., 1909; *The Magnificent Adventure,* 1916; *The Man Next Door,* Appleton, 1917; *The Passing of the Frontier,* Yale, 1918; *The Covered Wagon,* Grosset, 1922).

Nellie McClung's *Sowing Seeds in Danny* (an episodic account of twelve-year-old Pearlie Watson's life in Manitoba; similar to both the *Pollyanna* and *Elsie Dinsmore* books; published in New York by Doubleday).

L. M. Montgomery's *Anne of Green Gables* (a story about a young orphan girl, set in Prince Edward Island, Canada, illustrated by M. A. and W. A. J. Claus; published by Page; the sequels show Anne's growing up, her adulthood, and her children; *Anne of Avonlea,* Page, 1909; *Chronicles of Avonlea,* Page, 1912; *Anne of the Island,* Page, 1915; *Anne's House of Dreams,* Page, 1917; *Further Chronicles of Avonlea,* Page, 1920; *Anne of Windy Poplars,* Stokes, 1936; *Anne of Ingleside,* Stokes, 1939; the author's other work includes *Kilmeny of the Orchard,* Page, 1910; *The Story Girl,* Page, 1911; *The Golden Road,* Page, 1913; *Rainbow Valley,* Page, 1919; *Rilla of Ingleside,* Stokes, 1921; *Emily of New Moon,* Stokes, 1923; *Emily Climbs,* Stokes, 1925; *Emily's Quest,* Stokes, 1928; *Magic for Marigold,* Stokes, 1929; *Aunt Becky Began It,* Hodder, 1931; *A Tangled Web,* Stokes, 1931; *Mistress Pat,* Stokes, 1935; *Jane of Lantern Hill,* Stokes, 1937).

Peter Newell's *The Hole Book* (one of the author's books which features an alteration in format, in this case, a hole appears on every page and is incorporated into the illustration; the author was known as "the ink-blot man"; the author's other work includes *Topsys and Turvys,* Century, 1893; *The Slant Book,* Harper, 1910; *The Rocket Book,* Harper, 1912; the author also illustrated books for John Kendrick Bangs, Clifton Johnson, and Frank Stockton, as well as for *Harper's Weekly* and other magazines).

1909

Zane Grey's *The Lost Trail, A Story of Early Days in the Ohio Valley* (a popular "Western" appropriated by older children; published by Burt; the author's other work, published by Grosset except as noted, includes *Betty Zane*, 1903; *The Heritage of the Desert*, 1910; *Last of the Plainsmen*, 1911; *The Young Forester*, 1910; *The Young Lion Hunter*, Harper, 1911; *The Young Pitcher*, Harper, 1911; *Desert Gold*, 1912; *Ken Ward in the Jungle*, 1912; *Riders of the Purple Sage*, 1912; *The Light of Western Stars*, 1914; *The Lone Star Ranger*, 1915; *The Rainbow Trail*, 1915; *The Border Scouts*, 1918; *Raiders of Spanish Peaks*, 1918; *Majesty's Rancho*, 1920; *The Man of the Forest*, 1920; *The Red-Headed Outfield*, 1920; *The Mysterious Rider*, 1921; *The Day of the Beast*, 1922; *The Call of the Canyon*, 1925; *The Deer Stalker*, 1925; *The Thundering Herd*, 1925; *Don, the Story of a Lion Dog*, Harper, 1926; *Forlorn River*, 1927; *Fighting Caravans*, Harper, 1929; *Arizona Ames*, 1932; *The Drift Fence*, Harper, 1932; *The Roaring U.P. Trail*, 1932; *The Hash Knife Outfit*, 1933; *Code of the West*, Harper, 1934; *Knights of the Range*, 1936; *The Lost Wagon Train*, 1936; *An American Angler in Australia*, Harper, 1937; *King of the Royal Mounted and the Great Jewel Mystery*, Whitman, 1939; *King of the Royal Mounted*, Whitman, 1946; *King of the Royal Mounted and the Ghost Guns of Roaring River*, Whitman, 1946; *The Maverick Queen*, 1950; *The Dude Ranger*, Harper, 1951; *Captives of the Desert*, Harper, 1952; *Lost Pueblo*, 1954; *Black Mesa*, Harper, 1955). OHS

Gene Stratton Porter's *Girl of the Limberlost* (one of several popular "girls' novels," set in the great Limberlost Swamp of Indiana, which emphasizes the elements of nature; published in New York by Doubleday; the author's other work includes *The Song of the Cardinal*, Bobbs, 1902; *Freckles*, Grosset, 1904; *At the Foot of the Rainbow*, Grosset, 1908; *Birds of the Bible*, Grosset, 1909; *Music of the Wild*, Caton, 1910; *The Harvester*, Doubleday, 1911; *Laddie*, Grosset, 1913; *Michael O'Halloran*, Doubleday, 1915; *Friends in Feathers*, Doubleday, 1917; *The Keeper of the Bees*, Grosset, 1925; Gene is the nickname of Geneva Stratton Porter).

1910

Joseph Altsheler's *Horsemen of the Plains: A Story of the Great Cheyenne War* (one of the author's many popular books describing life on the frontier; illustrated by Charles Livingston Bull; published in New York by Macmillan; the author, noted for his coverage of great and meaningful periods of history, has been compared to James Fenimore Cooper; the author's other work, published by Appleton except as noted, includes *The Hidden Mine*, Tait, 1896; *The Sun of Saratoga: A Romance of Burgoyne's Surrender*, 1897; *A Soldier of Manhattan, and His Adventures at Ticonderoga and Quebec*, 1897; *The Herald of the West: An American Story of 1811-1815*, 1898; *The Rainbow of Gold*, Continental, 1898; *The Last Rebel*, Lippincott, 1900; *In Circling Camps: A Romance of the Civil War*, 1900; *In*

1910 *continued*

Hostile Red: A Romance of the Monmouth Campaign, Doubleday, 1900; *The Wilderness Road: A Romance of St. Clair's Defeat and Wayne's Victory,* 1901; *My Captive,* 1902; *Before the Dawn: A Story of the Fall of Richmond,* Doubleday, 1903; *Guthrie of the Times: A Story of Success,* illustrated by F. R. Gruger, Doubleday, 1904; *The Candidate: A Political Romance,* Harper, 1905; *The Young Trailers: A Story of Early Kentucky,* 1907; *The Forest Runners: A Story of the Great War Trail in Early Kentucky,* 1908; *The Recovery: A Story of Kentucky,* Lovell, 1908; *The Free Rangers: A Story of Early Days Along the Mississippi,* 1909; *The Last of the Chiefs: A Story of the Great Sioux War,* 1909; *The Riflemen of the Ohio: A Story of the Early Days Along "The Beautiful River,"* 1910; *The Quest of the Four: The Story of the Comanches and Buena Vista,* 1911; *The Scouts of the Valley: A Story of Wyoming and the Chemung,* 1911; *The Border Watch: A Story of the Great Chief's Last Stand,* 1912; *The Texan Star: The Story of a Great Fight for Liberty,* 1912; *Apache Gold,* 1913; *The Texan Scouts: A Story of the Alamo and Goliad,* 1913; *The Texan Triumph: A Romance of the San Jacinto Campaign,* 1913; *The Guns of Bull Run: A Story of the Civil War's Eve,* 1914; *The Guns of Shiloh: A Story of the Great Western Campaign,* 1914; *The Sword of Antietam: A Story of the Nation's Crisis,* illustrated by Charles L. Wrenn, 1914; *The Scouts of Stonewall: The Story of the Great Valley Campaign,* illustrated by Charles L. Wrenn, 1914; *The Forests of Swords: A Story of Paris and the Marne,* illustrated by Chalres L. Wrenn, 1915; *The Guns of Europe,* illustrated by Charles L. Wrenn, 1915; *The Rock of Chickamunga: A Story of the Western Crisis,* illustrated by Charles L. Wrenn, 1915; *The Hosts of the Air: The Story of a Quest in the Great War,* illustrated by Charles L. Wrenn, 1915; *The Star of Gettysburg: A Story of Southern High Tide,* illustrated by Charles L. Wrenn, 1915; *The Keepers of the Trail: A Story of the Great Woods,* illustrated by D. C. Hutchinson, 1916; *The Shades of the Wilderness: A Story of Lee's Great Stand,* illustrated by Charles L. Wrenn, 1916; *The Tree of Appomattox: A Story of the Civil War's Close,* illustrated by Charles L. Wrenn, 1916; *The Hunters of the Hills: A Story of the Great French and Indian War,* illustrated by D. C. Hutchinson, 1916; *The Eyes of the Woods: A Story of the Ancient Wilderness,* illustrated by D. C. Hutchinson, 1917; *The Rulers of the Lakes: A Story of George and Champlain,* illustrated by Charles L. Wrenn, 1917; *The Shadow of the North: A Story of Old New York and a Lost Campaign,* illustrated by Charles L. Wrenn, 1917; *The Great Sioux Trail: A Story of Mountain and Plain,* illustrated by Charles L. Wrenn, 1918; *The Lost Hunters: A Story of Wild Man and Great Beasts,* illustrated by Charles L. Wrenn, 1917; *The Masters of the Peaks: A Story of the Great North Woods,* 1918; *The Lords of the*

Wild: A Story of the Old New York Border, illustrated by Charles L. Wrenn, 1919; *The Sun of Quebec: A Story of a Great Crisis,* illustrated by Charles L. Wrenn, 1919). LC

Thornton Waldo Burgess's *Old Mother West Wind* (the first of a eight-volume series of popular books combining realism and fantasy in an attempt to explain natural phenomena; published in Boston by Little, Brown; illustrated by Harrison Cady; the author's other work, published by Little, Brown except as noted, includes *Mother West Wind's Children,* 1911; *The Boy Scouts of Woodcraft Camp,* Penn, 1921; *Mother West Wind's Animal Friends,* 1912; *The Adventures of Johnny Chuck,* 1913; *The Adventures of Reddy Fox,* 1913; *The Boy Scouts on Swift River,* Penn, 1913; *Mother West Wind's Neighbors,* 1913; *The Adventures of Jerry Muskrat,* 1914; *The Adventures of Mr. Mocker,* 1914; *The Adventures of Peter Cottontail,* 1914; *The Adventures of Unc' Billy Possum,* 1914; *The Boy Scouts on Lost Trail,* Penn, 1914; *The Adventures of Chatterer, the Red Squirrel,* 1915; *The Adventures of Danny Meadow Mouse,* 1915; *The Adventures of Grandfather Frog,* 1915; *The Adventures of Sammy Jay,* 1915; *The Boy Scouts in a Trapper's Camp,* Penn, 1915; *Mother West Wind "Why" Stories,* 1915; *The Adventures of Buster Bear,* 1916; *The Adventures of Old Man Coyote,* 1916; *The Adventures of Old Mr. Toad,* 1916; *The Adventures of Prickly Porky,* 1916; *Mother West Wind "How" Stories,* 1916; *Mother West Wind "When" Stories,* 1917; *The Adventures of Bobby Coon,* Little, 1918; *The Adventures of Jimmy Skunk,* Little, 1918; *Happy Jack,* 1918; *Mother West Wind "Where" Stories,* 1918; *The Adventures of Bob White,* 1919; *The Adventures of Ol' Mistah Buzzard,* 1919; *The Adventures of Poor Mrs. Quack,* 1919; *The Burgess Bird Book for Children,* 1919; *Mrs. Peter Rabbit,* 1919; *Bowser, the Hound,* 1920; *The Burgess Animal Book for Children,* 1920; *Old Granny Fox,* 1920; *Lightfoot the Deer,* 1921; *Tommy's Change of Heart,* 1921; *Tommy's Wishes Come True,* 1921; *Blacky the Crow,* 1922; *Whitefoot the Wood Mouse,* 1922; *The Burgess Flower Book for Children,* 1923; *Buster Bear's Twins,* 1923; *Billy Mink,* 1924; *Little Joe Otter,* 1925; *The Christmas Reindeer,* Macmillan, 1926; *Jerry Muskrat At Home,* 1926; *Cubby Bear Has a Mind of His Own,* Whitman, 1927; *Longlegs the Heron,* 1927; *Baby Possum's Queen Voyage,* Stoll, 1928; *Digger the Badger Decides To Stay,* Stoll, 1928; *Grandfather Frog Fools Farmer Brown's Boy,* Eggers, 1928; *Grandfather Frog Gets a Ride,* Stoll, 1928; *A Great Joke on Jimmy Skunk,* Stoll, 1928; *Happy Jack Squirrel Helps Unc' Billy,* Stoll, 1928; *The Neatness of Bobby Coon,* Stoll, 1928; *Peter Rabbit Learns to Use His New Coat,* Eggers, 1928; *Birds You Should Know,* 1933; *The Burgess Seashore Book for Children,* 1929; *The Wishing-Stone Stories,* 1924; *Tales from the Storyteller's House,* 1937;

1910 *continued*
The Big Thornton Burgess Storybook, Grosset, 1937; *While the Story-log Burns,* 1937; *Bobby Coon's Mistake,* Platt, 1940; *Paddy's Surprise Visitor,* Platt, 1940; *Peter Rabbit Proves a Friend,* Platt, 1940; *Reddy Fox's Sudden Engagement,* Platt, 1940; *A Robber Meets His Match,* Platt, 1940; *Young Flash the Deer,* Platt, 1940; *Little Pete's Adventure,* McLoughlin, 1941; *Animal Stories,* Platt, 1942; *Little Chuck's Adventure,* McLoughlin, 1942; *Little Red's Adventure,* McLoughlin, 1942; *On the Green Meadows,* 1944; *At Smiling Pool, A Book of Nature Stories,* 1945; *The Crooked Little Path,* 1946; *The Dear Old Briar Patch,* 1947; *Along Laughing Brook,* 1949; *Baby Animal Stories,* Grosset, 1949; *A Thornton Burgess Picture Story Book,* Garden City, 1950; *At Paddy Beaver's Pond; A Book of Nature Stories,* 1950; *The Littlest Christmas Tree,* Wonder, 1954; *Peter Rabbit and Reddy Fox,* Wonder, 1954; *Aunt Sally's Friends in Fur,* 1955; *Stories Around the Year,* Grosset, 1955). LC, UWi

Eleanor Hull's *The Boy's Cuchulain: Heroic Legends of Ireland* (a collection of retellings of the Irish Cuchulain saga and related cycles of stories based on and faithful to a variety of important sources; published in New York by Crowell).

E. Boyd Smith's *Chicken World* (a sensitive picture book that presents an unusual theme and treatment of the subject: life in a chicken yard; published in New York by G. P. Putnam; the author-illustrator's other work includes *My Village,* Scribner, 1896; *The Story of Pocahontas and Captain John Smith,* Houghton, 1906; *The Story of Noah's Ark,* Houghton, 1909; *The Seashore Book,* Houghton, 1912; *The Railroad Book,* 1913; *In the Land of Make Believe,* Holt, 1916; *The Country Book,* Stokes, 1924; *So Long Ago,* Mifflin, 1944).

1911

John Masefield's *Jim Davis* (a poetic adventure story filled with the spirit of the Devon coast; published in London by Wells, Gardner and Darton; the author's other work includes *Martin Hyde: the Duke's Messenger,* Wells, 1910; *A Book of Discoveries,* Wells, 1910; *The Midnight Folk,* Heineman, 1927; *The Box of Delights,* Heinemann, 1935).

Lucy Fitch Perkins's *The Dutch Twins* (the first of a series of realistic stories about twins in other lands; published by Houghton, Mifflin; the author also wrote stories about twins living in different historical periods; the author's other work, published by Houghton except as noted, includes *Robin Hood,* Stokes, 1906; *The Twenty Best Fairy Tales of Andersen, Grimm and Miss Muloch,* Stokes, 1907; *A Book of Joys,* McClurg, 1907;

In Shakespeare's Day, 1907; *The Japanese Twins*, 1912; *The Irish Twins*, 1913; *The Eskimo Twins*, 1914; *The Mexican Twins*, 1915; *The Cave Twins*, 1916; *The Belgian Twins*, 1917; *The Spartan Twins*, 1918; *The French Twins*, 1918; *The Scotch Twins*, 1919; *Cornelia*, 1919; *The Italian Twins*, 1920; *The Puritan Twins*, 1921; *The Swiss Twins*, 1922; *The Filipino Twins*, 1923; *The Colonial Twins of Virginia*, 1920; *The American Twins of 1812*, 1925; *Mr. Chick, His Travels and Adventures*, 1926; *The American Twins of the American Revolution*, 1926; *The Pioneer Twins*, 1927; *The Farm Twins*, 1928; *Kit and Kat, More Adventures of the Dutch Twins*, 1929; *The Indian Twins*, 1930; *The Pickaninny Twins*, 1931; *The Norwegian Twins*, 1933; *The Spanish Twins*, 1934; *The Chinese Twins*, 1935). CCBC

Caroline Snedeker's *The Coward of Thermopylae* (republished in 1912 as *The Spartan*, first of a series of historical novels set in ancient times; published by Doubleday except as noted; the author's other work includes an American period piece, *Downright Denecy*, 1927; *Perilous Seat*, 1923; *Theras and His Town*, 1924; *Beckoning Road*, 1929; *The Black Arrowhead*, 1929; *The Town of the Fearless*, 1931; *Uncharted Ways*, 1935; *Forgotten Daughter*, 1933; *White Isle*, 1940; *Luke's Quest*, 1947; *Triumph for Flavius*, Lothrop, 1954; *Lysis Goes to the Play*, Lothrop, 1962).

1912

Mary Grant Bruce's *Mates At Billabong* (one of a series of popular books set in Australia and often referred to as the "Billabong Books"; published by Ward; the Australian author's other work, published by Ward Lock except as noted, includes *A Little Bush Maid*, 1910; *Mates at Billabong*, 1911; *Timothy in Bushland*, 1912; *Glen Eyre*, 1912; *Norah of Billabong*, 1913; *Gray's Hollow*, 1914; *From Billabong to London*, 1915; *Jim and Wally*, 1916; *'Possum*, 1917; *Dick*, 1918; *Captain Jim*, 1919; *Dick Lester of Kurrajong*, 1920; *Rossiter's Farm*, Whitcombe and Tombs, 1920; *Back to Billabong*, 1921; *The Cousin from Town*, Whitcombe and Tombs, 1922; *The Stone Axe of Burkamukk*, 1922; *The Twins of Emu Plains*, 1923; *Billabong's Daughter*, 1924; *The Houses of the Eagle*, 1925; *Hugh Stanford's Luck*, Cornstalk, 1925; *The Tower Rooms*, 1926; *Robin*, Cornstalk, 1926; *Billabong Adventurers*, 1927; *Anderson's Jo*, Cornstalk, 1927; *Golden Fiddles*, 1928; *The Happy Traveller*, 1929; *Bill of Billabong*, 1931; *Road to Adventure*, 1932; *Billabong's Luck*, 1933; *"Seahawk,"* 1934; *Wings above Billabong*, 1935; *Circus Ring*, 1936; *Billabong Gold*, 1937; *Told by Peter*, 1938; *Son of Billabong*, 1939; *Karalta*, Angus and Robertson, 1941; *Billabong Riders*, 1942).

Howard Garis's *Uncle Wiggly's Adventures* (one of a series of popular books featuring the adventures of a rabbit; illustrated by Lansing Campbell and published by Fenno; the author's other work includes *The King*

1912 *continued*

of Unadilla, Ogilvie, 1903; *Isle of Black Fire,* Lippincott, 1904; *The White Crystals,* Little, 1904; *From Office Boy to Reporter,* Chatterton, 1907; *Larry Dexter, Reporter,* Grosset, 1907; *Larry Dexter's Great Search,* Grosset, 1909; *Dick Hamilton's Cadet Days,* Grosset, 1910; *Dick Hamilton's Fortune,* Grosset, 1910; *Johnny and Billie Bushytail,* Fenno, 1910; *Those Smith Boys,* Fenno, 1910; *Dick Hamilton's Steam Yacht,* Goldsmith, 1911; *Dick Hamilton's Football Team,* Goldsmith, 1912; *The Island Boys,* Fenno, 1912; *Jackie and Peetie Bow Wow,* Fenno, 1912; *Larry Dexter and the Bank Mystery,* Grosset, 1912; *Larry Dexter and the Stolen Boy,* Grosset, 1912; *Lulu, Alice, and Jimmie Wibblewobble,* Fenno, 1912; *Those Smith Boys on the Diamond,* Fenno, 1912; *Three Little Trippertots,* Graham, 1912; *Three Little Trippertots on Their Travels,* Graham, 1912; *Buddy and Brighteyes Pigg,* Burt, 1913; *Camp Fire Girls on the Ice,* Fenno, 1913; *Camp Fire Girls,* Fenno, 1913; *Uncle Wiggly's Fortune,* Burt, 1913; *Uncle Wiggly Longears,* Fenno, 1915; *Buddy and Bawly No-Tail,* Fenno, 1915; *Daddy Takes Us Hunting Birds,* Fenno, 1916; *Uncle Wiggly and Mother Goose,* Fenno, 1916; *Jacko and Jumpo Kinky-tail,* Burt, 1917; *Uncle Wiggly in the Woods,* Burt, 1917; *The Venture Boys Afloat,* Harper, 1917; *The Curlytops at Uncle Frank's Ranch,* Cupples, 1918; *The Curlytops on Star Island,* Cupples, 1918; *The Curlytops Snowed In,* Cupples, 1928; *Uncle Wiggly and Alice in Wonderland,* Fenno, 1918; *Uncle Wiggly on the Farm,* Burt, 1918; *The Venture Boys in Camp,* Harper, 1918; *Toodle and Voodle Flat-Tale,* Burt, 1919; *Rick and Ruddy; the Story of a Boy and His Dog,* Milton Bradley, 1920; *Uncle Wiggly and Baby Bunty,* Burt, 1920; *Uncle Wiggly's Rheumatism,* Burt, 1920; *Rick and Ruddy in Camp,* Milton Bradley, 1921; *The Curlytops and Their Playmates,* Cupples, 1922; *Rick and Ruddy Afloat,* Milton Bradley, 1922; *Uncle Wiggly, Indian Hunter,* Graham, 1922; *Uncle Wiggly's Ice Cream Party,* Graham, 1922; *Uncle Wiggly's June Bug Friends,* Graham, 1922; *Uncle Wiggly's Silk Hat,* Graham, 1922; *Uncle Wiggly's Woodland Games,* Graham, 1922; *The Curlytops in the Woods,* Cupples, 1923; *Rick and Ruddy Out West,* Milton Bradley, 1923; *The Adventures of Uncle Wiggly, the Bunny Rabbit Gentleman with the Twinkling Pink Nose,* illustrated by Lansing Campbell, Newark, N.J., Graham, 1924; *The Curlytops at Sunset Beach,* Cupples, 1924; *Rick and Ruddy on the Trail,* Milton Bradley, 1924; *Two Wild Cherries in the Woods,* Milton Bradley, 1924; *Uncle Wiggly and the Pirates,* Graham, 1924; *Uncle Wiggly at the Beach,* Graham, 1924; *Uncle Wiggly Goes Swimming,* Graham, 1924; *Uncle Wiggly on Roller Skates,* Graham, 1924; *Uncle Wiggly on the Flying Rug,* Graham, 1924; *Uncle Wiggly's Funny Auto,* Graham, 1924; *The Curlytops Touring Around,* Cupples, 1925; *Tom Cardiff's Circus,* Milton Bradley, 1926; *Tom Cardiff in the Big Top,* Milton Bradley, 1927; *The Uncle Wiggly Book,* Appleton,

1927; *Uncle Wiggly's Water-Spout,* Graham, 1927; *The Curlytops Growing Up,* Cupples, 1928; *Tuftoo the Clown,* illustrated by James Daugherty, Appleton, 1928; *Buddy and His Winter Fun,* Cupples, 1929; *Buddy on the Farm,* Cupples, 1929; *Buddy in School,* Cupples, 1929; *Chad of Knob Hill,* Little, 1929; *Uncle Wiggly and the Alligator,* Graham, 1929; *Uncle Wiggly's Ice Boat,* Graham, 1929; *Uncle Wiggly's Make Believe Tarts,* Graham, 1929; *Uncle Wiggly's Rolling Hoop,* Graham, 1929; *Uncle Wiggly's Squirt Gun,* Graham, 1929; *Uncle Wiggly's Wash Tub Ship,* Graham, 1929; *The Bear Hunt,* McLoughlin, 1930; *Buddy and His Chum,* Cupples, 1930; *Buddy at Rainbow Lake,* Cupples, 1930; *The Face in the Dismal Cavern,* McLoughlin, 1930; *The Gypsy Camp,* McLoughlin, 1930; *Mystery Boys in Ghost Canyon,* Milton Bradley, 1930; *The Mystery of the Brass Bound Box,* McLoughlin, 1930; *On the Showman's Trail,* McLoughlin, 1930; *Uncle Wiggly's Bungalow,* Burt, 1930; *Buddy and His Flying Balloon,* Cupples, 1931; *Buddy at Pine Beach,* Cupples, 1931; *The Curlytops at Happy House,* Cupples, 1931; *Mystery Boys at Round Lake,* Milton Bradley, 1931; *Uncle Wiggly's Airship,* Platt, 1931; *Uncle Wiggly's Icicle Spear,* Graham, 1931; *Uncle Wiggly's Jumping Boots,* Graham, 1931; *Uncle Wiggly's Travels,* Burt, 1931; *Buddy on Mystery Mountain,* Cupples, 1932; *The Curlytops at the Circus,* Cupples, 1932; *Buddy on Floating Island,* Cupples, 1933; *Rocket Riders Across the Ice,* Burt, 1933; *Rocket Riders in Stormy Seas,* Burt, 1933; *Uncle Wiggly's Picnic Party,* Burt, 1933; *Buddy and the Secret Cave,* Cupples, 1934; *Rocket Riders in the Air,* Burt, 1934; *Buddy and His Cowboy Pal,* Cupples, 1935; *Buddy and the Indian Chief,* Cupples, 1936; *Teddy and the Mystery Dog,* Cupples, 1936; *Teddy and the Mystery Monkey,* Cupples, 1936; *Uncle Wiggly's Auto Sled,* Whitman, 1936; *Uncle Wiggly's Holidays,* Whitman, 1936; *Uncle Wiggly's Visit to the Farm,* Whitman, 1936; *Buddy and the Arrow Club,* Cupples, 1937; *Teddy and the Mystery Cat,* Cupples, 1937; *Uncle Wiggly's Surprises,* Blue Ribbon, 1937; *Buddy At Lost River,* Cupples, 1938; *Teddy and the Mystery Parrot,* Cupples, 1938; *Buddy on the Trail,* Cupples, 1939; *Teddy and the Mystery Pony,* Cupples, 1939; *Uncle Wiggly's Automobile,* Platt, 1939; *Buddy in Deep Valley,* Cupples, 1940; *Teddy and the Mystery Deer,* Cupples, 1940; *Uncle Wiggly in the Country,* Platt, 1940; *Uncle Wiggly's Picture Book,* illustrated by Lansing Campbell, Platt, 1940; *Buddy At Red Gate,* Cupples, 1941; *Teddy and the Mystery Goat,* Cupples, 1941; *Buddy in Dragon Swamp,* Cupples, 1942; *Uncle Wiggly and the Little Tails,* Platt, 1942; *Buddy's Victory Club,* 1943; *Buddy and the G-Man Mystery,* Cupples, 1944; *Buddy and His Fresh-Air Camp,* Cupples, 1947; *Uncle Wiggly's Happy Days,* Platt, 1947; *Uncle Wiggly & Jackie and Peetie Bow Wow,* Platt, 1952; *Uncle Wiggly and His Friends,* Platt, 1955; the author's wife, Lilian Garis, also wrote many popular "girls" books, published by Grosset except as noted: *The Girl Scout Pioneers,* Cupples, 1920; *The Girl Scouts At Sea*

1912 *continued*

Crest, Cupples, 1920; *The Girl Scouts at Rocky Ledge,* Cupples, 1922; *Gloria: A Girl and Her Dad,* 1923; *Joan,* 1924; *Joan's Garden of Adventure,* 1924; *Nancy Brandon: Enthusiast,* Milton Bradley, 1924; *Connie Loring's Ambition,* 1925; *Connie Loring's Dilemma,* 1925; *Nancy Brandon: Idealist,* Milton Bradley, 1925; *Nancy Brandon's Mystery,* Milton Bradley, 1925; *A Girl Called Ted,* 1929; *Ted and Tony: Two Girls of Today,* 1929; *Sally for Short,* 1930; *Sally Found Out,* 1930; *Judy Jordan,* 1931; *Judy Jordan's Discovery,* 1931; *The Forbidden Trail,* 1933; *The Ghost of Melody Lane,* 1933; *The Tower Secret,* 1933; *The Wild Warning,* 1934; *Terror at Moaning Cliff,* 1935; *Dragon of the Hills,* 1936; *The Mystery of Stingyman's Alley,* 1938; *The Secret of the Kashmir Shawl,* 1939; *The Hermit of Proud Hill,* 1940; authors wrote many Stratemeyer Syndicate books). UMi

William Heath Robinson's *Bill the Minder* (story written and illustrated by well-known British artist; published by Constable; author has illustrated Andersen's *Fairy Tales* with brothers, T. H. Robinson and Charles Robinson and de la Mare's *Peacock Pie;* author-illustrator's other work includes *Uncle Lubin,* Dutton, n.d.).

James Stephens's *The Crock of Gold* (a poetic prose fantasy by an Irish author and poet, published by Small; the author's other work includes *The Charwoman's Daughter [Mary, Mary],* Macmillan, 1912; *The Adventures of Seumas Beg,* Macmillan, 1915; *Green Branches,* 1916; *Deirdre,* 1923; *The Collected Poems of James Stephens,* Macmillan, 1926; *The Outcast,* Faber, 1929; *Kings and the Moon,* Macmillan, 1938).

Jean Webster's *Daddy-Long-Legs* (a popular story of an orphan girl which appeared originally as a serial in the *Ladies' Home Journal,* April to September 1912; published in New York by Grosset; the author's other work includes *When Patty Went to College,* Century, 1903; *The Wheat Princess,* Century, 1905; *Jerry Junior,* Grosset, 1907; *Much Ado About Peter,* Doubleday, 1909; *Just Patty,* Century, 1911).

Dikken Zwilgmeyer's *Johnny Blossom* (translated from the Norwegian by Emile Poulsson; published in Boston by Pilgrim Press; a warm family story set in Norway; the author's other work includes *What Happened to Inger Johanne,* Lothrop, 1919, one of a series of books about small-town life in Norway).

1913

Eleanor H. Porter's *Pollyana* (a popular story of an orphan who learns to live with two spinster aunts; published in Boston by Page; illustrated by

Stockton Mulford; the author's other work includes *Cross Currents,* Wilde, 1907; *Miss Billy,* Page, 1911; *The Story of Marco,* Burt, 1911; *Miss Billy-Married,* Page, 1914; *Pollyana Grows Up,* Page, 1915; *Just David,* Grosset, 1916; *Across the Years,* Houghton, 1919; *Dawn,* Houghton, 1919; *Mary Marie,* Houghton, 1920).

Arthur Rackham's *Mother Goose. The Old Nursery Rhymes* (a collection of traditional rhymes with ninety-eight illustrations by Rackham, published by Heinemann; the illustrator's other work includes *Some British Ballads,* Constable, 1919, and *The Allies' Fairy Book,* Heinemann, 1916; illustrations for Martineau's *Feats on the Fjord,* 1899; the Lambs' *Tales from Shakespeare,* 1899; Swift's *Gulliver's Travels,* 1900; the Grimms' *Fairy Tales,* 1900; Dana's *Two Years Before the Mast,* 1904; Irving's *Rip Van Winkle,* 1905; Barrie's *Peter Pan,* 1906; Kipling's *Puck of Pook's Hill,* 1906; Carroll's *Alice's Adventures in Wonderland,* 1907; *Aesop's Fables,* 1912; Dickens's *A Christmas Carol,* 1915; Malory's *The Romance of King Arthur and His Knights,* 1917; Steel's *English Fairy Tales,* 1918; Evans's *Cinderella,* 1919; Milton's Comus, 1921; Hawthorne's *The Wonder Book,* 1922; Bianco's *Poor Cecco,* 1925; Irving's *The Legend of Sleepy Hollow,* 1928; Moore's *The Night Before Christmas,* 1931; Ruskin's *The King of the Golden River,* 1932; Andersen's *Fairy Tales,* 1932; Rossetti's *Goblin Market,* 1933; Browning's *The Pied Piper of Hamelin,* 1934; Ibsen's *Peer Gynt,* 1936; Grahame's *The Wind in the Willows,* 1940). PFL

James Willard Schultz's *Sinopah, the Indian Boy* (a story based on the traditions and customs of the Pikuni tribe of the Blackfeet with whom the author lived for a time; illustrated by E. Boyd Smith; published in New York by Houghton; the author's other work, published by Houghton except as noted, includes *My Life As An Indian: The Story of a Red Woman and a White Man in the Lodges of the Blackfeet,* illustrated with photos by George Bird Grinnell, Doubleday, 1907; *With the Indians in the Rockies,* illustrated by George Varian, 1912; *The Quest of the Fish-Dog Skin,* illustrated by George Varian, 1913; *On the Warpath,* illustrated by George Varian, 1914; *Apauk, Caller of Buffalo,* 1916; *Blackfeet Tales of Glacier National Park,* 1916; *The Gold Cache,* illustrated by George Varian, 1917; *Bird Woman (Sacajawea), the Guide of Lewis and Clark,* 1918; *Lone Bull's Mistake: A Lodge Pole Chief Story,* illustrated by George Varian, 1918; *Rising Wolf, the White Blackfoot: Hugh Monroe's Story of His First Year on the Plains,* illustrated by Frank E. Schoonover, 1919; *Running Eagle, the Warrior Girl,* 1919; *The Dreadful River Cave: Chief Black Elk's Story,* illustrated by Harold Cue, 1920; *In the Great Apache Forest: The Story of a Lone Boy Scout,* 1920; *The War-Trail Fort: Further*

1913 *continued*

Adventures of Thomas Fox and Pitamakan, illustrated by George Varian, 1921; *Siezer of Eagles,* illustrated by F. E. Schoonover, 1922; *The Trail of the Spanish Horse,* illustrated by George Varian, 1922; *Friends of My Life as an Indian,* 1923; *Plumed Snake Medicine,* illustrated by Frank E. Schoonover, 1924; *Sahtaki and I,* 1924; *Questers of the Desert,* illustrated by Frank E. Schoonover, 1925; *William Jackson, Indian Scout: His True Story Told by His Friend,* 1926; *Signposts of Adventure: Glacier National Park As the Indians Know It,* 1926; *Sun Woman: A Novel,* 1926; *Red Crow's Brother: Hugh Monroe's Story of His Second Year on the Plains,* illustrated by F. E. Schoonover, 1927; *A Son of the Navahos,* 1927; *In Enemy Country,* 1928; *Skull Head the Terrible,* illustrated by F. E. Schoonover, 1929; *The Sun God's Children,* with Jessie Louise Donaldson, illustrated by Winold Reiss, 1930; *The White Beaver,* illustrated by Rodney Thompson, 1930; *Alder Gulch Gold,* illustrated by Albin Henning, 1931; *Friends and Foes in the Rockies,* illustrated by Stockton Mulford, 1933; *Gold Dust,* illustrated by Stockton Mulford, 1934; *The White Buffalo Robe,* illustrated by F. E. Schoonover, 1936; *Stained Gold,* illustrated by F. E. Schoonover, 1937; *Short Bow's Big Medicine,* illustrated by Stockton Mulford, 1940).

1914

George Bird Grinnell's *Wolf Hunters* (the story of three soldiers who spend a winter on the plains, hunting wolves; published in New York by Charles Scribner; the author's work includes records of certain Native American histories and collections of folk tales; the author was one of three of the first white men to explore Glacier National Park; the author's other work includes *Pawnee Hero Stories and Folk Tales,* Forest, 1889; *Blackfoot Lodge Tales,* Scribner, 1892; *The Story of the Indians,* Appleton, 1895; the *Jack* series, seven volumes, published by Stokes: *Jack the Young Ranchman,* 1899, *Jack Among the Indians,* 1900, *Jack in the Rockies,* 1904, *Jack the Young Canoeman,* 1906, *Jack the Young Trapper,* 1907, *Jack the Young Explorer,* 1908, *Jack the Young Cowboy,* 1913, *The Punishment of the Stingy and Other Indian Tales,* Harper, 1901; *Trails of the Pathfinders,* Scribner, 1911; *Beyond the Old Frontier,* Scribner, 1913; *Blackfeet Indian Stories,* Scribner, 1913; *By Cheyenne Campfires,* Yale, 1926; the author was the editor of *Forest and Stream* from 1876 to 1911).

Jessie Willcox Smith's *Little Mother Goose* (a popular American edition of the traditional Mother Goose rhymes; published in New York by Dodd; the illustrator's other work includes illustrations for well-known editions of Stevenson's *A Child's Garden of Verses,* 1905; Moore's *'Twas the Night Before Christmas,* 1912; Alcott's *Little Women,* 1915; Kingsley's *Water Babies,* 1916; Spyri's *Heidi,* 1922).

Booth Tarkington's *Penrod* (a popular, humorous story about a boy's adventures; illustrated by Gordon Grant; first appeared in short story form in *Everybody's, Saturday Evening Post,* and *Cosmopolitan;* a sequel was *Penrod and Sam,* 1916; author's other work, published by Doubleday except where noted, includes *Seventeen,* Harper, 1916; the author received two Pulitzer prizes for his adult novels, *The Magnificent Ambersons,* Grosset, 1918, and *Alice Adams,* 1921; the author also wrote many plays and illustrated James Whitcomb Riley's *The Boss Girl,* 1886). CoU, PU

1916

Padraic Colum's *The King of Ireland's Son* (the first of this Irish author's poetic stories; published in New York by Holt; illustrated by Willy Pogany; the author's other work, published by Macmillan except as noted, includes *The Boy Who Knew What the Birds Said,* 1918; *The Children of Odin,* 1920; *The Golden Fleece and the Heroes Who Lived Before Achilles,* 1921; *The Children Who Followed the Piper,* 1922; *Island of the Mighty,* 1924; *Forge in the Forest,* 1925; *Voyagers,* 1925; *The Children's Homer,* 1925; *Myths of the World,* Universal, 1930; *Big Tree of Bunlahy,* 1933; *The Arabian Nights: Tales of Wonder & Magnificence,* 1935; *The Legend of Saint Columba,* 1935; *A Treasury of Irish Folklore,* Crown, 1954; *Roofs of Gold, Poems to Read Aloud,* 1964; *The Stone Victory and Other Tales,* McGraw, 1966; *The Girl Who Sat by the Ashes,* 1968; *The Six Who Were Left in a Shoe,* 1968).

Edmund Dulac's *Edmund Dulac's Fairy-Book* (a collection of fairy tales of the allied nations, illustrated by Edmund Dulac; published by Hodder; this illustrator's other work includes illustrations for Arthur Quiller-Couch's *The Sleeping Beauty,* Hodder, 1910; Nathaniel Hawthorne's *Tanglewood Tales,* Hodder, 1919; *The Poetical Works of Edgar Allan Poe,* Doran, 1921; Charlotte Bronte's *Jane Eyre,* Dent, 1922; Charlotte Bronte's *Villette,* Dent, 1922; Emily Bronte's *Wuthering Heights,* Dent, 1922; *Stories from Hans Christian Andersen,* Doran, 1923; *A Fairy Garland,* Scribner, 1930; Robert Louis Stevenson's *Treasure Island,* Garden City, 1930).

Blanche Fisher Wright's *The Real Mother Goose* (a popular "classic" American illustrated edition of the traditional nursery rhymes; published in Chicago by Rand).

1917

Cecil Aldin's *The White Puppy Book* (a collection of the illustrator's pictures of dogs which are full of life and reflect each dog's basic nature;

1917 *continued*

published in London by Milford; the illustrator's other work includes *The Mongrel Puppy Book,* Frowde, 1912).

Dorothy Canfield's *Understood Betsy* (a story in which a sickly city girl becomes healthy and happy after living for a while on a Vermont farm with relatives; illustrated by Ada C. Williamson; published in New York by Holt after appearing serially in *St. Nicholas* from November 1916 to July 1917; the author's other work includes contributions to *What Shall We Do Now? Five Hundred Games and Pastimes,* Stokes, 1907; with Sarah Scott, *On a Rainy Day,* Barnes, 1938; *Tell Me A Story: A Book of Stories to Tell Children,* University, 1940; *Something Old, Something New: Stories of People Who Are America,* Scott, 1949; *Paul Revere and the Minute Men,* Random, 1950; *Our Independence and the Constitution,* Random, 1950; *A Fair World for All: The Meaning of the Declaration of Human Rights,* with a foreword by Eleanor Roosevelt, Whittlesey, 1952; *And Long Remember: Some Great Americans Who Have Helped Me,* Whittlesey, 1959; the author's married name was Dorothy Canfield Fisher).

Johnny Gruelle's *Raggedy Ann Stories* (a popular collection of episodic tales about the house adventures of a rag doll; published in Chicago by Donahue; written in memory of the author's daughter, Marcella, who died at age fourteen [the original Raggedy Ann doll belonged to the author's sister before being passed on to Marcella]; the author's other work, published by Volland except as noted, includes *The Travels of Timmy Toodles,* Martin, 1916; *My Very Own Fairy Stories,* 1917; *The Funny Little Book,* Donahue, 1917; *Friendly Fairies,* 1919; *Little Sunny Stories,* 1919; *The Little Brown Bear,* 1920; *Raggedy Andy Stories; Introducing the Brother of Raggedy Ann,* 1920; *Eddie Elephant,* 1921; *Orphant Annie Story Book,* Merrill, 1921; *Johnny Mouse and the Wishing Stick,* Bobbs-Merrill, 1922; *The Magic Land of Noom,* 1922; *Raggedy Ann and Andy and the Camel with the Wrinkled Knees,* 1924; *Raggedy Ann's Alphabet Book,* 1925; *Raggedy Ann's Wishing Pebble,* 1925; *Beloved Belindy,* 1926; *The Paper Dragon; A Raggedy Ann Adventure,* 1926; *Raggedy Ann's Magical Wishes,* 1927; *Wooden Willie,* 1927; *The Cheery Scarecrow,* Donahue, 1929; *Marcella Stories,* Donahue, 1929; *Raggedy Ann in the Deep, Deep Woods,* 1930; *Raggedy Ann's Sunny Songs, Words, and Drawings,* Miller, 1930; *Raggedy Ann in Cookieland,* New York, 1931; *Raggedy Ann and Raggedy Andy's Lucky Pennies,* 1932; *Raggedy Ann in the Golden Meadow,* Whitman, 1935; *Raggedy Ann and the Lefthanded Safety Pin,* Whitman, 1935; *Raggedy Ann and the Magic Book,* Gruelle, 1939; *Raggedy Ann and the Golden Butterfly,* Gruelle, 1940; *Raggedy Ann and the Hoppy Toad,* McLaughlin, 1940; *Raggedy Ann Helps Grandpa Hoppergrass,* McLaughlin,

1940; *Raggedy Ann Goes Sailing,* McLaughlin, 1941; *Raggedy Ann and the Nice Fat Policeman,* Gruelle, 1942; *Raggedy Ann and Andy,* Saalfield, 1944; *Raggedy Ann in the Snow White Castle,* Gruelle, 1946; *Raggedy Ann's Adventures,* Saalfield, 1947; *Raggedy Ann and the Slippery Slide,* Saalfield, 1947; *Raggedy Ann's Mystery,* Saalfield, 1947; *Raggedy Ann and Marcella's First Day At School,* Wonder, 1952; *Raggedy Ann's Merriest Christmas,* Wonder, 1952; *Raggedy Andy's Surprise,* Wonder, 1953; *Raggedy Ann's Tea Party,* Wonder, 1954; *Raggedy Ann and the Golden Ring,* Bobbs, 1961; *Raggedy Ann and the Happy Meadow,* Bobbs, 1962; *Raggedy Ann and the Hobby Horse,* Bobbs, 1961; *Raggedy Ann and the Wonderful Witch,* Bobbs, 1961; the earliest books were illustrated by the author; after the author-illustrator's death, his brother Justin Gruelle, and his son Worth Gruelle, along with others, wrote and illustrated the series). UMI

Henriette Willebeek Le Mair's *Old Dutch Nursery Rhymes* (a collection of Dutch rhymes which include "Our Baby Prince" and "The Little Sailor"; published by McKay; illustrated in the de Monvel manner; the artist's other work includes illustrations for R. H. Elkins's verses in *The Children's Corner,* McKay, 1915, and *Little People,* McKay, 1916; A. E. Moffat's books of songs, *Little Songs of Long Ago,* McKay, 1912, *Our Old Nursery Rhymes,* McKay, 1913? and *What Children Sing,* Augener, 1915; Robert Louis Stevenson's *A Child's Garden of Verses,* McKay, 1926).

1918

O. Henry's *The Ransome of Red Chief, and Other O. Henry Stories for Boys* (a collection of popular short stories edited by Franklin K. Mathiews and illustrated by Gordon Grant; the author's other work includes many short story collections: *Cabbages and Kings,* McClure, 1904; *Four Million,* which contains "The Gift of the Magi," New York, 1906; *Heart of the West,* McClure, 1907; *The Trimmed Lamp, and Other Stories of the Four Million,* which contains "The Last Leaf," Doubleday, 1907; *The Gentle Grafter,* New York, 1908; *The Voice of the City: Further Stories of the Four Million,* Doubleday, 1908; *Options,* Doubleday, 1909; *Roads of Destiny,* Doubleday, 1909; *Whirligigs,* Hodder, 1910; *Sixes and Sevens,* Doubleday, 1911; *Rolling Stones,* Doubleday, 1912; *Waifs and Strays: Twelve Stories,* Doubleday, 1917; O. Henry was the pseudonym of William Sydney Porter).

Norman Lindsay's *The Magic Pudding* (Australian author's fantasy about a pudding that is able to turn into a variety of substances and is pursued by professional pudding thieves; published by Angus and Robertson).

1919

Daisy Ashford's *The Young Visitors* (a novel about Victorian high society which was written while author was a child, but published in her adulthood; with an introduction by James Barrie; published in England by George Doran).

Olaf Baker's *Shasta of the Wolves* (the story of an Indian boy who was adopted by a wolf; published in New York by Dodd; the author's other work includes *Dusty Star,* Dodd, 1922, in which a wolf is adopted by a boy).

Parker Fillmore's *Czechoslovak Fairy Tales* (a retelling of tales which the author first heard in a Czech settlement in New York City; published in New York by Harcourt; the author's other work includes *The Hickory Limb,* Lane, 1910; *The Rosie World,* Holt, 1914; *The Shoemaker's Apron,* Harcourt, 1920; *The Laughing Prince,* Harcourt, 1921; *Mighty Mikko,* Harcourt, 1922; *The Wizard of the North,* Harcourt, 1923; *The Stuffed Parrot,* Harcourt, 1931; *The Shepard's Nosegay,* Harcourt, 1958, a collection of eighteen tales selected by Catherine Love from the author's three folktale collections).

Albert Payson Terhune's *Lad: A Dog* (a popular heroic animal story; published in New York by E. P. Dutton; the author's other work includes *The Fighter,* Lovell, 1909; *Bruce,* Dutton, 1920; *Buff: a Collie,* Doran, 1921; *Black Gold,* Doran, 1921; *Wolf,* Doran, 1924; *Treve,* Doran, 1924; *The Way of a Dog,* Harper, 1934; *A Book of Famous Dogs,* Doran, 1937).

1920

Hilda Conkling's *Poems by a Little Girl* (sensitive nature poems written by a ten-year-old child; published in New York by F. A. Stokes; the author's other work, *Shoes of the Wind,* Stokes, 1922, was written when author was twelve; the child's mother was the poet Grace Conkling).

Thomas W. Rolleston's *The High Deeds of Finn, and Other Bardic Romances* (a collection of Gaelic romances retold in poetic prose; published in New York by Crowell; the author's other work includes *Myths and Legends of the Celtic Race,* Crowell, 1911).

1921

William Alvin Bowen's *The Old Tobacco Shop* (the story of a young boy who hears wonderful and astounding stories from the owners of a tobacco shop; published in New York by Macmillan; runner-up for the Newbery Medal; the author's other work includes *The Enchanted Forest,* Macmillan, 1920; *Solario the Tailor, His Tales of the Magic Doublet,* Macmillan, 1922; *Merrimeg,* Macmillan, 1923; *Philip and the Faun,* Little, 1926).

Bernard G. Marshall's *Cedric the Forester* (a thirteenth-century story of the brave deeds of a lowly forester's son; runner-up for the Newbery Medal; the author's other work, published by Appleton, includes *The Torch Bearer,* 1923; *Walter of Tinerton,* 1923; *Redcoat and Minuteman,* 1924; *Old Hickory's Prisoner; A Tale of the Second War for Independence,* 1925).

Lucy Sprague Mitchell's *Here and Now Storybook* (a collection of "awareness" stories for very young children, published in New York by E. P. Dutton, which were designed to stimulate sensory motor responses; although the stories were formulistic, the "awareness" idea influenced many authors and illustrators; the author's other work includes *Horses Now and Long Ago,* Harcourt, 1926; *North America,* Macmillan, 1931; *Stories for Children Under Seven,* Day, 1933; *Boats and Bridges,* Day, 1933; *Manhattan Now and Long Ago,* Macmillan, 1934; *Another Here and Now Storybook,* Dutton, 1937; *The Red, White and Blue Auto,* Scott, 1943; *Farm and City,* Heath, 1944; *Guess What's In the Grass,* Scott, 1945; *The Taxi That Hurried,* Simon, 1946; *The New House in the Forest,* Simon, 1946; *Fix It, Please!,* Simon, 1947; *A Year in the City,* Simon, 1948).

Hendrik Willem Van Loon's *The Story of Mankind* (an informational book which traces the origin and evolution of civilization; one of the first books of nonfiction to attempt to make learning inherently exciting; published by Boni and Liveright, awarded first Newbery Medal in 1922 for the most distinguished contribution to American literature for children written and published in America in the preceding year by an American resident or citizen; illustrated by the author; the author's other work includes *The Story of the Bible,* 1923; *Thomas Jefferson,* Dodd, 1932; *Van Loon's Geography,* Simon, 1932; *Ships and How They Sailed the Seven Seas,* Somerset, 1935; *The Arts,* Garden City, 1937; *Van Loon's Lives,* Simon, 1938; *The Story of the Pacific,* Harcourt, 1940; *Van Loon's Lives,* Simon, 1942; *Life and Times of Simon Bolivar,* Dodd, 1943; and a series of song books with Grace Castagnetta: *The Songs We Sing,* Simon, 1936; *Folk Songs of Many Lands,* Simon, 1939; *The Songs America Sings,* Simon, 1939).

1922

Margery Williams Bianco's *The Velveteen Rabbit* (a picture-book fantasy which explores the universal question, "What is real?"; illustrated by William Nicholson; published in New York by Doran; the author's other work includes *The Little Wooden Doll,* illustrated by Pamela Bianco, Macmillan, 1925; *Poor Cecco: The Wonderful Story of a Wonderful Wooden Dog Who Was the Jolliest Toy in the House Until He Went Out to Explore the World,* illustrated by Arthur Rackham, Doran, 1925; *The Apple Tree,* illustrated by Boris Artzybasheff, Doran, 1926; *The Adventures of Andy,* Doran, 1926; *The Skin Horse,* illustrated by Pamela Bianco,

1922 *continued*

Doran, 1927; *The Candlestick,* Doubleday, 1929; *Other People's Houses,* Viking, 1930; *The House that Grew Smaller,* illustrated by Rachel Field, Macmillan, 1931; *A Street of Little Shops,* Doubleday, 1932; *The Hurdy-Gurdy Man,* illustrated by Robert Lawson, Oxford, 1933; *The Good Friends,* Viking, 1934; *Winterbound,* illustrated by Kate Seredy, Viking, 1936; *Green Grows the Garden,* Macmillan, 1936; *Franzi and Gizi,* Messner, *1941; Penny and the White Horse,* Platt and Munk, 1949).

Richmal Crompton's *Just William* (the first of a series of popular British books about a middle-class English boy who is tough, scruffy, irreverent, and often the bane of his family's existence; the author's other work, published by Newnes and illustrated by Thomas Henry Ford except as noted, includes *More William,* 1923; *William Again,* 1923; *William the Fourth,* 1924; *Still William,* 1925; *William the Conqueror,* 1926; *William the Outlaw,* 1927; *William in Trouble,* 1927; *William the Good,* 1928; *William,* 1929; *William the Bad,* 1930; *William's Happy Days,* 1930; *William's Crowded Hours,* 1931; *William the Pirate,* 1932; *William the Rebel,* 1933; *William the Gangster,* 1934; *William the Detective,* 1935; *Sweet William,* 1936; *William the Showman,* 1937; *William the Dictator,* 1938; *William and A.R.P.,* 1939, reprinted as *William's Bad Resolution,* 1956; *William and the Evacuees,* 1940, reprinted as *William the Film Star,* 1956; *William Does His Bit,* 1941; *William Carries On,* 1942; *William and the Brain Trust,* 1945; *Just William's Luck,* 1948; *Jimmy,* 1949; *William the Bold,* 1950; *Jimmy Again,* illustrated by Lunt Roberts, 1951; *William and the Tramp,* 1952; *William and the Moon Rocket,* 1954; *William and the Space Animal,* 1956; *William's Television Show,* 1958; Richmal Crompton is the pseudonym of Richmal Crompton Lamburn).

Hugh Lofting's *The Voyages of Doctor Dolittle* (one of a series of humorous fantasies about an eccentric M.D., his unusual pets, and their adventures together; published in New York by F. A. Stokes; illustrated by the author; awarded Newbery Medal in 1923; the author's other work, published by Stokes except as noted, includes *The Story of Doctor Dolittle,* 1920; *Dr. Dolittle's Post Office,* 1924; *Dr. Dolittle's Circus,* 1925; *Dr. Dolittle's Zoo,* 1926; *Dr. Dolittle's Caravan,* 1927; *Dr. Dolittle's Garden,* Lippincott, 1928, *Dr. Dolittle in the Moon,* 1929; *Dr. Dolittle's Return,* 1933; *Dr. Dolittle and the Secret Lake,* Lippincott, 1949; *Dr. Dolittle and the Green Canary,* Lippincott, 1951; and *Dr. Dolittle's Puddleby Adventures,* Lippincott, 1953; non-Dolittle books include *The Story of Mrs. Tubbs,* 1923; *Noisy Nora,* 1929; *The Twilight of Magic,* 1931; *Gug-Gub's Book,* 1933; *Tommy, Tilly, and Mrs. Tubbs,* 1936; *Porridge Poetry,* 1924).

Carl Sandburg's *The Rootabaga Stories* (poetic "Midwestern" prose fantasies filled with beauty as well as the grotesque; illustrated by Maude and Miska Petersham; published in New York by Harcourt; followed by *Rootabaga Pigeons,* Harcourt, 1923; the author's books of poems for children include *Early Moon,* Harcourt, 1930; *Wind Song,* Harcourt, 1960; the author's biography for children is *Abe Lincoln Grows Up,* Harcourt, 1928, which is based on his five-volume adult biography of Lincoln). UI

Stewart Edward White's *Daniel Boone: Wilderness Scout* (a story about Boone's exploits; illustrated by Remington Schuyler; published in Garden City, N.Y., by Doubleday; the author's other work includes *The Westerners,* McClure, 1901; *The Claim Jumpers,* Appleton, 1902; *The Blazed Trail,* McClure, 1902; *The Forest,* Outlook, 1903; *The Mountains,* McClure, 1904; *Camp and Trail,* Outing, 1907; *The Riverman,* McClure, 1908; *The Grey Dawn,* Doubleday, Page, 1915; *Simba,* Doubleday, 1918; *The Long Rifle,* Doubleday, 1932; *Wild Geese Calling,* Doubleday, 1940).

1923

Enid Blyton's *Real Fairies: Poems* (one of the Irish author's numerous popular books for children, published by Saville; the author's other work includes *Child Whispers,* Saville, 1922; *The Enid Blyton Book of Fairies,* Newnes, 1924; *The Zoo Book,* Newnes, 1924; *Songs of Gladness,* Saville, 1924; *The Enid Blyton Book of Bunnies,* Newnes, 1925; *Silver and Gold,* Nelson, 1925; *The Book of Brownies,* Newnes, 1926; *Tales Half Told,* Nelson, 1926; *The Animal Book,* Newnes, 1927; *Let's Pretend,* Nelson, 1928; *Tarrydiddle Town,* Nelson, 1929; *Cheerio! A Book for Boys and Girls,* Birn, 1933; *Five Minute Tales: Sixty Short Stories for Children,* Methuen, 1933; *Letters from Bobs,* privately printed, 1933; *The Old Thatch,* Johnston, 16 vols., 1934-1935, 1938-1939; *The Red Pixie Book,* Newnes, 1934; *Ten Minutes Tales: Twenty-Nine Varied Stories for Children,* Methuen, 1934; *The Children's Garden,* Newnes, 1935; *The Green Goblin Book,* Newnes, 1935; shortened version, as *Feefo, Tuppenny, and Jinks,* Staples Press, 1951; *Hedgerow Tales,* Newnes, 1935; *The Famous Jimmy,* Muller, 1936; *Fifteen Minute Tales: Nineteen Stories for Children,* Methuen, 1936; *The Yellow Fairy* Book, Newnes, 1936; *Adventures of the Wishing Chair,* Newnes, 1937; *The Adventures of Binkle and Flip,* Newnes, 1938; *Billy-Bob Tales,* Methuen, 1938; *Mr. Galliano's Circus,* Newnes, 1938; *The Secret Island,* Blackwell, 1938; *Boys' and Girls' Circus Book,* News Chronicle, 1939; *The Enchanted Wood,* Newnes, 1939; *Hurrah for the Circus! Being Further Adventures of Mr. Galliano and His Famous Circus,* Newnes, 1939; *Naughty Amelia Jane!, Boys' and Girls' Story Book,* Newnes, 1940; *The Children of Cherry Tree Farm,* Country Life, 1940; *Children of Kidillin* (as Mary Pollock), Newnes, 1940; *The Little Tree House, Being the Adventures of Josie, Click, and Bun,* Newnes, 1940; as *Josie, Click, and Bun and*

1923 *continued*

the Little Tree House, 1951; *Mr. Meddle's Mischief,* Newnes, 1940; *Naughtiest Girl in the School,* Newnes, 1940; *The Secret of Spiggy Holes,* Blackwell, 1940; *Tales of Betsy-May,* Methuen, 1940; *Three Boys and a Circus* (as Mary Pollock), Newnes, 1940; *The Treasure Hunters,* Newnes, 1940; *Twenty Minute Tales,* Methuen, 1940; *The Adventures of Mr. Pink-Whistle,* Newnes, 1941; *The Adventurous Four,* Newnes, 1941; *Five O'Clock Tales,* 1941; *The Further Adventures of Josie, Click, and Bun,* Newnes, 1941; *The Secret Mountain,* Blackwell, 1941; *The Twins at St. Clare's,* Methuen, 1941; *The Children of Willow Farm,* Country Life, 1942; *Circus Days Again,* Newnes, 1942; *Happy Story Book,* Hodder and Stoughton, 1942; *Enid Blyton's Little Books,* Evans, 6 vols., 1942; *Five on a Treasure Island,* Hodder and Stoughton, 1942; *Hello, Mr. Twiddle,* Newnes, 1942; *I'll Tell You a Story,* Macmillan 1942; *I'll Tell You Another Story,* Macmillan, 1942; *Jolly John at Christmas Time,* Evans, 1942; *Mary Mouse and the Doll's House,* Brockhampton Press, 1942; *More Adventures on Willow Farm,* Country Life, 1942; *The Naughtiest Girl Again,* Newnes, 1942; *The O'Sullivan Twins,* Methuen, 1942; *Shadow the Sheep Dog,* Newnes, 1942; *Six O'Clock Tales: Thirty-Three Short Stories for Children,* Methuen, 1942; *Mischief at St. Rollo's* (as Mary Pollock), Newnes, 1943; *The Secret of Cliff Castle* (as Mary Pollock), Newnes, 1943; *Bimbo and Topsy,* Newnes, 1943; *The Adventures of Scamp* (as Mary Pollock), Newnes, 1943; *Dame Slap and Her School,* Newnes, 1943; *Five Go Adventuring Again,* Hodder and Stoughton, 1943; *Jolly John by the Sea,* Evans, 1943; *Jolly John on the Farm,* Evans, 1943; *The Magic Faraway Tree,* Newnes, 1943; *Merry Story Book,* Hodder and Stoughton, 1943; *More Adventures of Mary Mouse,* Brockhampton Press, 1943; *The Mystery of the Burnt Cottage,* Methuen, 1943; *The Secret of Killimooin,* Blackwell, 1943; *Polly Piglet,* Brockhampton Press, 1943; *Seven O'Clock Tales: Thirty Short Stories for Children,* Methuen, 1943; *Smuggler Ben* (as Mary Pollock), Werner Laurie, 1943; *Smuggler Term at St. Clare's,* Methuen, 1943; *The Toys Come to Life,* Brockhampton Press, 1943; *At Appletree Farm,* Brockhampton Press, 1944; *Billy and Betty at the Seaside,* Valentine and Sons, 1944; *A Book of Naughty Children,* Methuen, 1944; *The Boy Next Door,* Newnes, 1944; *The Dog That Went to Fairyland,* Brockhampton Press, 1944; *Claudine at St. Clare's,* Methuen, 1944; *Come to the Circus,* Brockhampton Press, 1944; *Eight O'Clock Tales,* Methuen, 1944; *Five Run Away Together,* Hodder and Stoughton, 1944; *The Island of Adventure,* Macmillan, 1944; *Jolly Little Jumbo,* Brockhampton Press, 1944; *Jolly Story Book,* Hodder and Stoughton, 1944; *Little Mary Mouse Again*, Brockhampton Press, 1944; *The Mystery of the Disappearing Cat,* Methuen, 1944; *Rainy Day Stories,* Evans, 1944; *The Second Form at St. Clare's,* Methuen, 1944; *Tales of Toyland,* Newnes, 1944; *The Three Golliwogs,* Newnes, 1944; *The Blue*

Story Book, Methuen, 1945; *The Brown Family,* News Chronicle, 1945; *The Caravan Family,* Lutterworth Press, 1945; *The Conjuring Wizard and Other Stories,* Macmillan, 1945; *The Family at Red Roofs,* Lutterworth Press, 1945; *Fifth Formers at St. Clare's,* Methuen, 1945; *Five Go to Smuggler's Top,* Hodder and Stoughton, 1945; *Hallo, Little Mary Mouse,* Brockhampton Press, 1945; *Hollow Tree House,* Lutterworth Press, 1945; *Jolly John at the Circus,* Evans, 1945; *The Mystery of the Secret Room,* Methuen, 1945; *The Naughtiest Girl Is a Monitor,* Newnes, 1945; *Round the Clock Stories,* National Magazine Company, 1945; *The Runaway Kitten,* Brockhampton Press, 1945; *Sunny Story Book,* Hodder and Stoughton, 1945; *The Teddy Bear's Party,* Brockhampton Press, 1945; *The Twins Go to Nursery-Rhyme Land,* Brockhampton Press, 1945; *Amelia Jane Again,* Newnes, 1946; *The Bad Little Monkey,* Brockhampton Press, 1946; *The Castle of Adventure,* Macmillan, 1946; *The Children at Happy House,* Blackwell, 1946; *Chimney Corner Stories,* National Magazine Company, 1946; *First Term at Malory Towers,* Methuen, 1946; *Five Go Off in a Caravan,* Hodder and Stoughton, 1946; *The Folk of the Faraway Tree,* Newnes, 1946; *Gay Story Book,* Hodder and Stoughton, 1946; *Josie, Click, and Bun Again,* Newnes, 1946; *The Little White Duck and Other Stories,* Macmillan, 1946; *Mary Mouse and Her Family,* Brockhampton Press, 1946; *The Mystery of the Spiteful Letters,* Methuen, 1946; *The Put-em-Rights,* Lutterworth Press, 1946; *The Red Story Book,* Methuen, 1946; *The Surprising Caravan,* Brockhampton Press, 1946; *Tales of Green Hedges,* National Magazine Company, 1946; *The Train That Lost Its Way,* Brockhampton Press, 1946; *The Adventurous Four Again,* Newnes, 1947; *At Seaside Cottage,* Brockhampton Press, 1947; *Five on Kirrin Island Again,* Hodder and Stoughton, 1947; *The Green Story Book,* Methuen, 1947; *The Happy House Children Again,* Blackwell, 1947; *Here Comes Mary Mouse Again,* Brockhampton Press, 1947; *The House at the Corner,* Lutterworth Press, 1947; *Little Green Duck and Other Stories,* Brockhampton Press, 1947; *Lucky Story Book,* Hodder and Stoughton, 1947; *More about Josie, Click, and Bun,* Newnes, 1947; *The Mystery of the Missing Necklace,* Methuen, 1947; *Rambles with Uncle Nat,* National Magazine Company, 1947; *The Saucy Jane Family,* Lutterworth Press, 1947; *A Second Book of Naughty Children: Twenty-Four Short Stories,* Methuen, 1947; *The Valley of Adventure,* Macmillan, 1947; *The Very Clever Rabbit,* Brockhampton Press, 1947; *The Adventures of Pip,* Sampson Low, 1948; *The Boy with the Loaves and Fishes,* Lutterworth Press, 1948; *Come to the Circus,* Newnes, 1948; *Bedtime Series,* Brockhampton Press, 2 vols., 1948; *Five Go Off to Camp,* Hodder and Stoughton, 1948; *How Do You Do, Mary Mouse,* Brockhampton Press, 1948; *Just Time for a Story,* Macmillan, 1948; *Jolly Tales,* Johnston, 1948; *Let's Have a Story,* Pitkin, 1948; *The Little Girl at Capernaum,* Lutterworth Press, 1948; *Mister Icy-*

1923 *continued*

Cold, Blackwell, 1948; *More Adventures of Pip,* Sampson Low, 1948; *The Mystery of the Hidden House,* Methuen, 1948; *Nature Tales,* Johnston, 1948; *Now for a Story,* Harold Hill, 1948; *The Red-Spotted Handkerchief and Other Stories,* Brockhampton Press, 1948; *The Sea of Adventure,* Macmillan, 1948; *The Secret of the Old Mill,* Brockhampton Press, 1948; *Six Cousins at Mistletoe Farm,* Evans, 1948; *Tales after Tea,* Werner Laurie, 1948; *Tales of the Twins,* Brockhampton Press, 1948; *Three Ran Away Together,* Brockhampton Press, 1948; *Third Year at Malory Towers,* Methuen, 1948; *We Want a Story,* Pitkin, 1948; *The Bluebell Story Book,* Gifford, 1949; *Bumpy and His Bus,* Newnes, 1949; *A Cat in Fairyland and Other Stories,* Pitkin, 1949; *The Circus Book,* Latimer House, 1949; *The Dear Old Snow Man,* Brockhampton Press, 1949; *Don't Be Silly, Mr. Twiddle,* Newnes, 1949; *The Enchanted Sea and Other Stories,* Pitkin, 1949; *Daffodil Story Book,* Gifford, 1949; *Good Morning Book,* National Magazine Company, 1949; *Five Get into Trouble,* Hodder and Stoughton, 1949; *Humpty Dumpty and Belinda,* Collins, 1949; *Jinky's Joke and Other Stories,* Brockhampton Press, 1949; *Little Noddy Goes to Toyland,* Sampson Low, 1949; *Mr. Tumpy and His Caravan,* Sidgwick and Jackson, 1949; *The Mountain of Adventure,* Macmillan, 1949; *The Mystery of the Pantomime Cat,* Methuen, 1949; *Oh, What a Lovely Time,* Brockhampton Press, 1949; *The Rockingdown Mystery,* Collins, 1949; *The Secret Seven,* Brockhampton Press, 1949; *A Story Party at Green Hedges,* Hodder and Stoughton, 1949; *The Strange Umbrella and Other Stories,* Pitkin, 1949; *Tales after Supper,* Werner Laurie, 1949; *Those Dreadful Children,* Lutterworth Press, 1949; *Tiny Tales,* Littlebury, 1949; *The Upper Fourth at Malory Towers,* Methuen, 1949; *Chuff the Chimney Sweep and Other Stories,* Macmillan, 1950; *The Astonishing Ladder and Other Stories,* Macmillan, 1950; *Enid Blyton's Little Book,* 6 vols., Brockhampton Press, 1950; *Five Fall into Adventure,* Hodder and Stoughton, 1950; *Hurrah for Little Nobody,* Sampson Low, 1950; *In the Fifth at Malory Towers,* Methuen, 1950; *The Magic Knitting Needles and Other Stories,* Macmillan, 1950; *Mister Meddle's Muddles,* Newnes, 1950; *Mr. Pink-Whistle Interferes,* Newnes, 1950; *The Mystery of the Invisible Thief,* Methuen, 1950; *The Pole Star Family,* Lutterworth Press, 1950; *The Poppy Story Book,* Gifford, 1950; *The Rilloby Fair Mystery,* Collins, 1950; *Round the Year Stories,* Coker, 1950; *Rubbalong Tales,* Macmillan, 1950; *The Seaside Family,* Lutterworth Press, 1950; *Secret Seven Adventure,* Brockhampton Press, 1950; *The Ship of Adventure,* Macmillan, 1950; *Six Cousins Again,* Evans, 1950; *Tales about Toys,* Brockhampton Press, 1950; *The Three Naughty Children and Other Stories,* Macmillan, 1950; *Tricky the Goblin and Other Stories,* Macmillan, 1950; *We Do Love Mary Mouse,* Brockhampton Press, 1950; *Welcome Mary Mouse,* Brockhampton Press, 1950; *What an Adventure,* Brockhampton

Press, 1950; *The Wishing Chair Again,* Newnes, 1950; *The Yellow Story Book,* Methuen, 1950; *Benny and the Princess and Other Stories,* Pitkin, 1951; *The Big Noddy Book,* Sampson Low, 1951; *The Buttercup Farm Family,* Lutterworth Press, 1951; *Buttercup Story Book,* Gifford, 1951; *Down at the Farm,* Sampson Low, 1951; *Father Christmas and Belinda,* Collins, 1951; *Five on a Hike Together,* Hodder and Stoughton, 1951; *The Flying Goat and Other Stories,* Pitkin, 1951; *Gay Street Book,* Latimer House, 1951; *Hello Twins,* Brockhampton Press, 1951; *Here Comes Noddy Again,* Sampson Low, 1951; *Hurrah for Mary Mouse,* Brockhampton Press, 1951; *Last Term at Malory Towers,* Methuen, 1951; *Let's Go to the Circus,* Odhams, 1951; *The Little Spinning Mouse and Other Stories,* Pitkin, 1951; *The Magic Snow-Bird and Other Stories,* Pitkin, 1951; *The Mystery of the Vanished Prince,* Methuen, 1951; *Noddy and Big Ears Have a Picnic,* Sampson Low, 1951; *Noddy and His Car,* Sampson Low, 1951; *Noddy Has a Shock,* Sampson Low, 1951; *Noddy Has More Adventures,* Sampson Low, 1951; *Noddy Goes to the Seaside,* Sampson Low, 1951; *Noddy Off to Rocking Horse Land,* Sampson Low, 1951; *Noddy Painting Book,* Sampson Low, 8 vols., 1951-1957; Noddy's House of Books, *Sampson Low,* 6 vols., 1951; *A Picnic Party with Enid Blyton,* Hodder and Stoughton, 1951; *Pippy and the Gnome and Other Stories,* Pitkin, 1951; *A Prize for Mary Mouse,* Brockhampton Press, 1951; *The Proud Golliwog,* Brockhampton Press, 1951; *The Runaway Teddy Bear and Other Stories,* Pitkin, 1951; *The Six Bad Boys,* Lutterworth Press, 1951; *A Tale of Little Noddy,* Sampson Low, 1951; *"Two-Wise" the Wonderful Wizard and Other Stories,* Pitkin, 1951; *Up the Faraway Tree,* Newnes, 1951; *Well Done, Secret Seven,* Brockhampton Press, 1951; *Bright Story Book,* Brockhampton Press, 1952; *The Circus of Adventure,* Macmillan, 1952; *Come Along Twins,* Brockhampton Press, 1952; *Five Have a Wonderful Time,* Hodder and Stoughton, 1952; *The Mad Teapot,* Brockhampton Press, 1952; *Mandy, Mops, and Cubby Find a House,* Sampson Low, 1952; *Mary Mouse and Her Bicycle,* Brockhampton Press, 1952; *Mr. Tumpy Plays a Trick on Saucepan,* Sampson Low, 1952; *The Mystery of the Strange Bundle,* Methuen, 1952; *Noddy and Big Ears,* Sampson Low, 1952; *Noddy and the Witch's Wand,* Sampson Low, 1952; *Noddy's Colour Strip Book,* Sampson Low, 1952; *Noddy Goes to School,* Sampson Low, 1952; *Noddy's Ark of Books,* Sampson Low, 5 vols., 1952; *Noddy's Car Gets a Squeak,* Sampson Low, 1952; *Noddy's Penny Wheel Car,* Sampson Low, 1952; *The Queer Mystery,* Staples Press, 1952; *The Rubadub Mystery,* Collins, 1952; *Secret Seven on the Trail,* Brockhampton Press, 1952; *Snowdrop Story Book,* Gifford, 1952; *The Very Big Secret,* Lutterworth Press, 1952; *Welcome Josie, Click, and Bun,* Newnes, 1952; *Well Done, Noddy,* Sampson Low, 1952; *Clicky the Clockwork Clown,* Brockhampton Press, 1953; *Five Go Down to the Sea,* Hodder and Stoughton, 1953; *Go Ahead Secret*

1923 *continued*

Seven, Brockhampton Press, 1953; *Gobo and Mr. Fierce,* Sampson Low, 1953; *Here Come the Twins,* Brockhampton Press, 1953; *Mandy Makes Cubby a Hat,* Sampson Low, 1953; *Mary Mouse and the Noah's Ark,* Brockhampton Press, 1953; *Mr. Tumpy in the Land of Wishes,* Sampson Low, 1953; *My Enid Blyton Story Book,* Juvenile Productions, 1953; *The Mystery of Holly Lane,* Methuen, 1953; *The New Big Noddy Book,* Sampson Low, 1953; *New Noddy Colour Strip Book,* Sampson Low, 1953; *Noddy and the Cuckoo's Nest,* Sampson Low, 1953; *Noddy at the Seaside,* Sampson Low, 1953; *Noddy's Cut-out Model Book,* Sampson Low, 1953; *Noddy Gets Captured,* Sampson Low, 1953; *Noddy Is Very Silly,* Sampson Low, 1953; *Noddy's Garage of Books,* Sampson Low, 5 vols., 1953; *The Secret of Moon Castle,* Blackwell, 1953; *Snowball the Pony,* Lutterworth Press, 1953; *Visitors in the Night,* Brockhampton Press, 1953; *Well Really Mr. Twiddle!,* Newnes, 1953; *The Adventure of the Secret Necklace,* Lutterworth Press, 1954; *The Castle Without a Door and Other Stories,* Pitkin, 1954; *The Children at Green Meadows,* Lutterworth Press, 1954; *Friendly Story Book,* Brockhampton Press, 1954; *Marigold Story Book,* Gifford, 1954; *Noddy Pop-Up Book,* Sampson Low, 1954; *Noddy Giant Painting Book,* Sampson Low, 1954; *Good Work, Secret Seven!,* Brockhampton Press, 1954; *Five Go to Mystery Moor,* Hodder and Stoughton, 1954; *How Funny You Are, Noddy,* Sampson Low, 1954; *Little Strip Picture Books,* Sampson Low, 1954; *The Little Toy Farm and Other Stories,* Pitkin, 1954; *Mary Mouse to the Rescue,* Brockhampton Press, 1954; *Merry Mister Meddle,* Newnes, 1954; *The Mystery of Tally-Ho Cottage,* Methuen, 1954; *Noddy and the Magic Rubber,* Sampson Low, 1954; *Noddy's Castle of Books,* Sampson Low, 5 vols., 1954; *Away Goes Sooty,* Collins, 1955; *Benjy and the Others,* Latimer House, 1955; *Bimbo and Blackie Go Camping,* Collins, 1955; *Bobs,* Collins, 1955; *Christmas with Scamp and Bimbo,* Collins, 1955; *Little Bedtime Books,* Sampson Low, 8 vols., 1955; *Neddy the Little Donkey,* Collins, 1955; *Sooty,* Collins, 1955; *Five Have Plenty of Fun,* Hodder and Stoughton, 1955; *Foxglove Story Book,* Gifford, 1955; *Gobo in the Land of Dreams,* Sampson Low, 1955; *Golliwog Grumbled,* Brockhampton Press, 1955; *Holiday House,* Evans, 1955; *The Laughing Kitten,* Harvill Press, 1955; *Mandy, Mops, and Cubby and the Whitewash,* Sampson Low, 1955; *Mary Mouse in Nursery Rhyme Land,* Brockhampton Press, 1955; *Mischief Again,* Harvill Press, 1955; *Mr. Pink-Whistle's Party,* Newnes, 1955; *Mr. Tumpy in the Land of Boys and Girls,* Sampson Low, 1955; *More Chimney Corner Stories,* Latimer House, 1955; *Noddy in Toyland,* Sampson Low, 1955; *Noddy Meets Father Christmas,* Sampson Low, 1955; *Ring o' Bells Mystery,* Collins, 1955; *The River of Adventure,* Macmillan, 1955; *Run-about Holidays,* Lutterworth Press, 1955; *Secret Seven Win Through,* Brockhampton Press, 1955; *The Troublesome Three,* Sampson Low, 1955; *You Funny Little Noddy!,* Sampson Low, 1955; *Be Brave, Little Noddy!,* Sampson Low, 1956; *Bom the Little Toy Drummer,* Brockhampton Press, 1956; *The Clever Little Donkey,* Collins, 1956; *Colin the Cow-Boy,* Collins, 1956; *A Day with Mary Mouse,* Brockhampton Press, 1956; *Animal Tales,* Collins, 1956; *Noddy Play Day Painting Book,* Sampson Low, 1956; *Five on a Secret Trail,* Hodder and Stoughton, 1956; *Four in a Family,* Lutterworth Press, 1956; *The Mystery of the Missing Man,* Methuen, 1956; *Noddy and His Friends,* Sampson Low, 1956; *Noddy's Nursery Rhymes,* Sampson Low, 1956; *Noddy and Tessie Bear,* Sampson Low, 1956; *The Noddy Toy Station Books,* Sampson Low, 5 vols., 1956; *The Rat-a-Tat Mystery,* Collins, 1956; *Three Cheers Secret Seven,* Brockhampton Press, 1956; *Bom and His Magic Drumstick,* Brockhampton Press, 1957; *Do Look Out, Noddy!,* Sampson Low, 1957; *Bom Painting Book,* Dean, 1957; *Five Go to Billycock Hill,* Hodder and Stoughton, 1957; *Mary Mouse and the Garden Party,* Brockhampton Press, 1957; *Mystery of the Strange Messages,* Methuen, 1957; *Noddy and Bumpy Dog,* Sampson Low, 1957; *Noddy's New Big Book,* Sampson Low, 1957; *Secret Seven Mystery,* Brockhampton Press, 1957; *The Birthday Kitten,* Lutterworth Press, 1958; *Bom Goes Adventuring,* Brockhampton Press, 1958; *Clicky Gets into Trouble,* Brockhampton Press, 1958; *Five Get into a Fix,* Hodder and Stoughton, 1958; *Mary Mouse Goes to the Fair,* Brockhampton Press, 1958; *Mr. Pink-Whistle's Big Book,* Evans, 1958; *My Big-Ears Picture Book,* Sampson Low, 1958; *My Noddy Picture Book,* Sampson Low, 1958; *Noddy Has an Adventure,* Sampson Low, 1958; *Puzzles for the Secret Seven,* Brockhampton Press, 1958; *Rumble and Chuff,* Juvenile Productions, 2 vols., 1958; *You're a Good Friend, Noddy!,* Sampson Low, 1958; *The Noddy Shop Book,* Sampson Low, 5 vols., 1958; *Noddy's Own Nursery Rhymes,* Sampson Low, 1958; *Bom and the Clown,* Brockhampton Press, 1959; *Bom and the Rainbow,* Brockhampton Press, 1959; *Hullo Bom and Wuffy Dog,* Brockhampton Press, 1959; *Mary Mouse Has a Wonderful Idea,* Brockhampton Press, 1959; *Noddy and Bunkey,* Sampson Low, 1959; *Noddy Goes to Sea,* Sampson Low, 1959; *Noddy's Car Picture Book,* Sampson Low, 1959; *Ragamuffin Mystery,* Collins, 1959; *Secret Seven Fireworks,* Brockhampton Press, 1959).

C. B. Falls's *C. B. Falls' ABC Book* (a popular American alphabet book with colored woodcuts of animals from zoo and farm; published in Garden City, N.Y., by Doubleday; the author-illustrator's other work includes *The First 3000 Years: Ancient Civilizations of the Tigris, Euphrates, and Nile River Valleys and the Mediterranean Sea,* Viking, 1960).

Charles Hawes's *Dark Frigate* (an exciting adventure novel with authentic history and seamanship; published in Boston by Little; the author was

1923 *continued*

awarded the Newbery Medal posthumously in 1924; the author's other work includes *Mutineers,* Atlantic, 1920; and *Great Quest,* Atlantic, 1921).

Grenville MacDonald's *Billy Barnicoat* (a fantasy set in Cornwall; published in London by Allen; the author is son of George MacDonald; the author's other work includes *The Magic Crook, or The Stolen Baby,* Vineyard; *Trystie's Quest or Kit King of the Pigwidgeons,* Vinyard, 1912; *Jack and Jill, a Fairy Story,* Dent, 1913; *Count Billy,* Dutton, 1928).

1924

Margery Clark's *The Poppy Seed Cakes* (realistic picture stories with Russian atmosphere for young children; published in Garden City, N.Y., by Doubleday; illustrated by Maude and Miska Petersham; Margery Clark is the pseudonym for Mary E. Clark and Margery C. Quigley).

Charles Finger's *Tales from Silver Lands* (a collection based on folktales gathered on the author's journeys through South America; published in New York by Doubleday; illustrated by Paul Honoré; awarded Newbery Medal in 1925; the author's other work includes *Courgeous Companions,* Longmans, 1929; *Our Navy,* Houghton, 1936; *A Dog at His Heel,* Harrap, 1936; *Cape Horn Snorter,* Houghton, 1939).

A. A. Milne's *When We Were Very Young* (the first of this British writer's collections of poems for children; published in London by E. P. Dutton; the author's other work includes a second book of poems, *Now We Are Six,* Dutton, 1927; two books of stories, *Winnie-the-Pooh,* Dutton, 1926; and *The House at Pooh Corner,* Dutton, 1928; all four books were illustrated by E. H. Shepard; the author's plays include *Make-Believe,* French, 1925; *Toad of Toad Hall,* French, 1929; and *The Ugly Duckling, A Play,* French, 1941; other works are: *Prince Rabbit* [and] *The Princess Who Could Not Laugh,* Dutton, 1926; *Once On a Time,* "a fairy tale for grown-ups," Hodder, 1917; *The Hums of Pooh,* Methuen, 1929; *The Christopher Robin Story Book,* Dutton, 1929; *The Tales of Pooh,* Dutton, 1930; *The Christopher Robin Birthday Book,* Methuen, 1930; *The Christopher Robin Verses,* Dutton, 1932, also published in 1958 as *The World of Christopher Robin; The Magic Hill and Other Stories,* Grosset, 1927; *The Princess and the Apple Tree,* Grosset, 1927; *The World of Pooh,* Dutton, 1957; *The Pooh Song Book,* Dutton, 1961; *Pooh's Birthday Book,* Dutton, 1962; *The Pooh Story Book,* Dutton, 1965; *The Christopher Robin Book of Verse,* Methuen, 1967).

Anne Carroll Moore's *Nicholas: A Manhattan Christmas Story* (a fantasy which gives the reader a picture of Clement Moore and his "Night Before

Christmas" country; published in New York by Putnam; the author's other work includes his editing of *Knickerbocker's History of New York,* Doubleday, 1928; *The Bold Dragoon and Other Ghostly Tales By Washington Irving,* Knopf, 1930; and *The Golden Goose,* Putnam, 1932; the author was children's book critic for *The Bookman,* 1918-1927; the *New York Herald Tribune Books,* 1924-1930; and *The Atlantic Monthly,* 1930-1958). PI

Vilhjalmur Stefansson and Violet Irwin's *Kak, the Copper Eskimo* (a story of an Eskimo boy's daily adventures by two Canadian authors; published in Toronto by Macmillan).

Gertrude Chandler Warner's *The Boxcar Children* (a popular adventure story published by Rand McNally; the author's other work, published by Whitman except as noted, includes *Surprise Island,* Scott, 1949; *The Yellow House Mystery,* 1953; *Mystery Ranch,* 1958; *Mike's Mystery,* 1960; *Blue Bay Mystery,* 1961; *The Woodshed Mystery,* 1962; *The Lighthouse Mystery,* 1963; *Mountain Top Mystery,* 1964; *Schoolhouse Mystery,* 1965; *Caboose Mystery,* 1966; *Houseboat Mystery,* 1967; *Snowbound Mystery,* 1968; *Tree House Mystery,* 1969; *Bicycle Mystery,* 1970; *Mystery in the Sand,* 1971; *Mystery Behind the Wall,* 1973; *Bus Station Mystery,* 1974; *Benny Uncovers a Mystery,* 1976).

1925

Dorothy Aldis's *Everything and Anything* (a collection of insightful verses about the everyday life of young children; published in New York by Minton; the author's other work includes *Here, There, and Everywhere,* Minton, 1927; *Jane's Father,* Minton, 1928; *Squiggles,* Minton, 1929; *Murder in a Hay Stack,* Farrar and Rinehart, 1930; *7 to 7,* Minton, 1931; *Any Spring,* Putnam, 1933; *Magic City,* Minton, 1933; *Hop, Skip and Jump,* Minton, 1934; *Their Own Apartment,* Putnam, 1935; *Time at Her Heels,* Houghton, 1937; *All the Year Round,* Houghton, 1938; *Poor Susan,* Putnam, 1942; *Cindy,* Putnam, 1942; *Dark Summers,* Putnam, 1947; *Miss Quinn's Secret,* Putnam, 1949; *We're Going to Town,* Bobbs, 1950; *Lucky Year,* Rand, 1952; *All Together: A Child's Treasury of Verses,* Putnam, 1952; *The Boy Who Cared,* Putnam, 1956; *Ride the Wild Waves,* Putnam, 1958; *Hello Day,* Putnam, 1959; *Quick as a Wink,* Putnam, 1960; *The Secret Place,* Scholastic, 1962; *Is Anybody Hungry?,* Putnam, 1964; *Dumb Stupid David,* Putnam, 1965; *Nothing Is Impossible: The Story of Beatrix Potter,* Atheneum, 1969).

Arthur Bowie Chrisman's *Shen of the Sea: Chinese Stories for Children* (a collection of stories about China based on the lore and wisdom of the old Chinese culture; published in New York by E. P. Dutton; illustrated

1925 *continued*

by Else Hasselriss; awarded Newbery Medal in 1926; the author's other work includes *The Wind that Wouldn't Blow: Stories of the Merry Middle Kingdom for Children and Myself,* Dutton, 1927; *Treasures Long Hidden, Old Tales and New Tales of the East,* Dutton, 1941).

Forrestine Hooker's *Cricket, A Little Girl of the Old West* (a historical novel based on family records and childhood memories; published in New York by Doubleday; the author's other work includes *Just George,* Doubleday, 1926; *The Garden of the Lost King,* Doubleday, 1929).

Grace Moon's *Chi-Wee* (the first of several stories of the everyday, realistic experiences of a Pueblo Indian girl; illustrated by author's husband, Carl Moon; published in New York by Doubleday; the author's other work includes *Indian Legends in Rhyme,* Stokes, 1916; *Lost Indian Magic,* Stokes, 1918; *Wongo and the Wise Old Crow,* Reilly, 1923; *Nadita,* Doubleday, 1927; *Runaway Papoose,* Doubleday, 1928; *The Magic Trail,* Doubleday, 1929; *The Missing Katchina,* Doubleday, 1930; *The Arrow of Teemay,* Doubleday, 1930; *Book of Nah-Wee,* with Carl Moon, Doubleday, 1932; *Tita of Mexico,* Stokes, 1934; *Shanty Ann,* Stokes, 1935; *Singing Sands,* Doubleday, 1936; *White Indian,* Doubleday, 1937; *Solita,* Doubleday, 1938; *Daughter of Thunder,* Macmillan, 1942; *One Little Indian,* Whitman, 1950).

Blanche Jennings Thompson's *All the Silver Pennies* (a popular collection of poems, including those published in earlier *Silver Pennies* volumes; illustrated by Winifred Bromhall; designed especially for use with elementary school children by their teachers; published in New York by Macmillan).

1926

Will James's *Smoky, the Cow Horse* (a realistic novel about the relationship between a man and a horse; written in the vernacular of the Western cowboy; illustrated by the author; published in New York by Scribner; awarded Newbery Medal in 1927; the author's other work, published by Scribner except as noted, includes *Cowboys North and South,* 1924; *The Drifting Cowboy,* 1925; *Cow Country,* 1927; *Sand,* 1929; *Lone Cowboy; My Life Story,* 1930; *Big Enough,* 1931; *Sun Up,* 1931; *Uncle Bill, A Tale of Two Kids and a Cowboy,* 1932; *All in the Day's Riding,* World, 1933; *The Three Mustangers,* 1933; *Young Cowboy,* 1935; *Home Ranch,* 1935; *In the Saddle with Uncle Bill,* 1935; *Scorpion, A Good Bad Horse,* 1936; *Cowboy in the Making,* 1937; *Look-See with Uncle Bill,* 1938; *Flint Spears; Cowboy Rodeo Contestant,* 1938; *The Dark Horse,* Grosset, 1939; *My First Horse,* 1940; *Horses I've Known,* 1940; *The American Cowboy,* 1942; *Book of Cowboy Stories,* 1951).

Arthur C. Parker's *Skunny Wundy and Other Indian Tales* (Seneca tales and other Indian stories retold by an Iroquois; illustrated by Will Crawford; published in New York by Doran; one of the earliest "authentic" books about Indians for children; the author's other work includes *Indian How Book,* Doran, 1927).

Howard Pease's *The Tattooed Man* (first of the popular "Tod Moran" mystery series, illustrated by Mahlon Blaine; published in New York by Doubleday; the author's other work includes *The Gypsy Caravan,* 1930; *Secret Cargo,* 1931; *Wind in the Rigging,* 1935; *Hurricane Weather,* Doubleday, 1936; *Captain Binnacle,* Dodd, 1938; *Jungle River,* Doubleday, 1938; *The Long Wharf,* Doubleday, 1938; *High Road to Adventure,* Doubleday, 1939; *Black Tanker,* Doubleday, 1941; *Thunderbolt House,* Doubleday, 1944; *Bound for "Singapore,"* Doubleday, 1948; *The Dark Adventure,* Doubleday, 1950; *Shipwreck,* Doubleday, 1957; *Mystery on Telegraph Hill,* Doubleday, 1961).

1927

Peggy Bacon's *The Lion-Hearted Kitten and Other Stories* (a collection of animal stories written and illustrated by the author; published by Macmillan; the author-illustrator's work includes *The True Philosopher and Other Cat Tales,* Four Seas, 1919; *Mercy and the Mouse and Other Stories,* Macmillan, 1928; *The Ballad of Tangle Street,* Macmillan, 1929; *The Terrible Nuisance and Other Tales,* Harcourt, 1931; *Mischief in Mayfield, A Sequel to the Terrible Nuisance,* Harcourt, 1933; *Off With Their Heads!,* McBride, 1934; *Cat-Calls,* McBride, 1935; *The Mystery at East Hatchett; or Eric the Pink,* Viking, 1939).

Dhan Gopal Mukerji's *Gay-Neck, The Story of a Pigeon* (a somewhat mystical story of a carrier pigeon's adventures in World War I with Indian soldiers in France, told from three viewpoints; illustrated by Boris Artzybasheff; published in New York by E. P. Dutton; awarded Newbery Medal in 1928; the author's other work, published by Dutton, includes *Kari, the Elephant,* 1922; *Caste and Outcaste,* 1923; *Jungle Beasts and Men,* Dutton, 1923; *Hari, the Jungle Lad,* 1924; *Ghoud the Hunter,* 1928; *Hindu Fables for Little Children,* 1929; *The Chief of the Herd,* 1929; *Bunny, Hound and Clown,* 1931; *The Master Monkey,* 1932; *Fierce-Face, the Story of a Tiger,* 1936).

Watty Piper's *The Little Engine That Could* (a popular picture-story of a little steam engine which determinedly climbs mountains saying, "I think I can, I think I can"; illustrated by George and Doris Hauman; published in New York by Platt and Munk; based on a story titled "The Pony Engine," by Mabel C. Bragg; the author's other work includes the retelling of *The*

1927 *continued*

Gingerbread Boy and Other Stories, 1927; Watty Piper is the pseudonym of Arnold Munk).

James Tippett's *I Live in a City* (poems about everyday urban life; the first of a series of this author's pocket-sized editions; illustrated by Elizabeth T. Wolcott; published in New York by Harper; the author's other work includes *I Go A-Traveling,* Harper, 1929; *I Spend the Summer,* Harper, 1930; *Henry and the Garden,* World, 1936; *Stories About Henry,* World, 1936; *Sniff,* Heath, 1937; *I Know Some Little Animals,* Harper, 1941).

1928

Mary Austin's *The Children Sing in the Far West* (a collection of poems about nature and Indians of the Southwest, which reveals the universality of childhood; illustrated by Gerald Cassidy; published in Boston by Houghton.

Wanda Gág's *Millions of Cats* (one of America's first outstanding picture books which completely integrates pictures and story; the author-illustrator's other work, published by Coward, includes *The Funny Thing,* 1929; *Snippy and Snappy,* 1931; *Wanda Gág's Story Book,* 1932; *ABC Bunny,* 1933; *Gone Is Gone,* 1935; *Growing Pains,* 1940; *Nothing At All,* 1941; illustrator and translator of *Tales from Grimm,* 1936; *Snow White and the Seven Dwarfs,* 1938; *Three Gay Tales from Grimm,* 1943; *More Tales from Grimm,* 1947; illustrator of Michael Wigglesworth's *Day of Doom,* first published by American News Company in 1857, published by Coward, 1929). UTA-L, UMi

Grace Hallock's *The Boy Who Was* (the story of Nino, the goatherd, who is given the gift of eternal youth and is able to tell about the part he has played in the exciting events of some changing civilizations; published in New York by Dutton; runner-up for the Newbery Award; the author's other work includes *The Riddle: A Play, Dramatizing Children's Health,* 1925; *May Day Festival Book,* American Child Health, 1926; *Petersham's Hill,* Dutton, 1927; *Hob o' the Mill,* Quaker Oats, 1929; *After the Rain; Cleanliness Customs of Children in Many Lands,* School Cleanliness Institute, 1930; *Birds in the Bush,* Dutton, 1930).

Eric Kelly's *The Trumpeter of Krakow* (a mystery novel set in fifteenth-century Poland; illustrated by Angela Pruszynska; published in New York by Macmillan; awarded Newbery Medal in 1929; the author's other work, published by Macmillan except as noted, includes *The Blacksmith of Vilno: A Tale of Poland in the Year 1832,* 1930; *The Golden Star of Halich: A Tale of the Red Land in 1362,* 1931; *The Christmas Nightingale: Three Christmas Stories from Poland,* illustrated by Marguerite De Angeli, 1932;

Three Sides of Agiochook: A Tale of the New England Frontier in 1775, 1935; *Treasure Mountain,* 1937; *At the Sign of the Golden Compass: A Tale of the Printing House of Christopher Plantin in Antwerp, 1576,* 1938; with Clara Hoffmanowa, *A Girl Who Would Be Queen: the Story and Diary of the Young Countess Krasinska,* illustrated by Vera Brock, McClurg, 1939; *On the Staked Plain,* 1940; *The Land of the Polish People,* Stokes, 1943; *From Star to Star,* n.p., 1944; *The Hand in the Picture,* Lippincott, 1947; *The Amazing Journey of David Ingram,* Lippincott, 1949; *In Clean Hay,* 1953; the author edited *Best Short Stories for Children,* 1939).

Vachel Lindsay's *Johnny Appleseed and Other Poems* (rhythmical poems which are distinctly American in theme and feeling; illustrated by George Richards; published in New York by Macmillan).

Chiyono Sugimoto's *Picture Tales from the Japanese* (stories which reflect Japanese customs and values; published in New York by F. A. Stokes; the author's other work includes *Japanese Holiday Picture Tales,* Stokes, 1933).

Elinor Whitney's *Tod of the Fens* (a historical novel set in England before Henry V came to the throne; published in New York by Macmillan; a runner-up for the Newbery Award; the author's other work includes *Tyke-y His Book and His Mark,* Macmillan, 1925; *Timothy and the Blue Cart,* Stokes, 1930; *Try All Ports,* Longmans, 1931; *The Mystery Club,* Stokes, 1933).

1929

Elsa Beskow's *Pelle's New Suit* (from the Swedish, a harmonious informational picture-story book describing the process of making clothes, from the wool on Pelle's pet sheep to the suit on his back; illustrated by the author; published in New York by Harper; the author's other work includes *Olle's Ski Trip,* Harper, 1928).

Rachel Field's *Hitty, Her First Hundred Years* (a fantasy recounting the adventures of a doll; illustrated by Dorothy Lathrop; published in New York by Macmillan; awarded the Newbery Medal in 1930; the author's other work includes *Taxis and Toadstools,* Doubleday, 1926; *Polly Patchwork,* Doubleday, 1928; *Calico Bush,* Macmillan, 1931; *Hepatica Hawks,* Macmillan, 1932; *The Pointed People,* Macmillan, 1933; *Branches Green,* Macmillan, 1934; *Christmas Time,* Macmillan, 1941; *Prayer for a Child,* Macmillan, 1944; *Poems,* Macmillan, 1957; *The Rachel Field Story Book,* Doubleday, 1958; author edited *The White Cat and Other Old French Fairy Tales,* illustrated by Elizabeth MacKinstry, Macmillan, 1928).

Marian Hurd McNeeley's *Jumping-Off Place* (the story of a family of children headed by a seventeen-year-old girl and how they make a home

1929 *continued*

for themselves on the Dakota prairie; runner-up for the Newbery Medal; published by Longmans; the author's other work, published by Longmans, includes, with Edith Stokely, *Miss Billy,* 1905; *Rusty Ruston,* 1928; *Winning Out,* 1931; *The Way To Glory,* 1932).

Elizabeth Miller's *Pran of Albania* (the story of an Albanian mountain girl who helps to save her country; runner-up for the Newbery Medal; published in New York by Doubleday; the author's other work includes *Children of the Mountain Eagle,* Doubleday, 1927; *Young Trojan,* Doubleday, 1931).

Felix Salten's *Bambi* (translated from the German by Whittaker Chambers; a poignant adult animal story appropriated by children; illustrated by Kurt Wiese; published in New York by Grosset; the author's other work includes *Bambi's Children,* Bobbs, 1938; *Perri,* Bobbs, 1938; *Renni, The Rescuer,* Bobbs, 1940; Felix Salten is the pseudonym of Siegmund Salzman).

Ella Young's *The Tangle-Coated Horse and Other Tales* (the stories of the Irish hero Fionn MacCumhal's childhood and youth as told by an Irish storyteller and scholar; runner-up for the Newbery Medal; published in New York by Longmans; the author's other work includes *Celtic Wonder Tales,* Longmans, 1923; *The Wonder Smith and His Son,* illustrated by Boris Artzybasheff, Longmans, 1927, runner-up for the 1928 Newbery Medal; *The Unicorn with Silver Shoes,* a tale of humans and the Pooka of fairyland, illustrated by Robert Lawson, Longmans, 1932).

1930

Herbert Best's *Garram the Hunter* (the story of the son of a West African hill tribe chieftan and his dog; published in New York by Doubleday; runner-up for the Newbery Medal; the author's other work includes *Son of the Whiteman,* Doubleday, 1931; *Garram the Chief,* Harper, 1932; *Flag of the Desert,* Viking, 1936; *Tal of the Four Tribes,* Doubleday, 1938; *Twenty-Fifth Hour,* Random, 1940; *Gunsmith's Boy,* Winston, 1942; *Young'un,* Macmillan, 1944; *Border Iron,* Viking, 1945; *Whistle, Daughter, Whistle,* Macmillan, 1947; *The Long Portage,* Viking, 1948; *Not Without Danger,* Viking, 1951; *Watergate, a Story of the Irish on the Erie Canal,* Winston, 1951; *Ranger's Ransom, A Story of Ticonderoga,* Aladdin, 1953; *Diane,* Morrow, 1954; *Desmond, the Dog Detective,* Viking, 1962; *Desmond and Dog Friday,* Viking, 1968). UOr

Elizabeth Coatsworth's *The Cat Who Went To Heaven* (a fanciful story about a cat, a poor Chinese artist, and a miracle; awarded Newbery Medal in 1931; illustrated by Lynd Ward; published in New York by Macmillan; the author's other work, published by Macmillan except as noted, includes

The Cat & the Captain, 1927; *Toutou in Bondage,* 1929; *The Sun's Diary,* 1929; *The Boy With the Parrot,* 1930; *Knock at the Door,* 1931; *Cricket & the Emperor's Son,* 1932; *Away Goes Sally,* 1934; *The Golden Horseshoe,* 1935; *Sword of the Wilderness,* 1936; *Alice-All-by-Herself,* 1937; *Dancing Tom,* 1938; *Five Bushel Farm,* 1939; *The Fair American,* 1940; *Tonio and the Stranger: A Mexican Adventure,* Grosset, 1941; *You Shall Have a Carriage,* 1941; *Forgotten Island,* Grosset, 1942; *Houseboat Summer,* 1942; *The White Horse,* 1942; *Thief Island,* 1943; *The Big Green Umbrella,* Grosset, 1944; *Trudy, the Treehouse,* 1944; *The Kitten Stand,* Grosset, 1945; *The Wonderful Day,* 1946; *Plum Daffy Adventure,* 1947; *Up Hill and Down,* Knopf, 1947; *The House of the Swan,* 1948; *Summer Green,* 1948; *The Little Haymakers,* 1949; *The Captain's Daughter,* 1950; *First Adventure,* 1950; *Door to the North,* Winston, 1950; *Dollar for Luck,* 1951; *The Wishing Pear,* 1951; *The Last Fort,* Winston, 1952; *Boston Bells,* 1952; *The Giant Golden Book of Cat Stories,* Simon, 1953; *The Giant Golden Book of Dog Stories,* Simon, 1953; *Old Whirlwind: A Story of Davy Crockett,* 1953; *Aunt Flora,* 1953; *Horse Stories,* Simon, 1954; *The Sod House,* 1954; *Mouse Chorus,* Pantheon, 1955; *Cherry Ann & the Dragon Horse,* 1955; *Hide & Seek,* Pantheon, 1956; *The Peddler's Cart,* 1956; *The Dog From Nowhere,* Row, 1958).

Ralph Hubbard's *Queer Person* (the story of an Indian grandmother who adopts a deaf and dumb child; runner-up for the Newbery Medal; published in New York by Doubleday; the author's other work includes *The Wolf Song,* Doubleday, 1935).

Eric Kästner's *Emil and the Detectives* (translated from the German by May Masse; a popular, well-written, realistic mystery; published in New York by Doubleday; the German author received the Hans Christian Andersen Award in 1960; the author's other work includes *Annaluise and Anton,* Cape, 1932; *The 35th of May,* Cape, 1933; *The Flying Classroom,* Cape, 1934; *Emil and the Three Twins,* Cape, 1935; *Lottie and Lisa,* Cape, 1950; *The Animals' Conference,* McKay, 1955).

Alice Lide and Margaret Johnson's *Ood-Le-Uk the Wanderer* (a story of the adventures of an Eskimo boy as he goes from Alaska to Siberia; published in Boston by Little; runner-up for the Newbery Medal; other work of these authors, who were sisters, includes *Pearls of Fortune,* Little, 1931; *Dark Possession,* Appleton, 1934; *Secret of the Circle,* Longmans, 1937; *Thord of Firetooth,* Lothrop, 1937; *Mystery of the Mahteb,* Longmans, 1942; *Wooden Locket,* Viking, 1953; *Lapland Drum,* Abingdon, 1955).

Alida Malkus's *The Dark Star of Itza* (a romantic story of Princess Nicti and her life in one of the Yucatan's lost cities; published by Harcourt;

1930 *continued*

runner-up for the Newbery Medal; the author's other work includes *Raquel of the Ranch Country,* Harcourt, 1927; *The Dragon Fly of Zuni,* Harcourt, 1928; *Pirate's Port, A Tale of Old New York,* Harper, 1929; *Timber Line,* Harcourt, 1929; *A Fight for the King: A Story of the Conquest of Yucatan and the Discovery of the Amazon,* Harper, 1931; *The Spindle Imp, and Other Tales of Maya Myth and Folklore,* Harcourt, 1931; *The Stone Knife Boy,* Harcourt, 1933; *Eastward Sweeps the Current,* Winston, 1937; *The Silver Llama,* Winston, 1939; *Along the Inca Highway,* Heath, 1941; *The Citadel of a Hundred Stairways,* Winston, 1941; *Constancia Lona,* Doubleday, 1947; *Chula of the Magic Islands,* Saalfield, 1948; *Colt of Destiny,* Winston, 1950; *Little Giant of the North, The Boy Who Won a Fur Empire,* Winston, 1952; *The Story of Louis Pasteur,* Grosset, 1952; *The Story of Good Queen Bess,* Grosset, 1952; *We Were There At the Battle of Gettysburg,* Grosset, 1955).

Stephen Meader's *Red Horse Hill* (a realistic story based on the author's own New Hampshire boyhood; published by Harcourt; the author's other work, all by Harcourt, includes *The Black Buccaneer,* 1920; *Down the Big River,* 1924; *Longshanks,* 1925; *Away To Sea,* 1931; *Lumberjack,* 1934; *Who Rides in the Dark?* 1935; *T-Model Tommy,* 1936; *Trap Lines North,* 1936; *Boy With a Pack,* 1937; *Bat, the Story of a Bull Terrier,* 1939; *Clear for Action,* 1940; *Blueberry Mountain,* 1941; *Shadow in the Pines,* 1942; *The Sea Snake,* 1943; *The Long Trains Roll,* 1944; *Skippy's Family,* 1945; *Jonathan Goes West,* 1946; *Behind the Ranges,* 1947; *River of the Wolves,* 1948; *Cedar's Boy,* 1949; *Whaler 'Round the Horn,* 1950; *Bulldozer,* 1951; *The Fish Hawk's Nest,* 1952; *Sparkplug of the Hornets,* 1953; *The Buckboard Stranger,* 1954; *Guns for the Saratoga,* 1955; *Sabre Pilot,* 1956; *Everglades Adventure,* 1957; *The Commodore's Cup,* 1958; *The Voyage of the Javelin,* 1959; *Wild Pony Island,* 1959; *Buffalo, Beaver,* 1960; *Snow on Blueberry Mountain,* 1961; *Phantom of the Blockade,* 1962; *The Muddy Road to Glory,* 1963; *Stranger on Big Hickory,* 1964; *A Blow for Liberty,* 1965; *Topsail Island Treasure,* 1966; *Keep 'Em Rolling,* 1967; *Lonesome End,* 1968; *The Cape May Packet,* 1969).

Elizabeth Morrow's *The Painted Pig* (story of a Mexican boy who wants a painted pig with a rosebud on its tail; illustrated by Rene d'Harnoncourt; published in New York by Knopf; the author's other work includes *Quatrains for My Daughter,* Knopf, 1931; *Beast, Bird and Fish, An Animal Alphabet,* Knopf, 1933; *A Pint of Judgement,* Knopf, 1939; *The Rabbit's Nest,* Macmillan, 1940; *Shannon,* Macmillan, 1940).

Anne Parrish's *Floating Island* (a story from a doll's point of view; illustrated by the author; published in New York by Harper; the author's other work includes *The Story of Appleby Capple,* Harper, 1950).

Arthur Ransome's *Swallows and Amazons* (a popular adventure story featuring a group of English children; published in London by Cape; the author was awarded the first Carnegie Medal in 1936 for *Pigeon Post,* Cape, 1935; the British Library Association awards the medal yearly to a children's book of outstanding merit published in the United Kingdom and written in English; the author's other work includes *The Thugs in Our Garden,* Treherne, ca. 1910; *Old Peter's Russian Tales,* Jack, 1916; *Aladdin and His Wonderful Lamp in Rhyme,* Nisbet, 1919; *The Soldier and Death,* Wilson, 1920; *Swallowdale,* Cape, 1931; *Peter Duck,* Cape, 1932; *Winter Holiday,* Cape, 1933; *Coot Club,* Cape, 1934; *We Didn't Mean to Go to Sea,* Cape, 1937; *Secret Water,* Cape, 1939; *The Big Six,* Cape, 1940; *Misee Lee,* Cape, 1941; *The Picts and the Martyrs,* Cape, 1943; *Great Northern,* Cape, 1947; *The Fool of the World and His Flying Ship,* Farrar, 1968, a tale taken from *Old Peter's Russian Tales,* illustrated by Uri Shulevitz, was awarded the Caldecott Medal, 1969).

Elizabeth Madox Roberts's *Under the Tree* (a collection of lyrical poems which reflect the author's childhood in Kentucky; illustrated by F. D. Bedford; published in New York by Viking, originally published by Huebsch in 1922; the author's other work includes *In the Great Steep's Garden,* Gowdy-Simmons, 1915; *The Time of Man,* Viking, 1926; *My Heart and My Flesh,* Grosset, 1927; *Jingling in the Wind,* Viking, 1928; *The Great Meadow,* Viking, 1930; *A Buried Treasure,* Doubleday, 1931; *The Haunted Mirror,* Viking, 1932; *He Sent Forth a Raven,* Viking, 1935; *Black Is My True Love's Hair,* Viking, 1938; *Song in the Meadow,* Viking, 1940; *Not By Strange Gods,* Viking, 1941).

Merriam Sherwood's *The Tale of the Warrior Lord* (translated from the Spanish edition of *El Cid,* retold by Ramon Menenday Pidal; published in London by Longmans).

Emma Gelders Sterne's *Loud Sing Cuckoo* (a story of life in England during Chaucer's time; published in New York by Duffield; the author's other work includes *No Surrender,* Duffield, 1932; *Amarantha Gay, M.D.,* Duffield, 1933; *The Calico Ball,* Dodd, 1934).

Sara Teasdale's *Stars Tonight* (a collection of lyrical nature poems; illustrated by Dorothy Lathrop; published in New York by Macmillan).

1931

Julia Davis Adams's *Mountains Are Free* (the story of William Tell in a new setting; runner-up for the Newbery Medal; published by Dutton; the author's other work, published by Dutton except as noted, includes *Swords of the Vikings,* 1927; *Vaino,* 1929; Stonewall, 1931; *Remember and Forget,*

1931 *continued*

1932; *No Other White Men,* 1937; *Peter Hale,* 1939; *The Sun Climbs Slowly,* 1942; *The Shenandoah,* Farrar, 1945).

Marjorie Allee's *Jane's Island* (the story of a girl's summer research efforts collecting laboratory specimens for her father; runner-up for the Newbery Medal; published by Houghton; the author's other work, all published by Houghton, includes *Susanna and Tristan,* 1929; *Judith Lankester,* 1930; *The Road to Carolina,* 1932; *Ann's Surprising Summer,* 1933; *A House of Her Own,* 1934; *Off to Philadelphia!* 1936; *The Great Tradition,* 1937; *The Little American Girl,* 1938; *Runaway Linda,* 1939; *The Camp at Westlands,* 1941; *Winter's Mischief,* 1942; *The House,* 1945; *Smoke Jumper,* 1945).

Laura Armer's *Waterless Mountain* (a novel which reveals the mystical side of Navaho life; illustrated by Sidney Armer; published by Longmans; the author was awarded the Newbery Medal, 1932; the author's other work includes *Dark Circle of Branches,* Longmans, 1933; *The Forest Pool,* Longmans, 1938).

Mary Gould Davis's *Truce of the Wolf and Other Tales of Old Italy* (one of the first collections of Italian folktales for American children; published in New York by Harcourt; the author's other work includes *The Three Golden Oranges and Other Spanish Folk Tales,* with Ralph Steele Boggs, Longmans, 1936).

Eleanor Farjeon's *Poems for Children* (a collection of fairy poems, portraits of children, poems about country life and city life, seasons; the 1951 edition included twenty additional poems; this British author's other work includes *Nursery Rhymes of London Town,* Duckworth, 1916; *All the Way to Alfriston,* Greenleaf, 1918; *Singing Games for Children,* Dent, 1918; *Gypsy and Ginger,* Dutton, 1920; *Martin Pippin in the Apple Orchard,* Collins, 1921; *Young Folk and Old,* High House, 1925; *Faithful Jenny Dove and Other Tales,* Collins, 1925; *Mighty Men,* Appleton, 1926; *Joan's Door,* Stokes, 1926; *Nuts and May, a Medley for Children,* Collins, 1926; *Come Christmas,* Collins, 1927; *Kaleidoscope,* Collins, 1928; *The Perfect Zoo,* McKay, 1929; *Collection of Poems,* Collins, 1929; *The King's Daughter Cries for the Moon,* Blackwell, 1929; *The Tale of Tom Tiddler,* Collins, 1929; five Martin Pippin books, Collins, 1930: *Mill of Dreams, Open Winkins, Proud Rosalind and the Hart's Royal, Young Gerald, King's Barn; Tales from Chaucer, the Canterbury Tales Done in Prose,* Hale, 1930; *Ladybrook,* Stokes, 1931; *The Old Nurse's Stocking Basket,* University of London, 1931; *Tom Cobble,* Blackwell, 1932; *Perkin the Peddler,* Faber,

1932; *The Fair of St. James,* Stokes, 1932; *Ameliaranne and the Magic Ring,* McKay, 1933; *Over the Garden Wall,* Stokes, 1933; *Ameliaranne's Prize Packet,* Harrap, 1933; *Jim at the Corner,* Blackwell, 1934; *The Old Sailor's Yarn Box,* Stokes, 1934; *Ameliaranne's Wash Day,* McKay, 1934; *Clumber Pup,* Blackwell, 1934; *The Children's Bells, a Selection of Poems,* Blackwell, 1934; *Ten Saints,* Oxford, 1936; *Jim and the Pirates,* Blackwell, 1936; *The Wonders of Herodotus,* Nelson, 1937; *Martin Pippin in the Daisy-field,* Joseph, 1937; *Sing for Your Supper,* Stokes, 1937; *One Foot in Fairyland,* Stokes, 1938; *Grannie Gray,* Dent, 1939; *Sussex Alphabet,* Pear Tree, 1939; *Miss Granby's Secret,* Joseph, 1940; *Brave Old Woman,* Joseph, 1941; *Magic Casements,* Allen and Unwin, 1941; *The New Book of Days,* Oxford, 1941; *Cherrystones,* Joseph, 1942; *The Fair Venetian,* Joseph, 1943; *Golden Coney,* Joseph, 1943; *Dark World of Animals,* Sylvan, 1945; *A Prayer for Little Things,* Houghton, 1945; *Ariadne and the Bull,* Joseph, 1945; *The Mulberry Bush,* Joseph, 1945; *The Starry Floor,* Joseph, 1949; *Mrs. Malone,* Joseph, 1950; *Poems for Children,* Lippincott, 1951; *Silver Sand and Snow,* Joseph, 1951; *The Silver Curlew,* Oxford, 1953; *The Little Bookroom,* Oxford, 1955; *Then There Were Three: Being Cherrystones,* Lippincott, 1958; *The Hamis Hamilton Book of Kings,* Hamish, 1964; *A Cavalcade of Kings,* Walk, 1965; *The Hamis Hamilton Book of Queens,* Walck, 1965; *Mr. Garden*, Walck, 1966; *The Wonderful Knight*, Kaye, 1967; *Around the Seasons*, Walck, 1969; with her brother Herbert Farjeon, *Kings and Queens,* Gollancz, 1932; *Heroes and Heroines,* Dutton, 1933; the author received the first Hans Christian Andersen Award, a medal given biennially since 1956 by the International Board on Books for Young People to an author and, since 1966, to one illustrator, in recognition of his or her entire body of work). LBC

Berta and Elmer Hader's *Farmer in the Dell* (a concept picture book about farm life with bold black and white illustrations; published in New York by Macmillan; the authors-illustrators' *The Big Snow,* Macmillan, 1948, was awarded the Caldecott Medal in 1949; the authors-illustrators' other work, published by Macmillan except as noted, includes *Wee Willie Winkie and Some Other Boys and Girls from Mother Goose,* 1927; *The Little Red Hen,* 1928; *The Old Woman and the Crooked Sixpence,* 1928; *The Story of the Three Bears,* 1928; *Picture Book of Travel,* 1928; *Two Funny Clowns,* Coward, 1929; *What'll You Do When You Grow Up?,* Longmans, 1929; *Berta and Elmer Hader's Picture Book of Mother Goose,* Coward, 1930; *Lions and Tigers and Elephants Too,* Longmans, 1930; *Under the Pig-Nut Tree: Spring,* Knopf, 1930; *Tookey,* Longmans, 1931; *Under the Pig-Nut Tree: Summer,* Knopf, 1931; *Picture Book of the States,* Harper, 1932; *Chuck-a-Luck and His Reindeer,* Houghton, 1933; *Spunky,* 1933; *Whiffy McMann,* Oxford, 1933; *Midget and Bridget,* 1934; *Jamaica Johnny,* 1935;

1931 *continued*

Billy Butter, 1936; *Green and Gold,* 1936; *Stop, Look and Listen,* Longmans, 1936; *The Inside Story of the Hader Books,* 1937; *Tommy Thatcher Goes to Sea,* 1937; *Cricket,* 1938; *Cock-A-Doodle-Do,* 1939; *Cat and the Kitten,* 1940; *Little Town,* 1941; *Story of Pancho and the Bull With the Crooked Tail,* 1942; *Mighty Hunter,* 1943; *Little Stone House,* 1944; *Rainbow's End,* 1945; *Skyrocket,* 1946; *Squirrely of Willow Hill,* 1950; *Lost in the Zoo,* 1951; *Little White Foot,* 1951; *The Friendly Phoebe,* Macmillan, 1953; *Wish on the Moon,* 1954; *Home on the Range: Jeremiah Jones and His Friend Little Bear in the Far West,* 1955; *Ding, Dong, Bell, Pussy's in the Well,* 1957; *Little Chip of Willow Hill,* 1958; *Mister Billy's Gun,* 1960; *Quack, Quack,* 1961; *Little Antelope: An Indian for a Day,* 1962; *Show in the City,* 1963; *Two Is Company, Three's A Crowd,* 1965). UOr

Eleanor Lattimore's *Little Pear* (one of a series of books about Chinese children for young readers; illustrated by the author; published in New York by Harcourt; the author's other work, published by Morrow except as noted, includes *Jerry and the Pusa,* Harcourt, 1932; *The Seven Crowns,* Harcourt, 1933; *Little Pear and His Friends,* Harcourt, 1934; *Turkestan Reunion,* Harcourt, 1934; *The Lost Leopard,* Harcourt, 1935; *The Clever Cat,* Harcourt, 1936; *Junior, A Colored Boy of Charleston,* Harcourt, 1938; *Jonny,* Harcourt, 1939; *The Story of Lee Ling,* Harcourt, 1940; *The Questions of Lifu: A Story of China,* Harcourt, 1942; *Storm on the Island,* 1942; *Peachblossom,* 1943; *First Grade,* 1944; *Bayou Boy,* 1946; *Jeremy's Isle,* 1947; *Three Little Chinese Girls,* 1948; *Davy of the Everglades,* 1949; *Deborah's White Winter,* 1949; *Christopher and His Turtle,* 1950; *Indigo Hill,* 1950; *Bells for a Chinese Donkey,* 1951; *The Fig Tree,* 1951; *Lively Victoria,* 1952; *Jasper,* 1953; *Wu, the Gatekeeper's Son,* 1953; *Holly in the Snow,* 1954; *Diana in the China Shop,* 1955; *Willow Tree Village,* 1955; *Molly in the Middle,* 1956; *Little Pear and the Rabbits,* 1956; *The Journey of Ching Lai,* 1957; *The Monkey of Crofton,* 1957; *Fair Bay,* 1958; *Happiness for Kimi,* 1958; *The Fisherman's Son,* 1959; *The Youngest Artist,* 1959; *Beachcomber Boy,* 1960; *The Chinese Daughter,* 1960; *Cousin Melinda,* 1961; *The Wonderful Glass House,* 1961; *The Bittern's Nest,* 1962; *Laurie and Company,* 1962; *Janetta's Magnet,* 1963; *The Little Tumbler,* 1963; *Felicia,* 1964; *The Mexican Bird,* 1965; *The Bus Trip,* 1965; *The Search for Christina,* 1966; *The Two Helens,* 1967; *Bird Song,* 1968; *The Girl on the Deer,* 1969).

Ethel Parton's *Melissa Ann* (first of six books set in Newburyport, Massachusetts, between 1800 and 1870, based on actual records as well as childhood memories; published in New York by Doubleday; the author's other work includes *The Mule of the Parthenon,* Doubleday, 1932; *Tabitha Mary,* Viking, 1933; *Penelope Ellen,* Viking, 1936; *Vinny Applegay,* Viking, 1937; *The Runaway Prentice,* Viking, 1939; *The Lost Locket,* Viking, 1940; *The House Between,* Viking, 1943; *The Year Without a Summer,* Viking, 1945).

Winifred Welles's *Skipping Along Alone* (a collection of imaginative lyrical poems combining realism and fantasy; illustrated by Marguerite Davis; published in New York by Macmillan).

1932

Nora Burglon's *Children of the Soil* (the story of a poor Scandinavian peasant family which delights in telling stories and believes in the importance of the "little people"; published in New York by Doubleday; runner-up for the Newbery Medal; the author's other work includes *The Keeper of the Herd,* reprinted from *Junior Life Magazine,* 1935; *Ghost Ship,* Little, 1936; *The Gate Swings,* Little, 1937; *Deep Silver,* Houghton, 1938; *Sticks Across the Chimney,* Holiday, 1938; *Lost Island,* Winston, 1939; *The Cuckoo Calls,* Winston, 1940; *Around the Caribbean,* Heath, 1941; *Diego Wins,* Random, 1941; *Shark Hole,* Holiday, 1943; *Slave Girls,* Stephen Paul, 1947).

Alice Crew Gall and Fleming Crew's *Wagtail* (one of a series of informational books in narrative form about animals and their natural habitats; illustrated by Kurt Wiese; published in New York by Oxford; the author's other work includes *Ringtail,* Oxford, 1933; *Flat Tail,* Oxford, 1935; *Little Black Ant,* Oxford, 1936; *Each in His Way,* Oxford, 1937; *Splasher,* Oxford, 1945; *Winter Flight,* Oxford, 1949).

Langston Hughes's *The Dream Keeper* (a collection of poems about the black experience as well as universal life experience; published in New York by Knopf; a collection of author's poems for children selected by Lee Bennett Hopkins and illustrated by Ann Grifalconi with woodcuts is entitled *Don't You Turn Back,* Knopf, 1969; the author's other work includes, with Arna Bontemps, *Popo and Fifina,* Macmillan, 1932; *The Ways of White Folks,* Knopf, 1934; *Simple Speaks His Mind,* Simon, 1950; *The First Book of Negroes,* Watts, 1952; *The First Book of Rhythms,* Watts, 1954; *Famous American Negroes,* Dodd, 1954; *Famous American Music Makers,* Dodd, 1955; *The First Book of Jazz,* Watts, 1955; *Famous Negro Music Makers,* Dodd, 1955; *The First Book of the West Indies,* Watts, 1956 [republished as *The First Book of the Caribbean,* 1965]; *Famous*

1932 *continued*
Negro Heroes of America, Dodd, 1958; *The First Book of Africa,* Watts, 1950, revised edition 1964). YU

Dorothy Lathrop's *The Fairy Circus* (a book of verse, illustrated by the author, which features fairies as circus performers; published in New York by Macmillan; the author-illustrator was awarded the first Caldecott Medal in 1938 for her illustrations for Helen Dean Fish's *Animals of the Bible,* Lippincott; the author-illustrator's other work, published by Macmillan, includes *The Little White Goat,* 1933; *The Lost Merry-go-round,* 1934; *The Snail Who Ran,* Stokes, 1934; *Who Goes There?,* 1935; *Bouncing Betsy,* 1936; *Hide and Go Seek,* 1938; *Presents for Lupe,* 1940; *Puppies for Keeps,* 1943; *The Skittle-Skattle Monkey,* 1945; *Angel in the Woods,* 1947; *Let Them Live,* 1951; *Puffy and the Seven Leaf Clover,* 1954; *Littlest Mouse,* 1955; *Follow the Brook,* 1960). LC

Elizabeth Foreman Lewis's *Young Fu of the Upper Yangtze* (the story of a young country boy who goes to Chungking to become a coppersmith's apprentice; published by Winston; awarded the Newbery Medal; the author's other work, published by Winston, includes *Ho-Ming, Girl of New China,* 1934; *China Quest,* 1937; *Portraits from a Chinese Scroll,* 1938; *When the Typhoon Blows,* 1942; *To Beat a Tiger, One Needs a Brother's Help,* 1956).

Maj Lindman's *Snipp, Snapp, Snurr and the Red Shoes* (from the Swedish; illustrated by the author; the first of a popular series of picture-story adventures of three brothers; all published in Chicago by Whitman, includes *Snipp, Snapp, Snurr and the Magic Horse,* 1933; *Snipp, Snapp, Snurr and the Buttered Bread,* 1934; *Snipp, Snapp, Snurr and the Gingerbread,* 1936; *Snipp, Snapp, Snurr and the Yellow Sled,* 1936; *Snipp, Snapp, Snurr and the Big Surprise,* 1937; *Flicka, Ricka, Dicka and the New Dotted Dresses,* 1939; *Flicka, Ricka, Dicka and the Three Kittens,* 1941; *Snipp, Snapp, Snurr and the Big Farm,* 1946; *Dear Little Deer,* 1953; *Snipp, Snapp, Snurr and the Reindeer,* 1957; *Flicka, Ricka, Dicka and the Big Red Hen,* 1960).

Eloise Lownsberry's *Out of the Flame* (a story of life at the Court of François as experienced by a young boy; published in New York by Longmans; runner-up for the Newbery Medal; the author's other work includes *Boy Knight of Reims,* Houghton, 1927; *Lighting the Torch,* Longmans, 1934; *A Camel for a Throne,* Houghton, 1941; *Gift of the Forest,* with Reginald Lal Singh, Longmans, 1942).

Laura E. Richards's *Tirra Lirra: Rhymes Old and New* (one of the earliest major collections of nonsense verse for children by an American writer; published by Little, Brown; illustrated by Marguerite Davis; the author's other work includes *The Little Tyrant,* Estes, 1880; *Five Mice in a Mousetrap, By the Man in the Moon, Done in the Vernacular, from the Lunacular,* Estes, 1880; *Our Baby's Favorite,* Estes, 1881; *Sketches and Scraps,* illustrated by Henry Richards, Estes, 1881; *The Joyous Story of Toto,* illustrated by E. H. Garrett, Roberts, 1885; the author was the editor of *Four Feet, Two Feet, and No Feet,* Estes, 1886; the author was the reteller of *Beauty and the Beast,* illustrated by Gordon Browne, Roberts, 1886, and of *Hop O' My Thumb,* illustrated by Gordon Browne, Roberts, 1886; with H. Baldwin, *Kasper Kroak's Kaleidoscope,* Nimo, 1886; *Tell-Tale from Hill and Dale,* Nims, 1886; *Toto's Merry Winter,* Roberts, 1887; *Queen Hildegarde: A Story for Girls,* Estes, 1889; *In My Nursery,* Roberts, 1890; *Captain January,* Estes, 1891; *Hildegarde's Holiday: A Sequel to Queen Hildegarde,* Estes, 1881; *Hildegarde's Home,* Estes, 1892; *Glimpses of the French Court: Sketches from French History,* Estes, 1892; *Melody: The Story of a Child,* Estes, 1892; *Narcissa; or, The Road to Rome [and] in Verona,* Estes, 1894; *Marie,* Estes, 1894; *When I Was Your Age,* Estes, 1894; *Five Minute Stories,* Estes, 1895; *Hildegarde's Neighbors,* Estes, 1895; *Jim of Hellas; or, In Durance Vele [and] Bethesda Pool,* Estes, 1895; *Nautilus, Estes, 1895; Some Say [and] Neighbors in Cyprus,* Estes, 1896; *Isla Heron,* Estes, 1896; *Hildegarde's Harvest,* Estes, 1897; *Three Margarets,* illustrated by E. B. Barry, Estes, 1897; *Love and Rocks,* Estes, 1898; *Margaret Montfort,* illustrated by E. B. Barry, Estes, 1898; *Rosin the Beau: A Sequel to "Melody" and "Marie,"* Estes, 1898; *Chop-Chin and the Golden Dragon,* Little, 1899; *The Golden Breasted Kootoo,* Little, 1899; *Peggy,* illustrated by E. B. Barry, Estes, 1899; *Quicksilver Sue,* illustrated by W. D. Stevens, Century, 1899; *Sun Down Songs,* Little, 1899; *For Tommy and Other Stories,* Estes, 1900; reteller of *Snow-White or the House in the Wood,* Estes, 1900; *Rita,* Estes, 1900; *Fernley House,* Estes, 1901; *Geoffrey Strong,* Estes, 1901; *The Hurdy-Gurdy,* Estes, 1902; *Mrs. Tree,* Estes, 1902; *The Golden Windows: A Book of Fables for Young and Old,* Little, 1903; *The Green Satin Gown,* Estes, 1903; *More Five Minute Stories,* illustrated by Wallace Goldsmith, Estes, 1903; *The Merryweathers,* illustrated by Julia Ward Richards, Estes, 1904; *The Armstrongs,* illustrated by Julia Ward Richards, Estes, 1905; *Mrs. Tree's Will,* Estes, 1905; *The Piccolo,* Estes, 1906; *The Silver Crown,* Little, 1906; *Grandmother: The Story of a Life that Never Was Lived,* Estes, 1907; *The Pig Brothers,* Little, 1908; *The Wooing of Calvin Parks,* Estes, 1908; *Florence Nightingale,* Appleton, 1909; *A Happy Little Times,* Estes, 1910; *Up to Calvin's,* illustrated by Frank T. Merrill, Estes, 1910; *On Board the Merry Sands,* illustrated by

1932 *continued*

Frank T. Merrill, Estes, 1911; *The Little Master,* Estes, 1913; *Miss Jimmy,* Estes, 1913; *Three Minute Stories,* illustrated by Josephine Bruce, Page, 1914; *The Pig-Brother Play-Book,* Little, 1915; *Elizabeth Fry,* Appleton, 1916; *Fairy Operettas,* Little, 1916; *Abigail Adams,* Appleton, 1917; *Pippin: A Wandering Flame,* Appleton, 1917; *A Daughter of Jehu,* Appleton, 1918; *Joan of Arc,* Appleton, 1919; *Honor Bright,* illustrated by Frank T. Merrill, Page, 1920; *In Blessed Cyprus,* Appleton, 1921; *The Squire,* Appleton, 1923; *Honor Bright's New Adventure,* illustrated by Elizabeth Withington, Page, 1925; *Star Bright: A Sequel to "Captain January,"* illustrated by Frank T. Merrill, Page, 1927; *Laura Bridgeman,* Appleton, 1928; *Merry-Go-Round: New Rhymes and Old,* Appleton, 1935; *Harry in England,* illustrated by Reginald Birch, Appleton, 1937; *I Have A Song To Sing To You: Still More Rhymes,* illustrated by Reginald Birch, Appleton, 1938).

Hildegarde Swift's *Railroad to Freedom* (a fictionalized biographical account of Harriet Tubman, a runaway black slave, who led other slaves to freedom before the Civil War; published in New York by Harcourt; illustrated by James Daugherty; the author's other work includes *Little Black Nose,* Harcourt, 1930; *Little Red Lighthouse and the Great Gray Bridge,* Harcourt, 1942; *Edge of April,* Morrow, 1957; *From the Eagle's Wing,* Morrow, 1962).

Eunice Tietjens's *Boy of the South Seas* (a story which captures the mystery and enchantment of life on a South Sea island as well as the daily life, customs, and ideals of the Polynesian inhabitants; runner-up for the Newbery Medal; published in New York by Coward; author's other work includes *Boy of the Desert,* Coward, 1928; *Romance of Antar,* Coward, 1929; *The Jawbreaker's Alphabet,* Boni, 1930; reteller, *The Gingerbread Boy,* Whitman, 1932).

Laura Ingalls Wilder's *Little House in the Big Woods* (the first of a series of semiautobiographical novels set on the American frontier; subsequent books trace Laura's growing up; illustrated by Helen Sewell; published by Harper; the author was the first recipient of the award named in her honor, the Laura Ingalls Wilder Award, 1954, given every five years, since 1960, in recognition of an author or illustrator whose books, published in the United States, have over a period of years have made a lasting and substantial contribution to literature for children; administered by American Library Association, Children's Services Division; the author's other work, published by Harper, and illustrated by Helen Sewell and Mildred Boyle except as noted, includes *Farmer Boy,* illustrated by Helen Sewell, 1933; *Little House on the Prairie,* illustrated by Helen Sewell, 1935; *On the Banks of Plum Creek,* 1937; *By the Shores of Silver Lake,* 1939; *The Long Winter,* 1940; *Little Town on the Prairie,* 1941; *These Happy Golden Years,* 1943; *The First Four Years,* illustrated by Garth Williams, 1971; with Rose Wilder Lane, *On the Way Home: The Diary of a Trip from South Dakota to Mansfield, Missouri in 1894,* 1962; edited by Roger Lea MacBride, *West from Home: Letters from Laura Ingalls Wilder, San Francisco 1915,* 1974; current editions of the "Little House" books are illustrated by Garth Williams). DPL, PPL

1933

Boris Artzybasheff's *Aesop's Fables* (an important illustrated edition of a "classic" done in dramatic woodcuts; published in New York by Viking; the author-illustrator's other work includes *Poor Shaydullah,* Macmillan, 1931; *Seven Simeons,* Viking, 1937).

Rosemary and Stephen Benét's *A Book of Americans* (sometimes satirical, occasionally poignant observations in verse about some important Americans; illustrated by Charles Child; published in New York by Farrar and Rinehart; Stephen Benét's other work includes [poetry] *The Ballad of William Sycamore, 1790-1880,* Hackett, 1923; *John Brown's Body,* Doubleday, 1941; *Ballads and Poems, 1915-1930,* Doubleday, 1931; [prose] *The Beginning of Wisdom,* Holt, 1921; *James Shore's Daughter,* Doubleday, 1934; [short stories] *Thirteen O'Clock: Stories of Several Worlds,* Farrar, 1937; *The Devil and Daniel Webster,* Countryman's Press, 1937; *Johnny Pye and the Fool-Killer,* Farrar, 1938; *Tales Before Midnight,* Farrar, 1939; [letters] *Stephen Vincent Benét on Writing: A Great Writer's Letters of Advice to a Young Beginner,* Green, 1964).

Erick Berry's *Winged Girl of Knossos* (a story about the exciting adventures of Inas, daughter of Daidalos, set in Crete during the time of Ariadne and Theseus; published by Appleton; runner-up for the Newbery Medal; the author's other work includes *Black Folk Tales,* retold from the Hausa, Harper, 1928; *Girls in Africa,* Macmillan, 1928; *Chang of the Siamese Jungle,* Dutton, 1930; *Penny Whistle,* Macmillan, 1930; *Mom Du Jos, The Story of a Little Black Doll,* Doubleday, 1931; *Humbro the Hippo and Little-Boy-Bumbo,* Harper, 1932; *Juma of the Hills, A Story of West Africa,* Harcourt, 1932; *Sojo, The Story of Little Lazybones,* Harper, 1934; *Strings to Adventure,* Lothrop, 1935; *Illustrations of Cynthia,* Harcourt, 1936; *Sunhelmet Sue,* Lothrop, 1936; *Cynthia Steps Out,* Goldsmith, 1937; *Homespun,* Lothrop, 1937; *Nancy Herself,* Goldsmith, 1937; *Honey of the Nile,* Oxford, 1938; *Humbo the Hippo,* Grosset, 1938; *Your Cup and Saucer,* Nelson, 1938; *Go and Find Wind,* Oxford, 1939; *One-String*

1933 *continued*

Fiddle, Winston, 1939; *Lock Her Through,* Oxford, 1940; *The Tinmaker of New Amsterdam,* Winston, 1941; *Whistle Round the Bend,* Oxford, 1941; *Hudson Frontier,* Oxford, 1942; *This Is the Land,* Oxford, 1943; *Hearthstone in the Wilderness,* Macmillan, 1944; *Harvest of the Hudson,* Macmillan, 1945; *The Little Farm in the Big City,* Viking, 1947; *Seven Beaver Skins,* Winston, 1948; *Forty-Seven Keys,* Macmillan, 1949; *The Road Runs Both Ways,* Macmillan, 1950; *Sybil Ludington's Ride,* Viking, 1952; *Hay-foot, Straw-foot,* Viking, 1954; *Green Door to the Sea,* Viking, 1955; Erick Berry is the pseudonym of Mrs. Evangel Allena Champlin Best). UOr

Jean de Brunhoff's *The Story of Babar* (translated from the French by Merle Haas; the first of a series of popular picture-story books about an elephant; published in Racine, Wisconsin, by Whitman; continued after author-illustrator's death by son, Laurent; the author-illustrator's other work includes *The Travels of Babar,* Methuen, 1934; *Babar the King,* Smith, 1935; *Babar's Friend Zephir,* Methuen, 1937; *Zephir's Holidays,* Random, 1937; *Babar at Home,* Methuen, 1938; *Babar and Father Christmas,* Random, 1940; *Babar's ABC,* Random, 1949; [Laurent] *Babar's Cousin, That Rascal Arthur,* illustrated by Merle Haas, Random, 1948; *Babar and the Professor,* Random, 1957; *Babar's French Lessons,* Random, 1965; *Serafina the Giraffe,* World, 1965; *Serafina's Lucky Find,* World, 1967; *Captain Serafina,* World, 1968).

Roger Duvoisin's *Donkey-Donkey* (an amusing picture story illustrated by the author, who is probably best known for his Petunia books; published in Racine, Wisconsin, by Whitman; reissued in 1976; the author-illustrator's other work includes *A Little Boy Was Drawing,* Scribner, 1932; *And There Was America,* Knopf, 1938; *The Christmas Cake in Search of Its Owner,* American Artists Group, 1941; *The Three Sneezes and Other Swiss Tales,* Knopf, 1941; *They Put Out to Sea; The Story of the Map,* Knopf, 1943, new edition, 1959; *The Christmas Whale,* Knopf, 1945; *Chanticleer, the Real Story of the Famous Rooster,* Grosset, 1947; *The Four Corners of the World,* Knopf, 1948; *Petunia,* Knopf, 1950; *A for Ark,* Lee and Shepard, 1952; *Petunia's Christmas,* Knopf, 1952; *Petunia Takes a Trip,* Knopf, 1942; *Petunia and the Song,* Knopf, 1953; *Easter Treat,* Knopf, 1954; *Two Lonely Ducks,* Knopf, 1955; *One Thousand Christmas Beards,* Knopf, 1955; *The House of Four Seasons,* Lothrop, 1956; *Petunia Beware,* Knopf, 1958; *Day and Night,* Knopf, 1960; *Veronica,* Knopf, 1961; *The Happy Hunter,* Lothrop, 1961; *Our Veronica Goes to Petunia's Farm,* Knopf, 1962; *Spring Snow,* Knopf, 1963; *Lonely Veronica,* Knopf, 1963; *Veronica's Smile,* Knopf, 1964; *Petunia, I Love You,* Knopf, 1965; *The Missing Milkman,* Knopf, 1967; *What Is Right for Tulip?,* Knopf, 1969).

Marjorie Flack's *The Story About Ping* (an animal picture-story book that incidentially introduces young children to the old Chinese culture; illustrated by Kurt Wiese; published in New York by Viking; the author's other work includes *Tartuk, an Arctic Boy,* Doubleday, 1928, with Helen Loman; *All Around the Town: The Story of a Boy in New York,* Doubleday, 1929; *Angus and the Ducks,* Viking, 1930; *Angus and the Cat,* Viking, 1931; *Angus Lost,* Viking, 1932; *Ask Mr. Bear,* Viking, *Wag-Tail Bess,* Doubleday, 1933; *Humphrey,* Doubleday, 1934; *Tim Tadpole and the Great Bullfrog,* Doubleday, 1934; *Christopher,* Doubleday, 1935; *Wait for William,* Houghton, 1935; *Topsy and Angus and the Cat,* Doubleday, 1935; *Up in the Air,* illustrated by Karl Larsson, Macmillan, 1935; *Topsy,* Doubleday, 1935; *What To Do About Molly,* illustrated by Larsson, *Macmillan,* 1936; *Willy Nilly,* Doubleday, 1936; *Walter, the Lazy Mouse,* Doubleday, 1937; *The Restless Robin,* Houghton, 1937; *Lucky Little Lena,* Macmillan, 1937; with Karl Larsson, *Pedro,* Macmillan, 1940; *Adolphus,* Houghton, 1941; *I See a Kitty,* illustrated by Karl's daughter, Hilma Larsson, Garden City, 1943; *The New Pet,* Doubleday, 1943; *Away Goes Jonathan Wheeler,* illustrated by Hilma Larsson, Garden City, 1944; *Boats on the River,* Viking, 1946; *Happy Birthday Letter,* Houghton, 1947).

Anne Kyle's *Apprentice of Florence* (a story of a young boy's romantic adventures in Florence during the time of the fall of Constantinople; published in Boston by Houghton; runner-up for the Newbery Medal; the author's other work includes *Crusader's Gold,* Houghton, 1928; *Prince of the Pale Mountains,* Houghton, 1929; *Red Sky Over Rome,* Houghton, 1938).

Louise Lamprey's *All the Ways of Building* (one of the author's many informational books that respect the child's intelligence and wide variety of interests; published in New York by Macmillan; the author's other work includes *In the Days of the Guild,* 1918; *Masters of the Guild,* Stokes, 1920; *Wonder Tales of Architecture,* Stokes, 1927; *The Treasure Valley,* Morrow, 1928; *The Tomahawk Trail,* Stokes, 1934; *The Story of Weaving,* Stokes, 1929; *The Story of Cookery,* Stokes, 1940; *Building an Empire,* Stokes, 1941; *Building a Republic,* Stokes, 1942; Great Days in America series, 1921-1926; Children of the World series, 1921-1928, published by Macmillan, includes books about children in the Congo, ancient Britain, Rome, Greece, Egypt, Gaul, and Russia).

Cornelia Meigs's *Invincible Louisa* (a biography of Louisa May Alcott; published by Little, Brown; awarded Newbery Medal in 1934; illustrated with photographs; the author's other work includes *The Kingdom of the Winding Road,* Macmillan, 1915; *Master Simon's Garden,* Macmillan,

1933 *continued*

1916; *The Steadfast Princess: A Play,* Macmillan, 1916; *The Windy Hill,* Macmillan, 1921; *Helga, the White Peacock: A Play,* Macmillan, 1922; *The New Moon: The Story of Dick Martin's Courage, His Silver Sixpence, His Friends in the New World,* Macmillan, 1924; *Rain on the Roof,* Macmillan, 1925; *As the Crow Flies,* Macmillan, 1927; *The Trade Wind,* Little, 1927; *Clearing Weather,* Little, 1928; *The Wonderful Locomotive,* Macmillan, 1928; *The Crooked Apple Tree,* Little, 1929; *The Willow Whistle,* Macmillan, 1931; *Swift Rivers,* Little, 1932; *Wind in the Chimney,* Macmillan, 1934; *The Covered Bridge,* Macmillan, 1936; *Young Americans: How History Looked to Them While It Was in the Making,* Ginn, 1936; *Railroad West*, Little, 1937; *The Scarlet Oak*, Macmillan, 1938; *Call of the Mountain,* Little, 1940; *Mother Makes Christmas,* Grosset, 1940; *Vanished Island,* Macmillan, 1941; *Mounted Messenger,* Macmillan, 1943; *The Two Arrows,* Macmillan, 1949; *The Violent Men: A Study of Human Relations in the First American Congress,* Macmillan, 1949; *The Dutch Colt,* Macmillan, 1952; *Fair Wind To Virginia,* Macmillan, 1955; *Wild Geese Flying,* Macmillan, 1957; *Mystery At the Red House,* Macmillan, 1961; *The Great Design: Men and Events in the United Nations from 1945-1963*, Little, 1964; *Glimpses of Louisa,* editor Little, 1968; *Jane Addams: Pioneer for Social Justice,* Little, 1970; *Louisa M. Alcott and the American Family Story,* Walck, 1971; books written under the pseudonym Adair Alton include: *The Island of Appledore,* Macmillan, 1917; *The Pirate of Jasper Peak,* Macmillan, 1918; *The Pool of Stars,* Macmillan, 1919; *At the Sign of the Heroes,* Century, 1920; *The Hill of Adventure,* Century, 1922).

Stafford Riggs's *The Story of Beowulf* (first important retelling of Beowulf for American children; illustrated by Henry C. Pitz; published in New York by Appleton-Century).

Sarah Schmidt's *New Land* (the story of a twin brother and sister who make a home for themselves in Wyoming; published in New York by McBride; the author's other work includes *The Secret of Silver Peak,* Random, 1938; *Shadow Over Winding Ranch,* Random, 1940; *The Hurricane Mystery,* Random, 1943; *Ranching on Eagle Eye,* McBride, 1943).

Elsie Singmaster's *Swords of Steel* (the story of a young boy who grows into manhood as he takes part in the Civil War and the Battle of Gettysburg; published in New York by Houghton; the author's other work, published by Houghton except as noted, includes *When Sarah Saved the Day,* 1909; *When Sarah Went to School,* 1910; *Katy Gaumer,* 1913; *Emmeline,* 1916; *Gettysburg,* 1916; *The Long Journey,* 1917; *Martin Luther,* 1917; *Basil*

Everman, 1920; *John Baring's House,* 1920; *Ellen Levis,* 1921; *Bennett Malin,* 1922; *The Hidden Road,* 1923; *A Boy at Gettysburg,* 1924; *Bred in the Bone and Other Stories,* illustrated by Elizabeth Shippen Green, 1925; *The Book of the Constitution,* Doran, 1926; *The Book of the United States,* Doran, 1927; *"Sewing Susie,"* 1927; *What Everybody Wanted,* 1928; *Virginia's Bandit,* 1929; *You Make Your Own Luck,* Longmans, 1929; *The Young Ravenals,* 1932; *The Magic Mirror,* 1934; *The Loving Heart,* 1937; *Stories of Pennsylvania,* Pennsylvania Book Service, 1937; *Rifles for Washington,* 1938; *Stories to Read at Christmas,* 1940; *A High Wind Rising,* 1942; *I Speak for Thaddeus Stevens,* 1947; *I Heard of a River,* illustrated by Henry C. Pitz, Winston, 1948; *The Isle of Que,* illustrated by Elmer Hader, Longmans, 1948).

1934

Ellis Credle's *Down, Down the Mountain* (a picture-story book about poor but industrious Appalachian children; published in New York by Nelson; the author-illustrator's other work, published by Nelson except as noted, includes *Pig-O-Wee,* Rand, 1935; *Across the Cotton Patch,* 1935; *Little Jeemes Henry,* 1936; *Pepe and the Parrot,* 1937; *The Flop-Eared Hound,* Oxford, 1938; *The Goat That Went to School,* Grosset, 1940; *Here Comes the Show Boat,* 1940; *Janie's Shoes,* Grosset, 1941; *Johnny and His Mule,* Oxford, 1948; *My Pet Peepolo,* Oxford, 1948; *Adventures of Tittletom,* Oxford, 1949; *Big Doin's on Razor Back Ridge,* 1956; *Tall Tales from the High Hills,* 1957; *Little Fraid, Big Fraid,* 1964; *Monkey See Monkey Do,* 1968; *Mexico, Land of Hidden Treasure,* 1967; *Little Pest Pico,* 1969).

Frank Dalby Davison's *Red Heifer* (an Australian writer's account of the encroachment of civilization on the Australian bush; published in New York by Coward-McCann).

Roderick Haig-Brown's *Ki-Yu: A Story of Panthers* (a Canadian author's account of the life-cycle of a panther on Vancouver Island; illustrated by Theyre Lee-Elliott; published in Boston by Houghton, also published in London by Collins under the title *Panther;* the author's other work includes *Starbuck Valley Winter,* Morrow, 1943; *Saltwater Summer,* Morrow, 1948; *Mounted Police Patrol,* Collins, 1954; *Captain of the Discovery: The Story of Captain George Vancouver,* Macmillan, 1956; *The Farthest Shores,* Longmans, 1960).

Margaret Thomsen Raymond's *A Bend in the Road* (the story of a young girl who rebels against her parents and runs away from home to make her own living; published in London by Longmans, Green).

1934 *continued*

Constance Rourke's *Davy Crockett* (a tale of the legendary hunter and hero of the Western frontier, illustrated by Walter Seaton; published in New York by Doubleday; runner-up for the Newbery Medal; the author's other Newbery runner-up book is *Audubon,* Harcourt, 1936).

Elizabeth Seeger's *Pageant of Chinese History* (the story of China's past, providing a sympathetic description of the people's lives; published in New York by Longmans; runner-up for the Newbery Medal; the author's other work includes *The Five Brothers of Mahabharta,* adapted from the English translation by Kisari Mohan, Day, 1948).

Monica Shannon's *Dobry* (a novel revealing Bulgarian farm life, customs, and costumes in a tender story; illustrated by Atanas Katchamakoff; published in New York by Viking; awarded Newbery Medal in 1935; the author's other work includes *California Fairy Tales,* Doubleday, 1926).

Pamela Travers's *Mary Poppins* (the first of a series of imaginative episodes centering on the antics of an extraordinary British nanny; published by Reynal and Hitchcock; illustrated by Mary Shepard; the author's other work includes *Mary Poppins Comes Back,* Reynal, 1935; *Moscow Excursion,* Reynal, 1935; *Happy Ever After,* Reynal, 1940; *I Go By Sea, I Go By Land,* Harper, 1941; *Mary Poppins Opens the Door,* Reynal, 1943; *Mary Poppins in the Park,* Harcourt, 1952; *The Fox at the Manger,* Norton, 1962; *Mary Poppins from A to Z,* Harcourt, 1962).

1935

Enid Bagnold's *National Velvet* (a popular horse story by a British author; published in London by Heineman; illustrated by Laurian Jones, the author's daughter; the author's other work includes *Alice and Thomas and Jane,* Heineman, 1930).

Carol Ryrie Brink's *Caddie Woodlawn* (the story of a young girl's growing up in Wisconsin in the 1860s; illustrated by Kate Seredy; awarded Newbery Medal in 1936; published in New York by Macmillan; the author's other work includes *Anything Can Happen on the River,* Macmillan, 1934; *Mademoiselle Misfortune,* Macmillan, 1936; *Baby Island,* Macmillan, 1937; *All Over Town,* Macmillan, 1939; *Lad With A Whistle,* Macmillan, 1941; *Magic Melons,* Macmillan, 1944; *Caddie Woodlawn, A Play,* Macmillan, 1945; *Narcissa Whitman,* Row, 1946; *Lafayette,* Row, Peterson, 1946; *Minty et Compagnie,* Easterman, 1948; *Family Grandstand,* Viking, 1952; *The Highly Trained Dogs of Professor Petit,* Macmillan, 1953;

Family Sabbatical, Viking, 1956; *The Pink Motel,* Macmillan, 1959; *Andy Buckram's Tin Men,* Viking, 1966; *Winter Cottage,* Macmillan, 1968; *Two Are Better Than One*, Macmillan, 1968). MPL, UMi

Eva Knox Evans's *Araminta* (the first of three books about a young black child; published in New York by Minton; the author's other work includes *Jerome Anthony,* Putnam, 1936; *Araminta's Goat,* Putnam, 1938; *Key Corner,* Putnam, 1938; *Emma Belle and Her Kinfolks,* Putnam, 1940; *The Lost Handkerchiefs,* Putnam, 1941; *Mr. Jones and Mr. Finnigan,* Oxford, 1941; *Something Different,* Heath, 1942; *A Surprise for Araminta,* Grosset, 1942; *Skookum,* Putnam, 1946; *Tim's Place,* Putnam, 1950; *The Story of Su-Su,* McKay, 1953; *Why We Live Where We Live,* Little, 1953).

Grey Owl's *The Adventures of Sajo and Her Beaver People* (one of the first books sympathetic to Indians, has an Indian female as a main character; published in Toronto by Macmillan; Grey Owl is the pseudonym of "Archie" George Stansfeld Belaney, an Englishman who lived with the Ojibways most of his adult life; his Indian name was Wa-Sha-Quon-Asin; this Canadian author's other work includes *Pilgrims of the Wild,* Dickson, 1935; *Tales of an Empty Cabin,* Dickson, 1936; *Tree,* Macmillan, 1937).

Inez Hogan's *Bear Twins* (one of a series of picture-story books about twin animals; illustrated by the author; published in New York by E. P. Dutton; the author's other work, published by Dutton except as noted, includes *The Black and White Lamb,* Macrae, 1927; *Sandy, Skip and the Man in the Moon,* Macrae, 1928; *The Little Toy Airplane,* Macrae, 1930; *The White Kitten and the Blue Plate,* Macmillan, 1930; *Nicodemus and His Little Sister,* 1932; *Nicodemus and the Houn' Dog,* 1933; *Nicodemus and the Little Black Pig,* 1934; *Elephant Twins,* 1936; *Nicodemus and His Gran'pappy,* 1936; *Twin Kids,* 1937; *Nicodemus and Petunia,* 1937; *Animal Tales from the Old North State,* 1938; *Nicodemus and His New Shoes,* 1938; *Kangaroo Twins,* 1938; *Four Funny Men,* 1939; *Mule Twins,* 1939; *Nicodemus and the Gang,* 1939; *Nicodemus and the New Born Baby,* 1940; edited with Mary Ellen Vorse, *Skinny Gets Fat,* Scott, 1940; *Twin Seals,* 1940; *Wakey Goes to Bed,* Scott, 1941; *Nicodemus Laughs,* 1941; *Twin Deer,* 1941; *Nappy Wanted a Dog,* 1942; *Nicodemus Runs Away,* 1942; *Bigger and Bigger,* Heath, 1942; *Monkey Twins,* 1943; *Listen Hitler! The Gremlins Are Coming,* 1943; *Nicodemus Helps Uncle Sam,* 1943; *Nappy Planted a Garden,* 1944; *Twin Colts,* 1944; *Nicodemus and the Goose,* 1945; *Nappy Chooses a Pet,* 1946; *Raccoon Twins,* 1946; *Nappy Has a New Friend,* 1947; *Read to Me About Nona, the Baby Elephant,* 1947; *Read to Me About Peter Platypus,* 1948; *Giraffe Twins,* 1948; *Nappy Is a*

1935 *continued*

Cowboy, 1949; *World Round,* 1949; *Runaway Toys,* 1950; *Read to Me About Charlie,* 1950; *Read to Me About the Littlest Cowboy,* 1951; *Twin Lambs,* 1951; *A Party for Poodles,* 1952; *We Are a Family,* 1952; *A Bear Is a Bear,* 1953; *Me* [poems], 1954; *Upside Down Book: A Story for Little Girls,* 1955; *Upside Down Book: A Story for Little Boys,* 1955; *Koala Bear Twins,* 1955; *The Little Ones,* 1956; *The Big Ones,* 1957; *The Littlest Satellite,* 1958; *Twin Kittens,* 1958; *The Littlest Bear,* 1959; *Twin Puppies,* 1959; *Little Lost Bear,* 1960; *Monkey See, Monkey Do;* 1960; *The Lone Wolf,* 1961; *Cubby Bear and the Book,* 1961; *Fraidy Cat,* 1962; *Twin Otters and the Indians,* 1962). ChPL

Philip D. Stong's *Honk: the Moose* (a humorous realistic animal story set in Minnesota; illustrated by Kurt Wiese; published in New York by Dodd, Mead; the author's other work includes *Farm Boy,* Doubleday, 1934; *Young Settler,* Dodd, 1938; *Cowhand Goes to Town,* Dodd, 1939; *Censored, the Goat,* Dodd, 1945; *A Beast Called an Elephant,* Dodd, 1955).

Louis Untermeyer's *Rainbow in the Sky* (the editor's first poetry collection for young people; published in New York by Harcourt; poet-editor's other work includes *Stars to Steer By,* Harcourt, 1941; *French Fairy Tales Retold,* Didier, 1945; *The Wonderful Adventures of Paul Bunyan,* Heritage, 1945; *All the French Fairy Tales,* Didier, 1946; *The Golden Treasury of Poetry,* illustrated by Joan Walsh Anglund, Golden, 1959; *Big and Little Creatures,* Golden, 1961; *Beloved Tales,* Golden, 1962; *Fun and Fancy,* Golden, 1962; *One and One and One,* Crowell, 1962; *Creatures Wild and Tame,* Golden, 1963; *Legendary Animals,* Golden, 1963; *Golden Treasury of Children's Literature,* Golden, 1966; *Merry Christmas: Legends and Traditions in Many Lands,* Golden, 1968; *Friend Indeed,* Golden, 1968).

1936

C. W. Anderson's *Billy and Blaze* (one of a series of popular realistic animal stories for young readers, published in New York by Macmillan; illustrated by author; the author-illustrator's other work, published by Macmillan except as noted, includes *And So to Bed,* Loring, 1935; *Blaze and the Gypsies,* 1937; *Blaze and the Forest Fire,* 1938; *Black Bay and Chestnut,* 1939; *Deep Through the Heart,* 1940; *Salute!,* 1940; *High Courage,* 1941; *Thoroughbreds,* 1942; *Big Red,* 1943; *Heads Up, Heels Down,* 1944; *A Touch of Greatness,* 1945; *All Thoroughbreds,* Harper, 1948; *Bobcat,* 1949; *Post Parade,* Harper, 1949; *Blaze Finds the Trail,* 1950; *Horses Are Folks,* Harper, 1950; *A Pony for Linda,* 1951; *Horse Show,* Harper, 1951; *Linda and the Indians,* 1952; *Turf and Bluegrass,* Harper, 1952; *The Crooked*

Colt, 1954; *The Smashers,* Harper, 1954; *Grey, Bay, and Chestnut,* Harper, 1955; *Blaze and the Thunderbolt,* 1955; *Colts and Champions,* Harper, 1956; *The Horse of Hurricane Hill,* 1956; *Afraid to Ride,* 1957; *Pony for Three,* 1958; *Blaze and the Mountain Lion,* 1959; *A Filly for Joan,* 1960; *Lonesome Little Colt,* 1961; *Complete Book of Horses,* 1963; *Blaze and the Indian Cave,* 1964; *The World of Horses,* 1965; *Before the Bugle,* 1965; *Great Heart,* 1965; *Twenty Gallant Horses,* 1965; *Blaze and the Lost Quarry,* 1966; *Another Man o' War,* 1966; *C. W. Anderson's Favorite Horse Stories,* 1967; *The Outlaw,* 1967; *Blaze and the Gray Spotted Pony,* 1968; *Blaze Shows the Way,* 1969).

Edward Ardizzone's *Little Tim and the Brave Sea Captain* (the first of the picture stories in Little Tim sea series; published in London by Oxford; this British author-illustrator was awarded the Kate Greenaway Medal for *Tim All Alone,* Walck, 1956; the medal has been given annually since 1957 by the British Library Association to the most distinguished work in the illustration of children's books published in the United Kingdom during the preceding year; the author-illustrator's other work includes *Lucy Brown and Mr. Grimes,* Oxford, 1937; *Tim and Lucy Go to Sea,* Oxford, 1938; *Nicholas and the Fast-Moving Diesel,* Eyre and Spottiswoode, 1947; *Paul, the Hero of the Fire,* Penguin, 1948; *Tim to the Rescue,* Oxford, 1949; *Tim and Charlotte,* Oxford, 1951; *Tim in Danger,* Oxford, 1953; *Johnny the Clockmaker,* Walck, 1960; *Tim's Friend Towser,* Walck, 1962; *Peter the Wanderer,* Oxford, 1963; *Diana and Her Rhinoceros,* Walck, 1964; *Tim and Ginger,* Walck, 1965; *Sarah and Simon and No Red Paint,* Constable, 1965; with Aingelda Ardizzone, *The Little Girl and the Tiny Doll,* Constable, 1966; *Tim to the Lighthouse,* Walck, 1968).

Helen D. Boylston's *Sue Barton, Student Nurse* (the first of a popular series of fictional accounts featuring various types of nursing; published in Boston by Little, Brown and Company; the author's other work, published by Little, Brown except as noted, includes *Sue Barton, Senior Nurse,* 1937; *Sue Barton, Visiting Nurse,* 1938; *Sue Barton, Rural Nurse,* 1939; *Sue Barton, Superintendent of Nurses,* 1940; *Carol Goes Backstage,* 1941; *Carol Plays Summer Stock,* 1942; *Carol Goes on Stage,* Lane, 1943; *Carol on Broadway,* 1944; *Carol on Tour,* 1946; *Sue Barton, Neighborhood Nurse,* 1949; *Sue Barton, Staff Nurse,* 1952; *Clara Barton, Founder of the American Red Cross,* Random, 1955).

Ralph Steele Boggs's *Three Golden Oranges* (romantic tales of Spain retold and collected by author with the assistance of Mary Gould Davis; illustrated by Emma Brock; published in New York by Longmans).

1936 *continued*

James Cloyd Bowman's with Margery Bianco's *Tales from a Finnish Tupa* (stories collected from one of the earliest printed sources of Finnish folktales; illustrated by Laura Bannon; published in Chicago by Whitman; the author was one of the first to give American children the tall tales of *Pecos Bill, the Greatest Cowboy of All Time,* Whitman, 1937; the author's other work includes *Mike Fink: The Snapping Turtle of the O-hi-oo and the Snag of the Mas-sas-sip,* Little, 1957).

Marguerite de Angeli's *Henner's Lydia* (the first of author-illustrator's several historical stories for middle-grade children; published in New York by Doubleday; the author-illustrator's popular *The Door in the Wall,* Doubleday, 1949, was awarded the Newbery Medal in 1950; the author's other work, published by Doubleday except as noted, includes *Ted and Nina Go to the Grocery Story,* 1935; *Ted and Nina Have a Happy Rainy Day,* 1936; *Petite Suzanne,* 1937; *Skippack School,* 1938; *A Summer Day with Ted and Nina,* 1940; *Thee, Hannah!,* 1940; *Elin's Amerika,* 1941; *Copper-Toed Boots,* 1943; *Yonie Wondernose,* 1944; *Turkey for Christmas,* 1944; *Bright April,* 1946; *Jared's Island,* 1947; *Just Like David,* 1951; *Marguerite de Angeli's Book of Nursery and Mother Goose Rhymes,* 1954; *Black Fox of Lorne,* 1956; *The Old Testament,* 1960; with Arthur de Angeli, *The Empty Barn,* Westminster, 1961; *Pocket Full of Posies,* 1961; *Marguerite de Angeli's Book of Favorite Hymns,* 1963; *The Ted and Nina Story Book,* 1965). PFL

Muriel Denison's *Susannah, a Little Girl with the Mounties* (the story of a little girl who helps the Canadian mounties bring in a "wanted" man; published in New York by Dodd, Mead).

Agnes Danforth Hewes's *Codfish Market* (the book reveals the part that trade played in the history of America; runner-up for the Newbery Medal; published in New York by Doubleday; the author's other work includes *Glory of the Seas,* a Newbery Medal runner-up, Knopf, 1933; *A Boy of the Lost Crusade,* Houghton, 1923; *Swords on the Sea,* Knopf, 1928; *Spice and the Devil's Cave,* Knopf, 1930; *The Golden Sleeve,* Doubleday, 1937; *The Sword of Roland Arnot,* Houghton, 1939; *The Iron Doctor,* Houghton, 1940; *Spice Ho!,* Knopf, 1941; *Jackhammer: Drill Runners of the Mountain Highways,* Knopf, 1942).

Idwal Jones's *Whistler's Van* (the story of a child's wonderful adventures with the gypsies in Wales, based on the author's childhood experiences; published in New York by Viking; runner-up for the Newbery Medal; illustrated by Zhenya Gay; the author's other work includes *The Splendid Shilling,* Doubleday, 1926; *China Boy,* Primavera, 1936; . . . *Black Bayou,* Duell, 1941; *High Bonnet,* Prentice-Hall, 1945).

Munro Leaf's *The Story of Ferdinand* (a "classic" animal picture-story book for young children; illustrated by Robert Lawson; published by Viking; the author's other work includes *Lo, the Poor Indian,* Mahoney, 1934; *Grammar Can Be Fun,* Stokes, 1934; *Manners Can Be Fun,* Stokes, 1936; *The Watchbirds,* Stokes, 1936; *Robert Francis Weatherbee,* Stokes, 1936; *Noodle,* Stokes, 1937; *Safety Can Be Fun,* Stokes, 1938; *Wee Gillis,* Viking, 1937; *Fair Play,* Lippincott, 1939; *John Henry Davis,* Stokes, 1940; *Let's Do Better,* Lippincott, 1945; *Sam and the Superdroop,* Viking, 1948; *Arithmetic Can Be Fun,* Lippincott, 1949; *History Can Be Fun,* Lippincott, 1950; *Geography Can Be Fun,* Lippincott, 1950; *Lucky You,* Lippincott, 1955; *Science Can Be Fun,* Lippincott, 1958; *Being an American Can Be Fun,* Lippincott, 1964).

Ruth Sawyer's *Roller Skates* (a child's adventures on the sidewalks of New York City in the 1890s; illustrated by Valenti Angelo; awarded Newbery Medal in 1937; published in New York by Viking; the author received the Laura Ingalls Wilder Award in 1965; the author's other work, published by Viking except as noted, includes *This Way to Christmas,* Harper, 1916; *Tale of the Enchanted Bunnies,* Harper, 1923; *Tono Antonio,* 1934; *Picture Tales from Spain,* Stokes, 1934; *The Year of Jublio,* 1940; *The Least One,* 1941; *The Long Christmas,* 1941; *The Christmas Anna Angel,* 1944; *Old Con and Patrick,* 1946; *The Little Red Horse,* 1950; *Maggie Rose, Her Birthday Christmas,* illustrated by Maurice Sendak, 1952; *Journey Cake, Ho!,* 1953; *A Cottage for Betsy,* Harper, 1954; *The Enchanted Schoolhouse,* 1956; *The Year of the Christmas Dragon,* 1960; with Emmy Molles, *Dietrich of Berne and the Dwarf-King Laurin: Hero Tales of the Austrian Tirol,* 1963; *Daddles: The Story of a Plain Hound-Dog,* Little, 1964; *Joy to the World: Christmas Legends,* Little, 1966).

1937

Esther Averill's *The Voyages of Jacques Cartier* (the title was revised to *Cartier Sails the St. Lawrence,* Harper, 1956; a distinguished biographical account of Cartier's historic journey; illustrated by Feodor Rojankovsky; the author's other work, published by Harper except as noted, includes, with Lila Stanley, *Powder: The Story of a Colt, a Dutchess, and the Circus,* Faber, 1933; *Flash: The Story of a Horse, a Coach-Dog, and the Gypsies,* Faber, 1934; *The Cat Club,* 1944; with Lila Stanley, *The Adventures of Jack Ninepins,* 1944; *Daniel Boone,* 1946; *The School for Cats,* 1947;

1937 *continued*

Jenny's First Party, 1948; *Jenny's Moonlight Adventure,* 1949; *King Philip: The Indian Chief,* 1950; *When Jenny Lost Her Scarf,* 1951; *Jenny's Adopted Brothers,* 1952; *How the Brothers Joined the Cat Club,* 1953; *Jenny's Birthday Book,* 1954; *Jenny Goes to Sea,* 1957; *Jenny's Bedside Book,* 1959; *The Fire Cat,* 1960; *The Hotel Cat,* 1969; *Eyes on the World,* Funk, 1969).

Arna Bontemps's *Sad-Faced Boy* (the story of the adventures of three black boys who travel from Alabama to New York; published in Boston by Houghton Mifflin; the author's other work includes, with Langston Hughes, *Popo and Fifina,* Macmillan, 1932; *You Can't Pet a Possum,* Morrow, 1934; *Black Thunder,* Macmillan, 1936; with W. C. Handy, *Father of the Blues,* Macmillan, 1941; *Golden Slippers,* Harper, 1941; with Jack Conroy, *The Fast Sooner Hound,* Houghton, 1942; *The Story of the Negro,* a Newbery Honor Book, Knopf, 1942; with Jack Conroy, *Slappy Hooper,* Houghton, 1946; with Jack Conroy, *Sam Patch, the High Wide and Handsome,* Houghton, 1951; *The Story of George Washington Carver,* Row, 1954; *Lonesome Boy,* Houghton, 1955; *Frederick Douglass: Slave, Fighter, Freeman,* Knopf, 1958; editor, *American Negro Poetry,* Hill, 1963; editor, *Great Slave Narratives,* Beacon, 1969).

John Brewton's *Under the Tent of the Sky* (the first of many collections of poems on a specific topic; published in New York by Macmillan; the editor also compiled, with Sara Brewton, *Talks to Young Adventurers,* Revell, 1938; *Gaily We Parade,* Macmillan, 1940; with Sara Brewton, *Bridled with Rainbows,* Macmillan, 1949; with Babette Lemon, Blanch Wellons, and Louise Abney, *Excursions in Fact and Fancy,* Laidlaw, 1949; with Lemon, Wellons, and Abney, *Your World in Prose and Verse,* Laidlaw, 1949; with Sara Brewton, *Christmas Bells Are Ringing,* Macmillan, 1951; *Poetry Time,* Upper Room, 1953; with Sara Brewton, *Sing a Song of Seasons,* Macmillan, 1955; *Birthday Candles Burning Bright,* Macmillan, 1960; *Laughable Limericks,* Crowell, 1965; with Sara Brewton, *America Forever New,* Crowell, 1967; *Shrieks at Midnight,* Crowell, 1969).

Frances Carpenter's *Tales of a Chinese Grandmother* (one of a series of "Grandmother" folktale collections from several countries; published in Garden City, New York, by Doubleday; illustrated by Malthe Hasselriis; the author's other work, published by Doubleday except as noted, includes *Sing a Song of Seasons,* illustrated by Flavia Gág, 1930; *Tales of a Basque Grandmother,* illustrated by Pedro Garmendia, 1930; *Tales of a Russian Grandmother,* illustrated by I. Bilbins, 1933; *Tales of a Swiss Grandmother,* illustrated by Ernest Biéler, 1940; *Tales of a Korean Grandmother,* 1947; *Wonder Tales of Dogs and Cats,* illustrated by Ezra Jack Keats, Doubleday, 1955; *Holiday in Washington,* Knopf, 1958; *The Elephant's Bathtub: Wonder Tales from the Far East,* 1962; *African Wonder Tales,* 1963; *The Mouse Palace,* McGraw-Hill, 1964).

Helen Dean Fish's *Animals of the Bible* (an informational book which presents an authentic picture of animals and plants found in biblical lands; illustrated by Dorothy Lathrop; awarded the first Caldecott Medal in 1938, for the most distinguished picture book for children by an American resident or citizen and published in America during the preceding year; published in New York by Stokes; the author's other work includes *Boy's Book of Verse* [editor], Stokes, 1923; *When the Root Children Wake Up,* Stokes, 1941; *Four and Twenty Blackbirds,* McClelland, 1947).

Eve Garnett's *The Family from One End Street* (a story about a family of modest means; awarded the Carnegie Medal; published in London by Muller; the author's other work includes a compilation of poems, *A Book of Seasons,* Oxford, 1952).

Mabel Robinson's *Bright Island* (the story of a young girl's devotion to the rugged life of the Maine seacoast and the friends she makes on and off Bright Island; published in New York by Random; the author's other work, published by Dutton, except as noted, includes *Dr. Tam O'Shanter,* 1921; *Little Lucia,* 1922; *Little Lucia and Her Puppy,* 1923; *All By Ourselves,* 1924; *Little Lucia's Island Camp,* 1924; *Little Lucia's School,* 1926; *Sarah's Dakin,* 1927; *Blue Ribbon Stories,* Macmillan, 1929; *Robin and Tito,* Macmillan, 1930; *Robin and Angus,* Macmillan, *Robin and Heather,* Macmillan, 1932; *Runner of the Mountain Tops,* Random, 1939; *Island Noon,* Random, 1942; *Bitter Forfeit,* Bobbs, 1947; *Back Seat Driver,* Random, 1949; *Strong Wings,* Random, 1951; *King Arthur and His Knights,* Random, 1953; *Skipper Riley, The Terrier Sea Dog,* Random, 1955).

Dr. Seuss's *And To Think That I Saw It on Mulberry Street* (the first of a series of nonsense picture-story books by a popular cartoonist who has been called the "Lear of the Twentieth Century"; published by Vanguard; Dr. Seuss is the pseudonym of Theodor Seuss Geisel; the author-iullustrator's other works, published by Random except as noted, many of which are controlled-vocabulary books, include *The 500 Hats of Bartholomew Cubbins,* Vanguard, 1938; *The King's Stilts,* 1939; *Horton Hatches the Egg,* 1940; *McElligot's Pool,* 1947; *Thidwick, the Big-Hearted Moose,* 1949; *Bartholomew and the Oobleck,* 1949; *If I Ran the Zoo,* 1950; *Scrambled*

1937 *continued*

Eggs Super!, 1953; *Horton Hears a Who,* 1954; *On Beyond Zebra,* 1955; *If I Ran the Circus,* 1956; *The Cat in the Hat,* Houghton, 1957; *How the Grinch Stole Christmas,* 1957; *The Cat in the Hat Comes Back,* 1958; *Yertle the Turtle and Other Stories,* 1958; *Happy Birthday to You!,* 1959; *One Fish, Two Fish, Three Fish,* 1960; *Green Eggs and Ham,* 1960; *The Sneetches and Other Stories,* 1961; *Dr. Seuss's Sleep Book,* 1962; *Hop on Pop,* 1963; *Dr. Seuss's ABC,* 1963; with P. D. Eastman, *The Cat in the Hat Dictionary, by the Cat Himself,* 1964; *Fox in Socks Knox in Box,* 1965; *I Had Trouble in Getting to Solla Sollew,* 1965; *The Cat in the Hat Songbook,* 1967; *The Eye Book,* 1968; *The Foot Book,* 1968; *I Can Lick 30 Tigers Today! and Other Stories,* 1969; *My Book About Me,* 1969; *I Can Draw It Myself,* 1970; *Mr. Brown Can Moo! Can You?,* 1970; *I Can Write,* 1971; *The Lorax,* 1971; under pseudonym Theo. LeSieg, *Ten Apples Up on Top,* 1961; *I Wish I Had Duck Feet,* 1965; *Come Over to My House,* 1966). UCLA *My House,* 1966). UCLA

Kate Seredy's *The White Stag* (a story based on an Hungarian legend; illustrated by the author; awarded Newbery Medal in 1938; published in New York by Viking; the author-illustrator's other work, published by Viking, includes *The Good Master,* 1935; *The Singing Tree,* 1939; *A Tree for Peter,* 1940; *The Open Gate,* 1943; *The Chestry Oak,* 1948; *Gypsy,* 1952; *Philomena,* 1955; *The Tenement Tree,* 1959; *A Brand New Uncle,* 1960; *Lazy Tinka,* 1962).

Noel Streatfeild's *Ballet Shoes* (the first of a series of adventure stories giving accurate information about careers; published in London by Dent; the author was awarded the Carnegie Medal for *The Circus Is Coming,* Dent, 1937; the author's other work includes *Tennis Shoes,* Random House, 1937; *Circus Shoes,* Random, 1939; *The Painted Garden,* Collins, 1949; *White Boots,* Random, 1951; *The Bell Family,* Collins, 1951; *New Town,* Collins, 1960; *Traveling Shoes,* Random, 1962; *Liz Goes to Russia,* Collins, 1963; *The Children on the Top Floor,* Random, 1964; *Let's Go Coaching,* Panther, 1965; *The Growing Summer,* Collins, 1965; *The First Book of Opera,* Watts, 1967; *The Family at Caldicott Place,* Random, 1968).

John Ronald Reuel Tolkien's *The Hobbit: or There and Back Again* (a high adventure fantasy by a British writer, based on the author's knowledge of Welsh legends and ancient Germanic languages; illustrated by the author; published in London by Allen and Unwin; a forerunner of the author's adult trilogy, *The Lord of the Rings,* Allen, which includes *The Fellowship of the Ring,* 1954, *The Two Towers,* 1954, and *The Return of the King,* 1955; the author's other work includes *The Adventures of Tom Bombadil,* Allen, 1962; *Smith of Wooton Major,* Houghton, 1967).

1938

Valenti Angelo's *Nino* (a story of the author-illustrator's childhood in Italy; illustrated by the author; published in New York by Viking; the author-illustrator's other work, all published by Viking, includes *Golden Gate,* 1939; *Paradise Valley,* 1940; *Hills of Little Miracles,* 1942; *The Bells of Bleecker Street,* 1949; *Marble Fountain,* 1951; *Acorn Tree,* 1958; *Angelino and the Barefoot Saint,* 1961; *The Tale of a Donkey,* 1966).

Florence and Richard Atwater's *Mr. Popper's Penguins* (a popular humorous story about penguins kept in a refrigerator; illustrated by Robert Lawson; published in Boston by Little, Brown; Richard Atwater wrote *Doris and the Trolls,* illustrated by John Gee, and published by Random in 1931).

Claire Huchet Bishop's *The Five Chinese Brothers* (a popular picture-story in folktale style in which each brother has a magical gift; illustrated by Kurt Wiese; published in New York by Coward-McCann; the author's other work includes *Pancakes-Paris,* Viking, 1947; *Blue Spring Farm,* Viking, 1948; *Twenty and Ten,* Viking, 1952; *All-Alone,* Viking, 1953; *Martin de Pores, Hero,* Houghton, 1954; *Twenty-Two Bears,* Viking, 1964; *Yeshu, Called Jesus,* Farrar, 1966).

Louise Crane's *The Magic Spear* (a collection of legendary stories of China's heroes, many of which have been adapted for theater and as such were favorites with Chinese children; illustrated by Yench 'i Tiao T'u; published in New York by Random House).

Phyllis Crawford's *Hello the Boat* (a story of the Ohio River life set in the early 1800s; published in New York by Holt; the author's other work includes *The Blot: Little City Cat,* Cape, 1930; *Elsie Dinsmore on the Loose,* Cape, 1930; *In England Still,* Arrowsmith, 1938; *Walking on Gold* Messner, 1940; *The Secret Brother,* Holt, 1941; *Last Semester,* Holt, 1942; *Second Shift,* Holt, 1943; *Let's Go!,* Holt, 1949).

Eleanor Doorly's *Radium Woman* (a biography for children based on Eve Curie's *Madame Curie;* illustrated with woodcuts by Robert Gibbings; awarded the Carnegie Medal; published in London by Heinemann; the author's other work includes *The Insect Man,* Appleton, 1937; *The Microbe Man,* Appleton, 1939; *The Story of France,* Cape, 1944).

1938 *continued*

Jeanette Eaton's *Leader By Destiny: George Washington, Man and Patriot* (one of a series of popular biographies for young people; illustrated by Jack M. Rose; published in New York by Harcourt; the author's other work includes *Story of Transportation,* Harper, 1927; *Story of Light,* Harper, 1928; *Daughter of the Seine,* Harper, 1929; *Young Lafayette,* Houghton, 1932; *Betsy's Napoleon,* Morrow, 1936; *Narcissa Whitman: Pioneer of Oregon,* Harcourt, 1941; *Lone Journey: The Life of Roger Williams,* Harcourt, 1944; *That Lively Man, Ben Franklin,* Morrow, 1948, illustrated by Henry C. Pitz; *Gandhi: Fighter Without a Sword,* Morrow, 1950; *Leaders in Other Lands,* Heath, 1950; *Washington, the Nation's First Hero,* Morrow, 1951; *Lee, the Gallant General,* Morrow, 1953; *Trumpeter's Tale: The Story of Louis Armstrong,* Morrow, 1955; *The Story of Eleanor Roosevelt,* Morrow, 1956).

Elizabeth Enright's *Thimble Summer* (an entertaining family story set on a Midwest farm; illustrated by the author; awarded Newbery Medal in 1939; published in New York by Farrar; the author's other work includes *Kintu,* Farrar, 1935; *The Sea Is All Around,* Farrar, 1940; *The Saturdays,* Farrar, 1941; *The Four-Story Mistake,* Farrar, 1942; *The Melendy Family,* Rinehart, 1944; *Then There Were Five,* Farrar, 1944; *Christmas Tree for Ludia,* Rinehart, 1951; *Spiderweb for Two,* Rinehart, 1951; *Gone-Away Lake,* Harcourt, 1957, *Return to Gone-Away Lake,* Harcourt, 1957; *Tatsinda,* Harcourt, 1963; *Zeeee,* Harcourt, 1965).

Thomas Handforth's *Mei Li* (a picture-story about a little girl in old China; the author-illustrator was awarded the Caldecott Medal in 1939; published in New York by Doubleday; the author's other work includes *Faraway Meadow,* Doubleday, 1939).

Florence Crannel Means's *Shuttered Windows* (a realistic novel about a northern black girl's adjustment when she goes to live with her grandmother on an island off South Carolina; published by Houghton; the author's other work, all published by Houghton except as noted, includes, with Harriet Culler, *Rafael and Consuelo,* Friendship, 1929; *A Candle in the Mist,* 1931; with Frances Riggs, *Children of the Great Spirit,* Friendship, 1932; *Ranch and Ring,* 1932; *Dusky Day,* 1933; *A Bowlful of Stars,* 1934; *Rainbow Bridge,* Friendship, 1934; *Penny for Luck,* 1935; *Tangled Waters,* 1936; *The Singing Wood,* 1937; *Adella May in Old Mexico,* 1939; *Across the Fruited Plains,* Friendship, 1940; *At the End of Nowhere,* 1940; *Children of Promise,* Friendship, 1941; *Whispering Girl,* 1941; *Shadow Over Wide Ruin,* 1942; *Teresita of the Valley,* 1943; *Peter of the Mesa,* Friendship, 1944; *The Moved-Outers,* 1945; *Great Day in the Morning,* 1946; *Assorted*

Sisters, 1947; *The House Under the Hill,* 1949; with Carl Means, *The Silver Fleece,* Winston, 1950; *Hetty of the Grande Deluxe,* 1951; *Carver's George,* 1952; *Alicia,* 1953; *The Rains Will Come,* 1954; *Sagebrush Surgeon,* Friendship, 1956; *Knock at the Door, Emmy,* 1956; *Reach for a Star,* 1957; *Borrowed Brother,* 1958; *Emmy and the Blue Door,* Judson, 1959; *Sunlight on the Hopi Mesas,* 1960; *But I Am Sara,* 1961; *That Girl Andy,* 1962; *Tolliver,* 1963; *It Takes All Kinds,* 1964; *Us Maltbys,* 1966; *Our Cup Is Broken,* 1969).

Marjorie Kinnan Rawlings's *The Yearling* (an adult realistic novel which presents the tender relationship between a boy and a deer; appropriated by children; illustrated by N. C. Wyeth; published in New York by Scribner; the author's other work, published by Viking except as noted, includes *The Secret River,* Scribner, 1955; *In and Out,* illustrated by Marguerite de Angeli, 1943; with Kurt Wiese, *Mr. Red Squirrel,* 1943; *Greylock and the Robins,* 1946; *Lost Dog Jerry,* illustrated by Morgan Dennis, 1952). UF

Tom Robinson's *Buttons* (a realistic picture-story about an alley cat; illustrated by Peggy Bacon; published in New York by Viking; the author's other work includes *Pete,* Viking, 1941; *Trigger John's Son,* Viking, 1949).

Hilda Van Stockum's *The Cottage at Bantry Bay* (the first of a series of popular family stories; presents life in Ireland; illustrated by the author; published in New York by Viking; the author's other work, published by Viking except as noted, includes *A Day on Skates,* Harper, 1934; *Francie on the Run,* 1939; *Kersti and St. Nicholas,* 1940; *Pegeen,* 1941; *Andries,* 1942; *Gerrit and the Organ,* 1943; *The Mitchells,* 1945; *Canadian Summer,* 1948; *The Angels' Alphabet,* 1950; *Patsy and the Pup,* 1951; *King Oberon's Forest,* 1957; *Friendly Gables,* 1958; *Little Old Bear,* 1962; *Winged Watchman,* Farrar, 1962; *Mogo's Flute,* 1966).

1939

Kitty Barne's *Visitors from London* (the story of a group of London cockney children who are evacuated to a Sussex farm; the author was awarded Carnegie Medal in 1940; published in New York by Dodd; the author's other work, published by Dodd except as noted, includes *The Easter Holidays,* 1935; *She Shall Have Music,* 1938; *Musical Honors,* 1939; *Family Footlights,* 1939; *We'll Meet in England,* Hamilton, 1942; *In the Same Boat,* 1945; *Dusty's Windmill,* 1949; *Secret of the Sand Hills,* Dodd, 1949; *Rosina Copper,* Evans, 1954; *Rosina and Son,* 1956).

Ludwig Bemelmans's *Madeline* (a popular picture-story written in rhyme and illustrated by the author, about a little Parisian girl who stands out from her eleven convent schoolmates because of her rambunctious person-

1939 *continued*

ality; published in New York by Simon and Schuster; the sequel, *Madeline's Rescue,* 1953, was the Caldecott Medal winner in 1954; published by Viking; the author-illustrator's other work, published by Viking except as noted, includes *Hansi,* 1934; *The Golden Basket,* 1936; *The Castle Number Nine,* 1937; *Quito Express,* 1938; *Fifi,* Simon, 1940; *Rosebud,* Random, 1942; *The Tale of Two Glimps,* Columbia Broadcasting System, 1947; *Sunshine,* Simon, 1950; *The Happy Place,* Little, 1952; *The Huge World,* Harper, 1954; *Christmas in Texas,* Nieman Marcus, 1955; *Madeline and the Bad Hat,* 1957; *Madeline and the Gypsies,* 1959; *Welcome Home!* Harper, 1960; *Madeline in London,* 1961; *Marina,* Harper, 1962).

Wilfred S. Bronson's *Chisel-Tooth Tribe* (one of the author's many books emphasizing animals' adaptations to their environment; published in New York by Harcourt, Brace; the author's other work, published by Harcourt except as noted, includes *Paddle Wings,* Macmillan, 1931; *Pollwiggle's Progress,* Macmillan, 1932; *Wonder World of Ants,* 1937; *Children of the Sea,* 1940; *Horns and Antlers,* 1942; *Turtles,* 1945; *Coyotes,* 1946; *Pinto's Journey,* Messner, 1948; *Cats,* 1950; *Freedom and Plenty: Ours to Save,* 1953; *Goats,* 1959; *Beetles,* 1963).

Margaret Wise Brown's *The Noisy Book* (one of a series of "awareness" picture books designed to stimulate sensory-motor responses in the young child; illustrated by Leonard Weisgard; published in New York by Scott; under the pseudonym of Golden MacDonald, the author wrote *The Little Island,* Doubleday, 1946, for which Leonard Weisgard, illustrator, was awarded the Caldecott Medal in 1947; the author's other work includes *Children's Year,* adapted from Y. Lacote's *Calendrier des Enfants,* illustrated by Feodor Rojankovsky, Harper, 1937; *When the Wind Blew,* illustrated by Rosalie Slocum, Harper, 1937; *Bumble Bugs and Elephants,* illustrated by Clement Hurd, Scott, 1938; *Fish with the Deep Sea Smile,* illustrated by Roberta Rauch, Dutton, 1938; *Little Fireman,* illustrated by Esphyr Slobodkina, Scott, 1938; *Streamlined Pig,* illustrated by Kurt Wiese, Harper, 1938; *Little Pig's Picnic and Other Stories,* illustrated by Walt Disney Studios, Heath, 1939; *The City Noisy Book,* illustrated by Leonard Weisgard, Scott, 1939; *Country Noisy Book,* illustrated by Leonard Weisgard, Scott, 1940; *Baby Animals,* Random, 1941; reteller, *Br'er Rabbit,* illustrated by A. B. Frost, Harper, 1941; *The Polite Penguin,* Harper, 1941; *The Poodle and the Sheep,* Dutton, 1941; *Seashore Noisy Book,* Scott, 1941; *Don't Frighten the Lion,* Harper, 1942; *Indoor Noisy Book,* Scott, 1942; *Night and Day,* Harper, 1942; *Runaway Bunny,* illustrated by Clement Hurd, Harper, 1942; under pseudonym of Golden MacDonald, *Big Dog, Little Dog,* Doubleday, 1942; *Child's Good Night Book,* illustrated by Jean Charlot, Scott, 1943; *The Little Chicken,* Harper, 1943; *The Noisy*

Bird Book, Scott, 1943; *SHHHhhh . . . . Bang,* Harper, 1944; *Red Light, Green Light,* Doubleday, 1944; *Little Lost Lamb,* Scott, 1945; *Whistle for the Train,* Doubleday, 1956; under pseudonym of Timothy Hay, *Horses,* Harper, 1944; with Rockbridge Campbell, *Willie's Walk to Grandmama,* Scott, 1944; *House of a Hundred Windows,* Harper, 1945; *The Little Fisherman,* illustrated by Dahlov Ipcar, Scott, 1945; *The Little Fur Family,* illustrated by Garth Williams, Harper, 1946; with Edith Hurd, *Man in the Manhole and the Fix-It Men,* Scott, 1946; *Bad Little Duckhunter,* Scott, 1947; *The First Story,* Harper, 1947; *Golden Egg Book,* illustrated by Leonard Weisgard, Simon, 1947; *Goodnight Moon,* illustrated by Clement Hurd, Harper, 1947; *The Winter Noisy Book,* Scott, 1947; *The Little Cowboy,* Scott, 1948; *Little Farmer,* Scott, 1948; *Wait Till the Moon Is Full, illustrated* by Garth Williams, Harper, 1948; *Five Little Firemen,* Simon, 1948; *Wonderful Story Book,* Simon, 1948; *The Golden Sleepy Book,* Simon, 1948; *The Important Book,* illustrated by Leonard Weisgard, Harper, 1949; *My World,* Harper, 1949; *A Pussycat's Christmas,* Crowell, 1949; *Two Little Trains,* illustrated by Jean Charlot, Scott, 1949; *Two Little Miners,* Simon, 1949; *The Color Kittens,* Simon, 1949; *Dark Wood of the Golden Birds,* Harper, 1950; *The Dream Book,* Random, 1950; *The Peppermint Family,* Harper, 1950; *The Wonderful House,* Simon, 1950; *Fox Eyes,* Pantheon, 1951; *The Quiet Noisy Book,* Harper, 1951; *The Summer Noisy Book,* Harper, 1951; *A Child's Good Morning,* Scott, 1952; *Christmas in the Barn,* Crowell, 1952; *The Duck,* Harvill, 1952; *Pussy Willow,* Simon, 1952; *Little Firemen,* 1952; *The Noon Balloon,* Harper, 1952; *Where Have You Been?,* illustrated by Barbara Cooney, Crowell, 1952; *Golden Bunny and 17 Other Stories and Poems,* Simon, 1953; *The Hidden House,* Holt, 1955; *The Friendly Book,* Simon, 1954; *The Little Fir Tree,* Crowell, 1954; *Little Indian,* Simon, 1954; *Wheel on the Chimney,* illustrated by Tibor Gergely, Lippincott, 1954; *Willie's Adventures,* Scott, 1954; *The Little Brass Band,* Harper, 1955; *Seven Stories About a Cat Named Sneakers,* Scott, 1955; *Young Kangaroo,* Scott, 1955; *Big Red Barn,* Scott, 1956; *David's Little Indian,* Scott, 1956; *Home for a Bunny,* Simon, 1956; *Three Little Animals,* Harper, 1956; *The Dead Bird,* illustrated by Remy Charlip, Scott, 1958; *The Train to Timbuctoo,* Simon, 1958; *Nibble, Nibble,* illustrated by Leonard Weisgard, Scott, 1959; *The Diggers,* Harper, 1960; *Four Fur Feet,* Scott, 1961; *On Christmas Eve,* Scott, 1961; *The Whispering Rabbit and Other Stories,* Golden, 1966; *Five Little Firemen,* 1967). WPL

James Daugherty's *Daniel Boone* (one of a series of illustrated biographies for older children; awarded the Newbery Medal; published in New York by Viking; the author-illustrator's other work includes *Andy and the Lion,* Viking, 1938; *Poor Richard,* Viking, 1941; *Abraham Lincoln,* Viking, 1943; *Landing of the Pilgrims,* Random, 1950; *Of Courage Undaunted: Across the Continent with Lewis and Clark,* Viking, 1951; *Marcus and Narcissa*

1939 *continued*
Whitman, Pioneers of Oregon, Viking, 1953; *Magna Charta,* Random, 1956; *Picnic,* Viking, 1958).

Ingri and Edgar Parin d'Aulaire's *Abraham Lincoln* (one of a series of distinguished picture-story biographies; awarded the Caldecott Medal in 1940; published in New York by Doubleday, Doran; the author-illustrator's other work, published by Doubleday except as noted, includes *The Magic Rug,* 1931; *Ola,* 1932; *Ola and Blakken and Line, Sine, Trine,* 1933; *The Conquest of the Atlantic,* Viking, 1933; *The Lord's Prayer,* 1934; *Children of the Northern Lights,* Viking, 1935; *George Washington,* 1936; *Animals Everywhere,* 1940; *Leif the Lucky,* 1941; *Star Spangled Banner,* 1942; *Don't Count Your Chickens,* 1943; *Wings for Per,* 1944; *Too Big,* 1945; *Pocahontas,* 1946; *Nils,* 1948; *Foxie,* 1949; *Benjamin Franklin,* 1950; *Buffalo Bill,* 1952; *The Two Cars,* 1955; *Columbus,* 1955; *The Magic Meadow,* 1958; *Ingri and Edgar Parin d'Aulaire's Book of Greek Myths,* 1962; *Ingri and Edgar Parin d'Aulaire's Norse Gods and Giants,* 1967).

Robert Davis's *Padre Porko* (the tales of the gentlemanly Spanish pig, collected from Spanish storytellers; illustrated by Fritz Eichenberg; published in New York by Holiday House; the author's other work, published by Holiday House, includes *Pepperfoot of Thursday Market,* 1941; *Hudson Bay Express,* 1942; *Gid Granger,* 1945; *France,* 1947; *Partners of Powder Lake,* 1947; *That Girl of Pierre's,* 1948).

Hardie Gramatky's *Little Toot* (the first of a series of popular picture stories for the very young about a personified tug boat; published by Putnam; the author-illustrator's other work, published by Putnam, includes *Hercules,* 1940; *Loopy,* 1941; *Creeper's Jeep,* 1948; *Sparky,* 1952; *Homer and the Circus Train,* 1957; *Bolivar,* 1961; *Nikos and the Sea God,* 1963; *Little Toot on the Thames,* 1964; *Little Toot on the Grand Canal,* 1968).

Carolyn Haywood's *"B" Is for Betsy* (one of a series of popular easy-reading books about life in a middle-class white neighborhood; illustrated by the author; published in New York by Harcourt; the author's other work, published by Morrow except as noted, includes *Two and Two Are Four,* Harcourt, 1940; *Betsy and Billy,* Harcourt, 1941; *Primrose Day,* Harcourt, 1942; *Back to School with Betsy,* Harcourt, 1943; *Here's A Penny,* Harcourt, 1944; *Betsy and the Boys,* Harcourt, 1945; *Penny and Peter,* Harcourt, 1946; *Little Eddie,* 1947; *Penny Goes to Camp,* 1948; *Eddie and the Fire Engine,* 1949; *Betsy's Little Star,* 1950; *Eddie and Gardenia,* 1951; *Mixed-Up Twins,* 1952; *Eddie's Pay Dirt,* 1953; *Eddie and His Big Deals,* 1955; *Betsy and the Circus,* 1956; *Betsy's Busy Summer,* 1956; *Eddie Makes*

Music, 1957; *Betsy's Winterhouse,* 1958; *Eddie and Lovella,* 1959; *Annie Pat and Eddie,* 1960; *Snowbound with Betsy,* 1962; *Here Comes the Bus,* 1963; *Eddie's Green Thumb,* 1964; *Robert Rows the River,* 1965; *Eddie, the Dog Holder,* 1966; *Betsy and Mr. Kilpatrick,* 1967; *Ever-Ready Eddie,* 1968; *Taffy and Melissa Molasses,* 1969).

Hubert Skidmore's *River Rising* (the story of a young man who teaches school in a Blue Ridge Mountains lumber camp in order to earn money for medical school; published in New York by Doubleday, Doran).

Gertrude Stein's *The World Is Round or A Rose Is a Rose* (the story of a child's adventures written in Stein's unique poetic style; British edition illustrated by Sir Francis Rose and published in London by Batsford; American edition illustrated by Clement Hurd and published by Scott).

Opal Wheeler and Sybil Deucher's *Franz Schubert and His Merry Friends* (one of a series of simplified biographies of famous musicians designed for young readers, published by Dutton, illustrated by Mary Greenwalt; the author's other work includes *Mozart, the Wonder Boy,* 1934; *Sebastian Bach, the Boy from Thuringia,* 1937; *Joseph Haydn, the Merry Little Peasant,* 1939; *Edward MacDowell and His Cabin in the Pines,* 1940; *Stephen Foster and His Little Dog Tray,* 1941; [Wheeler] *Ludwig Beethoven and the Chiming Tower Bells,* 1942; *Sing Mother Goose,* 1945; [Deucher] *Edward Grieg, Boy of the Northland,* 1946).

1940

Mary Jane Carr's *Young Mac of Fort Vancouver* (the story of a young boy's adventures at the Hudson's Bay Trading Post in the 1830s; runner-up for the Newbery Medal; published in New York by Crowell; the author's other work includes *The Magic of May,* Catholic Dramatic Co., 1928; *Children of the Covered Wagon,* Crowell, 1934; *Peggy and Paul and Laddy,* Crowell, 1936; *Top of the Morning,* Crowell, 1941). UOr

Babette Deutsch's *Heroes of the Kalevala* (translated from the Finnish by the author; illustrated by Fritz Eichenberg; published in New York by Messner; the author's other work includes *Walt Whitman, Builder for America,* Messner, 1941; *It's A Secret,* Harper, 1941; *The Welcome,* Harper, 1942; *Tales of Faraway Folk,* Harper, 1952; with Yarmolinsky, *More Tales of Faraway Folk,* Harper, 1963; *I Often Wish,* Funk, 1966).

Doris Gates's *Blue Willow* (a realistic story of a girl and her migrant-laborer family who eventually find security and a home of their own; illustrated by Paul Lantz; published in New York by Viking; the author's other work,

1940 *continued*

published by Viking, except as noted, includes *Sarah's Idea,* 1938; *Sensible Kate,* 1943; *Trouble for Jerry,* 1944; *North Fork,* 1945; *My Brother Mike,* 1948; *River Ranch,* 1949; *Little Vic,* 1951; *Becky and the Bandit,* Ginn, 1955; *The Cat and Mrs. Cary,* 1962; *The Elderberry Bush,* 1967).

Anna Gertrude Hall's *Nansen* (a biography of a famous scientist, explorer, and humanitarian; published in New York by Viking).

William Pene Du Bois's *The Great Geppy* (the story of an intelligent horse who solves the mystery of the Bott circus; illustrated by the author and published by Viking; the author-illustrator's other work includes his Newbery Medal book, *Twenty-one Balloons,* Viking, 1947, and other books published by Viking: *The Three Policemen or, Young Bottsford of Farbe Island,* 1938; *Peter Graves,* 1950; *Bear Party,* 1951; *The Giant,* 1954).

Clara Ingram Judson's *Boat Builder: The Story of Robert Fulton* (one of a series of well-researched fictionalized biographies of American heroes; illustrated by Armstrong Speery; published in New York by Scribner; the author has been called the "interpreter of America" for young people; recipient of the Laura Ingalls Wilder Award in 1960; the author's other work includes *Flower Fairies,* Rand, 1915; *Good-Night Stories,* McClurg, 1916; *Billy Robin and His Neighbors,* Rand, 1917; *Mary Jane, Her Book,* Grosset, 1918; *Mary Jane's Kindergarten,* Barse, 1918; *Mary Jane, Her Visit,* Barse, 1918; *Mary Jane Down South,* Barse, 1919; *Camp at Gravel Point,* Houghton, 1921; *Foxy Squirrel in the Garden,* Rand, 1921; *Garden Adventures in Winter,* Rand, 1921; *Garden Adventures of Tommy Tittlemouse,* Rand, 1922; *Jerry and Jean, Detectors,* 1923; *Virginia Lee,* Barse, 1926; *Alice Ann,* Barse, 1928; *Mary Jane in England,* Barse, 1928; *Mary Jane in Scotland,* Barse, 1929; *Mary Jane in France,* Grosset, 1930; *Mary Jane in Switzerland,* Barse, 1931; *Mary Jane in Italy,* Grosset, 1933; *Mary Jane in Spain,* Grosset, 1937; *Play Days,* Grosset, 1937; *Mary Jane's Friends in Holland,* Grosset, 1939; *Pioneer Girl,* Rand, 1939; *Virginia Lee's Bicycle Club,* Grosset, 1939; *People Who Came to Our House,* Rand, 1940; *Railway Engineer: The Story of George Stephenson,* Scribner, 1941; *Soldier Doctor: The Story of William Gorgas,* Scribner, 1941; *People Who Work Near Our House,* Rand, 1942; *They Came From Sweden,* Houghton, 1942; *Donald McKay, Designer of Clipper Ships,* Scribner, 1943; *People Who Work in the Country and the City,* Rand, 1943; *They Came from France,* Houghton, 1943; *They Came from Scotland,* Houghton, 1944; *Petar's Treasure: They Came from Dalmatia,* Houghton, 1945; *Michael's Victory: They Came from Ireland,* Houghton, 1946; *Lost Violin: They Came from Bohemia,* Houghton, 1947; *Reaper Man,* Houghton, 1948; *Summer Time,*

Broadman, 1948; *Green Ginger Jar: The Story of the Chinese in Chicago,* Houghton, 1949; *Abraham Lincoln, Friend of the People,* Follett, 1950; *City Neighbor,* Scribner, 1951; *George Washington, Leader of the People,* Follett, 1951; *Thomas Jefferson, Champion of the People,* Follett, 1952; *Theodore Roosevelt, Fighting Patriot,* Follett, 1953; *Andrew Jackson, Frontier Statesman,* Follett, 1954; *Mighty Soo,* Follett, 1955; *Mr. Justice Holmes,* Follett, 1956; *Benjamin Franklin,* Follett, 1957; *Pierre's Lucky Pouch,* Follett, 1957; *St. Lawrence Seaway,* Follett, 1959; *Andrew Carnegie,* Follett, 1964; *Admiral Christopher Columbus,* Follett, 1965).

Eric Knight's *Lassie Come Home* (a popular realistic animal story of a collie's return to home; set in Scotland and Yorkshire, England; illustrated by Cyrus Leroy Baldridge; published by Winston; appropriated by children).

Dorothy Kunhardt's *Pat the Bunny* (a popular cardboard participation book which invites the very young child to respond to tactile and other sensory stimuli; reminiscent of some nineteenth-century toy books; published by Simon; author's other work includes *Little Ones,* Viking, 1935; *David's Birthday Party,* Rand, 1940; *Billy the Barber,* Harper, 1961).

Robert Lawson's *They Were Strong and Good* (a picture book tracing the author's ancestors' journey to America; awarded the Caldecott Medal in 1941; illustrated by author; published in New York by Viking; the author-illustrator was awarded the Newbery Medal for the animal fantasy, *Rabbit Hill,* Viking, 1943; its sequel is *The Tough Winter,* 1954; the author-illustrator's other work includes *Ben and Me,* Little, 1939; *I Discover Columbus,* Little, 1941; *Watchwords of Liberty,* Little, 1943; *Country Colic,* Little, 1944; *Mr. Wilmer,* Little, 1945; *At That Time,* Viking, 1947; *Mr. Twigg's Mistake,* Little, 1947; *Robbut,* Viking, 1948; *Fabulous Flight,* Little, 1949; *Dick Whittington and His Cat,* Limited Editions, 1949; *Smeller Martin,* Viking, 1950; *McWhinney's Jaunt,* Little, 1951; *Edward, Hoppy and Joe,* Knopf, 1952; *Mr. Revere and I,* Little, 1953; *The Tough Winter,* Viking, 1954; *Captain Kidd's Cat,* Little, 1956; *Great Wheel,* Viking, 1957; the author-illustrator also illustrated Munro Leaf's *Story of Ferdinand,* 1936; Fish's *Four and Twenty Blackbirds,* 1937; Margery Bianco's *Hurdy-Gurdy Man,* 1937; Samuel Clemens's *The Prince and the Pauper,* 1937; Richard and Florence Atwater's *Mr. Popper's Penguins,* 1938; Eleanor Farjeon's *One Foot in Fairyland,* 1938; Leaf's *Gillis,* 1938; John Bunyan's *Pilgrim's Progress,* 1939; John Brewton's *Gaily We Parade,* 1940; Leaf's *Just for Fun,* 1940; Leaf's *Aesop's Fables,* 1941; Elizabeth Janet Gray's *Adam of the Road,* 1942; James Stephen's *Crock of Gold,* 1942; Andrew Lang's *Prince Prigio,* 1942; Patricia Teal's *Little Woman Who Wanted Noise,* 1943). PFL

1940 *continued*

Maud Hart Lovelace's *Betsy-Tacy* (the first of a series of books set in Minnesota at the turn of the century which traces the friendship of two girls through elementary school and high school and into adulthood; illustrated by Lois Lenski and published by Crowell except as noted; the author's other work includes *Betsy, Tacy and Tib*, 1941; *Betsy and Tacy Go Over the Big Hill*, 1942; *Betsy and Tacy Go Downtown*, 1943; *Heaven To Betsy*, illustrated by Vera Neville, 1945; *Betsy in Spite of Herself*, illustrated by Vera Neville, 1946; *Betsy Was a Junior*, illustrated by Vera Neville, 1947; *Betsy and Joe*, illustrated by Vera Neville, 1948; *Betsy and the Great World*, illustrated by Vera Neville, 1952; *Betsy's Wedding*, illustrated by Vera Neville, 1955).

Robert McCloskey's *Lentil* (the author's first book which is about a harmonica-playing, Hamilton, Ohio boy who "saves the day," illustrated by the author; the author's other work, published by Viking, includes Caldecott Medal winner *Make Way for Ducklings*, 1941; *Homer Price*, 1943; *Blueberries for Sal*, 1948; *Centerburg Tales*, 1951; *One Morning in Maine*, 1952; Caldecott Medal winner *Time of Wonder*, 1957; *Burt Dow, Deep-Water Man*, 1963; books illustrated by the author include Malcolmson's *Yankee Doodle's Cousin's*, 1941; Davis' *Tree Toad*, 1942; Bishop's *The Man Who Lost His Head*, 1942; Robinson's *Trigger John's Son*, 1949; Sawyer's *Journey Cake, Ho!*, 1953; White's *Junket*, 1955; and Robertson's *Henry Reed's Journey*, 1963; *Henry Reed's Baby Sitting Service*, 1966).

Clare Turley Newberry's *April's Kittens* (typical of the author-illustrator's many picture books which feature cats as the subject; author's other work, published by Harper, includes *Herbert and the Lion*, 1931; *Mittens*, 1936; *Babette*, 1937; *Barkis*, 1938; *Cousin Toby*, 1939; *Lambert's Bargain*, 1941; *Marshmallow*, 1942; *Pandora*, 1944; *What's That?*, 1946; *The Kittens' ABC*, 1946; *Smudge*, 1948; *T-Bone the Babysitter*, 1950; *Percey, Polly and Pete*, 1952; *Ice Cream for Two*, 1953; *Widget*, 1958; *Frosty*, 1961).

Esphyr Slobodkina's *Caps for Sale* (a popular picture story of a peddler's encounter with some clever monkeys; published by Scott; revised edition, 1947; illustrated by the author; the author-illustrator's other work includes *The Wonderful Feast*, Lothrop, 1955; *Little Dog Lost, Little Dog Found*, Abelard, 1956; *Behind the Dark Window Shade*, Lothrop, 1958; *Billie*, Lothrop, 1959; *Jack and Jim*, Abelard, 1961; *Pezzo, the Peddler and the Circus Elephant*, Abelard, 1968; *Flame, the Breeze and the Shadow*, Rand, 1969).

Armstrong Speery's *Call It Courage* a realistic, exciting account of how a Polynesian boy discovers his courage; illustrated by the author; awarded the Newbery Medal in 1941; published in New York by Macmillan; the author's other work includes *One Day with Manu,* Winston, 1932; *One Day with Jambi,* Winston, 1933; *One Day with Tuktu,* Winston, 1934; *All Sail Set,* Winston, 1935; *Wagons Westward,* Winston, 1936; *Little Eagle,* Winston, 1937; *Lost Lagoon,* Doubleday, 1939; *Storm Canvas,* Winston, 1944; *Hull Down for Action,* Doubleday, 1945; *Bamboo, the Grass Tree,* Macmillan, 1946; *The Rain Forest,* Macmillan, 1947; *Black Falcon,* Winston, 1949; *The Voyages of Christopher Columbus,* Random, 1950; *John Paul Jones, Fighting Sailor,* Random, 1952; *Thunder Country,* Macmillan, 1952; *Captain Cook Explores the South Seas,* Random, 1953; *All About the Arctic,* Random, 1957; *Pacific Islands Speaking,* Macmillan, 1957; *South of Cape Horn,* Winston, 1958; *All About the Jungle,* Random, 1959; *The Amazon,* Garrard, 1961; *Great River, Wide Land,* Macmillan, 1967).

Howard Spring's *Tumbledown Dick: All People and No Plot* (the story of a boy's adventures in Manchester with his uncles; published in New York by Viking; the author's other work includes *Heaven Lies About Us; A Fragment of Infancy,* illustrated by Fritz Kredel, Viking, 1939; *Fame is the Spur,* Collins, 1940; *Hard Facts,* Collins, 1944; *Dunkerley's,* Collins, 1946).

Mary Treadgold's *We Couldn't Leave Dinah* (the story of two children who become separated from their family during Nazi occupation of one of England's Channel Islands; awarded the Carnegie Medal; published in London by Cape; the American edition titled *Left Till Called For* was published in New York by Doubleday; the author's other work includes *Mystery of the Polly Harris,* Cape, 1949; *Running Child,* Cape, 1951).

1941

John Buchan's *Lake of Gold* (a time fantasy written by Canadian author and set in Canada's past; published in Boston by Houghton, Mifflin; author's other work includes *The Magic Walking Stick,* Houghton, Mifflin, 1932).

Ann Nolan Clark's *In My Mother's House* (a picture-story book in which a Navajo child explains what life is like in her house and village; published in New York by Viking; the author's other work includes *Who Wants to be a Prairie Dog?,* Phoenix, Ariz., Printing Dept., 1940; *Little Herder in Spring,* Phoenix Printing, 1940; *Little Boy With Three Names,* Chilocco, Okla., Printing Dept., 1940; *The Pine Ridge Porcupine,* Haskell Int. Printing Dept., 1941; *A Child's Story of New Mexico,* with Frances Carey, University, 1941; *The Slim Butte Raccoon,* United States Office of Indian Affairs, 1942; *Little Herder in Winter,* Phoenix Printing, 1942;

1941 *continued*

Little Herder in Summer, Phoenix Printing, 1942; *Buffalo Caller,* Row, Peterson, 1942; *Young Hunter of Picuris,* Chilocco Printing, 1943; *Little Navajo Bluebird,* Viking, 1943; *Bringer of the Mystery Dog,* Haskell Institute, 1943; *Singing Sioux Cowboy Reader,* United States Indian Service, 1947; *Magic Money,* Viking, 1950; *Little Herder in Spring, in Summer,* United States Indian Service, 1950; *Little Herder in Autumn, in Winter,* United States Indian Service, 1950; *Little Navajo Herder,* Haskell Institute, 1951; *The Secret of the Andes,* Viking, 1951; *Looking-for-Something,* Viking, 1952; *Blue Canyon Horse,* Viking, 1954; *Santiago,* Viking, 1955; *The Little Indian Pottery Maker,* Melmont, 1955; *Tia Maria's Garden,* Viking, 1963; *Medicine Man's Daughter,* Farrar, 1963; *Father Kino,* Farrar, 1963; *Bear Club,* Viking, 1965; *This for That,* Golden Gate, 1965; *Brother Andre,* Vision, 1965; *Summer Is for Growing,* Farrar, 1967; *Along Sandy Trails,* Viking, 1969).

Wesley Dennis's *Flip* (a popular horse story for beginning readers; illustrated by the author; published in New York by Viking; the author is best known as an illustrator of horses, especially for Marguerite Henry's *King of the Wind,* 1948; the author-illustrator's other work includes *Flip and the Cows,* Viking, 1942; Holiday, Viking, 1946; *Little-or-Nothing from Nottingham, Palomino and Other Horses,* World, 1950; *Flip and the Morning,* Viking, 1951; *Portfolio of Horses*, Rand, 1952).

Walter D. Edmonds's *The Matchlock Gun* (a historical thriller about a boy's defense of his family; presently controversial because it depicts Indians as savages; awarded the Newbery Medal in 1942; published in New York by Dodd, Mead; the author's other work, published by Dodd, Mead, includes *Tom Whipple,* 1942; *Two Logs Crossing,* 1943; *Wilderness Clearing,* 1944; *Cadmus Henry,* 1949; *Mr. Benedict's Lion,* 1950; *Corporal Bess,* 1952; *Hound Dog Moses and the Promised Land,* 1954; *Uncle Ben's Whale,* 1955; *They Had a Horse,* 1962).

Eleanor Estes's *The Moffats* (the first of a series of humorous, episodic accounts of family life around the turn of the century; the series, published in New York by Harcourt, is continued in *The Middle Moffat,* 1942, *Rufus M.,* 1943, and *Ginger Pye,* 1951, which was awarded the Newbery Medal in 1952; the author's other work includes *The Hundred Dresses,* 1944; *The Echoing Green,* Macmillan, 1947; *The Sleeping Giant,* 1948; *A Little Oven,* 1955; *Pinky Pye,* 1958; *The Witch Family,* 1960; *The Alley,* 1964; *Miranda the Great,* 1967).

Walter Farley's *The Black Stallion* (one of a series of realistic animal stories about a famous horse and his descendants; published by Random House;

the author's other work includes *Black Stallion Returns,* 1945; *Son of the Black Stallion,* 1947; *Island Stallion,* 1948; *Black Stallion and Satan,* 1949; *Blood Bay Colt,* 1950; *Island Stallion's Fury,* 1951; *Black Stallion's Filly,* 1952; *Black Stallion Revolts,* 1953; *Black Stallion's Sulky Colt,* 1954; *Island Stallion Races,* 1955; *Black Stallion's Courage,* 1956; *Black Stallion's Mystery,* 1957; *Black Stallion and Flame,* 1960; *Man o' War,* 1962; *The Black Stallion Challenged,* 1964; *The Horse That Swam Away,* 1965; *Black Stallion's Ghost,* 1969).

Genevieve Foster's *George Washington's World* (the first of a series of "world" biographies of famous Americans; published in New York by Scribner; the author's other work, published by Scribner except as noted, includes *Abraham Lincoln's World,* 1943; *Augustus Caesar's World,* 1947; *George Washington,* 1949; *Abraham Lincoln,* 1950; *Andrew Jackson,* 1951; *Birthdays of Freedom, Volume I,* 1952, and *Volume II,* 1957; *Theodore Roosevelt,* 1954; *When and Where in Italy,* Rand, 1955; *The World of Captain John Smith,* 1960; *World of Columbus and Sons,* 1965; *Year of Columbus, 1492,* 1969; *Year of the Pilgrims, 1620,* 1969).

Eva Roe Gaggin's *Down Ryton Water* (an action-filled story of the adventures of a Pilgrim family; runner-up for the Newbery Medal; published in New York by Viking; the author's other work includes *Jolly Animals,* Rand McNally, 1930; *An Ear for Uncle Emil,* Viking, 1939; *All Those Buckles,* Viking, 1945).

Holling C. Holling's *Paddle-to-the-Sea* (an informational narrative in picture-story book format that tells of Paddle's adventures as he floats from the Great Lakes to the sea; published in Boston by Houghton; illustrated by the author; the author's other work includes *Little Big Bye-and-Bye,* Vollard, 1926; *Claws of the Thunderbird,* Vollard, 1928; *Rocky Billy,* Macmillan, 1928; *Choo-Me-Shoo,* Buzza, 1928; *Twins Who Flew Around the World,* Platt, 1930; *Book of Cowboys,* Platt, 1932; *Book of Indians,* Platt, 1935; *Little Buffalo Boy,* Garden City, 1939; *Tree in the Trail,* Houghton, 1942; *Seabird,* Houghton, 1948; *Minn of the Mississippi,* Houghton, 1951; *Pagoo,* Houghton, 1957; author's wife, Lucille, helped research, write and illustrate the books).

H. A. Rey's *Curious George* (the first of a series of popular picture-story books about the antics of a monkey; published by Houghton; the author's other work, published by Houghton except as noted, includes *Zebrology,* 1937; *How the Flying Fishes Came Into Being,* 1938; *Raffy and the Nine Monkeys,* 1939; *Au Clair de la Lune, and Other French Nursery Songs,* Greystone, 1941; *How Do You Get There?,* 1941; *Uncle Gus's Farm,* 1942; *Uncle Gus's Circus,* 1942; *Tit for Tat,* Harper, 1942; *Elizabite: The Adven-*

1941 *continued*

tures of a Carnivorous Plant, Harper, 1942; *Christmas Manger,* 1942; *Cecily G. and the Nine Monkeys,* 1942; *Anybody At Home?,* 1942; *Where's My Baby?,* 1943; *Humpty Dumpty, and Other Mother Goose Songs,* Harper, 1943; *Feed the Animals,* 1944; with Margaret Rey, *Pretzel,* Harper, 1944; with Margaret Rey, *Spotty,* Harper, 1945; *Look for Letters,* Harper, 1945; with Margaret Rey, *Pretzel and the Puppies,* Harper, 1946; with Margaret Rey, *Billy's Picture,* Harper, 1948; *Mary Had A Little Lamb,* Penguin, 1951; *Katy No Pocket,* 1953; *Find the Constellations,* 1954; *See The Circus,* 1956; the Curious George series: *Curious George Takes A Job,* 1947; *Curious George Rides a Bike,* 1952; *Curious George Gets A Medal,* 1957; *Curious George Learns the Alphabet,* 1963; *Curious George Goes to the Hospital,* 1966).

Glen Rounds's *The Blind Colt* (a realistic story of a boy's devotion to a young colt who has been marked for death; illustrated by the author; published in New York by Holiday House; the author's other work, published by Holiday except as noted, includes *Ol' Paul, the Mighty Logger,* 1936; *Lumbercamp,* 1937, reissued as *Whistle Punk* in 1959; *Paydirt,* 1938; *Whitey's Sunday Horse,* 1943; *Whitey's First Roundup,* Grosset, 1943; *Whitey Looks for a Job,* Grosset, 1944; *Whitey and Jinglebob,* Grosset, 1946; *Stolen Pony,* 1948; *Rodeo,* 1949; *Whitey and the Rustlers,* 1951; *Hunted Horses,* 1951; *Whitey and the Blizzard,* 1952; *Buffalo Harvest,* 1952; *Lone Muskrat,* 1953; *Whitey Takes A Trip,* 1954; *Whitey Ropes and Rides,* 1956; *Swamp Life: An Almanac,* Prentice-Hall, 1957; *Whitey and the Wild Horse,* 1958; *Whitey's New Saddle,* 1960; *Beaver Business,* Prentice-Hall, 1960; *Wild Orphan,* 1961; *Whitey and the Colt Killer,* 1962; *Rain in the Woods,* World, 1964; *The Snake Tree,* World, 1967; compiler, *Boll Weevil,* Golden Gate, 1967; *The Treeless Plains,* 1967; *The Prairie Schooners,* 1968; compiler, *Casey Jones,* Golden Gate, 1968; *Wild Horses of the Red Desert,* 1969). UMi

Frances Clark Sayers's *Tag-Along Tooloo* (the story of a small girl's struggles to keep up with her sister; published in New York by Viking; the author is a noted librarian, storyteller, and critic).

Geoffrey Trease's *Cue for Treason* (one of this British author's many historical novels for young people; set in Tudor England; published by Blackwell; the author's other work includes *Bows Against the Barons,* International, 1934; *Comrades for the Charter,* Laurence, 1934; *Call To Arms,* International, 1935; *Walking in England,* Fenland, 1935; *Missing from Home,* Laurence, 1936; *The Christmas Holiday Mystery,* Black, 1937; *Mystery on the Moors,* Black, 1937; *Red Comet,* Laurence, 1937; *Detectives of the Dales,* Black, 1938; *The Dragon Who Was Different,*

Muller, 1938; *In the Land of Mogul,* Blackwell, 1938; *Such Divinity,*Chapman, 1939; *Only Natural,* Chapman, 1940; *Running Deer,* Harrap, 1941; *The Grey Adventurer,* Blackwell, 1942; *Black Night, Red Morning,* Blackwell, 1944; *Trumpets in the West,* Harcourt, 1947; *The Hills of Varna,* Macmillan, 1948; *Silver Guard,* Blackwell, 1948; *Fortune, My Foe—W. Raleigh,* Methuen, 1949; *The Mystery of Moorside Farm,* Blackwell, 1949; *No Boats on Bannermore,* Heineman, 1949; *The Secret Fiord,* Macmillan, 1949; *Tales Out of School,* Heinemann, 1949; *The Young Traveller in India and Pakistan,* Phoenix, 1949; *Under Black Banner,* Heinemann, 1950; *Enjoying Books,* Phoenix, 1951; *The Baron's Hostage,* Phoenix, 1952; *Web of Traitors,* Vanguard, 1952; *New House at Hardale,* Lutterworth, 1953; *The Seven Queens of England,* Vanguard, 1953; *The Silken Secret,* Blackwell, 1953; *Black Banner Abroad,* Warne, 1955; *Seven Kings of England,* Vanguard, 1955; *The Gates of Bannerdale,* Heinemann, 1956; *The Young Traveller in Greece,* Dutton, 1956; *Snared Nightingale,* Macmillan, 1957; *Escape To King Alfred,* Vanguard, 1958; *The Young Traveller in England and Wales,* Dutton, 1958; *So Wild the Heart,* Vanguard, 1959; *The Maythorn Story,* Heinemann, 1960; *Victory at Valmy,* Vanguard, 1960; *The Young Writer,* Nelson, 1961; *Follow My Black Plume,* Macmillan, 1963; *The Italian Story,* Macmillan, 1963; *Seven Stages,* Heinemann, 1964; *A Thousand for Sicily,* Macmillan, 1964; *Bent Is the Bow,* Nelson, 1965; *The Dutch Are Coming,* Hamish, 1965; *This Is Your Century,* Harcourt, 1965; *The Red Towers of Granada,* Macmillan, 1966; *The Grand Tour,* Holt, 1967; *The White Nights of St. Petersburg,* Macmillan, 1967; *The Runaway Serf,* Hamish, 1968; *Seven Sovereign Queens,* Heinemann, 1968; *Byron: A Poet Dangerous to Know,* Holt, 1969).

Virginia Watson's *Flags Over Quebec: A Story of the Conquest of Canada* (a historical novel set in Canada but written by an American author; illustrated by Harve Stein; published in New York by Coward; the author's other work includes under the pseudonym of Roger West, *Midshipman Days,* Houghton, 1913; *The Princess Pocahontas,* Penn, 1916; *With Cortez the Conqueror,* Penn, 1917; *With LaSalle, the Explorer,* illustrated by Henry C. Pitz, Holt, 1922; under the pseudonym of Roger West, *Through Many Waters,* Harper, 1944; *Trial of Courage,* illustrated by Marcia Brown, Coward, 1948).

1942

B. B.'s *The Little Grey Men* (the tale of the adventures of the last gnomes of Britain; illustrated by the author; awarded the Carnegie Medal in 1942; published by Scribner; the sequel was *Down the Bright Stream,* Eyre, 1948; the author's other work includes the fairy tale collections, *Meeting Hill,* Hollis, 1948, and *The Wind in the Wood,* Hollis, 1952; other stories include *Brendon Chase,* Hollis, 1944; *The Forest of Boland Light Railway,* Eyre,

1942 *continued*

1955; *The Wizard of Boland,* Ward, 1959; *The Whopper,* Benn, 1967; *At the Back o' Ben Dee,* Benn, 1968; *Ben the Bullfinch,* Hamilton, 1968; B. B. is the pseudonym of Denys James Watkins-Pitchford).

Conrad and Mary Buff's *Dash and Dart* (an animal picture book which presents the first year in the life of two fawns; published in New York by Viking; the author-illustrator's other work, published by Viking except as noted, includes The *Big Tree,* 1946; *Peter's Pinto,* 1949; *The Apple and the Arrow,* Houghton, 1951; *Magic Maize,* Houghton, 1953; *Hurry, Skurry, and Flurry,* 1954; *Hah-Nee of the Cliff Dwellers,* Houghton, 1956; *Dancing Cloud,* 1957; *Elf Owl,* 1958; *Forest Folk,* 1962; *The Colorado: River of Mystery,* Ritchie, 1968).

Virginia Lee Burton's *The Little House* (a poetic, informative picture-story account of the changes that come to a country house as the city grows up around it; awarded the Caldecott Medal in 1943; published in Boston by Houghton Mifflin; the author-illustrator's other work, published by Houghton, includes *Choo Choo,* 1935; *Mike Mulligan and His Steamshovel,* 1939; *Calico, the Wonder Horse,* 1941; *Katy and the Big Snow,* 1943; *Song of Robin Hood,* 1947; *Maybelle, the Cable Car,* 1952; *Life Story,* 1962).

Carl Carmer's *America Sings: Stories and Songs of Our Country's Growing* (a distinguished collection of stories and songs about some American legendary heroes; published in New York by Knopf).

Maureen Daly's *Seventeenth Summer* (a romance in which Angie Morrow grows emotionally during her summer holiday as she experiences her first love; published by Dodd).

Elizabeth Janet Gray's *Adam of the Road* (an adventure story set in thirteenth-century England; illustrated by Robert Lawson; awarded the Newbery Medal in 1943; published in New York by Viking; the author's other work includes *Meredith's Ann,* Doubleday, 1929; *Tilly-Tod,* Doubleday, 1929; *Meggy MacIntosh,* Doubleday, 1930; *Tangle Garden,* Doubleday, 1932; *Jane Hope,* Viking, 1933; *Young Walter Scott,* Viking, 1935; *Beppy Marlowe of Charles Town,* Viking, 1936; *Penn,* Viking, 1938; *Contributions of the Quakers,* Davis, 1939; *The Fair Adventure,* Viking, 1940; *Anthology with Comments,* Pendel, 1942; *Sandy,* Viking, 1945; under her married name of Elizabeth Gray Vining: *Windows for the Crown Prince,* Lippincott, 1952; *The World in Tune,* Harper, 1954; *The Virginia Exiles,* Lippincott, 1955; *Friend of Life: The Biography of Rufus M. Jones,* Lippincott, 1958; *The Cheerful Heart,* Viking, 1959; *Return to Japan,* Lippincott, 1960; *I Will Adventure,* Viking, 1962; *Take Heed of Loving*

Me, Lippincott, 1963; *Flora: A Biography,* Lippincott, 1966; *I, Roberta,* Lippincott, 1967).

Mabel Leigh Hunt's *Have You Seen Tom Thumb?* (a lively biography of the Barnum Circus's midget, Tom Thumb; runner-up for the Newbery Medal; published by Lippincott; the author's other work, published by Lippincott, except as noted, includes *Lucinda; A Little Girl of 1860,* 1934; *The Boy Who Had No Birthday,* 1935; *Little Girl With Seven Names,* 1936; *Susan Beware,* 1937; *Benjie's Hat,* 1938; *Little Grey Gown,* 1939; *Michel's Island,* 1940; *Billy Button's Butter'd Biscuit,* 1941; *John of Pudding Lane,* 1941; *Corn-belt Billy,* Grosset, 1942; *Peter Piper's Pickled Peppers,* 1942; *The Peddlar's Clock,* Grosset, 1943; *Young Man of the House,* 1944; *Sibby Botherbox,* 1945; *The Double Birthday Present,* 1947; *Such a Kind World,* Grosset, 1947; *Matilda's Buttons,* 1948; *The Wonderful Baker,* 1950; *The 69th Grandchild,* 1951; *Ladycake Farm,* 1952; *Singing Among Strangers,* 1954; *Miss Jellytot's Visit,* 1955; *Johnny-Up and Johnny-Down,* 1962).

Hope Newell's *Steppin and Family* (the story of a black child and his family; published by Hale; the author's other work includes *The Little Old Woman Who Used Her Head,* Nelson, 1938; *Cinder Ike,* Nelson, 1942; *The Story of Christina,* Harper, 1947; *The Little Old Woman Carries On,* Nelson, 1947; *A Cap for Mary Ellis,* Harper, 1953; *Penny's Best Summer,* Harper, 1954).

John R. Tunis's *All-American* (a sports story which deals with racial prejudice; one of a number of popular sports stories; published by Harcourt, Brace; the author's other work includes *American Girl,* Brewer, 1928; *Iron Duke,* Harcourt, 1938; *Duke Decides,* Harcourt, 1939; *Champion's Choice,* Harcourt, 1940; *Kid From Tomkinsville,* Harcourt, 1940; *Sport for the Fun of It,* Barnes, 1940; *Democracy and Sport,* Barnes, 1941; *The Writing Game,* Barnes, 1941; *World Series,* Harcourt, 1941; *Million-Miler,* Messner, 1942; *Keystone Kids,* Harcourt, 1943; *Lawn Games,* Barnes, 1943; *Rookie of the Year,* Harcourt, 1944; *Yea! Wildcats!,* Harcourt, 1944; *City for Lincoln,* Harcourt, 1945; *Kid Comes Back,* Morrow, 1946; *High Pockets,* Morrow, 1948; *Young Razzle,* Morrow, 1949; *The Other Side of the Fence,* Morrow, 1953; *Go, Team, Go!,* Morrow, 1954; *Buddy and the Old Pro,* Morrow, 1955; *American Way in Sport,* Duell, 1958; *Schoolboy Johnson,* Morrow, 1958; *Silence Over Dunkerque,* Morrow, 1962; *A Measure of Independence,* Atheneum, 1964).

1943

Pearl Buck's *The Water-Buffalo Children* (one of the author's realistic fiction books set in old China; published in New York by Day; the author's other work for children includes *The Dragon Fish,* Day, 1944; *The Big*

1943 *continued*

Wave, Day, 1948; *The Beech Tree,* Day, 1955; *Christmas Miniature,* Day, 1957; *Christmas Ghost,* Day, 1960; *Fairy Tales of the Orient,* Simon, 1965; *Matthew, Mark, Luke, and John,* Day, 1967).

Rebecca Caudill's *Barry and Daughter* (an historical novel with strong characterizations; published in New York by Viking; the author's other work includes *Happy Little Family,* Holt, 1947; *Schoolhouse in the Woods,* Winston, 1949; *Tree of Freedom,* Viking, 1949; *Up and Down the River,* Winston, 1951; *Saturday Cousins,* Winston, 1953; *House of the Fifers,* Longmans, 1954; *Susan Cornish,* Viking, 1955; *Time for Lissa,* Nelson, 1959; *Schoolroom in the Parlor,* Holt, 1959; *Higgins and the Big Scare,* Holt, 1960; *The Best-Loved Doll,* Holt, 1962; *A Pocketful of Cricket,* Holt, 1964; *A Certain Small Shepherd,* Holt, 1965; *Did You Carry the Flag Today, Charley?,* Holt, 1966; *My Appalachia,* Holt, 1966; with James Ayers, *Contrary Jenkins,* Holt, 1969; *Come Along!,* Holt, 1969).

Chih-Yi Chan's *The Good Luck Horse* (a Chinese legend retold by Chan and illustrated by Plato Chan; runner-up for the Newbery Medal; published by Whittlesey House; the author's other work includes *Magic Monkey,* written under the name of Christina Chan and illustrated by Plato Chan, Whittlesey, 1944).

Richard Chase's *The Jack Tales* (a collection of Appalachian tales derived from British folklore; published by Houghton; the author's other work includes *The Grandfather Tales,* Houghton, 1948; *Jack and the Three Sillies,* Houghton, 1950; *Wicked John and the Devil,* Houghton, 1951; *Billy Boy,* Golden Gate, 1966).

Antoine de Saint-Exupéry's *The Little Prince* (translated from the French; a literary fairy tale which reveals what a special child learns during his travels from planet to planet; published in New York by Harcourt).

David Ewen's *The Story of George Gershwin* (one of several fictionalized biographies of famous musicians for young people; published by Holt; the author's other work, published by Holt except as noted, includes *Haydn: A Good Life,* 1946; *The Story of Irving Berlin,* 1950; *The Story of Jerome Kern,* 1953; *Leonard Bernstein,* Chilton, 1960; *With a Song in His Heart: The Story of Richard Rogers,* 1963; *The Cole Porter Story,* 1965).

Esther Forbes's *Johnny Tremain* (a robust, realistic adventure story of a young man's development during the American Revolution; published by Houghton Mifflin; based on the author's research for her adult biography

Paul Revere and the World He Lived In, Houghton, 1942, which won the Pulitzer Prize for history).

Genevieve Fox's *Sir Wilfred Grenfell* (a convincing account by a Canadian author of Grenfell's childhood, his work in the London slums, and his great achievements in Labrador; published by Crowell; the author's other work includes *Border Girl,* Little, 1939).

Alice Kelsey's *Once the Hodja* (a collection of folktales about a Turkish Hodja; published by Longmans; the author's other work includes *Once the Mullah,* Longmans, 1954).

Lee Kingman's *Pierre Pigeon* (a story about Newfoundland home life, set in the rugged country of the lower St. Lawrence; published by Houghton; the author's other work includes *Ilenka,* Houghton, 1945; *The Rocky Summer,* Houghton, 1948; *The Best Christmas,* Doubleday, 1949; *Philippe's Hill,* Doubleday, 1950; *The Quarry Adventure,* Doubleday, 1951; *Kathy and the Mysterious Statue,* Doubleday, 1963; *Peter's Long Walk,* Doubleday, 1953; *Mikko's Fortune,* Ariel, 1955; *Magic Christmas Tree,* Ariel, 1956; *Secret Journey of the Silver Reindeer,* Doubleday, 1968).

Olive E. Knox's *By Paddle and Saddle* (the story of a sixteen-year-old Scottish boy who accompanies Sir George Simpson on his adventure-filled trip around the world in 1841; published in Toronto by Macmillan; the author's other work includes *Black Falcon,* Bouregy, 1955; *The Young Surveyor,* Ryerson, 1956).

Eric Linklater's *The Wind on the Moon* (a Scottish author's notable fantasy about two little English girls who embark on a career of naughtiness; awarded the Carnegie Medal in 1944; published in London by Macmillan; the author's other work includes *White Man's Saga,* Cape, 1929; *The Crusader's Key,* White Owl, 1933; *God Likes Them Plain,* Cape, 1935; *Ripeness Is All,* Farrar, 1935; *The Faithful Ally,* Cape, 1954).

Julia Sauer's *Fog Magic* (a fantasy about a Nova Scotian girl who through magic discovers an old fishing village; published by Viking; the author's other work includes *The Light at Tern Rock,* Viking, 1951; *Mike's House,* Viking, 1954).

Edwin Way Teale's *Dune Boy* (the autobiography of the early years of a well-known American naturalist, published by Dodd; the author's other work includes *The Boy's Book of Insects,* Dutton, 1939; *The Boy's Book of Photography,* Dutton, 1939).

1943 *continued*

James Thurber's *Many Moons* (a picture-story fantasy about a petulant princess who demands the moon; Louis Slobodkin, illustrator, awarded Caldecott Medal in 1944; published in New York by Harcourt; the author's other work includes *The Thirteen Clocks,* 1950; *The Wonderful O,* Simon, 1957).

1944

Alice Dalgleish's *The Silver Pencil* (the story of a young girl who wants to grow up to be a writer and teacher; runner-up for the Newbery Medal; published by Scribner; the author's other work, published by Scribner except as noted, includes *The Little Wooden Farmer and the Story of the Jungle Pool,* Macmillan, 1930; *The Blue Teapot, Sandy Cove Stories,* Macmillan, 1931; *The Choosing Book,* illustrated by Eloise Wilkin, Macmillan, 1932; *Relief's Rocker; A Story of Sandy Cove and the Sea,* Macmillan, 1932; *Christmas: A Book of Stories Old and New,* 1934; *Sailor Sam,* 1935; *The Smiths and Rusty,* illustrated by Berta and Elmer Hader, 1936; *Long Live the King!,* 1937; *Wings for the Smiths,* illustrated by Berta and Elmer Hader, 1937; *America Begins,* 1938; *The Gay Mother Goose,* illustrated by Francoise, 1938; compiler, *Once On A Time,* 1938; editor, *The Will James Cowboy Book,* 1938; *Happily Ever After,* 1939; *The Hollyberrys,* 1939; *The Young Aunts,* 1939; *A Book for Jennifer,* 1940; *Three from Greenaways, A Story of Children from England,* 1941; *Wings Around South America,* 1942; *Gulliver Joins the Army,* 1942; *They Live in South America,* 1942; with Margaret Suckley, *The True Story of Fala,* 1942; *The Little Angel, A Story of Old Rio,* 1943; joint compiler, *Childcraft,* Quarrie, 1945; *Along Janet's Road,* 1946; *Reuben and His Red Wheelbarrow,* Grosset, 1946; *The Enchanted Book,* 1947; *The Davenports Are at Dinner,* illustrated by Flavia Gág, 1948; *The Davenports and Cherry Pie,* 1949; *The Bears on Hemlock Mountain,* 1952; *The Courage of Sarah Noble,* 1954; *The Thanksgiving Story,* 1954; *The Columbus Story,* 1955; *The Fourth of July Story,* 1956; *Ride on the Wind,* 1956; *Adam and the Golden Cock,* 1959).

Florence Mary Fitch's *One God: The Ways We Worship Him* (an informational book describing the beliefs and rituals of the Catholic, Jewish, and Protestant faiths; with photographs chosen by Beatrice Creighton; published by Lothrop, Lee and Shepard; the author's other work, published by Lothrop, includes *Their Search for God,* 1947; *Allah, the God of Islam,* 1950; *A Book About God,* illustrated by Leonard Weisgard, 1953; *Child Jesus,* 1955).

Helen Garrett's *Angelo, the Naughty One* (a popular picture-story book about a Mexican boy; illustrated by Leo Politi; presently controversial because of negative stereotyping; published by Viking; the author's other work includes *Rufus Redtail,* Viking, 1947; *Brothers from North Bay,* Westminster, 1966).

May McNeer's *The Gold Rush* (one of the author's many well-researched informational books; illustrated by Lynd Ward; published by Grosset; the author's other work includes *Prince Bantam,* Macmillan, 1929; *Waif Maid,* Macmillan, 1930; *Stop Tim,* Farrar, 1930; with Charlotte Lederer, *Tales from the Crescent Moon,* Farrar, 1931; *Tinka, Minka, Linka,* Farrar, 1931; *The Story of the Great Plains,* Harper, 1943; *The Story of California,* Harper, 1944; *The Covered Wagon,* Grosset, 1944; *The Story of the Southern Highlands,* Harper, 1945; *The Golden Flash,* Viking, 1947; *The Story of Florida,* Harper, 1947; *The Story of the Southwest,* Harper, 1945; *California Gold Rush,* Random, 1950; *John Wesley,* Abingdon, 1951; *Up a Crooked River,* Viking, 1952; *Martin Luther,* Abingdon, 1953; *The Mexican Story,* Farrar, 1953; *War Chief of the Seminoles,* Random, 1954; *Little Baptiste,* Houghton, 1954; *America's Abraham Lincoln,* Houghton, 1957; *The Canadian Story,* Farrar, 1958; *Armed With Courage,* Abingdon, 1958; *My Friend Mac,* Houghton, 1960; *The Alaska Gold Rush,* Random, 1960; *America's Mark Twain,* Houghton, 1962; *The Hudson: River of History,* Garrard, 1962; with Lynd Ward, *Nic of the Woods,* Houghton, 1962; *The American Indian Story,* Farrar, 1963; *Profile of American History,* Hammond, 1964; *Give Me Freedom,* Abingdon, 1964; *The Wolf of Lamb's Lane,* Houghton, 1967; *Go, Tim, Go,* Random, 1968).

Lim Sian-Tek's *Folk Tales from China* (a collection of Chinese myths, legends, fairy and folk tales, romances, and historical legends designed to introduce Western children to Chinese literature; published by Daly; this Chinese writer's other work includes *More Folk Tales from China,* Daly, 1948).

Louise Hall Tharp's *Champlain, Northwest Voyager* (Canadian history is presented in exciting story form; published by Little, Brown; the author's other work includes *Company of Adventurers: The Story of the Hudson's Bay Company,* Little, 1946).

Tasha Tudor's *Mother Goose: Seventy-Seven Verses* (favorite nursery rhymes illustrated in watercolor; published by Oxford; the author-illustrator's other work includes *Pumpkin Moonshine,* Oxford, 1938; *Alexander the Gander,* Oxford, 1939; *A Is for Annabelle,* Oxford, 1954; *First Graces,*

1944 *continued*
Oxford, 1955; *1 is One,* Oxford, 1956; *Around the Year,* Oxford, 1957; *Becky's Birthday,* Viking, 1960; *Wings From the Wind,* Lippincott, 1964; *First Delights,* Platt and Munk, 1966; *Take Joy,* World, 1966; *More Prayers,* Walck, 1967).

Arthur Waley's *The Adventures of Monkey* (from the first seven chapters of the Chinese children's classic, *Monkey,* written by Wu Ch'eng-en in the seventeenth century; published in New York by Knopf).

Hugh Weatherby's *Tales the Totems Tell* (a collection of simplified versions of British Columbian Indian tales; illustrated by the author; published in Toronto by Macmillan).

1945

Carolyn Sherwin Bailey's *The Little Rabbit Who Wanted Red Wings* (a picture-book story which reaffirms a mother rabbit's love; illustrated by Dorothy Grider; published by Platt and Munk; the author's *Miss Hickory,* awarded the Newbery Medal in 1947, was illustrated by Ruth Chrisman Gannett and published by Viking in 1946; the author's other work includes *Stories for Sunday Telling,* Pilgrim, 1916; *Stories for Any Day,* Pilgrim, 1917; *Stories for Every Holiday,* Abingdon, 1918; *Once Upon a Time Animal Stories,* Bradley, 1918; *The Outdoor Story Book,* Pilgrim, 1918; *Everyday Stories,* Bradley, 1919; *Hero Stories,* Bradley, 1919; *The Enchanted Bugle and Other Stories,* Owen, 1920; *The Torch of Courage and Other Stories,* Bradley, 1921; *Flint,* Bradley, 1922; *Surprise Stories,* Whitman, 1923; *When Grandfather Was A Boy Stories,* Pilgrim, 1923; *The Wonderful Days,* Whitman, 1929; *Read Aloud Stories,* Bradley, 1929; *Li'l Hannibal,* Platt, 1938; *Country-Shop,* Viking, 1942; *Pioneer Art in America,* Viking, 1944; *Merry Christmas Book,* Whitman, 1948; *Old Man Rabbit's Dinner Party,* Platt and Munk, 1949; *Enchanted Village,* Viking, 1950; *Finnegan II, His Nine Lives,* Viking, 1953; *The Little Red Schoolhouse,* Viking, 1957; *Flickertail,* Walck, 1962). SCSC

Lorraine and Jerrold Beim's *Two Is a Team* (one of the first picture-story books advocating cooperation between blacks and whites on an equal basis; illustrated by Ernest Crichlow; published by Harcourt, Brace; the authors also wrote *Burrow That Had a Name,* Harcourt, 1939; Jerrold Beim's work includes *The Smallest Boy in the Class,* Morrow, 1949; *The Swimming Hole,* Morrow, 1951; *The Boy on Lincoln's Lap,* Morrow, 1955; *Trouble After School,* Harcourt, 1957).

Jean Bothwell's *Little Boat Boy* (the story of one child's life, set in India; published by Harcourt, Brace; the author's other work includes *River Boy of Kashmir,* Morrow, 1946; *Little Flute Player,* Morrow, 1949).

Betty Cavanna's *Going on Sixteen* (one of the author's many romances for young people; published by Westminster; the author's other work includes *Date For Diane,* Macrae Smith, 1945; *The Clue in the Blue,* Grosset, 1948; *Pick of the Litter,* Westminster, 1952; *First Book of Wild Flowers,* Watts, 1961; Betty Cavanna also writes under the pseudonyms Betsy Allen and Elizabeth Headley).

Georgene Faulkner and John Becker's *Melindy's Medal* (a popular realistic fiction account of a black child's daily adventures; published by Messner; Faulkner's other work includes *White Elephant, and Other Tales from Old India,* Wise, 1929; *Melindy's Happy Summer,* Messner, 1949; Becker's other work includes *New Feathers for the Old Goose,* Putnam, 1956).

Marguerite Henry's *Justin Morgan Had a Horse* (published by Wilcox and Follett, one of a popular series of horse stories illustrated by Wesley Dennis, who also illustrated the author's *King of the Wind,* Rand, 1948, which was awarded the Newbery Medal in 1949; the author's other work includes *Auno and Tauno,* Whitman, 1940; *Dilly Dally Sally,* Saalfield, 1940; *Alaska in Story and Pictures,* Whitman, 1941; *Argentina in Story and Pictures,* Whitman, 1941; *Brazil in Story and Pictures,* Whitman, 1941; *Canada in Story and Pictures,* Whitman, 1941; *Chile in Story and Pictures,* Whitman, 1941; *Mexico in Story and Pictures,* Whitman, 1941; *Panama in Story and Pictures,* Whitman, 1941; *West Indies in Story and Pictures,* Whitman, 1941; *Birds at Home,* Donohue, 1942; *Geraldine Belinda,* Platt, 1942; *Their First Igloo on Baffin Island,* Whitman, 1943; *A Boy and a Dog,* Follett, 1944; *Little Fellow,* Winston, 1945; *Robert Fulton, Boy Craftsman,* Bobbs-Merrill, 1945; *Australia in Story and Pictures,* Whitman, 1946; *Bahamas in Story and Pictures,* Whitman, 1946; *Bermuda in Story and Pictures,* Whitman, 1946; *British Honduras in Story and Pictures,* Whitman, 1946; *Dominican Republic in Story and Pictures,* Whitman, 1946; *New Zealand in Story and Pictures,* Whitman, 1946; *Virgin Islands in Story and Pictures,* Whitman, 1946; *Hawaii in Story and Pictures,* Whitman, 1946; *Benjamin West and His Cat, Grimalkin,* Bobbs, 1947; *Always Reddy,* McGraw, 1947; *Misty of Chincoteague,* Rand, 1947; *Little-or-Nothing from Nottingham,* McGraw, 1949; *Sea Star, Orphan of Chincoteague,* Rand, 1949; *Born to Trot,* Rand, 1950; *Album of Horses,* Rand, 1951; *Portfolio of Horses,* Rand, 1952; *Brighty of the Grand Canyon,* Rand, 1953; *Justin Morgan Had a Horse,* rev. ed., Rand, 1954; *Wagging Tails,* Rand,

1945 *continued*

1955; *Cinnabar,* Rand, 1956; *Black Gold,* Rand, 1957; *Muley-Ears, Nobody's Dog,* Rand, 1959; *Gaudenzia,* Rand, 1960; *Misty, the Wonder Pony,* Rand, 1961; *All About Horses,* Rand, 1962; *Five O'Clock Charlie,* Rand, 1962; *Stormy, Misty's Foal,* Rand, 1963; *White Stallion of Lipizza,* Rand, 1964; *Mustang,* Rand, 1966; *Dear Marguerite Henry,* Rand, 1969; *Dear Readers and Riders,* Rand, 1969).

Jesse Jackson's *Call Me Charley* (one of the first popular, realistic fiction books by a black writer; published by Harper; the author's other work includes *Anchor Man,* Harper, 1947; *Room for Randy,* Friendship, 1957; *Charley Starts From Scratch,* Harper, 1958).

James Kjelgaard's *Big Red* (one of a popular series of realistic dog stories; published by Holiday; the author's other work, published by Holiday except as noted, includes *Forest Patrol,* 1941; *Snow Dog,* 1948; *Wild Trek,* 1950; *Fire Hunter,* 1951; *Irish Red, Son of Big Red,* 1951; *Outlaw Red,* 1953; *Haunt Fox,* 1954; *Desert Dog,* 1956; *Wolf Brother,* 1956; *Swamp Cat,* Dodd, 1957; *Wildlife Cameraman,* 1957; *Double Challenge,* Dodd, 1957; *Boomerang Hunter,* 1960).

Ruth Krauss's *The Carrot Seed* (a popular concept book for young children which captures the young child's way of thinking; author's other work, published by Harper except as noted, includes *Good Man and His Wife,* 1944; *Great Duffy,* 1946; *Growing Story,* 1947; *Bears,* 1948; *Big World and Little House,* 1949; *Happy Day,* 1949; *Backward Day,* 1950; *Bundle Book,* 1951; *A Hole Is to Dig,* 1952; *A Very Special House,* 1953; *How to Make an Earthquake,* 1954; *I'll Be You and You Be Me,* 1954; *Charlotte and the White Horse,* 1955; with Crockett Johnson, *Is This You?* Scott, 1955; *I Want to Paint My Bathroom Blue,* 1956; *Birthday Party,* 1957; *Monkey Day,* 1957; *I Can Fly,* Golden, 1958; *Somebody Else's Nut Tree,* 1958; *Moon or a Button,* 1959; *Open House for Butterflies,* 1960; *Mama, I Wish I Was Snow,* Atheneum, 1962; *A Bouquet of Littles,* 1963; *Eyes, Nose, Fingers, Toes,* 1964; *The Cantilever Rainbow,* 1965; *The Little King, The Little Queen, The Littler Monster, and Other Stories You Can Make Up Yourself,* 1966; *This Thumbprint,* 1967; *What a Fine Day For . . . ,* Parents, 1967). YES

Lois Lenski's *Strawberry Girl* (one of a series of authentic regional realistic stories; awarded the Newbery Medal in 1946; published by Lippincott; the author-illustrator's other work includes *Shipping Village,* Stokes, 1927; *Jack Horner's Pie,* Harper, 1927; *A Little Girl of Nineteen Hundred,* Stokes, 1928; *Alphabet People,* Harper, 1928; *The Wonder City, A Picture Book of New York,* Coward, 1929; *Two Brothers and Their Animals Friends,* Stokes,

1929; *Two Brothers and Their Baby Sister,* Stokes, 1930; *The Washington Picture-Book,* Coward, 1930; *Spinach Boy,* Stokes, 1930; *Grandmother Tippytoe,* Stokes, 1931; *Benny and His Penny,* Knopf, 1931; *Arabella and Her Aunts,* Stokes, 1932; *The Little Family,* Doubleday, 1932; *Johnny Goes to the Fair, A Picture Book,* Minton, 1932; *The Little Auto,* Oxford, 1934; *Surprise for Mother,* Stokes, 1934; *Gooseberry Garden,* Harper, 1934; *Sugarplum House,* Harper, 1935; *Little Baby Ann,* Oxford, 1935; *The Easter Rabbit's Parade,* Stokes, 1936; *Phoebe Fairchild, Her Book,* Stokes, 1936; *A-Going to the Westward,* Stokes, 1937; *Baby Car,* Oxford, 1937; *The Little Sail Boat,* Oxford, 1937; *The Little Airplane,* Oxford, 1938; *Bound Girl of Cobble Hill,* Lippincott, 1938; *Oceanborn Mary,* Stokes, 1938; *Susie Mariar,* Oxford, 1939; *The Little Train,* Oxford, 1940; *Blueberry Corners,* Stokes, 1940; *Indian Captive: The Story of Mary Jemison,* Stokes, 1941; *Animals for Me,* Oxford, 1941; *The Little Farm,* Oxford, 1942; *Davy's Day,* Oxford, 1943; *Bayou Suzette,* Stokes, 1943; *Puritan Adventure,* Lippincott, 1944; *Let's Play House,* Oxford, 1944; *Spring Is Here,* Oxford, 1945; *Blue Ridge Billy,* Lippincott, 1946; *The Little Fire Engine,* Oxford, 1946; *Judy's Journey,* Lippincott, 1947; *Surprise for Davy,* Oxford, 1947; *Boom Town Boy,* Lippincott, 1948; *Mr. and Mrs. Noah,* Crowell, 1948; *Now It's Fall,* Oxford, 1948; *Cowboy Small,* Oxford, 1949; *Cotton In My Sack,* Lippincott, 1949; *Texas Tomboy,* Lippincott, 1950; *I Like Winter,* Oxford, 1950; *Papa Small,* Oxford, 1951; *Prairie School,* Lippincott, 1951; *We Live in the South,* Lippincott, 1952; *Peanuts for Billy Ben,* Lippincott, 1952; *Mama Hattie's Girl,* Lippincott, 1953; *On A Summer Day,* Oxford, 1953; *Corn-Farm Boy,* Lippincott, 1954; *We Live in the City,* Lippincott, 1954; with C. R. Bulla, *Songs of Mr. Small,* Oxford, 1954; *Project Boy,* Lippincott, 1954; with C. R. Bulla, *A Dog Came to School,* Oxford, 1955; *San Francisco Boy,* Lippincott, 1955; *Flood Friday,* Lippincott, 1956; *Big Little Davy,* Oxford, 1956; *Berries in the Scoop,* Lippincott, 1956; *We Live By the River,* Lippincott, 1956; with C. R. Bulla, *Songs of the City,* Marks, 1956; *Davy and His Dog,* Oxford, 1957; *Houseboat Girl,* Lippincott, 1957; with C. R. Bulla, *Little Sioux Girl,* Lippincott, 1958; with C. R. Bulla, *I Went for a Walk* [read-and-sing-book], Walck, 1958; *At Our House* [read-and-sing book] with C. R. Bulla, Walck, 1959; *Coal Camp Girl,* Lippincott, 1959; *We Live in the Country,* Lippincott, 1960; with C. R. Bulla, *When I Grow Up,* Walck, 1960; *Davy Goes Places,* Walck, 1961; *We Live in the Southwest,* Lippincott, 1962; *Policeman Small,* Walck, 1962; *Shoo-Fly Girl,* Lippincott, 1963; *The Life I Live,* Walck, 1965; *We Live in the North,* Lippincott, 1965; *High-Rise Secret,* Lippincott, 1966; *Debbie and Her Grandma,* Walck, 1967; *To Be a Logger,* Lippincott, 1967; *Lois Lenski's Christmas Stories,* Lippincott, 1968; *Deer Valley Girl,* Lippincott, 1968; *Debbie Herself,* Walck, 1969; *Debbie and Her Family,* Walck, 1969). IISU, UCB, UNCG, UO

1945 *continued*

Maud and Miska Petersham's *The Rooster Crows* (a collection of largely American nursery rhymes; awarded the Caldecott Medal in 1946; published by Macmillan, reissued in 1964 without sterotypic illustrations of blacks; the author-illustrator's other work includes *Miki,* Doubleday, Doran, 1929; *The Christ Child,* Doubleday, 1941; *The Box With Red Wheels,* Macmillan, 1949).

Becky Reyher's *My Mother Is the Most Beautiful Woman in the World* (a retelling of a popular Russian folktale; illustrated by Ruth Gannett; published by Hale).

Christine Weston's *Bhimsa, The Dancing Bear* (the story of an English boy who runs away with an Indian child and his trained bear; runner-up for the Newbery Medal; published by Scribner).

Appendix A.

American Periodicals for Children: A Chronological Checklist

"P" signifies periodicals still in print around 1979, the publication date of *Ulrich's International Periodicals Dictionary,* Eighteenth Edition. The earliest and latest dates of publication found in the *Union List of Serials,* Third Edition (1965), are recorded. Often the information sought was non-existent or conflicting, hence the numerous question marks. Lapses in publication are not noted and title changes and mergers are not given. Newspapers are sometimes included as well as magazines, but an attempt was made to exclude annuals. No distinction has been made between story papers, propaganda for special causes, weeklies vs. monthlies, secular magazines, and magazines designed for adults to use with children. The authors appreciate Harriett Christy's addition of over ninety American periodicals to their original list of over three hundred periodicals culled mainly from the third edition of the *Union List of Serials.*

1789	*Children*
1789	*Children's Magazine*
1797	*Youth's News Paper*
1802-1803?	*The Juvenile Magazine; or, Miscellaneous Repository of Useful Information*
1802	*Juvenile Olio*
1805	*The Fly; or Juvenile Miscellany*
1805-1867	*Youth's Magazine; or, Evangelical Miscellany*
1810-1812?	*Juvenile Mirror, or Educational Magazine*
1811-1813?	*Juvenile Magazine*
1811	*Juvenile Monitor*

1811-?	*Juvenile Repository*
1812-1816	*Juvenile Port-Folio and Literary Miscellany*
1813	*Youth's Repository of Christian Knowledge*
1819-1820?	*Juvenile Gazette*
1819?	*Juvenile Miscellany; or Friend of Youth*
1821	*Sunday Scholars' Magazine; or, Monthly Reward Book*
1822-1823	*Juvenile Museum*
1822-1823	*Youth's Monthly Visitor, or Instructive and Entertaining Miscellany of Useful Knowledge*
1823-1864	*The Teacher's Offering*
1823-1864	*Youth's Friend and Scholar's Magazine*
1823-1830	*Youth's Instructer [sic] and Guardian*
1824-1826	*Youth's Musical Companion*
1826-1834	*The Juvenile Miscellany*
1827-1846?	*Child's Magazine*
1827-1828	*Juvenile Gazette; Being An Amusing Repository for Youth*
1827-1828	*Juvenile Magazine*
1827-1929	*The Youth's Companion*
1828-1830	*Hive*
1828-1829?	*Juvenile Repertory*
1828-1895	*Youth's Journal*
1829-1874	*Children's Magazine*
1829-?	*Juvenile Monthly*
1829-1830	*Youth's Herald and Sabbath School Magazine*
1830-1833	*Infant's Magazine*
1830-?	*Juvenile Key*
1830-?	*Juvenile Reformer*
1830-?	*Juvenile Repository*
1830-?	*Mentor and Youth's Instructive Companion*
1830-1834	*Monthly Repository and Library of Entertaining Knowledge*
1831-1836?	*Family Pioneer and Juvenile Key*
1831-1832?	*Juvenile Magazine; and Youth's Monthly Visitor*
1831-?	*Scholar's Gazette*
1832	*Child's Cabinet*
1832-1833	*Juvenile Rambler*

1832-1834?	*The Rose Bud*
1832-1834	*Youth's Companion and Weekly Family Visitor*
1833-1844	*Parley's Magazine*
1833-1834?	*Juvenile Repository*
1834-?	*Child's Universalist Gazette and Monthly Visitor*
1834-1837	*Youth's Magazine*
1835-?	*Child's Gazette*
1835-1838?	*Juvenile Missionary Intelligencer*
1835-1836	*Youth's Lyceum and Literary Gazette*
1836-1838	*The Slave's Friend*
1836	*Youth's Guide*
1836	*Youth's Monitor and Monthly Magazine*
1837-1841?	*Youth's Cabinet*
1837	*Youth's Lyceum*
1837-1839	*Youth's Literary Messenger*
1838-1839	*Child's Companion*
1838-1841	*Youth's Magazine; A Monthly Miscellany*
1839-?	*Family and School Visitor*
1839-1842	*Youth's Mental Casket and Literary Star*
1839-1860	*Youth's Temperance Advocate*
1840-1843?	*The Juvenile Minstrel; for Sunday and Common Schools*
1840-1842	*Youth's Monitor*
1841-1843	*Cold Water Army*
1841-1872?	*Merry's Museum for Boys and Girls*
1841-1842	*Youth's Medallion*
1841-1921	*Sunday School Advocate*
1841-?	*Tutor: Boys' and Girls' Weekly Album*
1842-1846	*Boys' and Girls' Literary Bouquets*
1842-1871	*The Children's Magazine of General Knowledge*
1842-1846	*Boys' and Girls' Monthly Bouquet*
1842-?	*Every Youth's Gazette*
1842-1845?	*Juvenile Repository; Containing Lessons and Stories for the Young*
1842-1844	*Youth's Temperance Enterprise*
1843	*Boys' and Girls' Magazine*

1843-1858	*Child's Friend and Family Magazine*
1843-1850?	*Juvenile Wesleyan*
1843-1863	*New Church Magazine for Children*
1843-1859	*Youth's Penny Gazette*
1843-1848	*Youth's Penny Magazine*
1844-1845	*Bee*
1844-1852	*Golden Rule and Odd Fellows' Family Companion*
1844-1931	*Well-Spring*
1846-1851	*Child's Companion and Youth's Friend*
1846-?	*Encourager*
1846-?	*Golden Rule*
1846-1847?	*Satchel*
1846-1855	*Student*
1846?-1858	*Youth's Cabinet*
1846?-1858?	*Youth's Friend*
1847-?	*Judy*
1847-1848	*Boys' and Girls' Weekly Catholic Magazine*
1847?	*Mt. Vernon Enterprise*
1847-1848?	*The Playmate*
1847-1850	*Sunday Scholars' Mirror*
1847-?	*Young American's Magazine of Self-Improvement*
1848-1853	*Boys' and Girls' Journal, A Magazine for the People and Their Children*
1848-1857	*Boys' and Girls' Magazine and Fireside Companion*
1848?-?	*Fithian's Miniature Magazine*
1848-?	*Juvenile Gazette*
1848-?	*Young People's Mirror*
1848-1850	*The Scholar's Penny Gazette*
1849?-?	*The Boys' and Girls' Journal*
1849	*Bubble*
1849-1857	*Schoolfellow*
1850-1851?	*Juvenile Weekly Gazette*
1850-1853	*Pleasant Pages for Young People*
1850-1855	*The Youth's Dayspring*
1850-1851	*Youth's Monthly Magazine*

1851-?	*Mentor*
1851-1855	*Sunday School Visitor*
1852-1897?	*The Child's Paper*
1852	*Favorite*
1852-1855	*Schoolmate*
1852-1857	*The Youth's Casket*
1852-?	*The Youth's Instructor*
1853-1854	*Forest Garland*
1853-1868	*Forrester's Playmate*
1853-1855	*Little Traveler; A Monthly Paper for the Youth*
1853-1857	*Southern Boys' and Girls' Monthly*
1853?-1857	*The Standard-Bearer: An Illustrated Magazine for the Young*
1853	*Youth's Western Banner*
1854-1855	*Little Forester*
1854-?	*Little Juvenile Temperance Watchman*
1854-1868	*Little Pilgrim: An Illustrated Journal for Boys and Girls*
1854-1875	*The Little Pilgrim: A Monthly Journal for Boys*
1854-?	*Little Wolverine*
1854-?	*Youth's Galaxy*
1855-1860	*Children's Book of Choice and Entertaining Reading for Little Folks At Home*
1855-1872	*The Student and Schoolmate*
1856-1908	*Children's Visitor*
1856-1860	*Message Bird; A Monthly Literary Periodical*
1856-1858	*Pioneer*
1857-1858	*Boys' Monthly Gazette*
1857-1861	*Catholic Youth's Magazine*
1857-1858?	*Child's Magazine*
1857-1871	*Clark's School Visitor*
1857-1875	*Schoolday Magazine*
1859-1881	*All the Year Round*
1859-1861?	*Boys' and Girls' Own Magazine*
1859-1879?	*The Child At Home*
1859-1873	*Children's Friend*
?-1859	*Sargent's School Monthly*

1859-1860	*What Not*
1860-1863?	*Children's Friend*
1860-1862?	*The Children's Guest*
1860-1861	*Youth's Magazine*
[1862-1864 1866-1915]	*Children's Friend*
1862-1871?	*Child's World*
1862-1864?	*Little American*
1863-1864	*Boy's Miscellany; An Illustrated Journal of Useful and Entertaining Literature for Youth*
1863-1865?	*Children's Guide*
1863-1891?	*Children's New Church Magazine*
1863-1870	*Youth's Temperance Visitor*
1864-1872	*Youth's Visitor*
1865-1884	*Frank Leslie's Chimney Corner*
1865-1870	*Good Words*
1865-1870	*Hours at Home*
1865-1915	*Junior Life*
1865?-1867	*Little Bouquet*
1865-1875	*Little Corporal*
1865-1866	*Little Joker*
1865-1871	*Merry and Wise*
1865-1873	*Our Young Folks*
1866-1875?	*The Children's Friend; A Monthly Magazine. Devoted to the Best Interests of the Young*
1866-1872	*The Children's Hour; A Magazine for the Little Ones*
1866-1869?	*Child's Delight*
1866-1876	*Demorest's Young America*
1866-?	*Juvenile Instructor*
1866-1904	*Little Christian, A Sunday-School Paper for Boys and Girls*
1866	*Spare Hours*
1866-1917?	*Youth's Temperance Banner*
1867-1871	*Burke's Weekly for Boys and Girls*
1867-1874	*Children's Hour*
1867-1883	*Frank Leslie's Boy's and Girl's Weekly. An Illustrated Journal of Amusement, Adventure and Instruction*

1867	*Little Gleaner*
1867-1880	*The Nursery; A Monthly Magazine for Youngest Readers*
1867-1868	*Old Merry's Monthly*
1867-1875	*Oliver Optic's Magazine. Our Boys and Girls*
1867-1870	*Riverside Magazine for Young People*
1868-?	*Boys' and Girls' New Monthly Magazine*
1868-?	*Little Chief*
1868-?	*Lyceum Banner*
1868-1870	*Packard's Monthly*
1868-1887	*Young People's Magazine*
1869-1880	*Golden Hours: A Magazine for Boys and Girls*
1869-1877	*Little Folks*
1869-1870	*Onward*
1869?-1875?	*Scattered Seeds*
1870-1872	*American Boy's Magazine*
1870-?	*Infant's Delight*
1870-?	*One/Two*
1870	*Our Leisure Moments*
1870-1872	*Work and Play*
1870-1883	*Young Folks Monthly*
1870-1881	*Young Folks Rural*
1871-1875	*Children's Paper*
1871-1904	*Kind Words*
1871	*Our Schoolday Visitor*
1871-1873	*Our Young Folks Illustrated Paper*
1871-1909	*Young Israel. An Illustrated Monthly Magazine for Young People*
1872-?	*Boys' Ledger*
1872	*Schoolday Visitor Magazine*
1872-1931	*Story World*
1873-1874	*Boys' Own*
1873-1921	*Family Storypaper*
1873-1874	*Frank Leslie's Boys of America*
1873-?	*Girls and Boys of America*
1873-1939	*St. Nicholas*
1874?-1875?	*Scattered Seeds*

1874	*Pacific Youth*
1874-1896	*The Pansy*
1875-1885	*American Young Folks*
1875-1894	*Boys of New York; A Paper for Young Americans*
1875-1877	*Boys of the World. A Story Paper for the Rising Generation*
1875-1876	*Girls of Today*
1875-?	*Golden Rule*
1875-1886	*Little Folks*
1875	*Little People, An Illustrated Journal for Girls and Boys*
1875-1892	*Little Wide-Awake; An Illustrated Magazine for Children*
1875-1898	*Our Boys*
1875	*Schoolday Magazine, for All Homes and Schools*
1875-1930	*Sunbeam*
1875-1907	*Sunny South*
1875-1877	*Young Ireland; An Irish Magazine of Entertainment and Instruction*
1875-1893	*Wide Awake*
1876-1898	*Babyland*
1876-1893	*Children's Work for Children*
1876-P	*On the Line*
1877-1884	*Acanthus*
1877-1878	*Boys of Albany*
1877	*Boy's Own*
1877-?	*Child's Monthly*
1877-1885	*Good Times*
1877-1905	*Half-Dime Library*
1877-1900	*The Helper*
1877-1878	*New York Boys' Weekly*
1877	*Our Young People*
1877-1889	*Young Men of America*
1877-1893	*Treasure Trove*
1878-1879	*Boys' Leader; A Journal of Fact, Fiction, History and Instruction*
1878-1881	*Little Ones At Home*
1878-1893?	*Picture Gallery for Young Folks*
1878-?	*The Sunrise. A Magazine for Young Folks*

1879-1887   *Frank Leslie's Chatterbox*

1879-1899   *Harper's Young People*

1879-1959   *Our Own Magazine*

1879-1880   *Raindrops*

1880-1907   *Golden Days for Boys and Girls*

1880-1900   *Little Men and Women*

1880-?   *New York Boys*

1880-1881   *Our Boys' Paper . . . A Journal of Pure and Interesting Literature for Young People*

1880-1890   *Our Little Granger*

1880-1894   *Our Little Men and Women*

1880-1889   *Our Little Ones and the Nursery: Illustrated Stories and Poems for Little People*

1881-1883?   *Boys' Champion; An Instructive and Entertaining Journal for Young America*

1881-1882?   *Children's Museum, An Illustrated Monthly*

1882-1939   *Forward*

1882-1888   *Golden Argosy*

1882-1883?   *Juvenile Gleanings; or, Boys and Girls Bee Journal*

1882-?   *Young Folks Circle*

1884-1890   *Boys' Library of Sport, Story, and Adventure*

1884-1889   *Chautauqua Young Folks' Journal*

1884-1885   *Little . . . Bee, A Catholic Gatherer of Amusement and Instructive Reading*

1884-1900   *School and Home*

1885   *Good-time for Young People*

1885-1890   *Our Youth: A Paper for Young People and Their Teachers*

1885   *Youth's Treasury*

1886-1926   *Our Boys' Magazine*

1886-1907   *Sunshine for Youth: Also for All Those of All Ages Whose Hearts Are Not Withered*

1887   *Young People's Weekly*

1887-1890   *Young Idea*

1887-1914   *Young Idea*

1888-1911   *Golden Hours*

1888-1891   *Youth's Press*

1889-1898	*American Youth*
1889-1891	*Golden Weekly*
1889-1891	*The Look-Out. A Monthly Magazine for Young People*
1889	*The Sunny Hour*
1890-1904	*Baptist Union*
1890	*Boys' Holiday*
1890-1940	*Epworth Herald*
1890-1897	*Good News*
1890-?	*Our Little Friend*
1891-?	*Rosary*
1892-1903	*Child-Garden of Story, Song and Play*
1893-1948	*Current Events*
1893-1897	*Junior. A Juvenile Paper by Young Writers*
1893-1895	*The Lilliputian Magazine*
1893?-1895?	*Sunbeams; An Illustrated Monthly for Little Folks*
1893-P	*Wee Wisdom*
1894-1906	*Children's Missionary*
1894-1931	*Epworth Era*
1894-1906	*Gray Goose*
1894-1910	*Happy Days*
1894-1895	*Our Boys and Girls*
1894-1920	*Over Sea and Land*
1894-1908	*Star Monthly*
1895-1899	*Harper's Round Table: An Illustrated Journal of Amusement and Instruction*
1895-1897	*The Lark*
1896	*Little Chap: A Journal of Education and Literature*
1896-1912	*Tip Top Weekly; An Ideal Publication for the American Youth*
1897-1902	*Junior Munsey*
1897-1926	*Little Folks; An Illustrated Monthly for Youngest Readers*
1897-1899	*Our Boys and Girls*
1898-1916	*Junior Republic*
1898-1920	*Our Boys' and Girls' Own, An Illustrated Catholic Monthly*

1898-1908	*School Weekly*
1899-1929	*American Boy . . . Youth's Companion*
1899-1917	*Crittenton Magazine*
1899-1907	*Junior Naturalist Monthly*
1899-1901	*Our Boys and Girls*
1899-1907	*Pilgrim, A Magazine for the Home*
1899-?	*Up-To-Date Boys*
1900-1932	*Character Builder*
1900-1907	*Children of the United States*
1900-?	*Indian School Journal*
1900-1919	*Little Chronicle*
1900-P	*Round World*
1900-1902	*Story-teller. Tales True and Otherwise for Children of All Ages from 3-70*
1901-?	*Catholic School Journal*
1901-1904	*James Boys Weekly; Containing Stories*
1902-1911	*Association Boys; A Bi-Monthly Magazine*
1902-1935	*Boys' World*
1902-?	*Children's Friend*
1902-P	*Current Events*
1902-1949	*Girls' Companion*
1903-1907	*Boys and Girls; A Nature Study Magazine*
1903-1913	*Children's Magazine*
1903	*Fun Quarterly*
1903-1913	*Holiday Magazine*
1903-1903	*Just Fun, That's All*
1904-?	*Children's Magazine*
1905-P	*Story Friends*
1905-1913	*Youth's Outlook*
1906-1907	*Stories from Many Lands*
1907-1910?	*Children's Star Magazine*
1907-1939	*Youth's World*
1907-1913	*Uncle Remus; Home Magazine*
1908-1909	*Our Boy's Magazine*

1908-1921	*Visitor*
1909	*Wonderlands. The Young Folk's Magazine of the Baptist Missionary Society*
1909-1910	*Boy's Best Weekly*
1910-1924	*Boys' Magazine*
1911-P	*Boys' Life. The Boy Scouts Magazine*
1911-1916	*Child Life*
1912-1913	*Wee-Wee Winkie*
1914-1916?	*Childhood; A Monthly Magazine by, for and about Children*
1914-1932	*Children's Museum of Boston, Olmstead Park, Jamaica Plain Bulletin*
1914-?	*Our Boys*
1917-1920	*The Rally*
1918-P	*Four and Five*
1919-1925	*American Boy and Open Road*
1919-P	*Reach*
1919-1930	*Sunday School Friend*
1919-?	*Young Horizons*
1920-P	*American Girl*
1920-1925	*Boys of Today*
1920-1921	*The Brownie Book: A Monthly Magazine for Children of the Sun*
1920-P	*Senior Scholastic*
1921-1952	*Missionary Mail*
1921-P	*Child Life; Mystery and Science Fiction Magazine*
1922-P	*Voice of Youth*
1923-1928	*Child's Garden*
1925-1935	*Golden Book Magazine*
1925-1950	*Open Road for Boys*
1926-P	*Zoonooz*
1927-P	*American Newspaper Boy*
1927-?	*Boys' Monthly Magazine*
1927-?	*Children's Digest*
1927-P	*Current Science*
1927-?	*Juvenile World; A Newspaper Magazine for Young Folks*
1929-1935	*Children's Playmate*
1930-1976	*My Weekly Reader*

1930-1932	*Children's Playtime*
1930-P	*Jack and Jill*
1931-1935	*Sunrise. The Junior Quarterly Magazine of the Japan Evangelistic Band*
1932-P	*Children's Museum of Indianapolis Bulletin*
1932-1947	*Pilgrim Highroad*
1932-1940	*Young Israel; A Magazine for Jewish Boys and Girls of America*
1933-P	*Junior Astronomy News*
1933-P	*Picture Story Paper*
1934-?	*Junior State Report*
1935-1941	*Stories for the Little Child*
1936-P	*Junior Natural History Magazine*
1936-1954	*Story Parade*
1937	*Children's Digest*
1937-?	*The Child's Companion; A Weekly Magazine for Boys and Girls*
1937-P	*Junior Scholastic*
1938-P	*Jack & Jill*
1938-?	*Junior Naturalist, for the Preservation of Wildlife*
1938-1941	*Youth Today; the Month's Best Reading for Young People*
1939-P	*Junior Farmer and 4-H Enthusiast*
1939-1943?	*St. Nicholas: A Magazine for Boys and Girls*
1940-P	*World Over*
1941-P	*Children's Times*
1941-P	*News Citizen*
1941-P	*Plays*

Appendix B.

British Periodicals for Children: A Chronological Checklist

"P" signifies periodicals still in print around 1955, the publication date of the *British Union Catalogue of Periodicals,* and in some cases around 1963, the publication date of the *British Museum General Catalogue of Printed Books, Periodicals Index,* Vols. 183-186. Periodicals were culled from both of the above sources.

1757?	*The Young Misses' Magazine*
1788	*The Juvenile Magazine; or, An Entertaining and Instructive Miscellany for Youth of Both Sexes*
1792	*The Flagellant*
1799?	*The Minor's Pocketbook*
1799	*The Children's Magazine; or Monthly Repository of Instruction and Delight*
1799-1800	*The Young Gentleman's and Young Lady's Magazine*
1800-1801	*The Juvenile Library, The Monthly Preceptor or Juvenile Library*
1800-1801	*The Picture Magazine*
1801	*The Good Child's Cabinet of Natural History*
1802-1806	*Mrs Trimmer. The Guardian of Education*
1805-1867	*The Youth's Magazine or Evangelical Miscellany*
1809	*Juvenile Cabinet, or Magazine of Entertainment and Instruction*
1817-1855	*The Youth's Instructer [sic] and Guardian*
1819?	*The Juvenile Miscellany; or Friend of Youth*
1822-1823	*Youth's Monthly Visitor or Instructive and Entertaining Miscellany of Useful Knowledge*

1823	*The Youth's Miscellany of Knowledge and Entertainment*
1824-1831	*The Child's Companion; or Sunday Scholar's Reward*
1824-1922	*The Child's Companion, and Juvenile Instructor*
1824-1930	*The Children's Friend*
1824	*The New Youth's Magazine*
1825-1849	*The Sunday Scholar's Magazine and Juvenile Miscellany*
1826-1860	*The Children's Friend*
1827-1834	*Baptist Sabbath Scholar's Reward*
1827	*The Chimney Corner Companion*
1829-1834	*The Infant's Magazine*
1829-1838	*The Juvenile Forget Me Not*
1830	*Horae Juveniles*
1832-1845	*The Child's Magazine and Sunday Scholar's Companion*
1832	*Punchinello! or Sharps, Flats and Naturals: A Family Gazette of Fun*
1832	*The Boys' and Girls' Penny Magazine*
1833	*Juvenilia*
1833	*The Children's Weekly Visitor*
1833-1836	*The Protestant Dissenter's Juvenile Magazine*
1834-1844	*The Baptist Children's Magazine*
1834-1861	*The Children's Missionary Newspaper*
1836-1850	*Fisher's Juvenile Scrapbook*
1836	*Youth's Monitor and Monthly Magazine*
1838-1893	*The Children's Friend*
1838-1844	*The Children's Magazine of General Knowledge*
1838-1859	*The Children's Missionary Magazine of the United Presbyterian Church*
1839-1848	*The Children's Missionary Record*
1839	*The Juvenile Journal*
1839-1850	*The Missionary Repository for Youth*
1840	*Little—Go Monitor*
1840	*The Juvenile Gleaner: A Keepsake for the Young*
1840-1841	*The Little Magazine for Young Readers of Every Denomination*
1841-1847	*Child's Bethel Flag*
1841-1852	*Punch, or the London Charivari*
1842-1875	*Magazine for the Young*

1842-1843	*The Child At Home: An Illustrated Magazine for the Young*
1842-1851	*The Child's Own Book*
1842-1844	*The Children's Magazine of General Knowledge*
1842	*Every Youth's Gazette: A Semi-Monthly Journal*
1842	*Juvenile Magazine*
1842-1844	*Picture Magazine*
1843-1845?	*Children's Missionary and Sabbath School Record*
1843-1890	*Children's Missionary Juvenile Instructor*
1843-1844	*Youth's Biblical Cabinet*
1844?-1845	*Boys' and Girls' Monthly Bouquet*
1844-1845	*The Juvenile Miscellany of Facts and Fictions with Stray Leaves from Fairy Land*
1844	*The New Parley Magazine*
1844-1877	*News from Afar. Juvenile Missionary Magazine*
1844-1878	*The Wesleyan Juvenile Offering*
1845	*The Juvenile Christian's Remembrances*
1845-1846?	*The Juvenile Magazine Designed for the Use of Day and Sunday Schools*
1845-1908	*The Juvenile Missionary Herald*
1846-1916	*Early Days; or The Wesleyan Scholar's Guide*
1846-1854	*The Jewish Advocate, for the Young*
1847-1863	*The Children's Missionary Record of the Free Church of Scotland*
1847	*The Children's Monthly Garden of True Wisdom and Sound Knowledge*
1847-1848	*The Illustrated Juvenile Miscellany*
1847-1853	*The Snow Drop*
1848	*The Children's Guide and Garden of Wisdom and Knowledge*
1848	*The Juvenile Offering*
1848-1849	*The Playmate*
1849-1859	*The Juvenile Missionary Record*
1850-1893	*The Juvenile Instructor and Companion*
1851-1853	*Little Henry's Records of His Life-Time*
1851	*Primitive Methodist Children's Magazine*
1851-1893	*The Monthly Packet of Evening Readings for Younger Members of the English Church*

1851-1852	The Scholar's Friend
1851	Young Churchman; A Literary Magazine Designed Chiefly for the Youth of the Church of England in the Province of Canada
1852-1897	Child's Paper
1852	Leaves of Learning
1852	The Child's Cabinet
1852-1872	The Child's Own Magazine
1852-1859	The Friend of Youth, and Child's Magazine
1852-1853	The Wesleyan Juvenile Magazine
1853-1894	Erin's Hope
1853?	The Boys' and Girls' Journal
1853-1855	The Charm
1853-1854	The Juvenile: An Illustrated Penny Magazine for Children
1854	The Children's Bible and Missionary Box
1854	The Child's Visitor and Pleasing Instructor
1854	The Halfpenny Picture Magazine for Little Children
1854-1894	The Little Gleaner
1854	The Little Standard Bearer
1854-1940	Sunday At Home
1855-1857	Crumbs for the Lord's Little Ones
1855-1874	Boy's Own Magazine, An Illustrated Journal of Fact, Fiction, History and Adventure
1855-1864	The Children's Jewish Advocate
1855-1925	The Children's Paper
1855	The Pictorial Juvenile Penny Magazine
1855-1870	The Primitive Methodist Juvenile Magazine
1855-1882	The Sunday Scholar's Companion
1856-1857	Little England's Illustrated Newspaper
1856-1857	The Boy's Own Journal and Youth's Miscellany
1856-1862	The Young People's Pocket Book
1857-1858	The Boys' and Girls' Companion for Leisure Hours
1857	The Halfpenny Magazine
1857-1858	The Little Pilgrim
1858	The Child's Horn Book
1858-1861	The Companion for Youth

1858-1861	*The Sunbeam. A Little Luminary To Guide the Young to Glory*
1858	*The Youth's Instructor*
1858-1859	*Tracts for the Young*
1858-1861	*Young England's Illustrated Newspaper*
1859-1861	*Good News for the Little Ones*
1859-1863	*Kingston's Magazine for Boys*
1859	*The Boy's Own Times: Or, News of the World*
1859-1862	*The Little Child's Picture Magazine, in Easy Words*
1860-1894	*The Coral Missionary Magazine*
1860-1869	*The Sabbath Scholar's Treasury and Juvenile Missionary Record*
1860-1862	*Young Canada*
1860-1906	*Good Words*
1861-1901	*Juvenile Magazine and Young People's Record*
1862-1864	*Every Boy's Magazine*
1862	*Good News for Young People*
1862-1865	*Young England*
1863?-1886	*Ballantyne's Miscellany*
1863-1871	*Boy's Journal: A Magazine of Literature, Science, Adventure and Amusement*
1863	*The Boy's Penny Magazine*
1863-1868	*The Boy's Own Volume*
1863	*The Children's Journal*
1863-1875	*The Children's Prize*
1863-1865	*The Picture Magazine*
1864-1867	*The Boy's Friend*
1864-1868	*The Boy's Yearly Book. The Boy's Monthly Magazine*
1864-1890	*The Children's Record of the Free Church of Scotland*
1865-1871	*Merry and Wise. A Magazine for Young People*
1865-1866	*Monthly Readings for Young People*
1865-1866	*Routledge's Magazine for Boys*
1865-1866	*The Boy's Companion and British Traveller*
1865-1868	*The Boys' Own Pocket Book*
1865-1871	*The Children's Hour*
1866-1885	*Aunt Judy's Magazine*

1866	*Boy's Telegram. A Journal Devoted to the Instruction and Amusement of Youth in All Parts of the World*
1866-1867	*Father William's Stories*
1866-1879	*Kind Words for Boys and Girls*
1866	*Little Christian*
1866-1906	*Boys of England*
1866-1879	*The British Juvenile At Home, At Work, and At Play*
1866-1868	*The Children's Picture Magazine*
1866-1869	*The Infant's Magazine*
1866-1946	*The Chatterbox*
1866-1881	*Our Darlings; The Children's Treasury*
1867	*Sunday Reading*
1867-1903	*The Young Pilgrim*
1868-1872	*Good Words for the Young*
1868-1880	*The Children's Treasury*
1868-1876	*Young Men of Great Britain; A Journal of Amusing and Instructive Literature*
1869-1870	*Boys of the World; A Journal for Prince and Peasant*
1869-1888	*Gleanings for the Young*
1869-1883	*Good News for Young and Old*
1869	*The Glasgow Infant School Magazine*
1869-1871	*The Picture Magazine*
1869-1873	*The Young Gentleman's Magazine*
1869-1870	*The Youth's Gazette and Advertiser*
1870	*Every Child's Friend*
1870-1884	*My Sunday Friend*
1870-1874	*The Boy's Own Magazine*
1870-1873	*The Children's Treasure*
1870-1871	*The Chimney Corner*
1870-1873	*The Infant's Delight*
1870-1887	*The Little Missionary*
1870-1877	*The Monthly Rosebud*
1870-1871	*The Youth's Pictorial Treasure*
1870-1872	*The Youth's Play-Hour*
1871-1932?	*Little Folks; A Magazine for the Young*

1871-1876	*Our Young Folks Weekly Budget*
1871-1872	*The Juvenile and Bible Class Magazine*
1871-1872	*Young Ladies of Great Britain*
1872	*Boys' Own Picture Gallery*
1872-1877	*Good Things for the Young of All Ages*
1872	*Old Merry's Monthly*
1872	*Sunday Reading for the Young*
1872	*The Child's Own Magazine*
1872-1873	*The Young Scholar*
1873-1883	*Little Messengers for the Young*
1873-1900	*Primitive Methodist Children's Magazine*
1873	*The Boys' Serial*
1873-1900	*The Juvenile Magazine*
1873	*The Schoolboy's Journal*
1873-1876	*The Young Templar*
1874	*A Feast of Good Things*
1874-1889	*Every Boy's Magazine*
1874-1928	*Sabbath School Messenger*
1874-1877	*The Little Boy's Friend*
1874-1879	*The Peep-Show*
[1875-? 1877-1880]	*Golden Childhood*
1875-1892	*Little Wide-Awake: An Illustrated Magazine for Children*
1875	*The Boy's Athenaeum*
1875-1876	*The Boy's Standard*
1875	*The Little Girl's Treasure*
1876	*Merry Sunbeams*
1876-1877	*Our Boys' Journal*
1876-1921	*The Children's Messenger of the Presbyterian Church in England*
1876	*The Juvenile Temple*
1876-1917	*Young Days*
1876-1879	*Young Folks' Weekly Budget*
1877-1900	*Boys of London*
1877	*Little Ones At Home*
1877	*My Little Friend*

1877-1910	*Our Boys and Girls*
1877	*"Our Own"*
1877	*The Children's Visitor*
1878-1881	*Catholic Children's Magazine*
1878-1888	*Every Girl's Magazine*
1878	*The Children's Journal. For Schools and Bands of Hope*
1878	*The Daisy Picture Book*
1878	*The Keepsake Picture Book*
1879-1967	*The Boy's Own Paper*
1879-1882	*Boy's World*
1879	*Young Folks Budget*
1879-1884	*Young Folks*
1879-1887	*Missionary Pages for the Young*
1879-1884	*Winsome Words, the Help-One-Another Magazine for Boys and Girls*
1879-1890	*Young Naturalist*
1879-1959	*Our Own Magazine*
1880-1882	*Boys' Newspaper*
1880-1884	*The Children's Sunbeam*
1880-1908	*The Girl's Own Paper*
1880-1895	*The Jewish Advocate: A Quarterly Paper for the Young*
1880-1883	*The Missionary Juvenile and Illustrated Missionary News for Young People*
1880	*The Nursery. A Magazine for the Little Ones. Written Chiefly in Words of One or Two Syllables*
1880-1883	*The Union Jack. Tales for British Boys*
1880-1910	*Young Standard Bearer*
1881-1883	*Boys' Illustrated News*
1881-1883	*The Boys' Weekly Reader Novelette*
1881-1883	*Our Little Ones*
1881-1891	*The Little Papers and the MPS*
1881-1914	*The Rosebud. A Monthly Magazine of Nursery Nurture and Amusement*
1881-P	*Young Soldier*
1882-1891	*Juvenile Companion and Sunday School Hive*
1882	*Little Hearts and Little Hands*

1882	*The Boy Amateur*
1882-1886	*The Children's Own Paper*
1882-1883	*The Little Learner*
1882-1885	*The Scholar*
1882-1891	*Sunday School Hive and Juvenile Companion*
1882-1888	*Youth*
1883-1884	*After School Hours*
1883-1898	*Boys' Comic Journal. Stories of Fun, Adventure, and Romance*
1883-1884	*Pleasant Words*
1883-1903	*The Boys' & Girls' Companion*
1884	*Every Boy's Journal*
1884-1891	*The Boy's Leisure Hour*
1884-1891	*Young Folk's Paper*
1885-1891	*Harper's Young People*
1885-1890	*The Bairns' Annual*
1885	*The Boy's Champion Paper*
1885-1896	*The Child's Pictorial*
1885-1892	*The Children's Tidings*
1885-1892	*The Little One's Own Coloured Picture Paper*
1885	*Our Young People's Treasury*
1885-1891	*Young People*
1886-P	*Boy's Brigade Gazette*
1886-P	*Boys and Girls*
1886-1896?	*Children's Record*
1886-1889	*Little Star*
1886-1887	*Merry and Wise. A Magazine for Children*
1886-1926	*Our Boys Magazine*
1886	*Our Boys' Paper*
1886-1887	*The Ensign*
1886	*The Little Christian*
1887-1898	*Atalanta*
1887-1888	*Boys of the United Kingdom*
1887-1889	*Home and Fatherland: A Magazine for Boys and Girls*
1887-1923	*Our Little Dots*

1887	*The Sunrise. A Magazine for Young Folks*
1887	*The Young Scientist*
1887-1915	*Young Man*
1887-1919	*Young Man and Woman. An Illustrated Monthly Magazine*
1888	*The Young Man's Monthly Magazine*
1888-1890	*Beeton's Boy's Own Magazine*
1888-1901	*Boys of the Empire and Young Men of Great Britain*
1888-1889	*Boys' Guide, Philosopher and Friend*
1888-1889	*Boys' Popular Weekly*
1888-1889	*The Children's Illustrated Magazine*
1888-1894	*The Juvenile. A Magazine for the Young*
1888-1889	*Young Briton's Journal*
1889	*Golden Cords*
1889-1922	*The Bible Society Gleanings for the Young*
1889-1892	*The Boy's Champion Journal*
1889	*The Children's Hour*
1890-1893	*Children's Corner*
1890	*Children's Message*
1890	*Springtide. An Illustrated Magazine for Girls and Boys*
1890-1928	*The Boy's Graphic*
1890	*The Children's Guide*
1890	*The Juvenile Rechabite*
1890-1895	*Young People's Illustrated Weekly*
1890-1914	*Young People's Magazine*
1891-1900	*Children's World and Church*
1891-1896	*Old and Young*
1891-1893	*Our Children's Friend*
1891	*The Boy*
1891-1893	*The School of Authors. A Journal Devoted to the Interests of the Young*
1892-P	*Adventurer*
1892-1895	*African Tidings*
1892-1894	*Boys*
1892-1909	*Boys' Mail Bag*

1892-1895	*The Boys' Weekly Novelette*
1892-1900	*Childhood. A Monthly Magazine for Little Folks*
1892-1893	*The Children's Corner and the Young Crusader*
1892	*The Chimney Corner; or, At Home*
1892-1934	*Chums. A Paper for Boys*
1892	*Every Boy's Favourite Journal*
1892-1893	*Little One's Own*
1892	*Halfpenny Wonder*
1892	*Our Boys*
1892	*Sunny Hours for Children*
1892-1893	*The Girls' School Magazine*
1893	*Bits for Boys*
1893	*Jack Harkaway's Journal for Boys*
1893-1900	*Bright Eyes*
1893	*Catholic Girls' Magazine and Children's Corner*
1893-1894	*The Children's Corner and Catholic Girls' Magazine*
1893-1894	*Dean's Magazine*
1893-1898	*"Golden Nails"*
1893-1898	*The "Halfpenny Marvel"*
1893-1914	*Scholar's Own*
1893	*The Sunbeam. A Monthly Periodical for the Young Folks*
1893-1897	*Wee Willie Winkie*
1894-1895	*Aldine Garfield Boys' Journal*
1894	*The Golden Link*
1894	*The Junior-A Monthly Civil Service Paper for Boy Clerks*
1894-1904	*Our Bubble. A Colored Magazine for Boys and Girls*
1894	*Pluck*
1895-1900	*The B.B.*
1895-1931	*Boys' Friend*
1895	*The Boys of the Nation*
1895-1900	*Boy's Leader*
1895-1899	*The Children's Study*
1895	*Girl's Own Messenger*
1895-1896	*The Juvenile Outfitter*

1895-1897	*Our Boys*
1895-1937	*News from Afar*
1896-1897	*Children*
1896-1916	*Golden Sunbeams*
1896-1904	*Little Messenger*
1896	*The Children of the Hour. A Paper for the Few*
1896-1897	*Sunday Hours for Boys & Girls*
1897	*The Boy's Story-Teller*
1897	*The Boy's Welcome*
1897-1898	*Favourite Illustrated Penny Stories*
1897	*The Home Blessing. A Monthly Magazine for the Young*
1897-1905	*The Sunchildren's Budget. A Botanical Quarterly*
1897-1898	*Young Israel. A Magazine for Jewish Youth*
1898-1903	*The Children's Sunday*
1898	*The Girls' Favourite*
1898-1915	*Girl's Realm*
1898-1922	*The Marvel*
1899	*Boys of London and New York*
1899-1900	*Boys' Monster Weekly*
1899	*Boys' War News*
1899	*Children. Pictures and Stories for Little Ones*
1899-1900	*The Gem*
1899-1948	*Tiny Tots*
1899-1907	*Young People*
1900-1925	*Boys' Champion Story Paper*
1900-1905	*The Children's Garden*
1900-1901	*Playtime*
1900	*The Young Stamp Collector*
1901-1903	*Boys of Our Empire*
1901	*Girls' Sphere*
1901	*King's Own*
1901-1932	*Morning: A Magazine for Our Young Folk*
1902	*Baby's Pictorial*
1902-1929	*Boys' Realm*

1903	*Boys' Coloured Pictorial*
1903-1912	*Boys' Herald*
1903-1912	*Lotus Journal*
1903-1905	*The Young Scot*
1904	*Young Journalist and Author*
1905	*Every Boy's Monthly*
1905-1950	*Glad Tidings for the Young*
1905	*The Children's Gospel Magazine*
1906-1925	*"The Boy's Friend"*
1906-1911	*Good Words and Sunday School Magazine*
1906-1914	*The Children's Realm*
1906	*The Jabberwock*
1907	*Boys' Life*
1907-1910	*The Children's Pearl*
1907-1909	*The Gem*
1907-1920	*The Girls' Friend*
1907-P	*New Zealand School Journal*
1907	*Our Circle. A Magazine for Young People*
1907-1922	*Young Folks' Tales*
1908-1927	*Girl's Own Paper and Woman's Magazine*
1908-1915	*The Girls' Reader*
1908-1929	*The Magnet*
1909-1915	*Babyland*
1909-P	*Scouting*
1910-1919	*Our Little Paper*
1910-1911	*The Children's Encyclopedia Magazine*
1910-1915	*The Girls' Home*
1911-1922	*Boys' Best Story Paper*
1911-1914	*Children's Magazine*
1911	*Our Boys*
1911-1919	*The Children's Pulpit. A Comprehensive Library of Religious and Moral Instruction*
1911-1914	*The Wee Nipper*
1911-1916	*Words of Welcome*

1912-1913	*Cheer, Boys, Cheer*
1912	*The Children's Favourite*
1912-1922	*The Girls' Weekly*
1912-1920	*The Penny Popular*
1914-1915	*My Children's Magazine*
1914-P	*Our Boys*
1914	*Silver Wolf*
1915-1916	*Boys' and Girls' Own*
1915-1933	*My Magazine*
1916-1922	*Lloyd's Children's Story-Teller*
1917-1927	*The Kiddies' Magazine*
1919-1922	*Betty's Paper. Girls' Own Stories*
1919-1940?	*Boys' Cinema*
1919	*Boy's Weekly*
1919-P	*Children's Newspaper and Children's Pictorial*
1919-1920	*"Little Darkies" Budget*
1919-1922	*Girls' Own Stories*
1919-1940?	*Peg's Paper*
1919-1924	*Polly's Paper*
1919-1923	*Playtime*
1919	*The Sunday Fairy*
1919-1924	*Young Britain*
1920-1921	*The Greyfriars Boy's Herald*
1920-1931	*The Popular*
1921-1922	*The Boys' Herald*
1921-P	*Guide*
1922-1924	*Blue Bird*
1922	*The Boys' Magazine*
1922-1923	*Juvenile Life*
1922-1923	*Schoolgirl*
1922-1939	*The Schoolgirl's Weekly*
1922-1925	*The Young Quaker*
1922	*Youth*
1923-1925	*Boys' and Girls' Picture Newspaper*

1923	*The Children's Companion*
1923-1939	*Merry-Go-Round*
1923-1928	*Panpipes*
1923-1926	*Vanguard*
1924-1930	*Children's Pictorial*
1924-1942	*The Boys' Budget*
1924-1925	*The Mechanical Boy*
1924-1940	*Triumph. The Adventure Story Paper*
1924-P	*YSL Magazine*
1925-1928	*Bairns' Budget*
1925-1926	*The Children's Radio Magazine*
1925-1931	*Young Briton*
1926-1940	*The Quest*
1926-1930	*Young Folks' Evangel*
1927	*Young Folks' Reciter*
1928-1939	*Children's Weekly*
1928-P	*Council Fire*
1928-P	*Crusader*
1928-1929	*Live Girl Stories*
1928-1948	*The Children's Messenger of the Sacred Heart of Jesus*
1928-1930	*Woman's Magazine and Girl's Own Paper*
1929-1930	*Boys' Favourite*
1929-1930	*Girl Stories*
1930-1933	*Our Girls*
1932-P	*Canadian Guider*
1932-1939	*The Children's Greater World*
1933-1936	*Morning and Springtime*
1933-1938	*Sunshine Story Book*
1934-1935	*Boys' Broadcast*
1934-1950	*The Horizon*
1934-P	*Students' Digest*
1935	*Our Boys and Girls Weekly*
1938-1944	*The Children's Digest*
1935	*The Crystal*

1938-P	*Girl Crusader*
1938	*Horse and Heifer*
1938-1939	*Young Reekie*
1938-1944	*The Children's Digest*
1940-P	*Miracle Library*
1940	*Worldwide Evangelization Crusade*
1940-P	*Today's Generation*
1940-?	*World Wide Evangelization Crusade*
1940-P	*Young Warrior*
1941-1950	*Girl's Own Paper*

Appendix C.

Facsimiles and Reprints of Books Included in the Chronology
(with Key to Facsimile and Reprint Publishers)

[see Key to Facsimile and Reprint Publishers following]

Facsimiles and reprints were selected from publisher or museum catalogs published between 1968 and 1978.

Adams, Andy. *The Log of a Cowboy.* UM
The Adventures of A, Apple Pie. D
Aelfric. *Colloquy.* M
Alcott, Louisa May. "Will's Book" in *Louisa's Wonder Book.* CMU
Alger, Horatio. *From Canal Boy To President.* UM
Alger, Horatio. *Making His Way.* AN
Allingham, W. *Poems, Songs, Ballads and Stories.* AMS
Asbjörnsen, Peter Christian and Jörgen Moe. *Popular Tales of the North.* Translated by George Webbe Dasent
Asbjörnsen, Peter Christian. *Tales from the Fjeld.* AN
Aulnoy, Marie C., Comtesse d'. *"Tales of the Fairies in Three Parts, Compleat." As Extracted from the Second Edition in English of her "Diverting Works."* GAR
Austin, Mary. *The Basket Woman.* UM
Austin, Mary. *The Flock.* UM
Austin, Mary. *The Land of Little Rain.* UM
The Babee's Book: Medieval Manners for the Young; Done Into Modern English from Dr. Furnivall's Texts. CS
B. J. *The Merchants Avizo, verie necessarie for their Sons and Servants when they first send them beyond the Seas.* Da
Bailey, Carolyn Sherwin. *Stories for Every Holiday.* Gr
Baldwin, James. *The Story of Siegfried.* NE

Ballantyne, R. M. *Black Ivory; A Tale of Adventure Among the Slavers of East Africa.* MBI

Ballantyne, R. M. *Coral Island.* GAR

Ballantyne, R. M. *Hudson Bay, or Everyday Life in The Wilds of North America.* K

Barbauld, Anna L. A. *Hymns in Prose for Children;* 1781, bound with Hannah More's *Cheap Repository Tracts: The Shepherd of Salisbury Plain* (in 2 pts.), *The Two Wealthy Farmers* (in 7 pts.), *History of Tom White the Postillion* (in 2 pts.), *Black Gioles the Poacher and the History of Tawny Rachel the Fortuneteller* (3 pts.). GAR

Barrie, James M. *The Little White Bird, or Adventures in Kensington Gardens.* LIP

Bartholomaeus Anglicus. *De Rerum Proprietatibus.* J

Battledores. H

Battledores. St

Baum, L. Frank. *American Fairy Tales.* D

Baum, L. Frank. *John Dough and the Cherub.* S

Baum, L. Frank. *The Life and Adventures of Santa Claus.* D/s

Baum, L. Frank. *The Magical Monarch of Mo.* S

Baum,. L. Frank. *The Master Key.* HYP/S

Baum, L. Frank. *Queen Zixi of Ixor, The Story of the Magic Cloak.* S

Baum, L. Frank. *The Wonderful Wizard of Oz.* D/S

Belloc, Hilaire. *The Bad Child's Book of Beasts.* S

Belloc, Hilaire. *The Bad Child's Book of Beasts, More Beasts for Worse Children, A Moral Alphabet.* ID

Beowulf. CS

Berquin, Arnaud. *The Looking Glass for the Mind.* J

Blake, William. *Songs of Innocence.* D

Blake, William. *Songs of Innocence and Songs of Experience.* NE

Blake, William. *Songs of Innocence and Experience. Shewing the Two Contrary States of the Human Soul.* PY

Boethius, Anicus. *Consolacione Philosophie.* Translated by Geoffrey Chaucer. TO

Boethius, Anicus Manlius Severinus. *The Consolation of Philosophy.* UM

Boethius. *Philosophiae Consolationis.* J

Boreman, Thomas. *Description of Three Hundred Animals.* J

Boreman, Thomas. *Gigantick Histories of the Two Famous Giants of Guildhall.* GAR

Brooks, Noah. *Henry Knox, A Soldier of the Revolution.* Da

Bullokar, William. *Bullokar's Booke of Orthographie.* TO

Bunyan, John. *A Book for Boys and Girls or Country Rhymes for Children;* 1686, bound with Isaac Watts's *Divine Songs Attempted in Easy Language for the Use of Children;* 1715, bound with Thomas Foxton's *Moral Songs Composed for the Use of Children.* GAR

Bunyan, John. *Pilgrim's Progress from This World, To That Which Is To Come.* BRB

Burgess, Gelett. *Goops and How To Be Them.* D

Burgess, Gelett. *More Goops and How To Be Them.* D

Burgess, Gelett. *The Purple Cow and Other Nonsense.* D

Burnett, Frances H. *Little Lord Fauntleroy.* GAR

Burroughs, Edgar Rice. *At the Earth's Core; Pellucidar; Tanar of Pellucidar: Three Science Fiction Novels.* D

Burroughs, Edgar Rice. *The Land That Time Forgot; The Moon Maid.* D
Burroughs, Edgar Rice. *Pirates of Venus; Lost on Venus.* D
Burroughs, Edgar Rice. *Three Martian Novels: Thuvis, Maid of Mars; The Chessmen of Mars; The Master Mind of Mars.* D
Carroll, Lewis. *Alice's Adventures Underground.* D
Carroll, Lewis. *The Nursery Alice.* D
Caxton, William. *The Book of Curtesye.* K
Caxton, William. *The Historye of Reynart the Foxe.* PAR
Chaucer, Geoffrey. *Boethius's "De Consolatione Philosophiae."* OXP
Chaucer, Geoffrey. *Workes.* BRP
Child, F. J. *The English and Scottish Popular Ballads.* S
Cirker, Blanche. Five Great Dog Novels: *The Call of the Wild,* Jack London; *Rob and His Friends,* John Brown; *Bob, Son of Battle,* Alfred Ollivant; *Beautiful Joe,* Marshall Saunders; *A Dog of Flanders.* D
Clemens, Samuel L. *The American Claimant.* AMS
Coffin, Charles C. *Caleb Krinkle.* AN
Coffin, Charles C. *Four Years of Fighting.* AN
Comenius, John Amos. *Orbis Pictus.* OZ/DM
Comenius, John Amos. *Orbis Sensualium Pictus.* PSU
Comenius, John Amos. *Orbis, Sensualium Pictus . . . Or, A Picture and Nomenclature of All the Chief Things That Are in the World.* BRB
The Comic Adventures of Old Mother Hubbard and Her Dog. St
Cooper, James Fenimore. *The Borderers.* AMS
Cooper, James Fenimore. *The Chain Bearer.* AMS
Cooper, James Fenimore. *The Crater.* AMS
Cooper, James Fenimore. *Precaution.* AMS
Cooper, James Fenimore. *The Sea Lion.* S
Cooper, James Fenimore. *The Spy.* SB
Cooper, James Fenimore. *Tales for Fifteen.* SF
Cooper, James Fenimore. *The Water Witch.* AMS
Cooper, James Fenimore. *The Wept of Wish-Ton-Wish.* AMS
The Coverdale Bible. DAW
Cox, Palmer. *Another Brownie Book.* D
Cox, Palmer. *The Brownies: Their Book.* D
Cries of London As they Are Daily Exhibited in the Streets; 1775, bound with *Cries of New York;* 1808. GAR
Day, Mahlon. *New York Street Cries in Rhyme.* D
Day, Thomas. *The History of Little Jack;* 1788, bound with Mary Wollstonecraft's *Original Stories from Real Life.* GAR
Day, Thomas. *The History of Sanford and Merton.* GAR
Death and Burial of Cock Robin. St
DeFoe, Daniel. *The Life and Adventures of Robinson Crusoe.* ESV
DeMorgan, Mary. *On a Pincushion;* 1877, bound with Mary DeMorgan's *The Necklace of Princess Fiorimonde, and Other Stories,* 1880. GAR
Dickens, Charles. *A Christmas Carol.* UM
Dickens, Charles. *Life and Adventures of Nicholas Nickleby.* BRB
Dickens, Charles. *The Mystery of Edwin Drood.* HA

Dickens, Charles. *The Personal History, Adventures, Experience and Observation of David Copperfield.* AMS

Dodgson, C. L. *Lewis Carroll's Rhyme? and Reason?* GAR

Dodgson, C. L. *Lewis Carroll's Sylvie and Bruno.* GAR

Doyle, Arthur Conan. *The Adventures of Sherlock Holmes.* SB

Doyle, Arthur Conan. *The Hound of the Baskervilles.* SB

Doyle, Arthur Conan. *Memoirs of Sherlock Holmes.* SB

Doyle, Arthur Conan. *Memoirs of Sherlock Holmes.* GAR

Doyle, Arthur Conan. *The Return of Sherlock Holmes.* SB

Eastman, Charles. *Indian Boyhood.* D

Eastman, Charles. *Indian Scout Craft and Lore.* D

Edgeworth, Maria. *Moral Tales for Young People.* GAR

Edgeworth, Maria. *Ormond.* IU

Edgeworth, Maria. *The Parent's Assistant.* GAR

Edgeworth, Maria. *Tales and Novels.* GO

Edgeworth, Maria, and Richard Lovell. *Practical Education.* GAR

Eggleston, Edward. *The Hoosier School-Boy.* S

Eggleston, Edward. *The Hoosier Schoolmaster.* S

The English Bible, 1611. AMS

Ewing, Julianna H. *Lob-Lie-By-the-Fire;* 1874, bound with Julianna Ewing's *Jackanapes;* 1884, bound with *Daddy Darwin's Dovecot.* GAR

Ewing, Juliana H. *Mrs. Overtheway's Remembrances.* GAR

Ewing, Juliana H. *Six to Sixteen.* GAR

Exeter Book. *Old English Riddles.* AMS

Exeter Book. *Codex Exoniensis.* AMS

Fenn, Eleanor. *Fables in Monosyllables.* J

Fielding, Sarah. *Adventures of David Smple.* GAR

Finley, Martha. *Elsie Dinsmore.* AN/GAR

Foxe, John. *Acts and Monuments.* AMS

Franklin, Benjamin. *The Writings of Benjamin Franklin.* HA

"The Galloping Guide to the ABC" in *The Chapbook ABC's* selected by Peter Stockham. D

Gammer Gurton's Needle. AMS

Garland, Hamlin. *Boy Life on the Prairie.* UN

Gatty, Margaret. *Parables from Nature.* GAR

Gay, John. *Fables.* AMS

Gay, John. *Fables, and Fables Volume the Second.* BRB

Geoffrey of Monmouth. *Galfredi Monumentensis Historia Britonum.* F

Geoffrey of Monmouth. *A History of the Kings of Britain.* S

Godwin, William. *Fables Ancient and Modern.* GAR

"The Golden Pippin" in *The Chapbook ABC's* selected by Peter Stockham. D

Goodrich, Samuel G. *Tales of Peter Parley About America;* 1827, bound with William Snelling's *Tales of Travels West of the Mississippi.* By Solomon Bell, 1830. GAR

Goody Two Shoes; A Facsimile Reproduction of the Edition of 1766. M

Grahame, Kenneth. *Dream Days.* GAR

Grahame, Kenneth. *The Golden Age.* GAR

Grimm Brothers. *German Popular Stories Translated from the Kinder Und Haus Marchen.* BRB

Grimm Brothers. *Household Stories by the Brothers Grimm with Pictures by Walter Crane.* S

Grinnell, George Bird. *Blackfoot Lodge Tales: The Story of a Prairie People.* UN

Grinnell, George Bird. *By Cheyenne Campfires.* UN

Grinnell, George Bird. *The Cheyenne Indians.* CS

Grinnell, George Bird. *The Indians of Today.* AMS

Grinnell, George Bird. *The Last of the Buffalo.* AN

Grinnell, George Bird. *Pawnee Hero Stories and Folk-Tales.* S

Grinnell, George Bird. *When Buffalo Ran.* UO

Gutenberg Bible. CS

Haggard, H. Rider. *She; Allen Quatermain; King Solomon's Mines: Three Adventure Novels.* D

Hale, Lucretia. *The Last of the Peterkins, with Others of Their Kin and The Queen of the Red Chessmen.* D

Hale, Lucretia. *The Peterkin Papers.* D

Halliwell-Phillips, James O. *The Nursery Rhymes of England.* GR

Halliwell-Phillips, James O. *Popular Rhymes and Nursery Tales.* GR

Harris, Benjamin. *The Protestant Tutor, Instructing Youth and Others in the Compleat Method of Spelling, Reading, and Writing True English;* 1679, bound with *The New-England Primer, Enlarged;* 1737. GAR

Harris, Joel Chandler. *Daddy Jake, The Runaway.* AN

Harris, Joel Chandler. *Nights With Uncle Remus.* GR

Harris, Joel Chandler. *Uncle Remus.* SB

Hart, John. *Orthographic Conteyning the Due Order and Reason, Howe To Write or Paint Thimage of Mannes Voice, Most Like to the Life or Nature.* BRB

Henryson, Robert. *The Moral Fables of Robert Henryson.* AMS

The History of the Celebrated Nanny Goose, 1813; and *The History of Prince Renardo and the Lady Goosiana,* 1833. OS

Hodgson, Francis. *Lady Jane Grey.* GAR

Hornbook. H

Hough, Emerson. *The Web.* AN

Howitt, Mary. *Sketches of Natural History.* J

H. S. "The Picture Alphabet, for the Instruction and Amusement of Boys and Girls" in *The Chapbook ABC's* selected by Peter Stockham. D

Ingelow, Jean. *Mopsa the Fairy.* GAR

Irving, Washington. *Bracebridge Hall.* SHR

Irving, Washington. *Old Christmas.* SHR

Jack Juggler. AMS

Jacobs, Joseph, ed. *The Fables of Aesop.* SB

Jacobs, Joseph, ed. *The Most Delectable History of Reynard the Fox.* SB

James, Will. *Cow Country.* UN

James, Will. *Scorpion: A Good Bad Horse.* UN

Janvier, Thomas A. *Aztec Treasure House.* GP

Jewett, Sarah Orne. *A Country Doctor.* GP

Jewett, Sarah Orne. *The Country of the Pointed Firs and Other Stories.* S

Kipling, Rudyard. *Just So Stories.* SB
Knox, Thomas W. *The Boy Travellers in Australasia.* TU
Lang, Andrew. *The Arabian Nights Entertainments.* D/S
Lang, Andrew. *The Blue Fairy Book.* D/S
Lang, Andrew. *The Brown Fairy Book.* D/S
Lang, Andrew. *The Crimson Fairy Book.* D/S
Lang, Andrew. *The Green Fairy Book.* D/S
Lang, A. *The Grey Fairy Book.* D/S
Lang, Andrew. *King Arthur: Tales of the Round Table.* D/S
Lang, A. *The Lilac Fairy Book.* D/S
Lang, A. *The Olive Fairy Book.* D/S
Lang, Andrew. *The Orange Fairy Book.* D/S
Lang, Andrew. *The Pink Fairy Book.* D/S
Lang, Andrew. *The Red Fairy Book.* D/S
Lang, Andrew. *The Violet Fairy Book.* D/S
Lang, Andrew. *The Yellow Fairy Book.* D/S
Lily, William. *A Shorte Introduction of Grammar.* ScR
A Little Pretty Pocket-Book. Facsimile edition, with an introductory essay and
        bibliography by M. F. Thwaite. OXP
A Lytell Geste of Robyn Hode. Da
MacDonald, George. *At the Back of the North Wind.* GAR
MacDonald, George. *The Wise Woman or The Lost Princess.* GAR
Marryat, Frederick. *Masterman Ready.* GAR
Montgomery, Frances Trego. *Billy Whiskers: The Autobiography of a Goat.* D
Moore, Clement. *The Night Before Christmas.* D/UM
Mother Goose. *Mother Goose's Melodies.* D
Mure, Eleanor. *The Story of the Three Bears: A Manuscript.* OS
Newell, Peter. *The Hole Book.* TU
Newell, Peter. *The Rocket Book.* TU
The New England Primer; A History of Its Origin and Development. DM
New York Street Cries in Rhyme. D
Paget, Francis E. *The Hope of the Katzekopfs.* ScR
Parker, Arthur. *The Indian How Book.* D
Parley, Peter. *The Tales of Peter Parley About America.* D
Perrault, Charles. *Histories or Tales of Past Times.* GAR
Peter Piper's Practical Principles of Plain and Perfect Pronunciation Printed and
        Published with Pleasing Pretty Pictures According to Act of Parliament. D/St
"The Picture Alphabet" in *The Chapbook ABC's* selected by Peter Stockham. D/St
Power, Effie. *Bag O' Tales.* GR/S
Pyrnelle, Louise C. *Miss Lil' Tweetty.* AN
Raleigh, Sir Walter. *Works of Sir Walter Raleigh.* F
Richardson, Samuel. *Pamela; or, Virtue Rewarded.* GAR
Ritson, Joseph, ed. *Gammer Gurton's Garland, or The Nursery Parnassus; A*
        Choice Collection of Pretty Songs and Verses, for the Amusement of All
        Little Good Children Who Can Neither Read nor Run. NE
Ritson, Joseph, ed. *Robin Hood.* RL

Rossetti, Christina. *Sing-Song,* 1872, bound with Christina Rossetti's *Speaking Likenesses,* 1874, and *Goblin Market,* 1893. GAR

Ruskin, John. *The King of the Golden River.* D

Ruskin, John. *The King of the Golden River,* 1851, bound with Charles Dickens's *"A Holiday Romance" in 4 parts,* 1868, and Tom Hood's *Petsetilla's Posy,* 1870. GAR

"The Silver Penny, for the Amusement and Instruction of Good Children" in *The Chapbook ABC's* selected by Peter Stockham. D

Skinner, Cornelia Otis. *Footlights and Spotlights.* GNP

Stretton, Hesba. *Little Meg's Children.* J

Swift, Jonathan. *Gulliver's Travels.* SF

Swift, Jonathan. *Tale of a Tub.* AMS/GAR

Taylor, Jane and Ann. *Original Poems for Infant Minds,* 2 volumes, 1804-1805, bound with *Rhymes for the Nursery,* 1806. GAR

Templetown, Lady Elizabeth. *The Birthday Gift, or the Joy of a Doll.* OS

Topsell, Edward. *The Historie of Four-Footed Beastes.* TO

Topsell, Edward. *The History of Four-Footed Beasts and Serpents and Insects.* DC

Topsell, Edward. *The History of Serpents.* TO

Tyndale, William. *The New Testament.* PAR

Valentine and Orson: Facsimile of an 1822 Edition. OS

Watts, Isaac. *Divine Songs.* OXP

Watts, Isaac. *Reliquiae Juveniles Miscellaneous Thoughts in Prose and Verse.* SF

Weems, Mason L. *The Life of Washington the Great,* 5th edition, revised 1806, bound with William McGuffey's *The Eclectic First Reader,* 1836. GAR

Wiggin, Kate D. *Rebecca of Sunnybrook Farm.* GAR

Wilde, Oscar. *The Happy Prince and Other Tales,* 1888, bound with *A House of Pomegranates,* 1891. GAR

Wither, George. *Collection of Emblems, Ancient and Moderne.* BRB

Wollstonecraft, Mary. *Original Stories.* NE

Wollstonecraft, Mary. *Thoughts on the Education of Teachers.* NE

Yonge, Charlotte. *Abbeychurch.* GAR

Yonge, Charlotte. *The Daisy Chain.* GAR

Yonge, Charlotte. *The Heir of Redclyffe.* GAR

Yonge, Charlotte. *The Life of Sir Walter Scott.* NE

KEY TO FACSIMILE AND REPRINT PUBLISHERS

AMS   AMS Press, 56 East 16th Street, New York, NY 10003

AN   Arno Press, 3 Park Avenue, New York, NY 10016

BRB   British Book Center, c/o Pergamon Press, Fairview Park, Elmsford, NY 10523

CMU   Central Michigan University, Park Library, Lucile Clarke Collection, Mt. Pleasant, MI 48858

CS   Cooper Square Publishers, Inc., 59 Fourth Avenue, New York, NY 10003

D   Dover Publications, Inc., 180 Varick Street, New York, NY 10014

Da   Da Capo Press, 227 W. 17th Street, New York, NY 10011

DAW   William Dawson & Sons, Ltd., Back Issues Department, Cannon House, Folkstone, Kent, CT19 5EE, England

DM   Dr. Martin Sandig, Gmb. H., Nelkenstrasse 2, D-6229 Wallauf Bei Wiesbaden, West Germany

ESV   Editio Simile Verlag Gmb. H., Postfach 1949, 45 Osnabruck, West Germany

F   Lenox Hill Publishing, Burt Franklin, Publisher, 235 East 44th Street, New York, NY 10017

GAR   Garland Publishing, Inc., 545 Madison Avenue, New York, NY 10022

GNP   Greenwood Press, 88 Post Road West, Westport, CT 06881

GO   Georg Olms, Verlag Gmb. H., Hagentorwall 7, D-3200 Hildesheim, West Germany and 52 Vanderbilt Avenue, New York, NY 10017

GR   Gale Research Co., Book Tower, Detroit, MI 48226

H   The Horn Book, Inc., Dept. HB, Publications Division, 56 Main Street, Ashburnham, MA 01430

HA   Haskell House Publishers, Ltd., Box FF, Brooklyn, NY 11219

HYP   Hyperion Press, Inc., 45 Riverside Avenue, Westport, CT 06880

ID   Indiana University Press, 10th and Morton Streets, Bloomington, IN 47401

IU   Irish Academic Press, 3 Serpentine Avenue, Dublin 4, Ireland

J   Johnson Reprint Corporation, 111 Fifth Avenue, New York, NY 10003

M   Macmillan Publishers, 866 Third Avenue, New York, NY 10022

NB   University of Nebraska Press, 901 North 17th Street, Lincoln, NE 68588

NE   Norwood Editions, Box 38, Norwood, PA 19074

OS   Friends of the Osborne Collection, Toronto Public Library, Boys and Girls House, 40 St. George Street, Toronto 5, Ontario M5S 2E4 Canada

OXP   Oxford University Press, 200 Madison Avenue, New York, NY 10016

OZ   Otto Zeller, Verlagsbuchhandlung Gmb H., Jahnstrasse 15, 40 Osnabruck, West Germany

PAR David Paradine, Suite I Audley House, 9 North Audley Street, London, WIY 1 WF, England

PSU Pennsylvania State University Press, 215 Wagner Building, University Park, PA 16802

PY Pyramid Publications, Inc., 444 Madison Avenue, New York, NY 10022

RL Roman and Littlefield, 81 Adams Drive, Totowa, NJ 07512

S Peter Smith, Publisher, Inc., 6 Lexington Avenue, Magnolia, MA 01930

SB Schocken Books, Inc., 200 Madison Avenue, New York, NY 10016

ScR Scholarly Resources, 1508 Pennsylvania Avenue, Wilmington, DE 19806

SF Scholars' Facsimiles and Reprints, P.O. Box 344, Delmar, NY 12054

SH Hafner Press, Division of Macmillan Publishers, 866 Third Avenue, New York, NY 10022

SHR Sleepy Hollow Restorations, Tarrytown, NY 10591

St Anne and Peter Stockham, Images, 57 Barham Avenue, Elstree, Hertfordshire, England

TO Theatrum Orbis Terrarum Publishing Company, Keizersgracht 526, Amsterdam, Netherlands

TU Charles E. Tuttle, 28 South Main Street, Rutland, VT 05701

UM Books on Demand, University Microfilms International, Box 1467, Ann Arbor, MI 48106

UO University of Oklahoma Press, 1005 Asp Avenue, Norman, OK 73069

Bibliography
of Secondary Sources

Adams, Bess Porter. *About Books and Children.* Holt, 1953.

Albert, Edward. *A History of English Literature.* Crowell, 1923.

Allen, Agnes. *The Story of the Book.* Faber, 1952.

Allibone, S. A. *A Critical Dictionary of English Literature.* 5 vols. Lippincott, 1858-1872; reprint ed., Gale, 1965

Anderson, George. *The Literature of the Anglo-Saxon,* rev. ed. Princeton University Press, 1966.

Andrews, Siri, ed. *The Hewins Lectures 1947-1962.* The Horn Book, 1963.

Arber, Edward. *The Term Catalogues, 1668-1709 A.D.; with a Number for Easter Term, 1711 A.D. A Contemporary Bibliography of English Literature in the reigns of Charles II, James II, William and Mary, and Anne.* 3 vols., Professor Edward Arber, 1903-1906; reprint ed., Johnson, 1965.

Arbuthnot, May Hill. *Children and Books.* Scott, Foresman, 1947.

_____. *Children and Books.* 2nd ed. Scott, Foresman, 1957.

_____. *Children and Books.* 3rd ed. Scott, Foresman, 1964.

_____ , and Zena Sutherland. *Children and Books,* 4th ed. Scott, Foresman, 1972.

Aries, Philippe. *Centuries of Childhood: A Social History of Family Life.* Knopf, 1962.

_____ , and Edward Blishen, Phyllis Hostler, Dan Jacobson, Marghanita Laski, Colin MacInnes, Alastair Reid, Anthony Storr, Elizabeth Taylor, and Anthony Thwaite. *The World of Children.* Hamlyn, 1966.

Arnold, Arnold. *Pictures and Stories from Forgotten Children's Books.* Dover, 1969.

Avery, Gillian. *Nineteenth Century Children, Heroes and Heroines in English Children's Stories, 1780-1900.* Hodder, 1965.

Bader, Barbara. *American Picture Books from Noah's Ark to the Beast Within.* Macmillan, 1976.

Bainton, Roland H. *Early and Medieval Christianity.* Beacon, 1962.

Barchilon, Jacques, and Henry Pettit, eds. *The Authentic Mother Goose: Fairy Tales and Nursery Rhymes.* Swallow, 1960.

Baring-Gould, William S. and Cecil. *The Annotated Mother Goose: Nursery Rhymes Old and New, Arranged and Explained.* World, 1967.

Barry, Florence V. *A Century of Children's Books.* Methuen, 1922; reprint ed., Singing Tree Press, 1968.

Bator, Robert. "Out of the Ordinary Road: Locke and English Juvenile Fiction in the Eighteenth Century." In *The Great Excluded: Critical Essays on Children's Literature,* edited by Francelia Butler. Storrs, Connecticut, 1972. I: 46-53.

Beck, Robert Holmes. *A Social History of Education.* Prentice-Hall, 1965.

Bennett, H. S. *English Books and Readers, 1475-1557.* Cambridge University Press, 1969.

_____. *English Books and Readers, 1558-1603.* Cambridge University Press, 1969.

_____. *English Books and Readers, 1603-1640.* Cambridge University Press, 1969.

Bergman, Peter M. *The Chronological History of the Negro in America.* Harper, 1969.

Bishop, William. *A Checklist of American Copies of "Short-Title Catalogue" Books.* 2nd ed. University of Michigan Press, 1950.

Blanck, Jacob. *Peter Parley to Penrod: A Bibliographical Description of the Best-Loved American Juvenile Books.* Bowker, 1956.

_____. *Bibliography of American Literature.* 6 vols. Yale University Press, 1959.

Bland, David. *A History of Book Illustration,* rev. ed. University of California Press, 1969.

Blum, John M. *Yesterday's Children.* Houghton, 1959.

Bobbitt, Mary R. *A Bibliography of Etiquette Books Published in America Before 1900.* New York Public Library Bulletin, 1947.

Bolton, Theodore. *American Book Illustration; Bibliographic Check Lists of 123 Artists.* Bowker, 1938.

Books Known to Anglo-Latin Writers from Aldhelm to Alcuin. Cambridge University Press, 1936.

Brentano, Robert, ed. *The Early Middle Ages 500-1000.* Free Press of Glencoe/Collier-Macmillan Limited, 1964.

Briggs, Asa, ed. *Essays in the History of Publishing in Celebration of the 250th Anniversary of the House of Longman, 1724-1974.* Longman, 1974.

British Museum General Catalogue of Printed Books. 263 vols. Balding & Mansell, London and Wisbech, The Trustees of the British Museum, 1963.

British Union Catalogue of Periodicals. 4 vols. Butterworth, 1955-on.

Brockman, Bennett A. "Medieval Songs of Innocence and Experience." *Children's Literature: The Great Excluded,* edited by Francelia Butler. Storrs, Connecticut, 1973, II: 40-49.

Broderick, Dorothy. *Image of the Black in Children's Fiction.* Bowker, 1973.

Bronfenbrenner, Urie. *Two Worlds of Childhood: U.S. and U.S.S.R.* Basic Books, 1970.

Brooke, Iris. *English Children's Costume Since 1775.* Black, 1930.

Brooke, Z. N. *A History of Europe 911 to 1198*. Methuen, 1938.

Brosse, Jacques, Paul Chaland, and Jacques Ostier. *100,000 Years of Daily Life: A Visual History*. Golden, 1961.

Bullock, Alan, ed., with Sir Gerald Barry, Dr. J. Brownowski, James Fisher, Sir Julian Huxley. *World History: Civilization from Its Beginnings*. Doubleday, 1962.

Burchell, S. C. *Age of Progress*. Time, 1966.

Burke, W. J., and Will D. Howe. *American Authors and Books; 1640 to the Present Day*. Augmented and revised by Irving R. Weiss. Crown, 1943.

Butler, Marilyn. *Maria Edgeworth: A Literary Biography*. Oxford, 1972.

Butterworth, Charles. *The English Primers (1529-1545)*. Philadelphia, 1953.

Byrne, M. St. Clare. *Elizabethan Life in Town and Country*. Barnes, 1961.

Cable, Mary. *The Little Darlings: A History of Child Rearing in America*. Scribner's, 1975.

Cadogan, Mary, and Patricia Craig. *You're a Brick, Angela! A New Look at Girls' Fiction from 1839 to 1975*. Gollanez, 1976.

Cannon, William R. *History of Christianity in the Middle Ages*. Abingdon, 1960.

Carpenter, Charles. *History of American Schoolbooks*. University of Pennsylvania Press, 1963.

Chappell, Warren. *A Short History of the Printed Word*. Knopf, 1970.

Chrimes, S. B. *English Constitutional History*. Oxford, 1960.

A Chronicle of Boys' and Girls' House and a Selected List of Recent Additions to the Osborne Collection of Early Children's Books, 1542-1910, and the Lillian H. Smith Collection, 1911-1963, Toronto Public Library, 1966.

Churchill, Winston S. *A History of the English Speaking Peoples*. 4 vols. Dodd, 1966.

Clair, Colin. *A Chronology of Printing*. Praeger, 1969.

Cleaver, James. *A History of Graphic Art*. Philosophical Library, 1963.

Colbert, Margaret, ed. *Children's Books: Awards & Prizes*. Children's Book Council, 1971.

Colton, Joel G. *Twentieth Century*. Time, 1968.

Commire, Anne, ed. *Something About the Author*. 12 vols. Gale, 1971.

_____, Adele Sarkissian, and Agnes Garrett, eds., *Something About Yesterday's Authors*. 2 vols. Gale, 1977.

Coulton, G. G. *Medieval Panorama: The English Scene from Conquest to Reformation*. Norton, 1938.

Crouch, Marcus, comp. *Chosen for Children*. The Library Association, 1967.

Cruse, Amy. *The Victorians and Their Books*. Allen and Unwin, 1935.

Cunnington, Phillis, and Anne Buck. *Children's Costume in England, from the Fourteenth Century to the End of the Nineteenth Century*. Black, 1965.

Cusenza, Joan, comp. *The Eloise Ramsey Collection of Literature for Young People, A Catalogue*. Wayne State University and Detroit Public Libraries, 1967.

Dahl, Svend. *History of the Book*. Scarecrow, 1958.

Daniel-Rops, H. *The Church in the Dark Ages*. Translated from the French by Audrey Butler. Dent, 1959.

Darling, Richard L. *The Rise of Children's Book Reviewing in America, 1865-1881.* Bowker, 1968.

Darton, F. H. Harvey. *Children's Books in England: Five Centuries of Social Life.* 2nd ed. Cambridge University Press, 1958.

Davis, Dorothy R. *Carolyn Sherwin Bailey (1875-1961): Profile and Bibliography.* Eastern Press, 1967.

_____, comp. *The Carolyn Sherwin Bailey Historical Collection of Children's Books: A Catalog.* Southern Connecticut State College, The Columbia Printing Co., 1967.

Davison, Gustav. *First Editions in American Juvenilia and Problems in Their Identification.* Normandie House, 1939.

Dawson, Christopher. *The Formation of Christendom.* Sheed and Ward, 1967.

DeMause, Lloyd, ed. *The History of Childhood.* Harper, 1975.

Derby, James Cephas. *Fifty Years Among Authors, Books, and Publishers.* Carleton, 1884.

Diehl, Edith. *Bookbinding: Its Background and Technique,* Volume One. Kennikat, 1946.

Dodd, A. H. *Elizabethan England.* Putnam, 1974.

Downs, Robert B. *Famous Books: Ancient and Medieval.* Barnes and Noble, 1964.

Doyle, Brian, comp. and ed. *The Who's Who of Children's Literature.* Schocken, 1968.

Duggan, Alfred. *Growing Up in 13th Century England.* Pantheon, 1962.

Eames, Wilberforce. *Early New England Catechisms: A Bibliographical Account of Some Catechisms Published Before the Year 1800, for Use in New England.* Franklin, 1964.

Earle, Alice Morse. *Home and Child Life in Colonial Days.* Macmillan, 1969.

Early American Book Illustrators and Wood Engravers 1670-1870. A Catalog of a Collection of American Books Illustrated for the Most Part with Woodcuts and Wood Engravings in the Princeton University Library. Introduction by Sinclair Hamilton; foreword by Frank Weitenkampf. Princeton University Press, 1958.

Ede, Charles, ed. *The Art of the Book.* Studio Publications, 1951.

Egoff, Sheila. *The Republic of Childhood.* 2nd ed. Oxford, 1975.

_____. *Children's Periodicals of the Nineteenth Century: A Survey and Bibliography.* The Library Association, 1951.

Ellens, Richard Williamson. *Book Illustration: A Survey.* Kingsport Press, 1952.

Engen, Rodney K. *Kate Greenaway.* Crown, 1976.

_____. *Randolph Caldecott: "Lord of the Nursery."* Oresko Books, 1976.

_____. *Walter Crane As a Book Illustrator.* St. Martin's Press, 1975.

The English Catalogue of Books, Being a Continuation of the Original "London" and "British" Catalogues. 16 vols. The Publisher's Circular, 1801-1952.

Evans, Charles. *American Bibliography: A Chronological Dictionary of All Books and Pamphlets and Periodical Publications Printed in the U.S.* Volume 1 (1639, Volume 12 (Letter N.-1799; Volume 13 (1799-1800) completed by Clifford K. Shipton; Volume 14 (Index) compiled by Roger Patrell Bristol. American Antiquarian Society, 1955.

Eyre, Frank. *British Children's Books in the Twentieth Century.* Longmans, 1971.

Fairbank, Alfred. *The Story of Handwriting.* Watson-Guptill, 1970.

Farrar, Clarissa. *Bibliography of English Translations From Medieval Sources.* Columbia University Press, 1946.

Feaver, William. *When We Were Young: Two Centuries of Children's Book Illustration.* Thames and Hudson, 1977.

Fennelly, Catherine. *Town Schooling in Early New England, 1790-1840.* Old Sturbridge Village, 1962.

Field, Carolyn, et al., eds. *Subject Collections in Children's Literature.* Bowker, 1969.

Field, Mrs. E. M. *The Child and His Book.* 2nd ed. Wells Gardner, Darton, 1892; reprinted ed., Singing Tree Press, 1968.

Finley, Ruth E. *The Lady of Godey's, Sarah Josepha Hale.* Lippincott, 1931.

Fishel, Leslie H., Jr., and Benjamin Quarles. *The Negro American: A Documentary History.* Scott, Foresman, 1967.

Fisher, Dorothy Canfield. *Our Young Folks.* Harcourt, 1943.

Fisher, Margery. *Who's Who in Children's Books.* Holt, 1975.

Folmsbee, Beulah. *A Little History of the Horn-book.* Horn Book, 1942.

Fraser, James H., ed. *Society and Children's Literature.* Godine, with the American Library Association, 1978.

Freeman, Ruth S. *Children's Picture Books Yesterday and Today.* Century House, 1967.

Fryatt, Norma R., ed. *A Horn Book Sampler.* Horn Book, 1959.

Fuller, Muriel, comp. *More Junior Authors.* H. W. Wilson, 1963.

Gardner, Evelyn E., and Eloise Ramsey. *A Handbook of Children's Literature.* Scott, 1927.

Gardner, Ralph D. *Horatio Alger of the American Hero Era.* The Wayside Press, 1964.

Garnett, Richard, and Edmund Gosse. *English Literature: An Illustrated Record.* Vols. 1 and 2. Macmillan, 1935.

Gaskoin, C. J. B. *Alcuin: His Life and Work.* London, 1904.

Gillen, Molly. *The Wheel of Things: A Biography of L. M. Montgomery, Author of Anne of Green Gables.* Harrap, 1976.

Gillespie, Margaret C. *Literature for Children: History and Trends.* Brown, 1970.

Gillis, John R. *Youth and History, Tradition and Change in European Age Relations.* Academic Press, 1974.

Good, David, comp. *A Catalogue of the Spencer Collection of Early Children's Books and Chapbooks. Presented to the Harris Public Library.* Preston, 1947.

Good, H. G. *A History of Western Education.* Macmillan, 1960.

Gottlieb, Gerald, ed. *Early Children's Books and Their Illustration.* Godine, 1975.

Green, Roger L. *Tellers of Tales.* Rev. ed. Kaye and Ward, 1969.

_____. *Andrew Lang.* Ward, 1946.

Greene, David L., and Dick Martin. *The Oz Scrapbook.* Random, 1978.

Gruber, Frank. *Horatio Alger Jr., A Biography and Bibliography.* Grover James Press, 1961.

Halsey, Rosalie. *Forgotten Books of the American Nursery. A History of the Development of the American Story-Book.* Goodspeed, 1911; reprint ed., Singing Tree Press, 1969.

Hamilton, Ronald. *The Visitor's History of Britain.* Houghton, 1964.

Handlin, Oscar and Mary F. *Facing Life, Youth and the Family in American History.* Little, 1971.

Handover, P. M. *Printing in London from 1476 to Modern Times.* Harvard University Press, 1960.

Harnett, Cynthia. *Caxton's Challenge.* World, 1960.

Harrison, Frederick. *A Book About Books.* John Murray, 1948.

Harrison, Molly. *Children in History. Book Four. 19th Century.* Dufour Editions, 1962.

Hart, Roger. *English Life in the Seventeenth Century.* Putnam, 1970.

Harvey, Sir Paul, comp. and ed. *The Oxford Companion to English Literature.* 4th ed., rev. by Dorothy Eagle. Oxford, 1967.

Hassall, W. O., ed. *Holkham Bible Picture Book.* Dropmore, 1934.

_____. *How They Lived 55 B.C.-1485.* Blackwell, 1962.

Havighurst, Robert J., and Bernice L. Neugarten. *Society and Education.* 2nd ed. Allyn, 1962.

Haviland, Virginia. *The Travelogue Storybook of the Nineteenth Century.* Horn Book, 1950.

_____, comp. *Children's Literature: A Guide To Reference Sources.* Library of Congress, 1966.

_____, with Margaret Coughlan, comps. *Children's Literature: A Guide To Reference Sources.* First Supplement. Library of Congress, 1972.

_____ with Margaret Coughlan, comps. *Children's Literature: A Guide To Reference Sources.* Second Supplement. Library of Congress, 1977.

_____ with Margaret Coughlan, eds. *Yankee Doodle's Literary Sampler of Prose, Poetry, & Pictures.* Crowell, 1976.

Hazard, Paul. *Books, Children, and Men.* Translated from the French by Marguerite Mitchell. Horn Book, 1944.

Hearne, Michael Patrick. *The Annotated Wizard of Oz.* Potter, 1973.

Henry, Nelson B. *Social Forces Influencing American Education; The Sixtieth Yearbook of the National Society for the Study of Education.* Part II. The University of Chicago Press, 1961.

Herren, Dana T. *Early Children's Books.* S. R. Publishers Limited and Johnson reprint ed., Singing Tree Press, 1969.

Hewins, Caroline M. *A Mid-Century Child and Her Books.* Macmillan, 1926; reprint ed., Singing Tree Press, 1969.

Hewitt-Bates, J. S. *Bookbinding.* Dryad Press, 1967.

Horton, Rod W., and Herbert W. Edwards. *Backgrounds of American Literary Thought.* 3rd ed. Prentice-Hall, 1972.

Huck, Charlotte S. *Children's Literature in the Elementary School.* 3rd ed. Holt, 1976.

_____, and Doris Young Kuhn. *Children's Literature in the Elementary School.* 2nd ed. Holt, 1968.

Hunt, David. *Parents and Children in History: The Psychology of Family Life in Early Modern France.* Harper, 1972.

Hurlimann, Bettina. *Picture-Book World.* Translated and edited by Brian W. Alderson. Oxford, 1968.

_____. *Three Centuries of Children's Books in Europe.* World, 1968.

Jackson, W. T. H. *The Literature of the Middle Ages.* Columbia University Press, 1960.

Jacob, E. F. *The Fifteenth Century, 1399-1485.* Oxford, 1961.

Jacobus, Lee. "Milton's *Comus* as Children's Literature." *Children's Literature: The Great Excluded,* edited by Francelia Butler. Storrs, Connecticut, 1973. II: 67-72.

Jambeck, Thomas J. and Karen K. "Chaucer's Treatise on the Astrolabe: A Handbook for the Medieval Child." In *Children's Literature: The Great Excluded,* edited by Francelia Butler and Bennett A. Brockman. Storrs, Connecticut, 1974. III: 117-123.

James, Philip. *Children's Books of Yesterday.* Studio Publications, 1933.

Johannsen, Albert. *The House of Beadle and Adams and Its Dime and Nickel Novels; The Story of a Vanished Literature.* 3 vols. University of Oklahoma Press, 1970.

Jordan, Alice M. *From Rollo to Tom Sawyer and Other Papers.* Horn Book, 1948.

Keeman, Hugh T. "Children's Literature in Old English." In *The Great Excluded: Critical Essays on Children's Literature,* edited by Francelia Butler. Storrs, Connecticut, 1971. I: 16-20.

Kelly, R. Gordon. *Mother Was A Lady; Self and Society in Selected American Children's Periodicals 1865-1890.* Greenwood, 1974.

Kennedy, Charles. *The Earliest English Poetry: A Critical Survey of the Poetry Written before the Norman Conquest with Illustrative Translations.* London, 1943.

Kiefer, Monica. *American Children Through Their Books, 1700-1835.* University of Pennsylvania Press, 1948.

Kingman, Lee Joanna Foster, and Ruth Giles Lontoft, comps. *Illustrators of Children's Books, 1957-1966.* Horn Book, 1968.

Kujoth, Jean Spealman. *Best-Selling Children's Books.* Scarecrow Press, 1973.

Kunitz, Stanley J., and Howard Haycraft. *The Junior Book of Authors.* 2nd ed., rev. Wilson, 1951.

LaBeau, Dennis, ed. *Children's Authors and Illustrators: An Index to Biographical Dictionaries.* Gale, 1976.

Langer, William, ed. *An Encyclopedia of World History.* Houghton, 1948.

Lehmann-Haupt, Hellmut. *The Book in America.* 2nd ed. Bowker, 1951.

_____. *The Life of the Book.* Abelard-Schuman, 1957.

Levarie, Norma. *The Art and History of Books.* Heineman, 1968.

Linton, William J. *The History of Wood Engraving in America.* Estes, 1882.

A Little Pretty Pocket-Book, A facsimile with an introductory essay and bibliography by M. F. Thwaite. Oxford University Press, 1966.

Lofts, W. O. G., and D. J. Adley. *The Men Behind Boys' Fiction.* Baker, 1970.

Loomis, Roger. *Introduction to Medieval Literature Chiefly in England.* Columbia University Press, 1948.

Lownes, William Thomas. *The Bibliographer's Manual of English Literature.* 8 vols. New edition revised, corrected, and enlarged with an appendix by Henry Bohn. Bohn, 1864; reprint ed., Gale, 1967.

Mackie, J. D. *The Earlier Tudors, 1485-1558.* Oxford, 1952.

MacLeod, Anne Scott. *A Moral Tale, Children's Fiction and American Culture, 1820-1860.* Archon, 1975.

Mahoney, Bertha E., Louise Payson Latimer, and Beulah Folmsbee, comps. *Illustrators of Children's Books 1744-1945.* Horn Book, 1947.

Marshall, H. E. *English Literature for Boys and Girls.* Nelson, 1959.

Matthews, William, comp. *Old and Middle English Literature.* Appleton-Century-Crofts, 1968.

Maxwell, Barbara, comp. *Checklist of Children's Books, 1837-1876. Special Collections, Central Children's Department.* Free Library of Philadelphia, 1975.

McCallum, James Dow, ed. *English Literature: The Beginnings to 1500.* Scribner's, 1932.

McClinton, Katharine Morrison. *Antiques of American Childhood.* Bramhall, 1970.

McKisack, May. *The Fourteenth Century, 1307-1399.* Oxford, 1959.

McLean, Ruari. *Modern Book Design.* Faber, 1958.

————. *Victorian Book Design and Colour Printing.* 2nd ed. University of California Press, 1972.

McMunn, Meradith Tilbury, and William Robert McMunn. "Children's Literature in the Middle Ages." In *The Great Excluded: Critical Essays on Children's Literature,* edited by Francelia Butler. Storrs, Connecticut, 1972. I: 21-29.

McMurtrie, Douglas C. *The Book: The Story of Printing and Bookmaking.* Oxford University Press, 1943.

Meigs, Cornelia, Anne Thaxter Eaton, Elizabeth Nesbitt, and Ruth Hill Viguers. *A Critical History of Children's Literature: A Survey of Children's Books in English.* Rev. ed. Macmillan, 1969.

Meynell, Francis. *English Printed Books.* Collins, 1948.

Miller, Bertha Mahony, and Elinor Whitney Field, eds. *Caldecott Medal Books: 1938-1957; With the Artists' Acceptance Papers and Related Material Chiefly from the Horn Book Magazine.* Horn Book, 1957.

Miller, Daniel R., and Guy E. Swanson. *The Changing American Parent.* Wiley, 1958.

Miner, Robert G., Jr. "Aesop as Litmus: The Acid Test of Children's Literature." In *The Great Excluded: Critical Essays on Children's Literature,* edited by Francelia Butler. Storrs, Connecticut, 1972. I: 9-15.

Moore, Annie E. *Literature Old and New for Children: Materials for a College Course.* Houghton, 1934.

Morison, Samuel Eliot. *The Oxford History of the American People.* Volume 1, *Prehistory to 1789;* Volume 2, *1789 Through Reconstruction;* Volume 3, *1869-1963.* New American Library, 1972.

Moses, Montrose J. *Children's Books and Reading.* Kennerley, 1907.

Mott, Frank L. *A History of American Magazines, 1865-1885.* 5 vols. Harvard University Press, 1935.

Muir, Percy. *English Children's Books, 1600-1900.* Batsford, 1954.

————. *Victorian Illustrated Books.* Praeger, 1971.

Myers, A. R. *England in the Late Middle Ages.* Penguin, 1971.

National Union Catalog—Pre-1956 Imprints. Library of Congress, 1973.

Neuburg, Victor E., ed. *The Penny Histories: A Study of Chapbooks for Young Readers Over Two Centuries.* Harcourt, 1969.

Nisenson, Samuel. *The Dictionary of 1001 Famous People.* Lion Press, 1966.

Nordenfalk, Carl. *Celtic and Anglo-Saxon Painting, Book Illumination in the British Isles, 600-800.* George Braziller, 1977.

Oates, J. C. T., comp. *A Catalogue of the Fifteenth-Century Printed Books in the University Library.* 4 vols. Cambridge University Press, 1954.

O'Callaghan, Edmund Bailey, ed. *A List of Editions of the Holy Scriptures and Parts Thereof Printed in America Previous to 1860.* With an introduction and bibliographical notes by Edmund Bailey O'Callaghan. Mansell and Rowland, 1861; reprint ed., Gale, 1966.

Ogilvy, Jack. *Books Known to the English, 597-1066.* The Mediaeval Academy of America, 1967.

Orcutt, William Dana. *In Quest of the Perfect Book.* Little, 1926.

Osborne, John. *Britain.* Time, 1963.

Patrick, David, ed. *Chamber's Cyclopedia of English Literature.* Revised by J. Liddell Geddie. Chambers, 1938.

Paule, R. *The Life of Alfred the Great,* London, 1853. Includes "Orosius."

Pennell, Joseph. *The Illustration of Books.* Unwin, 1896.

Pinchbeck, Ivy, and Margaret Hewitt. *Children in English Society, from Tudor Times to the Eighteenth Century.* Vol. 1. Routledge and Kegan Paul, 1969.

_____. *Children in English Society, from the Eighteenth Century to the Children Act 1948.* Vol. 2. Routledge and Kegan Paul, 1973.

Pitz, Henry C. *Illustrating Children's Books, History, Technique, Production.* Watson-Guptill, 1963.

Pollard, Alfred W. *Old Picture Books.* Lenox Hill, 1902; reprint ed., Gale, 1970.

_____, G. R. Redgrave, et al. *A Short Title Catalogue of Books Printed in England, Scotland and Ireland, and of English Books Printed Abroad, 1475-1640.* The Bibliographical Society, 1926.

Powicke, Sir Maurice. *The Thirteenth Century, 1216-1307.* 2nd ed. Oxford, 1962.

Quayle, Eric. *The Collector's Book of Books.* Potter, 1971.

_____. *The Collector's Book of Children's Books.* Potter, 1972.

Quennell, Marjorie, and C. H. B. *Everyday Life in Roman and Anglo-Saxon Times, including Viking and Norman Times.* Putnam, 1959.

Quinnam, Barbara, comp. *Fables from Incunabula to Modern Picture Books.* The Library of Congress, 1966.

Ray, Gordon N. *The Illustrator and the Book in England from 1790 to 1914.* Pierpont Morgan Library, 1976.

Reid, Forrest. *Illustrators of the Eighteen Sixties.* Dover, 1975.

Reynolds, Quentin. *The Fiction Factory.* Street and Smith, 1955.

Rickert, Edith, comp. *Chaucer's World.* Columbia University Press, 1948.

Robertson, Ina, and Agnes Stahlschmidt. "Facsimiles of Historical Children's Books." *Library Trends,* 27/4: 531-527.

Roger-Marx, Claude. *Graphic Art: The 19th Century.* McGraw, 1962.

Rolfe, William J. *Shakespeare the Boy, with Sketches of the Home and School Life, The Games and Sports, The Manners, Customs and Folk-Lore of the Time.* Harper, 1896.

Roscoe, A. S. *John Newbery and His Successors.* Five Owls, 1973.

Rosenbach, A. S. W. *Early American Children's Books; with Bibliographical Descriptions of the Books in his Private Collection.* Southworth, 1933; reprint ed., Dover, 1971.

Ross, Eulalie Steinmetz. *The Spirited Life: Bertha Mahony Miller and Children's Books.* Horn Book, 1973.

Rowse, A. L. *The Elizabethan Renaissance.* Scribner's, 1971.

Sabin, Joseph. *Dictionary of Books Relating to America from its Discovery to the Present Time.* 2 vols. Bibliographical Society of America, 1928-1936.

Sadleir, M. *XIX Century Fiction.* 2 vols. Constable, 1953.

St. John, Judith. *The Osborne Collection of Early Children's Books,* Vol. I, 1566-1910. Toronto Public LIbrary, 1958.

_____, with Dana Tenny and Hazel I. MacTaggart. *The Osborne Collection of Early Children's Books.* Vol. II, 1476-1910. Toronto Public LIbrary, 1975.

Salter, Stefan. *From Cover to Cover: The Occasional Papers of Book Design.* Prentice-Hall, 1969.

Sayle, C. E., ed. *Early English Printed Books in the University Library, Cambridge, 1475-1640,* 4 vols. Cambridge University Press, 1900.

Schick, Frank L. *The Paperbound Book in America.* Bowker, 1958.

Schiller, Justin G. "Artistic Awareness in Early Children's Books." In *Children's Literature: The Great Excluded,* edited by Francelia Butler and Bennett A. Brockman. Storrs, Connecticut, 1974. III: 177-185.

_____. "Magazines for Young America: The First Hundred Years, *Columbia Library Columns* (May 1974): 24-39.

Sédillot, René. *The History of the World.* Translated by Gerard Hopkins. Harcourt, 1951.

Simon, Irving B. *The Story of Printing.* Harvey House, 1965.

Skeat, W. W., ed. *The Complete Works of Geoffrey Chaucer.* 6 vols. plus supplement Vol. 7. Oxford, 1894-1897.

Sloane, William. *Children's Books in England and America in the Seventeenth Century.* King's Crown Press, 1955.

Smith, Dora V. *Fifty Years of Children's Books 1910-1960: Trends, Backgrounds, Influences.* National Council of Teachers of English, 1963.

Smith, Elva S. *The History of Children's Literature. A Syllabus with Selected Bibliographies.* American Library Association, 1937.

Speare, Elizabeth George. *Child Life in New England, 1790-1840.* Old Sturbridge Village, 1961.

Steinberg, S. H. *Five Hundred Years of Printing.* Criterion, 1959.

Stenton, Doris Mary. *English Society in the Early Middle Ages.* Penguin, 1976.

Stenton, Sir Frank. *Anglo-Saxon England.* 2nd ed. Oxford, 1962.

_____. *The Oxford History of England.* Oxford, 1947.

Stephen, Sir Leslie, and Sir Sidney Lee, eds. *The Dictionary of National Biography.* Oxford, 1882; reprint ed., Gale, 1968.

Stillwell, Margaret. *Incunabula in American Libraries.* Bibliographical Society of America, 1940.

Stuart, Dorothy Margaret. *The Girl Through the Ages.* Harrap, 1933; reprint ed., Singing Tree Press, 1969.

_____. *The Boy Through the Ages.* Harrap, 1926; reprint ed., Singing Tree Press, 1970.

Sutherland, Zena, and May Hill Arbuthnot. *Children and Books.* 5th ed. Scott, Foresman, 1977.

Targ, William, ed. *Bibliophile in the Nursery: A Bookman's Treasury of Collector's Lore on Old and Rare Children's Books.* World, 1957.

Temple, Nigel, ed. *Seen and Not Heard: A Garland of Fancies for Victorian Children.* Dial, 1970.

Thomas, Alan G. *Fine Books.* G. P. Putnam, 1976.

_____. *Great Books and Book Collectors.* Putnam, 1975.

Thomas, Isaiah. *The History of Printing in America.* Isaiah Thomas, 1810; reprint ed., Weathervane, 1970.

Thompson, James Westfall. *The Medieval Library.* Hafner, 1957.

_____. *The Medieval Library.* University of Chicago Press, 1959.

Thompson, Susan Otis. *American Book Design and William Morris.* Bowker, 1977.

Thompson, Susan Ruth. *Kate Greenaway.* Wayne State University Press, 1977.

Thorndike, Joseph T., Jr., and Joseph Kastner. *Life's Picture History of Western Man.* Time, 1951.

Thorndike, Lynn. *The History of Medieval Europe.* Houghton, 1949.

Thorne, J. O. *Chambers's Biographical Dictionary.* St. Martin's Press, 1962.

Three Centuries of Nursery Rhymes and Poetry for Children; an Exhibition held at the National Book League, May 1973. Presented by Iona and Peter Opie. Oxford University Press, 1973.

Thwaite, Mary F. *From Primer to Pleasure in Reading: An Introduction to the History of Children's Books in England from the Invention of Printing to 1914 with an Outline of Some Developments in Other Countries.* Horn Book, 1972.

Townsend, John Rowe. *Written for Children: An Outline of English-language Children's Literature.* Rev. ed. Lippincott, 1975.

Trevelyan, G. M. *History of England.* 3 vols. Doubleday, 1926.

_____. *Illustrated English Social History.* 4 vols. Longmans, 1951.

Tuer, Andrew W. *History of the Horn Book.* Blom, 1968.

_____. *Pages and Pictures from Forgotten Children's Books.* Blom, 1968.

Turner, Ernest S. *Boys Will Be Boys; The Story of Sweeny Todd, Deadwood Dick, Sexton Blake, Billy Bunter, Dick Barton, et al.* with an introduction by C. B. Fry. Michael Joseph, 1948.

Union List of Serials. 3rd ed. H. W. Wilson, 1965.

Viguers, Ruth Hill, Marcia Dalphin, and Bertha Mahony Miller, comps. *Illustrators of Children's Books, 1946-1956.* Horn Book, 1958.

Watson, George, ed. *The Concise Cambridge Bibliography of English Literature.* 2nd ed. Cambridge University Press, 1965.

Watt, Robert. *Bibliotheca Britannica.* 4 vols. Constable, 1824.

Watts, Isaac. *Divine Songs.* With an introduction by J. H. Pafford. Oxford, 1971.

Weitenkampf, Frank. *American Graphic Art*. Macmillan, 1924.

———. *The Illustrated Book*. Bulletin of the New York Public Library, 1919. Library, 1919.

Welch, d'Alté. *A Bibliography of American Children's Books Printed Prior to 1821*. American Antiquarian Society and Barre Publishers, 1972.

Whalley, Joyce Irene. *Cobwebs to Catch Flies; Illustrated Books for the Nursery and Schoolroom, 1700-1900*. University of California Press, 1975.

White, R. J. *The Horizon Concise History of England*. American Heritage, 1971.

Wilds, Elmer H., and Kenneth V. Lottich. *The Foundations of Modern Education*. 3rd ed. Holt, 1961.

Wing, Donald. *A Short-titled Catalogue of Books in England, Scotland, Ireland, Wales, and British America and of English Books Printed in Other Countries 1641-1700*. 3 vols. Columbia University Press, 1945-1951.

Wishy, Bernard. *The Child and the Republic*. University of Pennsylvania Press, 1972.

Zengota, Eric, ed. *Children's Books in the Rare Book Division of the Library of Congress*. Volume 1, *Author*. Rowman and Little, 1975.

Index of Authors, Illustrators, Translators, and Early Publishers

Index of Titles Cited in the Chronology

About the Authors

JANE M. BINGHAM is Associate Professor of Education at Oakland University in Rochester, Michigan. Her book reviews and articles on children's literature have appeared in journals such as *Elementary English*, *Top of the News*, *The Reading Teacher*, and *Choice*.

GRAYCE SCHOLT teaches in the Language, Literature and Philosophy Division at Mott Community College in Flint, Michigan. Her book reviews and articles have appeared in journals such as *Language Arts*, the *CEA Critic*, the *Michigan Women's Studies Association Proceedings*, and *Choice*.